AF604296

half the sky

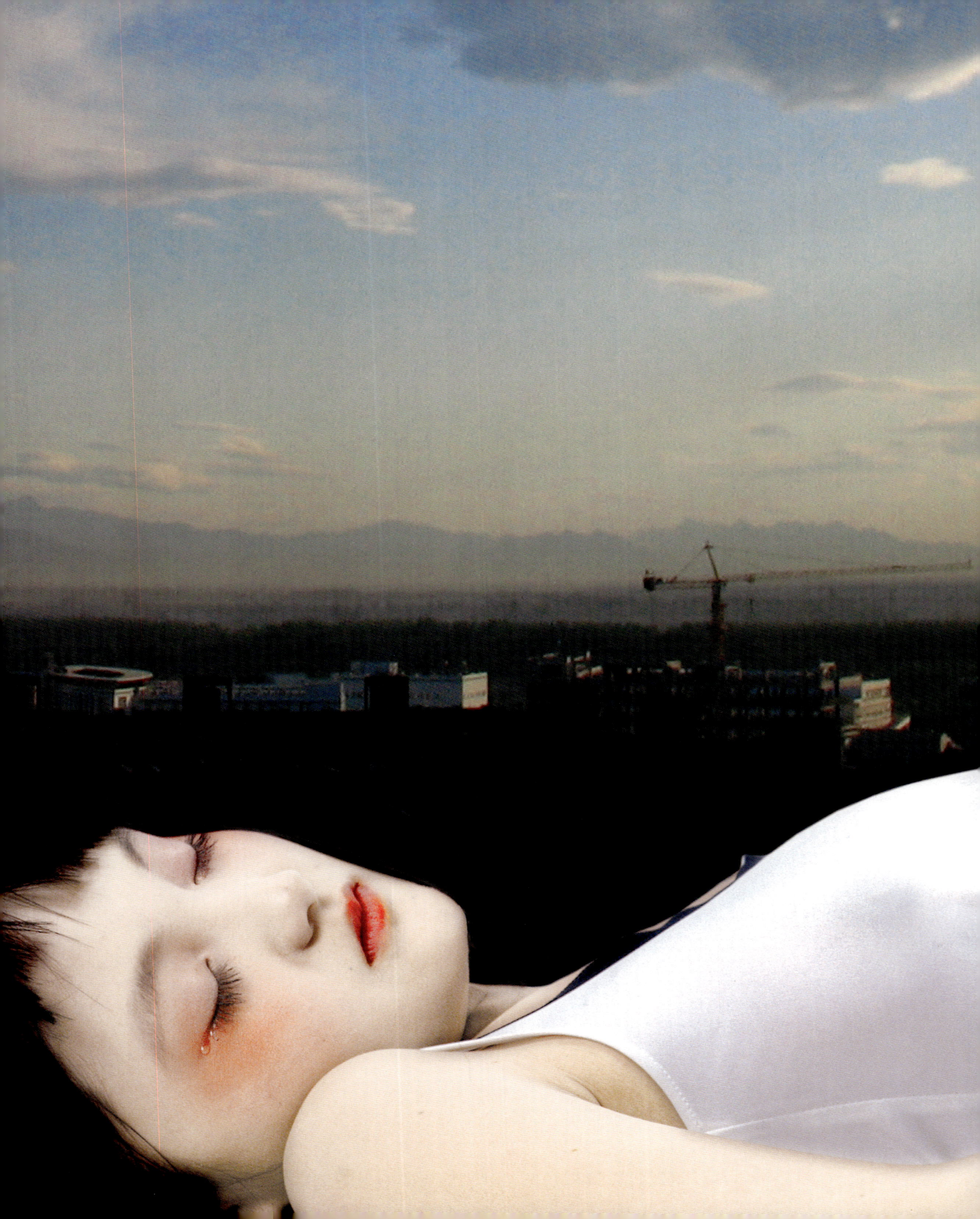

half the sky

luise guest

piper press

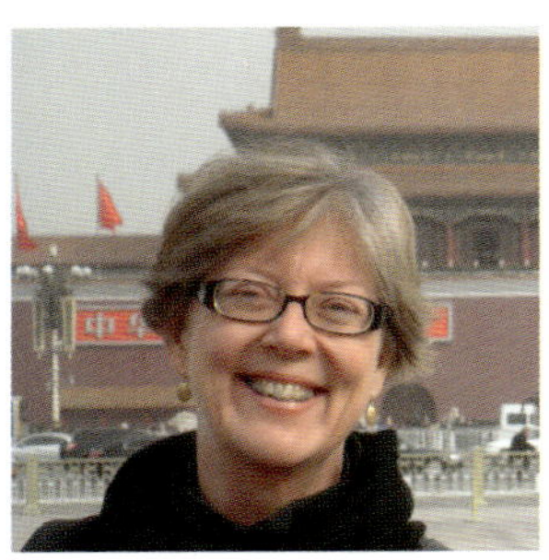

About the author
Art teacher, writer, researcher, and bad student of Chinese, Luise Guest writes regularly about contemporary Chinese art. Her blog, *An Art Teacher in China*, documents her adventures in the Middle Kingdom. Her articles and interviews have been published in a range of online and print art journals and web sites including *Creative Asia, Daily Serving, Randian, The Art Life, The Culture Trip* and the *Journal of Contemporary Chinese Art*.

front cover:
Bu Hua
AD 3012 – 8 (detail) 2012
giclée print
54 x 375 cm
image courtesy the artist

back cover:
Bu Hua
Brave Diligent (detail) 2014
silk wall carpet
200 x 300 cm
image courtesy the artist

title page:
Cui Xiuwen
Angel No. 13 (detail) 2006
type c photograph
100 x 119.5 cm
images courtesy and © Cui Xiuwen

Published by
Piper Press
37 Lower Fort Street
Dawes Point NSW 2000
www.piperpress.com.au

Printer: Toppan Printing Co. (Hong Kong)

Designer: by John Dunn

Editor: Julie Ewington

National Library of Australia
Cataloguing-in-Publication entry

Creator: Guest, Luise, author.

Title: Half the sky : conversations
with women artists in China /

Luise Guest.

ISBN: 9780980834741 (hardback)

Subjects: Artists, Chinese—21st century.

Artists—China.

Art, Chinese—21st century.

Dewey Number: 709.51

HALF THE SKY : Conversations with women artists in China

PROLOGUE

This book documents a series of conversations with women artists in China. My accounts of meetings in artists' homes and studios reveal a world in the process of transformation; the book is about a changing China, almost as much as it is about art. The truth is, I didn't expect to love China: my early travel desires were all too predictably focused on New York and Paris. But in recent years China has, most surprisingly, become a central part of my life. From my first tentative encounters with a society in flux, and the contemporary art being produced there, this fast-changing nation of more than 1.4 billion people[1] has gripped my imagination. It was, in fact, love at first sight.

What is it about China that makes foreigners fall under its spell? Despite apocalyptic air pollution, corruption, censorship and heavy-handed political control; despite barriers of language and culture, the Middle Kingdom exerts a strong attraction. China is wonderful and infuriating, beautiful and ugly, awe-inspiring and worrying in equal measures. What makes me return? It is the pull of history, the intriguing mix of optimism and cynicism, and the generosity of spirit of the Chinese people, as much as the quality of Chinese contemporary art. Since 2011 I have travelled to China many times, visited countless artists' studios, attempted to learn Chinese, and drunk more tea than I would ever have thought possible. In this book I have tried to convey some of the excitement that I feel each time I walk through the doors of Beijing Capital Airport, smell the dust from the Gobi Desert, jump into a taxi and hear that familiar rolled 'r' of the Beijing accent.

My Chinese journey began in 2006, when I introduced my high school art students to Ai Weiwei's *World Map* at the Biennale of Sydney. In the classroom, we looked at his Han Dynasty urns inscribed with Coca-Cola logos, his re-purposed, scrambled Qing Dynasty furniture and his provocatively raised middle finger in front of the Gate of Heavenly Peace, and the students were intrigued. I had never seen them respond with such interest to the work of a contemporary artist. I knew that, as a teacher, I was definitely onto something.

The art being produced in China today is extraordinary. Amidst a tornado of social change, artists have responded to the contemporary zeitgeist by inventing new visual languages, layers of coded meaning, and innovative forms. Chinese contemporary art (usually translated as *Zhongguo Dangdai Yishu*) emerged after the death of Mao Zedong in 1976. The collective madness of the Cultural Revolution had left bitterness and confusion in its wake. Under the economic reform policies of Deng Xiaoping, China was gradually opened up to what some older Chinese still call 'outside'. Thirty years of Soviet Socialist Realism and Mao-cult propaganda gave way to experimentation, innovation, and a postcolonial plundering of eclectic influences: from Duchamp to Damien Hirst; from Joseph Beuys to Pop Art; and from ancient (previously forbidden) Chinese painting and craft traditions to Japanese cartoons. The results were explosive.

My belief that contemporary art in China is unlike anything in the rest of the world is shared by international curators and scholars. Philip Tinari, director of Beijing's Ullens Centre for Contemporary Art, said:

> I have always believed that contemporary art is one area of contemporary culture in which China truly excels... While contemporary art can sometimes be a self-contained sphere, artists in China are exploring big ideas about their country and its place in the world in an open way that goes far beyond official culture.[2]

There is a history of 'art conversations' between Australia and China. The diplomatic relationship that developed from Gough Whitlam's ground-breaking visit to Beijing in 1971 was the starting point for mutually influential discourses between Chinese and Australian artists, curators and writers that have grown in depth and complexity over the intervening forty-five years. Australian audiences became aware of the new art from China soon after 1989, due at least in part to the sympathetic assistance of Australian Embassy officials and the actions of the Hawke Labor Government which allowed artists such as Guan Wei, Ah Xian, Shen Shaomin and others to settle in Australia, along with the 42,000 students who were granted permanent visas in the aftermath of the Tiananmen Square Massacre.

International exhibitions helped to spread the word that something momentous was happening in Chinese art. In Sydney, Claire Roberts curated an exhibition of seven artists at the Art Gallery of New South Wales in 1992, *New Art From China*. In 1993, at the Museum of Contemporary Art, *Mao Goes Pop: China Post 1989* introduced twenty-nine artists to Australian audiences. The influential Asia Pacific Triennial (APT) exhibitions at the Queensland Gallery of Modern Art brought art from China and the region into the consciousness of the Australian public in dramatic and influential ways from 1993. It is the APT that brought Ai Weiwei, Cai Quo-Qiang, and Song Dong to the attention of Australian audiences. APT4 focused on substantial bodies of work by sixteen artists, including Song Dong's *Stamping the Water* and *Writing Diary with Water*. It was at APT6 in 2009 that I began to seriously consider travelling to China to see some of this work for myself, in situ.

Other institutions that played an important role in this Australia–China conversation were the Sherman Gallery (later the Sherman Contemporary Art Foundation), the 4A Centre for Contemporary Asian Art, and the Ray Hughes Gallery, all of which pioneered the exposure of contemporary Chinese artists to Australian audiences. The Sherman Contemporary Art Foundation, under director Gene Sherman, developed influential projects, bringing significant artists from Asia to Australia. The first project, in 2008, was Ai Weiwei's *Under Construction*. 4A, under the inaugural leadership of Melissa Chiu, promoted in particular the contemporary art of transnational hybridity, and the work of Asian–Australian and diasporic artists. Ray Hughes travelled to China and began to show the work of artists from Beijing, Shanghai, Tianjin and Chongqing. It was at the Ray Hughes Gallery that collector and philanthropist Judith Neilson first encountered contemporary Chinese art.

After Neilson's White Rabbit Gallery opened in Chippendale in 2009, I became even more fascinated by the differences between contemporary art from China and elsewhere. Visiting the exhibitions at the White Rabbit, I began to understand the ability of Chinese artists to reference tradition, yet transform and reinvent it, layering past and present in works of breathtaking technical virtuosity. In 2011, with the assistance of a NSW Premier's Kingold Creative Arts Scholarship, I spent six weeks visiting galleries and studios in Beijing, Shanghai, Guangzhou and Hong Kong, interviewing artists, art writers, curators and gallerists. I met luminaries such as Wang Jianwei, Hu Jieming, Shi Qing and Yang Zhenzhong, and rising stars such as Wu Junyong, Liu Zhuoquan, Liang Yuanwei, Lu Yang and Shi Zhiying. Those first visits to the artists' villages on Beijing's outskirts in the cold winds of March and April introduced me to the feverish intensity of creation in China's art scene. Amidst my shock at finding a post-apocalyptic landscape of rubbish, rubble and partly demolished farmhouses, interspersed with statement museum and gallery buildings (often empty and abandoned), I discovered artists making extraordinary work.

In late 2012, I returned to Beijing and Shanghai, where I interviewed Li Tingting, Gao Rong, Dong Yuan and Lin Tianmiao. In late 2013, during a two-month Red Gate Gallery residency, I was 'embedded' in my favourite Beijing neighbourhood of Tuanjiehu. I interviewed artists, studied Chinese, ate too many noodles, watched the water calligraphers and ballroom dancers in Tuanjiehu Park each morning, and occasionally joined the retired ladies ('the aunties') in their vigorous dancing – and began to write this book. In 2014 I made two further trips to complete the interviews.

Half the Sky is the result of all those experiences in Beijing, Shanghai, Hangzhou, Xi'an, Chengdu, and Guangzhou. It developed from my conversations with Chinese artists, over a period of almost five years, and my growing conviction that, despite the constant stream of books and articles published in the field, there were fascinating stories yet to be told: the stories of contemporary women artists. It was Mao Zedong who said, 'Women hold up half the sky', but my experiences have revealed a gap between the egalitarian socialist dream and the realities for women today.

In 1998 in China, the popular song *Women are Tigers* warned men about powerful, bossy women.[3] In a patrilineal culture with a strong tradition of female subordination, to be a 'tiger girl' is to subvert expectations imposed from birth. Historically, and still today, Chinese women have struggled with this in various ways. Rural women in Hunan Province invented a secret written language, *Nüshu*, to write the emotional truths of their lives.[4] Some of the artists I encountered could be described as working in their own personal versions of Nüshu, developing a visual syntax to communicate their experiences as women. Others would reject such categorisation, working in a manner more influenced by Chinese traditional modes of image-making, or by internationalist art practice.

I wanted answers to my most pressing questions: What shapes the ways that these artists think about their practice? How do they navigate an artworld in post-Global Financial Crisis flux, in a society of such breathlessly rapid social transformation? How does the collectivist past influence the aspirational present? Artists of the post-Cultural Revolution generation are afforded opportunities never available to their older peers: they can study abroad; they are often savvy and entrepreneurial, positioning themselves cleverly in a global marketplace; they can connect with international artists, exhibitions and current debates with a click of a mouse or a sweep of a Smartphone. International curators seek them out. Chinese collectors are beginning to buy their works. What does all this mean for the state of contemporary art in China, and most especially for female artists, in an artworld which my experiences revealed to be a testosterone-fuelled domain, in which a handful of influential artists had developed reputations (and riches) like rock stars?

As I visited galleries and studios I had a growing belief in the importance of collecting the stories of three generations of women. Firstly, I was intrigued by those who had grown up during the Cultural Revolution, the tumultuous days of the 1980s, and the underground art scene leading up to the *China/ Avant-garde* exhibition of 1989. These women, many married to artists, architects or film-makers, experienced the excitement as well as the fear of those days, recalling clandestine meetings and secret exhibitions of 'apartment art'. Often, however, their participation was somewhat circumscribed. Qin Fengling, married to artist Wang Luyan, recalled that her role was to cook meals for the men, and to try to keep the noise down so the police did not arrive. Even today she finds it hard to acknowledge herself as an artist with a career as significant as her husband's.

Secondly, I heard the different stories of those who had been children in the 1980s, the first generation influenced by western popular culture during Deng Xiaoping's transformation of China. The world in which they came of age was one of increasing prosperity, as bicycles gave way to BMWs and China was overtaken by a spirit of get-rich-quick entrepreneurialism. Many artists in their thirties have mixed feelings about the dramatic changes they have witnessed, some expressing nostalgia for the apparently simpler world of their own childhood. And what of the new generation? Young artists for whom the Cultural Revolution seems as far distant as the Qing Dynasty often know nothing of events which galvanised the previous generation, such as the Tiananmen Square Massacre. They think of themselves as more global than Chinese. How do these different generational experiences influence their practice as artists?

The sheer number of artists working in China at any one time is almost unimaginable, and this book emerged from my conversations with more than thirty of them. They spoke willingly, often with surprising frankness, about their lives. In many cases they are more disturbed by the effects of the global art market on the authenticity and honesty of artists' production than with issues of political censorship – their concerns and interests are not necessarily those that western observers expect. Some are internationally famous, and others are as yet little known. Some have works in major private and public collections and others are emerging, seeking representation, teaching or working in a state enterprise as well as making art. I have selected artists whose work I believe in, who have interesting stories to tell, and who represent a diversity of artistic forms, backgrounds and conceptual intentions. No doubt some readers will question my choices, however, this group of artists is representative of the wider field. It includes painters and photographers, sculptors and performance artists, traditionalists and innovators, artists re-interpreting Chinese culture and tradition, and others whose gaze is focused on a world beyond. The separate stories of each artist are grouped to represent particular themes, traditions and tendencies in contemporary Chinese art.

Thoughtful, reflective, making considered and deliberate choices, they traverse difficult terrain. Sometimes they are ambushed by male colleagues who do not expect them to be serious. Sometimes, in a process familiar to women everywhere, they undermine or sabotage themselves. Drinking tea in their studios, I encouraged these women to talk about their lives, family histories and artistic ambitions. I wanted to provide a space in which they could express their ideas about what drives their work, in their own words (in most cases with the assistance of a translator), whilst at the same time I have endeavoured to place their work in art historical, social and political contexts.

I learned quickly to abandon notions of shared assumptions about gender. The history of feminism in China is entirely different to its western narrative, as will be its future trajectory. This was brought home to me in my second conversation with young Beijing artist Gao Rong, who works with embroidery, creating trompe l'oeil sculptures. Knowing that it may take us into difficult territory, I asked: 'You have made a choice to work with a traditionally female art form. You have taken something from the domestic sphere and put it into the high art sphere. In doing so are you intending to examine how our society values the work of women?' Gao Rong took the wind out of my sails, saying flatly, 'No. It's just that I am really good at embroidery, that's all.' I was to experience this conversational dead-end many times in China as I broached the subject of gender, or used the term 'feminism' in discussions with women artists. Many Chinese women see a western feminist paradigm as alien to their own experience. Some western commentators believe that feminism as a coherent political movement never emerged there,[4] but this is a gross over-simplification of a much more complex reality. A very specific Chinese history, embedded in colonialism, post-colonial discourses, and changing notions of gender after 1949 influenced masculine–feminine binaries. From foot-bound

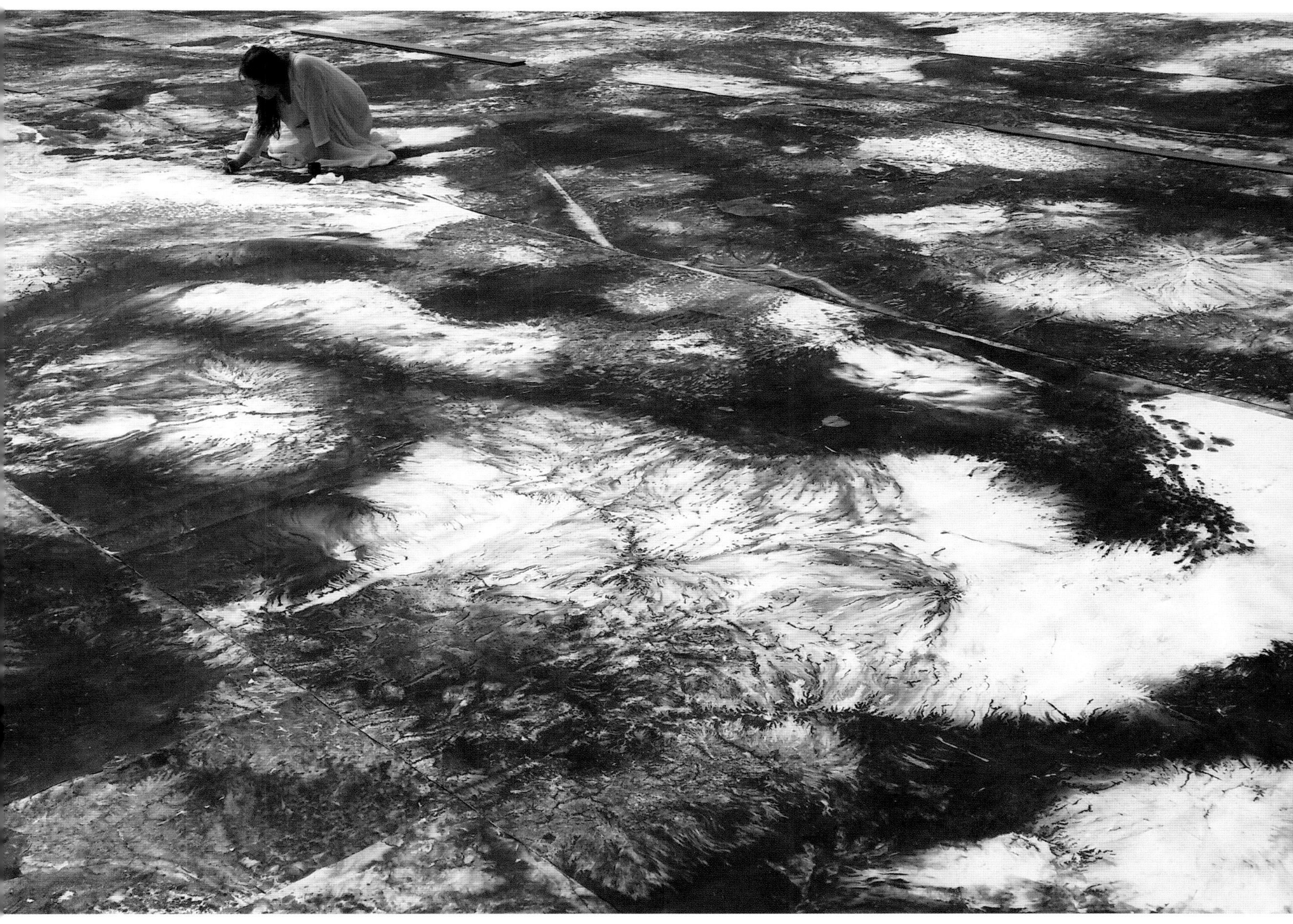

'little lotus' to the Modernist '*xin nuxing*' (new woman),[5] from revolutionary heroine to contemporary 'factory girl' operating in the global economy, Chinese women have experienced radical change in three generations.[5] It would be facile to expect that theories of gender would follow the same trajectory as in the West. I suspected in the end that Gao's reluctance to acknowledge a gendered reading of her practice was due more to wariness of being pigeon-holed, which, understandably, she resists. After a few such experiences I learned not to impose western paradigms on women who think very differently. They can speak for themselves. Despite our differences, however, in this cross-cultural dialogue between women, we found much common ground, and most of our conversations were punctuated by laughter.

Bingyi working on large-scale ink works
in the mountains outside Beijing
image courtesy the artist

NOTES

1 According to live information on http://www.worldometers.info/world-population/china-population/ accessed 1 November 2015

2 Tinari, Philip, interviewed for *Art Radar Journal* available at http://artradarjournal.com/2014/01/16/beyond-official-culture-philip-tinari-on-chinese-contemporary-art-interview/ accessed 19 January 2015. Philip Tinari is the director of the Ullens Center for Contemporary Art in Beijing, and the co-founder of *Leap: the International Art Magazine of Contemporary China*

3 Chen, Minglu, 2011, *Tiger Girls: Women and Enterprises in the People's Republic of China,* Routledge, UK, USA, Canada

4 See Chapter 8 for a discussion of *Nüshu* and its influence on two contemporary artists, Tao Aimin and Ma Yanling

5 For a useful discussion of Chinese feminism in the 20th century, see Barlow, Tani E (ed) *Gender Politics in Modern China* Duke University Press, Durham and London, 1993

INTRODUCTION

'Make the past serve the present and foreign things serve China' (Mao Zedong)

China is experiencing a whirlwind of change so rapid that its future trajectory is unforeseeable. Pundits proffer contradictory prophecies. Some confidently predict an economic crash: 'Any day now,' they have been saying for the last few years. Others suggest, with equal confidence, that China will at any moment achieve global dominance. Few would now forecast democratic reforms, given the hyper-vigilance of the internet censors and recent crackdowns on artists, writers, feminists and human rights lawyers. If there is any certainty in China, it is that change is constant, and that Chinese people – especially the younger generation – have become adept at navigating a fluxing, unpredictable world. Globalisation and urbanisation have swept away the revolutionary past, ushering in an unstable world characterised by continuing upheaval.

The rapid social change resulting from China's embrace of a free market economy – piously referred to by Communist Party officialdom as 'Socialism with Chinese characteristics' – brought unexpected personal freedoms to people accustomed to collectivism. Even the language changed, reflecting new realities. The word 'comrade' is now part of the lexicon of an emerging gay subculture, giving foreigners who learned their Chinese from Mao-era textbooks some potentially awkward moments. *New Yorker* reporter Evan Osnos points out that the word for 'ambition' in Chinese is 'ye xin' – literally, 'wild heart'. In the past this term had pejorative overtones, but in the new China the word exploded in popularity, appearing in self-help books, business courses, advertisements and TV dating shows.[1]

At the same time, the communications revolution changed people's lives dramatically. In 2004, China Mobile began to use the slogan 'My Turf, My Decision'[2] to promote its M-Zone mobile phone service to consumers between the ages of fifteen and twenty-five, linking the possibilities of communication with the dangerous notion of personal freedom. Two of the world's largest internet companies, Tencent and Baidu, are based in China. Internet dating, microblogging, and online shopping exploded in popularity. Despite Beijing's attempt to tightly control the online world with its Great Firewall, Chinese people embraced their new identities as 'netizens' with zeal. With all of these changes came tectonic shifts in the social geology.

Just as every aspect of society and social organisation has changed, so too has Chinese art. Critic Barbara Pollack was shocked by what she described as the '*über*-confidence' of the Chinese artists she encountered when she first travelled to China in the early years of this century. She asked Wang Qingsong to explain how he had succeeded in becoming a postmodern photographer, emerging from a culture that had been completely isolationist for thirty years under Mao. His reply is instructive: 'If you define modernism by art movements, that may seem true... But if you define modernism as grand utopian schemes promulgated by totalitarian leaders, then we were at the center of things and you Americans were on the sidelines.'[3]

Since its emergence in the years after Mao's death, Chinese contemporary art has continually reinvented itself, finding new audiences both inside and outside China. Arne Glimcher, founder of Pace Gallery,[4] believes the Western narrative is essentially ended, whilst the Chinese is just beginning. 'Just as China is the future, their art is the future... I'm not sure the West can compete,' he said in 2010.[5] Contemporary Chinese artists now have a reach far beyond China – their work has made a significant contribution to international art practices and discourses, in the process becoming a global commodity. Artists in China combine the acquired visual language of the international artworld with autochthonous art forms, materials and techniques. They are endlessly inventive in applying their own rich traditions and complex histories to new forms. Art critic Richard Vine quotes an old Maoist maxim: 'Make the past serve the present and foreign things serve China.'[6]

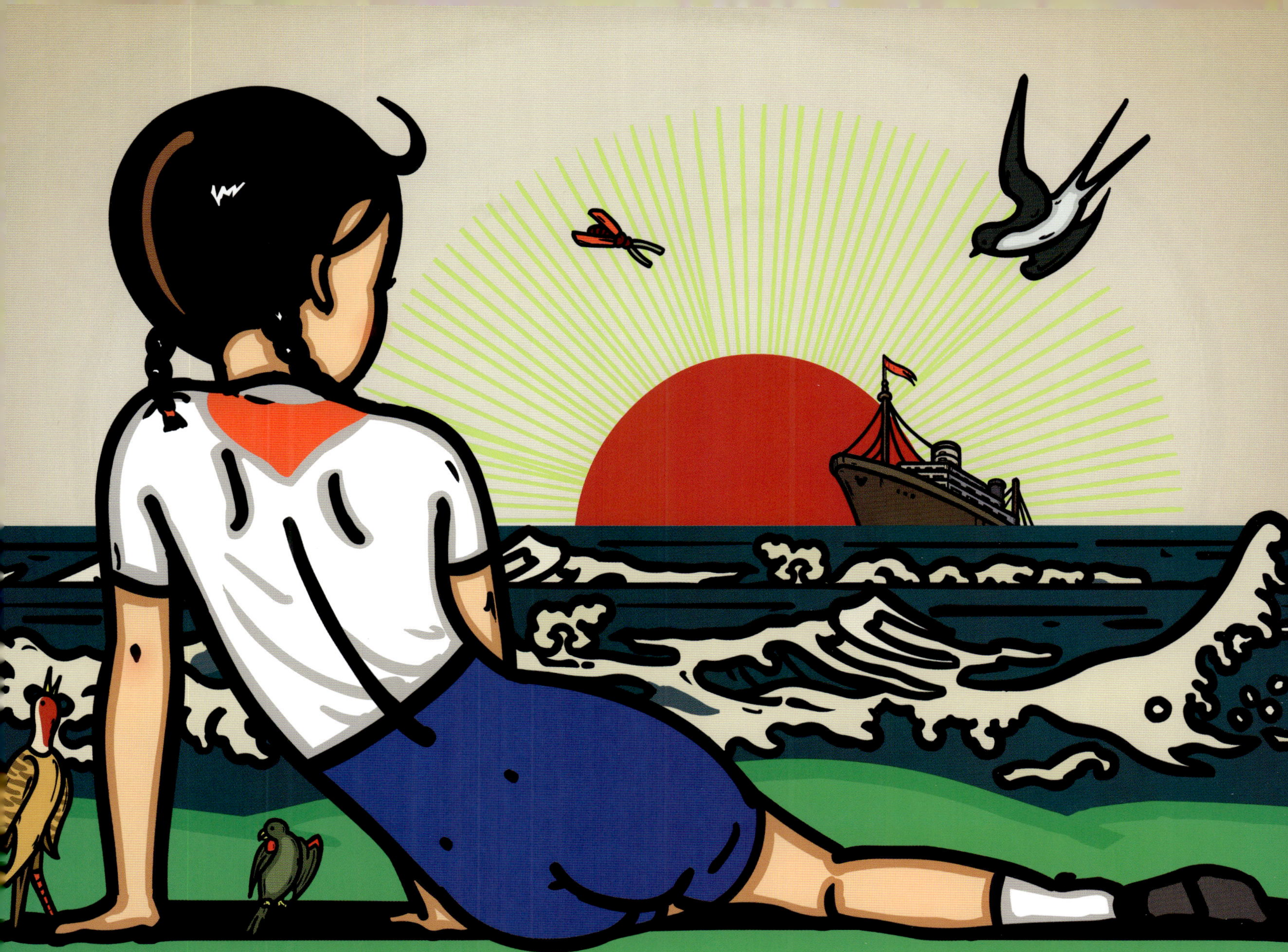

It is the specific historical, political and economic context of the People's Republic of China in a time of dramatic transformation that makes it particularly interesting. 'Art in China began on a clean slate after the Cultural Revolution,' says Glimcher.[7] The reality is a little more complex, but the astonishing fact is that a group of avant-garde artists, who emerged after the end of the Cultural Revolution and thirty years of Soviet Socialist Realism, discovered Modernism and Postmodernism all at once. They came blinking into the light of a globalising late twentieth-century world, and began almost immediately to develop inventive ways of combining traditional modes of expression with contemporary international art practices such as performance, photography and installation art.

The resulting collision of east and west, past and present, and tradition and innovation produced artists who applied their technical virtuosity, honed in the powerhouse Chinese art academies, to work that reflected on their own histories. The fact that labour and materials remain comparatively cheap allows artists to produce works on a scale of ambition almost unimaginable in Europe, the United States, or Australia. The art that emerged from China in the 1990s caught the attention of international audiences surprised by the ironic stance of the Political Pop and Cynical Realist painters. Today, beyond the post-traumatic stress syndrome of the Cultural Revolution generation, the work of younger artists resists easy categorisation. Creating work that is complex, diverse, and multi-layered, some have embraced new media, installation,

Bu Hua
Meet you at the end of the time 2012
giclée print on wood
60 x 84 cm
image courtesy the artist

performance and video, whilst others have developed new forms of painting and sculpture. They question old binaries between art and design, 'high' culture and commerce, in the process creating an entirely new sensibility. Themes of urbanisation, environmental destruction, rural poverty and new class divisions have emerged as preoccupations in contemporary Chinese art.[8]

This is the complex world of the artists who inhabit these pages. They are navigating new terrain, and their work charts this evolutionary process. It is sometimes a source of frustration to Chinese artists that western observers expect their artworks to be overtly political, in the manner of well-known 'dissident' artists such as Ai Weiwei, or those who first surged onto the international art scene in the wake of the Cultural Revolution. Cao Fei, who appears in Chapter 1, deflects such questions as rather uninteresting. For Hong Kong Art Basel, in March 2015, she created *Same Old, Brand New,* animated projections onto the ICC Tower on Victoria Harbour inspired by the 1980s video games of her childhood. Symbols of material aspiration – a house, a diamond, a happy couple – are crushed by a falling block. From an animated sea of skulls, the words 'Game Over' flash across the façade of the skyscraper, pointing to the cynicism of her generation. Interviewed for the *New Yorker*, Cao said, 'Criticizing society, that's the aesthetics of the last generation… When I started making art, I didn't want to do political things. I was more interested in subcultures, in pop culture.'[9] When I began to visit the studios of Chinese artists in early 2011, it was evident that the narrative of Chinese contemporary art generally told in the west is just part of a much more complex and more interesting picture, formed by economic developments and generational differences, international dialogues and diasporic journeys, as much as by politics.

Despite enormous social change and increasing cosmopolitanism, some aspects of traditional culture have proved resistant to change. Confucian family values are so deeply rooted that, in the absence of revolutionary ideology, they have resurfaced, promoted by authorities in the interests of social stability. The first time we met, the artist Lin Tianmiao said, 'There is no feminism in China.' I must have looked askance because she elaborated: 'Mao Zedong said that women hold up half the sky, but we have not arrived at that point yet.'[10] Mao did say that, and the Communists banned foot-binding, prostitution and concubinage as despised relics of the feudal past. Equality of the sexes was enshrined in law, as an essential step in building the socialist utopia. In 1955 Mao said, 'Enable every woman who can work to take her place on the labour front, under the principle of equal pay for equal work. This should be done as quickly as possible.'[11] As a result of these apparently enlightened policies, however, expressions of gender difference were suppressed for thirty years. In the Party's attempt to erase individualism, family relationships and sexual desire were subjugated to the needs of the state. In the post-Mao era, the sexual marketplace returned 'with a flourish,'[12] exemplified by a notorious video shot by Cui Xiuwen in the women's restrooms of a Beijing Karaoke Lounge.[13]

As the cradle-to-grave economic support of the 'iron rice bowl' was dismantled, women were disproportionately affected by the collapse of pension funds, subsidised or free education, and medical care. In the Chinese workplace, women have made gains in recent years, but in politics the presence of women is negligible, despite the inclusion of two women in the latest Politburo – the first time since the Cultural Revolution that it has not been entirely male.[14] In 2014, less than five percent of the party's central committee of two hundred officials were women, a figure lower than during Mao's reign.[15]

Issues of gender have dominated public conversation in recent years. 'What do women want?' wail media commentators, almost always referring to the (possibly apocryphal) young woman on a TV dating show who famously said that she would rather weep in a BMW than smile on the back of a bicycle. There is public angst over materialism, greed, and the loss of Confucian values, and the term *sheng nu* ('left-over woman'), referring to unmarried women over the age of twenty-seven is now common parlance. China's state-run feminist agency, the China All-Women's Federation, published a statement which has been quoted again and again: 'Pretty girls don't need a lot of education to marry into a rich and powerful family, but girls with an average or ugly appearance will find it difficult. These kind of girls hope to further their education in order to increase their competitiveness. The tragedy is, they don't realise that as women age they are worth less and less, so by the time they get their M.A or Ph.D., they are already old, like yellowed pearls.'[16]

In 2015, on the eve of International Women's Day, five young feminist activists were arrested and detained, facing charges of 'picking quarrels' and disturbing the social harmony. They were preparing to hand out leaflets protesting sexual harassment on public transport. Professor Wang Zhen, of the University of Michigan, has studied the modern and contemporary history of Chinese women. In a speech at the Brookings Institute on April 3, 2015, she discussed the tensions that gave rise to these events, and the limitations on NGOs working in China.[17] The 'Feminist Five' were later released, perhaps in part due to the international outcry. Wang Zhen suggests that the crackdown on feminist and human rights activists, part of a wider reaction against unwelcome western influence in education and social policy, might have the

unintended consequence of politicising a younger generation of students. That remains to be seen – feminism in China is very, very far from mainstream.

In the artworld, as elsewhere, women in China are dealing with complex social realities. Some female artists have achieved great success, establishing international careers. Recently there has been considerable interest in the work of women artists, with major survey shows of established artists such as Lin Tianmiao (at the Asia Society New York in 2012) and Yin Xiuzhen (at Pace Beijing in 2013), as well as curated shows such as Bowdoin College Museum of Art's *Breakthrough: Work by Contemporary Chinese Women Artists* in 2013. Yin Xiuzhen and Gao Rong were selected for the 2013 Moscow Biennale, Cao Fei for the 2015 Venice Biennale. There is no shortage of opportunities for audiences to engage with their work. Yet despite the global reputations of some artists in this book – and growing interest in all of them – they are not as well-known as their male counterparts.

Their stories are compelling. Liang Yuanwei recounted her experience as a young painter trying (and initially failing) to persuade any gallery to give her an exhibition. A gallery director told her, 'There are already too many female painters. You had better become a photographer.'[18] Her response was a notorious series of photographs, *Don't Forget To Say You Love Me When You Fuck Me*. By 2011, however, she was selected for the China Pavilion at the Venice Biennale, an experience she found troubling. She was left with a sense that she had been chosen to represent all women to make China look progressive in the eyes of the world. In 2014, she had a solo show at Pace Gallery in London – with her paintings. Liang's experiences serve to illustrate some of the contradictions that emerge in an investigation of gender in China. On one hand it might seem that female artists from the People's Republic are the flavour of the month. On the other hand, their work is known by a limited audience. In considering how they are positioned in the Chinese and international artworld, it is instructive to count the ratio of male to female artists in recent publications in the field. The result reveals a startling imbalance.[19]

In the hype and hustle of an over-inflated art market prior to the Global Financial Crisis, the gargantuan figures who reigned supreme in China were the Political Pop and Cynical Realist painters who had come to fame and fortune in the 1990s. In those heady days, when painters seemed to be making overnight reputations and huge international sales, female artists such as those interviewed for this book had been overshadowed by their male counterparts. Now, when the tropes of Pop-inspired Mao imagery seem tired, it is time for their work to be seen and their voices to be heard.

—Luise Guest, Sydney, November, 2015

NOTES

1 Osnos, Evan 2014 *The Age of Ambition: Chasing Fortune, Truth and Faith in the New China*, Farrar, Straus and Giroux, New York
2 ibid. (41) an account of the 'collision of two forces: aspiration and authoritarianism.'
3 Pollack, Barbara 2010 *The Wild East: An American Art Critic's Adventures in China*, Timezone 8, Beijing
4 Pace Gallery (London, New York and Beijing) is a contemporary art gallery representing many of the most significant international artists and estates. Founded by Arne Glimcher in Boston in 1960, Pace has introduced many renowned artists' work to the public.
5 Glimcher, Arne 2010, interviewed for *Blouin Art Info*, available at https://www.youtube.com/watch?v=W1Xz4WHLSYc accessed 5 November 2014
6 Vine, Richard 2011 *New China, New Art,* Prestel, Munich, London, New York, (9)
7 Glimcher, Arne 2010 interviewed for *Blouin Art Info*, available at https://www.youtube.com/watch?v=W1Xz4WHLSYc accessed 5 November 2014
8 Smith, Terry 2011 *Contemporary Art: World Currents*, Laurence King, London (165)
9 Cao Fei, interviewed by Christopher Beam, for 'Beyond Ai Weiwei: How China's Artists Handle Politics (Or Avoid Them)', *New Yorker*, March 27 2015 available at http://www.newyorker.com/news/news-desk/ai-weiwei-problem-political-art-china accessed 29 March 2015
10 In conversation with the writer, December 2012
11 Introductory note to 'On Widening the Scope of Women's Work in the Agricultural Co-operative Movement' (1955), '*The Socialist Upsurge in China's Countryside*' Chinese edition Vol. I
12 Mann, Susan L 2011 *Gender and Sexuality in Modern Chinese History*, Cambridge University Press (61–64)
13 Cui Xiuwen's work, *Lady's Room*, documented sex-workers with a hidden camcorder and caused a sensation. See Chapter 1 for a full discussion of the work and reactions to it.
14 http://www.reuters.com/article/2012/11/15/china-congress-politburo-idUSL3E8MF1VR20121115 Reuters report on Thursday November 15 2012 accessed 13 November 2014
15 Koyama, Jill 2014 'Feminism in China: Risky but Rising' *Ms Magazine* (Blog) August 25, 2014, available at http://msmagazine.com/blog/2014/08/25/feminism-in-china-risky-but-rising/ accessed 28 March 2015
16 Hong Fincher, Leta 2012 'China's Left-over Women' *New York Times*, October 11, 2012, quoting an item from the website of the All-China Women's Federation from March 2011, available at http://www.nytimes.com/2012/10/12/opinion/global/chinas-leftover-women.html?_r=0 accessed 28 October 2014
17 Wang Zhen interviewed for *China Change* on April 11 2015 available at http://chinachange.org/2015/04/12/detention-of-five-chinese-feminist-activists-at-the-juncture-of-beijing20-an-interview-with-professor-wang-zheng/ accessed 13 April 2015
18 In conversation with the writer, May 2011
19 For example, *From Heaven to Earth: Chinese Contemporary Painting* is a large and beautifully produced volume with text by art historian Lorenzo de Sassoli Bianchi. Of the nineteen featured painters, just one is female. An exhibition of the Rubell Family Collection, *28 Chinese Artists* in Miami in 2013 contained just two women, Fang Lu and Li Shurui. A major international survey show such as the Metropolitan Museum's 2013 *Ink Art: Past as Present in Contemporary China* included a ratio of only two female artists to thirty-three men.

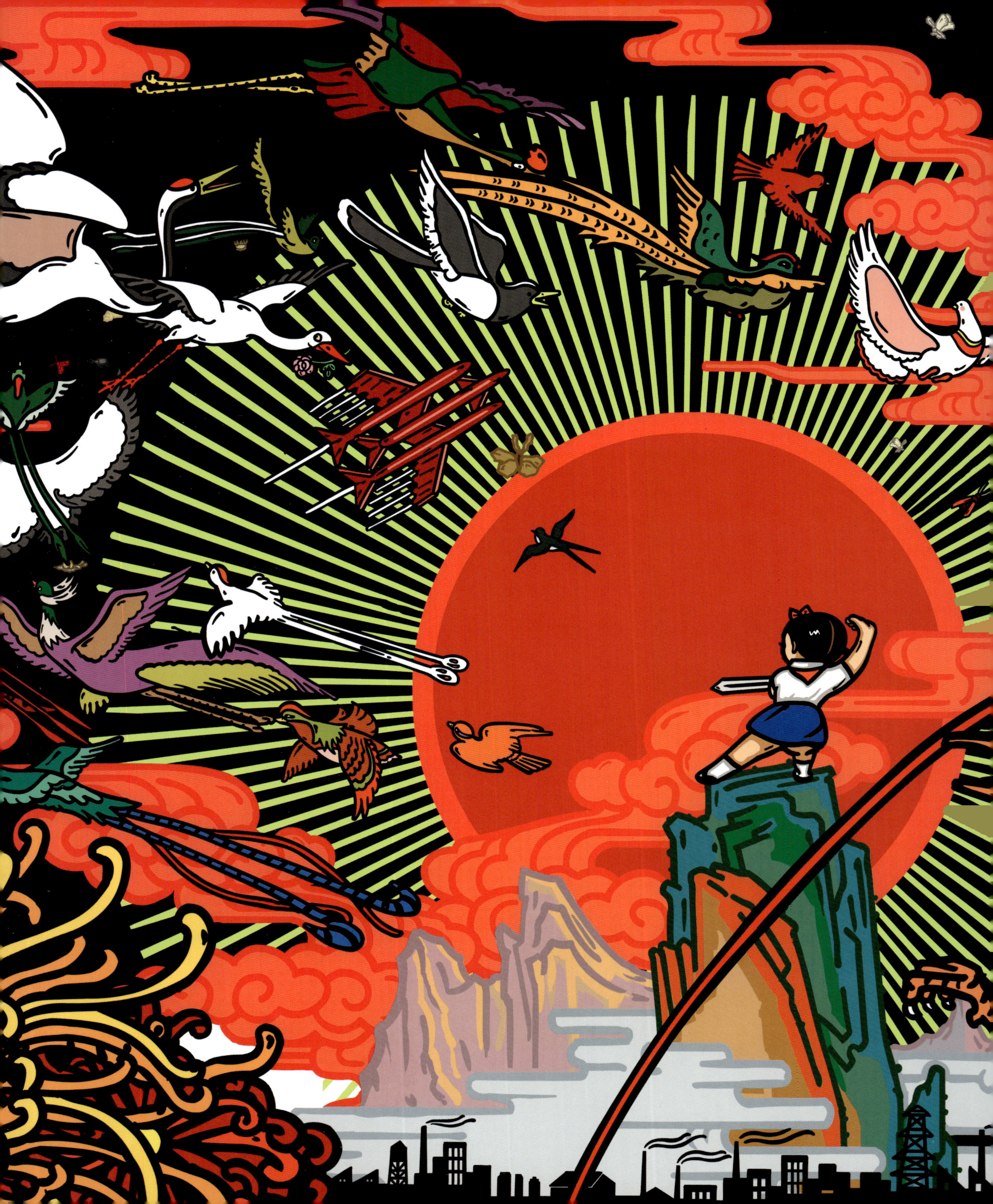

ALTER EGOS AND AVATARS
Bu Hua, Cui Xiuwen and Cao Fei

Dramatic economic development has resulted in the rapid unfolding of new possibilities and subjects for artists born into the generation who came of age in a new China. They have forged careers in a society that some believe has lost its way in a headlong rush to consumerist acquisition and the pursuit of wealth. Unlike the previous generation, for whom there were no galleries, and no art market in which to sell their work, artists today inhabit a globalised world in which Chinese contemporary art is a hot commodity. Amongst the new possibilities, this change brings its own pressures and paradoxes.

In encounters over five years with Chinese artists of this generation, some common themes emerged. They have a restless desire to blur boundaries – between fine art and design, between the artworld and the commercial marketplace, between genres and conventions of artistic practice, and between eastern and western modes of expression. These are artists who have little or no first-hand experience of the tragedy and bitterness of the Cultural Revolution, growing up during a period in which an isolationist Cold War mentality gradually collapsed. They are generally not making work about democratic freedoms, despite what some western commentators might wish and expect Chinese artists to do. They do, however, make reference in their work to the issues that concern them: from materialism and urbanisation to environmental degradation; from sexuality and motherhood to the impact of biotechnologies on the human body. Many are deeply interested in a revival of spirituality, in particular the traditions of Buddhism and Taoism.

The three artists featured in this chapter experienced the conformist collectivism of the Maoist era in their youth, but grew to adulthood in a society that was disconcertingly different, utterly transformed by the transition to a market economy and greater openness. Their response to this new China is to look backwards, with a degree of nostalgia, and also forwards, with considerable foreboding. Quick-wittedness and adaptability are required to negotiate the complexities of this brave new world. Reflecting upon the past and imagining the future, each has invented a second self, a *doppelganger* who mirrors her own journeys through a changing Chinese landscape. Bu Hua and Cui Xiuwen have each invented an alter ego – a 'Young Pioneer', a member of the Chinese children's organisation run by the Communist Youth League – to represent aspects of female experience. Cao Fei's approach is different. Her avatar, China Tracy, had adventures and encounters, even romantic liaisons, in the virtual world of Second Life.

Each of these artists mines her own female experience, while exploring disturbing facets of contemporary China. And each in her own way defies the limitations traditionally imposed upon Chinese women. Bu Hua's digital alter ego prances through a beautiful but nightmarish world of cities that never stop growing, like mutating cancerous cells. She expertly blends cuteness and pop culture influences with surrealism and satire. Cao Fei experiments freely with forms as diverse as digital media, video, and the virtual reality of Second Life; and genres ranging from the musical to the zombie movie. Cui Xiuwen has moved from figurative representations of female psychology to a consideration of the spiritual, the ineffable. Her most notorious work, *Lady's Room,* revealed the underbelly of life in the new Chinese mega-cities, when she covertly recorded the conversations of young hostesses in an upscale Beijing karaoke bar, revealing the mundane realities of prostitution and the pragmatism of the women in their 'private' space.

Women of China, a publication of the All-China Women's Federation, described *Lady's Room* as a work 'about the struggles of a young girl growing up in Beijing – or about the rugged roles women sometimes assume in China's rapidly evolving economy.'[1] This 'struggle' connects the work of three very different artists.

Bu Hua
Brave Diligent (detail) 2014
silk wall carpet
300 x 200cm
image courtesy the artist

BU HUA 卜桦

Beijing babes and fearless girls

In Beijing dialect the term *sa mi* means a fearless girl, confident and free from self-doubt. In fact, a girl with 'swagger' said Bu Hua, after conferring with my translator, also a Beijinger. The feisty, self-possessed, small female child she has brought to life in her digital still images, woodblock prints and animations is *sa mi*. Sassy and unafraid, pigtails swinging, she is sometimes depicted smoking a cigarette and staring bravely into the middle distance. In some works she is dressed like a schoolchild of the revolutionary past in a red Young Pioneer scarf and short skirt. In others she runs naked through a strange universe of towering flora and fauna. This character, a key protagonist in almost all Bu Hua's video and still images, is based on the artist as a child – a defiant Young Pioneer, red scarf flying. She bravely navigates the surreal landscape of the new China, encountering strange beasts, mystical forests, hideous pollution and rapacious developers, somehow emerging victorious. She is a more confident version of the artist herself, says Bu Hua, a fearless alter ego.

So who is she really, this brave little girl? 'This girl is wearing the school uniform that I wore when I was at school,' says Bu Hua. 'She is partly me but she has more emotional strength and more freedom.' She represents a yearning for a less complicated past – a nostalgia for a China that may be imaginary and idealised. Bu Hua has become deeply invested in her own creation:

> When I first started creating her all I thought about was creating a cute character, but with the emotion and process of painting I discovered I was in love with this nostalgic Beijing style. I tried different expressions and gestures on her but it didn't feel comfortable. A kind of expressionless look and a kind of 'swagger' came to characterise this girl. I followed my intuition and she took on a life of her own. She came into being in 2006/2007. Before that I was not doing so much painting, and was doing a lot more animation. But some people said to me, 'If all your work is animation then when the lights are out it's just an empty room.'[2]

Stung by this criticism, Bu Hua returned to painting, and to the creation of digital still images, and gradually her character took form. A clever combination of innocence and knowing, cuteness and cunning, playfulness and cynical parody, she fits a twenty-first century zeitgeist: 'I felt that this character is an actual person living in real life but [she] is really also an idealised version of myself. She knows this universe and the rules of this society like the back of her hand.' Through the character she has invented Bu Hua provides a dispassionate commentary on the contemporary world of Beijing and China.

Brave Diligent expresses the artist's anxiety about the social transformation and ecological destruction of China, fusing western and eastern traditions of art and design. The rising or setting sun is a recurring motif, an ironic inversion of how Mao Zedong was often pictured, framed in a nimbus of the sun's rays. Here it suggests an apocalyptic sense of doom. Darkness is coming. The fearless young protagonist, poised on a mountain top like a warrior, is framed by chrysanthemums, symbolising longevity in Chinese tradition, and auspicious coral-pink clouds. Far beneath her, on the horizon, a silhouetted city skyline, its factory chimneys belching smoke, is an ominous portent of the future. Eclectic influences from sources as diverse as Surrealism, Japanese 1920s modernity, contemporary anime and manga, and Art Deco design are evident here. Bu Hua loves Astro Boy and Salvador Dali equally. 'In modern China, how could you not be influenced by this fusion of west and east, this cultural invasion and "soft power"? I am just reflecting this reality,' she says.

Bu Hua was born in 1973, graduating from the Institute of Fine Art, Tsinghua University, Beijing, in 1995. Coming from a family of artists, her father a distinguished printmaker, she was immersed in art from an early age:

Bu Hua in her studio
image courtesy the artist

Bu Hua *(above right)*
Microcosmos 2014
acrylic on canvas
100 cm diameter
image courtesy the artist

Bu Hua *(above far right)*
Playing a Happy Game No. 1 2008
giclée print
100 cm diameter
image courtesy the artist and White Rabbit Gallery

Bu Hua *(right)*
The Water is Deep Here in Beijing I 2010
giclée print
75 x 120 cm
image courtesy the artist

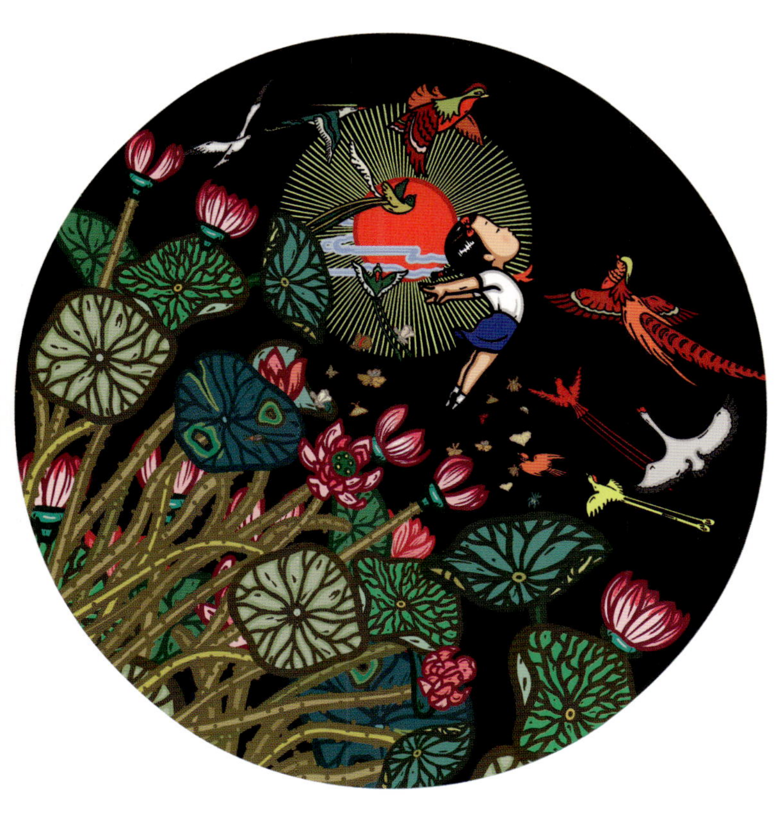

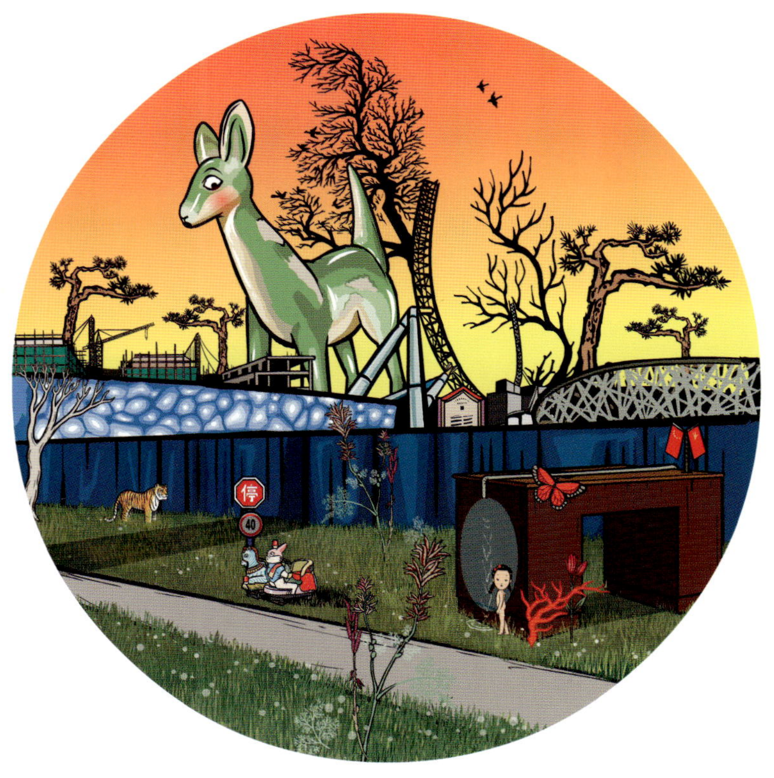
停
40

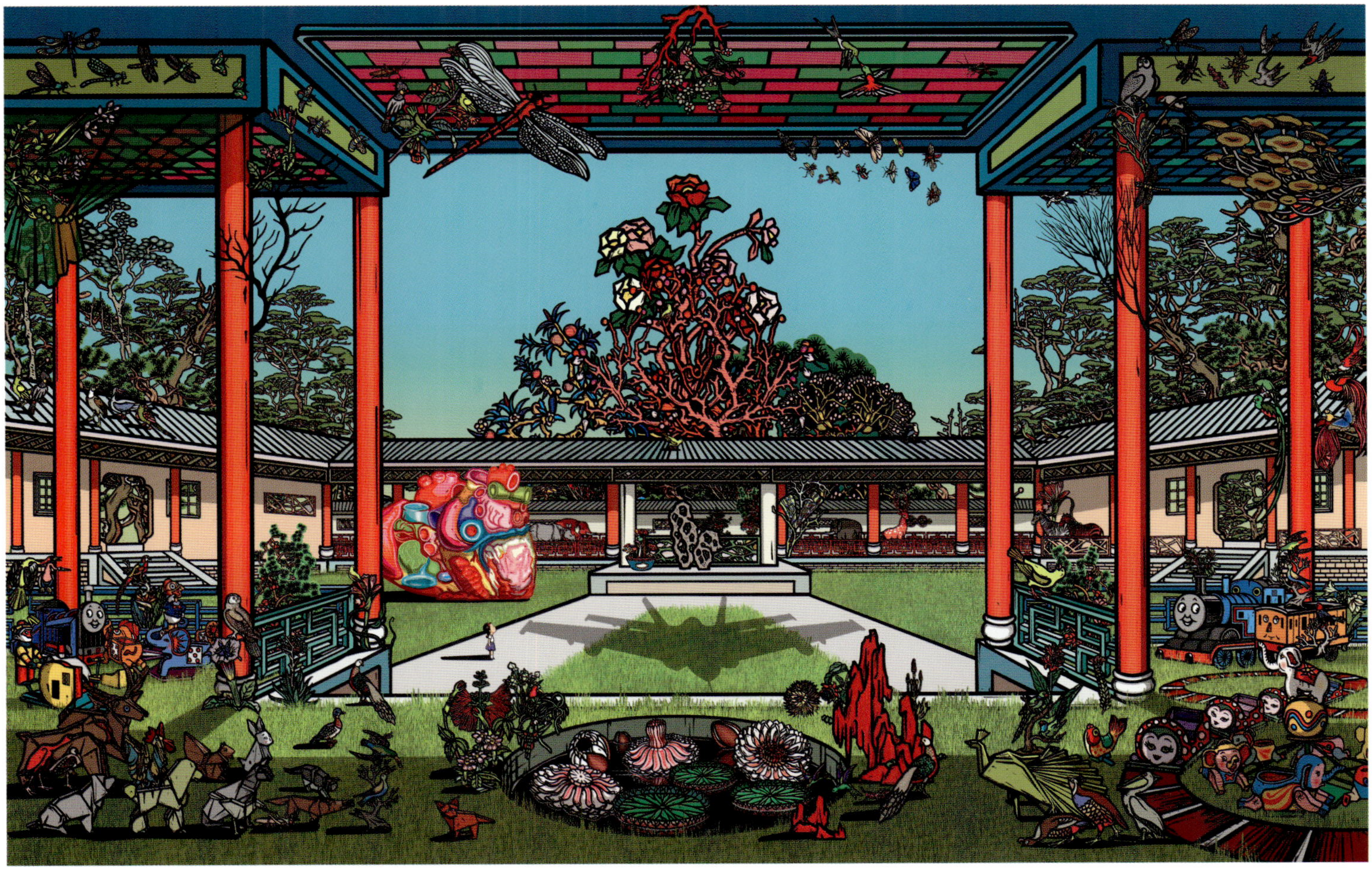

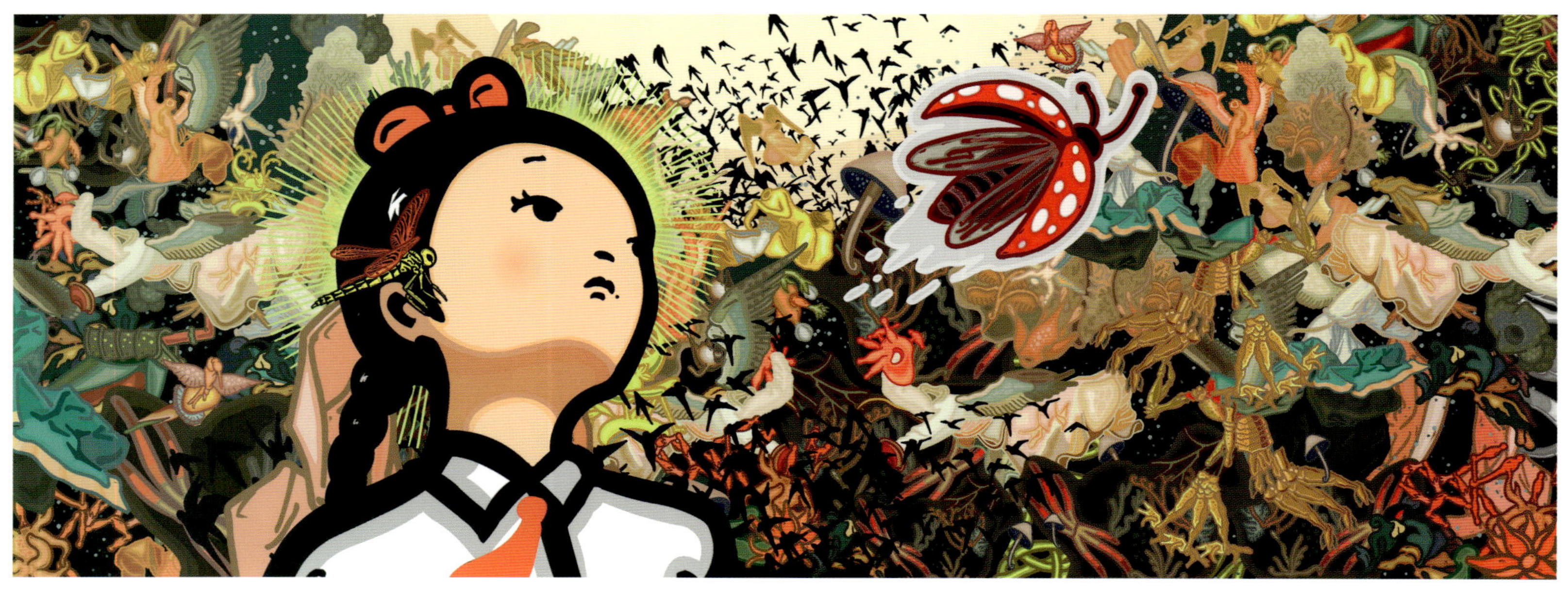

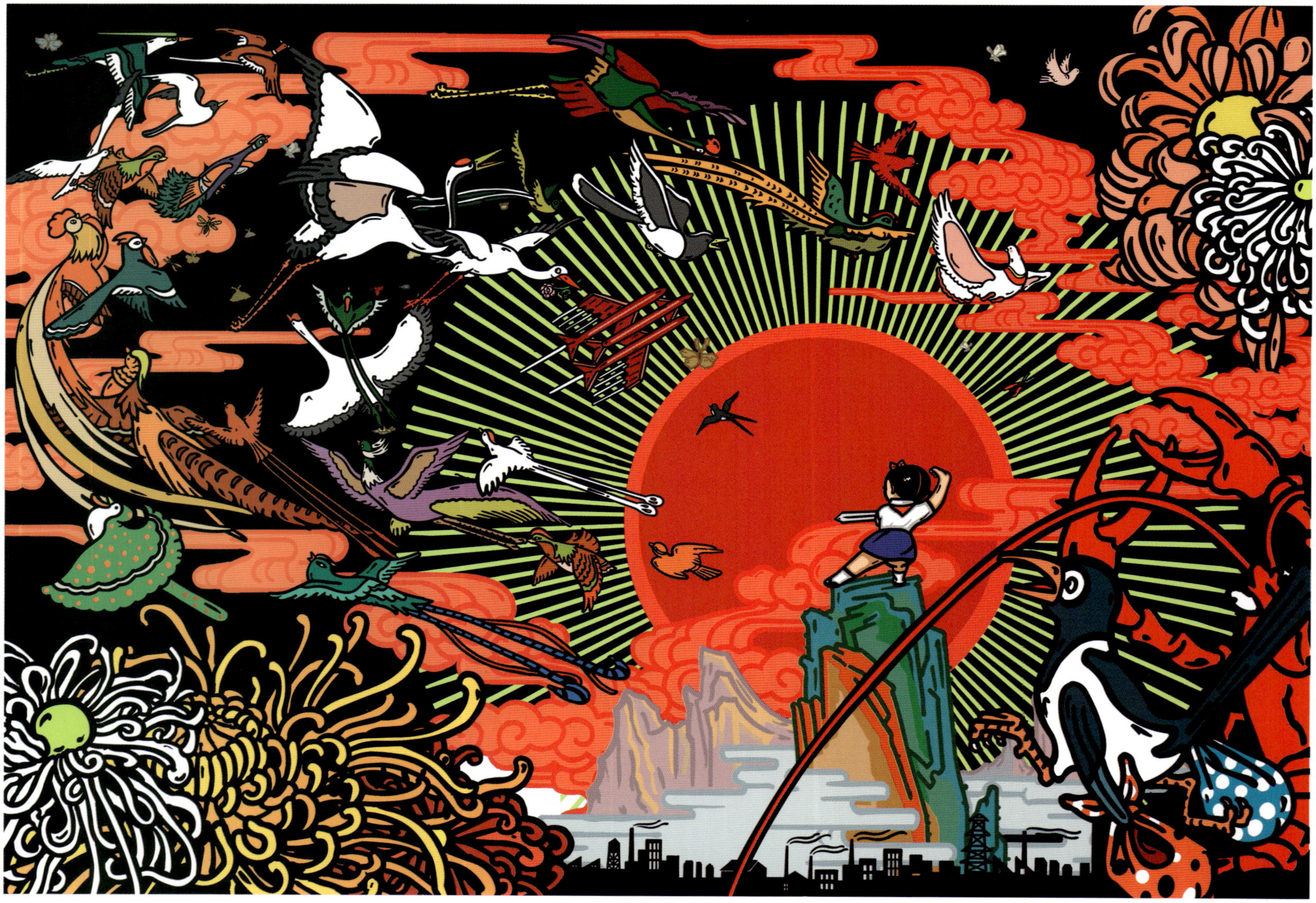

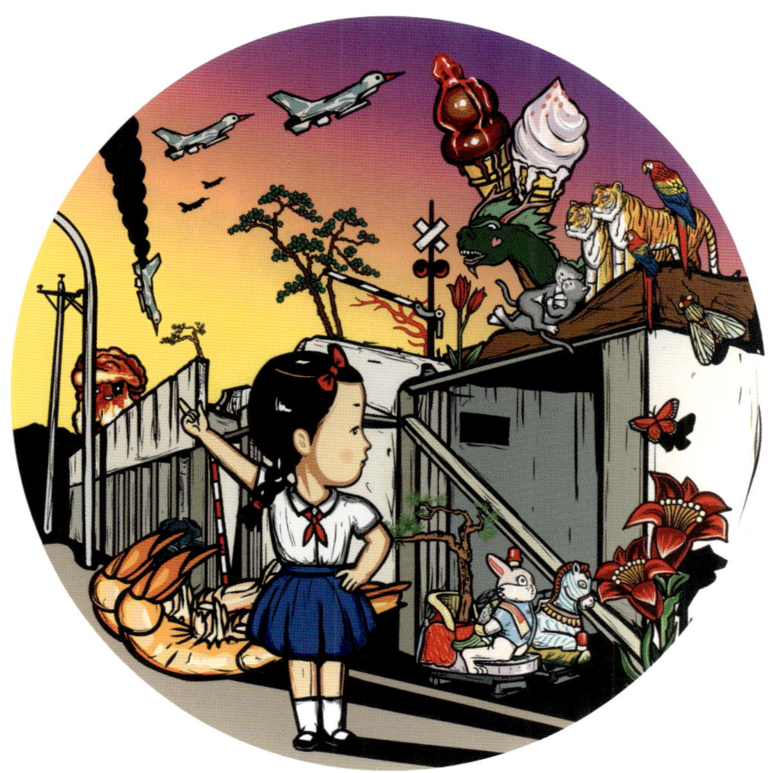

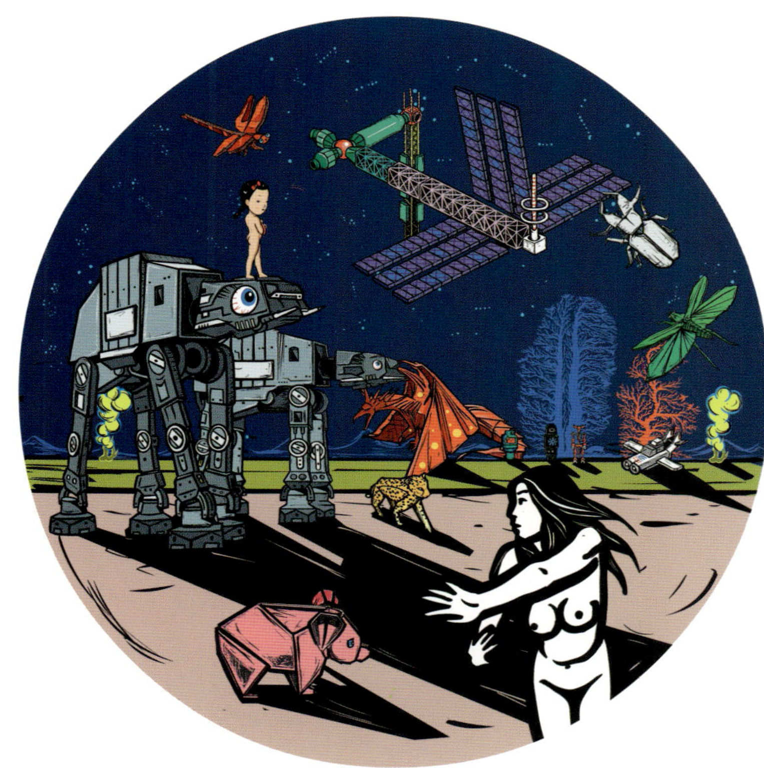

This is the story of how I started. I was born into a family that worked in the arts. My father was a printmaker who made woodcut prints in a traditional style – really detailed, really nice. So, since a very young age I was influenced by the environment in the family. Now when I analyse my love of line I realise it came from my father's influence and his woodblock prints. Lines were the language he used. This is why I really like clear, harsh distinct lines.

Art was a family tradition that she was expected to continue, an expectation that for a long time the young artist was reluctant to fulfil. 'My dad was a professor at the Central Academy for Art and Design, and so I went to a high school called "132 Art High School" to prepare me for that,' she says. Her art career had begun even earlier – she had designed a stamp at the age of ten, had a solo exhibition in Hong Kong at the age of twelve, and designed postcards for the former Ministry of Post and Telecommunications when she was sixteen. Then Bu Hua began her undergraduate degree at Tsinghua University's Institute of Fine Art. 'At the art academy my major was called "Decorative Arts". We were trained to paint wall paintings, and we learned how to use all kinds of materials – oil paint, acrylic, and even house paints.' She gave serious thought to following in her father's footsteps as a printmaker. But, 'you have to be so meticulous and careful as a printmaker,' she says. 'I was interested in creating the same effect in less time. Now I can imitate all kinds of effects using a computer. You can even imitate woodblock printing!'

After graduating in the mid-1990s Bu Hua struggled to find her own style, doubting her vocation:

In the year I graduated, my father died. Some exhibitions were organised in his honour in Germany so I went in his stead. The curator was interested in my works and my brother's as well as my father's. During these exhibitions in Germany I was painting a lot, but was finding that two-dimensional paintings were not expressive enough, so I started to explore other options. At that time the software to create animations was not available so I used my DV recorder to record a lot of small animations and began to write scripts for short live action movies.

In 1997 she encountered the stop-motion films of South African artist William Kentridge at *Documenta* in Kassel. Suddenly, she saw the possibilities of time-based work:

The reason I loved it was [that it was] this bridge between painting and animation, and I wanted so much to combine these two techniques. So in 2001 when it was first available I started using Flash software. I hadn't tried anything like that beforehand. I was actually [still] kind of obsessed with using charcoal to create still images but I didn't think I could do it.

Often described as a pioneer of digital animation in China, Bu Hua discovered the expressive possibilities of animation software, and she was one of the first to use it in an art context, understanding its potential to convey emotional truths about contemporary life in an engaging and dynamic way.

One of the first animations she produced using vector graphics software, *Cat*, in 2002, is a touching five-minute

Bu Hua *(top)*
AD 3012 – 8 2012
giclée print
54 x 375 cm
image courtesy the artist

Bu Hua *(bottom)*
Brave Diligent 2014
silk wall carpet
200 x 300 cm
image courtesy the artist

Bu Hua *(left)*
Beijing Babe Loves Freedom No. 1
2008
giclée print, 100 cm diameter
image courtesy the artist and White Rabbit Gallery

Bu Hua *(right)*
As Soon as China has a Space Station on the Moon it can Begin to Consider Establishing a Communist Party There No. 3 2008
giclée print, 100 cm diameter
image courtesy the artist and White Rabbit Gallery

narrative about the love between a cat and her kitten. The cat is murdered by gangsters and the tiny kitten bravely follows his mother into the underworld to try to bring her back to life. It's a dark story, expressed with her characteristic lightness of touch. Uploaded to an animation website, the short film was seen by thousands of viewers. Bu Hua won Best New Director Award at the 2003 China Qingdao International Animation Week and was short-listed by the 2004 Annecy International Animation Festival in France. She had found her visual language. Each frame of *Cat* is painterly, evoking German Expressionism in its emotive intensity and apparently gestural linear drawing. But it had not been as easy or spontaneous as it appears: 'The cat video was my tenth attempt. It was a whole process of learning the technology.'

When Bu Hua returned to the creation of still images – paintings and giclée prints combining her early training in painting and printmaking with her new knowledge of the possibilities of digital media – her work reveals a confident merging of genres and styles. *What is Left Belongs to You* focuses on a courageous girl riding triumphantly on a dinosaur through an impossibly fertile landscape, like a pigtailed warrior queen emerging from the ocean, accompanied by circling birds. A primeval glade of abundant foliage and opening flowers is punctured by a traffic sign. References to eclectic sources, including the flat decorative patterns of Japanese *ukiyo-e* woodblock prints, 1980s cartoons, and Chinese folk art can be discerned, but Bu Hua has created a visual language entirely her own. Maybe it is a post-apocalyptic world, or maybe just a dream.

There is a sense of innocence betrayed. 'On the surface it's very cute and very lovely,' she says, 'but underneath there is anxiety and pressure.' Bu Hua makes her social commentary in an oblique and metaphoric manner. *The Water is Deep Here in Beijing I* presents us with an apparently innocent world. A Chinese garden and its pavilions are crowded with origami animals, fairy-like creatures and children's toys, including Thomas the Tank Engine. The Young Pioneer, now minute like Alice in Wonderland, gazes skywards. We cannot see the object of her gaze, but the ground is darkened by the ominous shadow of a fighter plane. A giant multi-coloured heart, ventricles severed, lies on the grass behind her. What can this mean? The artist says her work has changed since she became a mother. On one hand there is a new lightness and playfulness, a delight in life and all its joys, but there is also the anxiety and fear of catastrophe that haunts every new parent.

Savage Growth, an animation shown at the 2008 Shanghai Biennale, employs her crisp graphic style in an allegory of industrialisation, pollution and militarisation. Bu's heroine, armed with a slingshot, takes aim at flocks of white birds which prove, on closer examination, to be military aircraft. Twisted trees grow out of pools of oil, and a row of sexy foxes (fox spirits, in Chinese lore, are dangerous seductresses) shimmy and sway backwards and forwards to a mechanical sound track like the rhythmic metallic noise of a factory assembly line. Bu Hua said, 'People in China pay a lot of attention to the past and the future, but it's really kind of forbidden to pay a lot of attention to what is happening now, in real life. So in *Savage Growth* I show this character's anxiety, and the fact that she cannot do much about change and development. I am showing what is happening in China at this exact moment, what is happening now.'

LV Forest, presented at the first Shenzhen Independent Animation Biennial, also features her young schoolgirl, dancing demurely at first and then riding on skeletal monsters, in a savage observation of China's rampant consumerism, competition and inequality. Graphically sexual, the work is a noir fairytale. Naked women fight each other, reminding us of news footage of wives attacking mistresses in the streets of Chinese cities, tearing off their clothes, slapping and kicking them. The black background is a metaphor for the bleakness of contemporary life. Despite the shiny promises of a capitalist consumerist paradise, it all turns to dust.

AD3012 was included in *Peach Blossom Spring: Cacotopia*, a curated exhibition shown in Guangzhou and Darwin in 2014. A traditional Chinese fable, *The Peach Blossom Spring* was written at a time of political instability and conflict, during the years between the collapse of the Han dynasty in 220 CE and the Sui dynasty's reunification of north and south in 589.[3] It recounts a simple fisherman's chance discovery of a Utopia at the end of a river (or spring) where people and animals live in harmony with nature, a kind of *Shangri-la*, removed from the outside world. Once he left this magical place, he was never able to find his way back there. A *cacotopia*, on the other hand, is an imagined place of the worst possible government: the opposite, in the corrupt and incompetent nature of its political institutions, of Thomas More's ideal commonwealth. Bu Hua reflects on aspects of our digital age, so pregnant with possibility, so filled with hope, and yet with such a sense of inevitable doom and despair at its centre. The charm and visual inventiveness of her images and animations almost disguises the seriousness of her intent, and her critical view of China's institutions.

Bu Hua retains a romantic view of the sublime nature of art: 'Art is not just my way of living, but also gives me a kind of spiritual peace. Some people turn to religion, but I guess you could say that art is my religion. I am not really a spiritual person but art is where I find my spirituality.' Her young protagonist is often represented with a halo-like nimbus surrounding her head. Bu Hua has created a saint for a postmodern Paradise Lost.

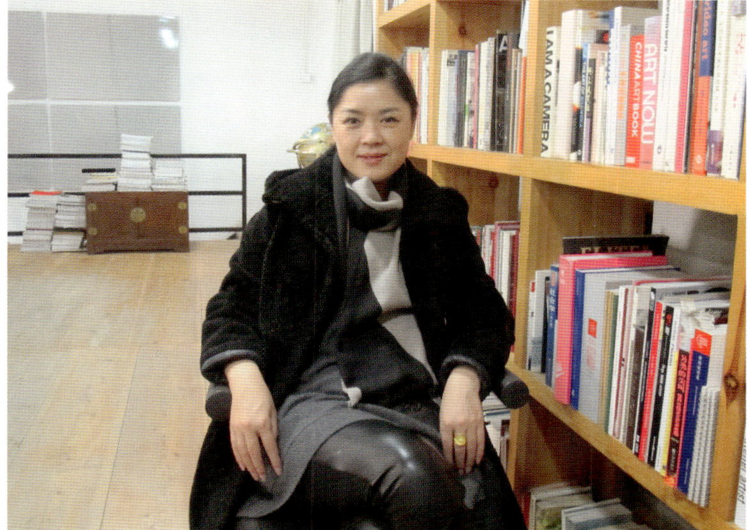

CUI XIUWEN 崔岫闻

Angels and Sirens

Cui Xiuwen is one of very few women identified by both Chinese and western commentators as a feminist artist. In conversation she revealed her reservations about this label, and some of the thinking behind new developments in her practice.

In 2002, her video *Lady's Room* was the subject of the first lawsuit in Chinese contemporary art. Her work shocked viewers with its frank documentation of prostitutes in the restroom of a Beijing nightclub, counting their money and arranging to meet clients. A teacher at the Guangzhou Academy of Fine Arts claimed that the shock he experienced when viewing this work at the Guangdong Art Museum affected his health. He demanded a refund of the admission fee, a public apology, and monetary compensation of RMB 20,000 (about USD 2,500).[4] When his first lawsuit was unsuccessful he lodged a second with the Guangzhou Intermediate People's Court. Aside from legal considerations, a passionate public discussion ensued about the legitimacy of art dealing with such subject matter, and the role of contemporary art in society, a discussion that continues.

Lady's Room explored the distinction between private and public space; how China's transformation affected the lives of young women forced to eke out a living in a harsh world. The supposedly private space of the women's restroom is colonised by working girls who are, by no stretch of the imagination, the 'good women' of Confucian tradition. By bringing the taboo reality of prostitution into the light of day, revealing sexual encounters to be pragmatic economic transactions, Cui Xiuwen catapulted herself into an identity as a controversial feminist artist. Curator Huang Du said, '[Cui's] work indicates that human beings have devolved. It is a piece with real social significance.'[5] The work positioned gender and sexuality at the forefront of discussion about the impact of social change. The artist herself said of her slice of social realism, 'You can feel that it is a situation before a battle.'[6]

Born in 1970 near Harbin, in China's far north, Cui Xiuwen trained as a painter. While completing her studies at Beijing's Central Academy of Fine Arts in the late 1990s, she began to produce works focused on the sexual awakening of young girls. However, it was the work she produced with a hidden camcorder in a public toilet that cemented her notoriety. In revealing the secret reality of young women approaching their sexual liaisons in a totally unemotional and business-like manner, she had ventured into highly contested territory.

At that time Cui was working with a group of four female artists, all trained in the Oil Painting Department of the Central Academy of Fine Arts. They called themselves the 'Sirens', a reference to women being perceived as either

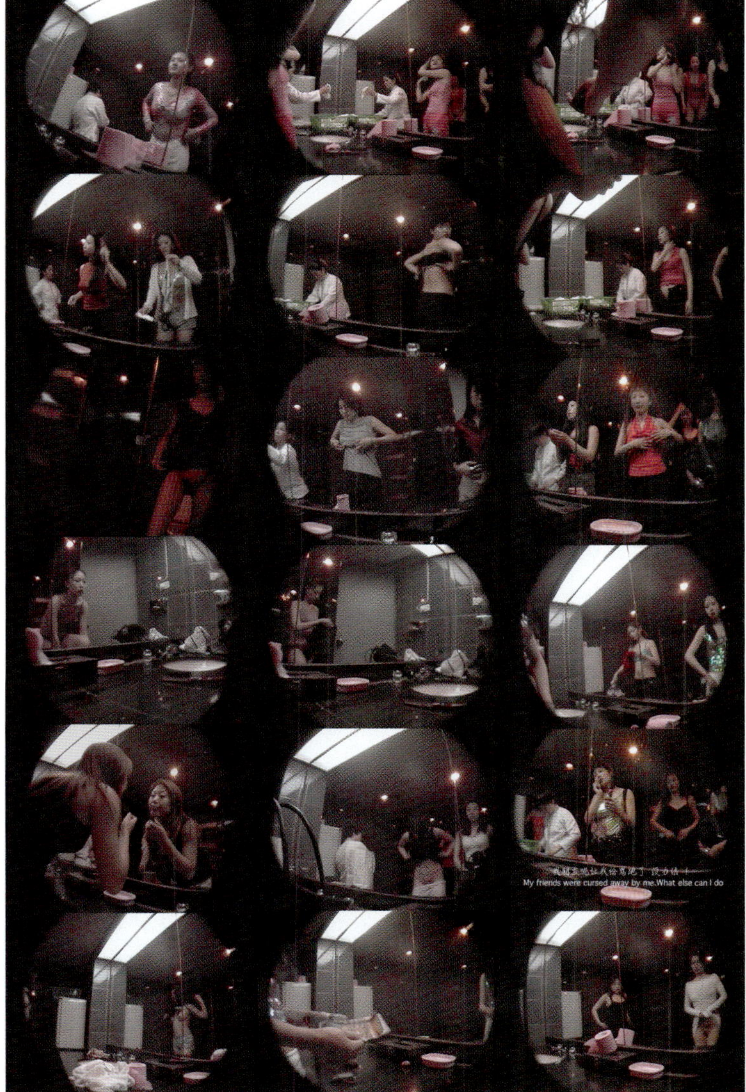

Cui Xiuwen in her Beijing studio
December 2014, photo LG

Cui Xiuwen
Lady's Room 2000
stills from video, 6 min 12 sec
image courtesy and © Cui Xiuwen

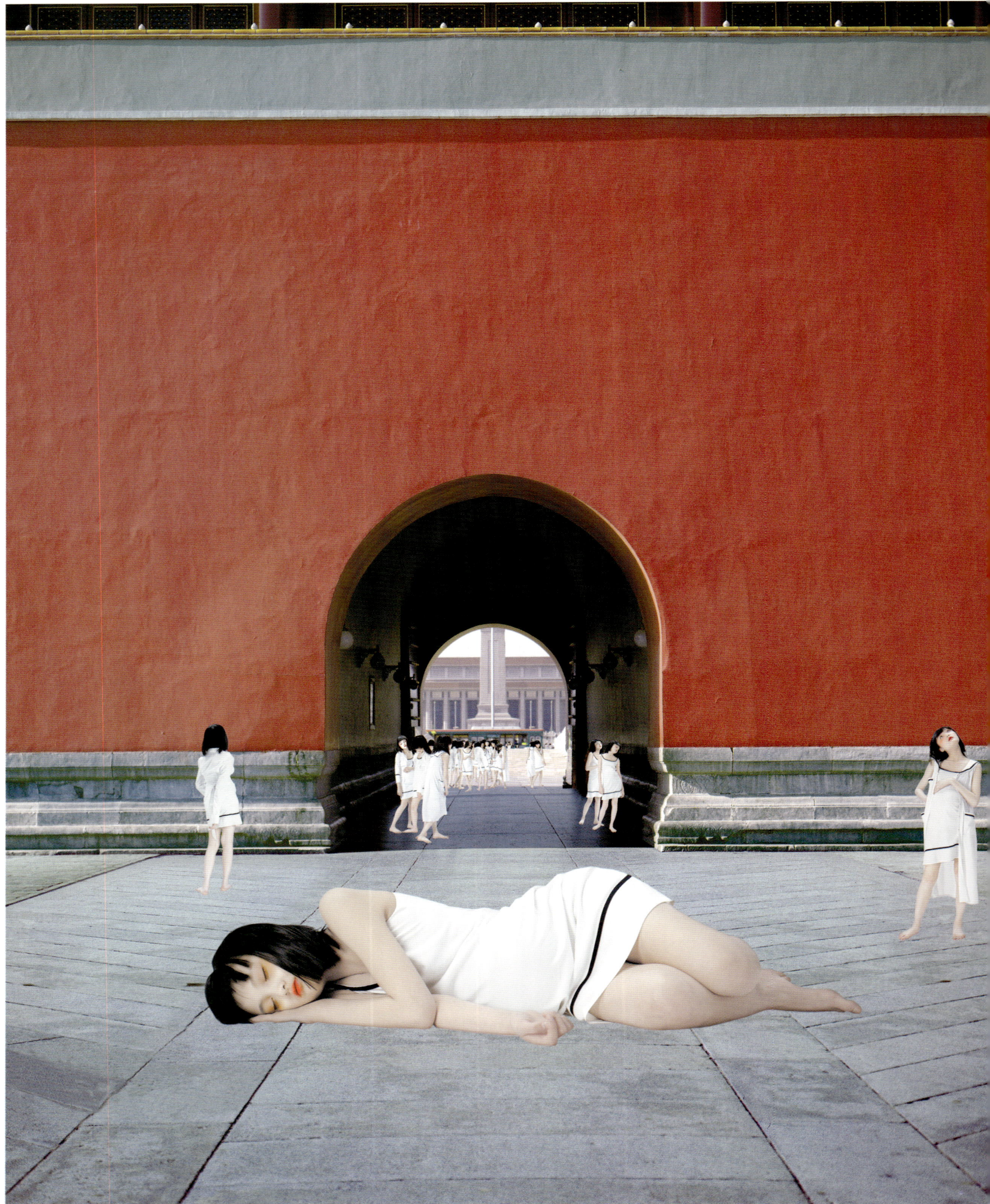

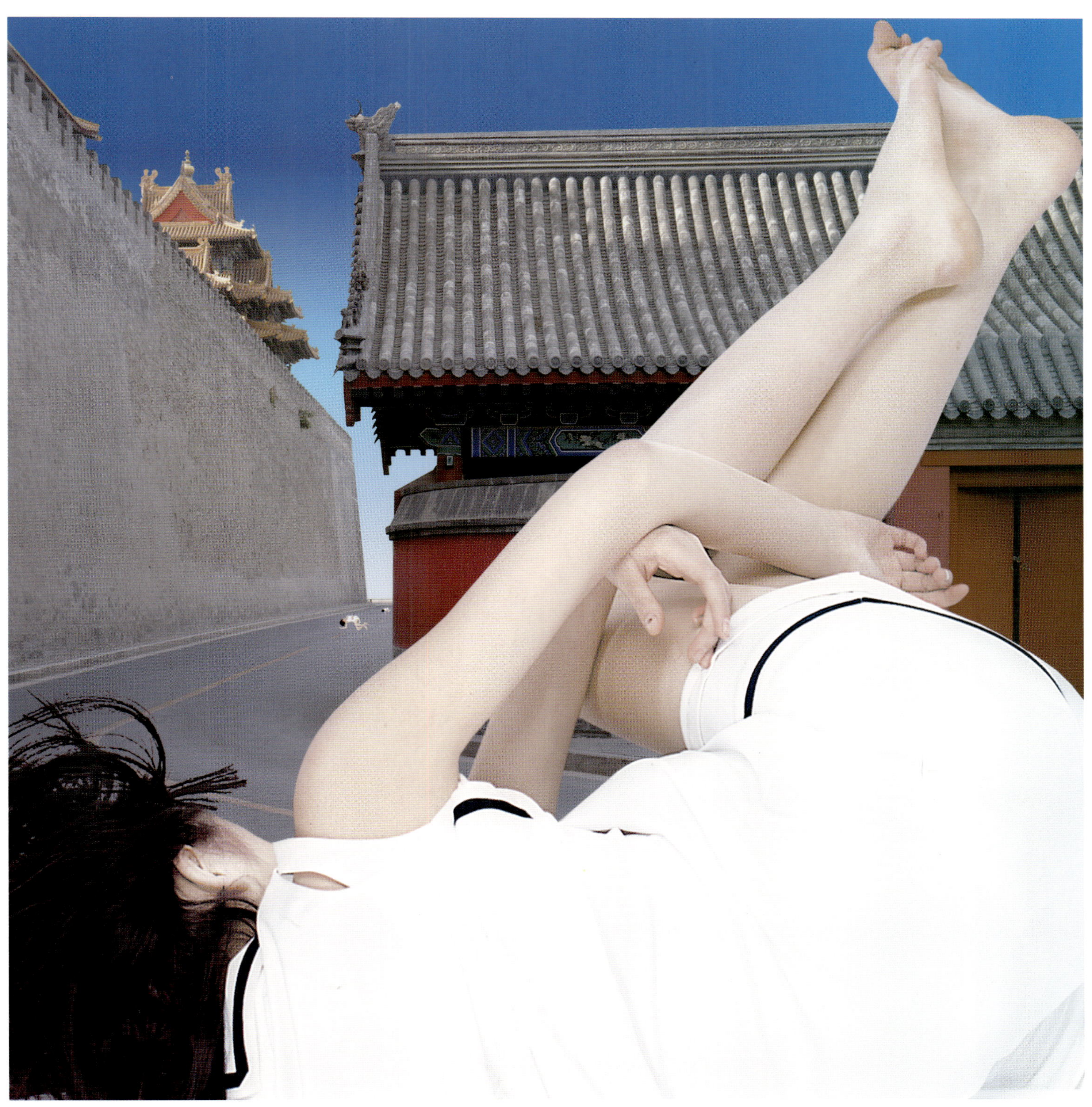

Cui Xiuwen *(left)*
Angel No. 11 2006
type c photograph
119.5 X 100 cm
image courtesy and © Cui Xiuwen

Cui Xiuwen *(above)*
Angel No. 8 2006
type c photograph
150 x 150 cm
image courtesy and © Cui Xiuwen

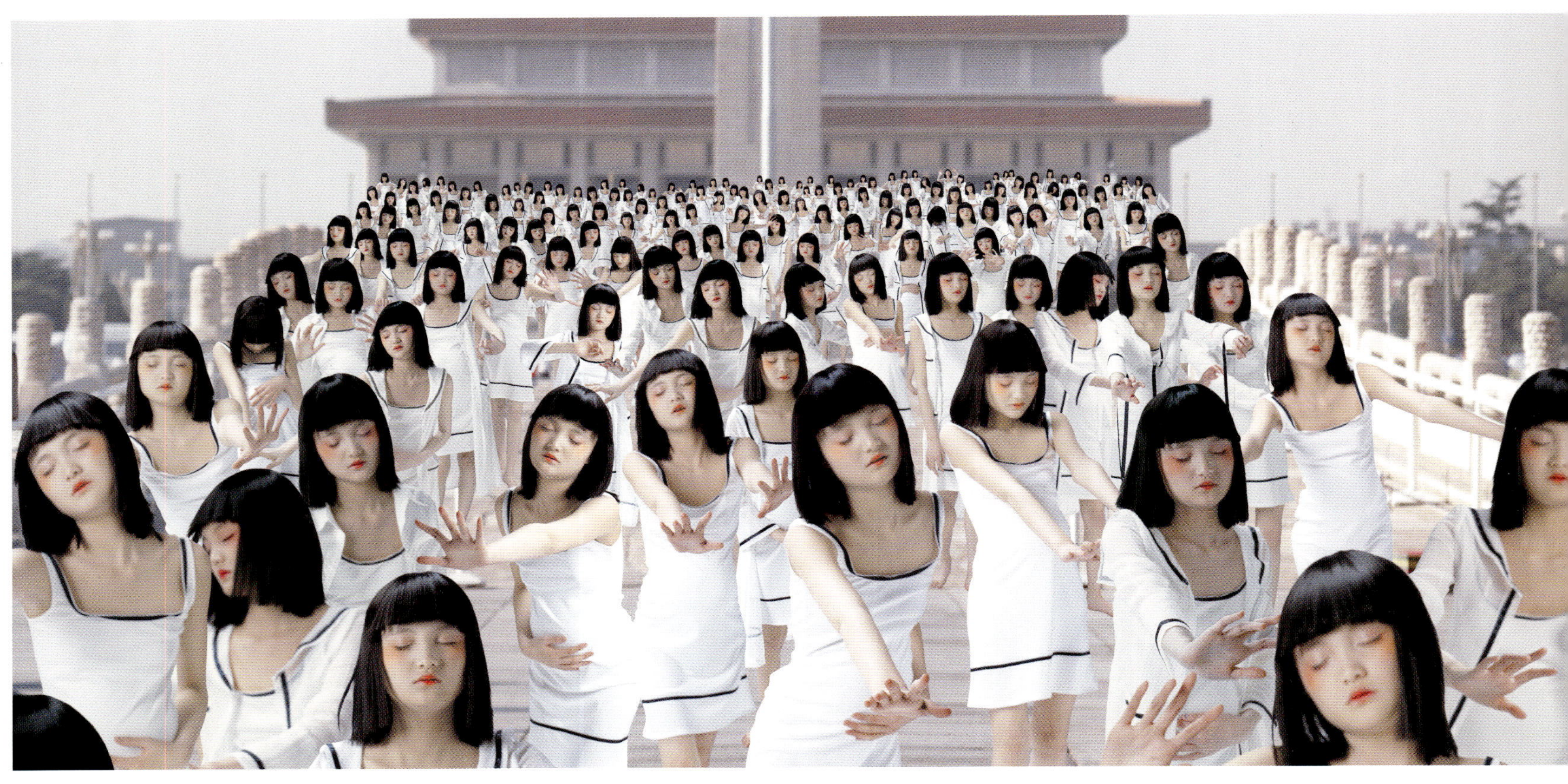

virtuous angels or devilish seductresses. In Homer's *Odyssey* Ulysses chained himself to the mast of his ship and blocked his ears so that he could not be seduced by the song of the sirens. Cui and her collaborators saw an analogy with Chinese women reclaiming a sexual identity after thirty years in which expressions of female sexuality had been, to all intents and purposes, taboo. The Sirens showed their figurative work in their own apartments, gaining the attention of other artists and a group of collectors, and a degree of notoriety.

One of these collectors invited Cui Xiuwen to visit a famous Beijing nightclub to see 'other modes of life.' In the bathrooms of the club women were engaged in so many different activities that she was astonished, she says:

> … to find that the function of a lady's room can be changed so dramatically by the people in it. I discovered that the girls working in the nightclub do so many things – they change their clothes, they take care of their children, they call their husbands, they count their money, they even borrow each other's lipsticks. Because of all these actions in that particular space the lady's room had a new function – quite outside of its usual function. That interested me and caught me by surprise.[7]

In her collaboration with fellow painters Li Hong, Feng Jyali and Yuan Yaomin, Cui had outspokenly criticised the legacy of Confucian restrictions on women's behaviour and aspirations. Her paintings had focused on sexuality, including the depiction of explicit male nudes (shocking at that time), and on female experience. She became interested in private female behaviour in public spaces, seen in her 2002 video work *Underground,* which focused on a young woman travelling in the Beijing subway who picks dry skin from her lips for twenty almost unbearable minutes.

In the mid-2000s Cui produced a body of work featuring adolescent and pre-adolescent girls dressed in the uniforms of Young Pioneers and posed against the red walls of the Forbidden City, or in Tiananmen Square. Like fading memories, they possess a disquietingly surreal atmosphere. Their young protagonist, an actress selected for her resemblance to the artist, is sometimes bruised and bloodied, a disturbing suggestion of potential or actual violence. The pubescent girl, no longer a child but not yet an adult, is dwarfed by claustrophobic walls and gates representing Chinese tradition. 'Red wall, white shirt, red scarf, blue-checked skirt. They occasionally bring up a particular kind of memory and sentiment,' says the artist.[8]

Cui Xiuwen
Angel No. 3 2006
type c photograph
138 x 290 cm
image courtesy and © Cui Xiuwen

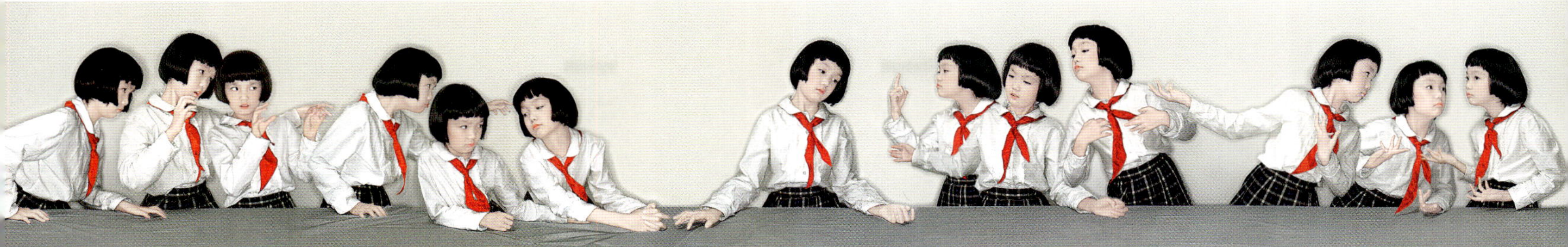

Cui Xiuwen repeated this potent symbolism throughout an important body of work. 'It's associated with a piece of the national flag, which represents honour and the sacrifice of brave soldiers. We wanted to defend the red scarf!' she says, laughing at the naivety of this passionately held childhood belief:

> This left a really strong impression from my childhood. We were only six or seven. I was a really good student, the first one in my class to wear the red scarf... These memories are very mixed. There are a lot of sorrows involved with this red scarf, like the time I mistakenly took a friend's red scarf instead of my own, and wore it home. This classmate and her sister came to my house, broke in, and accused me of stealing her new red scarf. This was very shocking to me. At that time I didn't understand the distinction between new and old things. It was traumatic.

There are personal stories and uncomfortable memories mixed with the sense of a larger historical narrative:

> To me, the red scarf represents a period in my memory, a mark of belonging to a certain generation, the desire to gain honour, the exciting and yet unsettling sentiment of being urged on by the martyrs who created the People's Republic, and even more so, the doubt and quest to identify the relationship between individual and group. Now I go back to the innocence of the youth as the source. Erase the whole process of growing up. Let the girl bear the consequence of history. Let her balance herself in the process of breaking up, converging, evolving, and duplicating.[9]

Memory can be an elusive thing, especially in a nation still dealing with traumatic events from the recent past. Sometimes it is slippery, ungraspable. At other times it is quite deliberately hidden. 'The colour of history is fading, people age, memory becomes vague and unreliable,' said the artist.[10]

Cui Xiuwen
The Three Realms (Sanjie) 2003
digitally manipulated type c print
96.98 x 560 cm and 60.61 x 350 cm
image courtesy and © Cui Xiuwen

Cui Xiuwen
Existential Emptiness No. 19 2009
type c photograph
240 x 153 cm
image courtesy Klein Sun Gallery NY and © Cui Xiuwen

The enforced conformity of the past becomes a nightmare vision. Many of Cui's paintings, videos and digital images are populated by rows of identical girls. Collectivism triumphs. The role of the individual human being in the revolutionary past was clear – you were a tiny cog in the great machine of socialism. But what place does the individual have in the apparently unstoppable juggernaut of mechanisation, urbanisation, globalisation? And what is the place of young women in this new society? Cui Xiuwen asks us to consider these questions.

Angel Number 3 features a young girl, nightmarishly replicated as a crowd of adolescent clones. Like somnambulists, they walk towards us with outstretched arms, suggesting that at a certain period of history, the Chinese people were sleepwalking. Cui says this series is about a time in her own life when she woke every day to a grey cloud of sadness, 'worse than today's Beijing smog.'

> This is about my own life experience. I would wake up and see the sky filled with this huge grey cloud which made me feel as if there was no hope. It's [also] about social conditions... part of the girl represents myself and part represents my criticism of society. That is why the girls are blind, and they are duplicated because they represent all the crises and problems of society.

Other works in the same series feature identical girls gathered in the courtyards of the Forbidden City, perhaps in the very courtyards where hundreds of imperial concubines lived enclosed and circumscribed lives. In *Angel No. 11* the girl in the foreground sleeps, oblivious to her surroundings. Like other images of sleeping women in art history, it evokes an uncomfortable sensation of voyeurism. Although Cui Xiuwen says that her work represents human concerns rather than focusing specifically on female experience, there can be no doubt that the core of her practice is focused on her own growth to adulthood in a period of dramatic social and ideological change. Her use of very young models as her subjects emphasises the atmosphere of existential doubt. That liminal zone of adolescence, characterised by a sense of yearning, becomes a metaphor for a changing national identity. The image of the sleeper, or the sleepwalker, represents the experience of Cui's generation, growing up in post-Mao China: the world that you see when you wake is profoundly unlike the world in which you fell asleep.

Existential Emptiness, a series of works from 2009, are scroll-like monochrome photographs representing aspects of female identity. Transcendent and spiritual, they were initially inspired by the artist's discovery of Japanese Bunraku Theatre. Her protagonist, now older, is accompanied in these images by a life-size doll/puppet who resembles her. A creepy Surrealist *doppelganger*, this puppet sat propped in a chair in the artist's studio throughout our conversation. The doll is a shadow version of the living girl, alluding to a lack of power, an absence of agency. In these images it is sometimes difficult to tell which is the living girl and which the puppet.

Cui Xiuwen explores binaries of body and soul, presence and absence, consciousness and unconsciousness. In a return to the bleak *Dong Bei* (north-east) landscapes of her youth, the photographs have been shot – over a period of some years - in the mountains of northern China. They evoke traditional *Shan Shui* (mountain and water) ink paintings in their subtle, muted tonalities. Even their compositional structure alludes to the sequential reading of a scroll. The figures are tiny in the vastness of the landscape, like classical paintings of lonely scholars in misty mountains. *Existential Emptiness No.19* is filled with yearning. The girl and her puppet shadow-self reach for each other but are destined to remain separate, isolated in their frozen, empty landscape, in a bleak metaphor for the inevitability of loneliness.

Cui Xiuwen's work has become increasingly abstract. She returned to painting with a body of work in 2014, *Reincarnation,* comprising works of varnished aluminium and acrylic on canvas, and video, presented as an installation. She identifies the change in her work as a shift from the physical to the psychological, and from thence to the spiritual. 'Like climbing a set of stairs,' Cui says. Her recent work is based on her study of Buddhism, and a growing desire to blur the boundary between artist and audience with works that provide viewers with an immersive experience. 'With a history of only thirty years of contemporary art it is a great challenge for Chinese artists to transcend themselves, to use concrete things to express abstract ideas,' she says. 'I try to transcend myself both in my practice and in a way of thinking, to find a breakthrough in consciousness.' Her 2015 New York exhibition at Klein Sun Gallery, *Awakening of the Flesh*, extended her visual representation of meditation and mysticism, an abstract language of colour and form.

Cui Xiuwen's changing practice reflects her lived experience of change in China. After Maoist ideology was discredited in the 1980s and 1990s, the soul-searching and bitterness of her generation as they came to terms with their loss of certainty resulted in works exploring childhood memories. A more lyrical approach followed, with the *Existential Emptiness* series evoking enduring Chinese traditions and a search for beauty in landscapes that symbolise particular states of mind. Latterly, pure abstraction indicates the artist's emerging quest for spiritual growth, and an adaptation of the traditions and philosophies of Buddhism to make sense of an uncertain present.

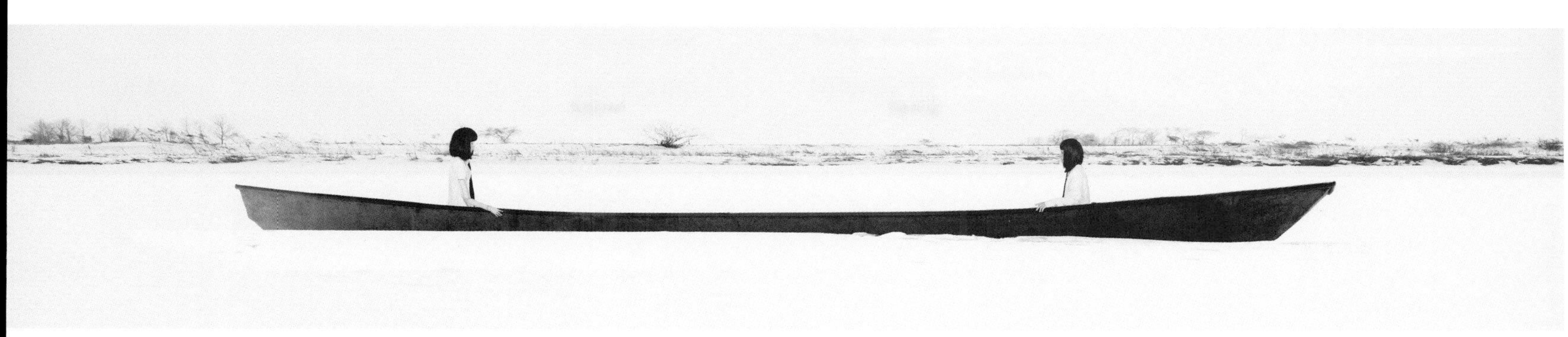

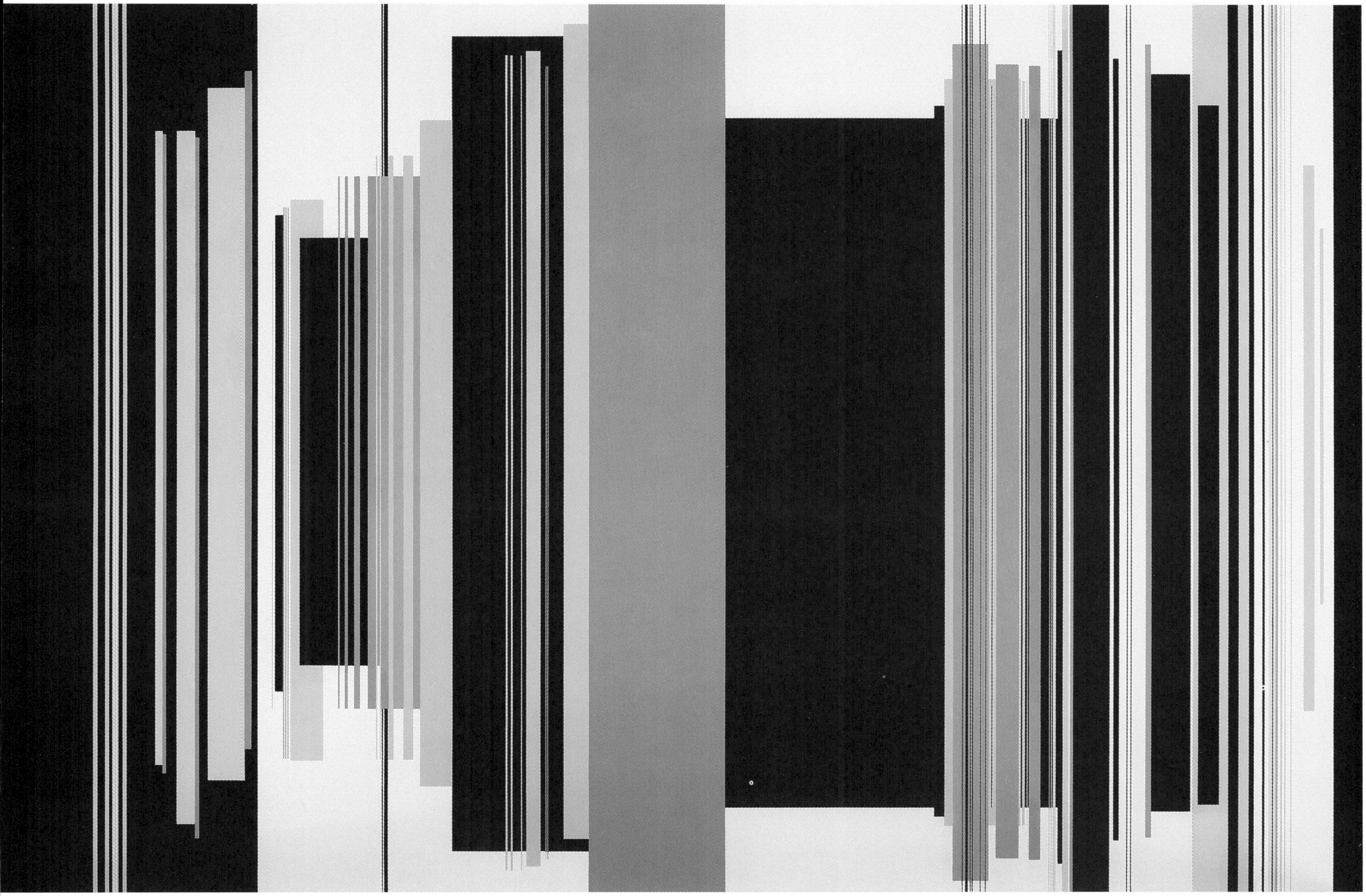

Cui Xiuwen *(top)*
Existential Emptiness No. 11 2009
type c photograph
58 x 300 cm
image courtesy Klein Sun Gallery NY
and © Cui Xiuwen

Cui Xiuwen
Reincarnation No. 9 2014
acrylic on canvas
180 x 280 cm
image courtesy Klein Sun Gallery NY
and © Cui Xiuwen

CAO FEI 曹斐

Magical Metropolises

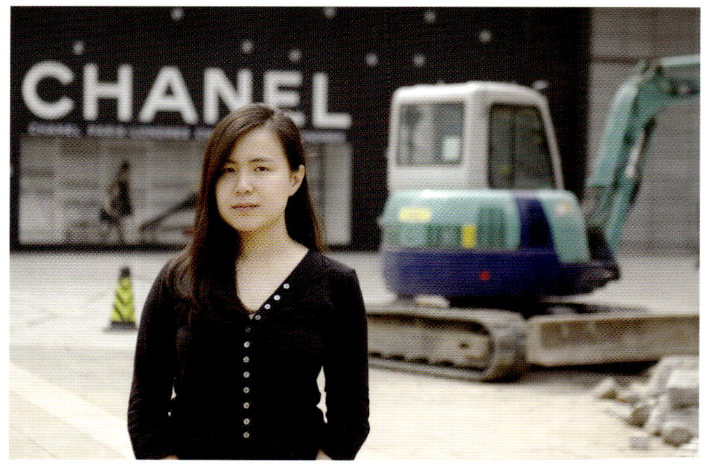

In 1959 when Hollywood diva Ava Gardner was shooting the post-apocalyptic drama *On the Beach,* she famously declared that Melbourne was the perfect place to make a movie about the end of the world. In 2015, Beijing seems an even more appropriate location, particularly on those days when the particulate pollution reduces visibility to almost zero and masked people navigate the city through a shrouding fog. Cao Fei, who moved to Beijing from China's south, saw the dystopian possibilities, creating a surreal forty-seven minute drama featuring zombies and real estate agents among a cast of odd and eccentric Beijing characters. *Haze and Fog* was shot entirely in the suburbs where the artist now lives. Known for her love of popular culture, performance, and the exploration of virtual realities, her inversion of the tropes of a B-grade cinematic genre is a logical development.

I spoke with Cao Fei one afternoon before she picked up her children from school. Inevitably, our conversation turned to motherhood and how it had changed her practice and her view of the world. This factor is not often mentioned in accounts of her work, but the change is discernible, and Cao Fei referred to it throughout our discussion. The impact of this key female life experience was to be repeated in many of my conversations with artists. As Cao explained the ideas that prompted her recent works, she emphasised her sense of dislocation and homesickness in moving from the south of China to the cold grey north, and the additional isolation of finding herself at home with small children.

Cao Fei has pioneered video, new media and virtual reality in a witty and often collaborative practice. Born in Guangzhou to artist parents in 1978, her work explores the dissonance between fantasy and reality in a fluid, rapidly changing world. Her experiences growing up in the 1980s and '90s, the period in which southern China became the world's factory, have provided rich material for her work. She has explored the imaginary identities of factory workers and the subculture of Cosplay, in which people dress up as their favourite superhero, anime or videogame character and engage in extended role-playing. She identifies key influences on her early work: 'Pop culture, Hong Kong TV, music, Japanese Anime – but less than for my kids! The impact of western culture at the end of the 1980s and the beginning of the 1990s was just starting.'

A long-term project in which she explored the possibilities of virtual reality was a response to the contemporary experience of urban life. In the online fantasy world of Second Life, she created an avatar – an idealised version of herself named China Tracy. In 2007 she presented *i.MIRROR – A Second Life Documentary Film by China Tracy* in the China Pavilion at the Venice Biennale. The work was shown in the pavilion's garden, inside a cloud-like tent. In a dreamlike immersive environment, audiences could watch China Tracy's adventures in an alternative, parallel universe. Despite the apparent freedom of the artist's avatar there is a sense of isolation and detachment. China Tracy is as alone as Bu Hua's alter-ego, the Young Pioneer, in her fight against the terrifying monsters of the modern metropolis.

The next iteration of this project, *RMB City,* explored consumerism and materialism. This work was created in Beijing, a city in which it took a long time for Cao Fei to feel comfortable. Her imaginary city, surrounded by water, is a hybrid of communism, capitalism and socialism, a construction which appropriates the architectural icons of Chinese cities, such as Beijing's 'Bird's Nest' stadium, all condensed into one, indistinguishable megalopolis. She satirises the Chinese obsession with real estate, a theme which is developed in her 2013 video, *Haze and Fog*. Like Cui Xiuwen and Bu Hua, her satire is playful, yet sharply pointed. *RMB City*'s Gate of Heavenly Peace replaces Mao's portrait with a panda, and a giant sculpture of Mao floats just offshore, an ironic version of the Statue of Liberty. Living in Beijing, where billboards on every construction site promise, 'This is my Chinese Dream' in giant letters, Cao Fei's skewering of political posturing and opportunistic corruption is refreshing. She financed the project by selling RMB City property in 'real estate offices.' RMB had art museums, nightclubs and versions of well-known 'statement' buildings such as Beijing's notorious 'pair of pants' CCTV tower.

In a conversation with curator, Hans-Ulrich Obrist, during the 2015 Hong Kong Art Basel art fair, Cao Fei reflected on her motivations. During her first years in Beijing she was living a rich and vibrant online life, creating *RMB City*, and

Cao Fei, 2008
photograph by Judy Zhou
image courtesy the artist

adventuring in the persona of China Tracy, she explained, while her life in the real world seemed 'boring and sad.'[11]

Cao is interested in the lives of workers in the Pearl River Delta, China's manufacturing hub, and the locus of China's transformation into a new kind of society. The factories in southern China have been a magnet for a generation of young migrant workers, who have arrived in their millions seeking a better life. Her continuing interest in the intersection between the reality of ordinary daily life for these people, and their inner fantasy world, is represented in her award-winning SIEMENS Art Project of 2006, *What Are You Doing Here*? Cao Fei traced the daily lives of workers at the Osram Light Bulb Factory in Foshan, where she stayed from October 2005 to April 2006. One element of this ambitious, long-term work is a video entitled *Whose Utopia*, for which she invited the workers to perform a dance to the music of their choice, against the background clatter of the assembly line. The video opens with the workers performing their repetitive daily tasks, as if they themselves are part of this massive industrial machine. In the second part a small group act out their own personal fantasy identities as ballerina, hip-hop dancer, guitarist, or peacock dancer. These are other kinds of avatars, which the artist suggests are necessary to survive the pressures of the everyday. The video closes with portraits of individual workers gazing straight at the camera, defying us to see them as mere cogs in the machinery of China's economic miracle.

Whose Utopia is wonderfully funny and touching, making its point with empathy and wit. Cao Fei conducted surveys with the workers in the factory and developed an ongoing dialogue with them, posing the question, 'What are you doing here?' Collecting their dreams and aspirations, she created installations, small theatrical performances and videos that were shown in the factory. The work is a genuine collaboration with the participants, who were actively involved in the process, and a manifestation of the 'social sculpture' promoted by Joseph Beuys in the 1970s – 'socially collaborative, participatory, dialogical, and relational art'.[12] Cao stresses that her project is not intended to be an exposé of working conditions or an overtly political work:

> Rather, it attempts to look at and examine a particular kind of reality from multiple angles—how workers are on the lookout for the opportunity to survive; where they are now versus the kinds of dreams they have; their experiences growing up; their nostalgia or memory of their hometowns, their traditional Chinese families, their life experiences living inland, and how they migrated into urban life; and their hopes and aspirations for the future.[13]

Essentially, Cao Fei says, the Siemens Project, like all her work to date, is 'all about the zeitgeist.'[14]

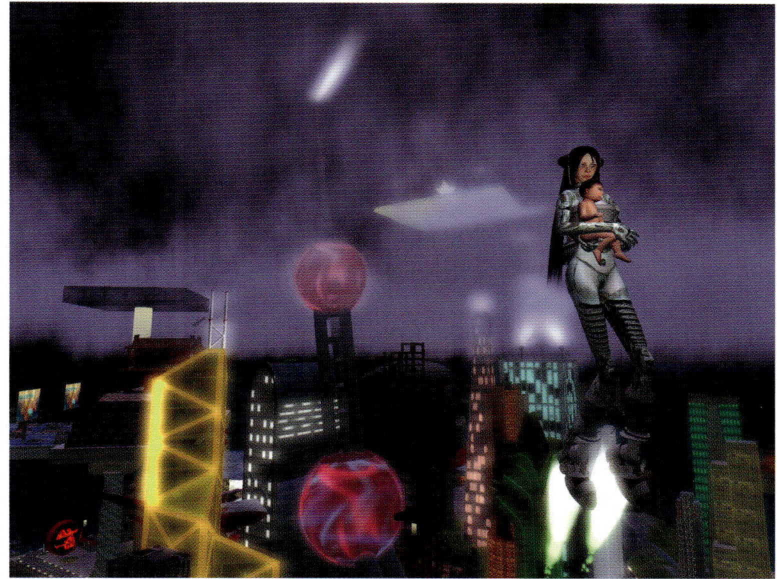

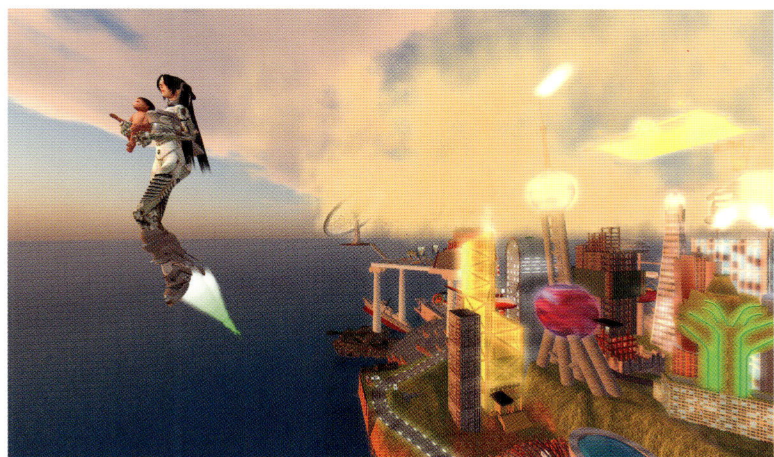

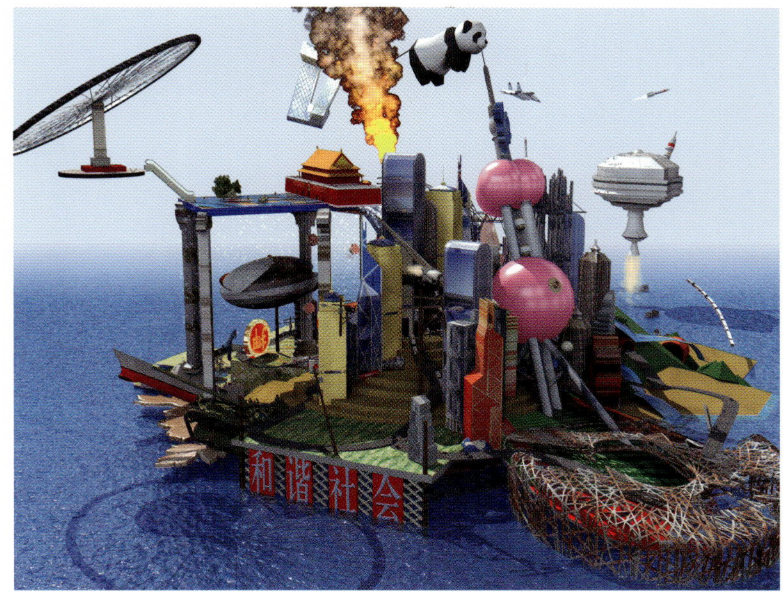

Cao Fei (SL: China Tracy) *(top, middle)*
Live in RMB City: Online Project in Second Life 2009
machinima 24 min 50 sec
image courtesy Cao Fei and Vitamin Creative Space

Cao Fei (SL: China Tracy) *(bottom)*
RMB City Planning: Online Project in Second Life 2007–11
digital video, 10 mins
image courtesy Cao Fei and Vitamin Creative Space

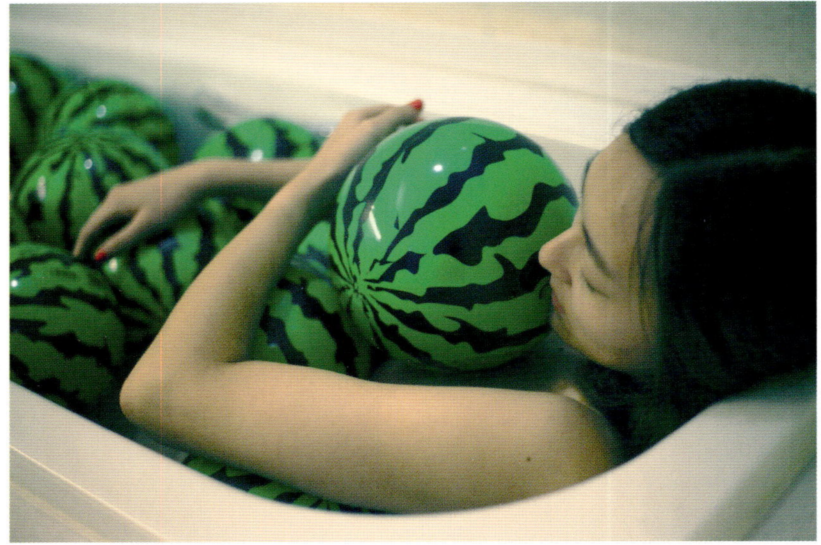

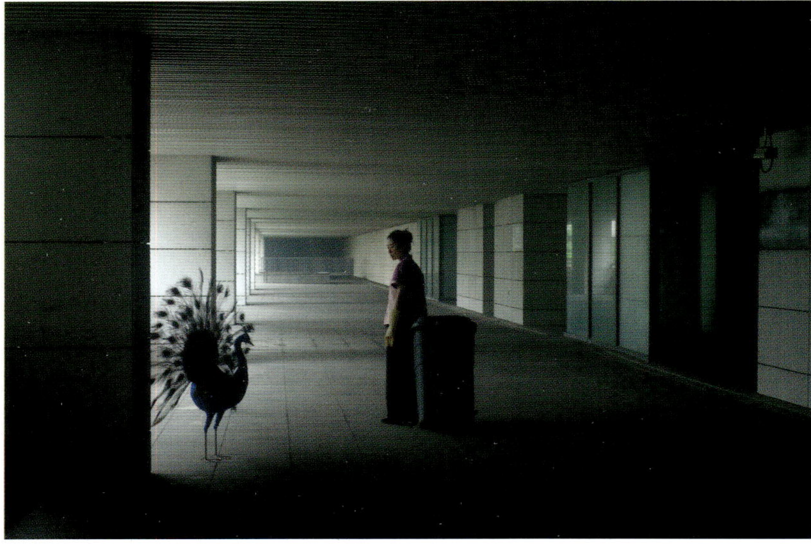

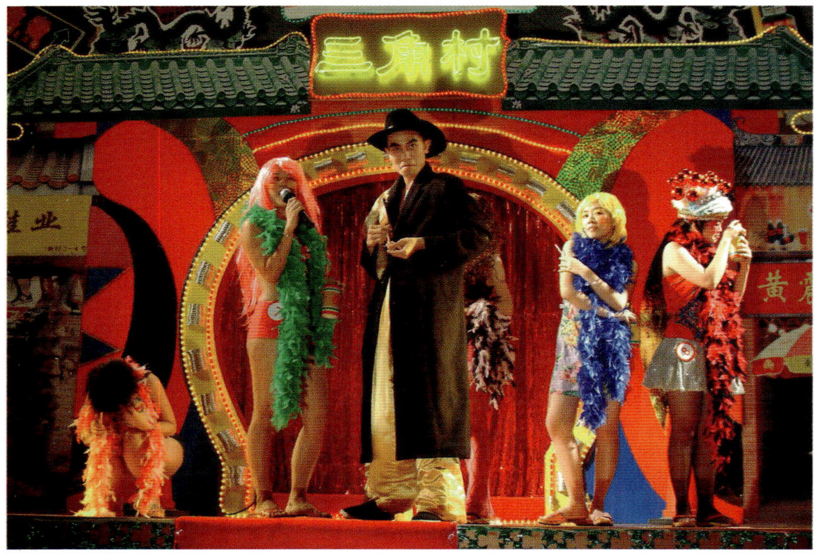

Cao Fei *(top and middle)*
Haze and Fog 2013
digital video 46 min 30 sec
image courtesy the artist
and Vitamin Creative Space

Cao Fei *(bottom)*
PRD Anti-heroes 2005
performance
image courtesy the artist
and Vitamin Creative Space

In the same year Cao produced *PRD (Pearl River Delta) Anti-Heroes*, a video work that appears to be a cross between a corny variety show, a Cantonese farce (which the artist admits she loved watching on TV, growing up in Guangzhou) and a revolutionary opera. A non-professional cast takes the role of female factory workers and other anti-heroes including mistresses, beggars, fortune-tellers and sellers of pirated DVDs. The video opens with a conga line of factory girls singing, 'Nowadays working in a garment factory is a way of making money. It is such a lovely job which can make cash quickly.' The comedy is broad, in a style familiar to Chinese television audiences, and the acting is far from subtle. The characters are anonymous and unsung heroes with ambition, living by their wits.

Cao Fei skewers people's preoccupation with climbing the ladder of material success, in the 'new' China. The fiction is that with a self-sufficient spirit of entrepreneurialism, any ordinary person can become one of the new breed of Chinese tycoons – an understandable narrative of aspiration in a country where the cradle-to-grave state support of the 'iron rice bowl' gave way to a harsh insistence on self-reliance. Today's dramatic disparity between rich and poor has been reflected in Cao Fei's work since she arrived in Beijing. She has become interested in social class, in relationships between the new rich and those who serve them – an army of cleaners, nannies, drivers, security guards, manicurists and beauticians, real estate agents and sex workers.

While breastfeeding her second child, Cao obsessively watched the American TV series *The Walking Dead*. She wryly observed that during this period she had a lot of time to think and dream as she pushed a pram around her neighbourhood. 'I think it's quite interesting, the idea of a dead city,' she says. 'I like the idea of making a video about an anti-Utopia.' In fact, she says, this is really an 'anti-anti-Utopia' that reverses the commonly held assumptions and conventions of the genre. She decided that the most appropriate vehicle for her ideas was a zombie movie. Unlike most zombie movies, however, 'It's about how the *people* are the living dead while the zombies are alive – more alive than the living people. This is my feeling, living in this city in the past few years.' As a sleep-deprived parent Cao was more than usually attuned to the rhythms of her neighbourhood, to liminal zones between the real and imaginary, night and day, sleep and wakefulness. She was homesick for southern China, and finding Beijing less than comfortable. Her screenplay is based on observations of the people in her neighbourhood, and her increasingly lurid speculations about their secret lives in a city of toxic mist.

Cao has been observing Beijing with the clear gaze of the newcomer since 2006, when she arrived from Guangzhou.

Moving from the south of China was hard, and she struggled to feel at home, in an unforgiving environment. 'At the beginning I worked on the virtual project so I didn't need to touch the ground. I was always floating in the virtual world. Then I had two kids. That brought me back to reality!' She spent a lot of time at home, feeling a little lost, adrift in Beijing. Her feelings are distilled in *Haze and Fog*:

> Some of it is my sad feelings about life. I watch different characters in my district. I take my kids to the supermarket and watch the security guards, I watch people in the gardens. It wasn't like research for a project, this was my life, and I slowed down and took lots of time. You can feel the heartbeat.

'Is this really how you see Beijing?' I asked. 'Not just Beijing, but maybe the whole country,' Cao Fei replied. 'People are stuck. They are living statues. The people are all the same whatever their social class. In the film you can see the city like a ghost city – empty real estate, [full of] excess.' There are moments of humour, but this is a damning portrayal of a lost place full of lost people, who seem unable to connect with each other. There is no dialogue, and an evocative tango soundtrack enhances the strange atmosphere. Cao Fei is interested in the films of Federico Fellini, and the oeuvre of independent Chinese filmmaker Jia Zhangke, whose films, including *Still Life*, a disquieting narrative about two people searching for their spouses in the environs of the Three Gorges Dam, reflect China's transformation.

Haze and Fog is compelling from its opening sequence. Apartment buyers arrive at an empty, de Chirico-like plaza where real estate agents are spruiking newly built apartments. They run over a cyclist, who turns into a zombie and staggers away. The middle-class buyers are oblivious to his plight, and to the humanity of the bored real estate agents. In Cao Fei's bleak vision old notions of a common humanity have given way to an individualism that leaves each of her characters utterly alone, alienated from each other. The 'haze' of the title refers to more than the pollution in Beijing. It mirrors the collective psychological 'haze' of its inhabitants – their inability to see clearly impedes human connection and any vision for the future.

Cao Fei uses her cast – the cleaners and maids, security guards, delivery boys, bored housewives and nouveau riche home buyers – as a means to examine the ills of a society in which traditional Confucian values and revolutionary idealism are replaced by materialism and envy. Class divisions are glaringly obvious. The presence of a peacock and a tiger, repeated motifs suggesting the dissonance between nature and culture, are strange and unsettling. Together with a magical realist mise-en-scène and languid cinematography they place the work firmly in the realm of allegory, linking her narrative with Chinese tradition and mythology.

Memorable characters – the isolated old man on his walking frame; the bored housewife who chops off her own finger in a moment of savagery and is then shown having a manicure, lying listlessly on her sofa; the maid trying on the stiletto heels of her employer; the prostitute who changes costumes quickly in apartment block fire-stairs in between clients – reveal aspects of the new China. She pays homage to cinematic conventions, from the bleak urban landscape of Jean Luc-Godard's *Alphaville* to a parody of the Hollywood musical, in which her zombies dance manically through the deserted aisles of the supermarket. She is interested in fantasy lives, the 'magic reality' in which we all really live, most especially perhaps those people inhabiting a city in such continual flux as Beijing. People in China reinvent themselves all the time, but in the process, says the artist, they risk losing important parts of their culture, their moral compass and their identity.

Blending fantasy with real life, *Haze and Fog* is a logical development from Cao's earlier works, most particularly her *Cosplay* series. Depicting a subculture in which she herself was a participant, she made videos and photographs depicting young people dressed as video-game characters, enacting fantasy battles in the urban landscape of Guangzhou. The artist says, 'I was quite young – twenty four! I was part of the subculture in Guangzhou, they were my friends, and I asked them to be involved with me in video and performance.' Cao agrees that she was interested in revealing the rich fantasy life of people in the urban space: 'Yes, you can see the connection with *RMB City* – the city landscape and the life of people in the city. How they live on the inside. I was interested in performance, in the costumes and in the drama.' This blurring of reality and fantasy, as her characters bring their new personae into mundane lives at home with their parents, reveals disillusionment with the world they have inherited, and the gap between generations.

The rift between two Chinese generations was explored poignantly in an extended 2005 interview with her own father, a successful traditional sculptor, still making work in his eighties. Cao Fei's parents were artists and teachers, and she grew up in the midst of the art academy when Soviet Socialist Realism was still the accepted style, despite the changes beginning to filter through the country:

> I lived in the academy school, in my parents' studio, using the clay and other materials. I was always surrounded by lots of [their] students, so it influenced me. Those were times of the traditional way [in art]. That might be why I went to the opposite way – there was too much of the Russian style of painting and sculpture, which I reacted against.

Her video records her father creating sculptures of revolutionary heroes, creating in the process a narrative of her personal history that mirrors the bigger narrative of China.

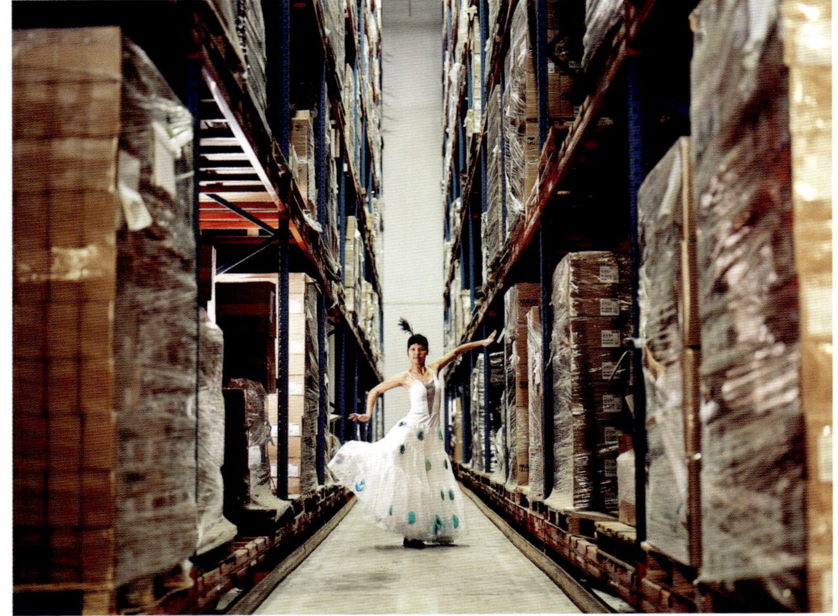

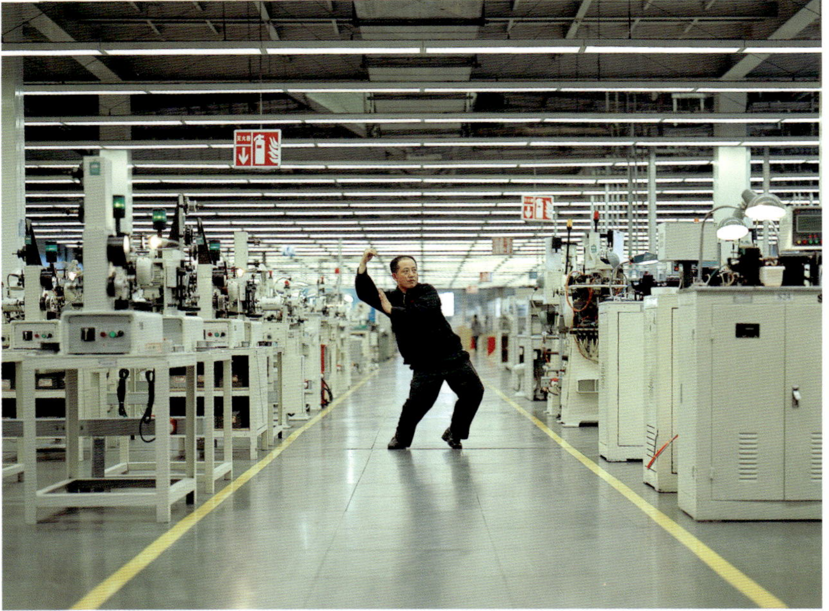

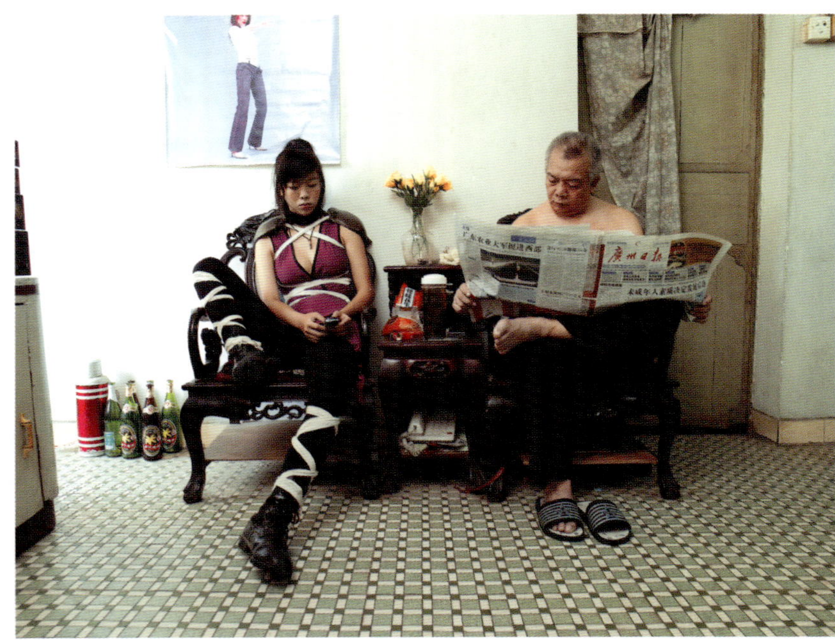

Cao Fei is interested in 'magical metropolises'.[15] After *Haze and Fog*, she began to develop a work inspired by the French film *Hiroshima Mon Amour* and its themes of memory and forgetting. In 2014 she made *La Town*, which centres on a ruined city after a mysterious unnamed disaster. Cao found tiny figurines intended for use in model train sets which gave her the power to be a 'real director', moving a large cast of characters around on a table, using stop motion to create a parallel universe that even contained an art museum, as all utopian cities should. The sound track is darkly noir, with echoes of Hitchcock and horror, adding further atmosphere to the surreal glimpses of tiny plastic figures engaged in acts of inexplicable violence, or standing bewildered in the rubble, with neon signs flickering. Each new development in her practice explores binaries of memory and amnesia, light and dark, utopia and dystopia, visible and invisible.

For Hong Kong Art Basel 2015, Cao Fei projected the arcade game imagery of her childhood onto the ICC Tower that dominates the skyline, thus merging her own individual memories and desires with the city's, and by extension, with China's national aspirations. Ironically, she employs the latest digital animation techniques to represent a nostalgic past, an elegy to a time when people were filled with hope. Using imagery from 1980s video games such as Mario Brothers and Pac-Man, Cao alludes to our collective memories of technology and popular culture, imagining a future in which the social media of today becomes a library of 'artefacts' like the superseded VHS videotapes and computer floppy disks of the recent past. She was intrigued to see *Same Old, Brand New* represented on social media, as her intervention into the public urban space was photographed by thousands of people for their own Instagram, Tumblr and Facebook accounts. This was an inversion of *RMB City*, she believed – a real artwork, in a real city, became a virtual entity online.[16]

If we believe that art holds up a mirror and reflects our world back to us, then the world represented by Bu Hua, Cui Xiuwen and Cao Fei is a place of paradox. It is filled with humour, wit and pathos, but also with increasing levels of anxiety. Each of these artists reveals not just her own personal preoccupations but also some of the themes and concerns common to their generation. Distanced from the collectivist past, they have embraced the pluralist possibilities of the present whilst remaining clear-sighted about its dangers.

NOTES

1 'The Colors of Cui Xiuwen' republished from *Artzine China* 24 April 2009 http://www.womenofchina.cn/womenofchina/html1/people/artists/10/476-1.htm accessed 26 November 2014

2 Unless otherwise acknowledged, all quotes from Bu Hua are from her conversation with the writer, in October 2013

Cao Fei *(top and middle)*
My Future is Not a Dream 2006
from the series ***Whose Utopia***
digital video 20 min 6 sec
image courtesy the artist
and Vitamin Creative Space

Cao Fei *(bottom)*
A Ming at Home 2004
from the series ***Cos Players***
type c photograph, 76.5 x 102 cm
image courtesy the artist
and Vitamin Creative Space

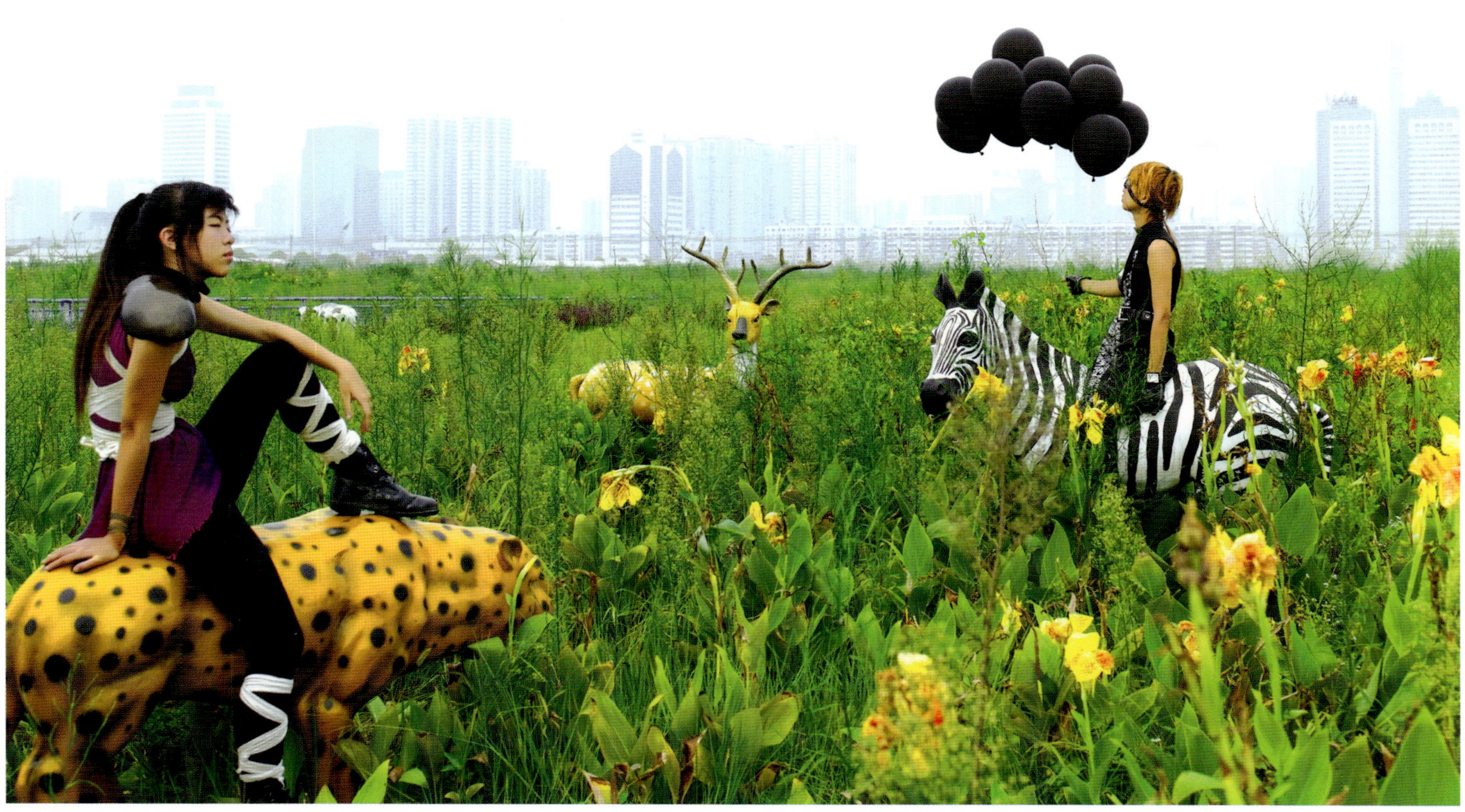

3 http://afe.easia.columbia.edu/ps/china/taoqian_peachblossom.pdf accessed 18 January 2015
4 *Beijing Today*, Issue 113, 2003, http://issuu.com/beijingtoday/docs/2004-01-02/6 accessed 26 October 2014
5 ibid.
6 Cotter, Holland 2008 'China's Female Artists Quietly Emerge', *New York Times*, 30 July 2008 available at http://www.nytimes.com/2008/07/30/arts/design/30arti.html?pagewanted=all&_r=1& accessed 6 November 2014
7 Unless otherwise acknowledged all quotes from Cui Xiuwen are from her conversation with the writer in December 2014
8 Cui Xiuwen, http://www.cuixiuwen.com/ accessed 6 November 2014
9 ibid.
10 ibid.
11 Chang, Charlotte 2015 'Art Basel Hong Kong 2015: Conversations with Cao Fei' available at http://artradarjournal.com/2015/03/20/art-basel-hong-kong-2015-conversations-with-cao-fei/ accessed 29 March 2015
12 Beuys is most famously remembered for two things: the theoretical hypothesis of 'social sculpture,' and the statement 'everybody is an artist.' See Rojas, Laurie, 'Beuys' Concept of Social Sculpture and Relational Art Practices Today' in *Chicago Art Magazine*, http://chicagoartmagazine.com/2010/11/beuys%E2%80%99-concept-of-social-sculpture-and-relational-art-practices-today/ (accessed 18 January 2015) for a cogent summary of his key ideas and their influence on contemporary artists today. Beuys' philosophy proved a significant influence on a generation of Chinese contemporary artists, acknowledged in the important 2013 exhibition at Beijing's Ullens Centre for Contemporary Art *Social Sculpture: Beuys in China*
13 Tinari, Philip 2013 'Cao Fei: Coming Up Hip Hop and Questioning Utopia' (transl. Xiaotong Wang) *Art 21* available at http://www.art21.org/texts/cao-fei/interview-cao-fei-coming-up-hip-hop-and-questioning-utopia accessed 9 November 2014
14 Unless otherwise acknowledged all quotes from Cao Fei are from her conversation with the writer in April 2014
15 A phrase used often in my conversation with the artist, in April 2014
16 Chang, Charlotte 2015 'Art Basel Hong Kong 2015: Conversations with Cao Fei' available at http://artradarjournal.com/2015/03/20/art-basel-hong-kong-2015-conversations-with-cao-fei/ accessed 29 March 2015

Cao Fei
A Mirage 2004
from the series ***Cos Players***
type c photograph, 76.5 x 102 cm
image courtesy the artist
and Vitamin Creative Space

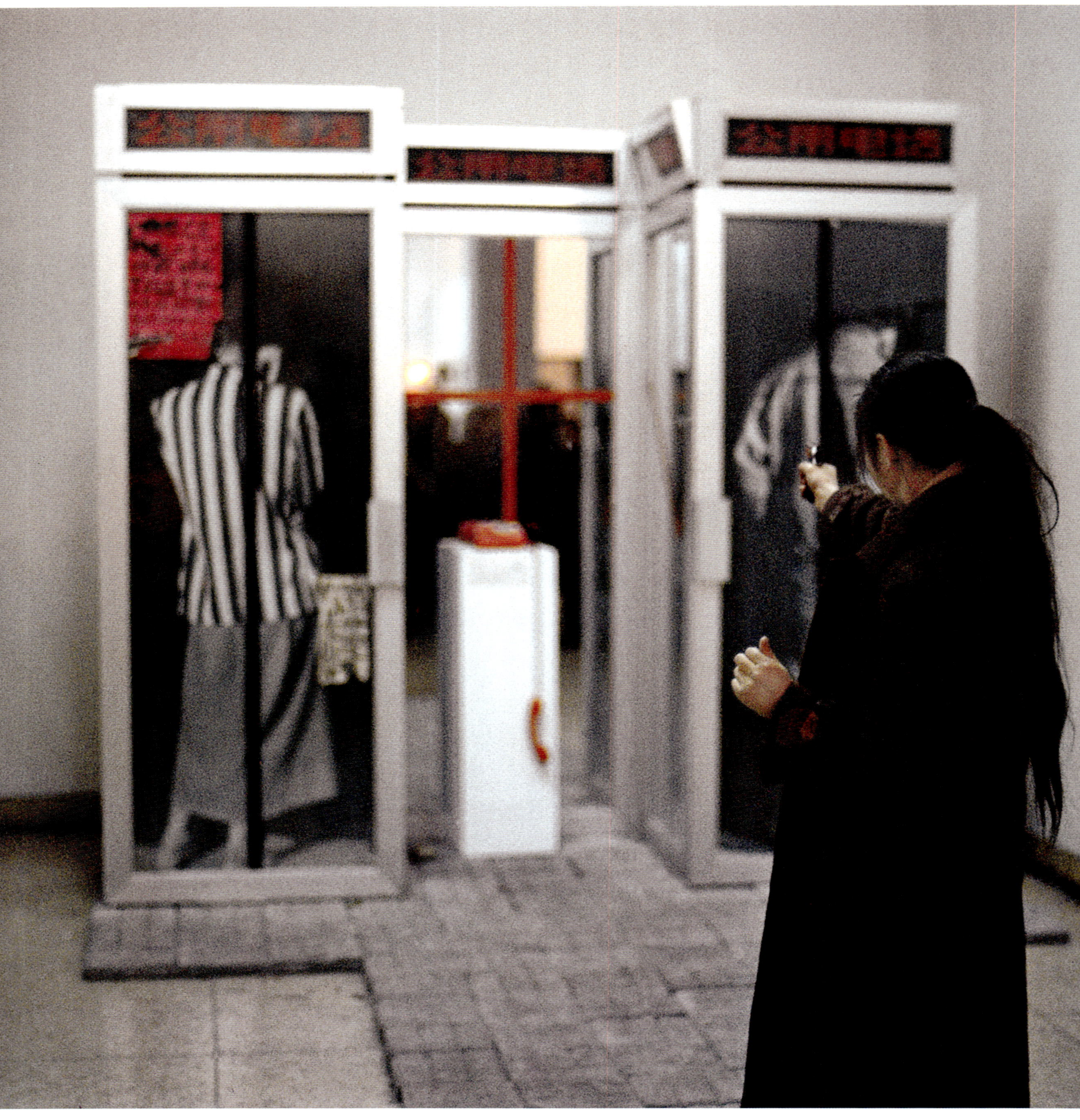

TWO GUNSHOTS IN BEIJING

China/Avant-garde and Xiao Lu 肖鲁

The previous chapter introduced three artists who came of age in a world of relative personal freedom, mass communication, and growing private wealth. Now we look back, to a very different China, when these potent social forces were at a nascent stage of development, to trace contemporary art in its earliest manifestations as China began to open up to the outside world after the Cultural Revolution. A controversial event that took place at the opening of a significant exhibition in Beijing in 1989 serves as a useful starting point for a journey through recent Chinese art history.

What actually happened in the National Art Museum of China, at about 11 o'clock in the morning on February 5, 1989? Accounts from eye witnesses and those of the main protagonists differ: not only do they contradict each other, but over time they even contradict themselves. The artwork at the centre of this drama has been interpreted in radically different ways. The only thing on which everyone can agree is that Xiao Lu, a young, unknown artist, suddenly pulled out a gun in the crowded gallery space and fired two shots into an installation consisting of two telephone booths. There are many questions to be unravelled here. Was this her own work, or one created with another artist who later became her partner? Had they planned it together, or was it a spontaneous act? Did the curators know it was about to happen, or were they as shocked as the audience? Was it a deliberately political act at a highly charged time in Beijing, or a purely subjective expression of emotion by a troubled young woman? Everything surrounding her subversive action is contested territory even now, twenty-five years later.

The event in question took place at the opening of the largest exhibition of ground-breaking contemporary art ever to be presented in China, *China/Avant-garde*, which the curators intended to 'launch a new wave of avant-garde assaults against the art establishment,'[1] just a few short months before army tanks rolled into Tiananmen Square to crush the student demonstration which had occupied the centre of Beijing since April.

Art history – and the compelling narratives by which we understand it – is sometimes constructed by particular, singular exhibitions. Often it is only with hindsight that their real significance is understood. And so it was in Beijing, in 1989, a year which was to become forever etched in memory by the entry of armed troops into Tiananmen Square, where they opened fire on unarmed civilians. The months leading up to this tragic turn of events, however, saw the culmination of a period of relaxed government control of art and literature and increasing openness – a period of excitement, energy and optimism. The writer Linda Jaivin, who spent much of the 1980s and 1990s living in Beijing, recalls the period before the crackdown as 'that time when everything was hopeful.'[2]

The term 'Chinese contemporary art' ('*Zhongguo Dangdai Yishu*') refers to artistic production since the end of the Cultural Revolution, after 1976. Art historian Gao Minglu, who played a pivotal role in the events of this time, positions the zeitgeist of this era, its '*Shidai Jingshen*', as the equivalent of modernity in the narrative of modern Chinese history.[3] Not to be confused with western modernity (despite some obvious parallels), Gao links the development of modernity and postmodernity in China with the pragmatism of Deng Xiaoping's Reform and Opening period[4] in the late 1970s and 1980s, and his promulgation of the 'Socialism with Chinese characteristics' that continues to transform Chinese society today. Deng, who famously said, 'White cat, black cat, as long as it catches mice it is a good cat,' emphasising his preference for efficiency above revolutionary idealism, exemplifies a model of the modern which has established a 'permanent condition of contemporaneity'[5] at its core.

There are inherent problems in transferring western assumptions about modernity and postmodernity to a Chinese context. Art historian John Clark argues that the Chinese

Xiao Lu
Dialogue (detail) 1989
photographic documentation of installation
and performance at *China/Avant-garde*
90 x 120 cm
image courtesy the artist

tendency from the 1980s to 'counter-appropriate' from western modernism and postmodernism, in a playful and ironic disregard of the origins and meanings of the western sources, opposes the notion of one kind of modernism transferred to another, entirely different, postcolonial cultural context.[6] Paul Gladston points out that it would be wrong to assume that contemporary Chinese art is merely a 'localized variant of postmodernism.' To imagine that western modernity and postmodernity are culturally authoritative and universally applicable is to position other cultural traditions as the oriental 'other.' In contrast, within mainland China there is a 'widely held and durable belief in the existence of an essential, spatially bounded, Chinese national-cultural identity as well as in the potential manifestation of that identity through indigenous cultural practices including those associated with contemporary Chinese art.'[7]

Theoretical interpretations aside, at precisely the time that the concept of the avant-garde was in its death throes in the west during the 1970s, replaced by the doubt and deconstruction of postmodernity, it flourished in China. We could call it 'avant-gardism with Chinese characteristics': in its concern with 'closing the gap between art and real space' (the space of the art market, the exhibition space, the spaces of academia, the political arena, the studio space, and the conceptual space between artists and audiences) it is fundamentally different from its western counterpart.[8] The Cultural Revolution had severed China's intellectual connections to the outside world and its own cultural history and traditions. Afterwards, there was an enormous thirst for knowledge of what had been happening internationally.

When twenty-six-year-old Xiao Lu fired two pistol shots into the work she had created with Tang Song (although the truth of his degree of involvement is doubtful, as we shall see) it seemed both transgressive and potentially transformative. Gao Minglu, a curator of that significant exhibition, recalls events surrounding the opening on the eve of the Spring Festival: 'At about 11.10am on 5 February 1989, about two hours after the opening of the *China/Avant-garde* Exhibition, Xiao Lu, standing in the ground floor exhibition hall, suddenly raised a handgun and fired two shots at her own installation work, *Dialogue*. The sound of these gunshots not only shook the National Art Museum of China, it also attracted widespread attention among the Chinese and international media. The *China/Avant-garde* exhibition was immediately closed by the Public Security. At that moment Xiao Lu became a public figure who stirred both China and the world.'[9] Taking place just four months prior to June 4 1989, the event came to be seen, not just as a challenge to the conservatism of the artworld in China, but as a gauntlet thrown down to official authority, and a precursor to the unfolding tragedy of Tiananmen. Xiao Lu's action became part of the 'agitation and frenzy' of the time.[10] For an event that had lasted only for a few hours, the ripples spread outwards for a long time to come.

The two artists made a public announcement: 'As the people involved in the handgun incident at the opening of *China/Avant-garde* we believe this to be a purely artistic event. We believe that art naturally carries with it the artist's different understandings of society. But, as artists, we are not interested in politics. Rather, what interests us is the artistic and social value of art itself, as well as the way in which we can use a suitable form to create and to extend and deepen our understanding of art.'[11] Their disavowal of any political intention and an emphasis on 'art for art's sake' was disingenuous. At this time of heightened political turmoil in Beijing, and, indeed throughout China, the artists could not fail to be aware of the atmosphere in which they were enacting their artistic 'intervention'. There had been a growing demand for social and political change, a feeling of optimism, and an increasing freedom of public discourse allowing a more open discussion of issues such as official corruption.

Following her gunshots the exhibition was closed immediately and the iron gates in front of the museum – so close to Tiananmen Square and the heart of political power – were shut, leaving the artists and a large audience outside with crowds of onlookers. Foreign and Chinese reporters carried out impromptu interviews with members of the public. A car full of armed riot police arrived on the scene, departing in some haste once the number of TV crews and journalists' cameras became evident.[12] The media sensation ensured that the exhibition's second opening a few days later drew even greater crowds, attracting not only artists and the cultured elite but also ordinary people, curious to see what the fuss was about.

Eyewitness accounts convey the iconoclastic flavour of the times: 'There was a lot of weird stuff going on in that cavernous Beijing museum back in February 1989. A young man was throwing condoms to a group of people gathered around him; a guy in red was washing his feet in a basin plastered with images of Ronald Reagan; a long-haired man was selling fresh shrimps to a crowd of customers. Strange things were scattered around: lumps of gnarled plastic resembling human intestines; rotting surgical gloves preserved under glass; a poster announcing that a man's death sentence had been carried out was plastered on a wall of photographs. And then, suddenly, two gunshots rang out,' said video artist Zhang Peili in an interview with art historian Francesca Dal Lago ten years later.[13] 'Everybody knew that we were making history. We were totally invested in our roles as actors on a stage where anybody could suddenly become a star,' he said, acknowledging that the exhibition represented an unprecedented relaxation of the restrictions placed on artistic freedom of expression by the Chinese government. Although the show was closed after the furore of the shooting incident, the authorities allowed it to re-open twice more before the official closing date two weeks later, an uncharacteristic indecision which indicates the internal division of the Politburo itself at that time, torn between reformists and hardliners.

China scholar Don J. Cohn, who was also present, describes the exhibition as China's coming-out party for postmodern art, with an atmosphere unlike anything before: 'The early spring air was filled with soot and the men wore their hair at shoulder-length, giving the scene a distinctly bohemian feel. While the exhibition of nearly three hundred artworks was set in a museum designed and still managed in Stalinist fashion, it gave Chinese visitors – especially those forty and older whose lives were traumatically altered and their minds shell-shocked by the Cultural Revolution – the impression that they were treading on forbidden, even foreign territory. One could sense their trepidation as they entered the great hall on the ground floor, and read the incomprehension in their eyes as they stood before works of art that nothing in their lives had prepared them for. They blushed, for example, at the sight of the hanging sculpture of inflated balloons and medical gloves explicitly resembling human genitals, the Gao Brothers' *Mass in the Midnight* (1989), and craned their necks in wonder at Xu Bing's huge ceiling installation *Book From the Sky* (1987–91), with its thousands of playfully sabotaged Chinese characters printed with hand-carved woodblocks.'[14]

The idea for organising a large-scale exhibition of New Wave Art had first been mooted in 1986, during a conference on avant-garde art that took place in the city of Zhuhai, in Guangdong Province. There was, predictably, internal dissension between different factions of the organising body.[15] One of the curators, Li Xianting, felt conflicted. Uneasy about the stringent limitations applied by the National Art Museum, which included a ban on performance art and on any works with explicit sexual content, and anxious about the limited time available to organise such a massive show, he wondered about the curatorial purpose. 'At that point I already felt that it would be impossible to realise an avant-garde approach.'[16]

Despite these reservations, or perhaps because of them, Li decided that the only way forward was to 'build a certain atmosphere with a sense of freshness and provocation unlike that of any exhibition the general public had ever seen.'[17] He describes clandestine arrangements (and many secret long distance phone calls) to invite radical groups such as Xiamen Dada to present forbidden performance works. From this distance the entire affair seems to have had the chaotic energy of Dada gatherings in the Cabaret Voltaire in Zurich at the beginning of the twentieth century, at another heightened and politically sensitive time. Wang Deren angered Huang Yong Ping by scattering condoms around at the opening, some of which covered his work. In response to Huang's complaints, Wang declared, 'Huang Yong Ping is a fake Dadaist!'[18]

The intensity of the atmosphere, after forty years of censorship, was a heady mix of fear and jubilation, 'an exciting, explosive atmosphere.'[19] Li Xianting describes what happened next. Xiao Lu and Tang Song had concealed from him their plans to create a performance work around Xiao's installation, so it was particularly shocking: 'When the gunfire occurred, I became immediately conscious of the sensitive social psychology that these gunshots embodied. After having been constrained for so long, a new mentality yearned to be set free.'[20]

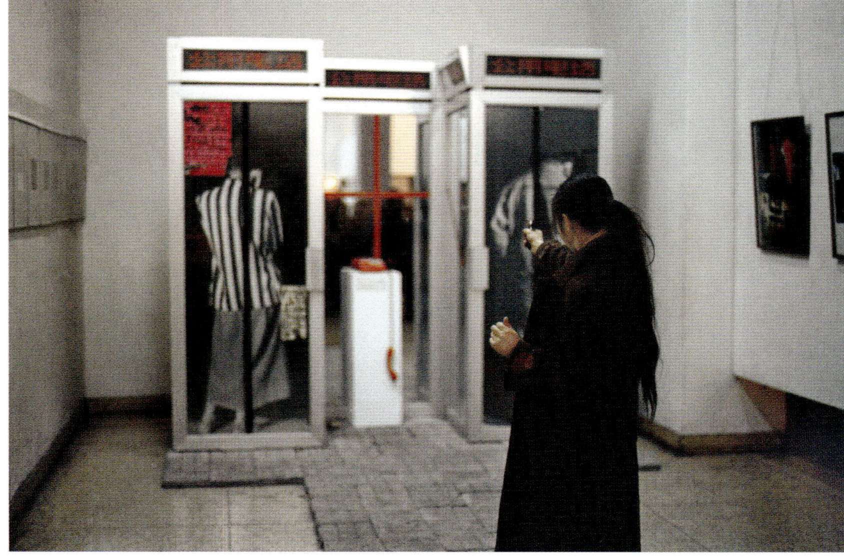

Despite the conditions insisted upon by the National Art Museum, and the internal dissension within the organising committee, the *China/Avant-garde* exhibition is remembered as perhaps the single most important event in the history of contemporary art in China, not just for its size but also its social impact. Wu Hung recalls: 'The National Art Gallery was transformed into a solemn installation: long black banners, extending from the street to the exhibition hall, bore the emblem of the exhibition – a "No U-Turn" traffic sign – signalling "no turning back." The feeling of heroism was closely related to the political situation of the time: three months later, student demonstrations broke out in Tiananmen Square. Because of the radical redirection of Chinese contemporary art in the aftermath of the demonstrations, the *China/Avant-garde* exhibition represented both the climax and the end of the avant-garde art movement in 1980s China.'[21]

Xiao Lu
Dialogue 1989
photographic documentation of installation
and performance at *China/Avant-garde*
90 x 120 cm
image courtesy the artist

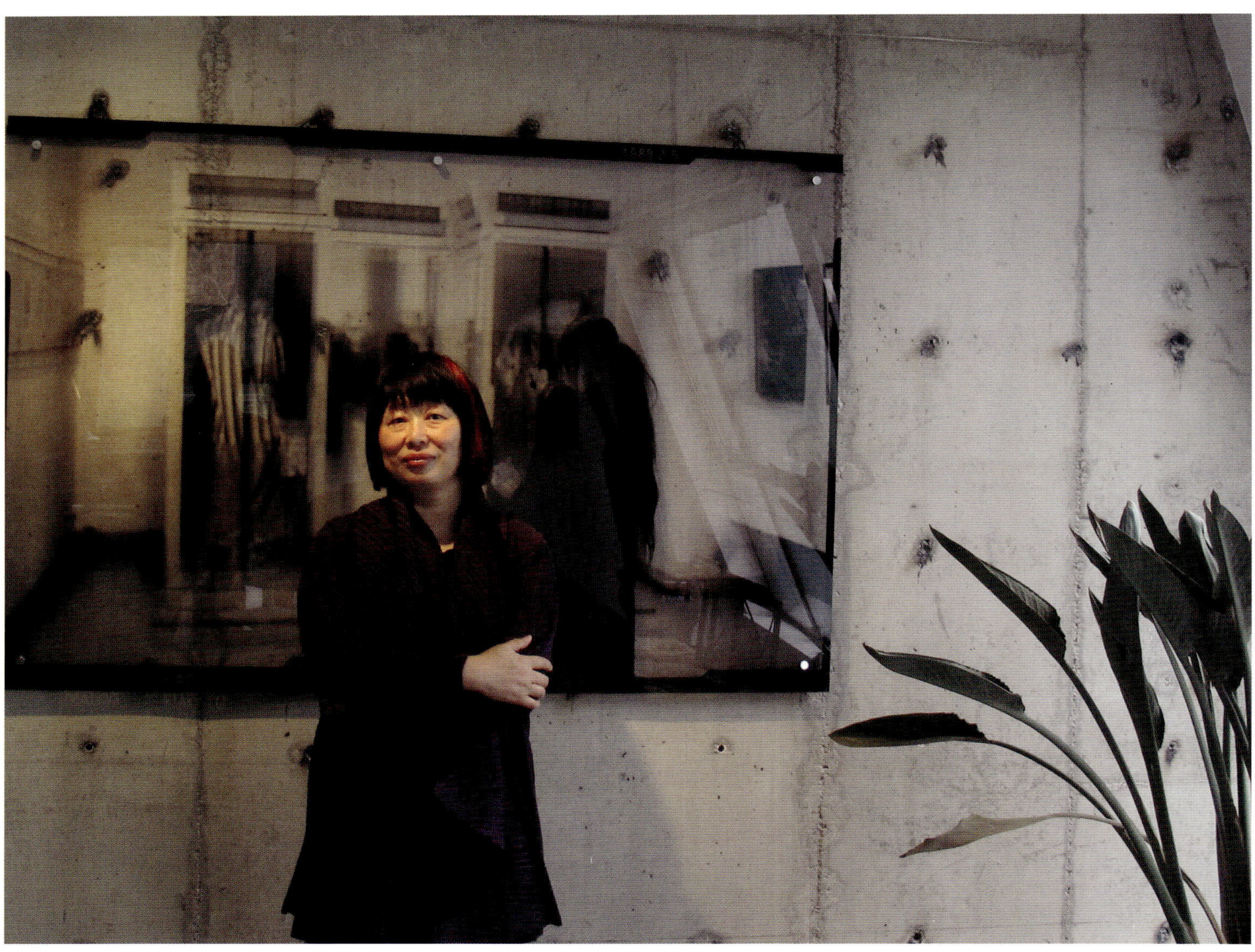

After the 'June 4 Incident', as the events of Tiananmen are often described in China, Xiao Lu moved to Australia, where Tang Song later joined her after being dramatically smuggled out of China through Hong Kong.[22] *China/Avant-garde* became part of pro-democracy movement mythology, but was also shrouded in mystery, even to the point of who should be credited with authorship of the performance work – was it Xiao Lu, Tang Song, or the friend who had lent her the gun? Fifteen years after the events, and after the disintegration of their relationship, Xiao Lu made an effort to set the record straight, claiming sole authorship of the work in her autobiographical novel, *Dialogue*. An outpouring of vitriol was directed towards her by former friends, acquaintances and even people only peripherally involved in the art scene. Gao Minglu interprets the way that her actions in reclaiming the work were viewed: 'She had become a "bad woman" who was subverting the grand historical narrative of avant-garde art.'[23]

Gao describes *Dialogue* as, 'undoubtedly one of the most iconic works in the history of Chinese contemporary art.'[24] In the late 1980s performance art was a form of oppositional and radical practice by artists who had discovered the work of Western practitioners such as Joseph Beuys. Painters and sculptors too were experimenting with new forms. The 1985 *'Art New Wave'* label describes a period of exuberant experimentation, in which radical groups with a variety of manifestoes and political/artistic positions flourished across twenty-three provinces and major cities. The artists were young, many still at art school, with a fervent desire

Xiao Lu at home in Beijing, April 2014
photo LG

to rediscover their modernist roots, interrupted by more than thirty years of artistic conservatism and heavy-handed insistence upon Soviet socialist realism.[25]

Duchamp and Dada were inspirational for artists such as the members of the 'Xiamen Dada' group, resulting in notorious performances such as *Burning Works* (1986) in which they set fire to a pile of their own oil paintings in front of the Xiamen City Art Gallery of the Masses. It is hard to imagine such an event taking place today, but at that time commercial considerations were non-existent. In a statement drafted for the event their spokesman, Huang Yong Ping, pointed out that the purpose of burning their artworks was to de-emphasise the materiality of art and emphasises its spirituality: 'The fact that collecting art does not exist in China may be a good thing: an artist can therefore do whatever he likes with his works and does not have to be careful with them.'[26] In 1987 Huang created *The History of Chinese Painting and the History of Western (Modern) Painting Washed Together in a Washing Machine for Two Minutes*. The title describes the work. Two art history books, from opposing cultural traditions, are washed together, with the resulting pulp displayed in an unattractive pile. For *China/Avant-garde*, Huang proposed an absurd and impossible action: to literally pull the museum off its foundations, exposing the National Art Museum of China as a morally bankrupt edifice of repressive state apparatus.[27]

Xiao Lu's gunshots were not the first performance work in contemporary Chinese art, and not the most outrageous. In being enacted on the central stage of the National Art Museum, however, and in attracting the attention of Chinese and Western media, Xiao Lu became, at least for that moment, a star of the avant-garde narrative. Even so, her radical act has largely been interpreted by commentators outside China as a minor footnote in the development of a performative genre in Chinese contemporary art, dismissed by Thomas Berghuis as an ill-advised action by 'two young artists seeking attention.'[28] Her work itself was hi-jacked in a manner familiar to female artists now and in the past, often described as co-authored by Tang Song. With hindsight, Gao Minglu believes that Xiao's gunshots have been consistently misunderstood, in large part due to the media attention they generated. Fired by a female artist, the shots became part of a narrative not of the artist's construction – instead they became a new construct of subjective feminine anger and emotion. The work has been interpreted in diverse ways, but the artist herself has been a mostly silent presence, forever frozen at that decisive moment, her back to the audience, sighting down the barrel of the gun.

In the spring of 2014, I met Xiao Lu at her home, a minimalist concrete structure of her own design in a new art zone on Beijing's outskirts, and asked her to tell me about *Two Gunshots Fired at the Installation, Dialogue* in her own words. Initially reluctant – it must be irritating in your fifties to be forever defined by an act of youthful defiance twenty-five years ago – she warmed to the subject and provided some new insights into this much-disputed narrative. Recalling her motivations for the shooting, Xiao said:

> So many years later, it's hard to remember. I had a series of emotions before that performance. It was not because of an idea. It was an emotion. You may have a lot of ideas but you must use that idea that is most in accordance with what you want to express. Back in '88 I was thinking about shooting (the sculpture) and in '89 I still wanted to do it; it just seemed a very natural thing, and the circumstances allowed me to do it.[29]

The work had been germinating for a while. In 1988 Xiao began her final semester at the Zhejiang Fine Arts Academy in Hangzhou, where she was studying oil painting, and where her father was the Principal of the college. Influenced by pioneering Bulgarian artist and visiting professor Maryn Varbanov, whose impact on contemporary Chinese art has been acknowledged by numerous artists including Gu Wenda,[30] she began to experiment, combining painting with sculptural materials. Robert Rauschenberg's work had been shown in Beijing in 1985, suggesting new possibilities for combining 2D and 3D forms and using 'found' materials. Varbanov evidently wasn't interested in fostering the self-esteem of his students. When Xiao eagerly showed him her new paintings, he said, 'Throw all of them on the rubbish tip!' He advised her to break away from the limitations of the painted surface, to use whatever materials would express her own personal response to the world as she experienced it.[31]

Xiao Lu recalls the late 1980s as an exciting time of passionate discussions of art and ideas; a time when it seemed that young artists wanted to throw away the past and abandon Chinese traditions, emulating western styles. Huang Yong Ping had himself graduated from the Zhejiang Fine Arts Academy some years earlier, and Hangzhou had experienced its share of radical young artists making a splash. Gu Wenda explains the influence of Professor Varbanov on a generation of young Chinese artists, and his recommendation of a rather different approach: 'At that time… most Chinese artists just wanted to embrace Western techniques and styles. But Varbanov knew that you can have modern materials and modern techniques but you also need to find your own unique Chinese vocabulary…Today it's normal for artists to talk about bridging East and West and cultural exchange, but for many avant-garde artists [at that time] the key point was to embrace the West and throw out the traditional. But he saw something different. He could see both sides. He was a pioneer.'[31] With Varbanov's encouragement Xiao Lu decided to make an

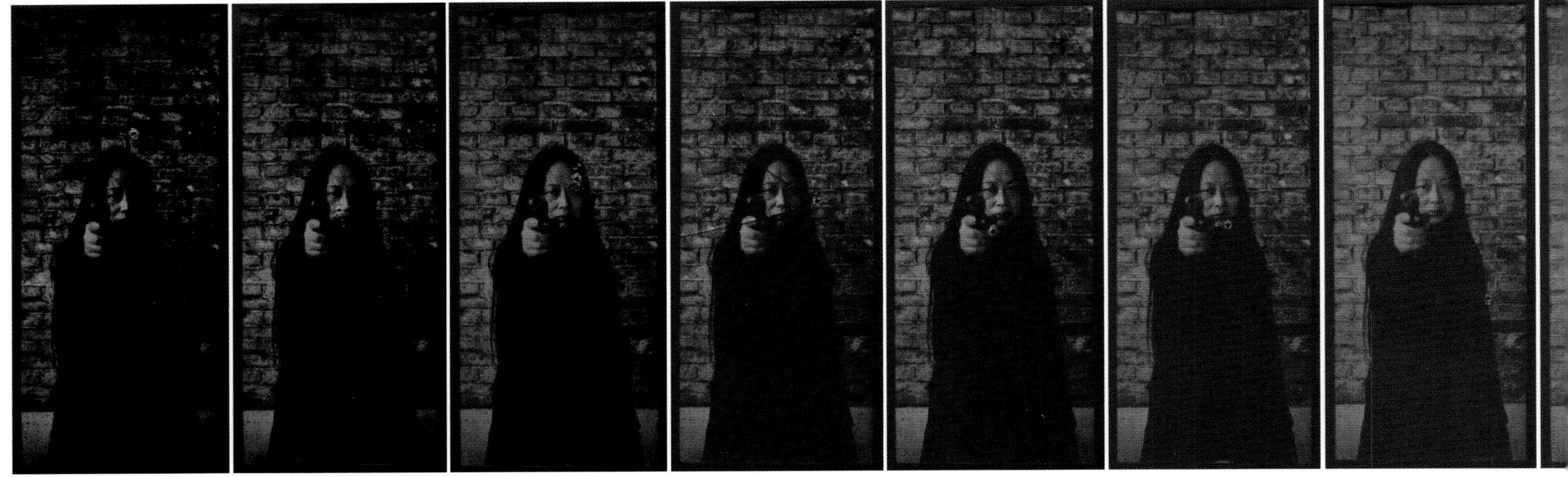

installation for her graduation work, rather than exhibit her paintings. This was a controversial move, and in the end, to appease her father, she was forced to submit oil paintings as well, just to prove that she could work in the medium she was supposed to be studying.

Her graduation piece was inspired by what Xiao Lu had come to see as the impossibility of communication across the gender divide: 'As soon as I thought about a dialogue between male and female I felt flustered. Men – to hell with them!'[32] In her autobiographical 'novel' she remembers calling the old man (a friend of her father's, and her godfather) who had seduced her as a young girl, accusing him of ruining her life. He hung up on her, and she was left stranded in the phone booth, telephone receiver dangling from her hand, weeping hysterically. This humiliating moment was the decisive factor in the creation of her work, which may be interpreted as a kind of *'J'accuse'* – a pointed message to this man and others that she believed had wronged her. 'Just as I left the phone booth, a picture appeared before my eyes – specifically and artistically formed: the telephone booth, a male-female conversation, a dangling telephone receiver, an engaged signal... it had found its format.'[33]

The work was exhibited at the graduation show, later appearing on the cover of *Xin Meishu (New Art),* the magazine of the Zhejiang Fine Arts Academy. As Xiao Lu tells it, her inclusion in the *China/Avant-garde* exhibition was something of an accident, and a surprise. She received a letter informing her that the work had been accepted, later discovering that a classmate had entered slides of her work to the organising committee. 'There seemed to be no rhyme or reason in someone who had just graduated being invited to participate in such a grand exhibition,' she said.[34] She agonised over whether she should carry out the plan that had been germinating since the previous year, the idea of shooting her own work as a defiant surprise performance in the hallowed space of the art museum. The night before the opening, she borrowed a gun from an old friend. Xiao Lu describes the moments before and after the gunshots:

> I walked up to my work, saw my reflection in the mirror. There was only the slightest moment of doubt. For a split second I lowered my head. Everything around me came to a standstill, the air congealed. I heard the leaping of my pulse. I heard the gunshot ringing in my ears again, heaven and hell, mortal hatred and exhaustion, suffocation in my chest... I savagely raised my head, raised the gun in my hands, looked straight at my reflection in the mirror, the barrel of my gun aimed at myself... The shooting left bullet holes in the mirror.[35]

Under the spell of romantic love, she allowed Tang Song to take credit for the work, despite the fact that the installation had been exhibited in Hangzhou long before the exhibition in Beijing, and that she had planned the shooting for months beforehand. She had met Tang Song for the first time when she arrived in Beijing for the exhibition, she recalls. 'At that moment, a man entered my life. A misunderstanding, a woman's fears and illusions, and her silence for the sake of love, allowed him to appear as a co-curator of the work.'[36] Looking back at her own youthful self, Xiao seemed at a loss to explain her fifteen-year silent acquiescence. The influential art magazine *Zhongguo Meishu Bao* credited Tang Song equally

Xiao Lu
15 Gunshots from 1989 to 2003 1989–2003
photographs documenting performance
fifteen of 100 x 45 cm
image courtesy the artist

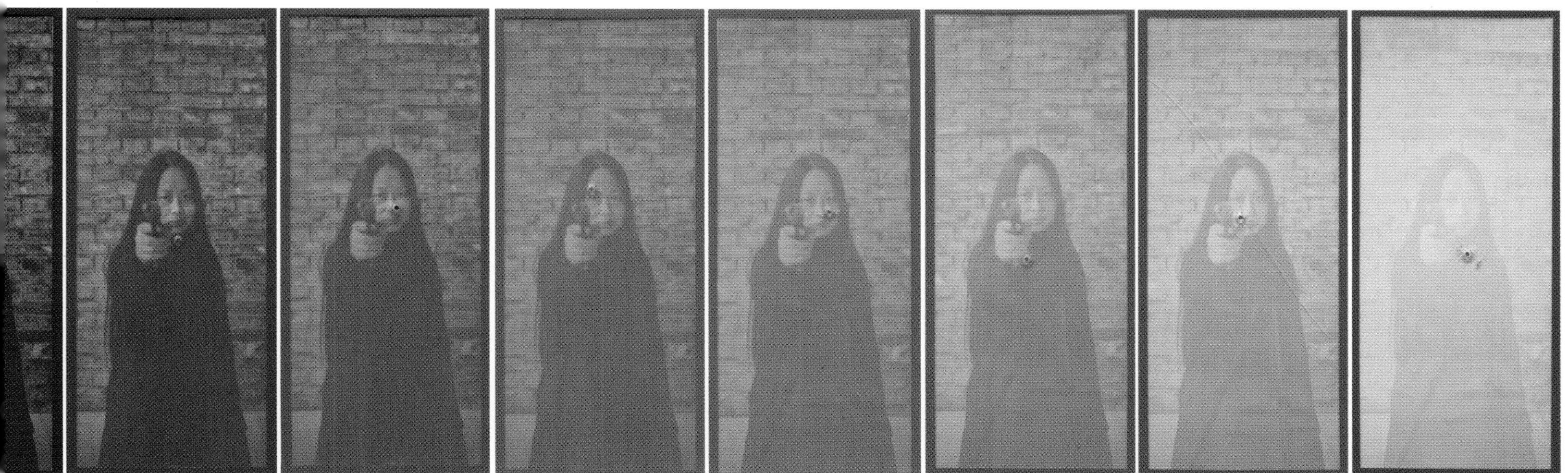

with Xiao Lu. In an interview with *Art Asia Pacific* magazine, Li Xianting, the deputy editor of *Meishu Bao*, presented his own version of the events. He had written an article in 1989 based on interviews with the two artists:

> Xiao Lu and Tang Song fired gunshots at their installation of a man and a woman in separate telephone booths, a piece entitled *Dialogue* (1989). The artists hailed from high-ranking military families, and Xiao's father was also director of a provincial art academy. To stage the performance, they had stolen the guns and bullets from their parents; part of the concept of the work was to criticize their own status as children of the privileged class.[37]

Apart from the source of the gun and the issue of who created the installation, Xiao Lu denies that 'criticism' was ever a part of her intention. She sees the work as entirely personal, even confessional, based on a private emotional impasse, rather than overtly political: 'This complex and paradoxical emotional state is the original notion that produced the work.'[38]

There are as many theories about Xiao Lu's real intentions as there are artists and critics who have a stake in the avant-garde narrative in China. Perhaps all it shows is the suspect nature of memory and the hopeless unreliability of eyewitnesses. Gao Minglu says:

> When the shots were fired that day in the museum everyone immediately suspected that it was performative violence and a challenge to the law. Chinese citizens are not permitted to carry guns, and even less so to fire them in public settings... very naturally, the media, and especially the foreign media, thought immediately of politics and national ideology. But in truth, Xiao Lu's gunshots came first and foremost from her own doubtful attitude towards modernity (the bright, clean surfaces of the telephone booths.)[39]

Here is yet another interpretation of the work as a critique of modernity and China's transformation. Gao Minglu acknowledges, however:

> The original author of this work was Xiao Lu, but the interpretations which followed were not hers... After the gunshots, the interpretation of *Dialogue* no longer belonged to her, but to society.[40]

It may not have been her intention, but her gunshots catapulted her into a world in which gendered social and political readings of her action were inevitable.

Even the various accounts of what transpired after the exhibition was closed down are contradictory. Xiao Lu remembers handing herself over to police later that day, to ensure that nobody else was blamed for her action. She was released a little later. Others tell the story differently. 'They were arrested and beaten up by the police,' Li Xianting recounts. 'Then they were released a day or two later when high-positioned people went to see them. The artists exposed the inequality of Chinese law through an art event.' When he was asked for the *Art Asia Pacific* interview in 2010 if he had known in advance that Xiao and Tang would fire live ammunition, Li contradicts his own earlier account at the time

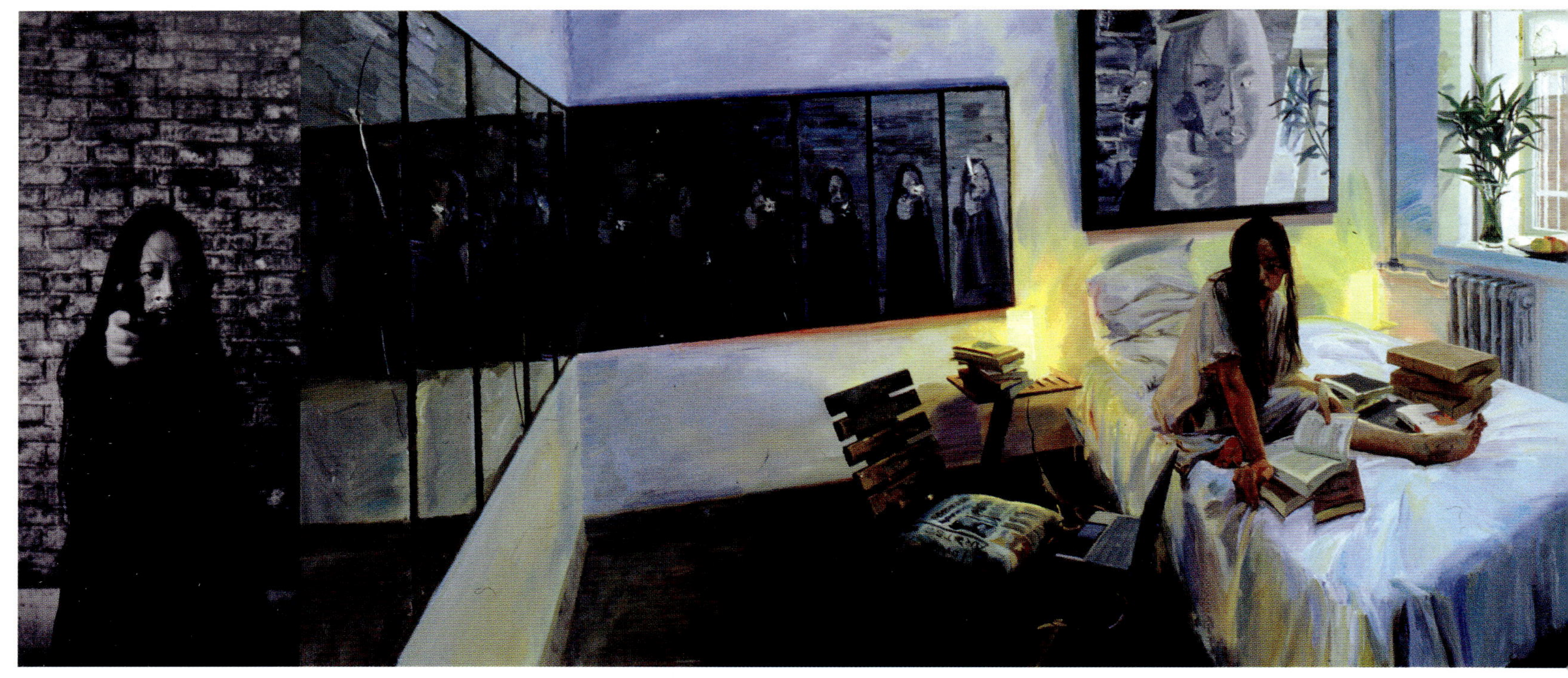

of the incident in which he said he was shocked and taken by surprise: 'I overheard a little bit. Most people didn't know. I kept it secret.'[41] Despite numerous attempts since 2004 by Gao Minglu and Xiao Lu herself to reclaim her authorship, the work is still described as a collaboration in numerous articles and on some current websites. Eminent critic and historian Wu Hung credits the two artists jointly, and describes the work as a 'premeditated shooting incident.'[42] Why is this story so obfuscated by mutually contradictory interpretations?

Xiao Lu spoke out only in 2004, after breaking up with Tang Song, with whom she had spent years in Sydney, and with whom she had returned to China. And what became of him? He has continued to work as an artist in Beijing since his return to China. An exhibition of his abstract paintings at Boers-Li Gallery in Beijing in 2013, *Eulogy – In Memory of Hans van Dijk*, included a photograph of the artist being dragged away from the National Museum in 1989. After his release from his short imprisonment Tang wrote a letter to van Dijk, the art historian and curator who had a major influence on artists such as Tang Song in the late 1980s and 1990s, in which he asserted yet another set of intentions for the act. Writing in *Leap* magazine, Fiona He describes it:

> He had taken blame for his partner Xiao Lu's gunshot at their installation, *Dialogue* – the renegade artist objects to the common claim of the gunshot being a mere piece of destructive performance art, but rather, 'A provocation to the media, a disruption of the audience's visual and auditory experience, a contestation to the law, a rebellious act against art education in China and an impulsive decision propelled by China's New Wave movement.'[43]

What is the significance of Xiao Lu's work now, after so many years, and in the context of an utterly different China? It would be easy to interpret *Two Gunshots* as the angry, rebellious act of a girl abused by an adult in a position of trust. Xiao could not openly speak about her experiences and believed no-one would understand her distress. She had been thinking about using a gun in the art arena for a long time. Although it is tempting to see Xiao's transition to installation and performance art as a rejection of her father and his adherence to Soviet socialist realist painting, which was also the artistic modus operandi of her abuser, to do so would be to deny the complexity of the artist's work and her awareness of the nuances of contemporary art practices of the time. It may well have been a cathartic act – 'the manifestation of an inner demand'[44] according to the artist – but it was also an artwork planned in the context of a growing awareness of international contemporary art practices.

Shooting the gun in the gallery was a symbolic attack on authority in all its forms: the patriarchal authority of her

Yu Hong
She: Performance Artist 2005
oil on canvas
150 x 68 cm and 150 x 300 cm
image courtesy the artist

father and godfather, and the authority of the privileged revolutionary caste to which her family belonged. Xiao Lu herself seems a little uncertain, from this distance of time, of her real intentions. To some she has said that although she herself had no explicit political intentions with the gunshots, the fact that it has become layered with such meanings is inevitable.[45] In conversation she emphasises the subjective nature of *Dialogue* as a confessional artwork, feminist in intent and a precursor to her continuing body of performance work and her interest in women's rights. 'Each artist [in *China/Avant-garde*] had their own thought process in making their artwork, but how that artwork is associated with society is out of your control,' she said, agreeing that her own work had taken on a life of its own, and perhaps a deeper meaning and a different significance than the one she originally intended.

The work stands now as a social document of a particular time and place, a case study of the influences of western artists and theorists on the development of avant-garde art in China, and, perhaps most importantly, as one of only a few overtly and explicitly feminist works in contemporary Chinese art. Gao Minglu identifies it as 'the most sophisticated and controversial work in the *China/Avant-garde* exhibition, as well as in Chinese contemporary art history.'[46]

Xiao Lu wrote five letters to Gao Minglu between February and March 2004, in an attempt to reclaim authorship of her work. He encouraged her, believing that not only was it her right as the artist, but that it was vital for a younger generation of artists to 'rediscover the complex context of this historical event made by a particular female individual.' In 2003 she had appropriated her own work, creating a new performance piece. Fifteen gunshots were fired (at a gun club – the only place where Chinese people are legally permitted to fire a gun) into photographs of the original event. A re-creation with a difference, she directs her anger against her own younger, acquiescent self. With one bullet for each year of her fifteen-year relationship with Tang Song, fired into the iconic image of the artist aiming a pistol, she metaphorically freed herself from his control and reasserted her identity and agency.

What is one to make of all the claims and counter-claims, the contradictory accounts and interpretations of events? Love betrayed, a traumatised girl sexually abused by a trusted adult, a woman ignored and belittled, or the old story of a man claiming a woman's work as his own? Perhaps the doubt is due to the genuine confusion and muddle of a volatile time in history. So many years later, memories are faded and the dramatis personae, having taken up their entrenched positions, maintain them at all costs. The last word on the subject must belong to Xiao Lu herself. In a 2004 performance, *A Dialogue about Dialogue,* Xiao cut off her long hair in front of her own 1989 telephone booth installation. Recalling her thoughts she wrote:

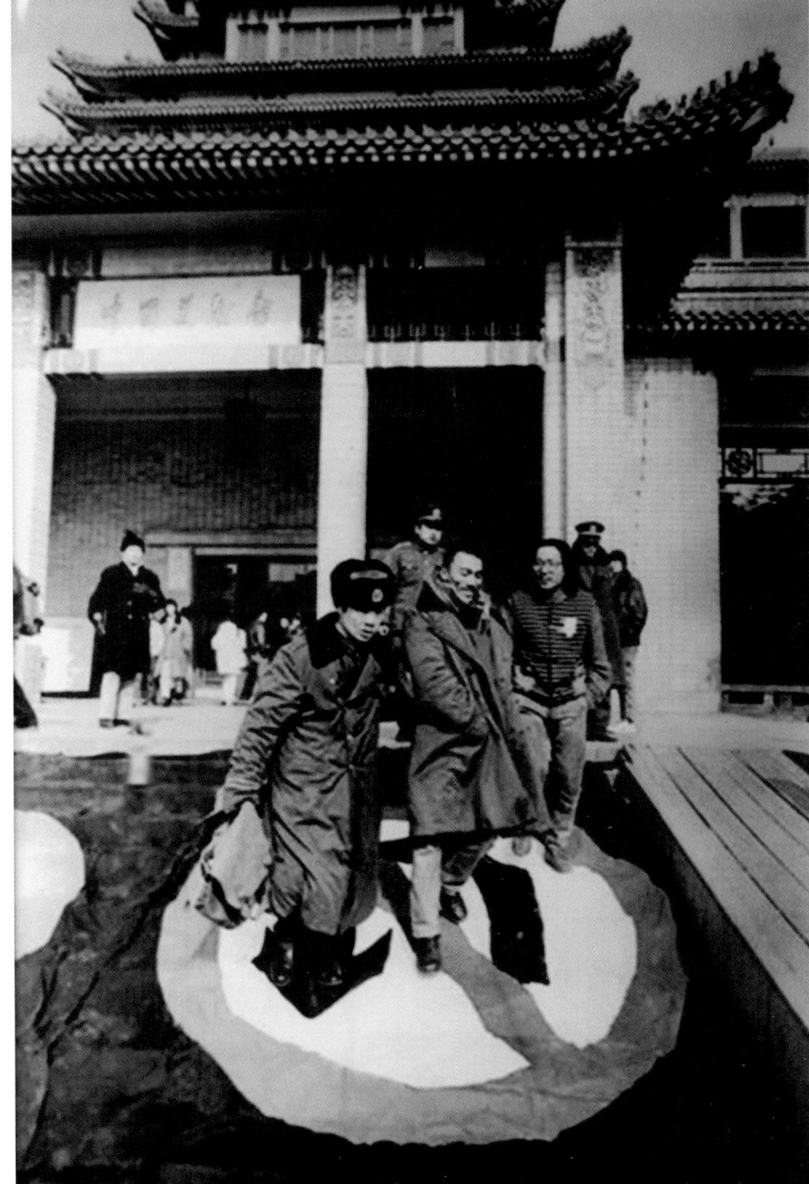

Fifteen years ago, after I fired those two shots at the National Art Museum of China, Beijing, the art museum was closed.
Fifteen years ago, after the report of the gunshot, he was drawn into the "gunshot incident".
Fifteen years ago, I didn't know how to explain, and he became a spokesperson for this work.
Fifteen years ago, when I was bewildered by the gun, "love" seemed to have come to me.
For fifteen years I didn't say a word about this work.
Today, after fifteen years, I have finally spoken the words I wanted to say as an artist.[47]

Tang Song
Real and Fake 2.6.1989–3.20.2013
black and white print
120 x 80cm
image courtesy the artist and Boers-Li Gallery Beijing

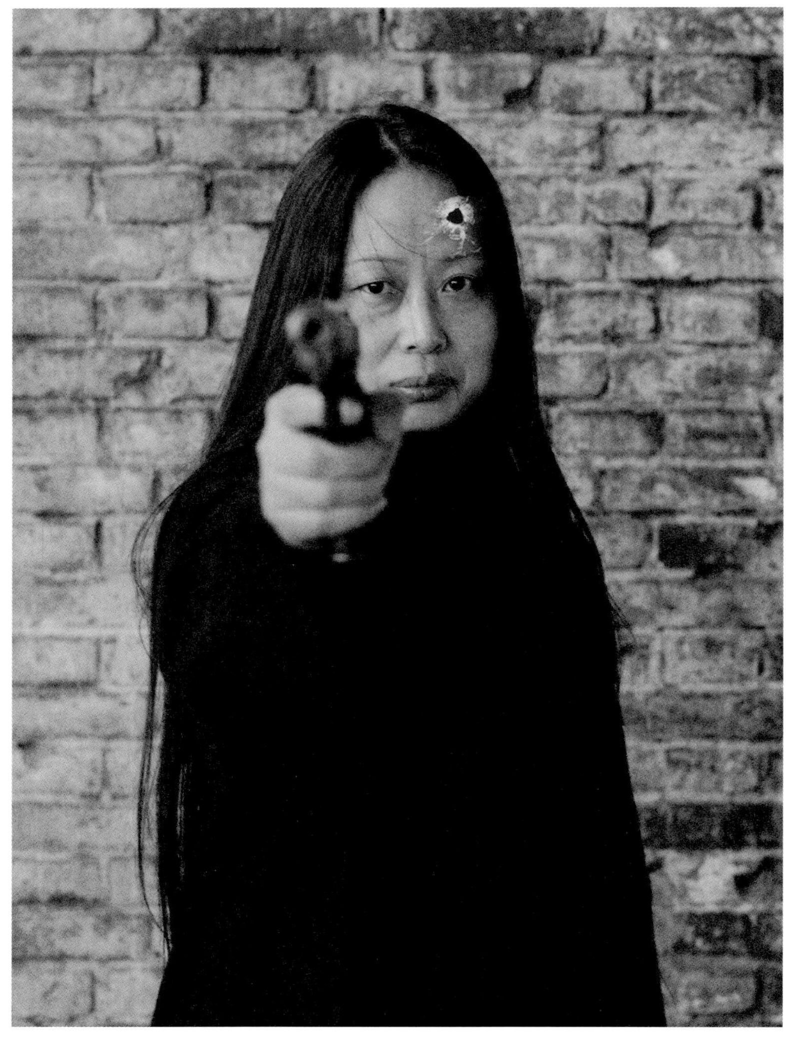

Xiao Lu
15 Gunshots from 1989 to 2003 (detail) 1989–2003
photographs documenting performance
fifteen of 100 x 45 cm
image courtesy the artist

AFTER THE GUNSHOTS

After the crackdown on the pro-democracy demonstrators, the *China/Avant-garde* exhibition was repeatedly attacked by authorities as a manifestation of bourgeois liberalism – even condemned as a small Tiananmen Square of the artworld. Gao Minglu was informed that he 'needed to study Marxism at home' and was prohibited from editing, publishing, lecturing and travelling outside Beijing.[48] A year later he went to the United States as a visiting scholar. Huang Yong Ping went to Paris, Gu Wenda and Xu Bing to the United States, and a group of artists obtained visas to stay in Australia. In an unlikely turn of events Xiao Lu found herself drawing caricatures of tourists in Sydney's Kings Cross for twenty dollars a portrait. She said, 'For those few months [in early 1989] China was totally different. After June 4 everything changed. 1989 was a turning point. For *China/Avant-garde* – so many of the artists were connected with June 4, joining the demonstrators in the streets.' She worries that the younger generation know nothing of these events. In Chinese history each successive dynasty erased all traces of the preceding rulers. In the case of a generation of avant-garde artists and activists, the subsequent transformation of China, and the Chinese economic miracle which saw the rise of the art stars of the 1990s, has overshadowed their achievements. Huang Zhuan summarised its fleeting nature: 'The moment the exhibition was over, another storm of passion swept the whole country. When that storm died down, it was already the 1990s. Then, the exhibition was just like an answer to a curtain call. After the 1990s, the entire world had changed, changed to a time of pursuing material comforts and a time of consumption.'[49] It was like a dream from which the country had awoken, and the avant-garde art of the 1980s disappeared without a trace.

NOTES

1 Wu Hung, with assistance of Wang, Peggy, *Contemporary Chinese Art: Primary Documents* MOMA 2010 (113)
2 Jaivin, Linda, speaking at the Sydney Writers' Festival, 9 June 2014, in conversation with Amy Tan, recorded for ABC radio available at http://omnyapp.com/shows/books-arts-daily-separate/a-love-affair-with-china-amy-tan-and-linda-jaivin accessed 13 June 2014
3 Gao Minglu, *Total Modernity and the Avant-Garde in Twentieth Century Chinese Art*, 2011 Massachusetts Institute of Technology Press (1)
4 Economic reforms introducing market principles began in 1978 and were carried out in two stages. See Vogel, Ezra F., available at http://www.eastasiaforum.org/2011/09/27/china-under-deng-xiaopings-leadership/ accessed 19 January 2015
5 Gao Minglu, *Total Modernity and the Avant-Garde in Twentieth Century Chinese Art*, 2011 Massachusetts Institute of Technology Press (1)
6 Clark, John 'Is the modernity of Chinese art comparable? An opening of a theoretical space', *Journal of Art Historiography* 10, June 2014; available at https://arthistoriography.wordpress.com/10-jun-2014/ (accessed 1 May 2015) and *Asian Modernities: Chinese and Thai art of the 1980s and 1990s*, 2010, Power Publications, Sydney
7 Gladston, Paul, 'Deconstructing Gao Minglu: critical reflections on contemporaneity and associated exceptionalist readings of contemporary Chinese art' *Journal of Art Historiography* 10 June 2014 available at https://arthistoriography.wordpress.com/10-jun-2014/ accessed 2 May 2015
8 Gao Minglu, *Total Modernity and the Avant-Garde in Twentieth Century Chinese Art*, 2011 Massachusetts Institute of Technology Press (1)
9 Xiao Lu, with Foreword by Gao Minglu (transl. by Archibald McKenzie) *Dialogue* pp. vii–viii, Hong Kong University Press 2010
10 ibid.
11 Hang Jian and Cao Xiao'ou (transl. by Jiayun Zhuang) 'A Brief

Account of China Avant-Garde' (1989) in Wu Hung, with assistance of Wang, Peggy, *Contemporary Chinese Art: Primary Documents* MOMA 2010, 121–26, originally published as 'Zhongguo Xiandai Yishuzhan Ceji' in *Meishu* (Art) 256, no.4 (1989) 5–9
12 ibid.
13 Del Lago, Francesca, 'The Avant-garde has its Moment of Glory', *Time* magazine, 1999, available at http://content.time.com/time/world/article/0,8599,2054554,00.html#ixzz2WHSeBk1Y accessed 14 January 2014
14 Cohn, Don. J, 'Shots Heard Round Beijing' in *Art Asia Pacific*, 2009, available at http://artasiapacific.com/Magazine/65/ShotsHearRoundBeijing accessed 19 January 2014
15 Wu Hung, *Contemporary Chinese Art: Primary Documents*. MOMA 2010 (113)
16 Li Xianting, (transl. Kristen Loring) Confessions of a China/Avant-Garde Curator, in *Contemporary Chinese Art: Primary Documents*. MOMA 2010, (116) originally published as 'WoZuowei Zhongguo Xiandai Yishuzhan chouzhanren de zigongzhuang' in *Meishu Shilun* (Art History and Theory) 1989 No. 3
17 ibid.
18 Hang Jian and Cao Xiao'ou 'A Brief Account of China/Avant-Garde' (1989) in *Contemporary Chinese Art Primary Documents* (Wu Hung Ed.) Museum of Modern Art New York 2010 pp 121–26. Orig. published as 'Zhongguo Xiandai Yishuzhan Ceji' in *Meishu* (Art) 256. No. 4 (1989) 5–9
19 Li Xianting, (transl. Kristen Loring) 'Confessions of a China/Avant-Garde Curator', in *Contemporary Chinese Art: Primary Documents*. MOMA 2010, (116) originally published as 'WoZuowei Zhongguo Xiandai Yishuzhan chouzhanren de zigongzhuang' in *Meishu Shilun* (Art History and Theory) 1989 No. 3
20 ibid. (120)
21 Wu Hung, with assistance of Wang, Peggy, *Contemporary Chinese Art: Primary Documents*. MOMA 2010 (113)
22 Xiao Lu, with Foreword by Gao Minglu (transl. by Archibald McKenzie) *Dialogue* pp. vii–viii, Hong Kong University Press 2010
23 ibid. (xi)
24 ibid. (vii–viii)
25 Wu Hung with assistance of Wang, Peggy, *85 Art New Wave*, in *Contemporary Chinese Art: Primary Documents*. MOMA 2010 (51)
26 Xiamen Dada 'Statement on Burning' 1986, reproduced by Fei Dawei (transl. Tzu-Wen Cheng) in 'Two Minute Wash Cycle: Huang Yong Ping's Chinese Period' 2005 available at http://visualarts.walkerart.org/oracles/details.wac?id=2453&title=Writings accessed 9 June 2014
27 Huang Yong Ping in conversation with Jane De Bevoise at MOMA New York, October 15 2010, transcribed for Asia Art Archive, available at http://www.aaa-a.org/programs/conversation-with-huang-yongping/ accessed 9 June 2014
28 Berghuis, Thomas J, *Performance Art in China* 2006 Timezone 8, Beijing (91)
29 Unless otherwise acknowledged all quotes from Xiao Lu are from her conversation with the writer in April 2014
30 O'Dea, Madelyn, 'Perpetual Motion, The Life and Times of Maryn Varbanov', in *Leap: the Art Magazine of Contemporary China* 1 August 2010
31 ibid.
32 Xiao Lu (transl. by Archibald McKenzie) *Dialogue*, Hong Kong University Press 2010 (60)
33 ibid. (62)
34 ibid. (79)
35 ibid. (89)
36 ibid. (4)
37 Cohen, Andrew, 'Off the Page', *Art AsiaPacific*, Issue 71, Nov/Dec 2010, available at http://artasiapacific.com/Magazine/71/OffThePageLiXianting accessed 9 June 2014
38 In conversation with the writer, April 2014, and 'Xiao Lu', self-edited and self-published catalogue 2013
39 Gao Minglu (transl. Philip Tinari) 'The Sound of Gunshots Half a Life's Dialogue: On Xiao Lu's Dialogue' in *Xiao Lu 1989–2013*, self-edited self-published catalogue
40 ibid.
41 Cohen, Andrew, 'Off the Page', *Art AsiaPacific*, Issue 71, Nov/Dec 2010 available at http://artasiapacific.com/Magazine/71/OffThePageLiXianting accessed 9 June 2014
42 Wu Hung, *Contemporary Chinese Art*, Thames and Hudson, 2014, London (87)
43 He, Fiona, 'Tang Song, Eulogy – In Memory of Hans Van Dijk' *Leap Magazine* Issue 21, available at http://leapleapleap.com/2013/07/tang-song-elegy-in-memory-of-hans-van-dijk/ accessed 9 June 2014
44 Xiao Lu, transl. by Archibald McKenzie, *Dialogue*, Hong Kong University Press 2010 (4)
45 Wen, Philip 'Gunshots that Foreshadowed a Massacre: An interview with Xiao Lu', *Sydney Morning Herald*, 31 May–1 June 2014
46 Gao Minglu, *Total Modernity and the Avant-Garde in Twentieth Century Chinese Art* 2011 Massachusetts Institute of Technology Press (162)
47 Xiao Lu (transl. Archibald McKenzie), 5 May 2004, 798 Studio Beijing, reproduced in *Xiao Lu*, self-published catalogue
48 Gao Minglu, *Total Modernity and the Avant-Garde in Twentieth Century Chinese Art*, 2011 Massachusetts Institute of Technology Press (166)
49 available at http://www.artspeakchina.org/mediawiki/1989_Avant-Garde Exhibition_%E5%89%8D%E5%8D%AB%E8%89%BA%E6%9C%AF%E5%B1%95 accessed 9 June 2014

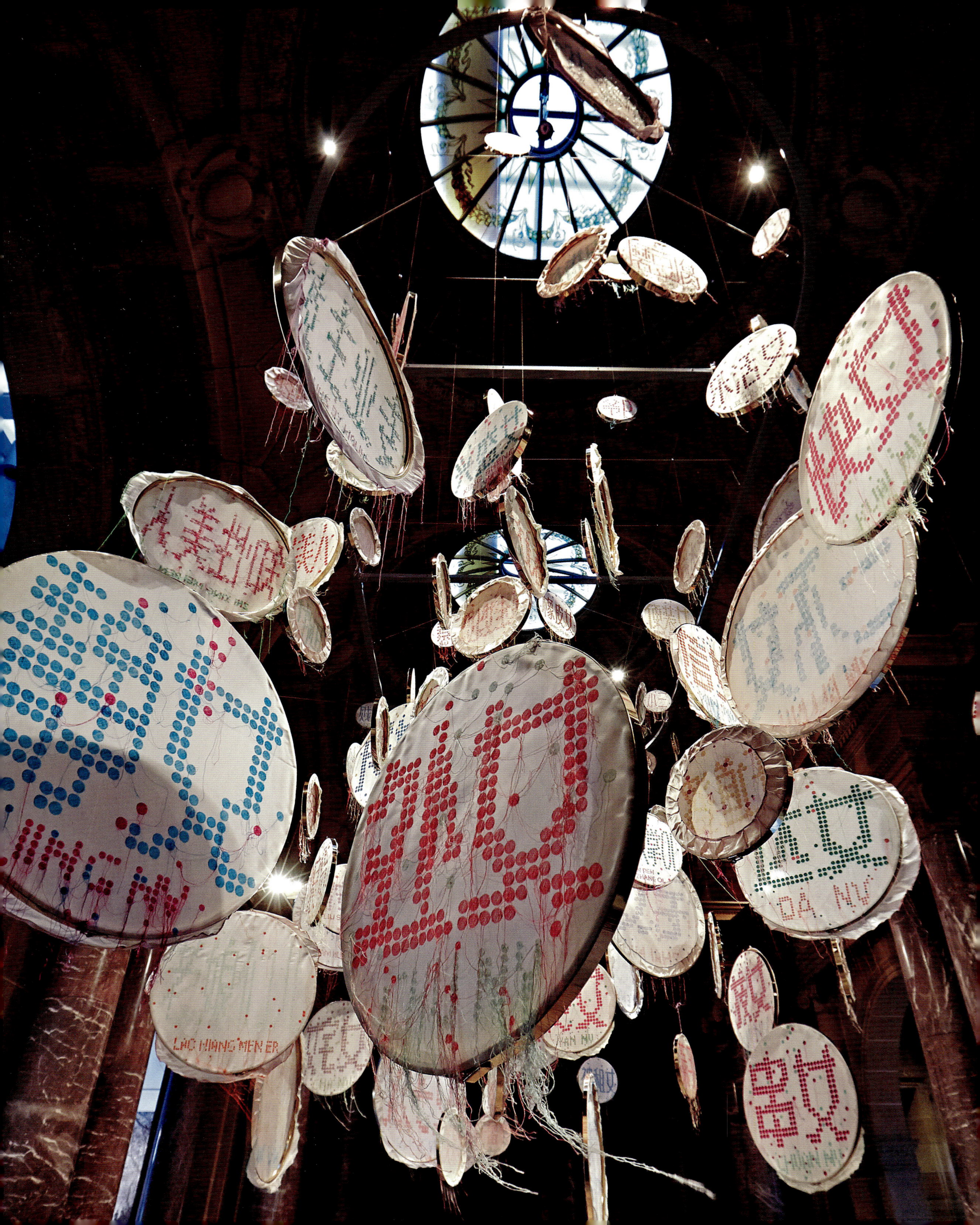
LAO NIANG MEN ER

NEEDLE AND THREAD: MATERIAL PRACTICES

Gao Rong, Lin Jingjing, Lin Tianmiao and Yin Xiuzhen

Mao Zedong once famously said, 'A revolution is not a dinner party, or writing an essay, or painting a picture, or doing embroidery...' [1] In revolutionary times perhaps it is unsurprising that he would speak contemptuously of a traditional handicraft performed mostly by women. Yet in China the history of embroidery is long and important, a history reflected in the work of the four artists in this chapter.

The feminist art movement of the 1970s re-valued traditionally female craft practices. In a gendered approach to the high/low reshuffle of the times, the domestic was deliberately brought into the cultural sphere of the gallery as a political act. Artists such as Miriam Schapiro, Louise Bourgeois and Judy Chicago punctured the art establishment, 'stitching' women into the discourse. Are Chinese artists working with textiles familiar with these antecedents, or are they operating from within an entirely different paradigm? Conversations with four artists of different generations and backgrounds provide some surprising answers.

Traditional practices: flowers of the field and silken cocoons

Raising silkworms and spinning silk from their cocoons had been practised from ancient times.[2] Originally, embroidery was practised by both male and female professionals, only later becoming associated with womanly refinement in the imperial courts of the Song Dynasty. By the Ming Dynasty it had become an almost entirely female occupation, thus to a large extent excluded from the masculine category of 'art'.[3] The Ming embroiderers were famous in their own right, but considered as amateur artisans rather than professional artists. Embroidery was synonymous with virtue,[4] in part because over time it became an art made almost entirely by women.

With the establishment of the People's Republic of China in 1949 some traditions of embroidery and textiles became associated with a despised feudal past. Folk arts – by the people and for the people – were initially exempted from this taint. In Hunan Province, for example, embroidery had flourished in the period after the Sino-Japanese war and the establishment of the People's Republic in 1949. Fifteen thousand embroiderers worked in its embroidery shops in the late 1940s. Mao believed that art and design should 'serve the people' and daily necessities such as embroidered bed linen, tablecloths and baby clothing were produced at low prices, with a flourishing export market to the Soviet Union. Before the Cultural Revolution, themes of Hunan embroidery consisted of animals, flowers, fairy tales, and legends. After 1966 these motifs were vilified as feudal, and the production of Hunan embroidery plummeted. Many famous embroiderers were exiled to the countryside and forced to do farm work, while some were appointed to create propaganda artworks depicting approved subjects and themes.[5]

The harsh realities of Chinese life in the 1950s and 1960s necessitated a utilitarian approach to the act of sewing. The *Four Musts* – products representing success and status – were a watch, a radio, a bicycle and a sewing machine. These were expensive possessions, almost out of reach of ordinary people. Children received new clothes only at Spring Festival time, and women skilfully patched and re-patched old clothes. Today, craft skills such as embroidery are fast becoming endangered, despite attempts to revive them. We should be careful not to romanticise gendered traditions and cultural practices, nor see them through the soft-focus lens of nostalgia. However, each of these artists reflects on ways in which Chinese society is homogenising through globalisation, with a consequent loss of important cultural traditions.

From Lin Tianmiao's exploration of sexuality, and the ageing and decay of the body, to Yin Xiuzhen's memories embodied in old clothing; from Lin Jingjing's stitched-over memories and sutured roses to Gao Rong's embroidered replicas of banal objects, each subverts and reinvents traditional forms. Working with thread and textiles in experimental ways, these

Lin Tianmiao
Badges 2009
white silk satin, coloured silk threads, gold embroidery
frames made of stainless steel, dimensions variable
collection Gene & Brian Sherman, Sydney
installation view, AGNSW 2015
Photo: Jenni Carter, AGNSW

artists challenge the hegemony of painting and sculpture, communicating personal memories and cultural identities through the everyday materials of women's work. Lin Tianmiao and Yin Xiuzhen grew up during the Cultural Revolution, but the fall-out from that period of collective madness affected the families of the younger artists, too. There are connections, direct and indirect, between the hardships of recent Chinese history and the act of sewing.

This chapter could have been subtitled *Mothers and Daughters* – the relationships between the four artists and their mothers have powerfully influenced their lives. Like the traditional practitioners of *Nüshu* ('Women's Writing') – a form of secret written script known only by women and passed from mother to daughter in remote rural regions of Hunan Province – they employ a visual syntax of fabric and thread.[6] *Nüshu* was taught to female children by their mothers and grandmothers, written into letters between women, inscribed into cloth bound books, embroidered onto handkerchiefs, and stitched onto fans. Gao Rong, Lin Jingjing, Lin Tianmiao and Yin Xiuzhen have created a contemporary form of 'women's writing' in their work.

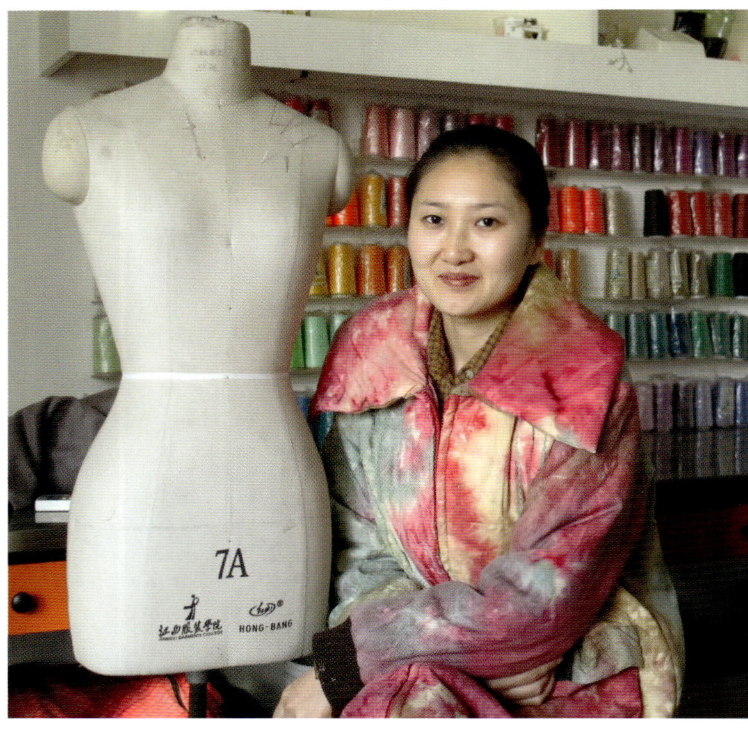

GAO RONG 高蓉

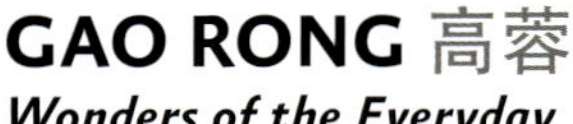

Wonders of the Everyday

Gao Rong transforms banal things into objects of delight and wonder. Stitching onto fabric wrapped around armatures of sponge stiffened by steel and wire, she creates hyper-real sculptures, applying her skill with the needle to represent the quotidian, saying, 'I want to show my responses to everyday life in a very particular and distinctive way.' Electricity fuse boxes, public telephones and bus timetables, water-damaged cardboard boxes, apartment doorways – even a cheap three-wheeled taxi-cab and (literally) the kitchen sink – are replicated with extraordinary accuracy. 'I am a sculptor who uses embroidery, not an embroiderer,' she says.

Born in 1986 in Inner Mongolia, Gao Rong graduated from Beijing's Central Academy of Fine Arts in 2010. Her discovery of Tracey Emin's confessional, narrative appliqué quilts prompted her to abandon more conventional sculptural techniques while she was still a student. Emin's rebelliousness appealed to her: 'I liked the way her work showed her private life, and how she broke free of tradition.' Gao takes a gentler, more discreet approach to inserting her own life into her work. She is not so interested in the confessional and autobiographical: 'I don't want to only show my individual life. My own shadow is there, but I want to make artwork that is about more than that. Not just me.'[7]

In her workroom, filled with spools of rainbow-coloured thread, she gazed out the window to a vista of endless rows of apartments stretching to the fog-obscured horizon. Quietly she explained that she is reinventing the *nu hong* tradition of embroidery to become a new visual language. The name is said to be derived from the story of an emperor's daughter in the Zhao Dynasty who spent seven days and seven nights embroidering dragons onto her father's robes. Gao Rong, too, is a dutiful Chinese daughter. Connections with family are immensely important to her, exemplified by *The Static Eternity*, a full-size replica of her grandparents' house in Inner Mongolia. Gao's mother is her occasional assistant, confidante and companion, a collaborator in the passing on of traditions between generations of mothers and daughters.

Gao Rong's grandmother taught her the traditional embroidery of her native Shaanxi Province. Sent to Inner Mongolia during the Cultural Revolution, she supported her seven children by exchanging embroidery for food. Gao says, 'Heritage is not just a technique, but a spirit of survival handed down from one Chinese woman to another.' In rural areas of Shaanxi Province the folk art appliqué technique is known as *buduihua*. Approximately one hundred designs make up the traditional repertory, rich in symbolism, and drawn from ancient legends and folk tales. Similar to paper-cutting in the simplicity of its style, the stitching techniques are passed from generations of rural women to their daughters.[8] Gao explains that Shaanxi stitching is not like the more famous

Gao Rong in her Beijing studio
October 2013, photo LG

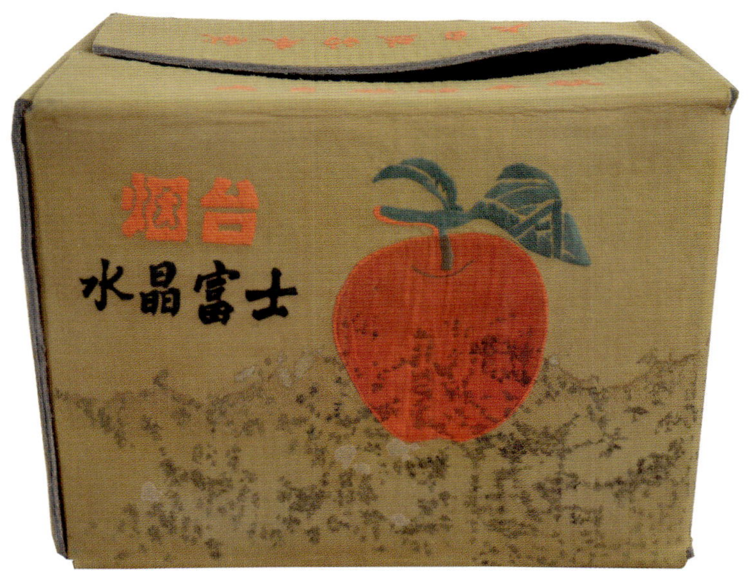

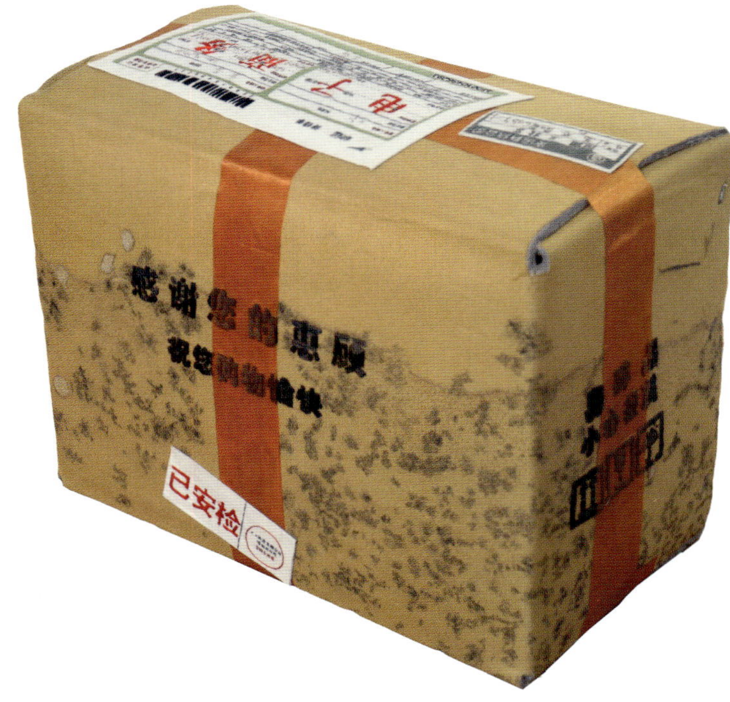

embroidery from Suzhou: 'It's plainer and more representative of local culture.' As a child she was always making things from fabric, such as dolls' clothes, finding sewing a natural form of expression which she longed to continue when she began studying sculpture, far from home and lonely in Beijing. 'Because I want to find the roots and origins of my visual language I thought of my grandmother sewing when I was a child. In the act of sewing there is a connection with my mother and my grandmother.' Gao's work is deliberately and intentionally feminine, applying a craft traditionally practised by women: 'I want to reinvent embroidery. I want to find more possibilities. These traditions are very long, and different in all parts of China. I want to make new and different things.' But, she adds, it is not just about craft skills: 'I also add the heart.'

Relationships between women across generations play a significant role in her practice. Apart from her mother, who helps with large projects, her grandmother, now deceased, is a constant presence in her thoughts and memories. But Gao Rong now needs more assistance with her large-scale ambitious installations than her immediate family can provide. For her replica of her grandmother's house, *The Static Eternity,* she was assisted by four workers, as well as a carpenter, her mother and her boyfriend. She has since taught the embroidery technique to rural women whom she employs when they can be spared from the fields. Unlike many contemporary artists in China, who delight in cheap labour and fabrication costs to produce work on an enormous scale, Gao wants all her work to bear the marks of her own hand:

> In China when artwork is commercial or mass-produced, people put less heart into it. I don't want my work to be influenced by that aspect of Chinese culture. I don't want my work to be like that. I want to put my heart into every stitch.

Level 1/2 Unit 8 Building 5 Hua Jiadi Bei Li simulates the entry to the typical Beijing apartment where she lived as a student. With its rusty water pipe, fuse box, security door, stencilled advertisements and footprints on the wall, it appears astonishingly real, but every single detail is embroidered fabric. Evocative and nostalgic, it's a memory of her student days, which may have been rather Spartan, but were also exciting, as she forged her independence in the huge city:

> I try to show *my* condition and *my* life. As a student I felt I did not have a clear social status, living in a new city, and I wanted to show my feelings. Coming from Inner Mongolia to the city of Beijing had a really strong impact on me. At first I felt very excited, but also life was quite difficult, and there were hardships. It was more about adapting to a life where I had to support myself away from my parents, alone in a new city. I missed my parents.

Gao Rong
After July 21st – Box No. 1 and ***No. 2*** 2013
embroidery, cloth, foam
43 x 32 x 26 cm; 34 x 25.5 x 18 cm
images courtesy Klein Sun Gallery, NY and © Gao Rong

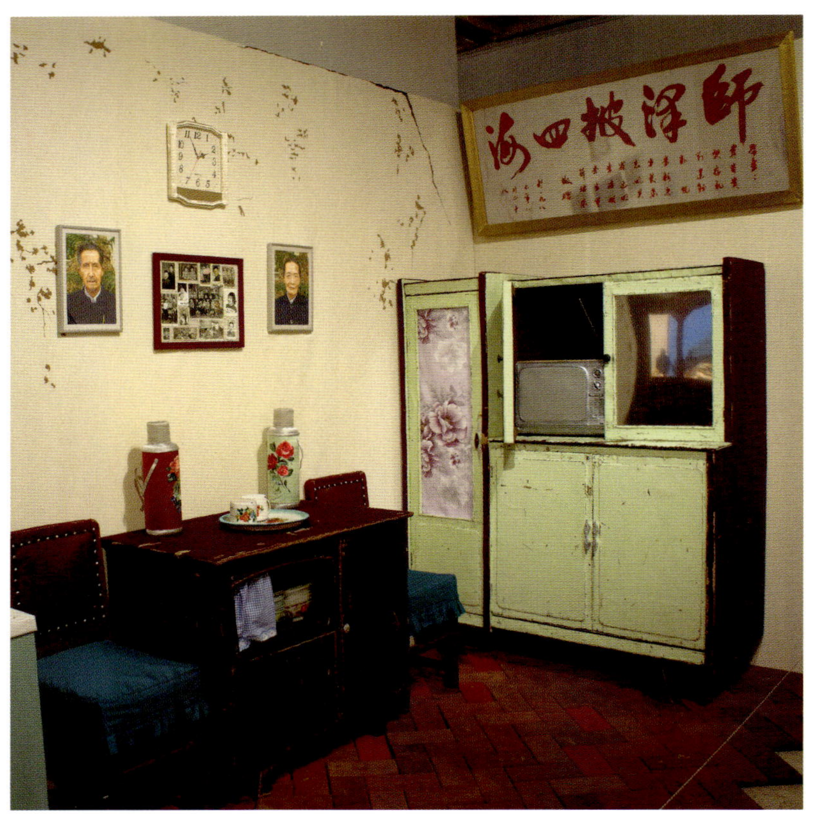

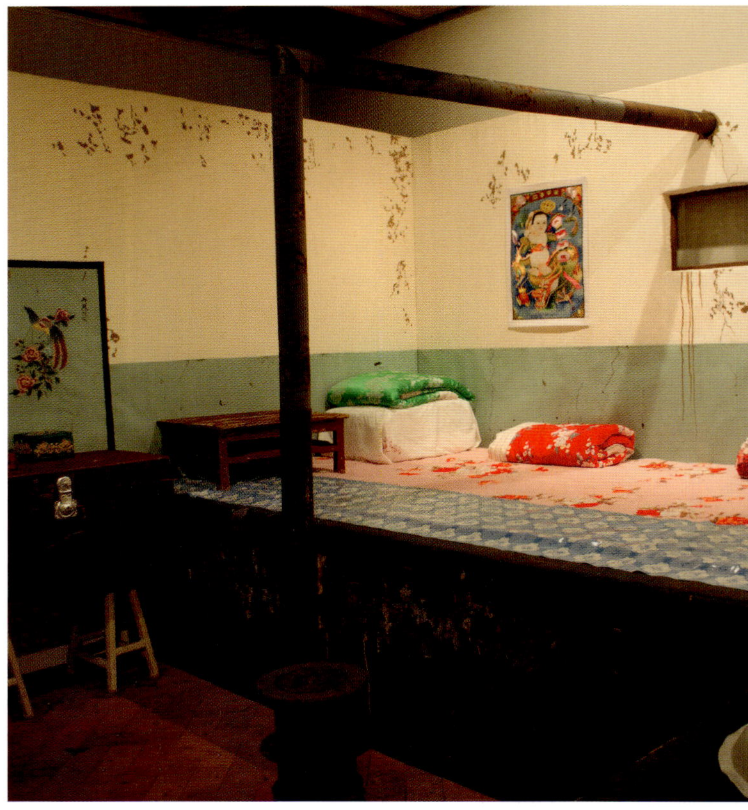

Gao Rong describes her generation as 'adrift in Beijing', lost in a city where everything is happening at warp speed. Her response is to look very closely at apparently mundane objects, seeing in them a greater meaning. A set of battered green apartment mailboxes, a bus stop, a mildew-stained shower room, a kitchen sink filled with soaking dishes - all are imbued with significance. Works such as this reflect her homesickness. She stitched an actual letter of her own into one of the mailboxes, where it remains. One day, she says, it might be opened. Focusing her attention on things that are about to become obsolete, Gao says:

> I want to record things from daily life that may not exist in the future. The passage of time is not always recorded, but it can be recorded through art and through this kind of embroidery... The history of objects is on their surface. I make a creative choice when I see a surface that lends itself to embroidery. I want to use embroidery to represent the tracks of time passing by on wood and steel.

The city she came to know as a student is being erased by relentless development and demolition. In her painstaking replication of stains, grime, rust and mould on the surfaces of mundane objects, she makes us look anew at the unexpected visual pleasure of the everyday. 'I want to show an illusion of reality because sometimes, just to be real is not real enough. Being real is not just about the form or the surface but on a much deeper level, when it also shows something about me.'

Guangzhou Station comments on the materialism of contemporary culture, a phenomenon Gao Rong finds 'objectionable'. She embroidered fake designer handbags with realistic food, coffee and make-up stains, and stuffed them with replicas of mundane daily necessities. A Louis Vuitton bag is filled with a giant oozing tube of toothpaste, another with an outsize tub of instant noodles, or a packet of washing powder. These works comment sardonically on 'material girls' blindly following fashion, collecting such bags as evidence of social status and success, but they also remind us of the factory girls on the production lines of southern China who make them. 'My work has always been concerned with the living conditions of people around me,' says the artist.

I Live in Beijing, Gao Rong's 2013 New York solo show, featured stained packing boxes, a shower room with mildewed tiles, and a water-damaged battered sofa, documenting apparently unimportant details of life. *What Type of Car Can a Motor-Tricycle be Exchanged For?* is a nostalgic memorial to cheap, three-wheeled taxis, disappearing in twenty-first

Gao Rong
The Static Eternity 2012
cloth, wire, sponge, cotton, steel support and board, 516 x 460 x 70 cm
image courtesy the artist and White Rabbit Gallery

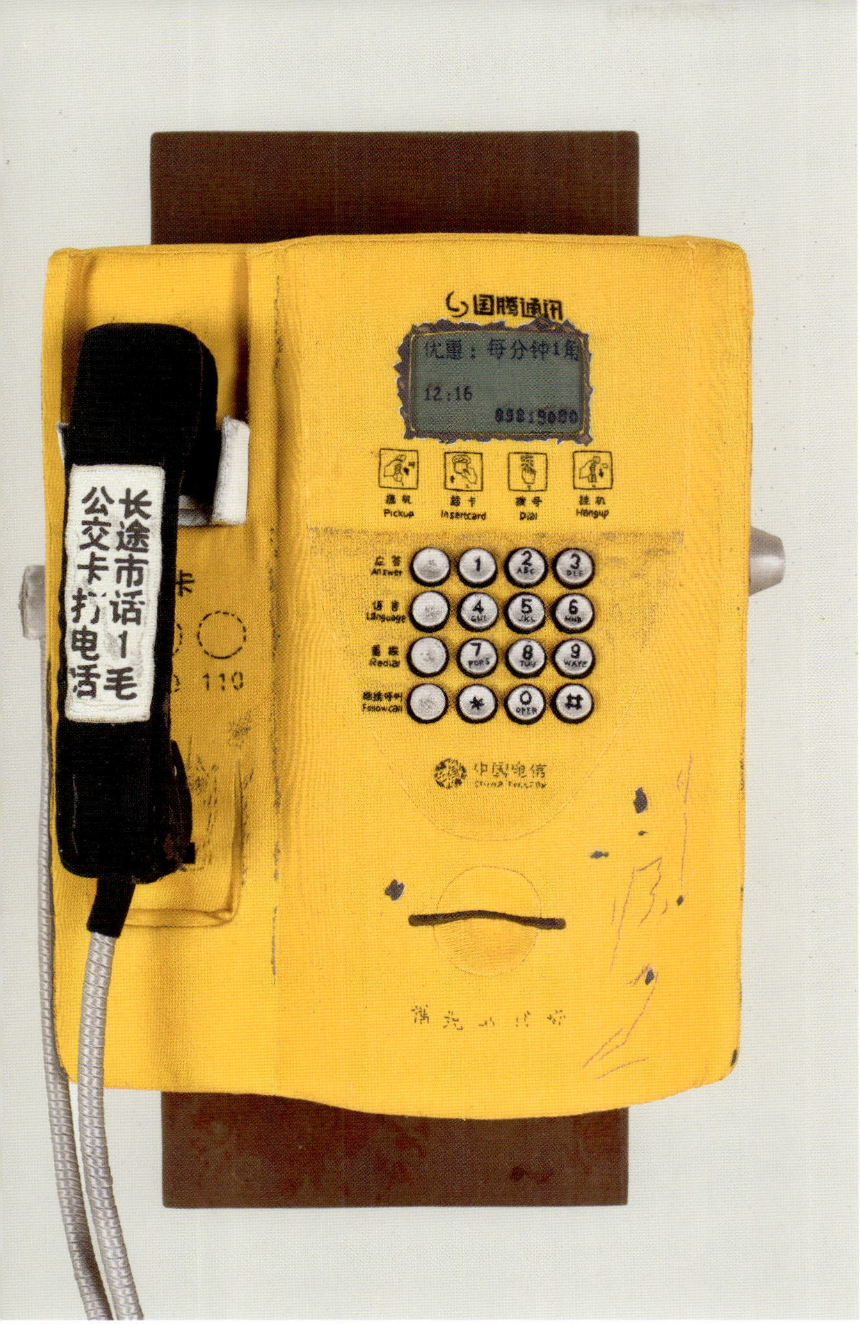

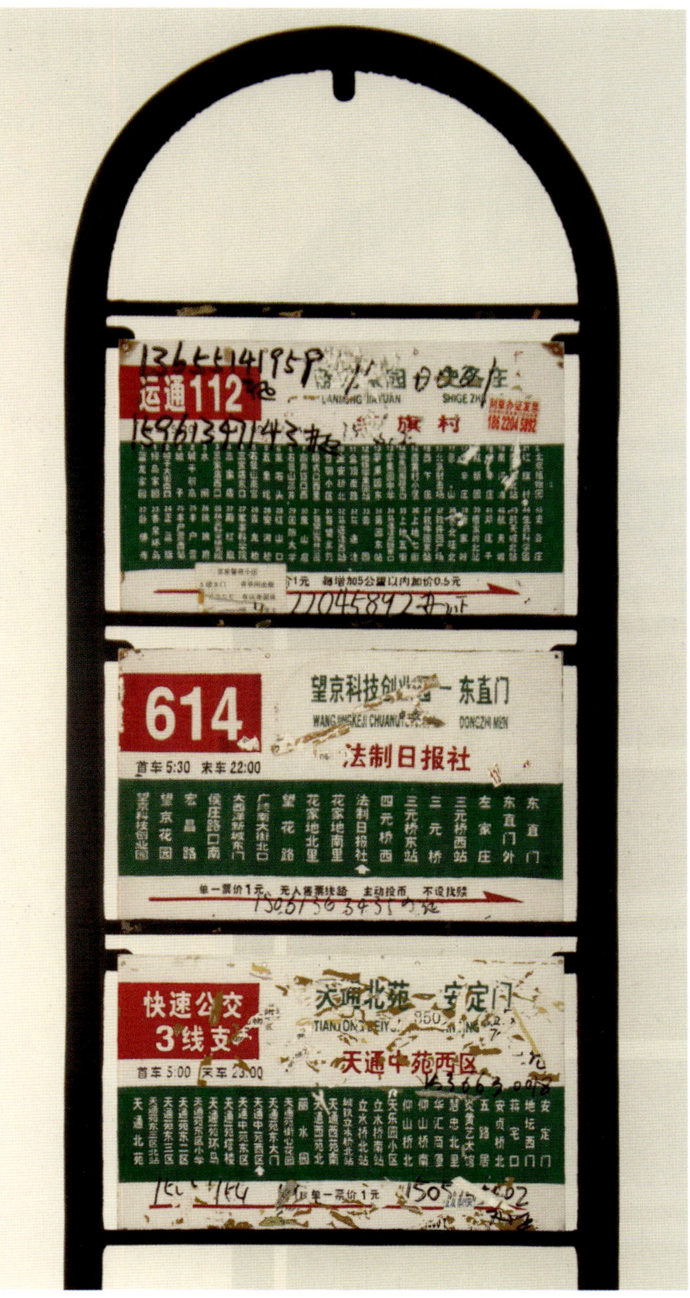

century Beijing. The title alludes to her half-joking ambition to join the ranks of newly-qualified Chinese drivers: 'As a student I used to ride in the beng-beng taxis a lot because I didn't have much money... Maybe if I can sell the artwork I will actually be able to buy a car!' Her embroidered bus stop represents the three bus routes she travelled each day to the Central Academy. Covered with timetables and the stencilled phone numbers of people with things to sell and services to offer, it is an evocative slice of ordinary life. A love for the grimy, fluxing energy of Beijing is evident in all her work.

The Static Eternity, in contrast, re-created her grandmother's tiny traditional home (long since demolished) in Inner Mongolia. To replicate it accurately she visited relatives living in similar houses, taking precise measurements and making drawings. She pored over old photographs, interviewed elders, and examined bricks and timber. Gao Rong was not present when her grandmother passed away, which saddens and disturbs her. She tried to make her mother remember every tiny detail, even the damp areas on the walls and the rust on the pipes: 'I wanted it as original as possible.' The work is enormously touching in its painstaking evocation of a simple family life. From enamel mugs and thermos flasks to battered furniture and ancestor portraits, everything was created with embroidered fabric. 'I wanted audiences to think it's the real thing,' she says. Gao's work speaks of memory and the beauty inherent in the ordinary moments of life.

Gao Rong
Communicate by Phone 1 2012
sponge, cloth, wire, board
20 x 48 x 28cm
image courtesy the artist and
Klein Sun Gallery, NY. © Gao Rong

Gao Rong
Station 2011
fabric, thread, sponge, metal frame
255 x 100 x 3 cm
image courtesy the artist and
White Rabbit Gallery

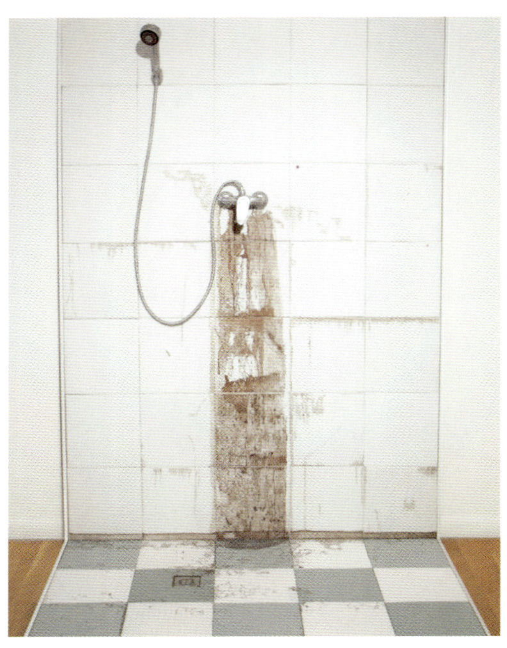

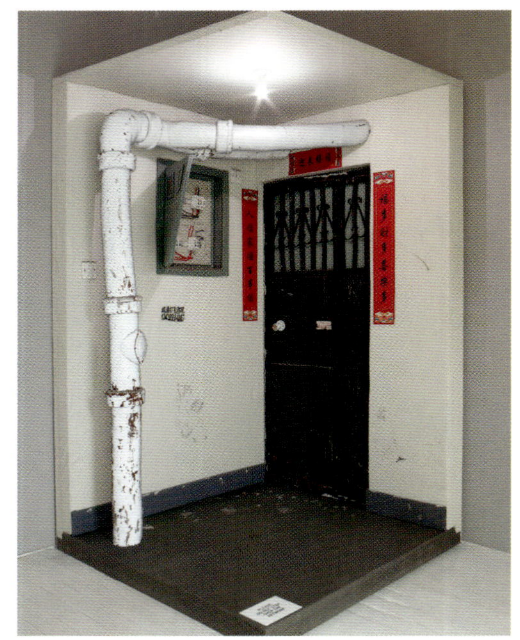

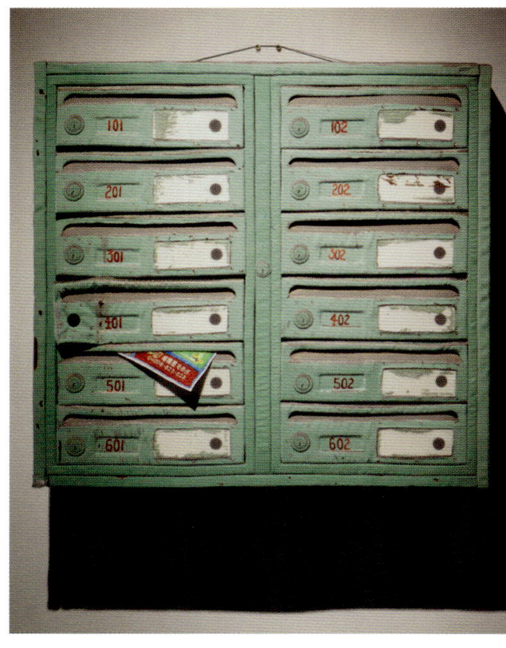

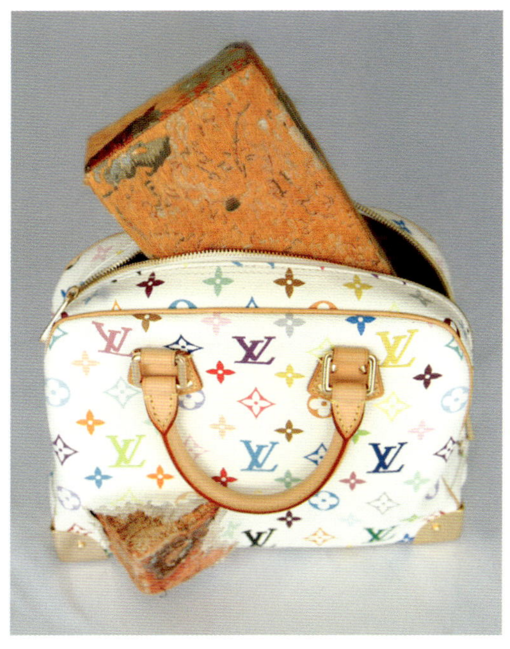

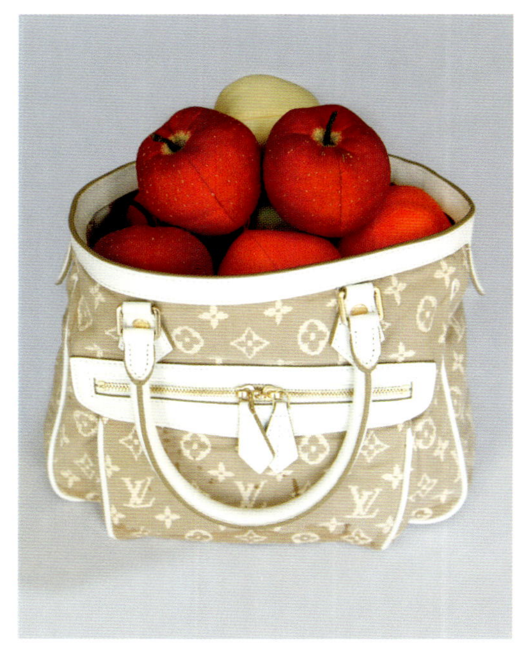

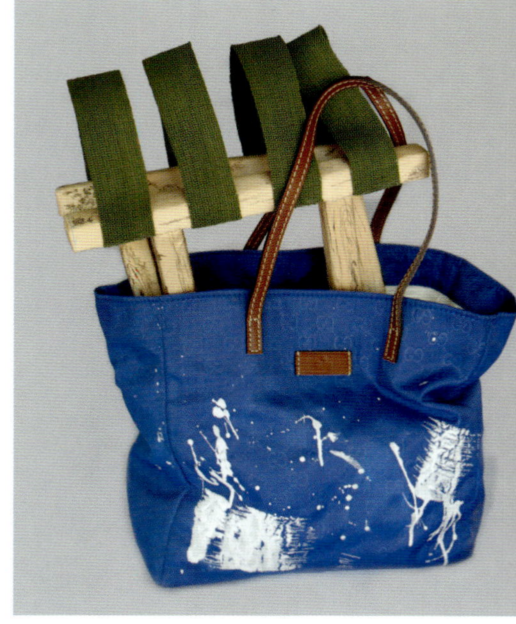

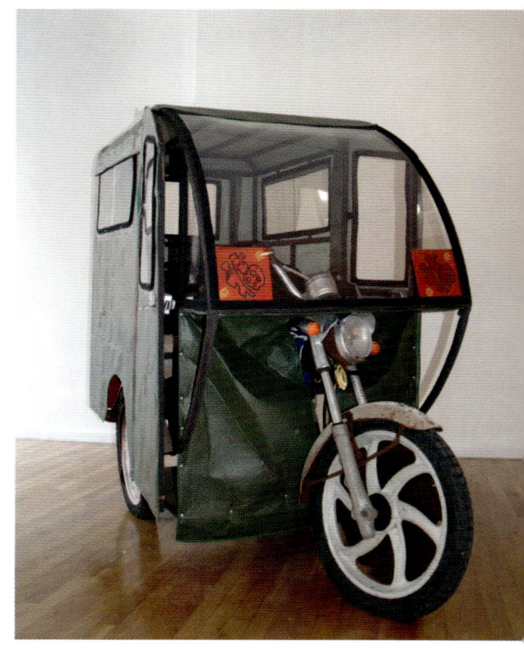

Gao Rong *(top left)*
Winter – Bathroom Wall 2013
embroidery, cloth, wooden board, foam
120 x 155 x 155 cm
image courtesy the artist and
Klein Sun Gallery, NY. © Gao Rong

Gao Rong *(top cente)*
Level 1/2 Unit 8 Building 5
Hua Jiadi Bei Li 2010
embroidery, cloth, wooden board,
foam
250 x 155 x 155 cm
image courtesy the artist and
White Rabbit Gallery

Gao Rong *(top right)*
Mailbox 2011
embroidery, cloth and foam
68 x 70 x 21 cm
image courtesy the artist and
Klein Sun Gallery, NY. © Gao Rong

Gao Rong *(middle row)*
Guangzhou Station (details) 2013
copy bags, cloth, embroidery,
sponge
dimensions variable
images courtesy the artist

Gao Rong *(bottom)*
What Type of Car Can A Motor-Tricycle be Exchanged For? 2013
embroidery, cloth, wood, foam,
iron shelf, leather, and plastic
180 x 195 x 95 cm
image courtesy the artist and
Klein Sun Gallery, NY. © Gao Rong

Gao Rong
Some Days Later 2014
Cloth, thread, latex foam, steel
115 x 53 x 50 cm
image courtesy the artist and
White Rabbit Gallery

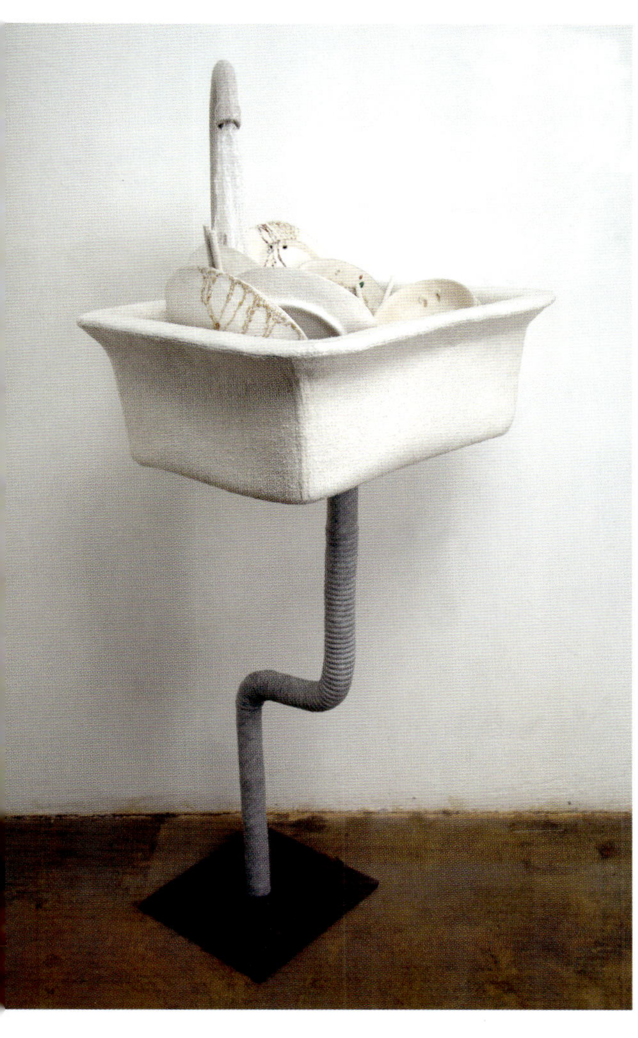
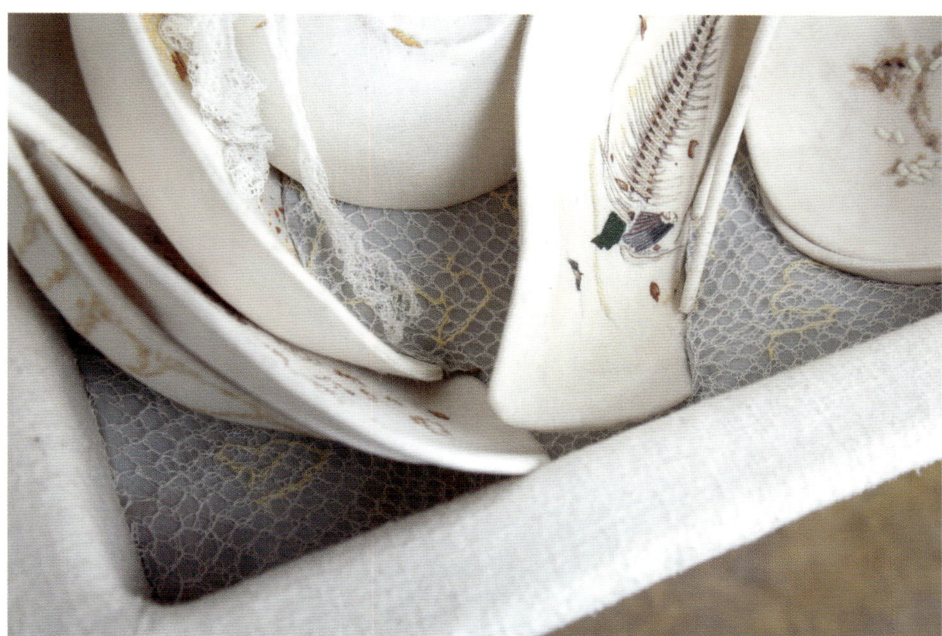
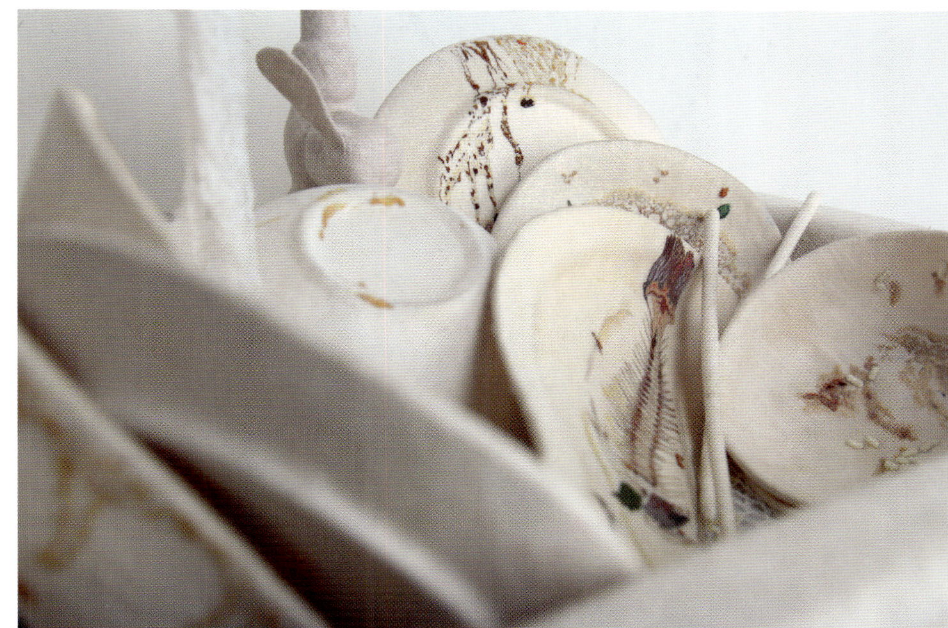
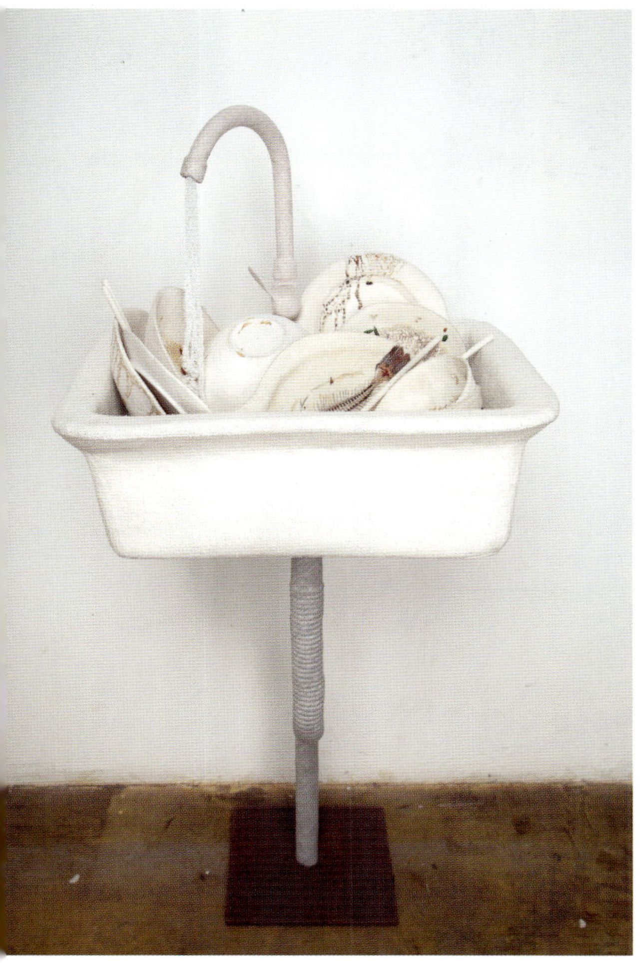
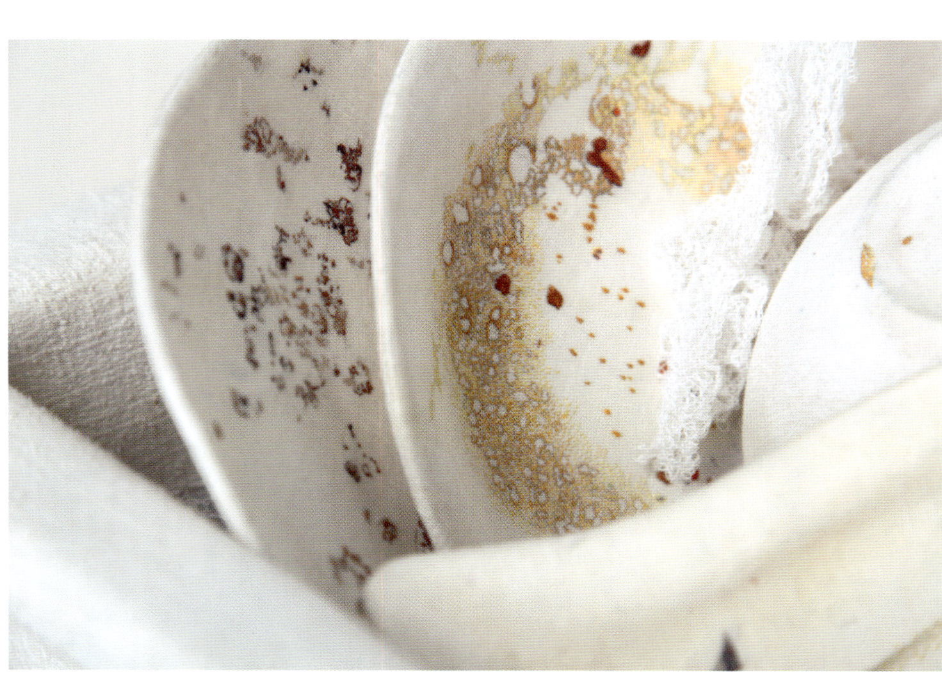

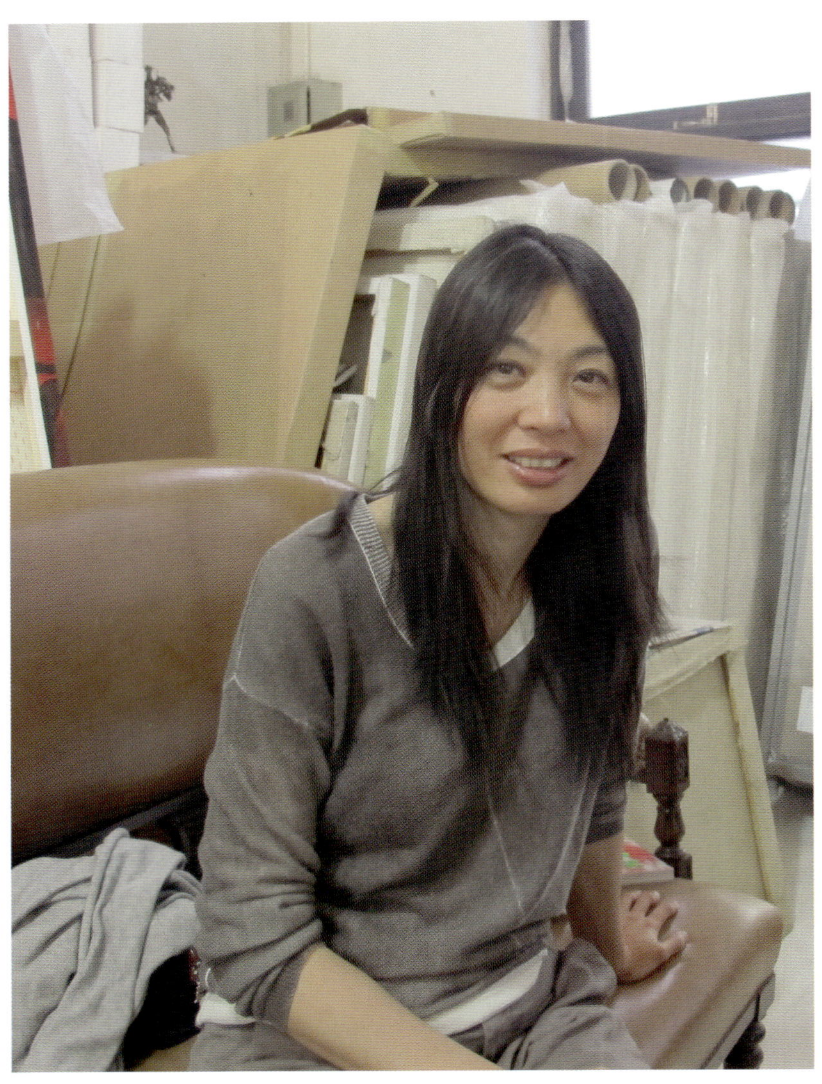

LIN JINGJING 林菁菁

The Realm of Paradox

As a young girl, Lin Jingjing yearned to discover a world beyond her neighbourhood. She rode her bicycle as far as she could in each direction, a little further each week. 'It wasn't about distance, it was about time,' she says, recalling her adventures speeding through the countryside. 'To get home before dark, I knew if I rode for four hours I needed four hours to get back.'[9] Similarly, as an artist she has travelled in new directions, discovering the unexpected along the way. She identifies these first, small journeys as the start of her interest in time-based work. Lin has always been curious to discover the world, travelling overseas independently from her early twenties. She quotes an old Chinese saying: 'It is better to travel ten thousand miles than to read ten thousand books.' She has been travelling restlessly since her early twenties.

Lin Jingjing's travels, and her voracious reading of philosophy and literature, inspire her practice. Born in 1970, she graduated from Fujian Normal University in 1992 before heading to Beijing's Central Academy of Fine Arts for postgraduate study. Her work crosses traditional boundaries. Trained as a painter, but now working in photomedia, installation and performance, she examines the paradoxes of our contemporary reality. *Never Ever* is inspired by a real event – a mishap that occurred as she disembarked from a plane. As she stood on the steps leading to the tarmac the plane unexpectedly rolled away, leaving her standing at the top of a flight of stairs leading into empty space. Lin began to think of it as a symbolic event: a flight of stairs going nowhere seemed an apt metaphor for China's economic growth, which has transformed the lives of so many, with such profound and far-reaching social upheaval. Lin's monochrome paintings and photographic works depicting people and places are layered with colourful threads, an artificial intervention in the surface that mirrors the artifice and alienation of society in the twenty-first century.

Part of a body of work entitled *Nobody knows I was there, Nobody knows I was not there...* the *Public Memories* series (2011–12) reproduces photographic images of public and private events in bright colours, selected areas on each canvas neatly stitched with rows of thread. The stitches conceal parts of the painted image, suggesting the unreliability of memory. Photographic images from past and present – group portraits, award ceremonies, movie stills and political images – are partially eradicated, reminding us of the doctored photographs that falsified events during China's twentieth-century history. Selected faces and figures are obliterated by Lin's neat stitches. These works speak of the fragility of memory, and the malleability of truth.

The act of stitching through the canvas (a task both physically difficult and immensely tedious) reminds us that it is generally women who are the guardians of family history and collective memory, doing the hard work of maintaining generational ties. Remembering or forgetting is a conscious act. In *Public Memory 2* the photographs are absent and only the threads remain. The work juxtaposes public and private, remembering and forgetting, concealing and revealing. Some of Lin's selected 'memories' are publicity photographs, whilst others are banal images found on randomly selected internet sites. Lin uses her own photographs, family snapshots, official photographs and vernacular photography found on the internet – four quite different photographic languages. She alludes to the problematic history of photography in China, for thirty years used solely for propaganda purposes, a discourse of political manipulation.

The formal public spaces of Chinese cities, and their monumental architecture, are represented in her body of work, *Promise Again for the First Time*. Sometimes they contain people who appear disconnected from their environment, and

Lin Jingjing in her Beijing studio, Caochangdi
December 2014, photo LG

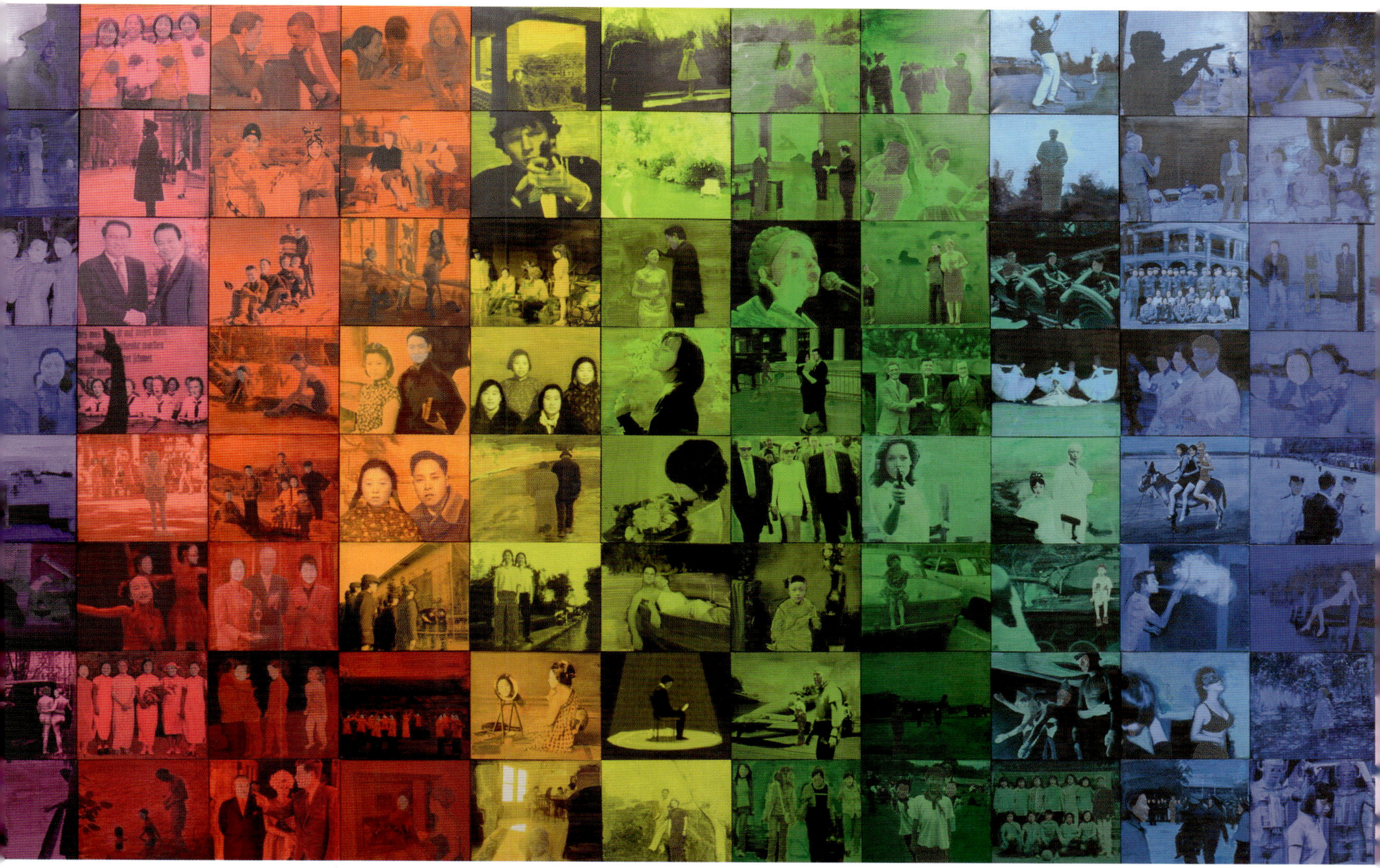

from each other. Sometimes, as in *Sunshine Sunshine Sunshine 5*, deserted spaces with crowd barriers suggest the inevitability of surveillance and the possibility of terror. The people in Lin Jingjing's urban landscapes are witnesses to – and survivors of – contemporary life, and the pain and fear which cloud transitory moments of joy and pleasure. *My Promise for Your Happiness* shows a male figure carrying a bunch of roses through gritty urban scenes, an ambiguous narrative. We wonder about the recipient, and whether Lin's protagonist is making a declaration of love or seeking forgiveness. Brightly coloured stitching denies the photographic reality of her canvases, making us question the 'truth' of the painted image. Lin Jingjing sees contemporary Chinese citizens as victims of abundance, greed and social control.

Unlike most Chinese artists, trained at hothouse art high schools, Lin Jingjing's path was atypical. Planning a career as a writer, she suddenly changed her mind after a chance encounter in her final year of high school. She was editing the school magazine and became friends with the art teacher responsible for its design, visiting his studio to select images:

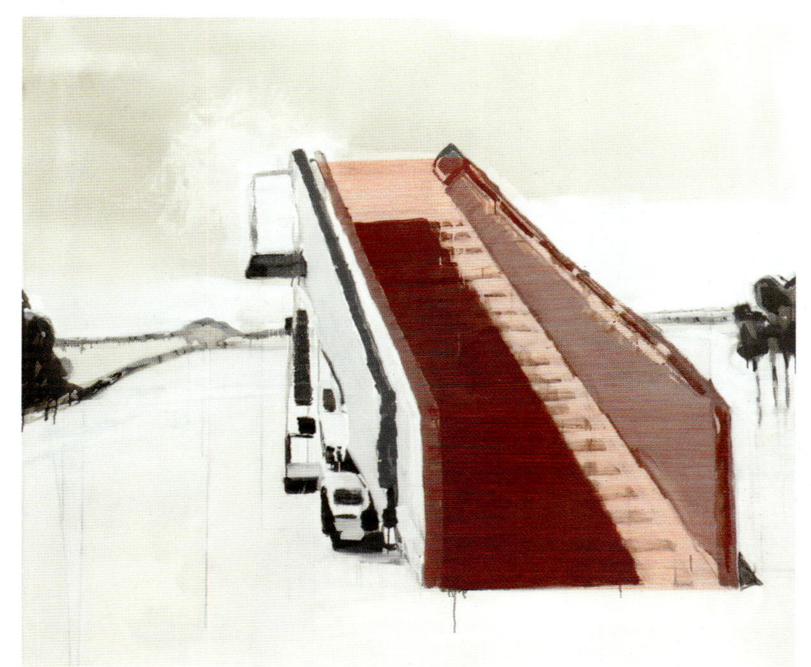

Lin Jingjing
Public Memory 1 2011
mixed media on canvas
88 works each 38 x 46 cm
image courtesy the artist and De Sarthe Gallery Beijing and Hong Kong

Lin Jingjing
Never Ever 2014
oil on canvas
150 x 180 cm
image courtesy the artist

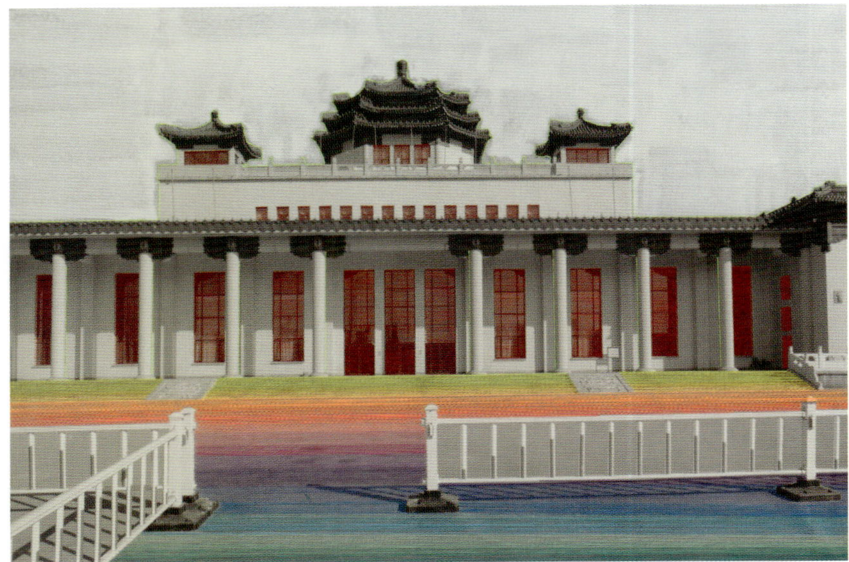

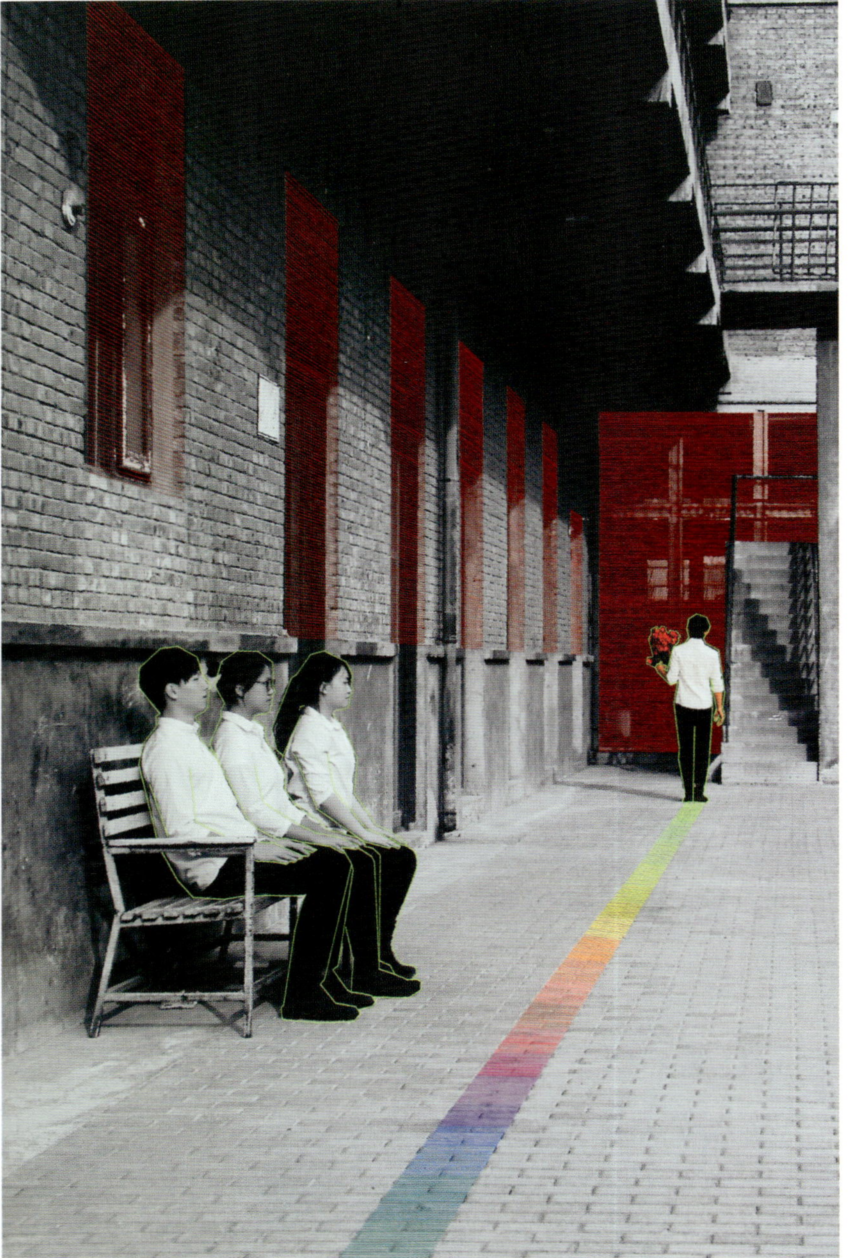

> He had music on, he was drawing, and I looked at all his books, all the philosophy books that I loved. So I thought, '*This* is my life! Forget about being a writer!' I had always loved drawing, but I never knew anyone who studied art, so it had never crossed my mind.

Unsurprisingly her scientist parents were horrified at this sudden change of heart in the very last months of high school. Lin managed to win them over:

> My mother is a very special woman, very educated, very open-minded, very intelligent. I told her, 'This is my dream. I cannot do anything else.' She said, 'OK, if this is really your dream, even though I don't like it, I have no choice. I must help you.'

Once enrolled in the art academy, Lin Jingjing realised she had seriously underestimated the difficulty of making up for lost time, competing with students who had been developing their technical skills for years:

> Compared to all the other kids I was like a loser. I was used to doing very well in all my subjects at school. It was miserable. I thought I had no hope. I realised that I had made a mistake, and I thought I would never be able to catch up.

With a temporary summer job as a designer she decided to abandon her studies. Her mother said, 'You told me this was your dream. Now you want to quit? I will not let you quit!' During her third year she experienced an epiphany:

> I realised there is something I *can* do, even without the same training as the other kids. They are so well trained that they cannot break out of it. Because I don't have that training, in fact, I am free. I can start to do things that are not like anyone else's works. Somehow I began to feel I had unlimited possibilities. It slowly started to connect with what I had been doing in my writing. I realised that in art you really are creating something, it is not just a skill.

Lin Jingjing's interest in writing and philosophy influenced her developing practice. As a postgraduate student at the Central Academy of Fine Arts in Beijing she began to paint abstract canvases, 'like poetry':

> At that time nobody was really doing that so it got media attention and sold well. It was very easy. But after a few years it became *too* easy and I was bored. I started to lose interest. So I stopped. I was very young, early twenties. I said to myself, if I am bored now I cannot possibly continue in this way, [so] I had to do something to change. I stopped painting for a while... My father was very angry, he said, 'You give up school, you give up the writing and now you give up painting? What is wrong with you that you give up so easily?'

Lin Jingjing *(top)*
All I Need is Sunshine Sunshine Sunshine 5 2014
print, acrylic and thread on canvas
80 x 120 cm
image courtesy the artist

Lin Jingjing *(bottom)*
My Promise for Your Happiness 2013
mixed media
200 x 135 cm
image courtesy the artist

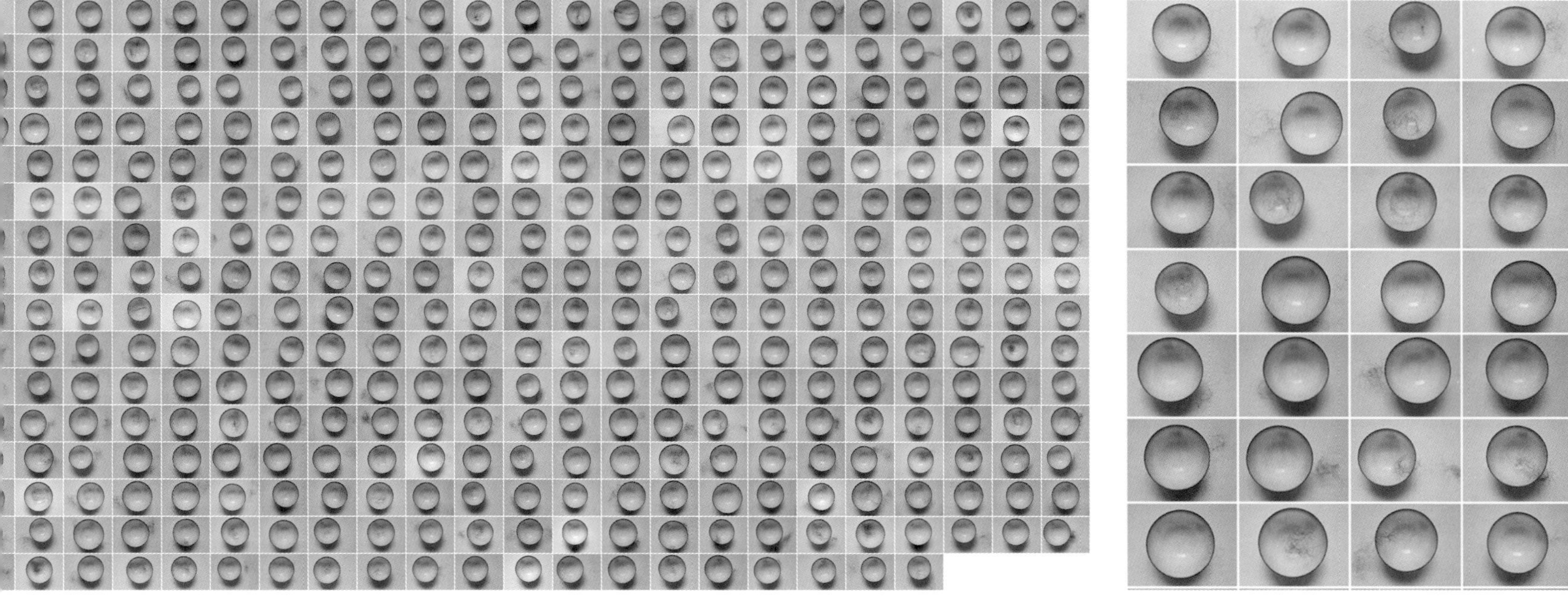

In this hiatus period Lin began to travel, and to experiment. Photography interested her – its ability to document ephemeral moments was intriguing. She developed the idea of recording paradoxical moments:

> I started with a photo series. I was starting to notice that in the morning when you brush your hair you lose a little – some falls out. I took photographs of this hair every day. I did that for a year, three hundred and sixty-five days, as one photo work. Is it part of you or not part of you? Is it connected or not connected? You think, '*Why I am recording this*?' If I don't record it, it's gone completely. It also comes back to the time-based thing – this is the first work that made me realise that this really interests me.

My 365 Days, like a contemporary *Vanitas*, records the loss of youth and the inevitable ravages of time. During this period she returned to writing:

> Thinking, questioning, philosophy... At this point I realised why I stopped writing and [then] stopped painting. I realised that what I was looking for all those years was the freedom to use whatever material you want to express your idea. I can write, I can paint, I can use different materials. Wow, this is magic!

As a small child Lin had visited her parents' laboratory and had seen them create extraordinary things, effecting chemical transformations: 'I thought they were magicians! They mix things, make things change colour. Magic! I went to school and told everyone that my parents were magicians.' The school principal invited them to come and perform magic for the children, and the illusion died:

> They said, 'No, no – we are not magicians!' I was so disappointed but also so embarrassed in front of my classmates. So I said, 'OK maybe *they* are not magicians but *I* am going to be a magician!'

Lin's technique of stitching across the surfaces of painted and photographic images transforms them. Banal images now evoke the frail and mutable nature of lived experience. Lin does not use sewing in her work because of childhood memories:

> When I was small I did no handiwork – I was like a boy! [I was out] climbing trees... I was never familiar with it. My mother knew how to use the sewing machine. One day I asked her to show me how to do it and I was doing it all wrong, and she was a little bit upset and after that I never wanted to touch it.

She returned to the use of needle and thread much later, as a deliberate element of her conceptually layered works rather than for any inherent qualities of the medium:

> I choose stitching because it gives me an interesting connection. The needle is repairing something, but at the same time destroying it. I realised many years ago that sewing on the one hand is like fixing, but on the other hand... the needle, it's very violent! It is back to the paradox. All the materials I choose are full of paradox.

Lin Jingjing's performance, video, and photographic works explore binaries – beauty and cruelty, wounds and healing, life and death. Barely-opened long-stemmed roses are stitched closed. They are fleshy, suggesting sexuality and fertility, until you see the sutures:

Lin Jingjing
My 365 Days 2003
photographic documentation
250 x 1200 cm
images courtesy the artist

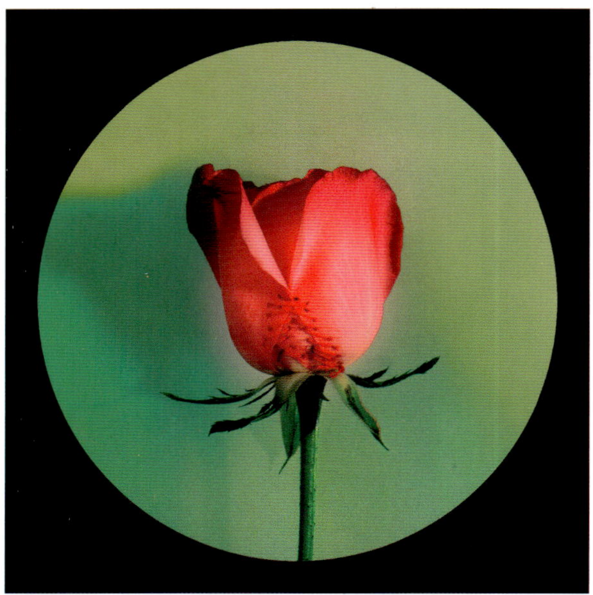

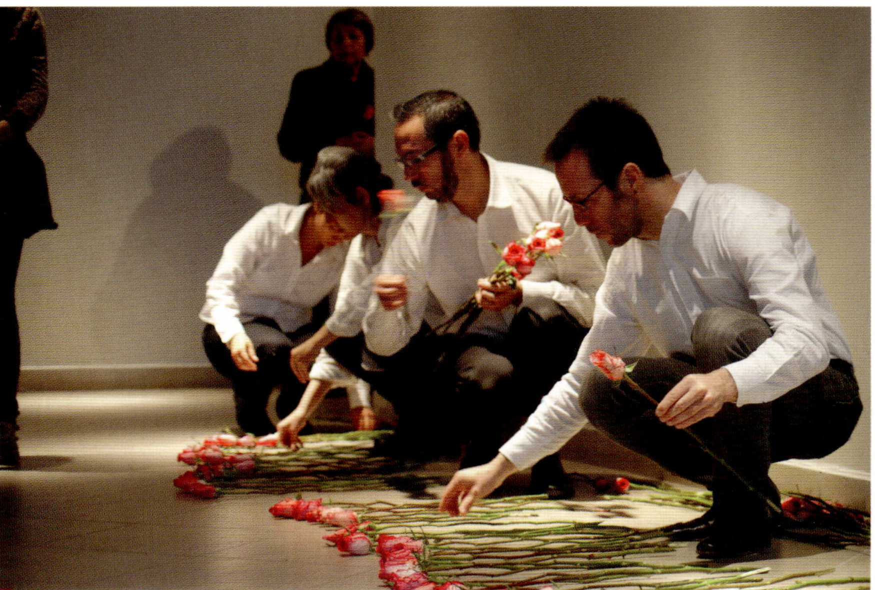

> I use roses not because they are a symbol of love, but because of the thorns. The thorns are there for protection, but at the same time how can you protect yourself? When the roses open they are moving towards death. When you stitch them together you are stopping death but at the same time you are damageing them. The suturing of the roses evokes cruelties enacted upon the body.

In site-specific performances Lin directs others to sew the roses, then they are placed in locations of symbolic significance, or handed to passers-by. In Chile, the work was performed in Concepcion, devastated by the tsunami following the 2010 earthquake. Volunteers stitched three thousand pink roses in a space divided into two halves, one side for the sewing and the other an empty space with theatrical lighting where the roses could be placed. Without prompting, Lin's actors laid them down in the form of a road. It became a cathartic act of healing.

Other works relate to secrets; to the hidden histories held within families. *Nobody knows I was there, Nobody knows I was not there: Private Memory* is a traditional Chinese medicine chest with ninety drawers, each containing a family photograph. Yellowing images depicting relatives of the artist are placed like precious artefacts on beds of cotton, suggesting a respectful honouring of the collective past. But in every photograph there is a hole where the faces should be. They are, literally, defaced. The work represents the fracturing of family ties during the Cultural Revolution, the transience of human lives and relationships, the erosion of trust, and a melancholy sense of loss. Lin says that if the photographs are kept in the chest, and the drawers are closed, nobody know they are there: 'It's quite similar to our memory system which allows you to remember many things but only when you pull out that drawer.'[10]

For an ongoing project, *Color of Memory,* Lin Jingjing asks complete strangers to tell her three things: their most painful memory, an object they associate with it, and the colour it evokes. She makes a small painting of the object in the specified colour, with a text transcribing the questions and answers. The stories are so heartbreaking that Lin has become uncertain about continuing the project. A woman loses her three-year-old daughter in a shopping mall and the child is never seen again, presumably kidnapped. This is the first time she has been able to speak of it for twenty years. A young girl's fractured relationship with a stern father is healed with a gift. On that day she finds out that he has incurable cancer. A wife receives a letter from her husband's pregnant girlfriend and terminates her own pregnancy. Lin Jingjing sees people who have suffered traumatic events as fragile, yet also strong, living by sheer courageous force of will.

Her own mother's story provided the inspiration for this project, and she was one of the first participants in the work. Before the Cultural Revolution, Lin's wealthy grandparents took their children to safety overseas, leaving their eldest daughter behind, to 'take care of things.' She was still a schoolgirl. In the chaos and terror that ensued their property was confiscated, Lin's mother was imprisoned, then sent to do farm labour in the countryside. The next time she saw her own mother was thirty years later. There are many stories like this in Chinese families, secret sorrows only now coming to light. Lin admires her mother enormously:

> My mother is a fantastic woman – a great sense of humour, very calm, very strong-minded, and she is so funny. We are like friends. But look at how difficult a life she had! I wanted to do something about that. After you go through all of these difficulties, what is it that changes you? I realised that when people have been through these difficulties something really powerful happens in their

Lin Jingjing
Rose (from the series *Rose Rose*) 2011
photographic print
60 x 60 cm
image courtesy the artist

Lin Jingjing
Rose Rose 2011
documentation of performance at Chile National Art Museum, Concepcion, Chile, 3 October 2011
image courtesy the artist

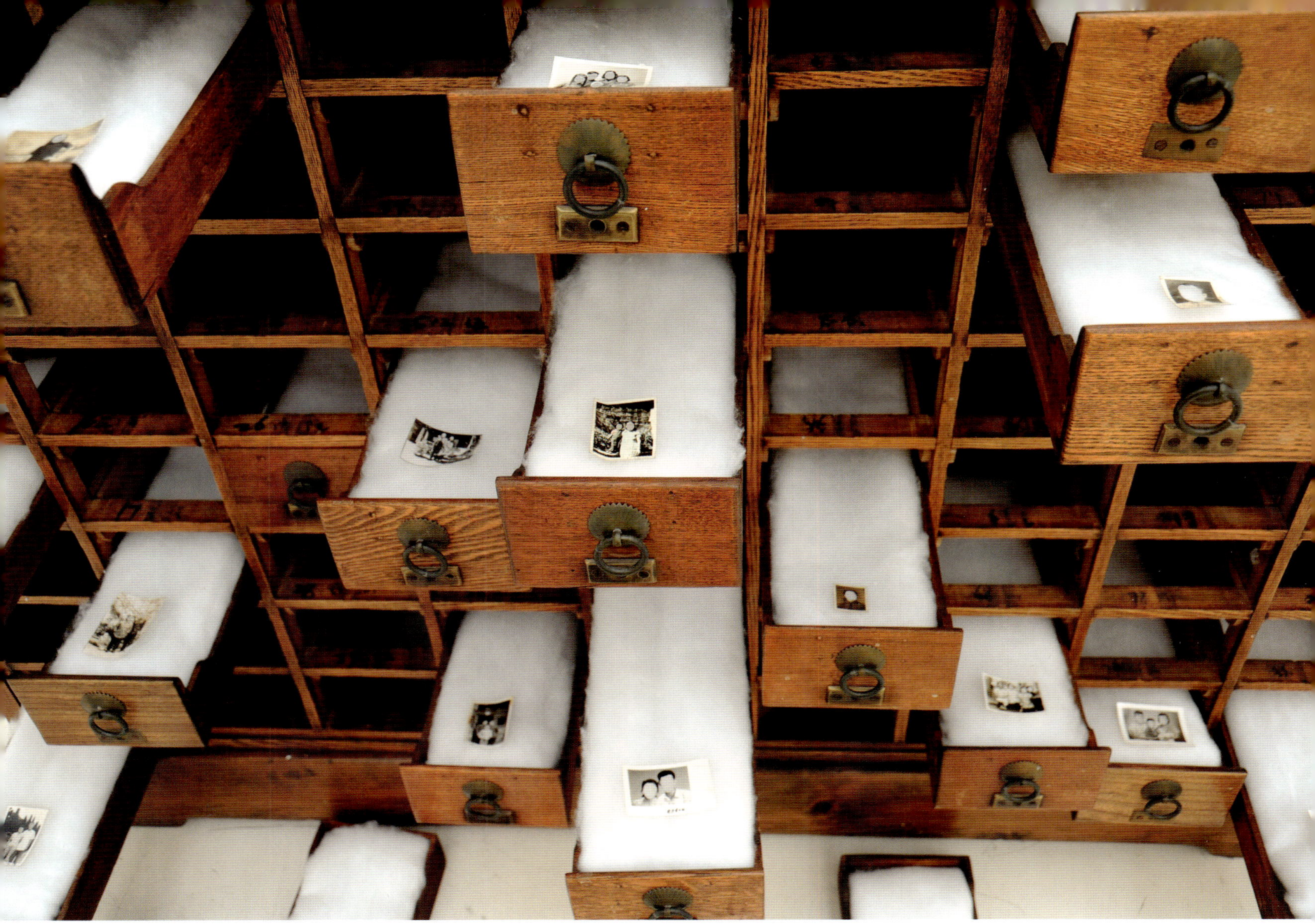

attitude. So I started to talk to more people. It was difficult. Even with the first question my mother said, 'Which bad memory? There are so many.' I want to understand how pain can affect a person. I realised it was actually much more powerful than I had planned. I never know what people are going to tell me or how they will react. So in a way we both give one hundred percent trust to each other and neither of us has control – there are so many things that have happened to people that you could not expect and not guess.

In the paintings that result from this cathartic process Lin stitches the object named by the person onto the canvas before applying paint, representing memory as something tangible, tactile, but always partially obscured. Whether the memories recounted are recent, or from a painful past, they are almost always about love, the loss of love, or missed opportunities for love: 'I want to show there is no difference between the past and now – there is something in common even though it's a different time.'

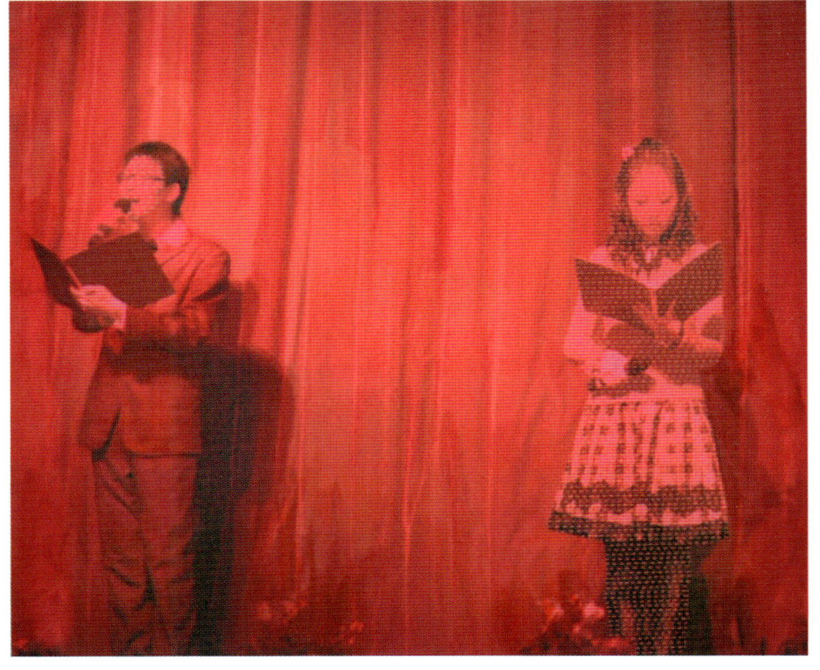

Lin Jingjing
Nobody knows I was there, Nobody knows I was not there: Private Memory 2009
medicine drawers, cotton, photographs
image courtesy the artist

Lin Jingjing
Nobody Knows I was There, Public Memory 2013
mixed media on canvas
135 x 162 cm
image courtesy the artist

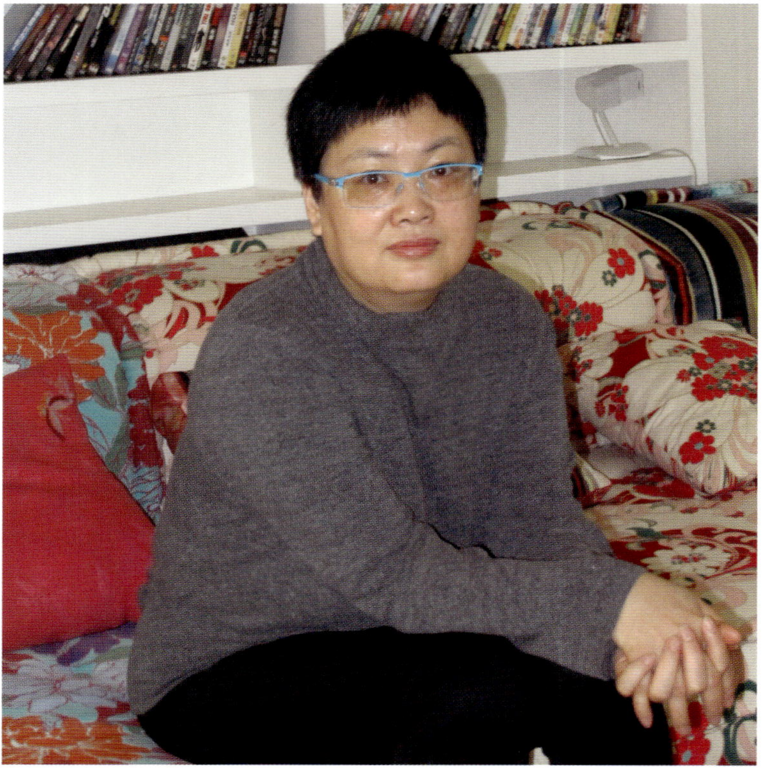

LIN TIANMIAO 林天苗

Bound and Unbound

Lin Tianmiao is sometimes described as one of the few feminist artists in China, a description she is inclined to reject. Born in Taiyuan, Shanxi, in 1961, Lin's father is a traditional painter and her mother was a dancer. In the 1980s, with her husband, video artist Wang Gongxin, she moved to New York, where she worked as a textile designer. When they returned to Beijing in the mid-1990s it was to textiles – cotton, silk, and felt – that she turned when she began to make her first sculptures and installations.

There is a dark undercurrent in Lin Tianmiao's work, a sense of the frailty of the body and the fragility of relationships. Childhood memories of her mother sewing prompted her to develop a unique technique she calls 'thread winding.' She binds cotton or silk thread tightly around found and manufactured objects, a metamorphosis of wrapping and transforming. Now, she believes, there is a greater awareness of the significance and meaning of the 'raw materials' of art: 'Artists look back to tradition and want to experiment with the physical nature of their materials. Nowadays life is so complex we don't even know how to sew buttons, so working with fabrics is a return to a simpler past,' she says.[11] These materials connect us with the physical world and with bodily realities: birth, motherhood, sexuality, illness and ageing.

Lin Tianmiao's mother was sent to the countryside for three years during the Cultural Revolution. During this time she learned how to spin and sew, discovering the relationship between labour and the natural world, a process of material transformation that she passed on to her daughter. Complex, powerful memories of her mother sewing were bound up with that tumultuous period in China's recent history. Much of her work has in turn centred upon her own experience of motherhood:

> Becoming a wife and mother changes you dramatically, both emotionally and physically. Motherhood makes you strong, and also very, very sensitive. You have to become stronger and also enlarge your whole approach to life. You're affected by traditional social values in which women are secondary – you can be knocked down by that.

In her early works Lin used white cotton thread, which has a particular meaning for her generation. State-owned *danwei* – the work units to which every citizen belonged – supplied some workers with white cotton work gloves. These became valuable commodities because in the hands of a skilful sewer, 'the threads from a pair of socialist worker's gloves could be unwound, washed, and knitted into charming *xiaozi*, "petit bourgeois" things: sweaters, hats, doilies and table cloths, sofa throws, or curtains.'[12] As a child Lin helped her mother with this transformational unwinding and rewinding of white cotton thread. One of her first major installations, *Bound and Unbound,* consists of eight hundred household objects wrapped with white thread, arranged like archaeological discoveries. A threateningly large pair of scissors endlessly snipping thread is nightmarishly projected above them. Lin created this installation in 1997 when she had only recently given birth to her son and had returned from America to a very different China. Urbanisation and westernisation were transforming the world she had known. Many of the domestic objects she chose to 'wrap' and transform – a hot water bottle, a sewing machine, a coal briquette stove – were rapidly becoming obsolete. Her poetic metamorphosis transformed the ordinary into strangely surreal forms – a *memento mori* for a disappearing way of life.

Chatting suggests elemental communication between women, the intimacy but also the claustrophobia of female friendships. A group of naked women stand in a circle, as if in a communal bathhouse. They are fleshy, their sagging breasts and stomachs suggesting the weight of time and experience. Their heads are replaced by box-like objects fronted by screens, and a disturbing soundtrack combines women's soft voices and laughter with vomiting sounds and other grunts and moans: a primal non-language, incomprehensible, increasing the sense of disquiet.

Lin Tianmiao at home in Songzhuang, December 2012, photo LG

Lin Tianmiao *(top left)*
Mother's!!! 2008
polyurea, silk, cotton threads
dimensions variable
image courtesy the artist

Lin Tianmiao *(top right)*
Focus Series No.2 2007
lithograph on handmade paper with mixed media, 130 x 100 cm
image courtesy the artist and White Rabbit Gallery

Lin Tianmiao *(bottom left and right)*
Bound and Unbound 1997
white cotton thread, 800 household objects, video projection, sound
dimensions variable
images courtesy the artist

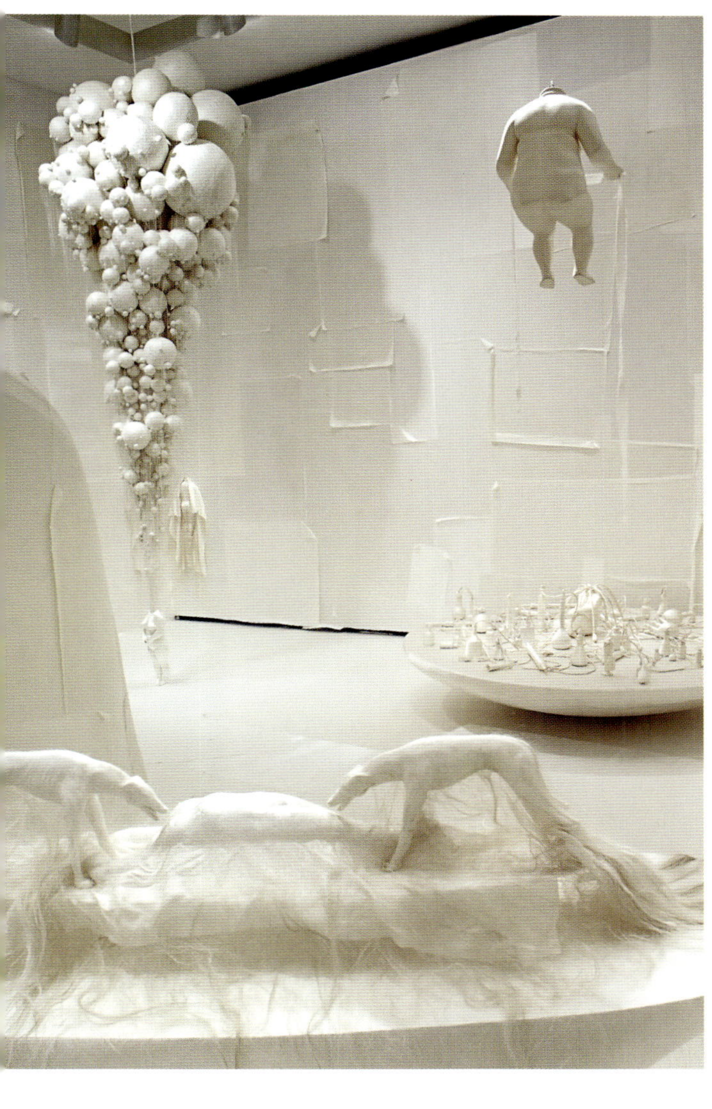

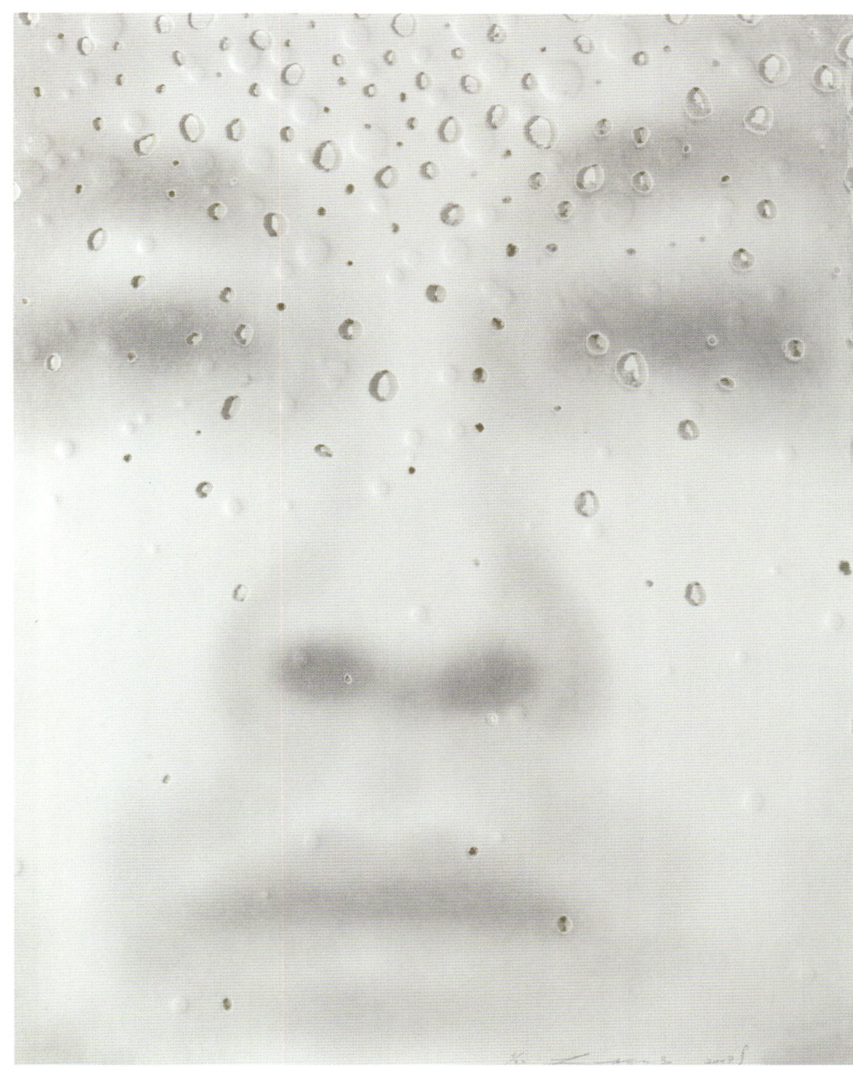

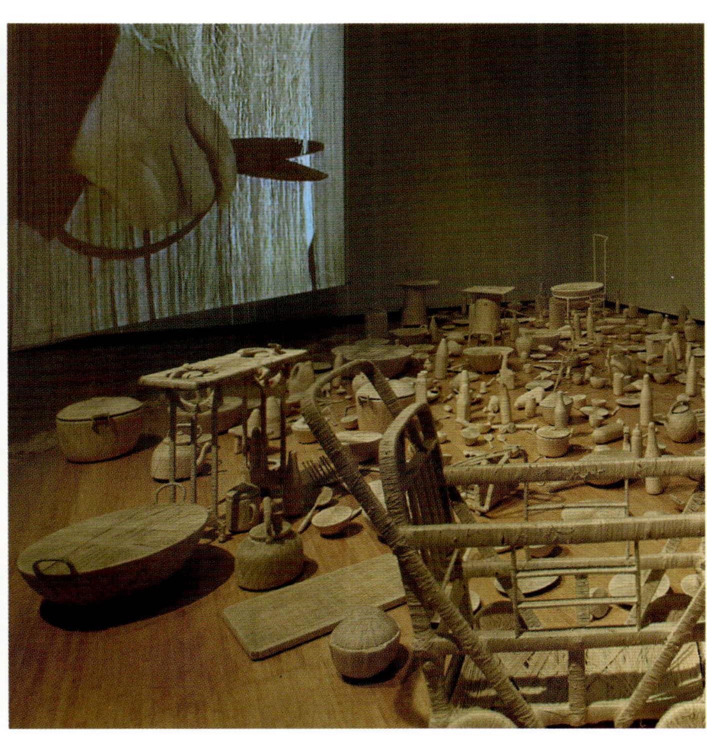

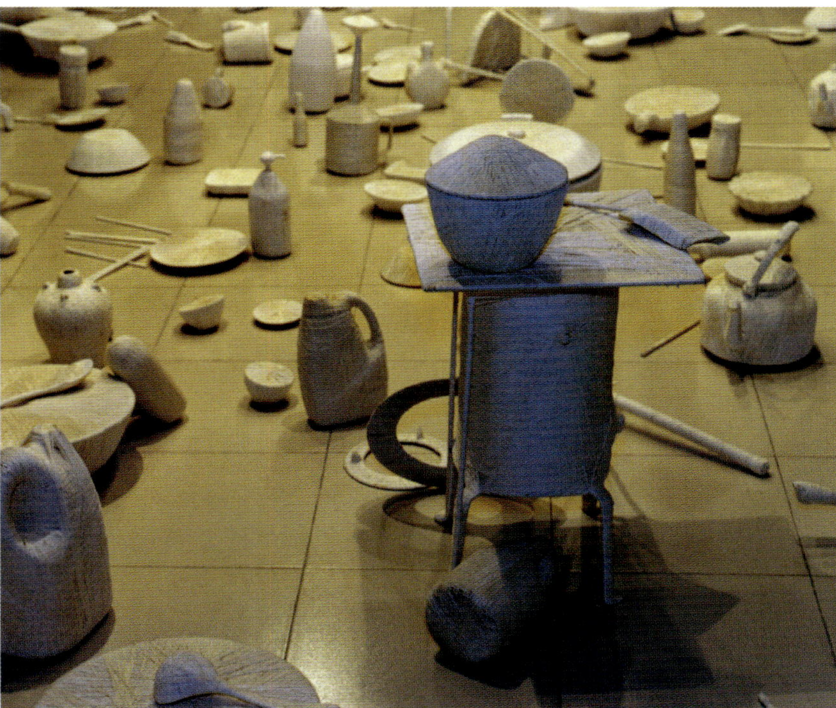

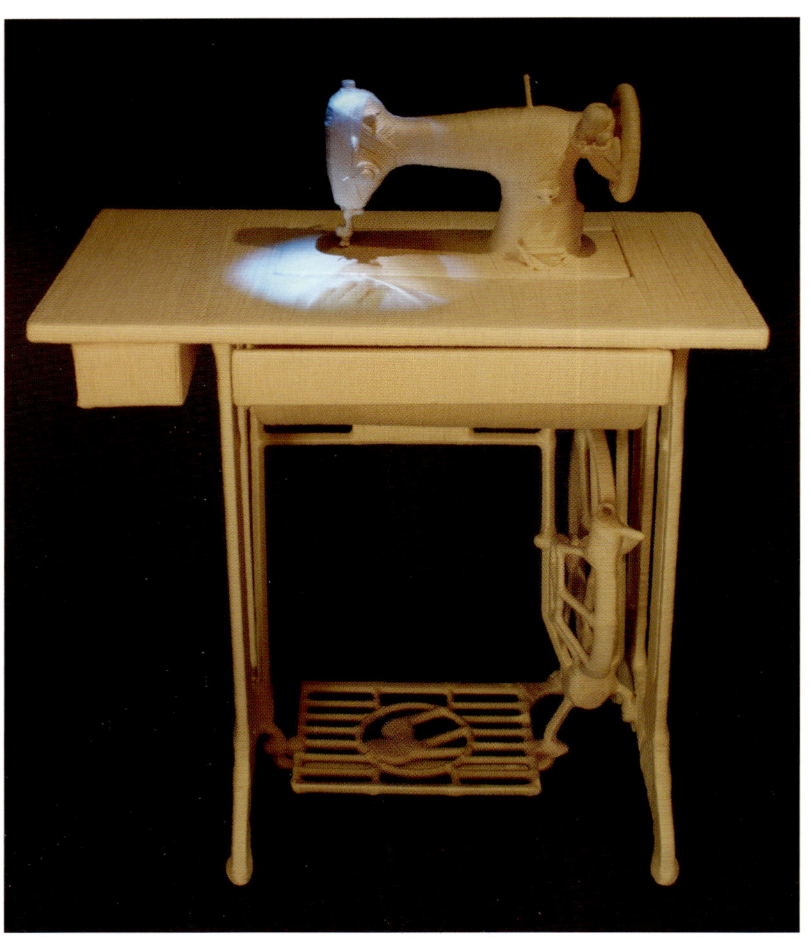

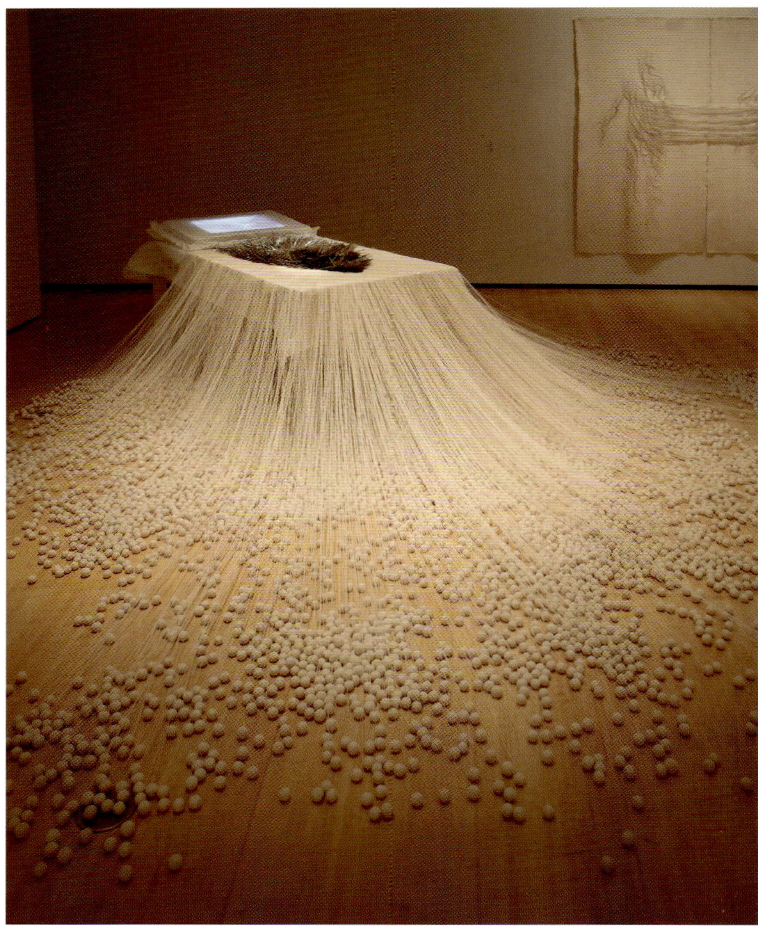

Her work is not a conscious response to feminist theory: 'I think feminism is from the West,' she says. 'Look at the photos of the Communist Party congress – there are no women! My own feminism comes from a basic instinct – I believe as women we have to get stronger by ourselves. I don't think there is any feminism in China. Mao said that women hold up half the sky, but we have not reached that level.' Nor does she see herself as a mentor for younger women artists: 'Being an artist is a very personal and often a lonely thing.'

Lin Tianmiao's practice is at once intensely subjective – based on deep feelings about her relationships, her past and her world - and at the same time grounded in knowledge of Chinese and western art history. She explores subtle and shifting relationships between large and small, male and female, aggression and tenderness.

One of her first substantial works, *The Proliferation of Thread Winding* (1995) features a bed from which cascade balls of wound thread, made sinister by twenty thousand steel needles embedded into the mattress. More recently she has begun to use bones. 'I believe that the bone is the only perfect object left in the world,' she told curator Melissa Chiu before her retrospective exhibition at Asia Society New York. 'The most interesting thing about bones is that they lead us to face our mortality.'[13] *More or Less the Same* features synthetic bones fused with hand tools such as pliers, tin snips, spray guns, hammers and trowels wrapped in grey silk thread. *The Same* employs silks in a vibrant rainbow of colour to transform the bone/tools into resplendently decorative forms. Critic Sun Yunfan interpreted this tension between the beautiful and grotesque as Lin's critique of growing materialism and conspicuous consumption in China – the obscene displays of opulence that are increasingly common.[14] Lin herself has said her work is 'a calm observation of contemporary society.'[15] The process of binding natural forms is like bonsai – a deliberate distortion that conforms to imposed ideals of beauty. Foot-binding, creating the desired 'lotus foot' through cruelly painful mutilation, springs to mind.

Lin's use of silk reflects her focus on the physical, and on the body. Silk has many associations in China. At different times it has been a measure of wealth, a symbol of the imperial past, a sign of social status, and a bargaining chip with western nations. Silk is bound to nature, to the lifecycle of the silkworm and the mulberry leaves upon which they feed. Smooth, shiny, slippery, it possesses great tensile strength. It reminds us of the natural processes that her mother confronted during the Cultural Revolution when she learned to spin, weave and sew.

Lin Tianmiao
***Bound and Unbound** (detail)* 1997
white cotton thread, 800 household objects, video projection, sound
dimensions variable
images courtesy the artist

Lin Tianmiao
The Proliferation of Thread Winding 1995
white cotton thread, rice paper, 20,000 needles (12–15 cm in length)
bed, video player, TV monitor
dimensions variable
image courtesy the artist

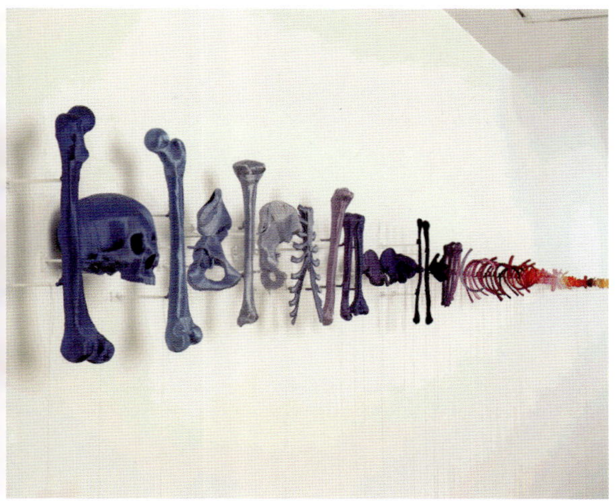

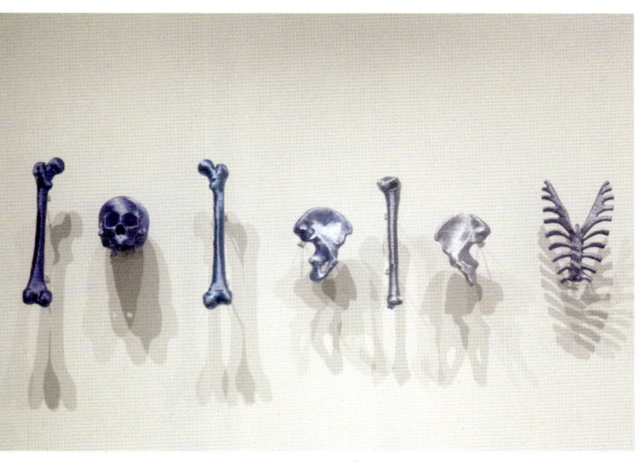

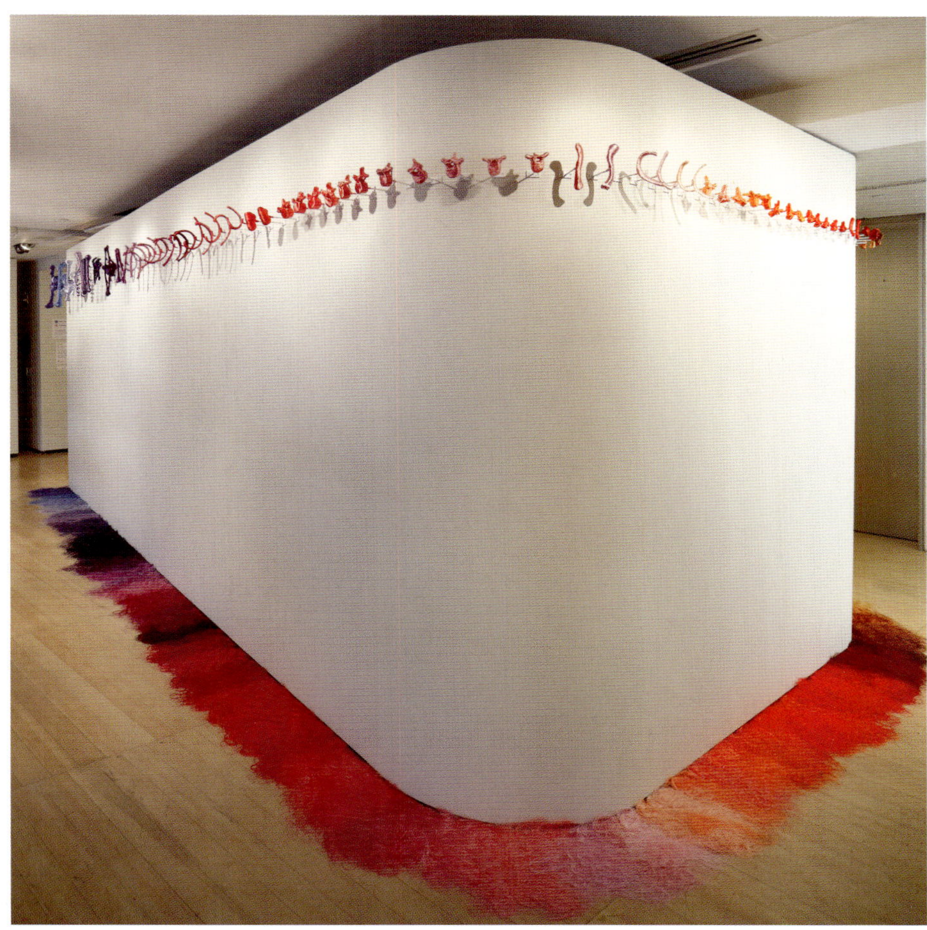

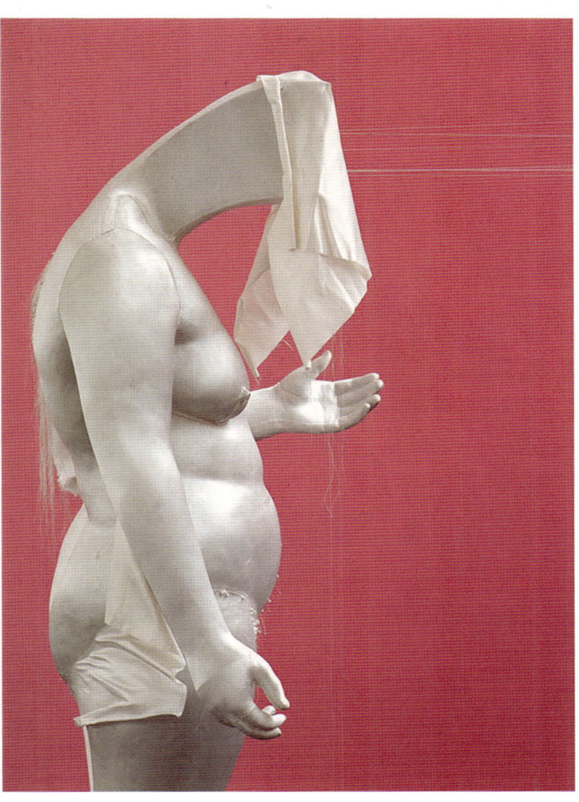

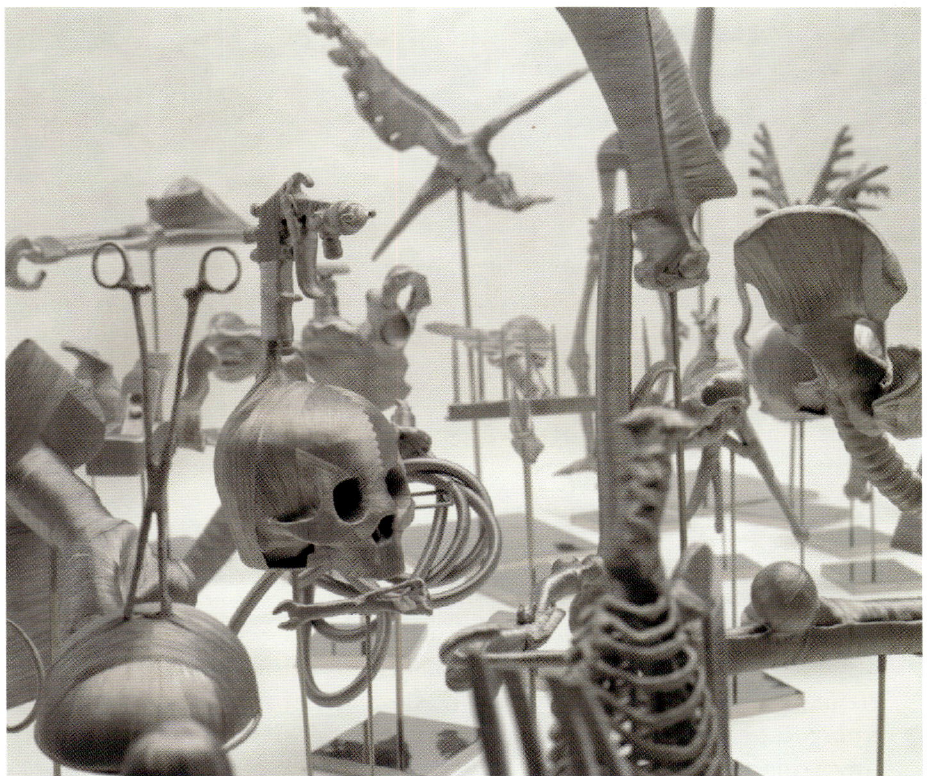

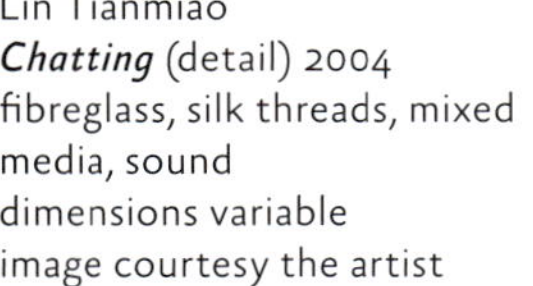

Lin Tianmiao
Chatting (detail) 2004
fibreglass, silk threads, mixed media, sound
dimensions variable
image courtesy the artist

Lin Tianmiao *(top and top left)*
All the Same 2011
installation view and details
coloured silk threads, synthetic skeletons, metal constructions
approximately 15 metres long
images courtesy the artist

Lin Tianmiao *(bottom)*
More or Less the Same 2011
installation view, silk threads, synthetic skeletons, metal constructions
image courtesy the artist

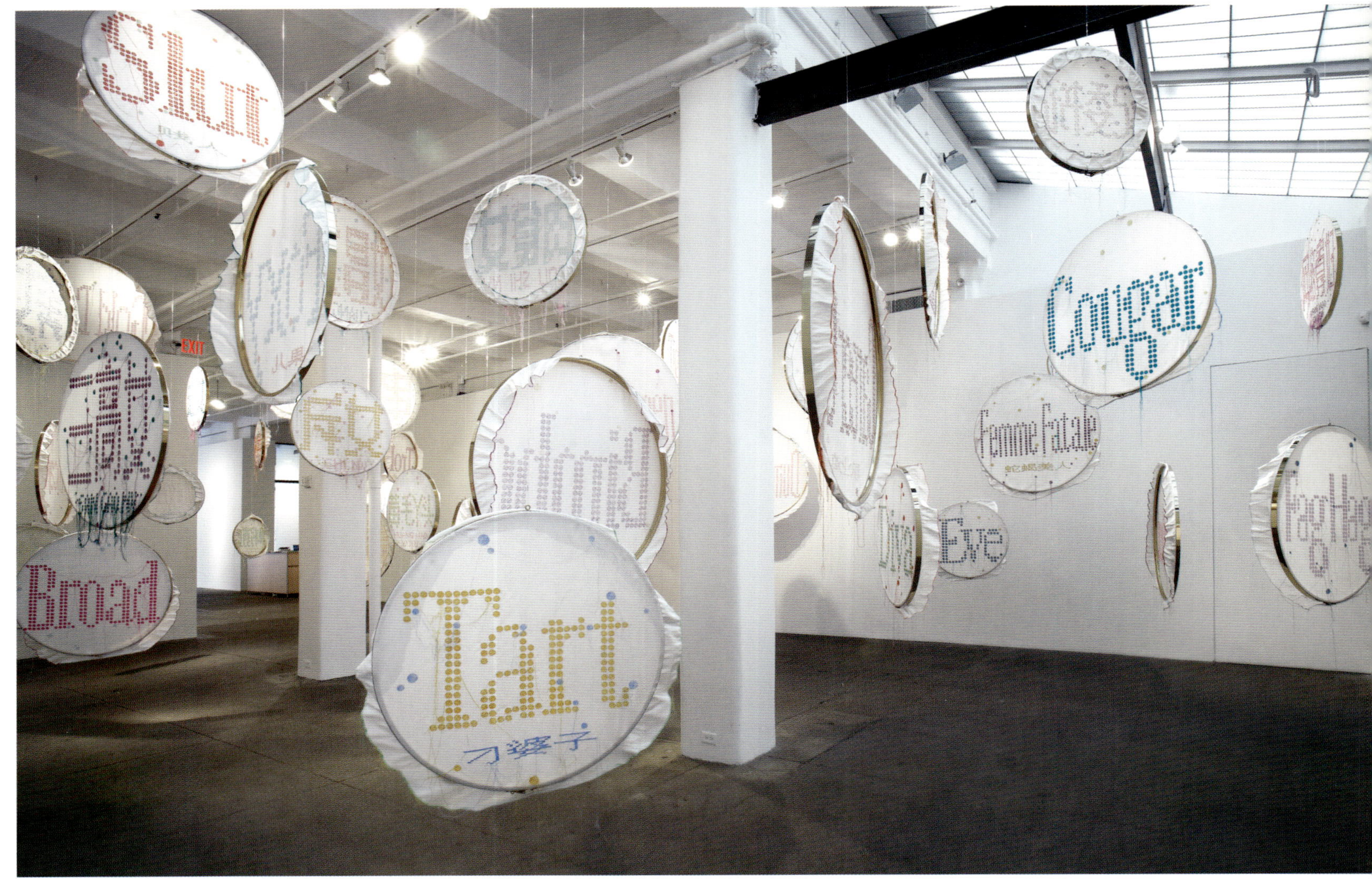

The colour pink has appeared in Lin's work since 2004. At once fleshy and artificial, it suggests multiple associations – childhood innocence, gendered 'girl' symbolism and pleasure. The conjunction of pink silk thread with bones and other relics such as dead tree branches creates an uncomfortable dissonance, forcing us to confront our feelings about difficult subjects. The pink colour is often raw, artificial, even slightly repellent. Recent works, most particularly those created since the death of the artist's mother, evoke the *Vanitas* tradition, although Lin's work focuses on transformation and metamorphosis. The works are not morbid, even when they are meditations on ageing or illness. Despite the shiny pink or white satin in some, the ethereal threads and gauze-like veils of fabric in others, they possess a certain earthiness. Lin Tianmiao nominates Louise Bourgeois, who faced female bodily realities uncompromisingly, as her favourite artist and strongest influence.

Like Bourgeois, Lin has always had an interest in textiles, and her experiments with materials such as hair, felt and cashmere recognise their elemental power. 'The materials take on a life of their own,' she says. In June 2011 the artist's mother died of cancer. Afterwards she started to see some of the motifs of her work – the balls connected by threads to each other, or the matted webs of silk threads and felt – as representing the growth of cancerous cells in the body. Lin Tianmiao often returns to memories of her childhood, of her mother sewing and knitting: 'Life was so much simpler in the past.'

Lin Tianmiao is interested in the power of language to construct female identity. *Badges* presents words applied only to women, words such as witch, tart, trophy wife, whore, leftover woman, phoenix lady, and cougar, in Chinese and English. Stitched on silk, hanging from the ceiling in large embroidery hoops, they question how women are perceived

Lin Tianmiao
Badges 2011–12
white silk, coloured silk thread, painted stainless steel
embroidery frame, sound component
dimensions variable
Installation view, Galerie Lelong, New York, 2012
image courtesy the artist

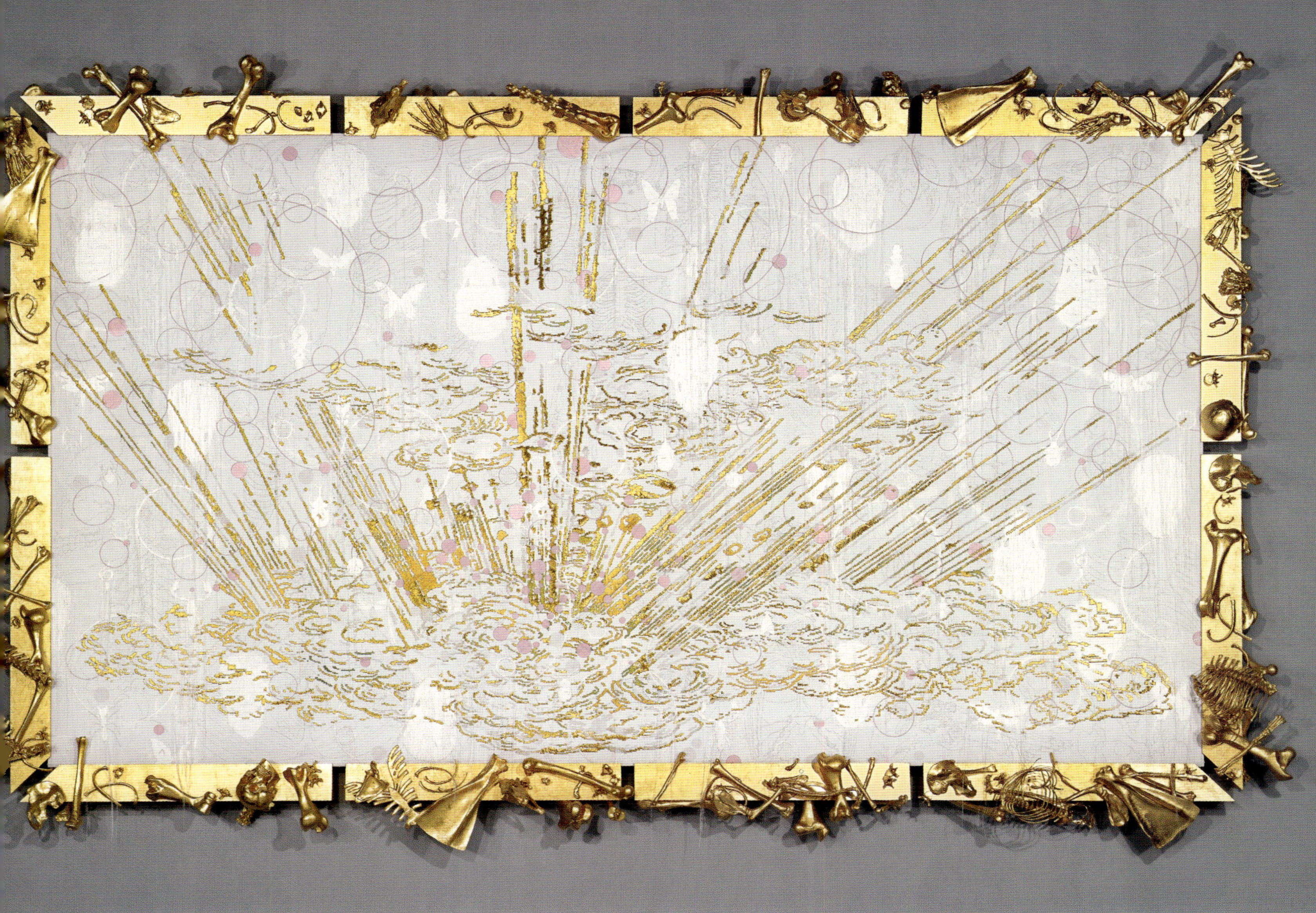

and defined. During our conversation in the enormous studio she shares with Wang Gongxin, I observed a team of assistants seated at long tables stitching the next series of badges, silent and focused. She began the *Badges* series with historical research. In the 1716 Manchu *Kangxi* dictionary she found only two or three hundred words describing women and the roles they played in society, mostly obsolete and relating to courtesans and concubines. Today, new words are coined every week. They emerge from the pop cultures of Japan, Hong Kong and Taiwan and the postings of Chinese 'netizens'. Some cannot easily be translated – 'Mandarin Duck Lady', 'Fox Spirit' and 'Reliable Lady' are culturally specific. Others have penetrated the discourse even beyond China. The term *sheng nu* (leftover woman) has gained enormous currency in the Chinese vernacular. It describes an over-educated, unmarried women over the age of twenty-seven, a pariah figure.

Lin Tianmiao is interested in a broad range of social issues. *The Same for N Times* presents a vast explosion, framed by gold-foiled bones. The work was started in 2011, after the disaster at the Fukushima nuclear power plant in Japan. Lin began to think about radiation and biological mutations, the development of new and altered life forms. She is disturbed by many aspects of contemporary China, including food safety scandals, catastrophic pollution, and corruption. Despite her critical appraisal of what China has become, she could not become an artist until she had returned from America: 'It is my country, and it creates such strong feelings in me.' She likens the experience of returning to China as an intangible force pushing her to find her own artistic vocabulary. At its heart, her work is about processes of transformation. Through the artist's alchemy, unpromising materials such as real or synthetic bones, balls of thread, tree branches, and plastic tools suggest the deepest mysteries of life.

Lin Tianmiao
The Same for N Times 2011
embroidery, silk, cotton, linen, golden silk thread, wooden frame, resin, polyurea, gold leaf
325 x 520 x 45 cm
Image courtesy the artist

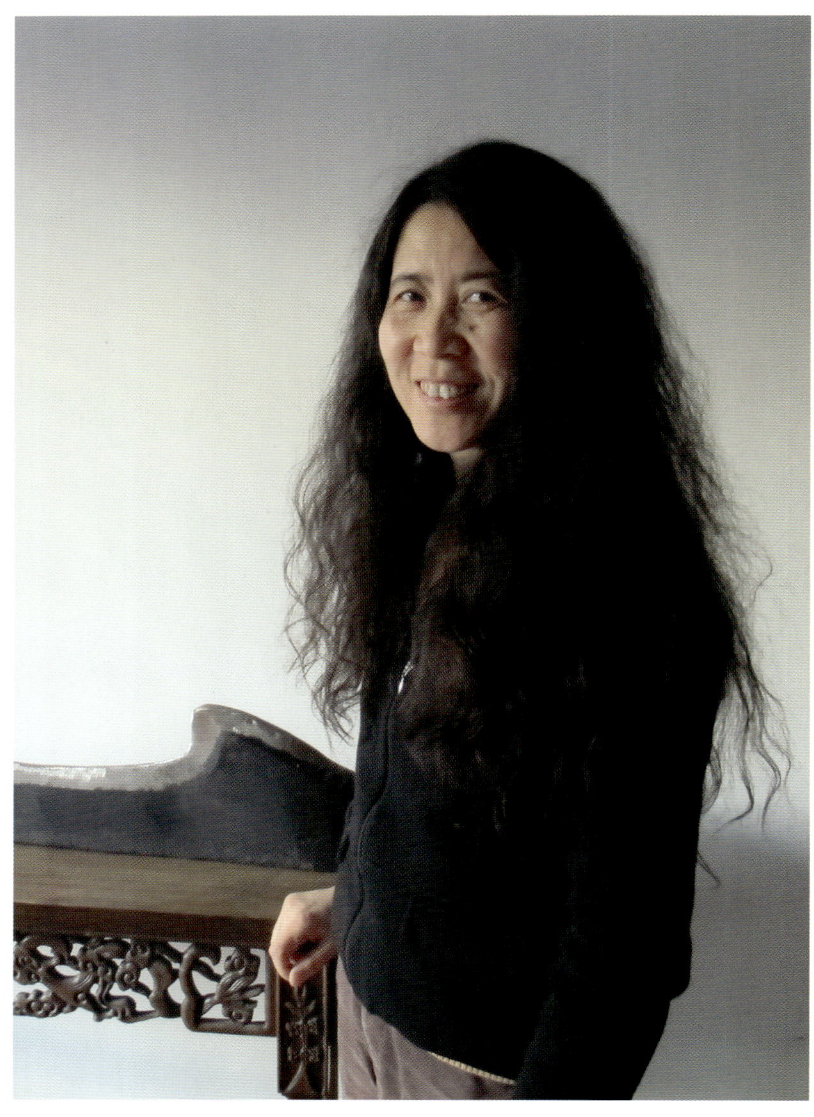

YIN XIUZHEN 尹秀珍

The Collective Subconscious

To reach the rural house and studio where Yin Xiuzhen and her husband Song Dong live and work, you follow a cryptic text message directing you to take an exit past Beijing's sixth ring road, cross a railway line, and then look for landmarks like stone bridges, trees and red gates. My driver was horrified, moaning, 'This isn't Beijing, this is the countryside!' Indeed, you are close to the Great Wall. Arriving, finally, at their metal door, you enter past stacks of winter cabbages to the barking of dogs and the sound of distant trains. The artist couple's monumentally scaled works are stored in a vast space, some wrapped in plastic, and some in packing crates. They work on their own separate projects but often collaborate: in 2013, for instance, *The Way of the Chopsticks* transformed a historic Philadelphia mansion into an immersive three-story multimedia installation.

Yin XIuzhen at home in Beijing
November 2013
photo LG

The first collaboration between the pair began in 2002. They were approaching their tenth wedding anniversary and awaiting the birth of their daughter. They had agreed that the metaphor of a pair of chopsticks – 'useless when separated and nearly omnipotent when combined'[16] – represented their marriage and their art practice. Yin Xiuzhen recalled: 'Song Dong and I were eating dinner... We talked about the idea of chopsticks, and we were excited about it. We thought our relationship is like a pair of chopsticks, helping each other and yet independent of each other.'[17] For these artists, life and art are inextricably connected. The first presentation of the work revealed the differences between the two. Song Dong created a metal chopstick conveying a story from the classic Ming Dynasty novel *Journey to the West*. Yin Xiuzhen's, in contrast, embodied some of the characteristics which have come to typify her practice – it was like a giant textile trouser leg which unzipped to reveal a pile of household objects. In the next version, in 2006, Song Dong's metal chopstick was imprinted with ancient maps of Beijing's central axis, whilst Yin Xiuzhen's was covered with nylon and topped by stuffed fabric versions of iconic city buildings.

Memory – personal and collective – informs all Yin's work. Memories of her Beijing childhood and youth, of difficult times during the Cultural Revolution, and the excitement and anxiety of the early 1990s, are represented in her choice of materials. The softness of fabric is juxtaposed with steel and plastics. She says, 'In a rapidly changing China, "memory" seems to vanish more quickly than everything else. That's why preserving memory has become an alternative way of life.'[18] Critic Hou Hanru explains her intentions: 'she collects, recycles and transforms objects and images which recall the most intense moment of conflicts between sentimental, often female, souls and the turmoil of social revolutions in recent Chinese history.'[19]

Using second-hand objects, especially old clothing and shoes, Yin explores personal memory, nostalgia, and the transformation and Westernisation of China. In a self-titled work from 1998 she inserted identity photographs of herself at different ages into the innersoles of ten pairs of identical handmade cloth shoes of the type once worn by all Chinese women. She sewed the shoes with her mother, an act of communing between generations of women, reinforcing familial bonds.

Clothing is a recurring material, embedded with personal meaning. Yin remembers waiting impatiently beside the family sewing machine as her mother transformed unwanted fabric from the factory where she worked into new clothes for her children at Spring Festival time. Clothes are a second skin, she says, evoking powerful emotions: 'Not just personal experiences but the history of a country.' *Dress Box* consists of her own childhood garments stacked inside a wooden case. Yin poured cement into the box, petrifying the clothes and all the memories they held. Only the top garment is visible, a pink dress handmade by her mother. Like Lin Jingjing's medicine drawers filled with old photographs, *Dress Box* preserves the pain and joy of the past. Never merely nostalgic, her work suggests the journeys of generations of women. In the past Chinese women took their personal possessions – bridal quilts and linens – from their parents' home to their husband's. In contrast, this case was made by Yin's father for her older sister when she was sent to do farm labour, like millions of 'educated youth' all over China, under Mao's policy of rustication. Later, Yin took the same case when she went to teachers' college.

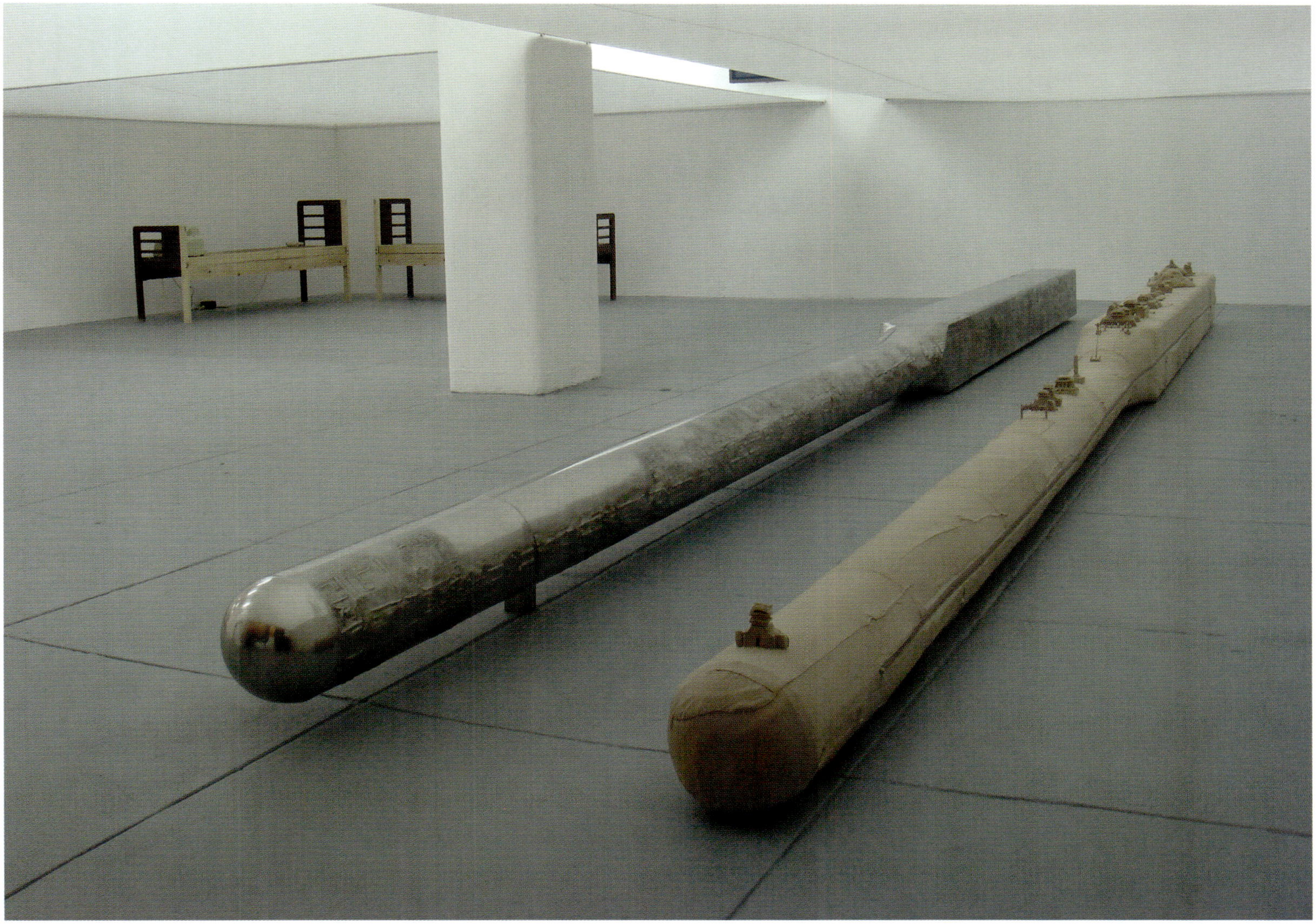

Born in 1963 in Beijing, Yin Xiuzhen remembers the years of her childhood with less bitterness than others of her generation. She found it 'quite exciting' as a schoolgirl,

Yin Xiuzhen (with Song Dong)
Chopsticks 2006 (***Kuai Zi*** 2006)
stockings, foam, thread, stainless steel
each 795 x 30 x 30 cm
image courtesy the artists

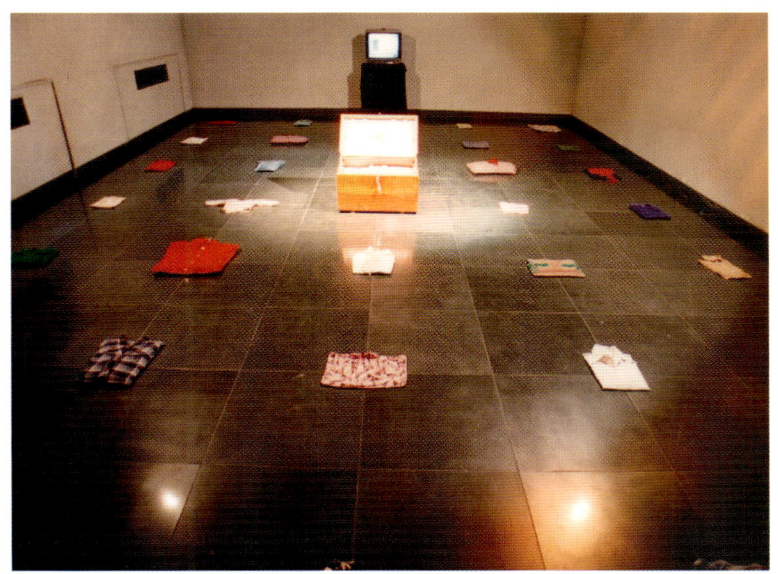

Yin Xiuzhen
Dress Box 1999 (installation view)
clothes worn by the artist over three decades, cement, an old home-made dress box, copper plate, television
dimensions variable
image courtesy and © Yin Xiuzhen

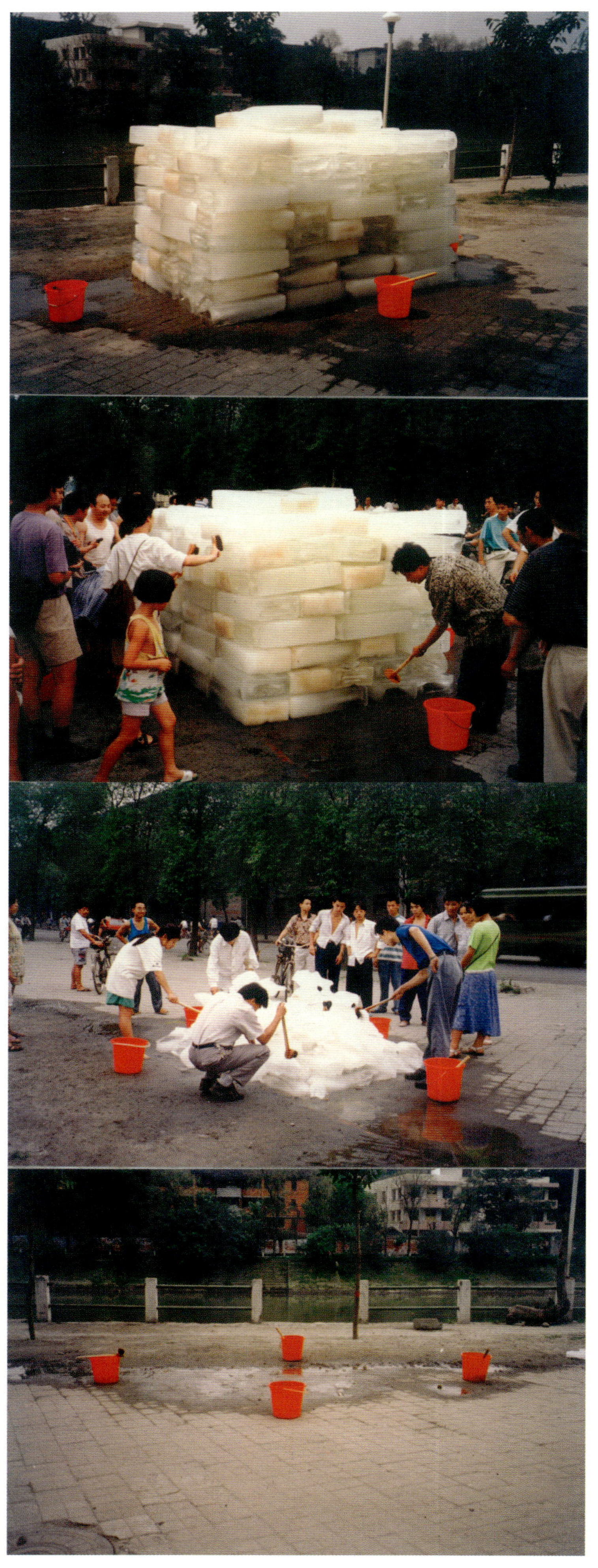

especially when, after a certain point, all classes were cancelled and schools closed: 'I was so young it didn't have a huge impact on me. Maybe it's a horrible memory for adults but for children it was fun. We were watching people doing strange things... We had to recite Mao's sayings before every class.' She carried two satchels to school, one just for Mao's *Little Red Book*, which would be placed with great care on one side of the desk, pencil box in the middle, and school exercise books on the other side. 'My childhood was happy but when I grew up and looked back I could see how horrible that time was. It was a kind of religion, a kind of Mao worship. We truly believed that the collective good was more important than the individual's desires or wishes.'[20]

In 1989 Yin graduated from Capital Normal University with a degree in painting, and began work as a high school art teacher. She was constantly in trouble with school authorities for sins against propriety such as allowing students to listen to music. During her ten-year teaching career she began to make installation and performance work with other artists, including her husband. Chinese artists were discovering the outside world: 'It was exciting because we were young, and things were forbidden and underground, and we liked the rebelliousness.'

Yin Xiuzhen remembers travelling in buses to clandestine performance art events in rural areas outside Beijing. The artists were always being watched, so despite the remote locations it wasn't unusual for the police to arrive and confiscate cameras, destroying film of the events. There were no commercial galleries in China at that time. Artists worked in their homes, then called all their friends to see their work: 'So you would see the same old faces all the time. Not like today when there are so many galleries and so many exhibitions. In the nineties we all went to see everything!' Song Dong and Yin Xiuzhen were key figures in this 'apartment art' of the 1990s, as were other artist couples such as Lin Tianmiao and her husband Wang Gongxin; and Qin Fengling and Wang Luyan. Gao Minglu describes the flavour of this period: 'They made their homes the stronghold of personal space, where they created and exhibited a large number of small-scale installations made of cheap materials and embracing the concept of randomness.'[21]

Yin Xiuzhen and Song Dong – still both working as art teachers – formed *The Wooden Stool Group*, meeting in their tiny living room to share and discuss their works. One of Yin's Fluxus-inspired works from that time, *Androgynous Sweater*, was made by taking their knitted sweaters apart and joining them together. While Song Dong was ritually performing *Writing Diary with Water*, Yin Xiuzhen planned her own significant performance, *Washing the River*, re-created on the Derwent

Yin Xiuzhen
Washing the River 1995
documentation of performance
Funan River, Chengdu, China
Image courtesy and © Yin Xiuzhen

Yin Xiuzhen *(right and overleaf)*
Collective Subconscious (Blue) 2007
minivan, stainless steel, used clothes, stool, music
140 x 190 x 1420 cm
image courtesy the artist and Beijing Commune

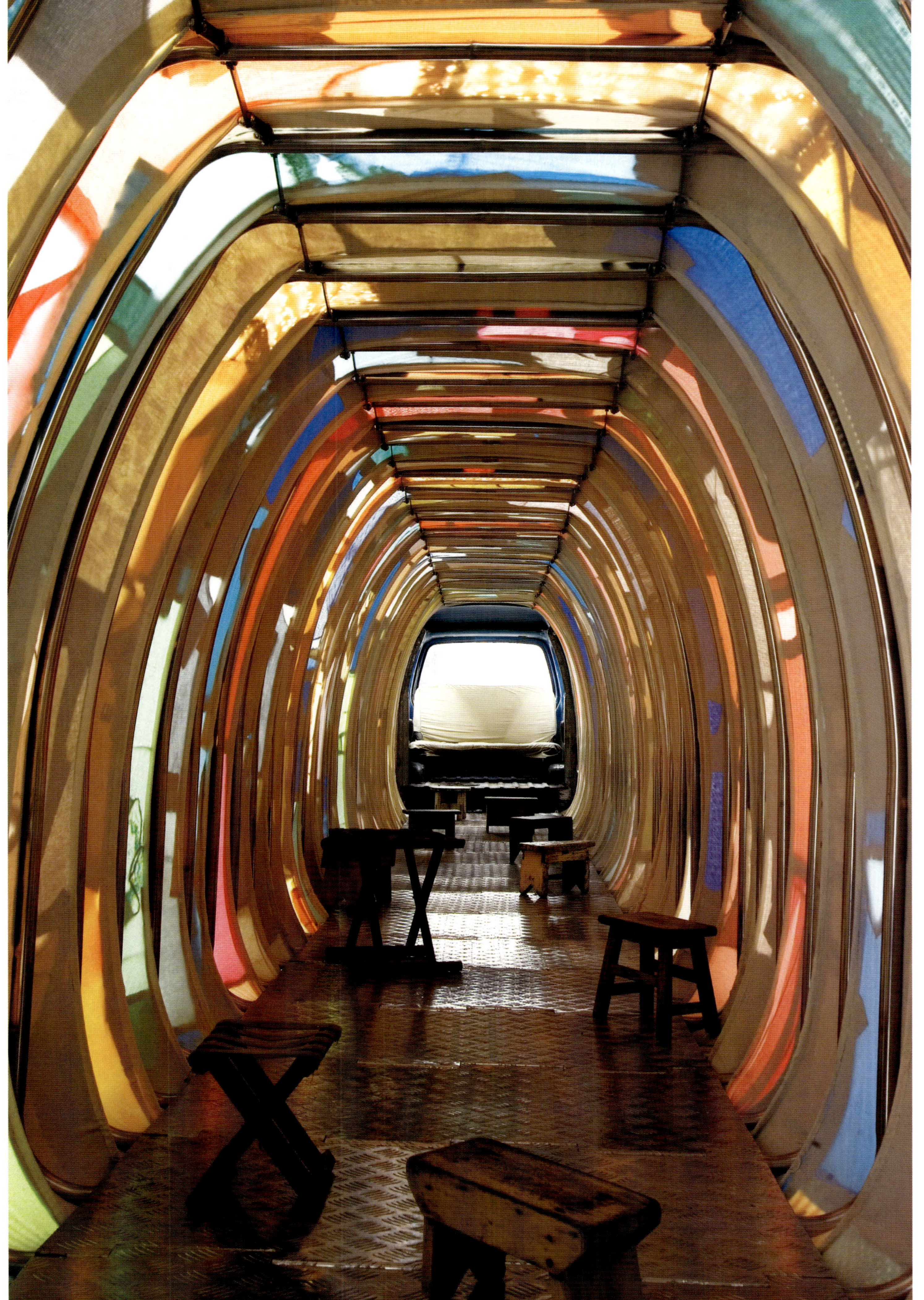

River in Hobart in 2014. For the original 1995 performance she invited passers-by to scrub blocks of ice made from the water of a polluted river in Chengdu, Sichuan Province, returning the 'cleansed' melted water back into its source, an indication even at this early stage of her engagement with environmental issues.

Suffering constant disapproval from education authorities, Yin Xiuzhen finally resigned in 1999, when she was awarded a year-long studio residency in Bad Ems, Germany. She had begun to travel abroad from 1997, discovering the global phenomenon of contemporary art. When she was an art student and the library received a Russian art book about Impressionism it was considered so precious that the students had to wear gloves to read it, and queue for the privilege. However, China was changing. Yin Xiuzhen identifies two exhibitions that influenced her ideas: in 1985 Robert Rauschenberg shook Beijing's hermetic avant-garde artworld, and in 1989, the year she graduated, *China/Avant-garde* was a watershed.[22]

Yin Xiuzhen focuses on memory – on the shift from a collectivist past to an individualist and materialist present. *Collective Subconscious* explores the desires of the individual versus the collective experiences of her youth. A minivan of the type called a *xiao mian* (little loaf of bread) is cut in half and connected by a concertina-like armature wrapped in a quilt made of four hundred items of discarded clothing collected from friends and relatives. Just as the possession of a sewing machine symbolised prosperity in Yin Xiuzhen's childhood, vans like these indicated material prosperity and entrepreneurship (they were used as private taxis) in the 1990s. Yin transforms the symbol of private success into a public space. The audience sits inside on little stools, listening to a popular song of the nineties, *Beijing Beijing*. It is a gently nostalgic work, but Yin's alarm at the rampant greed and environmental destruction of today's China undercuts its charm.

Yin Xiuzhen and Song Dong belong to the first generation of Chinese artists since 1949 to participate in global culture. *Portable Cities* documents travel to cities such as San Francisco, Sydney, Vancouver, Paris, Dusseldorf and Berlin, via the symbol of the suitcase. Closed, they appear to be ordinary cases. Opened, they reveal pop-up cityscapes, sometimes accompanied by sound recordings made on location. Each miniature metropolis is made of second-hand clothing previously worn by the citizens of that city, in a wry comment on globalisation and the increasing homogenisation of the planet, as well as a reference to Yin's opportunities for travel outside China from the late 1990s.

Portable Cities remind us of Yin Xiuzhen's love for Duchamp and Rauschenberg. Like Duchamp's *Boite en Valise* (a 'portable museum' that allowed him to carry his life's work in a box) the *Portable Cities* issue a tongue-in-cheek challenge to the seriousness of the artworld. Duchamp's willingness to reproduce his works in miniature stemmed from his belief that there was nothing inherently sacred about a work of art, that the idea behind an art object was more important than the object itself.[23] Working as a conceptual and performance artist with Song Dong in the 1990s, Yin Xiuzhen embraced these ideas, together with Rauschenberg's intention to work 'in the gap between art and life.'[24] The surprise interiors of her suitcases reveal Yin's delight in her new freedom to experience what the world has to offer, but they also suggest that you take your past with you wherever you go. In that sense they are not so far removed from the earlier *Dress Box*. With wit and poignancy, Yin confronts the way that past and present collide in a society that appears to be on fast-forward.

In 2001 Yin Xiuzhen was commissioned by the Siemens Corporation to create a large-scale sculpture of a plane made from the discarded clothing of their employees. She completed

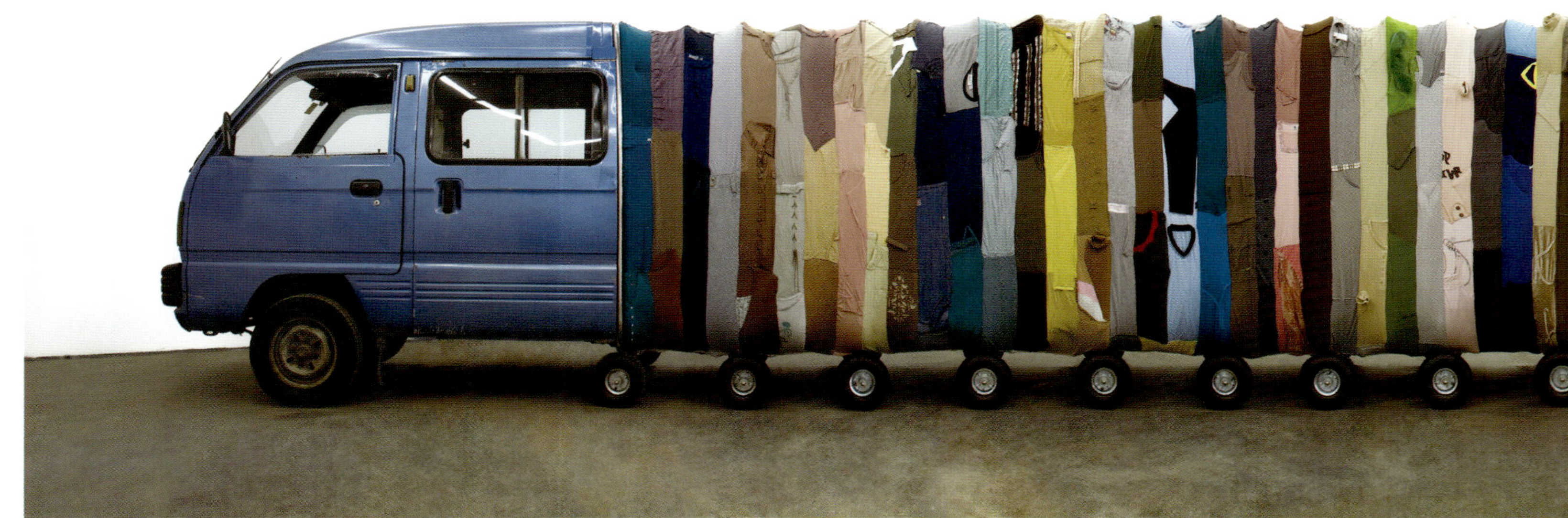

the work in August. One month later, the terrorist attack on the Twin Towers changed everything. The clothing used in the work now seemed to take on the character of a memorial. Yin began to make more planes, and the ongoing project *International Flight* has continued to take on new meanings: after the tragic aviation disasters of 2014 and 2015, audiences will not be able to see these works in the same way. The juxtaposition between the homespun, handcrafted nature of her materials and the old clothes piled on the ground beneath is chilling in this new context.

Yin Xiuzhen creates allegories for the contemporary world. *Nowhere to Land,* at Pace Beijing in 2013, expressed her unease with the expansionist thrust of Chinese modernisation. The title work appears at first sight to consist of huge upturned aeroplane wheels and landing gear. A closer look reveals that it is assembled from prosaic domestic objects creating the illusion of high-tech machinery, and covered with used clothing. Does this represent China's twenty-first century trajectory of growing wealth and global power? At this point, no-one can guess where the plane will land.

Thought, a massive brain made entirely of blue fabric, is similarly ambiguous. Audiences are invited to crawl into the enticing space within, a restful chamber lined with shades of blue. The work reflects the desire for respite from the constant clamour and stress of the modern world, contrasting public and private spheres, individual and collective experience. It also suggests brainwashing and constant surveillance, even within the family unit, evoking a past in which children were encouraged to betray their parents to the authorities. Today we are accustomed to constant electronic surveillance. 'What is really private space?' asks Yin Xiuzhen. With the tactile familiarity of clothing, she invites us to consider our deepest fears and our most heartfelt desires.

Gao Rong, Lin Jingjing, Lin Tianmiao and Yin Xiuzhen use the materials and techniques of everyday life to reflect on their experiences (specifically, their experiences as women) in a fluxing, unpredictable world. The choice to use needle and thread or second-hand clothing can be interpreted in multiple ways, which may at times be at odds with the artist's own stated intent. When Yin Xiuzhen's work was exhibited in Dusseldorff, Germany, in 2012, audiences interpreted her use of clothing as a comment on China's manufacturing industry and a critique of China's industrialisation, a reading which Yin explicitly denies.[25] Similarly, Gao Rong denies any feminist intent in using the materials and techniques of domestic labour, and Lin Jingjing says her act of sewing has nothing to do with 'women's work'. Nevertheless, in their very materiality, each artist embodies their own femaleness, as well as reflecting on broader concerns such as environmental destruction and the high social cost of progress.

Two of the four artists, Lin Tianmiao and Yin Xiuzhen, were included in *Global Feminisms*, the inaugural exhibition at the Elizabeth A. Sackler Center for Feminist Art in the Brooklyn Museum, curated by Maura Reilly and Linda Nochlin with the stated aim of presenting 'a multitude of feminist voices from across cultures.'[26] While it is important to acknowledge the doubts expressed by these and other women artists about what a twenty-first century Chinese feminism might be, and to recognise that it may look very different from western versions, their use of textiles nonetheless places female experience at the centre of their practice. We can trace commonalities in their responses to universal experiences of family, motherhood, sexuality and ageing, and discern the differences that emerge from the particularities of their lived experience.

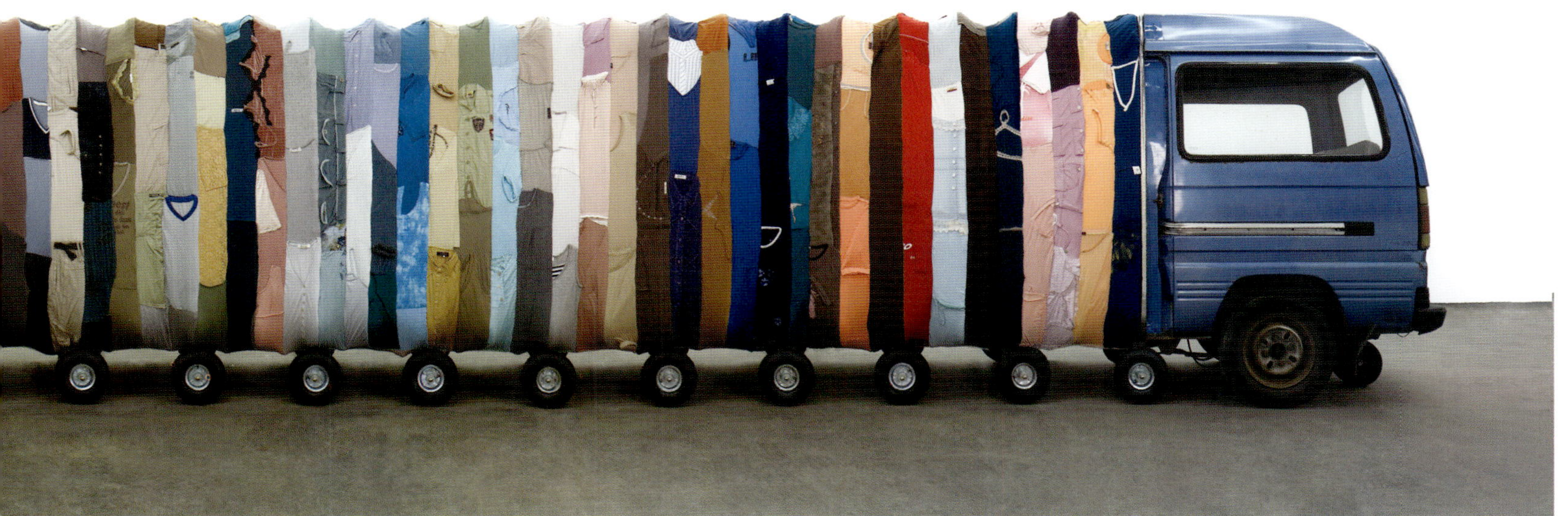

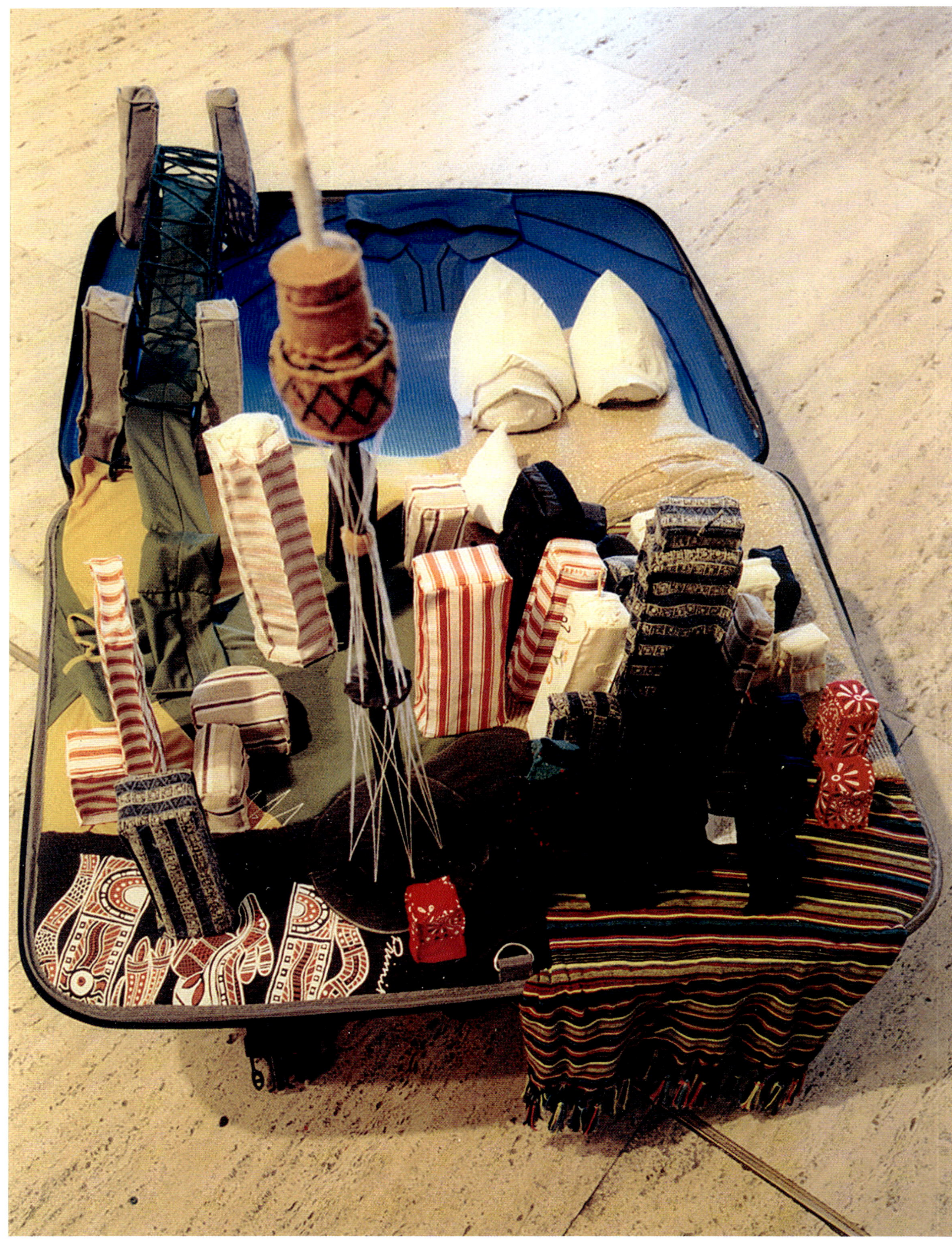

NOTES

1 Quentin, David & Baggins, Brian 1966 'Quotations from Chairman Mao Tse-Tung' (sic) 'Report on an Investigation of the Peasant Movement in Hunan' Peking Foreign Languages Press, Mao Tse Tung Internet Archive (marxists.org) 2000 available at http://www.marxists.org/reference/archive/mao/works/red-book/ accessed 23 July 2014

2 Embroidery and textiles were found in the sacred Buddhist caves along the Silk Road. In an indication of the extent of this history, Craig Clunas describes the thirty-five complete blankets and garments recovered from a tomb of around 300 BCE at Mashan in Hubei Province, featuring interlaced dragons, tigers and birds. Clunas, Craig 2009 *Art in China* 2nd edition Oxford University Press (28–29)

3 Clunas, Craig 2009 *Art in China* 2nd edition Oxford University Press (185)

4 Tsui, Shu Chin, 2013 *Breakthrough: Work by Contemporary Chinese Women Artists*, Bowdoin College Museum of Art, Cambridge

5 Que Zhang 2013 'The Future of a Fading Chinese Tradition: Hunan Embroidery' *IOSR Journal of Humanities and Social Science (IOSR-JHSS)* Volume 12, Issue 5, Jul–Aug 2013 (97–106) notes that after the Cultural Revolution, 'In the entire province of Hunan, there were only one thousand two hundred embroiderers and nine painters left in the embroidery industry.'

6 McLaren, Anne E., 1996 'Women's Voices and Textuality: Chastity and Abduction in Chinese Nüshu Writing' in *Modern China,* 22 (4) (382–416).

7 Unless otherwise acknowledged all quotes from Gao Rong are from her conversations with the writer, in Beijing in December 2012 and November 2013

8 Dimond, V. Scott 2013 *Stories Joyfully Embroidered: Shaanxi Folk Textiles from Northern China* available at http://www.sama-art.org/media/documents/Catalogues-ChineseTextiles.pdf accessed 14 July 2014

9 Unless otherwise acknowledged all quotes from Lin Jingjing are from her conversations with the writer, in Beijing in November 2013 and December 2014

10 Xu Liuliu 2011 'Artist Puts Private Life on Display' *Global Times* 16 June 2011 available at http://www.globaltimes.cn/content/661845.shtml accessed 18 July 2014

11 Unless otherwise acknowledged all quotes from Lin Tianmiao are from her conversation with the writer, in Beijing, in December 2012

12 Sun Yunfan 2012 'Interview: Lin Tianmiao on Art, Influence, and "Bodily Reaction" as Inspiration' available at http://asiasociety.org/blog/asia/interview-lin-tianmiao-art-influence-and-bodily-reaction-inspiration accessed 4 July 2014

13 Chiu, Melissa and Lin Tianmiao 2012 'A conversation with the writer' in *Bound and Unbound* Asia Society New York

14 Sun Yunfan 2012 'Interview: Lin Tianmiao on Art, Influence, and 'Bodily Reaction as Inspiration' available at http://asiasociety.org/blog/asia/interview-lin-tianmiao-art-influence-and-bodily-reaction-inspiration accessed 4 July 2014

15 Lin Tianmiao in conversation with Heather Russell for Artnet

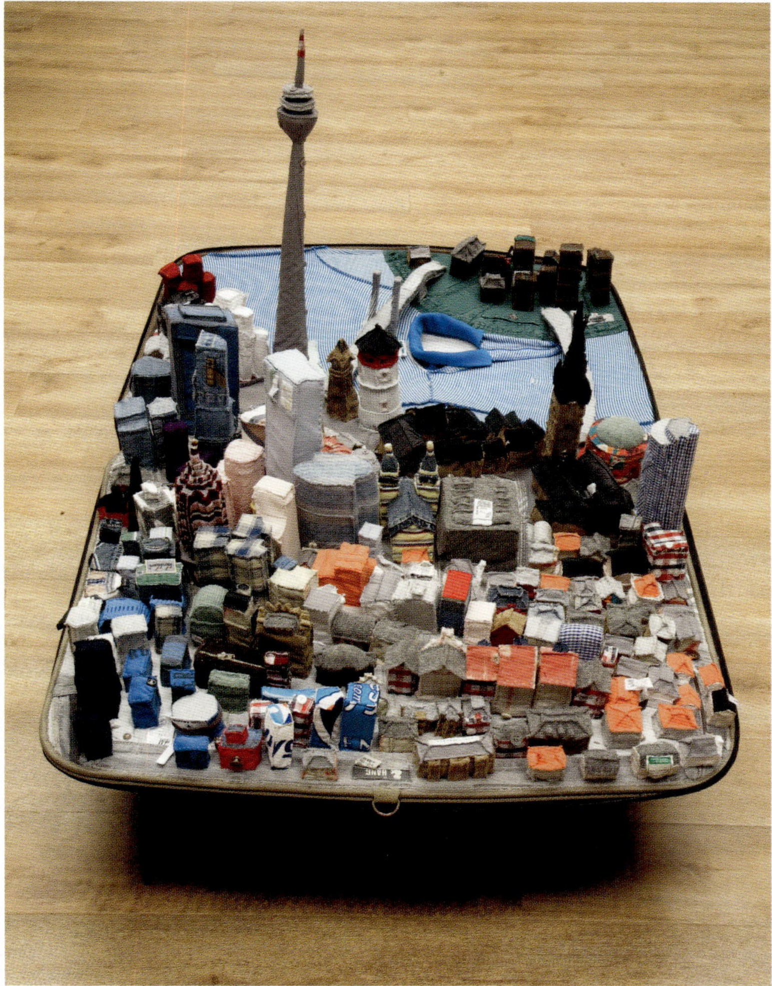

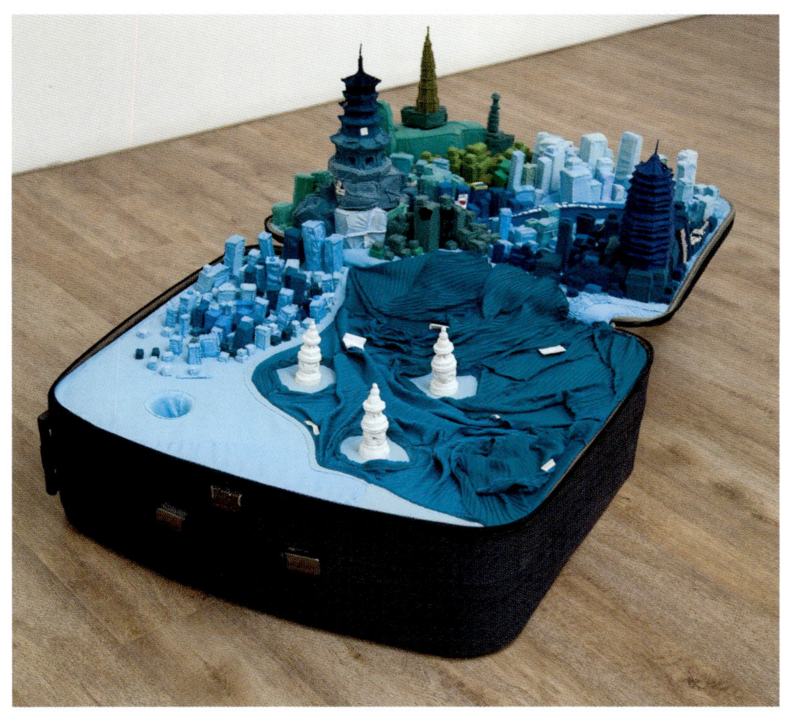

Yin Xiuzhen
Portable Cities – Sydney, Dusseldorf and ***Hangzhou*** 2007
suitcases, used clothes, light, map, sound
images courtesy Pace Beijing and © Yin Xiuzhen

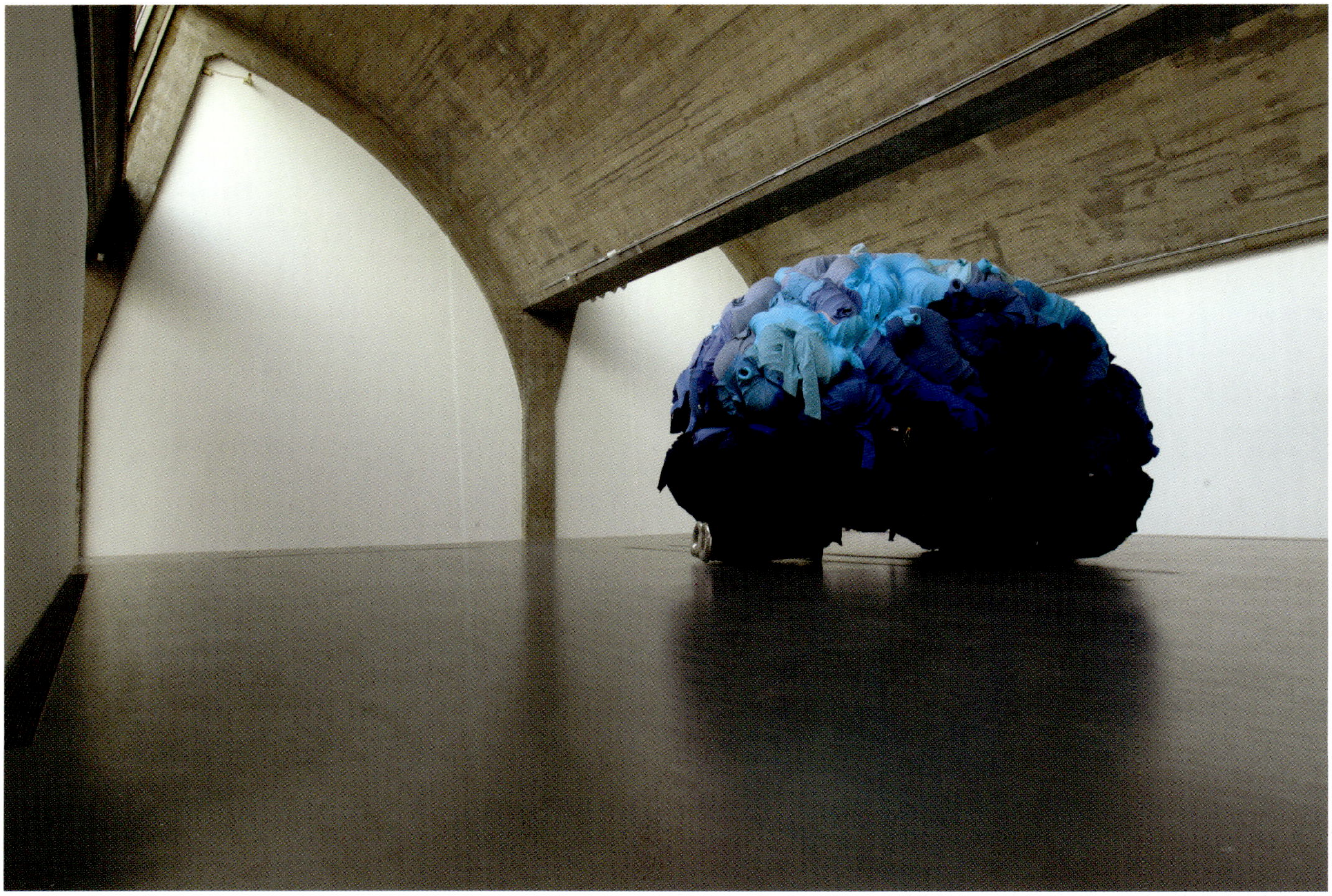

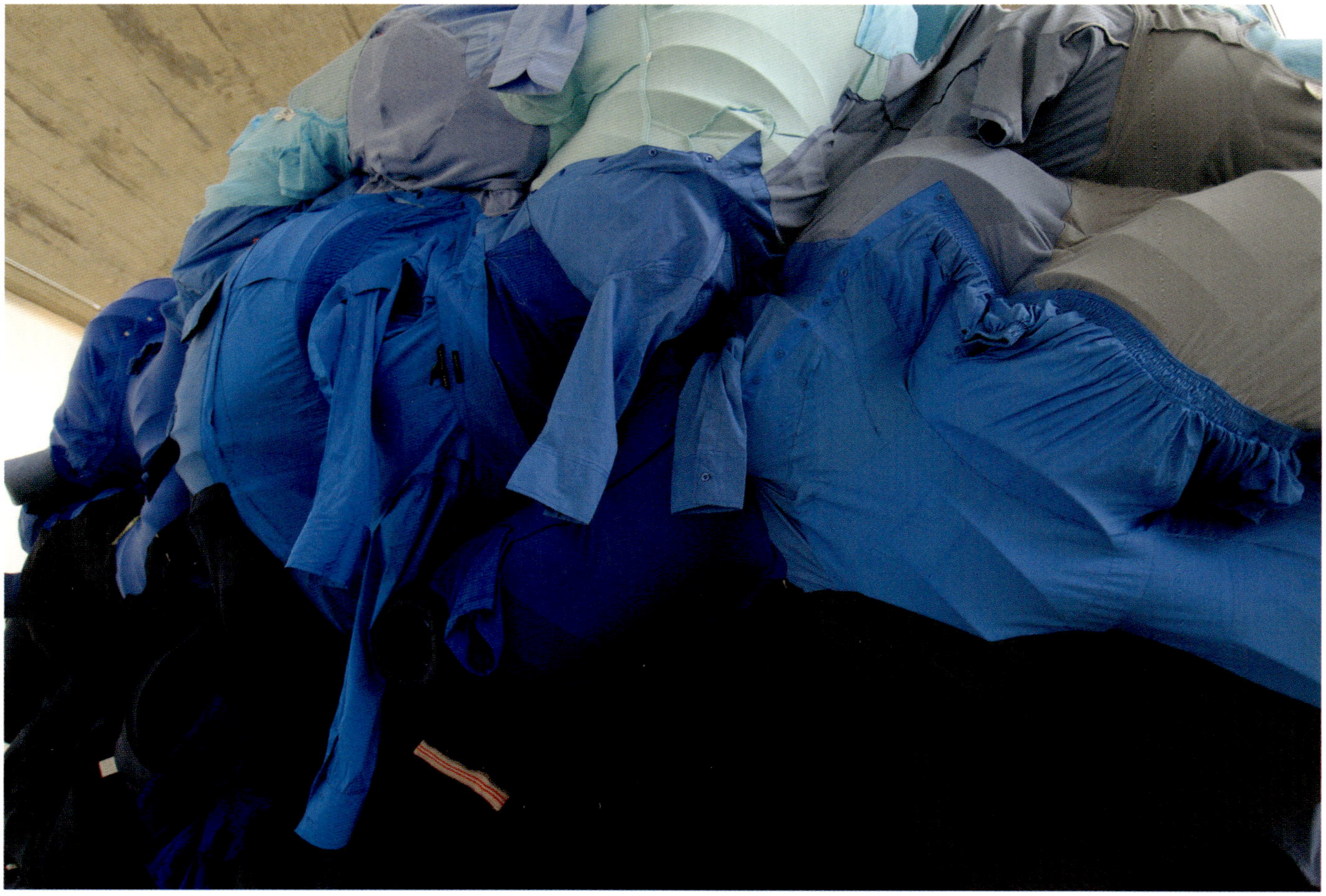

13 Dec 2013 available at http://news.artnet.com/art-world/an-interview-with-lin-tianmiao-and-wang-gongxin-52483 accessed 19 July 2014

16 Tinari, Philip 2011 'Song Dong and Yin Xiuzhen's Way of Chopsticks' in *The Way of Chopsticks III* Chambers Fine Art, Beijing

17 Yin Xiuzhen 2011 *The Way of Chopsticks III* Chambers Fine Art, Beijing (19)

18 Yin Xiuzhen, Pace Gallery Beijing website available at http://www.pacegallery.com/artists/520/yin-xiuzhen accessed 18 July 2014

19 Hou Hanru 1999 'One Year Not at Home: 1999 in Bad Ems Germany' Kunstlerhaus Schloss Balmoral, Bad Ems

20 Unless otherwise acknowledged all quotes from Yin Xiuzhen are from her conversation with the writer, in Beijing in November 2013

21 Gao Minglu 2011 *Total Modernity and the Avant-garde in Contemporary Chinese Art*, MIT Press, Cambridge (284)

22 See Chapter 2 for a full account of *China/Avant-garde*

23 Taylor, Michael, in a lecture at the Hood Museum of Art on 4 April 2012, available at http://hoodmuseum.dartmouth.edu/exhibitions/theboxinavalise/ accessed 20 July 2014

24 Jones, Jonathan 2008 'How Robert Rauschenberg Brought Art to Life' the *Guardian* available at http://www.theguardian.com/artanddesign/jonathanjonesblog/2008/dec/16/robert-rauschenberg-pollock-rothko accessed 20 July 2014

25 Bailey, Stephanie 2013 'Yin Xiuzhen: A Material World' in *Yishu Journal of Contemporary Chinese Art* Vol 12 (2) March/April 2013

26 Reilly, Maura 2007 'Towards Transnational Feminisms' in *Global Feminisms: New Directions in Contemporary Art* Merrell, London, New York (Brooklyn Museum) (15)

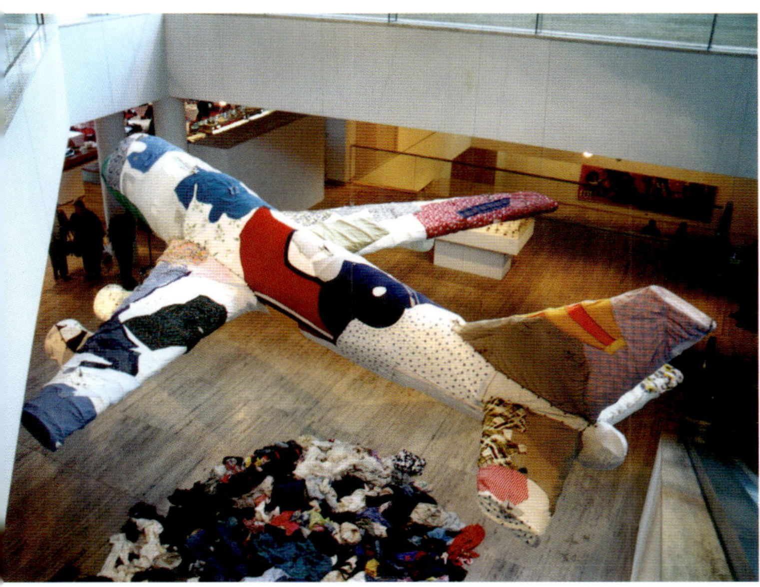

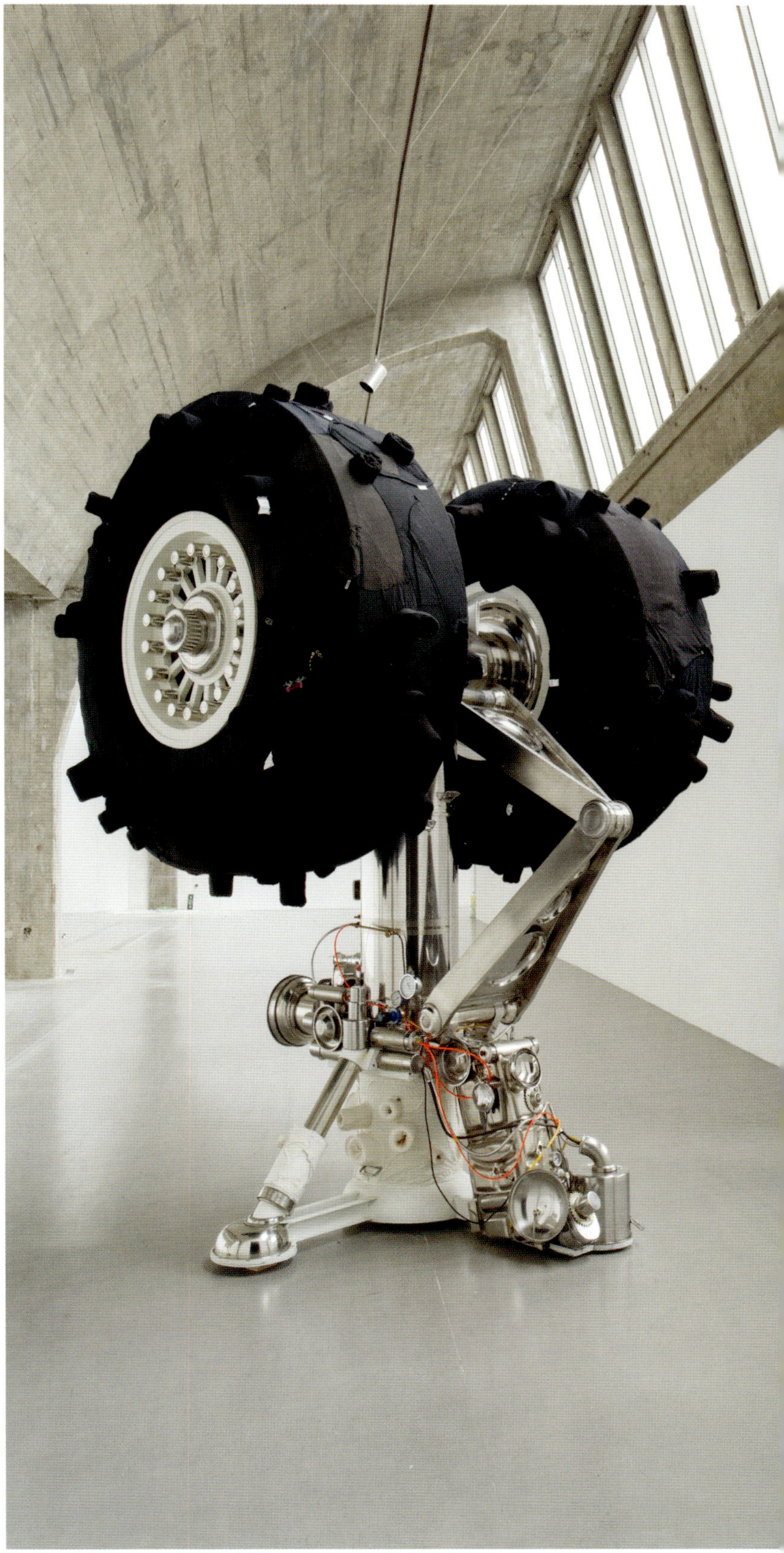

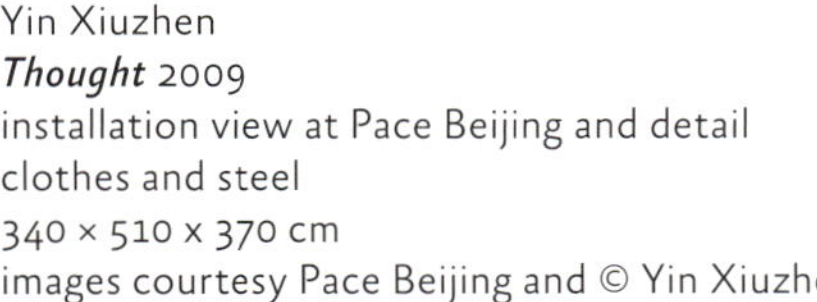

Yin Xiuzhen
Thought 2009
installation view at Pace Beijing and detail
clothes and steel
340 x 510 x 370 cm
images courtesy Pace Beijing and © Yin Xiuzhen

Yin Xiuzhen
International Flight 2001–04
installation view at 14th Biennale of Sydney 2004
steel frame, used clothes
700 x 600 x 150 cm
image courtesy the artist

Yin Xiuzhen
Nowhere to Land 2012
used clothes, steel, stainless steel,
daily objects
330 x 240 x 210 cm
image courtesy Pace Beijing and © Yin Xiuzhen

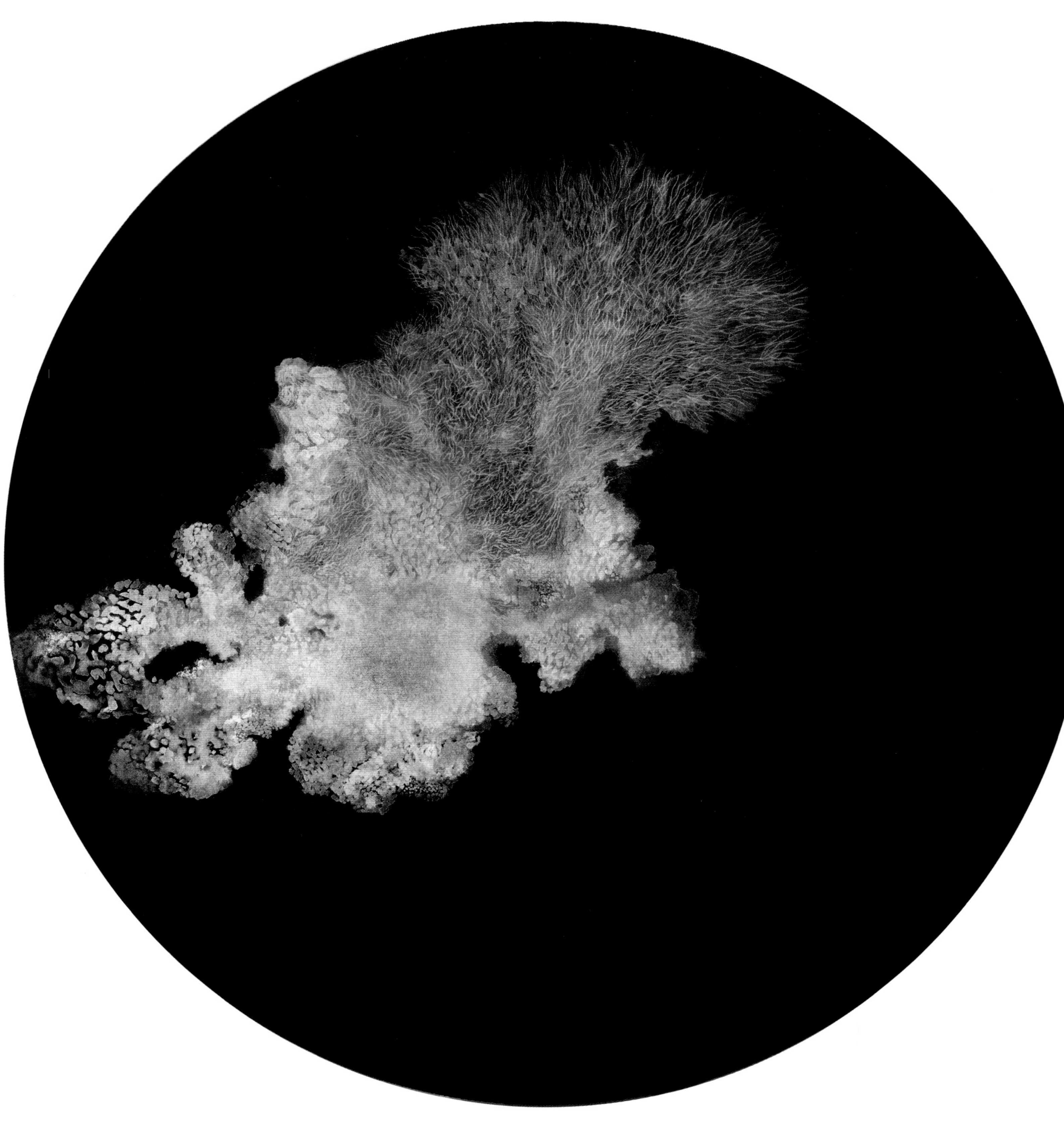

'BLACK AS LACQUER': REINVENTING INK

Li Tingting, Shi Zhiying, Gao Ping and Bingyi

It is not possible to discuss Chinese art without considering the mark of the brush dipped in ink. Fundamental to Chinese calligraphy and painting for more than two millennia, its techniques and methods have been astonishingly constant. Writing with some form of black ink on surfaces such as silk, stone, bamboo and wood can be traced back as far as the Spring and Autumn periods (722–480 BCE). Made with carbon and animal glue, the properties of Chinese ink allow artists to produce works of great expressive power with limited means. It can be diluted to the most delicate shades of grey, capable of infinitely nuanced and subtle mark-making.

By the eleventh century the ability to write beautiful calligraphy was one of the criteria for recruitment into the ranks of government officials through the civil service examinations. Those who succeeded became a powerful and influential elite, 'responsible for maintaining the moral and aesthetic standards established by the political and cultural paragons of the past.'[1] These scholar officials, the 'literati', knew that it was through their accounts, recorded in beautiful script, that their emperor would be judged by future generations.

The literati became amateur artists upon retirement, devoting themselves to poetry and painting, contemplation of their beautifully designed gardens, and other gentlemanly pursuits. They were not interested in literal representation, preferring an understated simplicity, with deft use of the brush developed through disciplined years of practice in calligraphy. Their works were animated and expressive, even to a twenty-first-century eye accustomed to the gestural mark-making of a modernist idiom. For scholar officials trying to distance themselves from the realpolitik of the imperial court, creating ink paintings of birds and flowers could 'bring comfort to their hearts,' says art historian Lin Ci, an endearing image of the lonely scholar contemplating his garden.[2]

The significance of calligraphy and ink painting in Chinese history continues to resonate. Contemporary artists reinvent ancient traditions in diverse ways. Bringing the aesthetic and conceptual underpinnings of ink painting to works in other media such as oil paint, sculpture, video – even performance art – has ensured the tradition remains vital. From Xu Bing's radically re-imagined landscapes made from backlit garden debris and rubbish, to Gu Wenda's ethereal curtains of text made of human hair, or Yang Yongliang's digitally animated landscapes, contemporary artists have ensured that the ink tradition has remained vital. They revere their cultural heritage, but at the same time freely experiment with it. Their works reference tradition and convention, yet speak to the contemporary world with a rich layering of past and present that is one of the most distinctive features of contemporary Chinese art.

Throughout history, Chinese artists have copied, reinvented and transformed past models of art, and ink painting is no exception. Current discourses about its significance in contemporary art acknowledge its importance. Chang Tsong-Zung has likened the significance of '*shui mo*' (water/ink) painting in recent times to the politicisation of Abstract Expressionism in the Cold War America of the 1950s, in the sense that an artistic medium is used to create a 'new supra-national identity.'[3] Chang believes it should be called '*shu hua*' (calligraphy painting) in recognition of the importance of calligraphy as a parallel practice. Despite this link with history and national pride, however, the boundaries of ink painting – what it is and what it might be – are as blurred as a misty Song Dynasty scroll depicting water and mountains.

Artists still work with ink on paper in the time-honoured manner, but as curator Britta Erickson points out, you can now also find the paper without the ink, the ink without the paper – even sometimes just the memory of the gesture in artists' documentation of performative work.[4] Explaining the current international fascination with new forms of ink

Bingyi
The Luminaries 2015
40 x 40 cm
ink on paper
image courtesy the artist

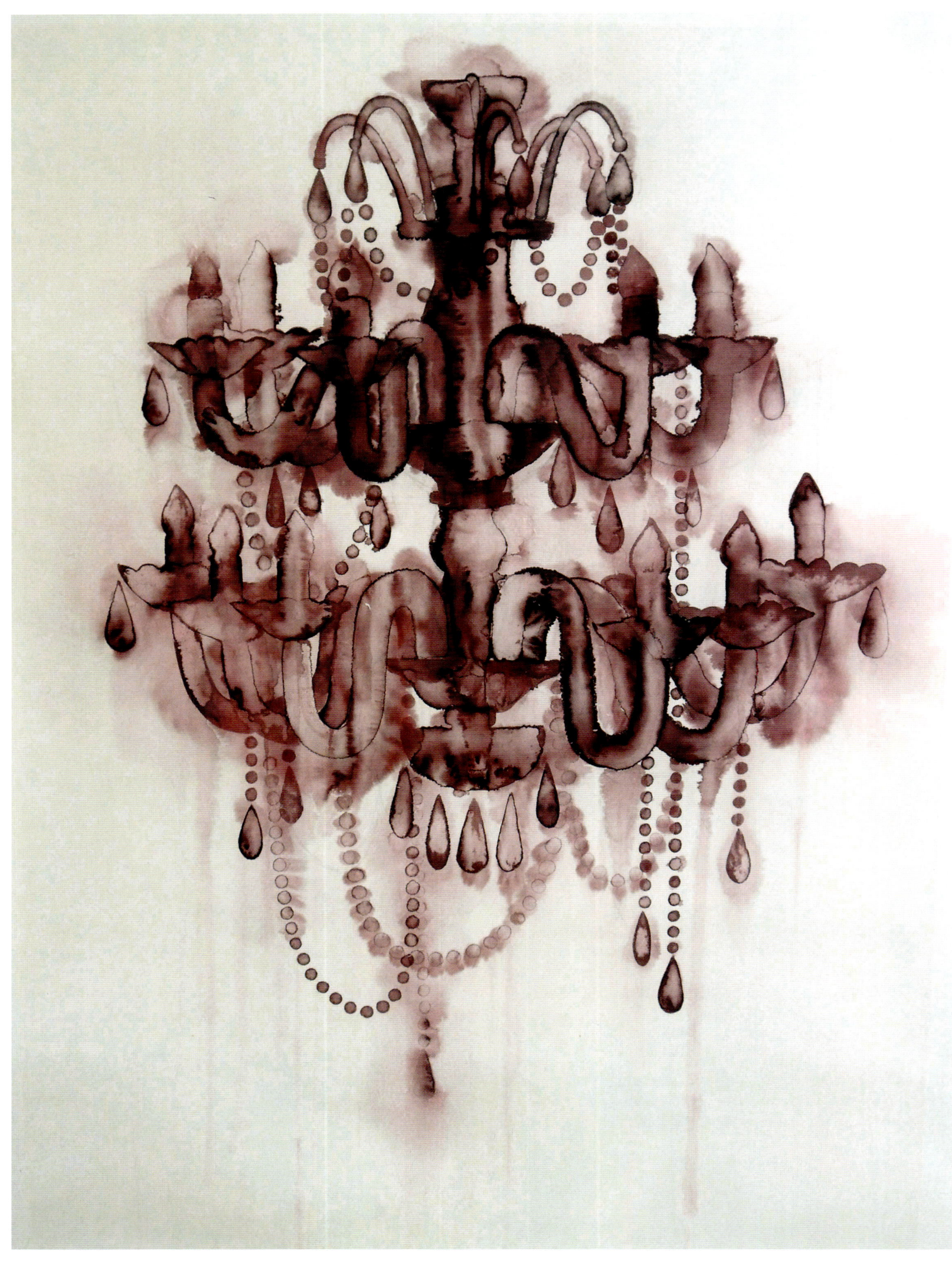

painting she said, 'Perhaps people are remembering what a perfect trio of materials ink, brush, and paper are, their harmonious interaction honed over the centuries. Of essential importance, too, is the artist's highly trained body, working in conjunction with ink, brush, and paper. It takes patience and a calm mind both to create and to fully appreciate the best ink painting: perhaps people are ready for this, and tired of art that can be digested in a couple of seconds.'[5] That unique combination of body, mind and spirit is central to the practice of artists working in, or transforming, ink traditions today.

Shanghai painter Shi Zhiying and Beijing-based artists Li Tingting, Gao Ping and Bingyi have incorporated their love for literati ink traditions into a contemporary practice. Their work acknowledges the history of *shui mo* (ink and water) in innovative ways that represent their own ideas and beliefs.

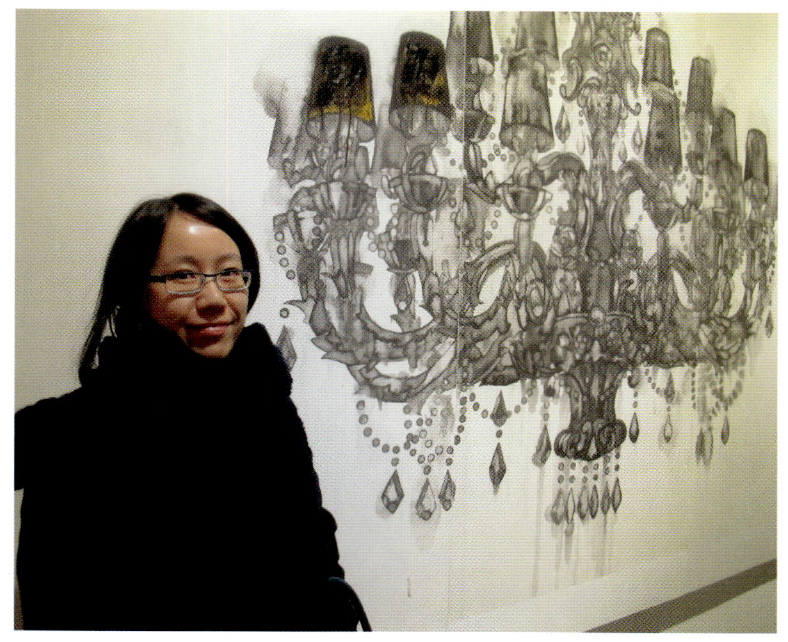

LI TINGTING 李婷婷

Shoes, Sofas and Chandeliers

Li Tingting uses Chinese ink, brush and paper in the classical manner, sometimes in the traditional form of a scroll – but with a surprising twist. Despite her admiration for the ink masters, she represents non-traditional subjects, and in early paintings she used vivid pink ink, drawing considerable attention to her work whilst she was still a student. Her early success influenced her to switch from an academic path leading towards a PhD in Chinese art history, and a future in academia, to the more uncertain path of the artist. Li's decision horrified her parents, teachers of mathematics and science. Even now they remain a little mystified as to why her paintings don't look more like the works of the old masters she spent years studying. Li says, 'They don't understand what I am painting, and why is it not perfect, they say, "Why all these drips of paint?"'[6]

Born in Shanxi Province in 1982, Li graduated from Beijing's Renmin University in 2007 and now lives and works in Beijing. As a small child she loved to paint and draw, copying anything she could find. During her teenage years access to art books was limited, but she discovered Matisse and his simplicity of line and form, identifying a connection with the dexterous calligraphic brush mark of the literati painters. Today, she experiments to see how far the ink tradition can be pushed into new and hybrid forms. Rather than painting scholar rocks, plum blossom, or bamboo, Li paints mass-produced consumer goods, furniture and household items, documenting the transformation of Chinese culture. Her depictions of ethereal feminine accessories and solid formal furnishings signify China's new wealth.

Travelling overseas and visiting European galleries, Li's discovery of abstract paintings by Cy Twombly inspired a new direction in her work, which became more overtly gestural. The result, after a period of intense experimentation, was a series representing grandiose items of furniture, with expressive marks, drips and stains soaking the paper. Floral upholstered armchairs and overstuffed sofas, lacquered Chinese chests and opulent chandeliers float in amorphous spaces with dribbles of ink running down the surfaces.

Li Tingting initially focused on 'feminine' subject matter such as handbags, shoes and dresses, but in a deliberate effort not to be pigeon-holed or stereotyped, she began to include banal objects associated with contemporary life and mass production, such as disposable plastic water bottles and light bulbs. Her *Shoes* series of 2007–08 may be interpreted as a feminist response to societal pressure on women to adopt an overtly feminine identity. The artist politely denies this reading of her work, insisting that she wanted to celebrate her life as a young woman.

Other works represent teddy bears, fruits, and flowers – even sunflower seeds. Cascading shapes spill down the surface of her paper in a deceptively spontaneous manner. In actuality the process of working with traditional inks, balancing wet and dry brushstrokes, is exacting and painstaking. Li Tingting surprises through her choice of bright colour and her contemporary choice of subjects, whilst at the same time she pays homage to the Chinese ink tradition. Seventeenth century ink master Shi Tao's oft-quoted insistence, 'The brush and Ink should follow the times,' an assertion of individual vision opposed to the orthodox forces of historicism, reveals that the alignment of contemporaneity and ink painting is not new.[7]

Li Tingting
Chandelier 2012
ink on rice paper
97 x 130 cm
image courtesy the artist

Li Tingting with her work, Beijing, December 2012, photograph LG

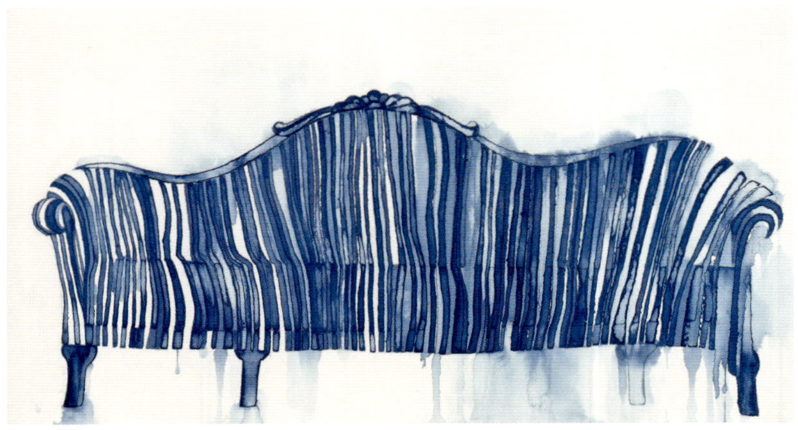

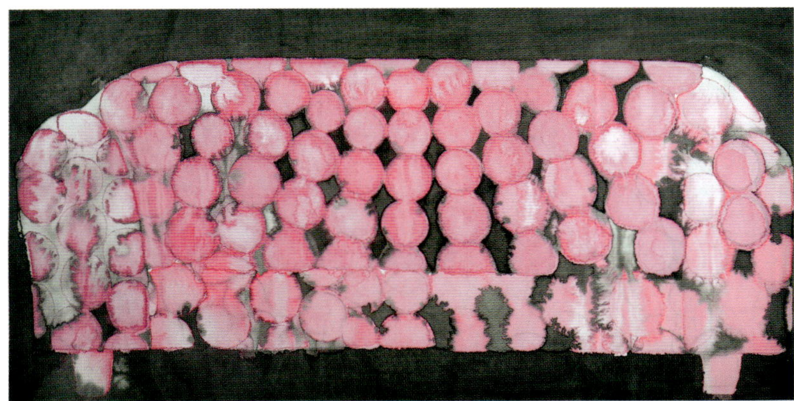

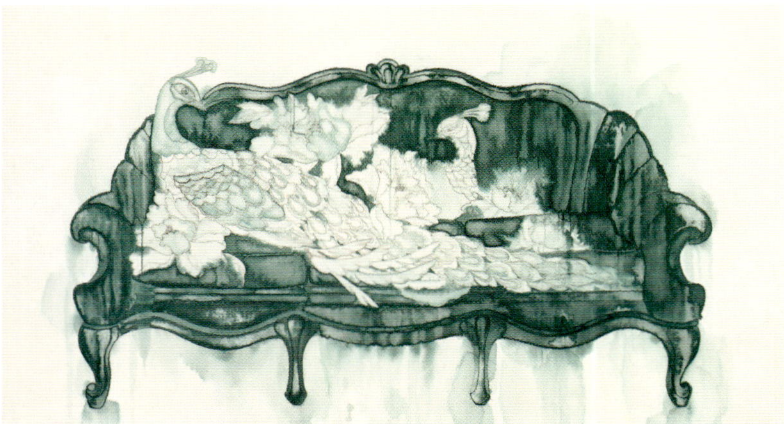

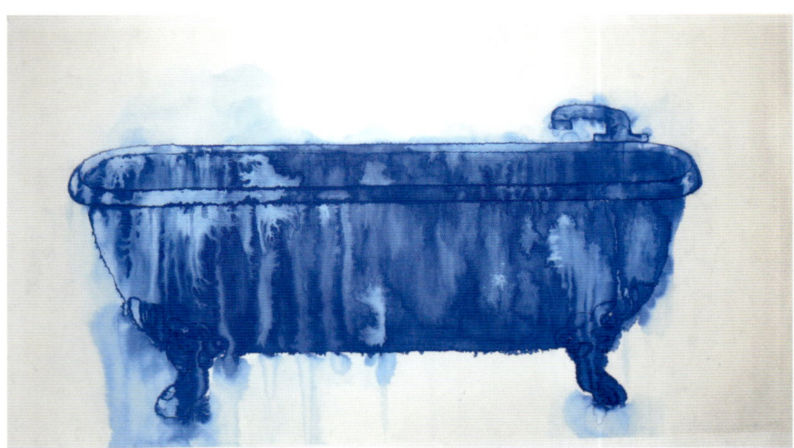

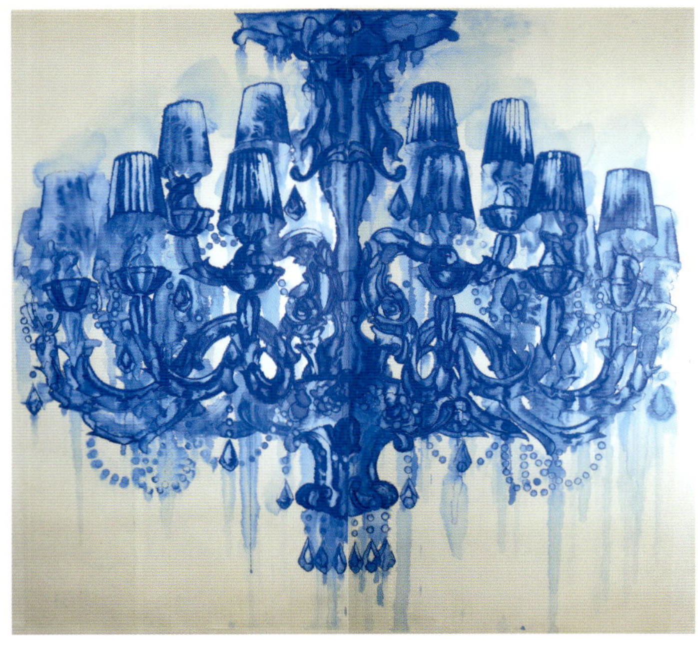

In Li's early scroll-like paintings, the objects appear as delicate and ethereal as traditional misty mountains, until we realise they are a jumble of light bulbs, plastic bottles, high-heeled shoes, or abandoned toys. They may be read as beautiful, transcendent images of abundance, or as a commentary on meaningless consumption and waste in an increasingly wealthy society. She aims to make something new using the visual language of the past.

Like the handscrolls and album leaves produced by scholarly artists of imperial times, Li Tingting's paintings are deeply connected to the act of writing:

> My new paintings [of antique Chinese furniture] are influenced by calligraphy. The details and textures, the lines and the mark-making are more calligraphic in comparison with the earlier scrolls and the chandelier works. I am studying the ancient calligraphy from the caves and the strong, hard, pure characters engraved into stone. For the last two years I have been studying this and practising every day... imitating the ancient calligraphy. In these new works the lines have more power.

Li Tingting is fascinated by the Forest of Stone Steles, dating mostly from the Tang Dynasty, that miraculously survived the Cultural Revolution. Like many Chinese artists, Li has made a pilgrimage to Xi'an, where they are housed in a former Confucian temple, and has studied the rubbings made of the ancient calligraphy. The continuation of Chinese tradition is very important to her, and she is exploring ways to further develop the calligraphic influence in her painting, which has become stronger and more dramatic in comparison to her earlier, delicately grey and rose-coloured paintings of

Li Tingting
***Sofa** series (three works)* 2013
Bathtub 2014
ink on rice paper
97 x 182; 69 x 137; 97 x 182; 97 x 182 cm
images courtesy the artist

Li Tingting
Crystal Lamp 2012
ink on rice paper
182 x 194 cm
image courtesy the artist

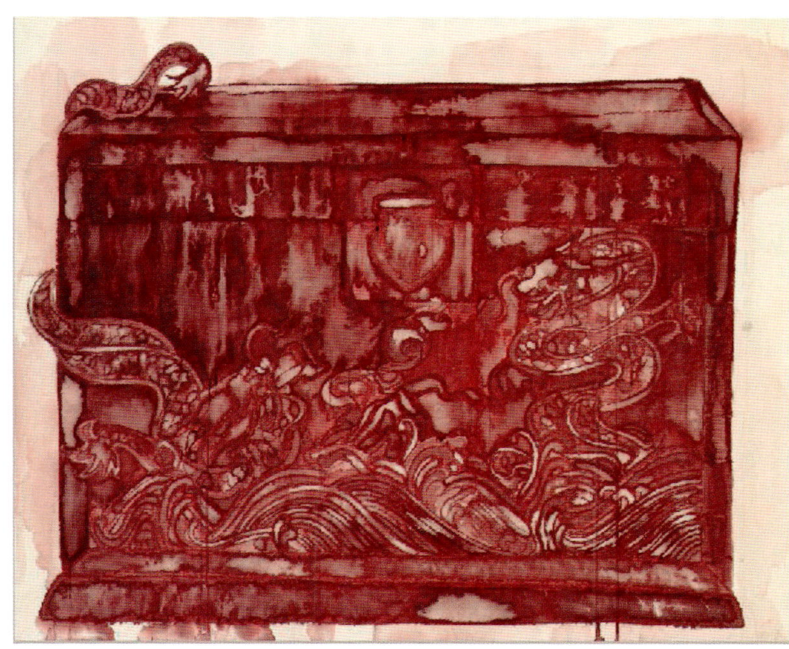

translucent shoes, handbags, dresses, and champagne glasses. Like the literati painters who preceded her, Li feels she could spend a lifetime mastering her medium. A series of Buddhist reliquaries, containers for prayers and sutra scrolls, is painted with inks in natural vegetable colours, not the artificial colour of mineral pigments. They represent the search for meaning and spirituality that is an important element of the zeitgeist in today's China, a backlash against the emptiness of materialism.

Li Tingting expresses disdain for those who would classify female painters as merely 'feminine' and delicate: 'I want to express strong stuff. I want to reduce things to their essential and simple form but still have strong meanings. To make things complex is easy, but to reduce and make things simple is the hardest thing. My new works are stronger paintings. I am looking at Chinese history, using strong shapes and strong colours.' She has been examining the Buddhist frescoes from the Mogao Caves. 'The classical masterpieces can be viewed over and over again and every time you see something new and learn something new,' she says.

Since giving birth to her child, Li Tingting has returned to painting with a new sense of urgency. She has no interest in painting autobiographical, confessional works, or revealing her personal feelings in obvious or literal ways. There are clues in the paintings, however. Her focus is on the domestic and the everyday, and she skilfully manipulates her brush to record bathtubs and sofas, children's toys and clothing. The acclaimed ink painter Peng Xiancheng said, 'For me there is no boundary between art and life.'[8] Li TIngting may not be painting waterfalls and mountains, but just as surely as the ink masters of the past, with her delicate depictions of the ordinary and the mass-produced she is recording the seismic shifts in Chinese culture.

Li Tingting
Chest 2013
ink on rice paper
97 x 91cm
image courtesy the artist

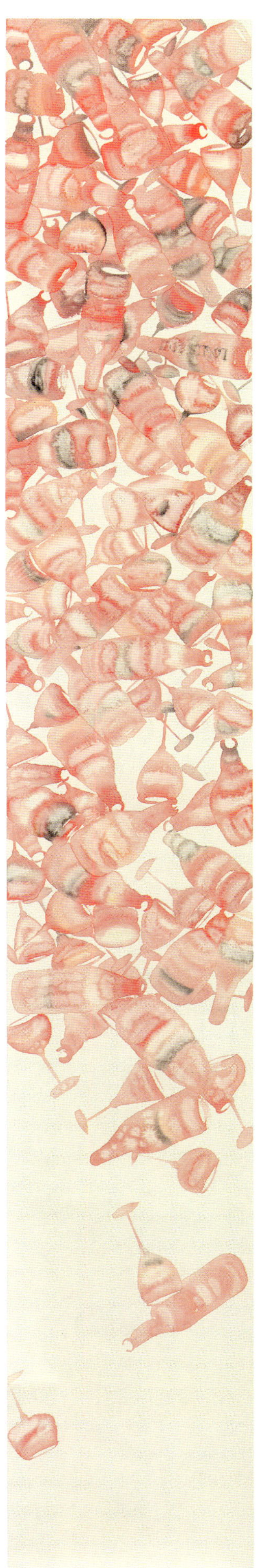

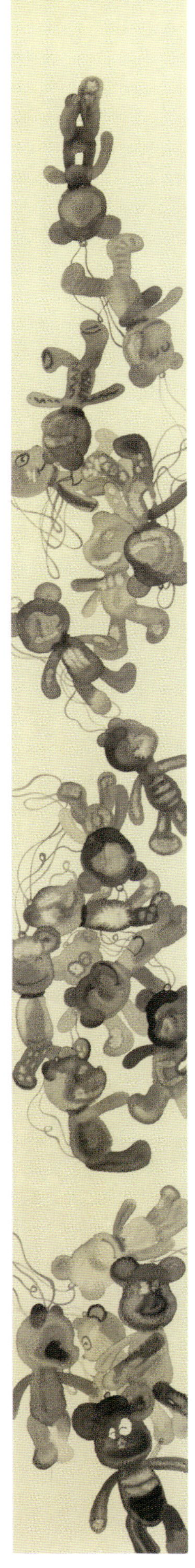

Li Tingting
Bottle Series 2006; ***Toy Series*** 2006
Chinese ink on rice paper
261 x 53 cm; 249 x 43 cm
images courtesy the artist and
White Rabbit Gallery

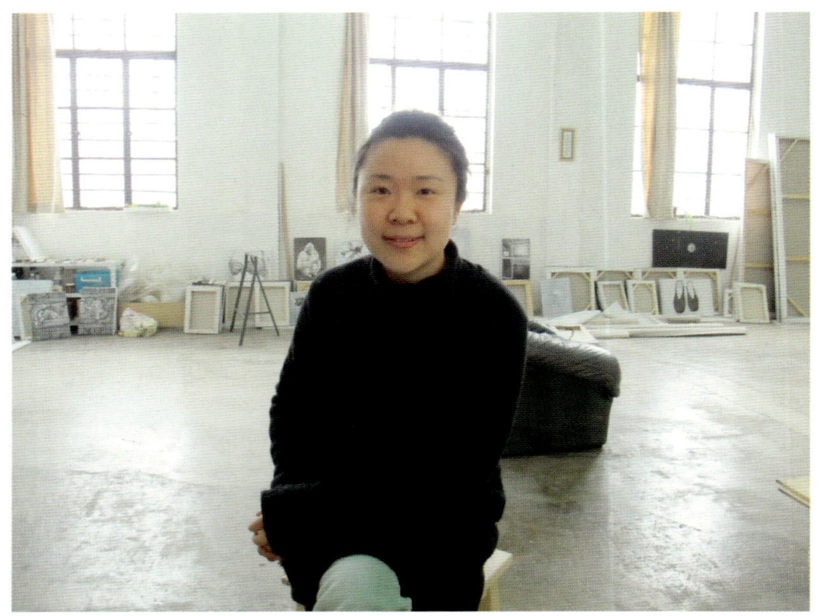

SHI ZHIYING 石至莹

Grains of sand in the Universe

Shanghai painter Shi Zhiying works mostly with oil paint on canvas, yet her paintings also reference the ink masters of the past. Best known for immersive monochrome oil paintings of subjects such as vast expanses of ocean, or lawns in which each separate blade of grass bends to the wind, she has also experimented with ink on paper. The connecting thread is her Buddhist belief, central to her life and her painting. Despite its contemporary appearance, her work is informed by her reading of Buddhist scripture, her love for ancient art and religious artefacts, and her deep understanding of Chinese tradition.

Shi Zhiying's studio in Shanghai's outer suburbs is a large, quiet space; very, very cold when I have visited her in three successive Chinese winters. Chinese artists are hardy beings. A chair is positioned in the centre of the room where she sits to reflect on her work. Canvases in various stages of completion are propped around the walls and on easels, and the smell of oil paint and turpentine is tangible evidence of intense creation. Working on a large scale with thin washes of blackish oil paint, she creates images of vastness that from a distance appear photographic. Close-up, you see the dribbles and stains of paint and the expressive mark of the brush. Every work reveals her restrained control of her medium.

Born in Shanghai in 1979, as a child Shi Zhiying learned calligraphy. Later, as an art student in the late 1990s and early 2000s, studying in the Oil Painting Department of the Fine Arts College of Shanghai University, she decided that ink-painting was an irrelevant relic of the past, preferring to pore over the work of modern masters such as Cézanne and Gauguin. Much later, trying to develop her own unique vision, she realised that she had been wrong. It took her some years to find a visual language that combines western and eastern techniques and expresses her own view of the world. In recent years Shi Zhiying has visited Suzhou to study traditional ink paintings and learn from master painters of the past, but her work is also informed by her travels to New York and Europe, and to South East Asia.

Her technique, stripped of inessential elements such as colour, developed almost by accident. For a while after she graduated from university, overwhelmed by different influences, western and Chinese, Shi Zhiying lost her belief in her ability to say anything new or original in her painting. On a trip to America, she regained her confidence. Her architect husband was studying there, and she travelled to meet him in California. Visiting a lighthouse on the west coast, she looked down at the vast ocean below and experienced an overwhelming sensation that she had vanished from the world. This uncomfortable but, she emphatically insists, not unpleasant experience prompted her to study Buddhist scriptures. It seemed to her a clear message that she should return to her traditions, and she began to look for subjects that could reveal essential truths about the nature of the world.

She began taking photographs of the Pacific Ocean, removing the colour. The blue of the ocean and the sky seemed 'fake' – the absence of colour seemed to reveal a greater truth. At that time Shi Zhiying saw Japanese photographer Hiroshi Sugimoto's black-and-white seascapes. His belief that looking at the ocean is a 'voyage of seeing' akin to visiting one's ancestral home[9] echoed her own feeling. From photographs, sketches and studies Shi Zhiying began to paint the large canvases of seas and oceans which brought her to the attention of curators and collectors. She calls them 'Sea Sutras'.

These paintings of sublime vistas remove unnecessary detail, focusing our attention on the immensity of the ocean – an immersive, almost overwhelming, experience for the viewer. In Shi Zhiying's works, we see familiar imagery – the ocean, a raked path, or an expanse of lawn – in new ways. She works slowly, often making several studies and small versions of a painting before transferring the image to a large canvas. Using very thin washes of oil paint, she controls the drips and dribbles and stains of paint, always aiming for an internal truth. In conversation she likened her particular method of painting to the practice of meditation, 'a slow and peaceful process that takes a long time to develop.'[10]

In contrast to these big, ambitious canvases, Shi also paints smaller works representing objects of daily life: a bowl of rice, a plate of food, some discarded clothing, a pair of shoes. Beautifully observed, their lack of colour imbues them with

Shi Zhiying in her studio, Shanghai, May 2011, Photo LG

Shi Zhiying
Zen Garden No. 2 2010
oil on canvas
200 x 300 cm
image courtesy the artist

Shi Zhiying,
***Rice** (study)* 2011
oil on canvas
100 x 100 cm
image courtesy the artist

Shi Zhiying
High Heels 2013
oil on canvas
30 x 40 cm
image courtesy the artist

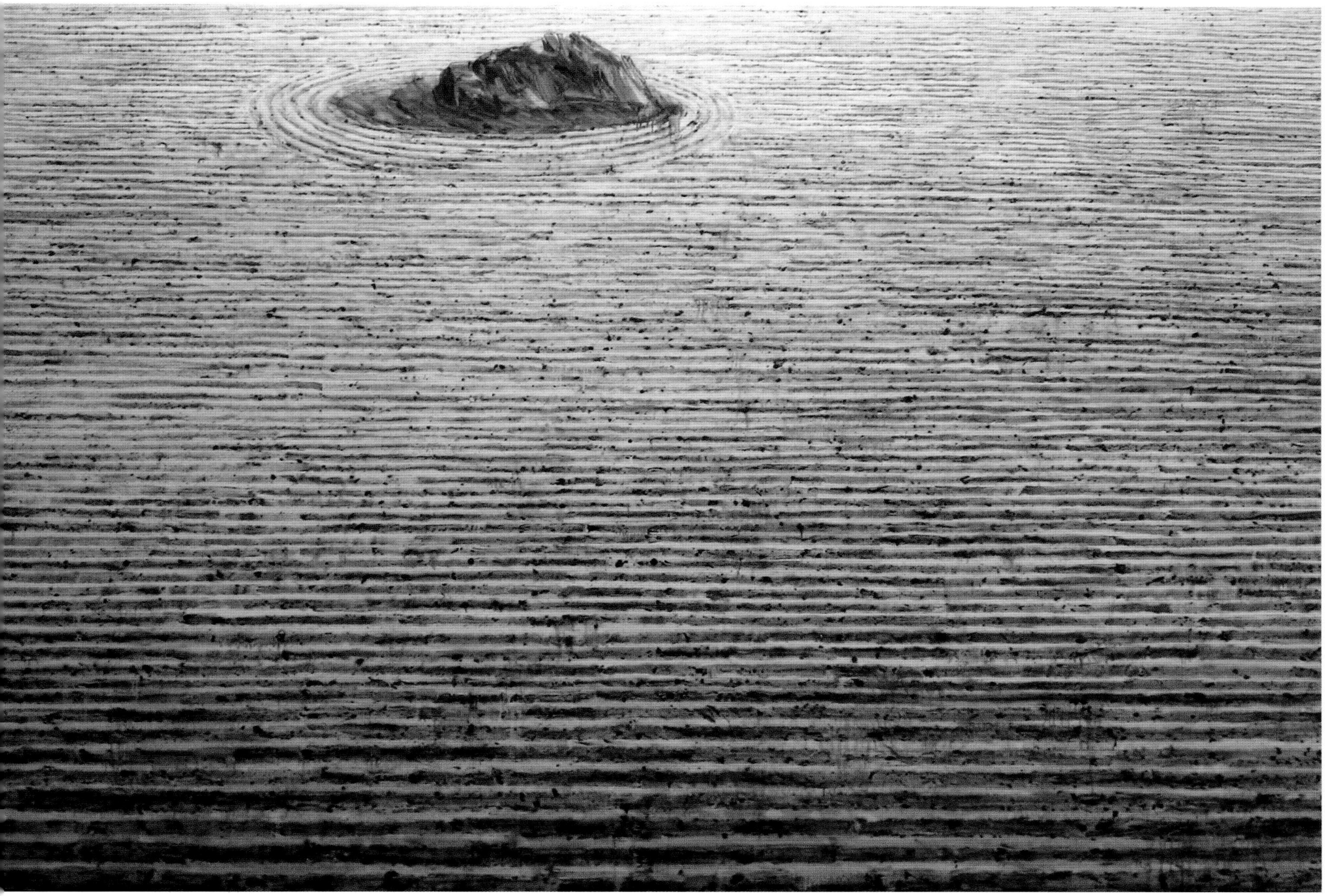

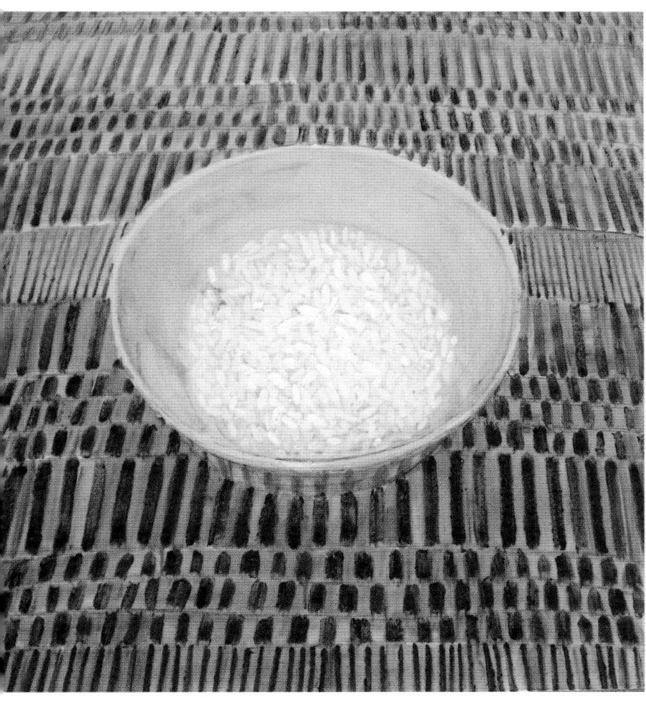

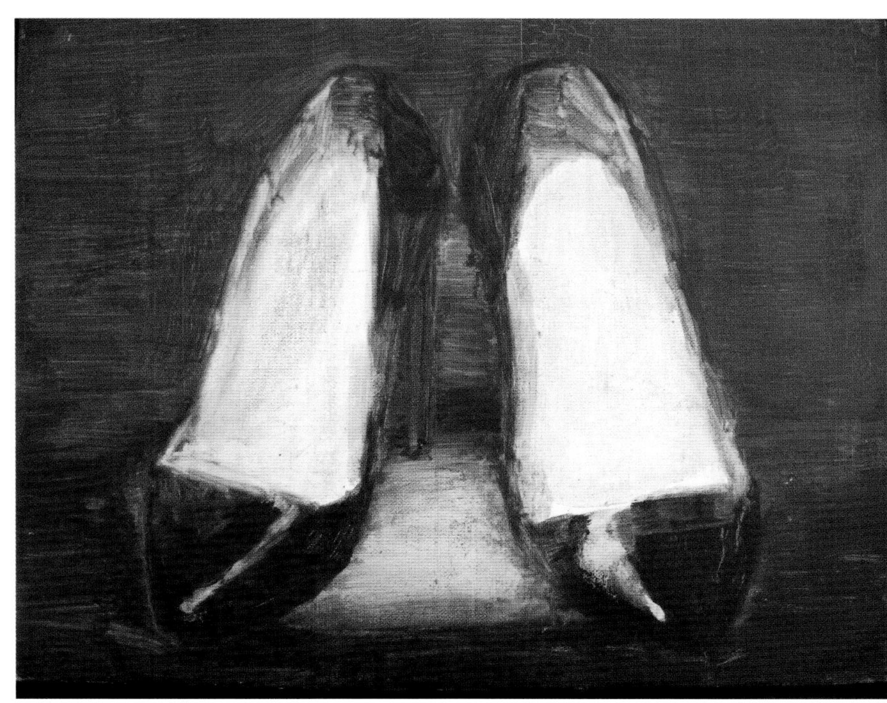

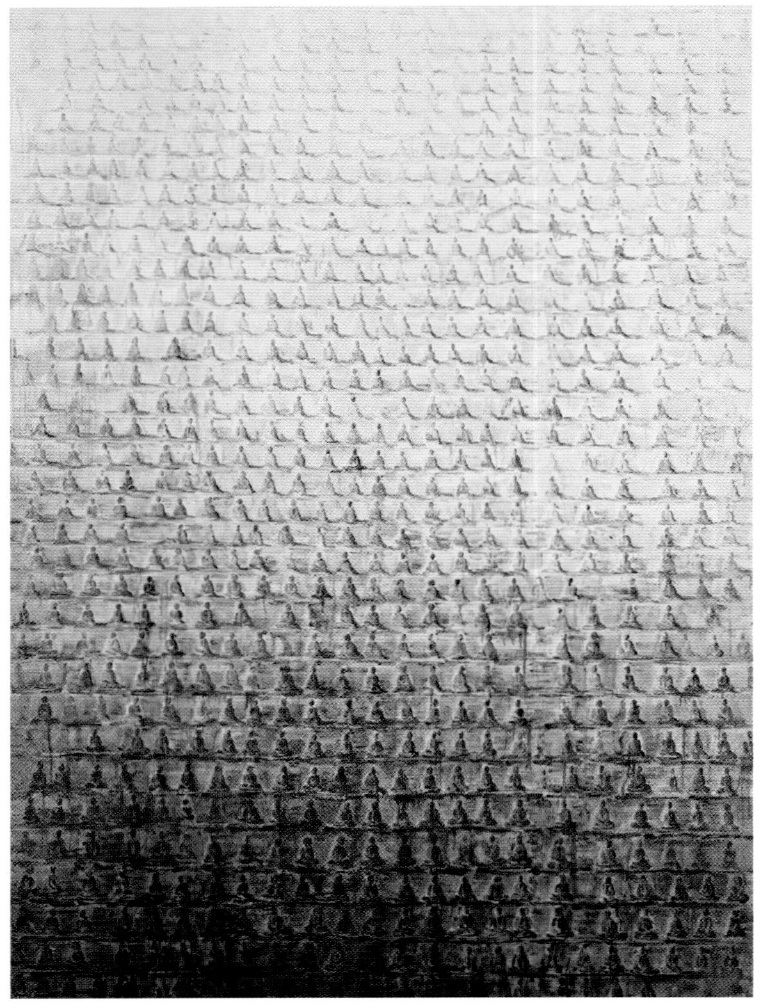

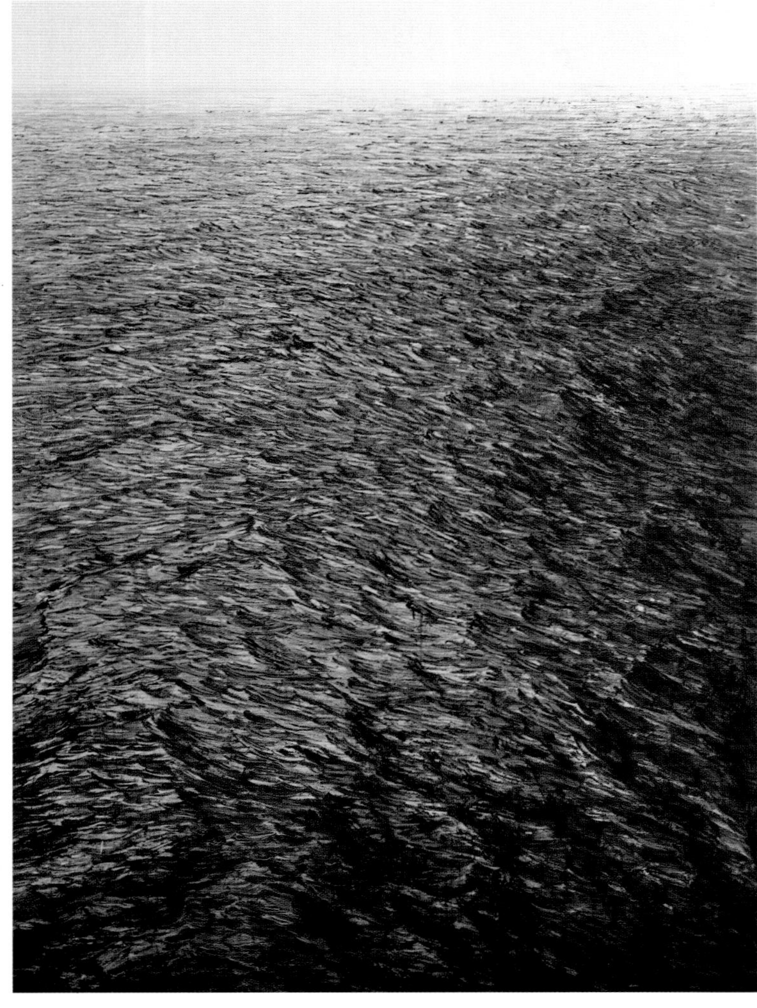

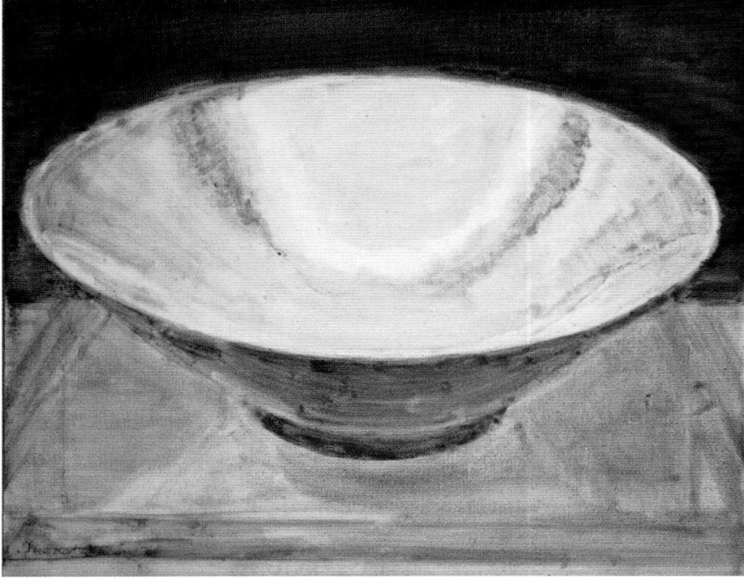

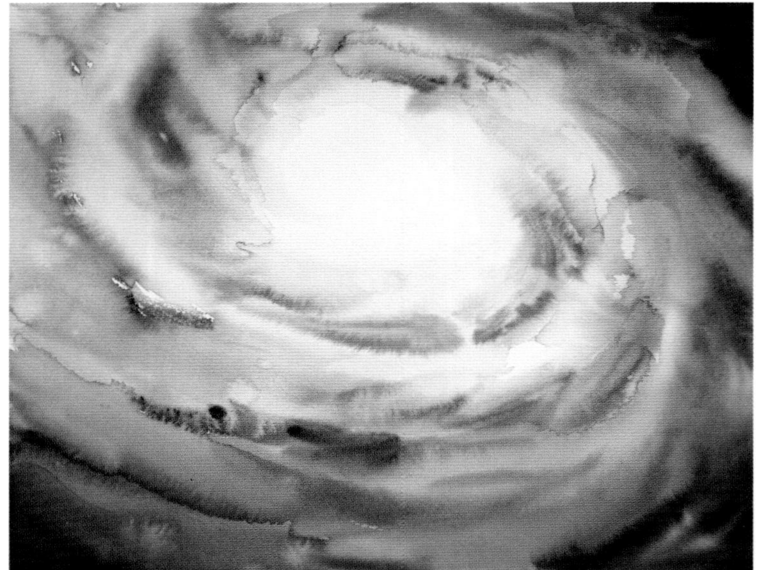

Shi Zhiying
Cave of Ten Thousand Buddhas 2013
oil on canvas
240 x 180 cm
image courtesy the artist

Shi Zhiying
Egg-white Glazed Porcelain Bowl 2013
oil on canvas, 40 x 50 cm
image courtesy the artist

Shi Zhiying
The Pacific Ocean 2011
oil on canvas
240 x 180 cm
image courtesy the artist

Shi Zhiying
The Universe No. 2 2012
oil on canvas
40 x 50 cm
image courtesy the artist

a compelling stillness. Filling the canvas, her high-heeled shoes represent the appeal of feminine adornment and also its darker, fetishised shadow. Ironically perhaps, her painting of a pair of designer stiletto heels was destined for an exhibition sponsored by a fashion magazine. Shi says she is both drawn to and repelled by the current Chinese obsession with designer brands, and the overtly performative display of femininity found in popular culture. She has been influenced by the monochrome paintings of Yan Peiming, most famous for enormous black or red portraits of Mao Zedong, and by Zhang Enli, who focused on objects of the everyday, finding in the works of these fellow Shanghainese painters a spirit like her own.

Like the literati painters, who pushed the expressive possibilities of ink tonalities from jet black to the palest, most subtle and transparent washes of grey, she is able to create nuanced, painterly surfaces enlivened with gestural marks, stains and drips. There are hints of Burnt Umber, Paynes Grey and Indigo in the dark washes behind large carved Buddha figures in recent paintings. Successive planes and shapes are laid down in layers, building up facets that become a fully realised and modelled form, whether representing a rock, a plate of cheese, a pair of high heeled shoes or an ancient carved deity.

In 2012 Shi Zhiying painted a series of ink-on-paper works inspired by Italo Calvino's 1983 novel *Mr Palomar*. She wanted to use Chinese ink on paper to represent Mr Palomar's quest to discover universal truths and the nature of existence. The 'big questions' of the book, such as speculations about the nature of the cosmos, lend themselves to her subtle, sweeping areas of ink and wash. Mr Palomar sees the whole universe in the blades of grass growing in his lawn. Just as the individual waves and drops of water in Shi's oceans represent a sense of the infinite, so too do her paintings of Mr Palomar's 'infinite lawn', the raked pebbles of traditional Zen gardens, and the individual grains of rice in a bowl. In 2015, she exhibited works inspired by Herman Hesse's 1943 novel, *The Glass Bead Game*, applying the properties of watercolour and oil paint to represent temporal celestial bodies. The title of the exhibition, *I Don't Pretend to Understand the Universe*, is a quote from Einstein, an allusion to the artist's quest for meaning in the events and objects of daily life.

Whether her subject is quotidian or sublime, Shi Zhiying's sense of the oneness of all things in the universe underpins her imagery, and her painterly techniques. She visited Xi'an in 2012 to see Tang Dynasty artefacts in the museum, and made a pilgrimage to the famous Mogao cave paintings of Dunhuang in Gansu Province, a religious and cultural crossroads on the Silk Road. Known as the 'Caves of the Thousand Buddhas', this is one of the best preserved and most extensive collections of Buddhist painting and sculpture in the world, miraculously escaping the wholesale destructions of the Cultural Revolution. Many books with colour plates of the frescoes now lie around the tables and benches in her studio, pages bookmarked and covers stained with oil paint.

When we met for a third time, in the winter of 2013, we looked through these books together, a large canvas with a partially completed draped figure leaning against the wall behind us. Shi Zhiying showed me images of Buddha in various guises, flying apsaras, and other deities, pointing out their complex draperies and their subtle faded colours, dominated by viridian greens and rose pink. Explaining why these paintings are so important to her, she said:

> It's another kind of time and space, very different from our time and space. It is much larger... we can feel we are a very tiny grain of sand in the universe. This makes me feel [that] I am nothing... When I feel that I am nothing, I can hold everything, and everything can hold me – it's a good feeling.

Her approach to painting references *wu wei*, a Taoist concept that means non-action, an in-the-moment mindfulness. Clarifying her earlier analogy, Shi says, 'Painting is not meditation. Painting is painting. But it can be *like* meditation because I do it carefully, honestly and truthfully.'

In Shi Zhiying's paintings of Buddhist reliquaries and traditional Chinese vessels, bowls and sculptural forms, at once solid in form and ethereal, lies a desire to distil the true essence of each tangible object. Beneath her large canvases depicting fields of grass, ancient weathered Buddhist caves, or shifting patterns of wind and water, lies a hidden narrative about the complexity and connectedness of the universe and all it contains. Buddhist scripture advises eliminating all that is inessential in order to distil the essence. 'Simplicity is reality,' she says.

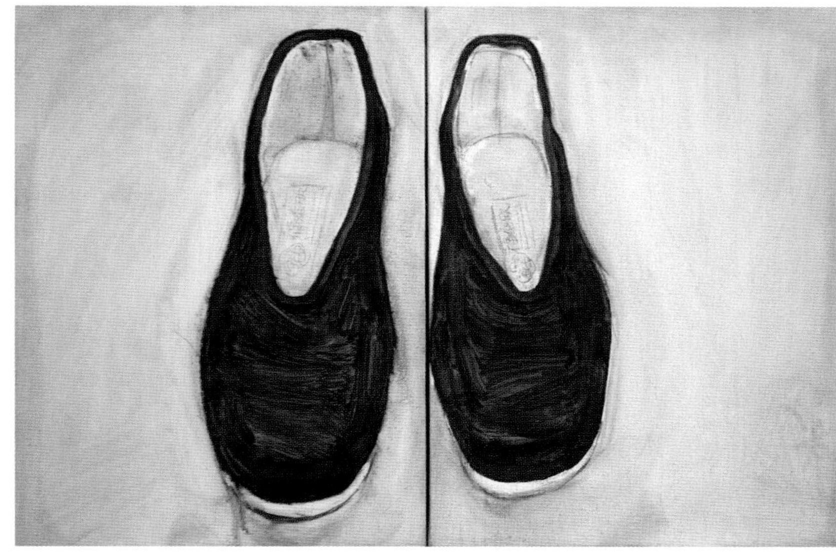

Shi Zhiying
The Odd Cloth Shoes 2010
oil on canvas
30 x 40 cm
image courtesy the artist

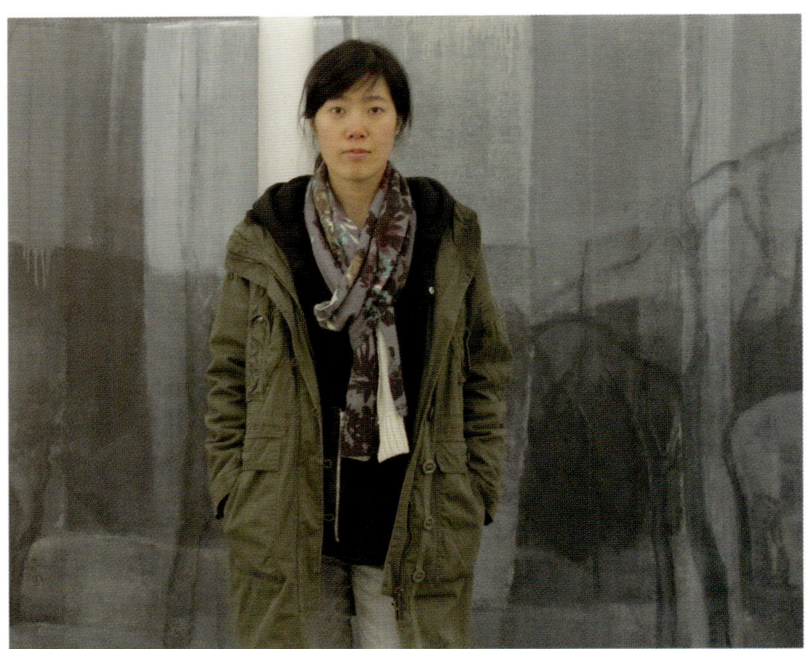

GAO PING 高平

Tiny Things

Like Shi Zhiying, Gao Ping works mostly in monochrome. She spends silent days painting in her studio on the outskirts of Beijing, or in a smaller space in Ditan Park, near the Lama and Confucius temples. The first element of her practice results in delicate ink paintings on Chinese paper of what she calls 'the tiny things'. People, domestic objects, furniture and toys float in a vast space, defined by deft marks of the brush. They appear to be spontaneous, intuitive works. On the contrary, says Gao, every mark is deliberate and carefully placed. She alternates these smaller works with bold experimental paintings, some on canvas and some on paper, mixing Chinese ink with oil and acrylic pigments and mediums. Sometimes layers are scraped back to reveal underpainting, sometimes she uses stencils, sgraffito and layers of glaze that drip and stain across the surface. All her work possesses the same paradoxical combination of fragility and strength as the artist herself.

Arriving in Beijing from Shandong Province in the mid-1990s to study at the Central Academy of Fine Arts, Gao was horrified by the destructive power of the capital – the constant demolition and transformation of neighbourhoods, the wholesale destruction of history, the relentless noise and appalling pollution. This alienation found its way into her work, and she completed a series of dark, gloomy canvases. Today, she still finds the city an overwhelming place, and like many Beijing residents she worries about the way that 'progress' excuses the eradication of history. Seeking peace, Gao walks at night in the calm of Ditan Park. Its ordered landscape of avenues, walls and formal gardens recurs in her work. In the late evening it is still busily populated by men with their caged birds, card-players, dancers, singers, walkers and water calligraphers, and she enjoys encountering others along its avenues and shaded paths, as well as the rare experience of solitude.

These quiet experiences in the midst of a chaotically busy city stay in her memory in an almost photographic manner, as she draws freely and quickly onto large sheets of heavy paper. The first mark is the hardest, she says, but after that it flows almost effortlessly. This is quite unlike the meticulousness of her more traditional ink paintings, which may look spontaneous but in reality are utterly controlled and deliberate. Gao layers her paintings until they are a palimpsest of washes, gestures and ghostly forms, combining the finely judged brush marks of her ink painting with a range of experimental painterly techniques. Some of the most interesting surfaces reveal unorthodox combinations of materials. Thinned washes of acrylic are brushed over the Chinese ink underneath, in a process akin to a wax resist. These works are moody, atmospheric and subtle, glimpses of Beijing seen through its omnipresent haze and mist. Happiest when working in her studio, Gao says 'Drawing is in my heart. It is the thing that makes me who I am.'[11] The life of an artist in Beijing is lonely, she says, but painting is like a secret language, creating mysterious layers that reveal themselves slowly to those willing to take the time to look carefully.

Using hand cut stencils on some works, Gao creates areas patterned like traditional Chinese carved window screens seen in the pavilions bordering lakes in public parks and gardens. During this process, images emerge from her unconscious mind, not images of observed reality, rather 'a kind of vague trace on the surface of the paper without clear definition.'[12] Gao transforms the mundane – a bridge, a teapot, a window, a branch of blossom seen in the park – into something mysterious and other-worldly. In some works subtle hints of colour underlie the dominant greys and blacks which remind us that Chinese ink is, after all, formed from soot. In others she plays with high-key blocks of viridian green and rose pink.

Large, ambitious canvases merge western and eastern influences. Reminiscent of the visual language of *Shan Shui* painting, they also evoke the Symbolists, most particularly Odilon Redon, and the softness of forms found in the paintings of Marlene Dumas, whom Gao admires. These lyrical works employ a subtle grisaille in which translucent washes are layered to create depth. Ambiguous landscapes represent an ideal world: a place of harmony and retreat from the city; a response to her distress at Beijing's constant transformation of familiar places in a never-ending process of demolition and renewal. Gao invents a different, calmer world in her paintings.

Gao Ping in her Beijing studio,
December 2012, Photo LG

Gao Ping
Untitled 2012
oil on canvas
50 x 65 cm
image courtesy the artist
and China Art Projects

Gao Ping
Untitled 2012
oil on canvas
50 x 65 cm
image courtesy the artist
China Art Projects

Gao Ping
Landscape 3 2010
oil on canvas
150 x 350 cm
image courtesy the artist and
China Art Projects

Gao Ping returns often to look at traditional Chinese ink masters: there are postcards and prints pinned on her walls, and a jumble of books scattered around the studio. But she is also interested in an eclectic list of contemporary artists, from Antony Gormley to Nan Goldin.

Gao Ping puts 'all her life' into her ink paintings – her contemporary approach to an ancient form. She believes that for Chinese artists the traditions of ink painting are 'like the ground under your feet'. She admires the early Qing Dynasty painter Ba Da Shenren, who famously observed that there were 'more tears than ink' in his paintings. His expressive landscapes achieve a balance between stillness, space and closely observed detail, and Gao Ping returns to them often. She finds his work both sad and 'calm in heart', a description which equally applies to her own work. Tiny, lonely figures or objects on the paper create a dynamic relationship between their forms and the space they inhabit. Her deep understanding of traditional painting is evident in the 'rightness' of her placement and the confidence of her mark-making. Gao's work is grounded in her idiosyncratic observations of people, places and events, from the potted plants in her courtyard to the tottering stacks of boxes and plastic bottles left outside every front door for the recyclers.

With a photographic eye, Gao stores up memories of people and things she observes in daily life, until, in the solitude of the studio they spring back to life under her deft brush – a weary figure leaning sideways on a park bench, a feisty girl in jeans talking on a mobile phone, a gathering of men in suits. Together with her characteristic subjects of sad, abandoned toys, and collections of chairs, lamps or electric fans, they suggest a population in a state of flux. She believes tiny things are often overlooked in the busy rush of modern life, but are sometimes more important than the large and obvious. The delicate restraint of her ink marks gives them a sense of impermanence, as if they could dissolve, or transform into something else altogether.

Gao Ping describes her experience of living in the urban madness of Beijing as one of loss and sadness. There is humour, however, to be found in her wry observations of unexpected details – she has a keen sense of the absurd and finds much in modern life to amuse her. Recent paintings of handbags reveal her sardonic observation of the materialism of today's world, the obsessive purchase by young Chinese consumers of designer-brand bags, shoes and clothing.

Tiny female figures, some nude, some clothed, explore loneliness. *Still Life – Girls* contains four minute figures: an overtly sexy one in black stockings, an exhausted one slumped flat on her back, and two who turn away from the viewer. Their outlines are softly blurred. They are touching and whimsical, as are her representations of lonely toys, pot plants, plates of food, figures seated on park benches, shabby gardens and

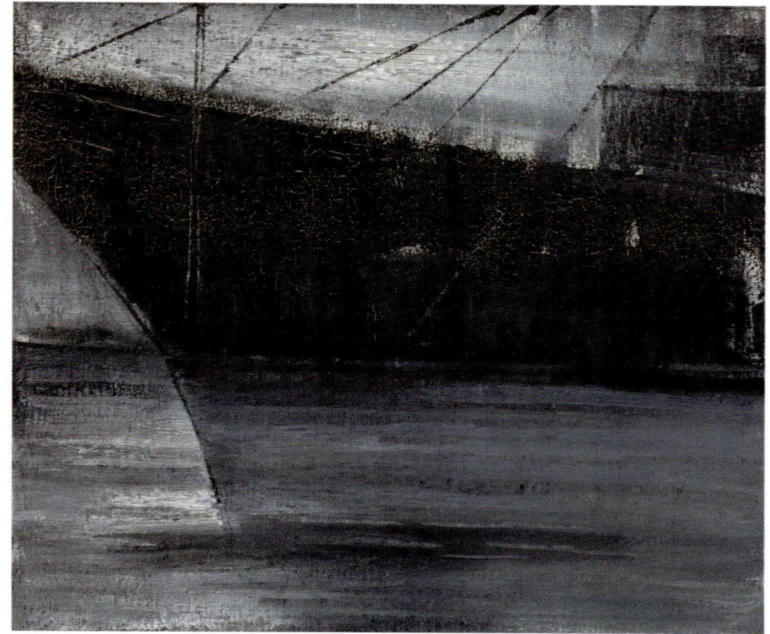

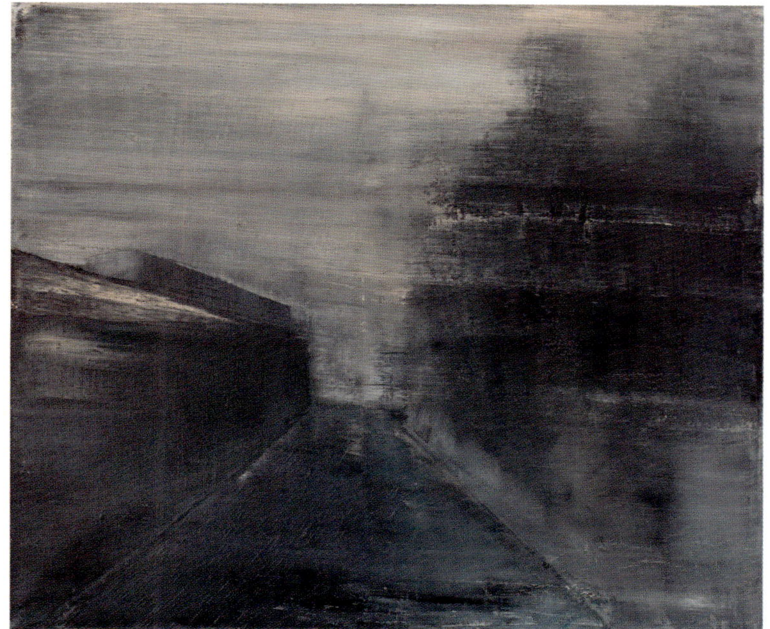

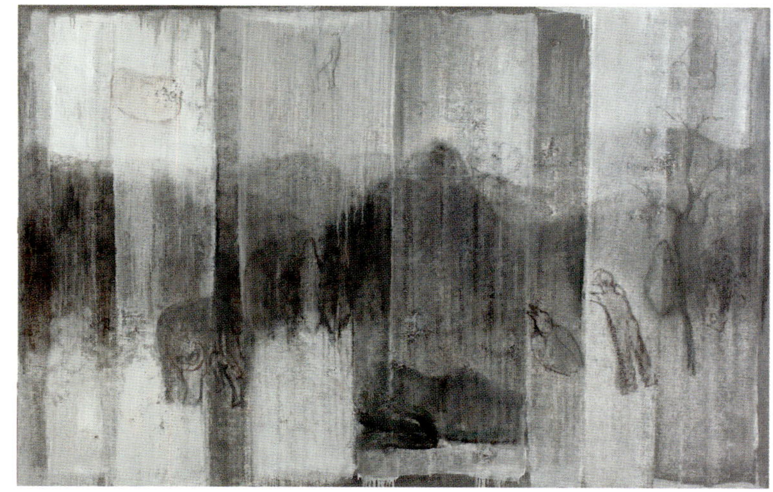

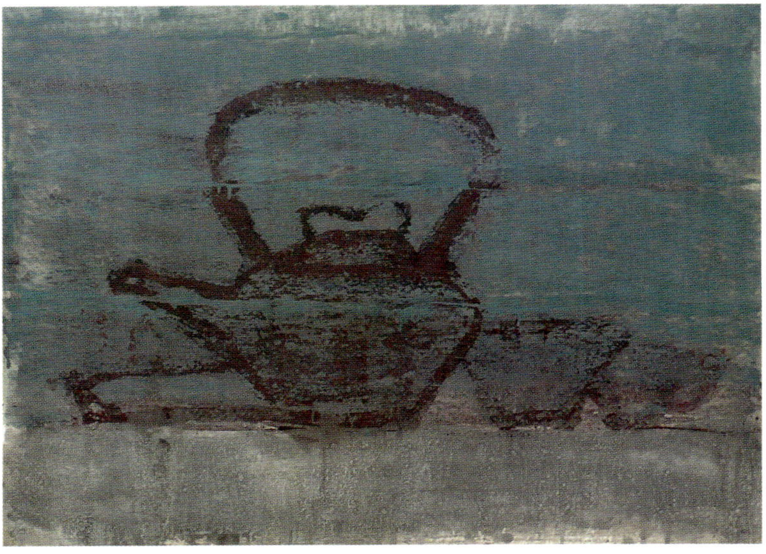

simple houses. These 'tiny things' are unassuming and modest, yet astutely observed. The drooping leaves of a pot plant, the bamboo handle of a teapot, the wonky leg of a chair – all are truthfully represented in minimal strokes of the brush that reveal the inner life of these mundane objects.

Gao Ping always knew she wanted to be an artist, from her earliest experiments with watercolour in middle school, and her first exposure to ink and brush. She was interested even then in the traditions of Chinese painting, inspired by a teacher who taught his students to use the brush to paint bamboo in the traditional manner, one side darker and the other lighter. Western oil painting learned at high school was followed by years of study in her hometown, and later at Beijing's prestigious Central Academy of Fine Arts, with its notoriously difficult entrance requirements. She was trained in what she describes as 'free style painting', fortunate to have escaped the prevailing Russian method ('very brown, using colour like soy sauce!' she says) and the classic academic oil painting studio. There was no choice – students were directed to a specific studio and learned techniques and conventions as directed by their teachers.

After she graduated in 1997, like all young artists, she had to find her own style. 'Because if you can't find your own self, your own thinking, your own voice, what is the point? But I am not clever,' she says, laughing, 'So I have to just work slowly, slowly in my own way, and it takes a long time to find my way.' Outside the formal drawing classes at the art academy, Gao had been using ink to record tiny, quick observations of the world around her – animals, birds, buildings and people, city landscapes: 'all my thinking.' This daily practice is the foundation of her work:

> Sometimes I can't paint, and I just think. Sometimes the first mark is very hard. Once I start, though, no matter what the difficulties were, I can solve them and just keep painting. It's part of me, part of my life. If I didn't paint for a while I would feel nervous. I think if I don't paint I would have doubts about myself… it's a space for me, for living and for thinking. I need to paint to make energy.

Gao is very aware of the way in which painters of the 1990s such as Zhang Xiaogang lit what she describes as a 'big fire.' She acknowledges that politics (including the politics of gender) and art are intertwined:

> Things have changed. Now the politics is more open, and female artists have more opportunities. But things change slowly over time. I think this time now, in this moment, is OK. You can have a space, and time to think about art. In the 1970s they talked about men and women being equal… but even now it is not equal.

Discussing other Chinese women artists and their different approaches to issues of gender, she says that sometimes she worries that she is not strong enough. In the end, though:

> Female artists have their own way to solve this problem. A different way for each individual person… you cannot change the time, or the country, or the age that you live in, you have to work within and influence that. You can change it through your work. It's not like a simple problem you can solve. It's like two overlapping circles. Some female artists need to be strong, like warriors, some female artists are not like that and are in a situation that is changed by the times.

'Which kind of artist are you?' I asked her. Gao laughed and replied, 'Sometimes the warrior kind!'

Gao Ping
UN 14 2012
oil on canvas
30 x 35 cm
image courtesy the artist and China Art Projects

Gao Ping
Teapot and Cups 2013
acrylic and ink on paper
50 x 100 cm
image courtesy the artist and China Art Projects

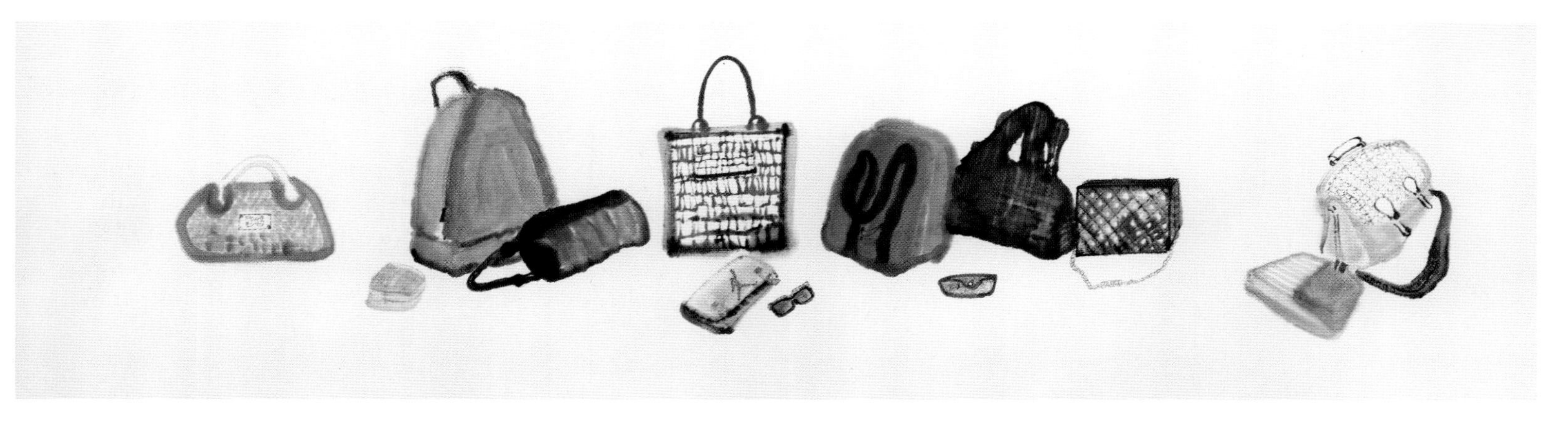

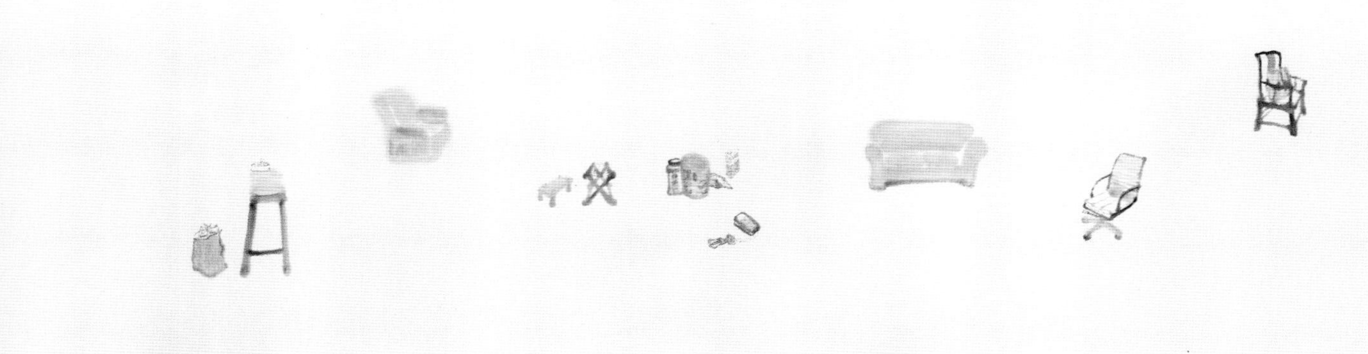

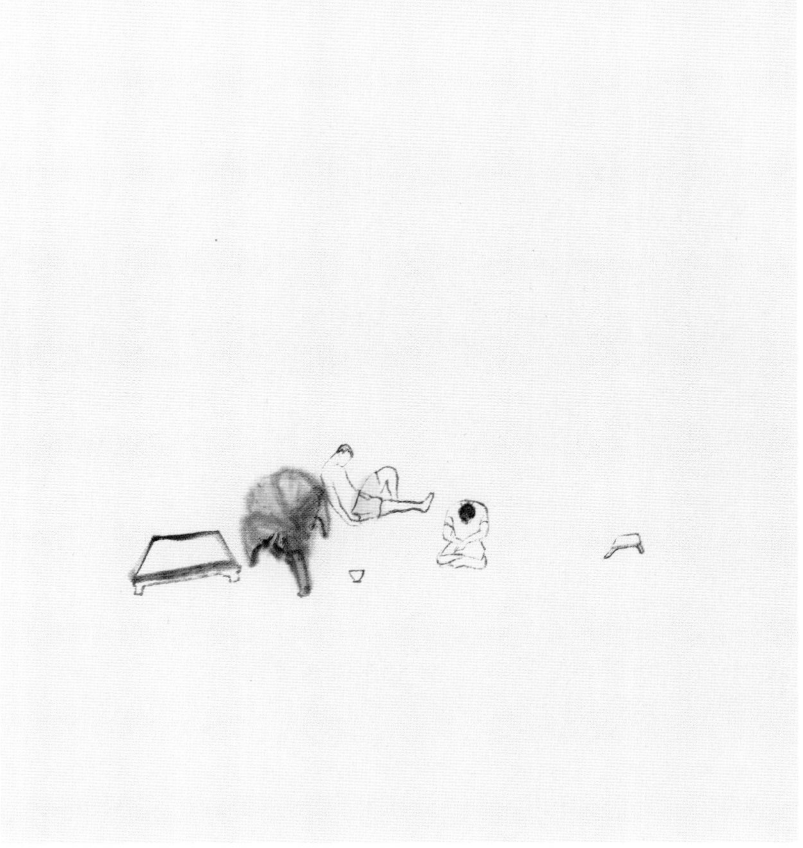

Gao Ping *(top and middle)*
Gathering – Bags 2011
Gathering – Chairs 2011
Chinese ink on rice paper
each 62 x 245 cm
images courtesy the artist and
China Art Projects

Gao Ping *(bottom)*
Still Life – Girls 2011
Time 2011
Chinese ink on rice paper
45 x 36 cm; 48 x 45 cm
images courtesy the artist and
China Art Projects

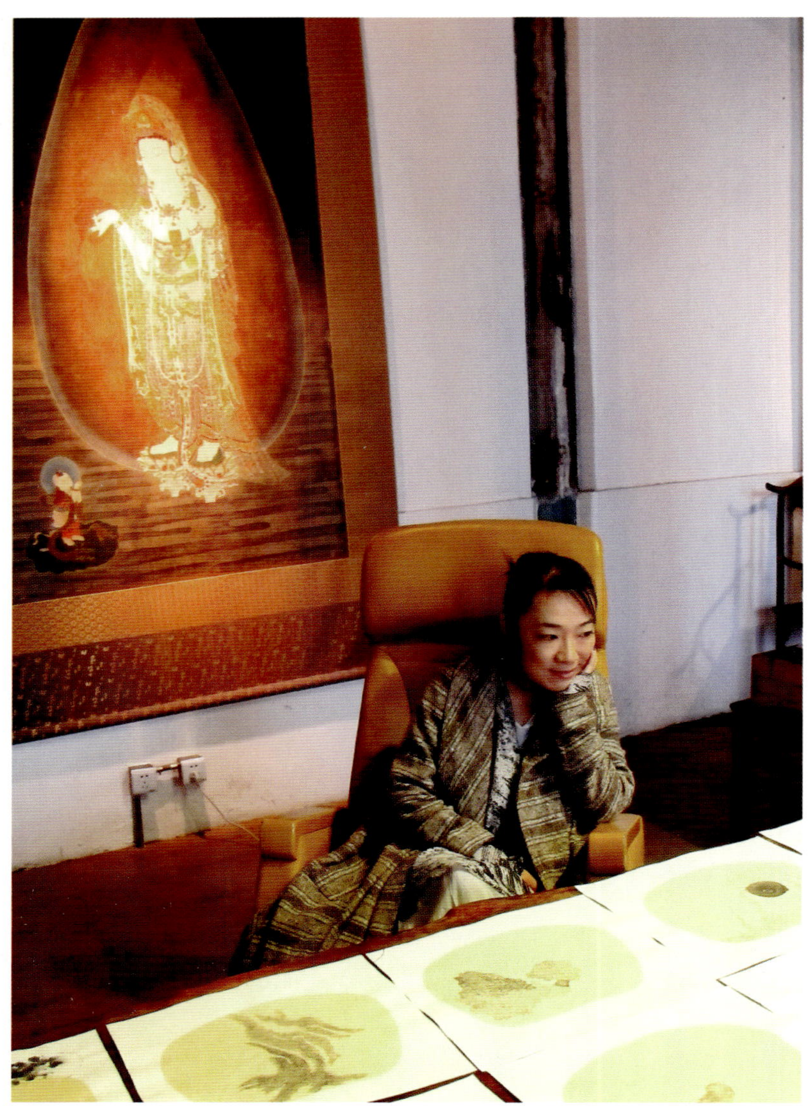

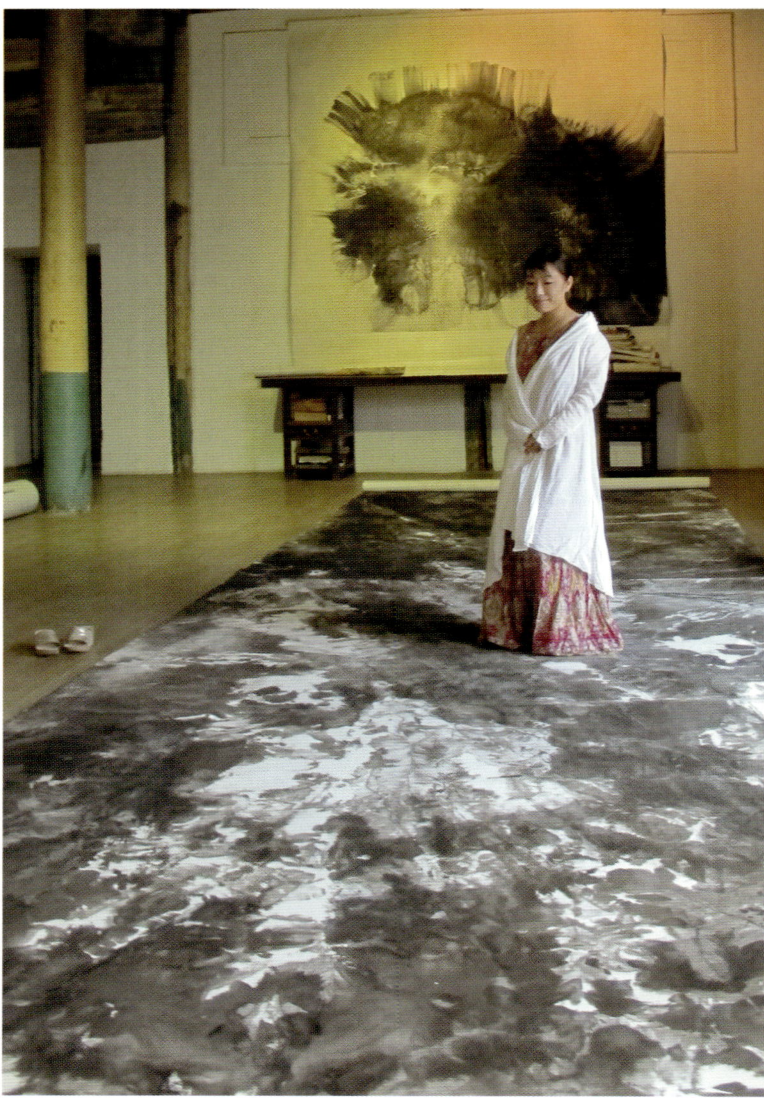

BINGYI 冰逸

The Postmodern Literati

Bingyi Huang (usually known simply as 'Bingyi') currently lives and works in a Yuan Dynasty temple on the ancient central axis of Beijing, near the famous Drum and Bell Towers, not far from the Forbidden City. Once across the stone threshold and through the heavy wooden doors, the shouts of street vendors, and the honking horns of motorcycles and cars in the narrow laneways of this traditional hutong neighbourhood, recede. There is tranquillity: orchids in large pots, and birds fluttering in cages. The vast studio, with its enormous timber pillars, coffered ceiling and antique furniture, reveals a long history – an appropriate space for an artist such as Bingyi, equally conversant with obscure details of Chinese history and international contemporary art practices.

Becoming a practising artist after switching from biomedical engineering to art history, along the way studying computer programming, music and finance, polymath Bingyi describes her painting idiom as a 'search for the sublime.' Not the European sublime, in which humans are passive observers of the power of nature, but a specifically Chinese notion informed by Buddhist beliefs and intensive art historical research – her doctorate at Yale was a study of the Han Dynasty. 'I lived with the Han for seven years,' she says, 'I *was* them!' Through art, she believes, 'One can embody the notion of eternity. If you can feel and express eternity and transience, then you are approaching a much higher level of metaphysics.'[13]

Bingyi began painting in her mother's living room in 2006. 'I always wanted to become an artist,' she says. 'What lies in the heart of humans is a desire to express. We all wish to express, but the question becomes, "What is your embodiment? What is your medium?" It was completely inside of me, completely contained. One could say that it's fate, but we Chinese have a different way of perceiving that.' When we met in 2013, she had just returned from some months painting in the mountains outside Beijing. Her assistants carefully unrolled a thirty-metre long painting that revealed her unique approach, fusing ink painting with land art,

Bingyi in her Beijing studio
October 2013 and April 2014
photographs LG

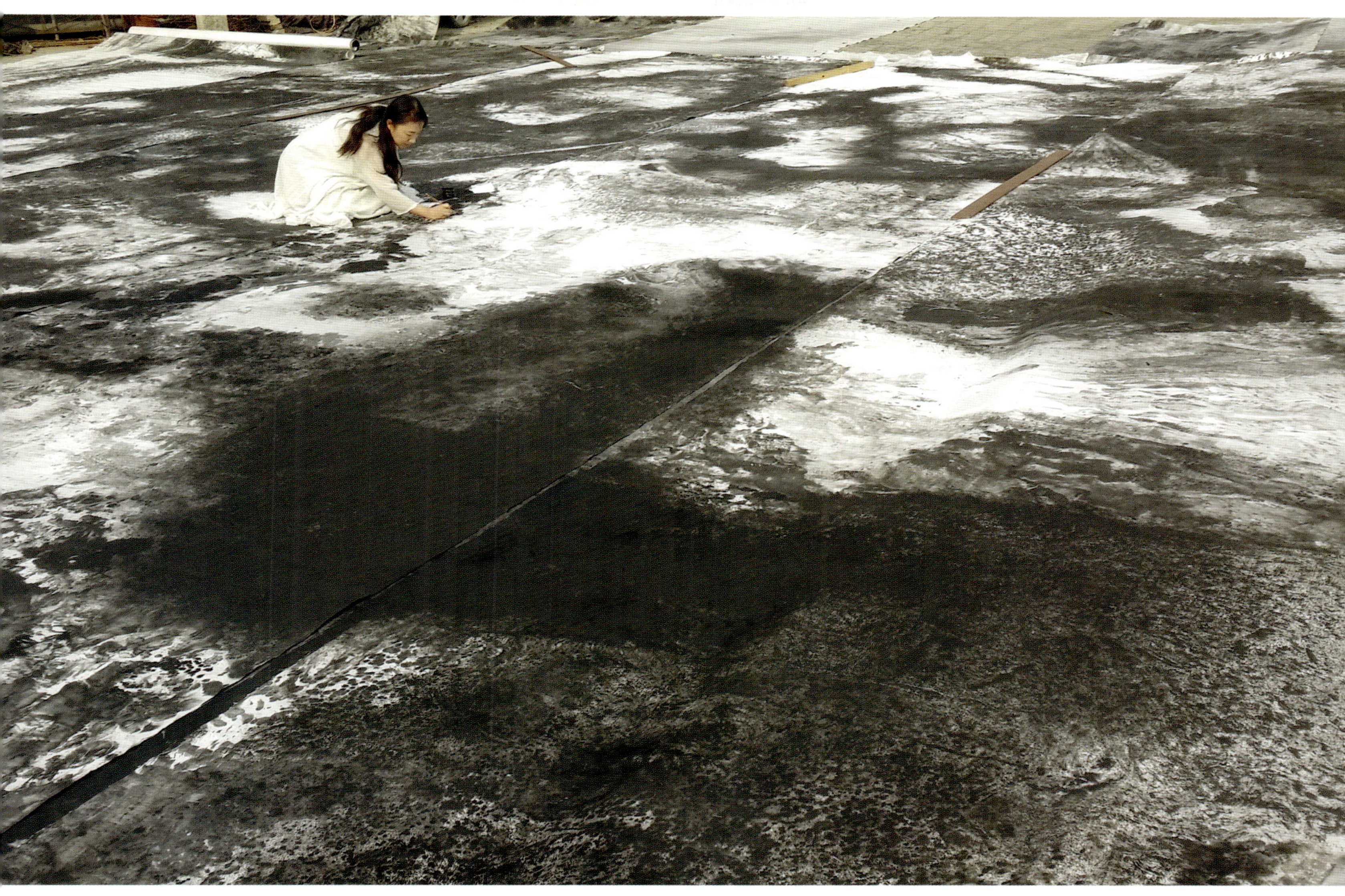

installation art, and performance art. Produced on a vast scale, her ink paintings become immersive site-specific installations:

> I seem to have unlimited curiosity towards the world. I want a different kind of relationship to what I look at, how I look at things, what I do. For instance I invented every single type of technology, or devices, or instruments, or methods, for my paintings. Even the paper is a special order – the chemicals we put in to make it dry or wet, to make it able to absorb humidity or temperature. It's not only scientific but also philosophical. I treat the material as an expression.

Bingyi is hostile to the current fashion for what is often called 'Contemporary Ink', and the many international exhibitions and auction sales that have created such interest. 'I couldn't care less about the art market, about auction prices, it's boring,' she said emphatically. 'In my case it's not about reinterpreting Chinese traditional ink painting. If you *are* truly *shan shui* you don't need to think about it. If you *are* the being, you don't need to think about the being. You just are.' She defines her work as intensely spiritual. 'It's the universe working through me,' she says, 'and sometimes it's that space between human hand and God's hand.' Bingyi aims to fuse classical painting traditions with a twenty-first century sensibility:

> The values of *shan shui* are rotten and decadent and indulgent because it's been repeated over and over again. To really give life to *shan shui* you must use a much larger question to reinterpret it. All those ethical and aesthetic questions have been asked so many times before. The reason people say I have given life to ink painting is because I am not really dealing with ink painting at all. I am dealing with the biggest, most perpetual problems that any species has to ask itself. I am dealing with detachment. So now it [my painting] has a completely different meaning. That is what makes these paintings relevant and what makes them meaningful.

Bingyi sees the world in micro and macro perspectives, perhaps due to her scientific background. In her daily practice of making small ink paintings, the series she calls *Fairies,*

Bingyi working on large-scale ink works
in the mountains outside Beijing
image courtesy the artist

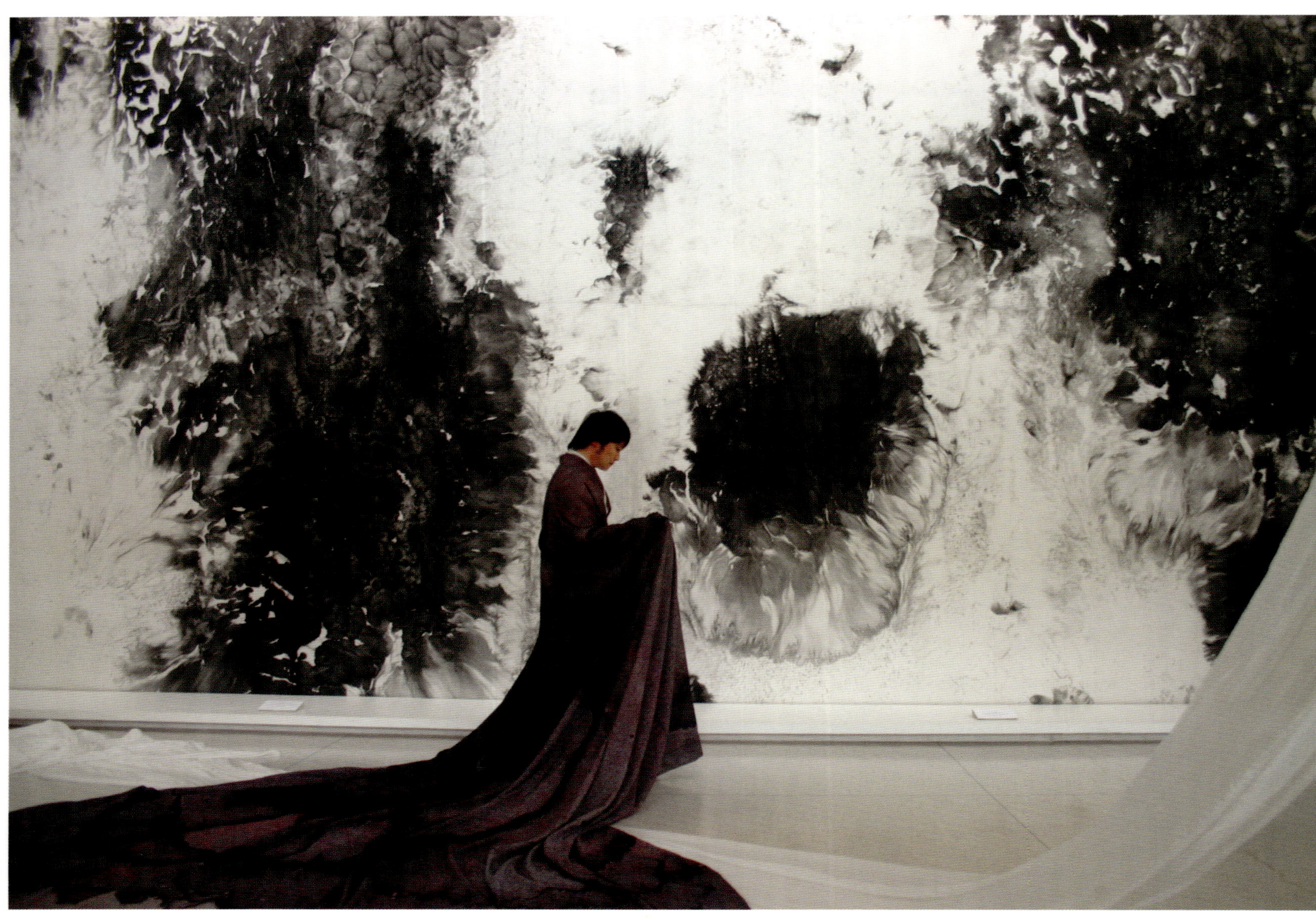

she examines tiny, apparently insignificant elements of the natural world. In contrast, her major projects are on a vast scale. Ink paintings one hundred and fifty metres long, presented to audiences in a theatrical manner that includes operatic performances, dance and reading from her own poetry, take the tradition of the scholar painters and poets in a new direction:

> I am not dealing with classicism. I am not dealing with the schools or the processes [of historical painting]. No – that's not what I am interested in at all. I paint an entire world view. Micro to macro? Yes. The *Fairies* series – now there are five hundred of them, and once I reach 1000 it's a complete encyclopaedia of stories. But the most fundamental thing is that it's a view of the world through my eyes.

These small ink-on-paper works are like album leaves from the scholar painting tradition. Her subjects include insects, acorns, scallions, the cocoons of silk worms, walnuts, a cloud devouring the moon, the buds of flowers, a silk knot, a willow tree. 'Like ghosts,' she says. Painting daily like the calligraphers of the past, in a meditative, deliberate process requiring great control of fine brushes, Bingyi is the modern-day embodiment of a tradition that was closed to women. They are in the form of fans, a classical allusion representing dreams. The contemporary world is here too, with images such as a plastic bag flying through the air in the wind. 'It's really about the energy of *qi*,' says Bingyi. By the end of our first meeting they were spread out along the full length of an enormous table in the temple, one delicate, subtle image after another, revealing the expressive quality of the calligraphic mark. The paintings are accompanied by her own poetry, in the same manner as the literati painters. One such is titled *Flow*:

Bingyi *(above and opposite)*
Cascade *(detail of installation with performers)* 2010
ink, household cleaners and water on paper, 13 x 20 metres
David and Alfred Smart Museum of Art, The University of Chicago
images courtesy the artist

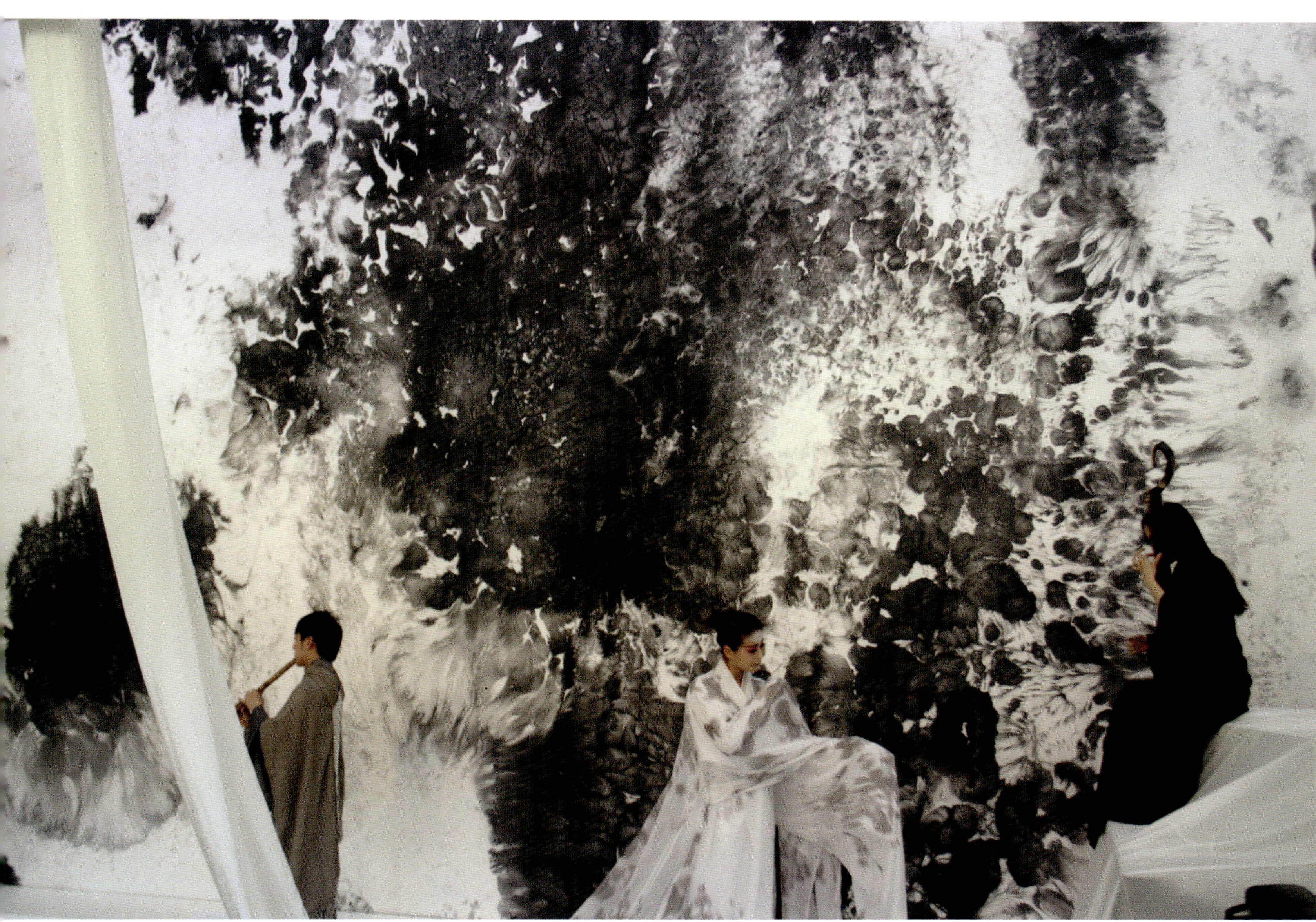

The world completes itself
As the river appears
Then I come to realise: I am the river
I flow over the world as I am never completed.

Bingyi loves poetry, and selected her first college in the United States, Mount Holyoke, from which she graduated in 1998, on the basis that it was the alma mater of Emily Dickinson, her favourite poet. (Bingyi's mother, a doctor as well as a calligrapher and translator, was the first to translate Dickinson's poetry into Chinese.) She had gone to the United States seeking 'a different kind of freedom' after unhappy experiences at school and university in China.

Always different, Bingyi graduated high school at the age of fifteen. Like other academically gifted students, she struggled to fit in:

> I was such a rebel. Whenever the bell rang I would just stand up and leave, I was out and wandering. I was catching butterflies. My biggest mission at that time was to speak to insects. Adults were a bit mystified... The way I looked at everything was so different and unique. They could feel that liberty was breeding in me. I was *so* weird, like perpetually on LSD! I had no boundaries. Teenage years were such an enormously difficult time. But poetically different. You look at the world in a different way. In your entire adolescence, when everyone else is dealing with hormones and dating, you are thinking about butterflies. But you are very lonely and sad. At school it was a bitter struggle. I was relocated from class to class because I couldn't get along with anyone, I had no proper social skills and I was too weird.

After she went to the United States, she says, she had to 'rebuild my entire value system on my own.'

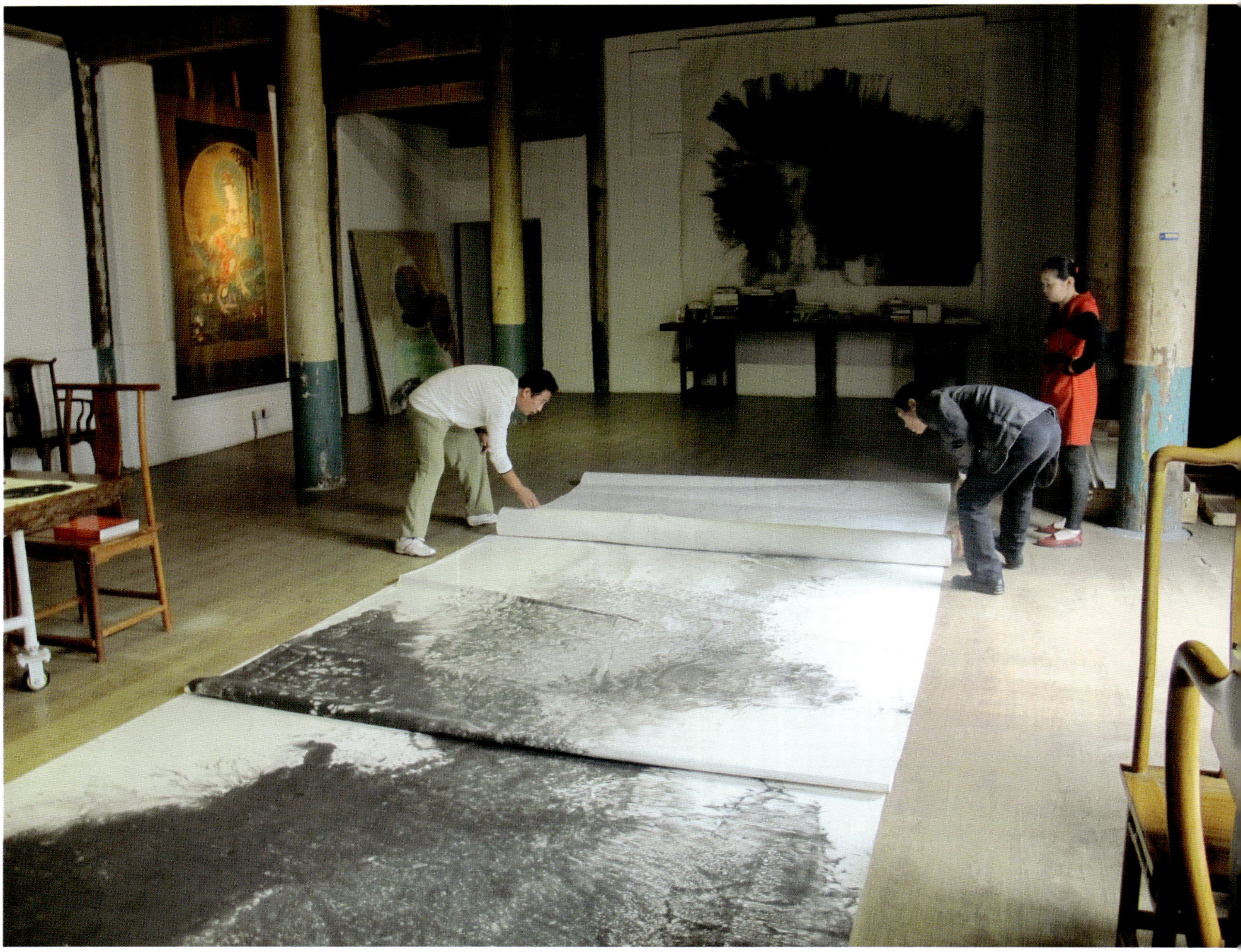

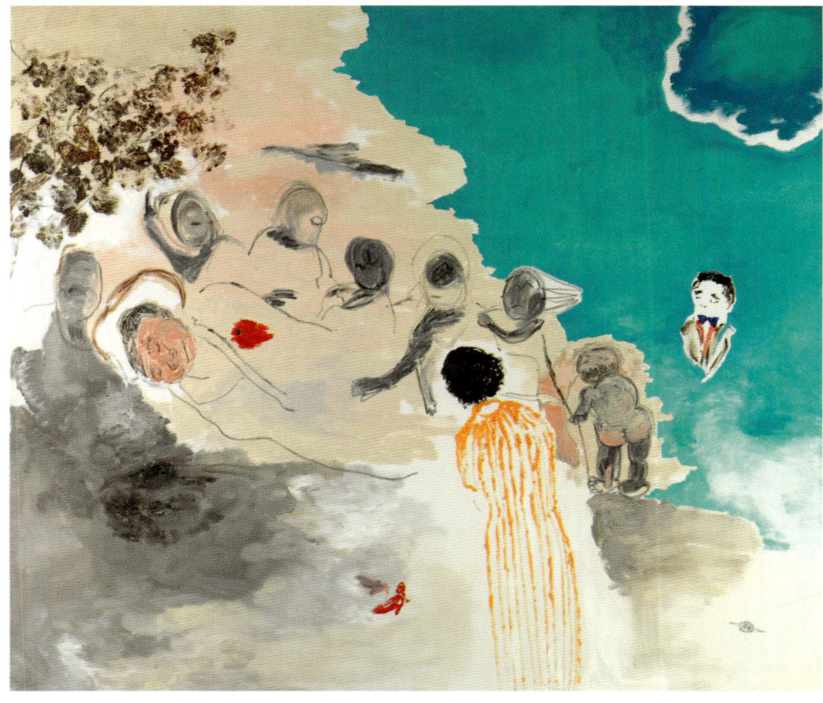

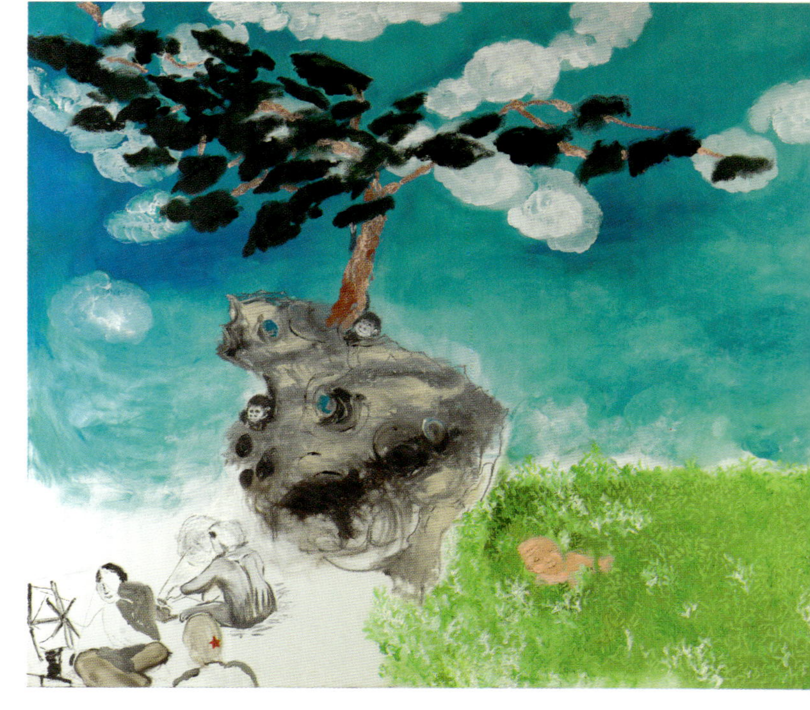

Earlier figurative paintings are expressionist, delicate works revealing aspects of the artist's own life. A serious accident in 2009 left her badly burned and subject to a series of medical interventions and operations. That same year, she painted *I Watch Myself Dying,* a work that expresses the horror of this experience: the artist's fragile body lies on the operating table, whilst her soul hovers above, somewhere past the bright surgical lights, watching. *Six Accounts of a Floating Life* is similarly revealing. Inspired by an eighteenth century memoir by Shen Fu, a wandering scholar who took to the road after the death of his wife, it is intended to be read like a traditional narrative scroll, its separate episodes recounting scenes of her childhood and early adulthood. In the vignette dealing with romantic love and desire a naked couple appear as if in the Garden of Eden, sharing a single set of organs. Inevitably, tragedy follows, and a sense of incompleteness – there are five images in this series, not six.

The transition to ink came about through a commissioned work. *Cascade*, a site-specific work commissioned in 2010 for the lobby of the Smart Museum in the University of Chicago, was thought to be the largest ink-on-paper work ever created, exploring personal and mythological subject matter in a reinvention and transformation of traditional brush techniques. Curator and critic Wu Hung visited Bingyi in 2009, having seen earlier forty-metre oil paintings, and proposed that she create a work for the site: 'I went and looked to see if I could attach an oil painting to that ceiling and found it was impossible. That is how I came to use rice paper and ink painting. I investigated the chemistry of the paper, its humidity and temperature. I needed to research the science, because in ink painting you control the image by controlling these factors.' Until this moment, Bingyi had never worked with ink. In creating *Cascade* she made reference to a Buddhist temple named *Zhihuihai* (The Ocean of Wisdom) in Beijing's Summer Palace, which has similar proportions to the Chicago site. The work refers to elements in nature – wind, fire, mountains, earth and water – and to human and animal DNA. An artist highly conversant with both western and eastern traditions, conventions and theories, Bingyi describes these site-specific works as 'Like Walter de Maria inverted. I was very early on interested in this idea of land art. We all breathe through nature don't we? We *are* nature! I am someone who is willing to cover my own world with a vision. It's not about big or small, it's about what size is needed to have that universal touch.'

Bingyi's monumental approach to ink painting has transformed the Chinese tradition of viewing a scroll, pored over section by section as each new part is unrolled, a private and leisurely experience of contemplation. The experience of Bingyi's site-specific works, in contrast, is theatrical and immersive. Yet she sees herself as continuing a particular scholarly tradition. 'Elegant gatherings' (called *yaji*) were meetings where learned scholars exchanged ideas through poetry, calligraphy, music, and painting. *Yaji* were themselves depicted in many classical paintings. *Elegant Gathering in the Apricot Garden,* an early Ming handscroll by Xie Huan, shows a gathering of eight bureaucratic colleagues in a lushly planted garden on April 6, 1437, ostentatiously engaged in the scholarly pursuits of writing calligraphy and examining paintings.[14] It is a practice that fascinates Bingyi:

> It's the connection between poetry, calligraphy, painting and music – these divine games. I compose operas, I write thousands of pieces, and songs and sutras. When you do all of these things together as a body of work it's the ultimate spiritual exercise of beauty. That's very classic! And also very universal.

'Could you be described as a postmodern literati painter?' I asked. 'Yes! I often gather friends and we send each other poetry. We do it on Facebook. I post a poem and someone responds with a poem and it's happening every single day. That makes me an ultimate literati!'

Journey to the Centre of the Earth, created for a site in Essen, Germany, a mining region of dramatic mountainous landscapes, is an ink painting of one hundred and fifty metres in length – a length which equals the depth of the shaft of the first mine. It developed from meticulous research. Weather, geology, geography, history and sociology were all considered in planning the project. Bingyi began her research in Germany and then moved into the mountains outside Beijing for two months, camping in forty-five degree heat to make the work. With four assistants, she worked on the painting section by section, applying ink to the paper with tools that would astonish the traditional literati painters. Her assistants even created a pond large enough to make the sheets of paper that make up the vast scroll. 'I was standing between the heaven and the earth,' says the artist. Dealing with the extreme physical discomfort of the conditions, even finding herself covered with mosquito bites, was all part of her practice. 'I could feel I was no different than a mosquito, I was no different than a toad. That's eternity – you are so minimal, you are nothing. And that is the sublime.'

Bingyi defines her process as opposite to traditional notions of landscape painting, in which the artist is observing and recording nature:

> Nature is just a projection of the universe. It's conceptual, it's land art, it's performance art. It's a ritual I perform between Heaven and Earth. I am not a shaman, I am just a human, but this ritual is relational between the universe and the individual, it's a kind of sublime. It's intensely primal. It raises questions about our fundamental being – what is pain, what is suffering, what is loneliness.

Bingyi's assistants unroll a 30-metre ink painting,
Beijing, October 2013, photograph LG

Bingyi
Six Accounts of a Floating Life *(Parts 4 and 5)* 2008
oil on canvas
each 90 x 160 cm
images courtesy the artist and White Rabbit Gallery

Notions of the artist as a high priestess enacting powerful rites would ordinarily seem far-fetched, but such is the strength of Bingyi's self-confidence and the scale of her ambitious works that one is swept along by her enthusiasm.

Large-scale site-specific works, such as *Journey to the Centre of the Earth* and *Cascade* (which also included an operatic performance with original music and costumes designed by the artist), feature what appears to be spontaneous mark-making on an epic scale, reminiscent of Jackson Pollock and his dance-like movements around his abstract expressionist canvases, inspired by North American Indian shamanism and Navajo sand-painting rituals. 'No!' says Bingyi, explaining that her careful control, and the meticulous planning of every element positions her as the polar opposite of a gestural abstractionist. She acknowledges that Wu Hung, who first suggested the possibility of ink painting to Bingyi, has connected her work with the western tradition of Abstract Expressionism and action painting. 'Of course I see that connection,' she says. 'But in the work of Jackson Pollock what's important is really that horizontal plane as opposed to the vertical. It's the gesture, the speed, the expression. In my work it's really the image. My work is not abstract.'

Bingyi likens her process to researching a complex novel, composing passages of music, or writing a computer program. For *The Shape of the Wind: In Fuchun Mountain* (2012) she created a scroll work almost three metres wide and one hundred metres long on handmade rice paper, to be shown inside the nave of St Johannes- Evangelist Church in Berlin:

> I went to Berlin and… I saw the church where it was to be shown and [in my mind] I saw fire, because that church was burned during the war. Then I thought about a famous Chinese painting [the Ming Dynasty scroll, *Dwelling in the Fuchun Mountains*] that was burned into two halves. One classical painting in two pieces – one in the Taipei Museum and one in a Chinese museum. This became a bigger metaphor when you think of Berlin. So I decided the location [where I would create the work] had to be the Fuchun River where that original classical painting was made. So it alludes to the historical moment but really allegorically it is about now. And about survival.

The paper to create this work had to be specially made to order in Anhui Province, as it was to be the exact length of the circumference of the mountain itself. 'It's not just about a problematic nexus between east and west but also time and space,' she says. 'Once the painting is burned it creates a different kind of abstract story, about conflict and war and the scars that result. How do you come to terms with that scar?'

Bingyi herself is badly scarred as a result of her accident:

> Fire has a very specific meaning for me, and the scars are all on my body. At that time in 2010 I was healing, and dealing with fire myself. So [like my earlier work] it is still profoundly autobiographical. The notion of survival is so important in human ethical development. This makes us divine, and closer to the sublime. And at the heart of that is love. It's very poetic but also very basic.

She identifies the interconnectedness of all things in the universe as the idea that most interests her. She asks:

> How can you not think about these things? What I am interested in is not dynamics on the personal level, it's more like dynamics on the species level. How do we convey ourselves as a species? Humans are such an arrogant, blind group of creatures that we forget how minimal, how primal, how limited we are. We keep taking and taking from the world but we forget that we are not here to take… Why are we here? At a species level, in the eye of the universe, what are we? Are we dust? Are we marks? Are we traces? Whatever we may be we are not the centre of the earth.

In their different ways Shi Zhiying, Gao Ping, Li Tingting and Bingyi exemplify the experimental approach that Chinese artists bring to their own history, their willingness to adapt the past to the needs of the present. Applying the viscous qualities of oil paint glazes to evoke the subtle nuances of ink on paper; representing the quotidian details of urban daily life; referencing western Modernist idioms; or developing performative interpretations of the gesture of the brush in site-specific installations: the ink tradition is alive and well in numerous guises. Art historian Chen Anying identifies the discontinuous nature of present day Chinese society as the chief rationale for a tendency to 'revert to tradition.'[15] Sometimes this re-examination of Chinese tradition implies a deliberate rejection of western art and international influences. In the practice of these four artists, however, it fuses aspects of global contemporary practice with the scholarly traditions of ancient China.

NOTES

1 Hearn, Maxwell 2008 'Chinese Painting' in *Heilbrunn Timeline of Art History*, The Metropolitan Museum of Art, New York http://www.metmuseum.org/toah/hd/chin/hd_chin.htm accessed 11 July 2014

2 Lin Ci 2006 (transl. Yan Xinjian & Ni Yanshuo) *The art of Chinese painting: capturing the timeless spirit of nature*, China Intercontinental Press, Beijing

3 Chang Tsong-Zung 2011 'Ink Painting in the Age of New Wave', in *A New Thoughtfulness in Contemporary China: Critical Voices in Art and Aesthetics*, Huber, Jorg & Zhao Chuan (eds) Hong Kong University Press (20)

4 Erickson, Britta 2012 interviewed for the *New York Times* in

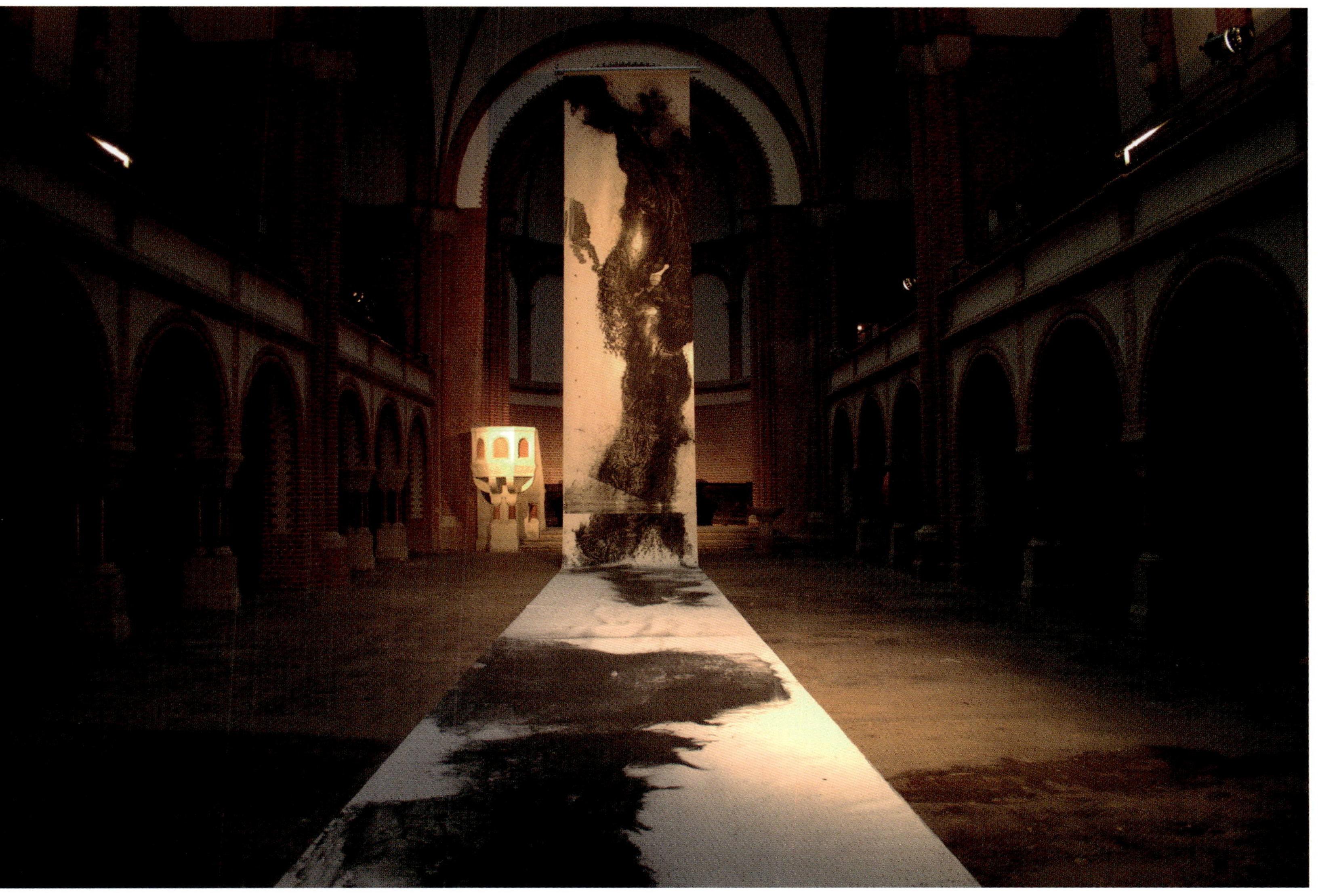

relation to the 2012 exhibitions *Modern Chinese Ink Paintings* at the British Museum, *Ink: The Art of China* at the Saatchi Gallery and *Revolutionary Ink: The Paintings of Wu Guanzhong* at the Asia Society New York available at http://www.nytimes.com/2012/11/01/arts/ancient-art-tellschinas-modern-tale.html?_r=0 accessed 5 April 2014 and further discussed in an email with the writer 22 October 2014

5 Erickson, Britta, in an email to the writer, 31 December 2014

6 Unless otherwise acknowledged all quotes from Li Tingting are from her conversations with the writer in Beijing in December 2012 and April 2014

7 See http://www.bergerfoundation.ch/highlights/Shitao/shitao.html for a discussion of Shi Tao's paintings and his published theories of painting, and http://en.cafa.com.cn/when-brush-and-ink-speak-peng-xiancheng-talks-about-chinese-painting.html for a discussion by artist Peng Xiancheng of their significance today (both accessed 6 April 2014)

8 Peng Xiancheng 2012 'When Brush and Ink Speak: Peng Xiancheng Talks About Chinese Painting' available at http://en.cafa.com.cn/when-brush-and-ink-speak-peng-xiancheng-talks-about-chinese-painting.html accessed 6 April 2015

9 http://www.sugimotohiroshi.com/seascape.html accessed 30 December 2014

10 Unless otherwise acknowledged, all quotes from Shi Zhiying are from her conversations with the writer in Shanghai in April 2011, December 2012 and December 2013

11 Unless otherwise acknowledged all quotes from Gao Ping are from her conversations with the writer in Beijing in March 2011, December 2012, October/November 2013, April and December 2014 and in Sydney in 2012

12 Gao Ping 2013 – her own description for the solo exhibition at Yun Gallery, 798, Beijing

13 Unless otherwise acknowledged all quotes from Bingyi are from her conversations with the writer in Beijing in October 2013 and April 2014

14 Burkus-Chasson, Anna 2002 'Between Representations: The Historical and the Visionary in Chen Hongshou's "Yaji"' in *The Art Bulletin* Vol. 84, No. 2 (June 2002) (315–33)

15 Chen Anying 2011 'Literati Painting: Reflections Across Discontinuities', in *A New Thoughtfulness in Contemporary China*, Jorg Huber & Zhao Chuan (eds) Hong Kong University Press (59)

Bingyi
The Shape of the Wind: In Fuchun Mountain 2012
ink on Chinese paper
2.65 x 160 metres
image courtesy the artist

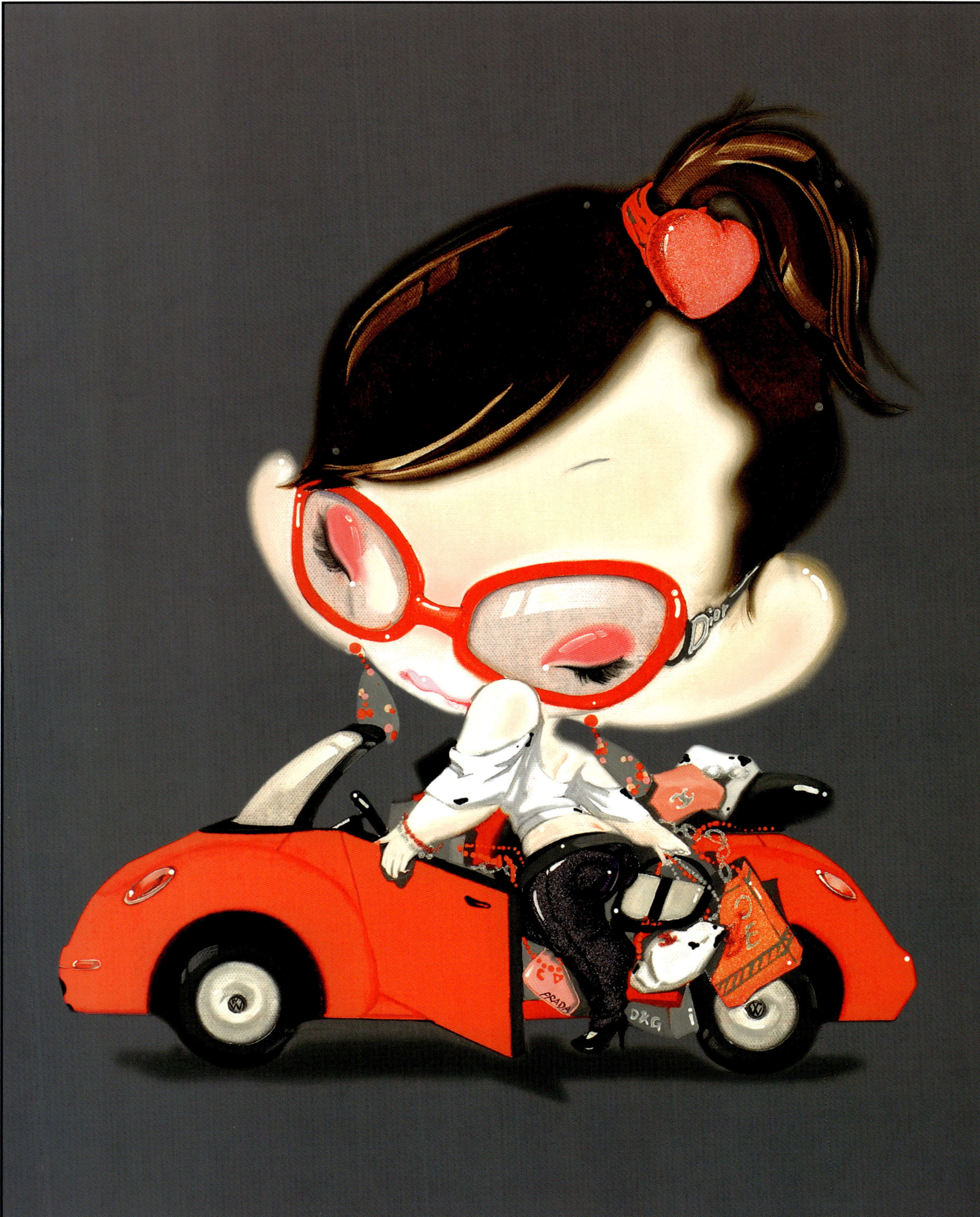
Dior
PRADA

PAINTING THE ZEITGEIST

Yu Hong, Xie Qi and Han Yajuan

Twenty-first century China seems to me like Florence or Rome at the height of the Italian Renaissance. This is not an entirely outlandish comparison – there are similarities. There is the get-rich-quick-at-all-costs entrepreneurialism, and the palpable excitement of a fast-changing society. There is the class of wealthy patrons for whom art legitimises their wealth, there are scholarly artists who work alone, and industrial-scale artists' studios employing artisans and labourers fabricating artworks on a massively ambitious scale. The free exchange of new ideas? Well, yes and no. Artists know they walk a fine line in relation to political content in their work, and most are very adept at doing so. The art of contemporary China exhibits all the complexity, inventiveness, and manic energy of a society in flux. Artists who navigate the tricky cultural and political landscape of Beijing today are treading some of the same ground as those who dealt with the Medici family or the Borgia Popes.

In spite of authoritarian control which ebbs and flows, creating a sense of uncertainty and a tendency to self-censor, and the knowledge that government officials prefer art that celebrates Chinese culture without examining its history too closely, artists have responded to the 'new' China in diverse ways. The dislocating experience of a transforming world requires a new kind of art. Two major directions are evident in contemporary painting: practice grounded in classical Chinese traditions; and painting that reveals the influence of western academic and avant-garde painting from the earliest days of Chinese modernism and its revival in the 1980s. There are artists exploring abstraction, and evidence that this emergent trend will become more significant, but figuration continues to dominate.

Modernity and the Western Influence on Chinese Painting

The history of western-style painting (*xi hua*) in China was always contentious. Traditional Chinese painting was transformed during the eighteenth and nineteenth centuries due to the impact of missionaries and traders. Later, Chinese artists travelled and studied abroad. Lin Fengmian, Liu Haisu and Wu Daiyu studied in France, and were influenced by Impressionism and the emerging avant-garde styles of Post-impressionism and Fauvism. With other returnees, they took up teaching positions in Chinese art schools and became oracles for the developing knowledge of western art, filled with the Utopian idealism of early Modernism. In their urgent desire to move away from 'literati' painting, they saw western painting techniques as a form which could convey new ideas for a new society. These new ideas did not go unchallenged. At the 1929 National Exchange exhibition those supporting the Modernists came into open conflict with Xu Beihong, a celebrated exponent of French academic Realism. He responded to the works of the Modernists with sarcasm, saying, 'Manet is mediocre, Renoir is vulgar, Cézanne is shallow, Matisse is inferior.'[1]

The political connections between the Eurocentric proponents of avant-garde painting and Nationalist politics, as well as their rejection of colonialism and the dominance of the old scholar class, were clear. During the 1930s a number of artist groups such as the Storm Society and the Chinese Independent Artists Association in Shanghai were actively promoting change. They tended to see traditional Chinese art as symptomatic of a closed, inward-looking society poisoned by feudalism and colonialism, positioning western modernism in contrast as progressive.

A number of female artists studied alongside men in the 1920s and 1930s, some travelling to Paris to study the new modernist styles. One of the most successful was Pan Yuliang, who exhibited her work in Shanghai in the first exhibition of Chinese female painters. Her style was described as 'fierce' and she did not conform to the restrained emphasis on beauty and delicacy expected of female artists.[2] She was influenced by Post-impressionism but combined this with a simplicity of

Han Yajuan
Travel Alone 2007
oil on canvas
60 x 50 cm
image copyright © Han Yajuan

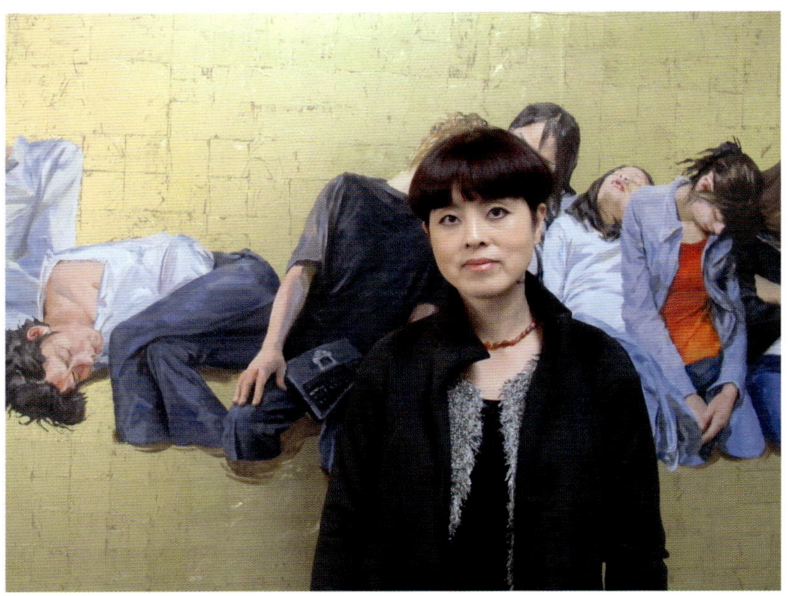

form derived from ink painting, prolifically creating a body of work numbering more than four thousand paintings.

The appreciation of modern art was restricted to a very small group of urban intellectuals, mostly in Shanghai. Traditional ink painting and highly conventional academic realism remained the dominant styles.[3] There was virtually no market for modern art in China before the establishment of the People's Republic. After 1949, any western form of artistic expression other than Soviet Socialist Realism was considered decadent and capitalist, so much so that at the first (illegal) exhibition of the 'Stars' ('*Xing Xing*') group of artists in Beijing in 1979, the artists held banners declaring, '*Kathe Kollwitz* is our banner-bearer, Pablo Picasso is our pioneer,[4] in a radical rejection of Socialist art. The Stars Group (Craig Clunas suggests that 'Sparks' is a better translation[5]) confronted the forces of officialdom through the medium of painting in oils, in a Modernist idiom.

Oil painting proved extraordinarily popular in this period after Mao's death, and in Chinese art academies to this day – although challenged in recent years by photography, installation and new media. In the Reform and Opening period after 1978, and through the 1980s and 1990s, significant experimental abstract painting occurred in different urban loci; however, for a variety of reasons, figurative genres have continued to dominate. The extraordinary degree of technical accomplishment resulting from the rigorous academic training in Chinese art schools has continued to produce new forms of realist painting.

Artists such as Yu Hong, Xie Qi and Han Yajuan have inherited the figurative tradition of 'western-style' oil painting, with its emphasis on moral and psychological truthfulness. They are also navigating artworld power-dynamics. Since the 1990s there have been a number of large-scale, state-sanctioned exhibitions of work by women artists, as well as numerous smaller curated shows. The problem is the same one that became an ideological battleground in the west in the 1970s and early 1980s. Curators construct a narrative that identifies particular characteristics in art by women: art that explored personal experience, autobiography and self-discovery dominated the discourse, a limiting codification that tended to deny other possibilities. To view the work of each of these painters solely through the lens of gender is to misrepresent their intentions in important ways. Han Yajuan, the youngest of the three, sees it as essentially irrelevant to her practice, as does Xie Qi. Yu Hong paints monumental history paintings in addition to her series of self-portraits exploring female experience. Autobiography is only part of the story.

YU HONG 喻红

A New Classicism

Born in Xi'an in 1966, Yu Hong entered the Central Academy of Fine Arts in 1984, after attending its affiliated high school. Although the heady experimental days of the 'Stars' group took place while she was still a teenager, she directly witnessed the dramatic changes brought about by the 1985 New Wave art movement which culminated in the 1989 *China/Avant-garde* exhibition. She felt the excitement and anticipation of 'a new window opening'[6] and participated in intense discussions of philosophy, western art, new media and new ideas. After graduation she became known (together with her husband, acclaimed painter Liu Xiaodong) as one of the New Realist painters, working in a highly personal, painterly style of figuration. She has said, 'I am recording my life as it happens, and that involves my family and friends.'[7]

Entering the Oil Painting Department of the Central Academy of Fine Arts when it had only recently re-opened after the Cultural Revolution, she learned a method of figurative painting in which the influences of European academic painting, Soviet-style painting and classical Chinese painting were equally significant. Her mother, who also graduated from that same 'Third Studio' in the Oil Painting Department, becoming an art editor in a publishing house, a painter of socialist realist propaganda images [8] – and later herself a teacher of oil painting at Minzu University – was a major influence on her life and work. Yu's parents encouraged her to paint and draw, and from early childhood through to her days in the CAFA-affiliated high school, she learned ink painting at the Children's Palace in Beijing, which inculcated a love of Chinese art traditions. In her childhood, at a time of great privation and hardship, Yu Hong had access to art

Yu Hong in her Beijing studio, April 2014, photograph LG

materials and to Soviet art magazines with pictures of western-style paintings, an unimaginable luxury for other children. 'I grew up in this environment so I felt I was destined to become an artist,' she says.

Yu Hong finds poetry in everyday life, in her acute observation of momentary gesture and body language, in ordinary people caught unawares, or sometimes posing for the camera. She applies her technical virtuosity to monumental works in which the quotidian is transformed, gaining a powerful significance which makes us see ordinary moments in new ways.

She has clear memories of the excitement of the 1980s in the Beijing artworld, a time when it appeared great change was about to happen in China. She worked hard every morning in the studio, painting from the model and learning the rigorous technique that is the hallmark of her painting today. In the afternoons, she and her fellow students would go to art lectures, discuss philosophy and contemporary art with their professors, or attend exhibitions that were held clandestinely in the apartments of foreign diplomats. There were no galleries, no art market. At that time CAFA's campus was in the centre of Beijing, and compared to its gargantuan size today it was a tiny institution: 'Just like a family. We all knew each other, we met our professors every day because they lived on the campus.'

Since the birth of her daughter in 1994, Yu has produced one self-portrait and one portrait of her child on a yearly basis, revealing the passage of time and the journey of the mother-daughter relationship. In the two paintings made in her twenty-ninth year, in the first she is pregnant, and has given birth in the second to her daughter, Liu Wa. Yu Hong says, 'I started this project after I had a baby and wanted to make works about life in this way. I wanted to develop a series about feminism, and a group of people from different social classes.' She reflects on her experience as a woman, and as a mother. 'It has a really big impact. *Witness and Growth* is about my motherhood role. Women have a different attitude to the world – we tend to focus more on their own experience and feelings.' Yu Hong believes art by women differs from the work of men: 'Of course it depends on the individual – there are some female painters who look more at the outside world and some men vice versa. But in general, women have a more... benign outlook.' She thinks women tend to focus on psychology and relationships rather than on the events of the external world, and in many of her works that internal dynamic has been her focus.

She – Performance Artist (reproduced on page 42) references a highly-charged and memorable moment – the shooting by performance artist Xiao Lu of her own installation, *Dialogue,* at the *China/Avant-Garde* exhibition in 1989.[9] Yu was present at this seminal moment in the history of contemporary

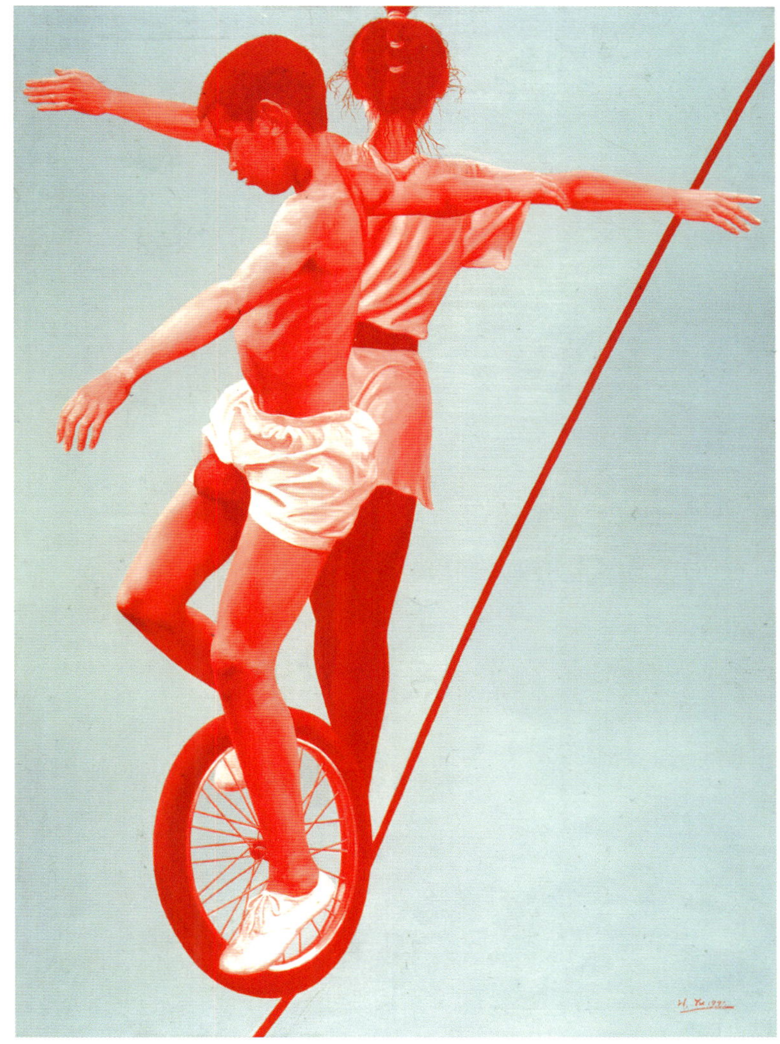

Chinese art: 'While I was at the performance in 1989, I did not actually see Xiao Lu make the gunshots as the crowd was too large and I couldn't see through them. But yes, this was the work that inspired the painting.'[10] To represent this event is courageous, as accounts of it descended into vitriolic blame, vicious gossip, and a gendered narrative which positioned Xiao Lu as 'a woman scorned'.

Xiao Lu and Yu Hong were classmates at the CAFA-affiliated High School, 'so we know each other quite well and admire each other. I've always followed her artwork with interest, so for the artist portrait in the *She* series, it was natural that I thought of her,' she says. Yu Hong identifies the *China/Avant-Garde* exhibition, and Xiao Lu herself, as highly influential. 'The Chinese avant-garde movement really embodied not only China, but also the era – it strongly brought about the unique qualities of China. Xiao Lu's work is a strong personal symbol.'[11] Yu had always wanted to paint Xiao Lu, seeing her as exemplifying the contradictions inherent in femaleness and

Yu Hong
Tightrope Walking 1991
oil on canvas
130x97cm
image courtesy the artist

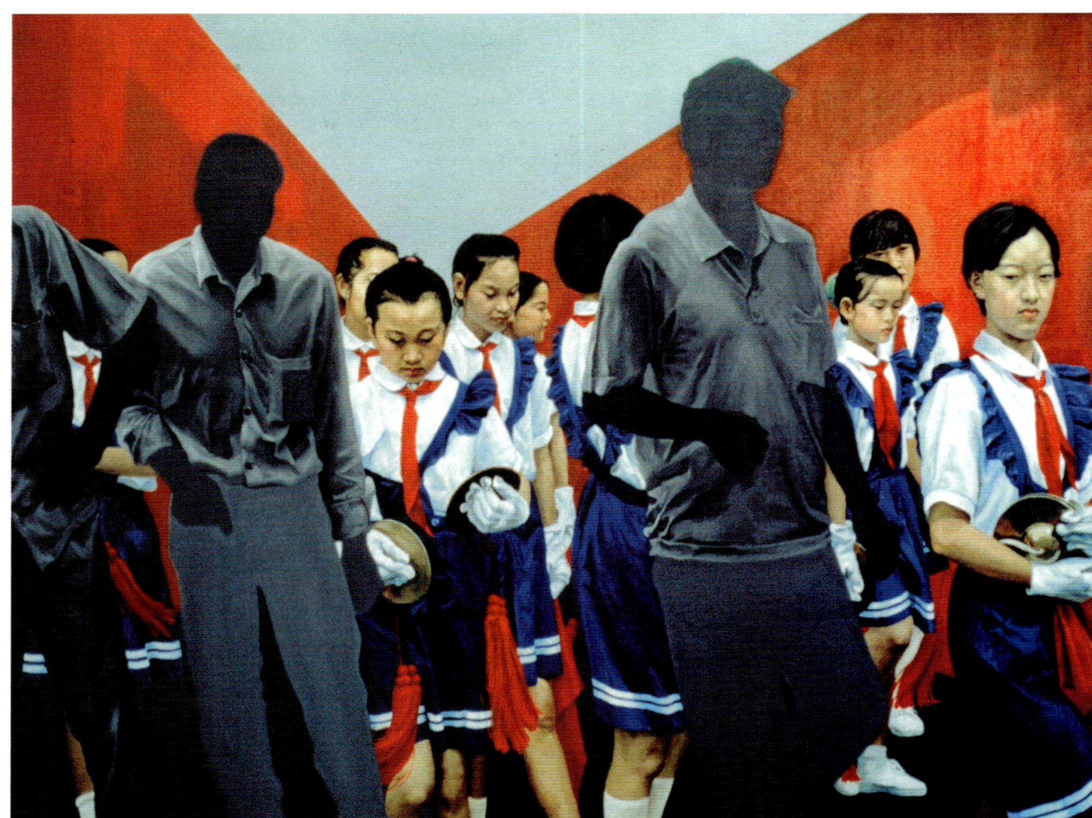

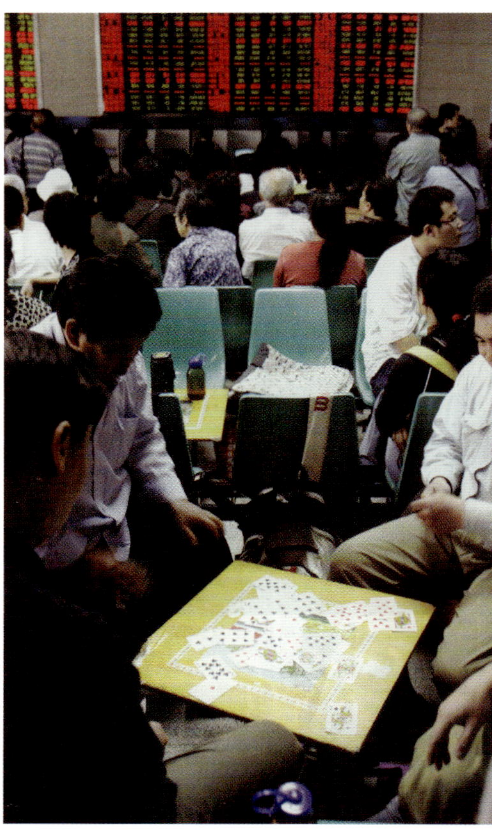

femininity. 'Her life has many legendary stories... her artworks really embody this shocking power,' she says. Yu Hong has painted Xiao in the domestic space of a bedroom, surrounded by repeated images of her defining moment. A solitary figure, she appears small and fragile, in contrast to the image of female aggression which has entered art history, creating a reputation that Xiao Lu has struggled to move beyond.

Lu Jie, founder of Beijing's Long March Space, identifies Yu's ongoing *Witness to Growth* series, as 'an articulation of the connection between the individual and the history of the era.'[12] The entire series consists of two paintings for each year of her life, since her birth in 1966 at the start of the Cultural Revolution. Yu compares her own childhood with the very different experiences of her daughter, in what seems like a different universe. A painterly investigation of China's recent history, each self-portrait is developed from a photograph of the time and paired with another, taken from official publications – the vernacular snapshot beside the photographic apparatus of state propaganda. 'It seemed that painting the old photographs enabled me to physically touch the past,' said Yu Hong.[13] The 1968 photograph celebrating the production of the famous propaganda poster *Chairman Mao Goes to Anyuan* is juxtaposed with two-year-old Yu Hong proudly wearing a Mao badge, walking hand-in-hand with her mother in the park. We recognise in these transitory moments fleeting passages of our own lives, captured in fading photographs. They are highly specific and personal, but at the same time absolutely universal.

These paintings question the verisimilitude of the photographic image, traditionally viewed as more truthful than painting. In China photography has a contested and complex history – photographic veracity was manipulated to serve the interests of party and state. By juxtaposing photographs published as historical 'evidence' with her own life and memories, Yu Hong reveals contradictory intersections of private and public memory, bearing witness. There is irony mixed with the nostalgia, but it is carefully considered. The use of photographs brings the past sharply into focus. For some it is a memory almost too painful to bear, recalling a time of fanaticism and collective madness, whereas for others the memories are more benign. In China the act of remembering is always politically charged. Yu Hong believes it is vitally important that artists should reflect social change, 'especially for artists of my generation who lived through a period of China changing very dramatically.'

Yu's paintings often feature empty backgrounds of gold leaf, in which her keenly observed figures float like Renaissance saints – if saints wore blue jeans and high heels. They seamlessly integrate different cultural conventions. *Romance of Spring*, created for an exhibition at Boston's Museum of Fine Arts

Yu Hong
Young Pioneers 1990
oil on canvas
137 x 184cm
image courtesy the artist

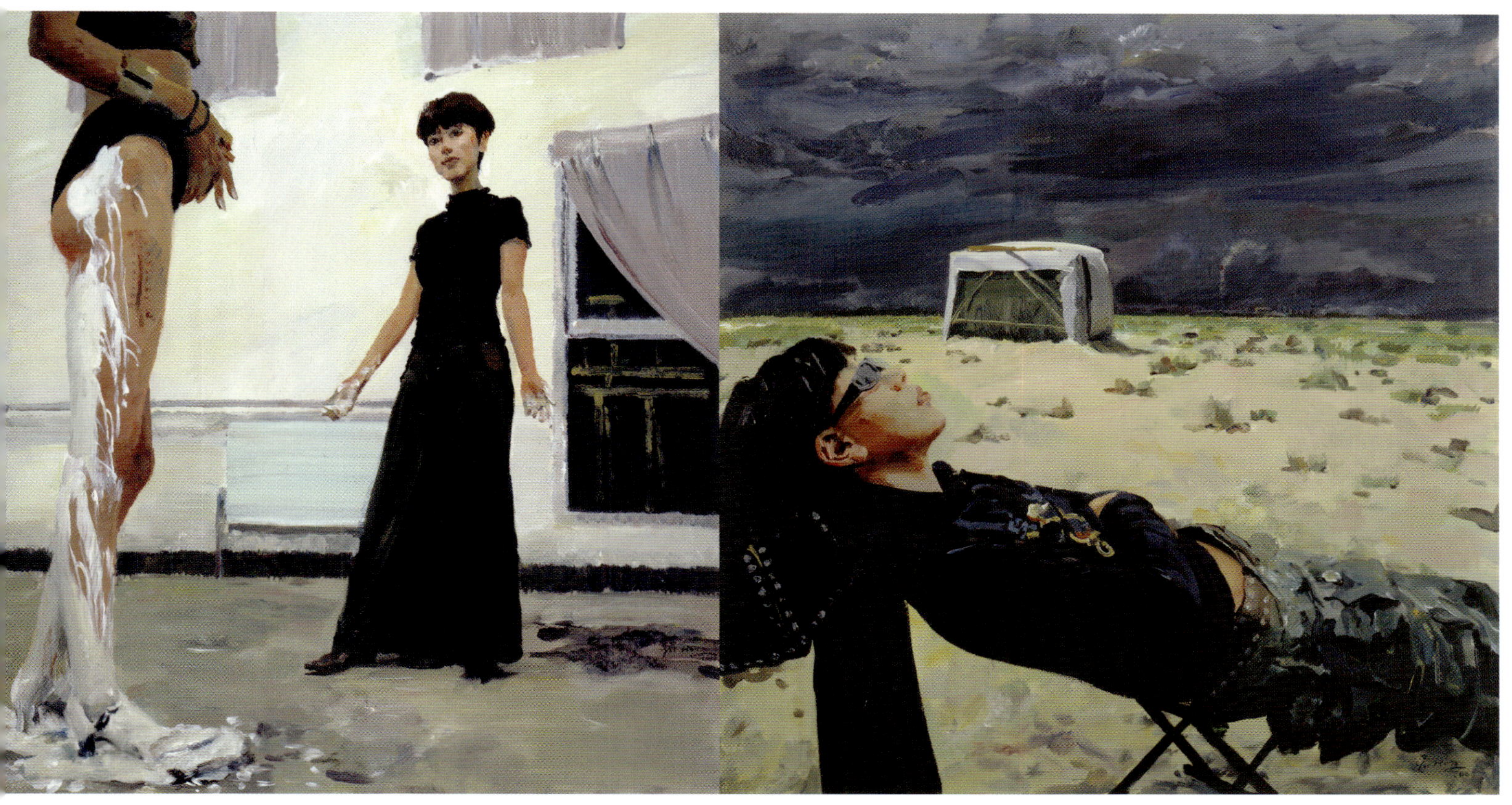

entitled *Fresh Ink: Ten Takes on Chinese Tradition*, subverts a masterpiece from the Northern Song. In Yu's transformation, the classical painting attributed to Emperor Huizong, *Court Ladies Preparing Newly Woven Silk*, becomes a two-way dialogue with the traditions of Chinese painting. Writer Hao Sheng explains: 'The old historicizes the new while the new offers a fresh interpretation of the old.'[14]

Yu produced a work on long, hanging panels of silk, and later a second painting, a horizontal polyptych. The artist herself, wearing paint-spattered trousers, appears on the far right-hand side. The court ladies in the original, engaged in collaborative labour in their comfortable interior space, are replaced by young women stretching out the actual Song scroll, observed by two children and one seated older woman carrying a fan, in the same positions as the original.

They are disconnected from each other and from the empty gold background on which they float. Alienated, uncommunicative, they represent social dislocation and the loneliness of life in today's world. This may be why some writers have described Yu Hong as possessed of a cool and clinical gaze capable of dissecting the social realities of our age.[15] Yu, a little stung by this, says, 'Maybe every artist has some problem with society and shows anxiety or criticism. I was being to some extent critical, perhaps – but not cynical.'

The monumental six metre high *Ladder to the Sky* is derived from a twelfth century Orthodox icon, *The Ladder of Divine Ascent from Saint Catherine's Monastery on Mount Sinai*, depicting monks ascending the ladder towards Heaven, some tempted by demons and falling into the mouth of Hell. In Yu Hong's version the figures climbing the ladder, or falling from it, are real characters from her daily life in Beijing. The work may be read as a reflection on the struggle to succeed in today's China, a society of winners and losers in stark contrast to the egalitarian idealism of the past:

> In my version I removed the religious content and instead painted Chinese people from all walks of life standing on or climbing up a narrow ladder. Some people are going up, some are coming back down, and others are simply sitting down to take a rest.[16]

Yu Hong asks us to examine our assumptions about society: 'I re-examine the painting from a modern perspective, strip away its religious character and replace it with contemporary people and situations.'[17] She sees the contemporary world as fragmented, the certainties and grand narratives of the past replaced by doubt and distrust. Encountering hieratic representations of gods and mortals in tombs and temples on a trip to Egypt, Yu saw a similarity with her method of painting figures disconnected from each other, and from their surroundings.

Yu Hong
Witness to Growth, Work, 41 Years Old
photoprint (first panel) and oil on canvas
triptych, 100 x 275 cm overall
image courtesy the artist

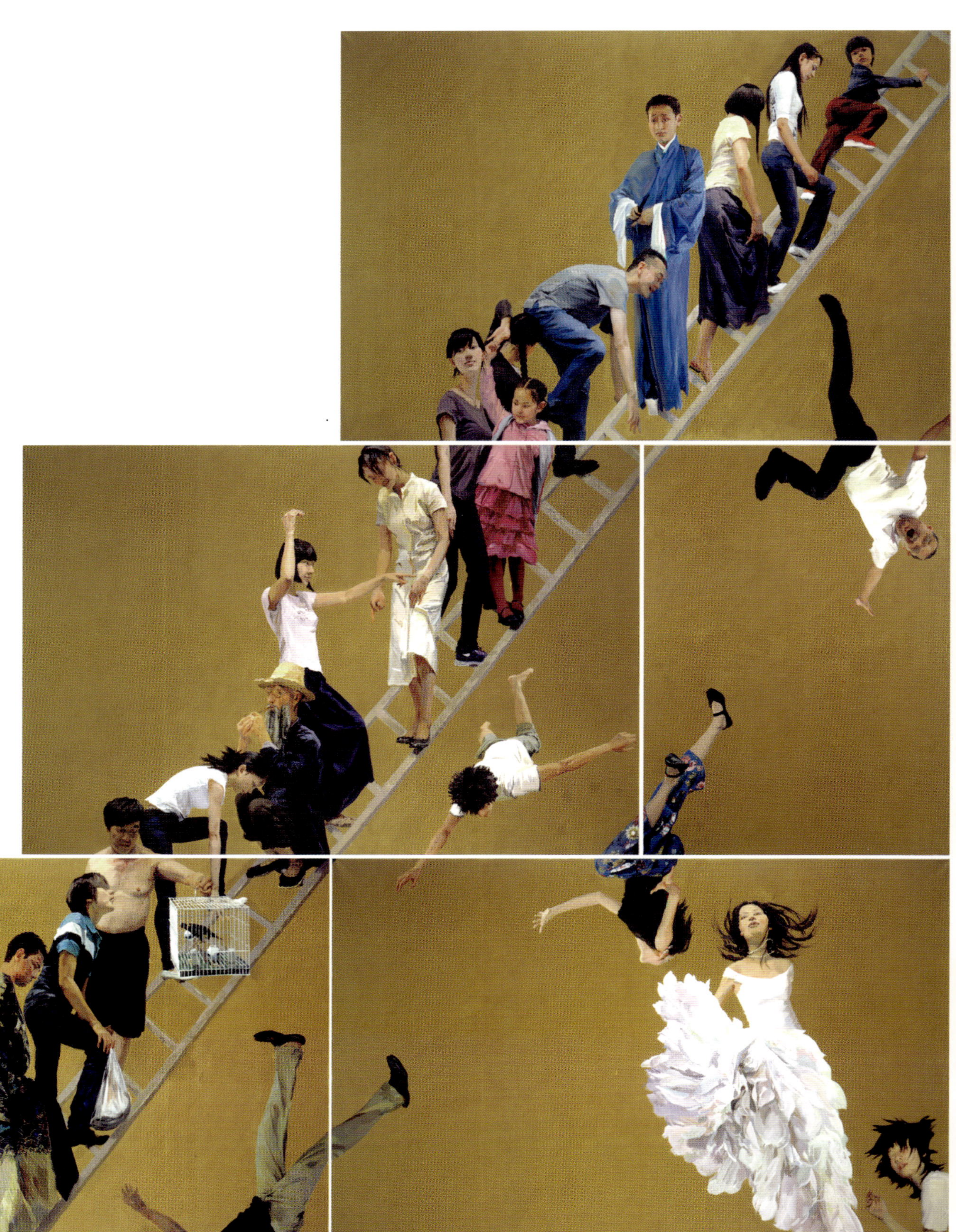

Yu Hong
Ladder to the Sky 2008
acrylic on canvas
600 x 600 cm
image courtesy the artist

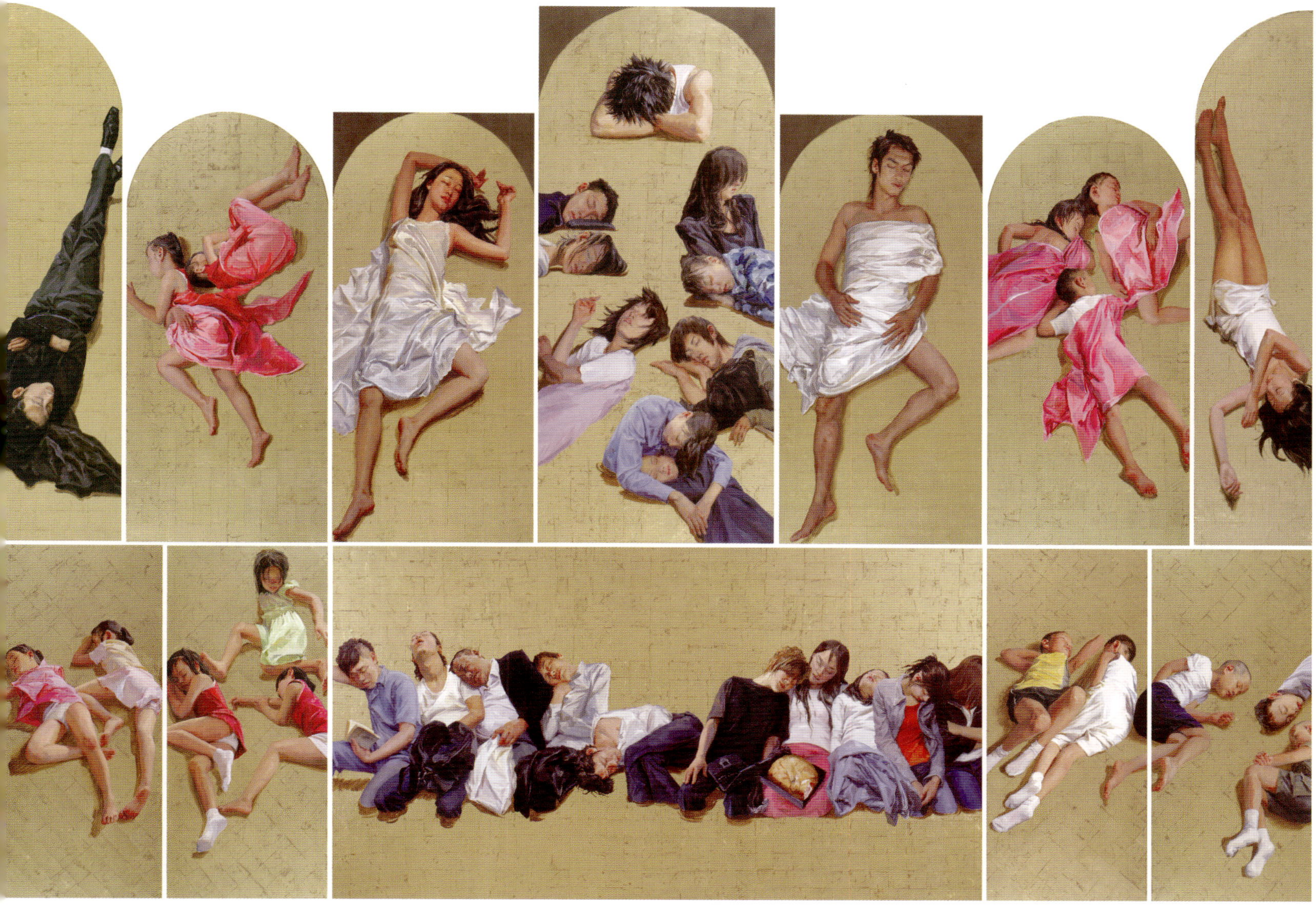

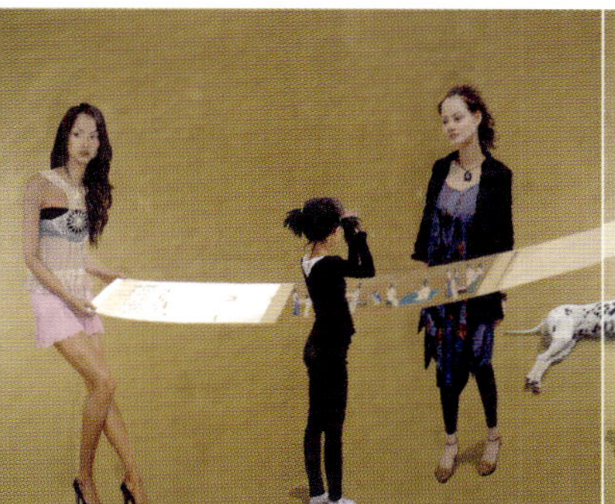
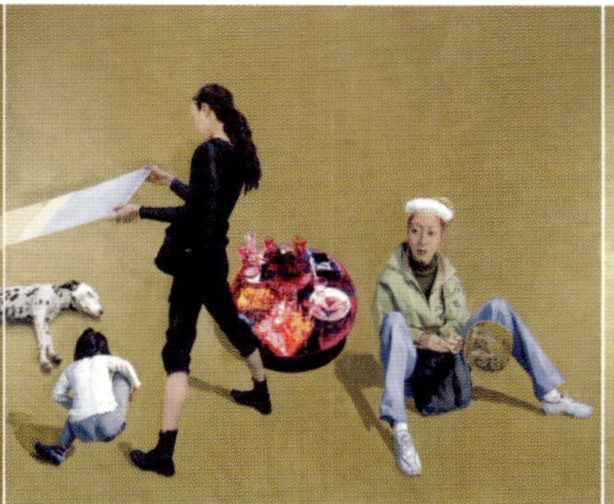
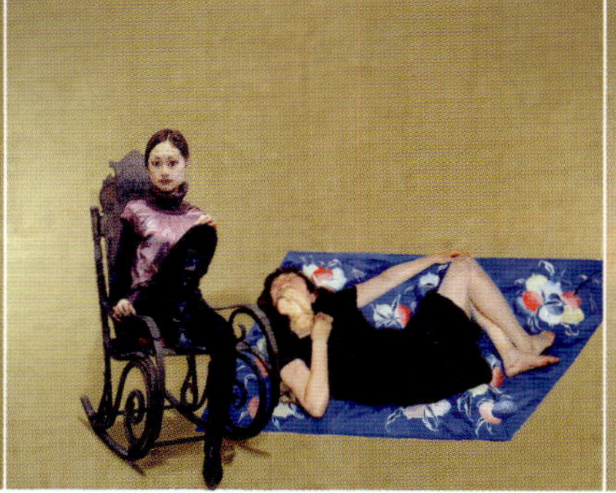
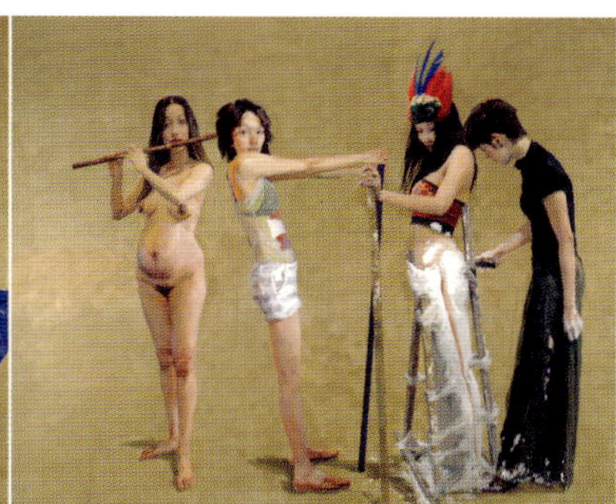

Yu Hong
One Hundred Years of Repose 2011
gold leaf, acrylic on canvas
418 x 600 cm, 12 panels
image courtesy the artist

Yu Hong
Romance of Spring 2008
acrylic on canvas
250 x 1200 cm
image courtesy the artist

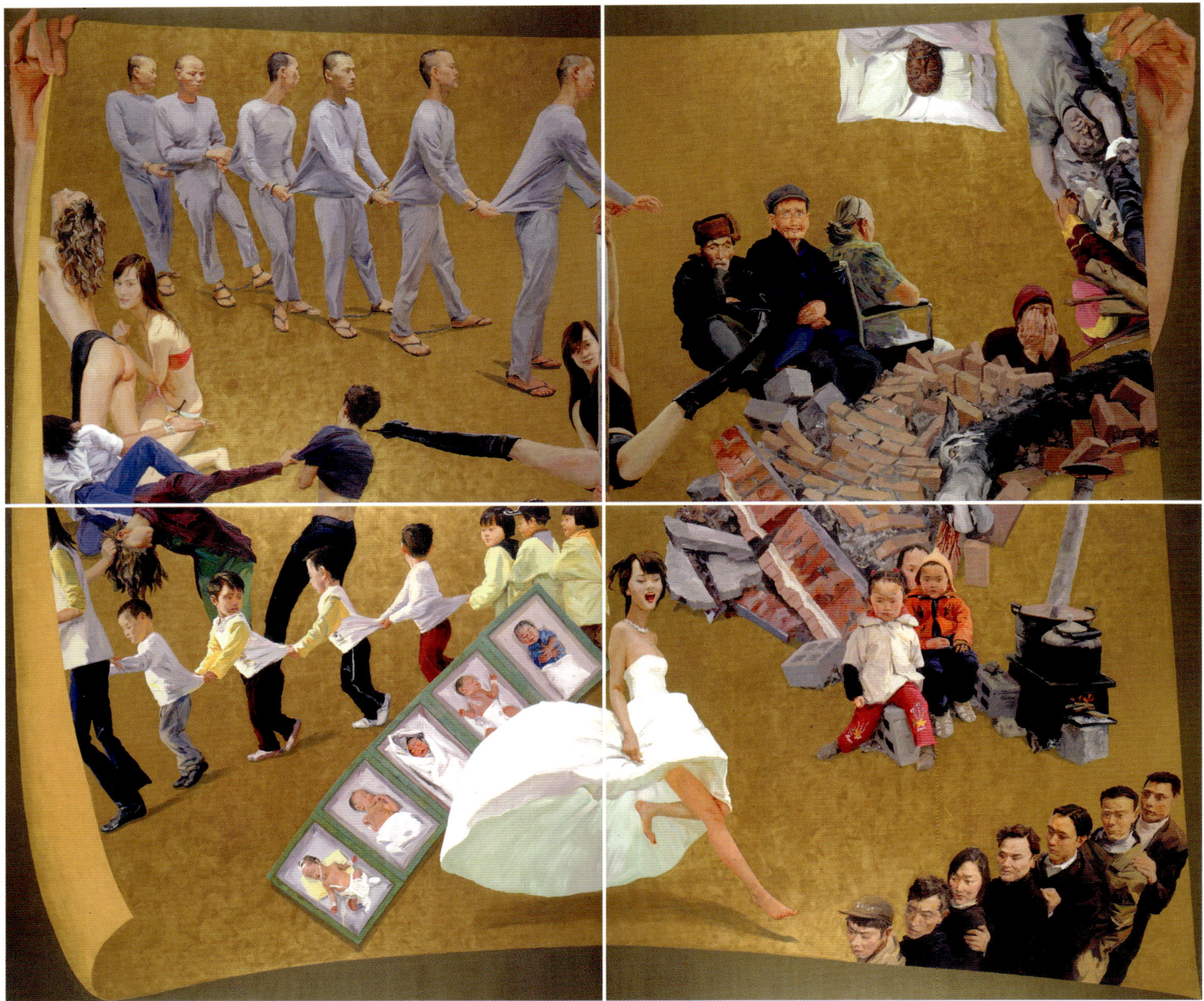

Yu Hong describes the relationship she creates between the figures and the background of *Ladder to the Sky*, and *One Hundred Years of Repose* (a later work referencing Van Eyck's *Ghent Altarpiece*) as 'a kind of estrangement from their daily environment.' She says:

> [The] shadows underneath – can you see? They suggest maybe that the people are trapped in the sand or the mud so they are fixed in this position, which gives you a feeling of helplessness. The gold is a traditional colour with many meanings in classical Chinese painting and in the west – authority, religion, faith, money.'

She is reticent about her specific intention with these gold backgrounds, which inevitably evoke notions of the sacred for a western viewer, but acknowledges that they are intended to suggest the universality of human experience, transcending language and culture. Likewise, her references to canonical western masterpieces in these postmodern history paintings deliberately blur cultural boundaries and conventions.

Photographs remain the starting point for many works. In the past she used her own photographs – staged images as well as family photographs – but now more often searches for images on line. She stores thousands of images, waiting for the

Yu Hong
Sky Curtain 2010
acrylic on canvas
500 x 600cm
image courtesy the artist

right opportunity to use them in a new composition. Due to their sometimes poor image quality she will often re-stage and re-shoot the selected photograph with models in the studio.

Yu Hong fuses influences from sources as diverse as Egyptian tomb painting, Northern Renaissance altarpieces, Baroque frescoes, and the Buddhist murals of the Dunhuang caves, inventing a visual vocabulary entirely her own. Britta Erickson has pointed out that in one particular respect Yu Hong's work is highly unusual. It has been rare in the history of Chinese art for a female point of view to be represented in such an 'understanding and understated manner.'[18] Her work has often been examined through the lens of gender, but it can also be understood as recording time, particularly the ways women experience time as a cyclical bodily phenomenon.

In the paintings of Yu Hong, whose own grandmother had bound feet, women silenced by convention and cultural expectations are depicted as strong characters. Entirely unsentimental, despite her belief that women artists are 'more poetic', Yu turns her gaze on a subject that has preoccupied recent discourse in China – the ways in which social relationships, within the family and beyond it, have been transformed. Her muses are her friends, her family, her daughter and most especially, the artist herself. Yu Hong acknowledges that the female undergraduates she teaches will have a harder road to travel than their male counterparts. The artworld can be harsh and unforgiving, she says: 'It is a fact that girls face more difficulties on graduation. But then again, if they can be so easily stopped they must not have enough motivation.'

XIE QI 谢其
Money, Money

Born in Chongqing in 1974, Xie Qi makes works that are lushly layered and seductive. Her impressive technique results in translucent glazed, smeared, dripped and dribbled layers of oil paint, ambiguous images in which figures and landscapes seem to appear out of the mist. A 2011 series inspired by Madame Bilan de Linphel, a Beijing fashion designer and drag queen, possesses a Beardsley-like fin-de-siecle sense of tragedy. She comments satirically on aspects of contemporary China. If the gold leaf backgrounds in Yu Hong's canvases symbolise wealth and power, Xie's choice to paint actual money speaks even more emphatically about China's culture of consumerism. In a 2014 series her primary subject is the Chinese *Renminbi* bank note, its iconic image of Mao Zedong emerging from scumbled veils of paint. What could be more appropriate in today's China than currency, the literal embodiment of the dramatic social change that has taken place since the 1980s, the symbol of an emerging global superpower?

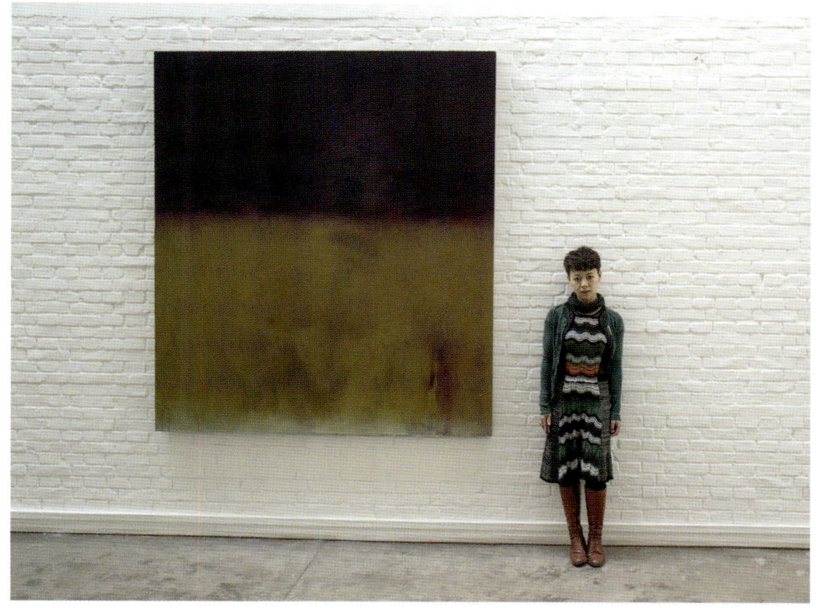

Xie Qi at Pékin Fine Arts April 2014
image courtesy Pékin Fine Arts and © Xie Qi

Rich rust-red, bruised purple, and viridian green dominate. The drips and lines of paint running across each canvas suggest the constant folding, crumpling and unfolding of paper currency as it passes from hand to hand. Ghostly imagery hints at buildings, figures, and landscapes. In some works the architecture of the revolutionary past emerges as if seen through thick fog. Mysterious and ethereal, these paintings possess a melancholy beauty. In *So Green (Mao on 50 Yuan)* the Chairman is only partially visible behind semi-transparent curtains of colour, as if vanishing into the past. There is a sense of loss here, an acknowledgement of the layering of history. Xie Qi describes her practice as 'a long period of nurturing and waiting' while her images form at a subconscious level. She works spontaneously, sometimes from photographs and sometimes drawing directly onto the canvas with colour, building up layers and wiping back, rebuilding the surface and destroying it again. It is a process of intuitive recognition of the emergence of the image. 'I allow a lot of accidents,' she says.[19]

Xie Qi's work is informed by emotive responses to people, events and ideas. Although she now lives and works in Beijing, the famous swirling mists of her birth city of Chongqing permeate her paintings. Wu Hung has noted that Sichuan oil painters of the post-Cultural Revolution 'Scar Painting' movement focused on a 'lost generation' of Chinese youth, expressing their melancholy as well as a new hopefulness.[20] They sought a visual language that would enable them to express new truths in what they imagined would be an entirely different China. Their soul-searching continues today in the practice of another generation of painters. In traditional Chinese art, meaning is never on the surface; rather it is subtly encoded in images of landscape, mountains and water. Xie Qi says she aims not to directly reflect the situation of life in China today, but a distorted or refracted

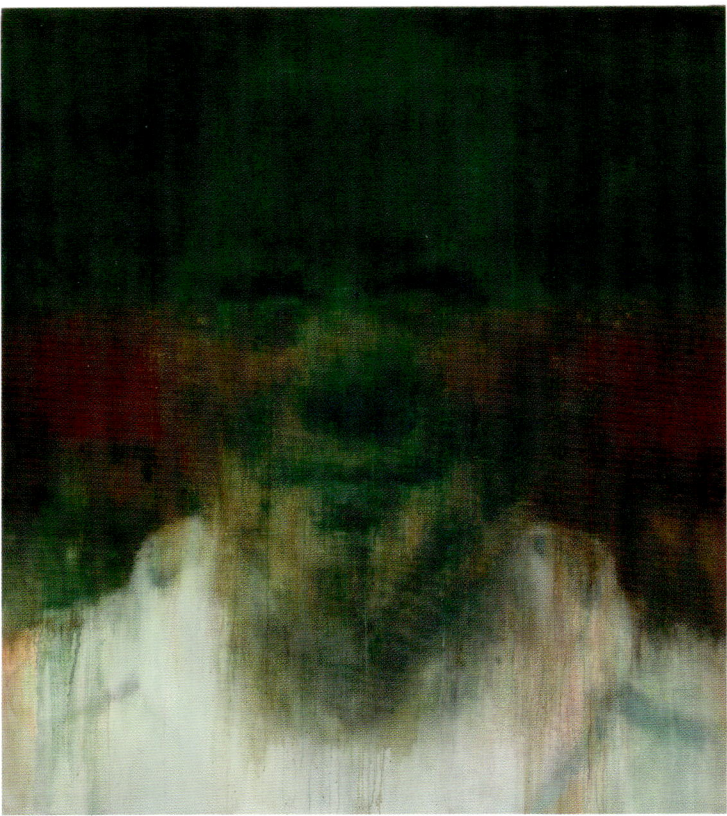

image.[21] Her sardonic artist's eye observes the rapacious greed of her society, as well as the unexpected beauty in the everyday. In a painting such as *50 RMB* Mao looms from behind her ethereal layers of paint like a vengeful ghost.

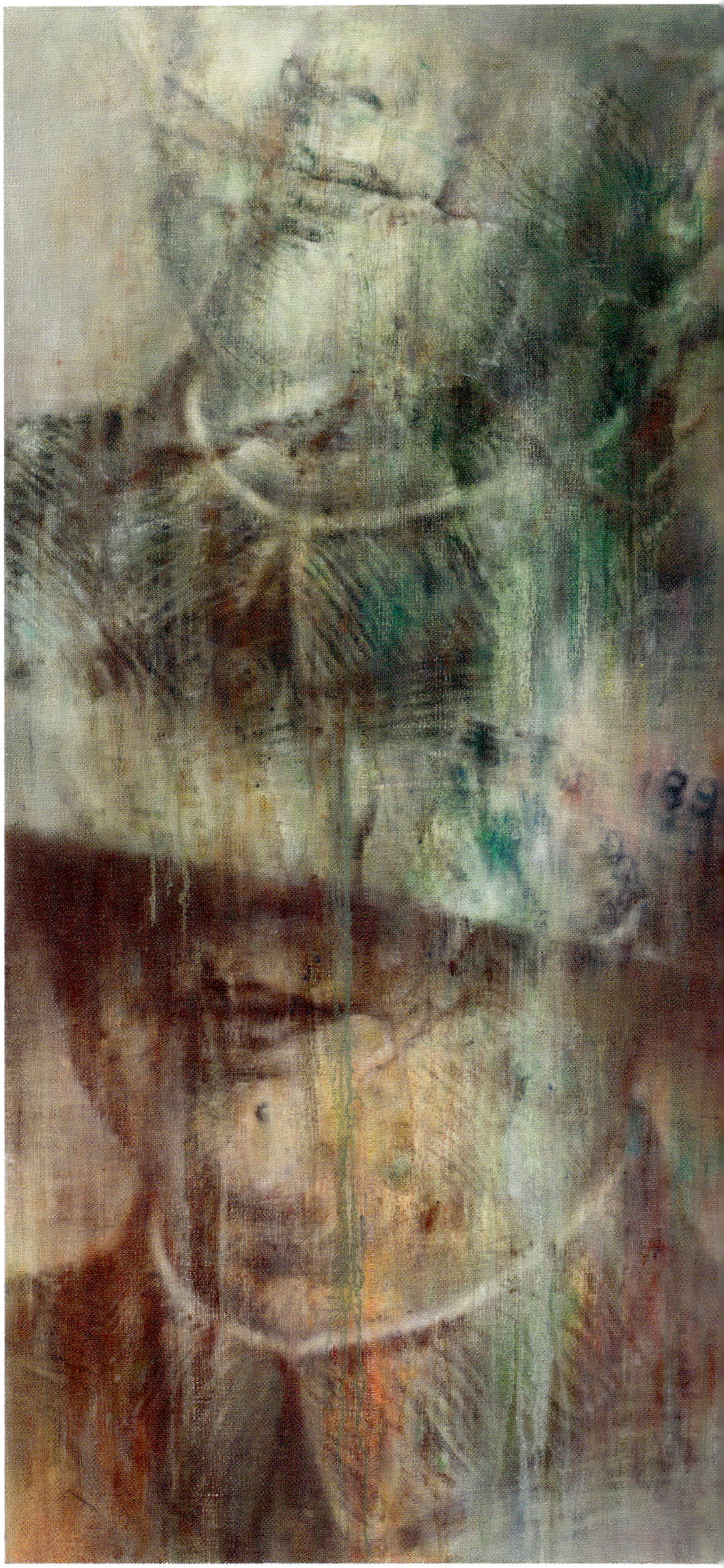

She does not see these paintings as a critique of the money-hunger that many observers believe has poisoned Chinese society. Rather, she says:

> Using the Chinese currency as a motif was about finding something that everybody touches every single day – the most basic, the most utilitarian act of everyday life. So somehow the money also brings people back to associations with events in their lives – it acts as a trigger to bring back emotions and memories of different experiences of their lives, whether they are looking at the landscapes on the notes, or the figures.

Speaking of the image of Mao which recurs in these paintings, she says:

> I like the absurdity of it. You start from this very noble and serious historic image which gets rumpled and crumpled and dirty, is shoved into people's pockets, and gets thrown around.

Xie Qi
So Green (Mao on 50 Yuan) 2012
oil on canvas
200 x 180 cm
image courtesy the artist and Pékin Fine Arts

Xie Qi
One and Two RMB Yuan 2012
oil on canvas
150 x 70 cm
image courtesy the artist and Pékin Fine Arts

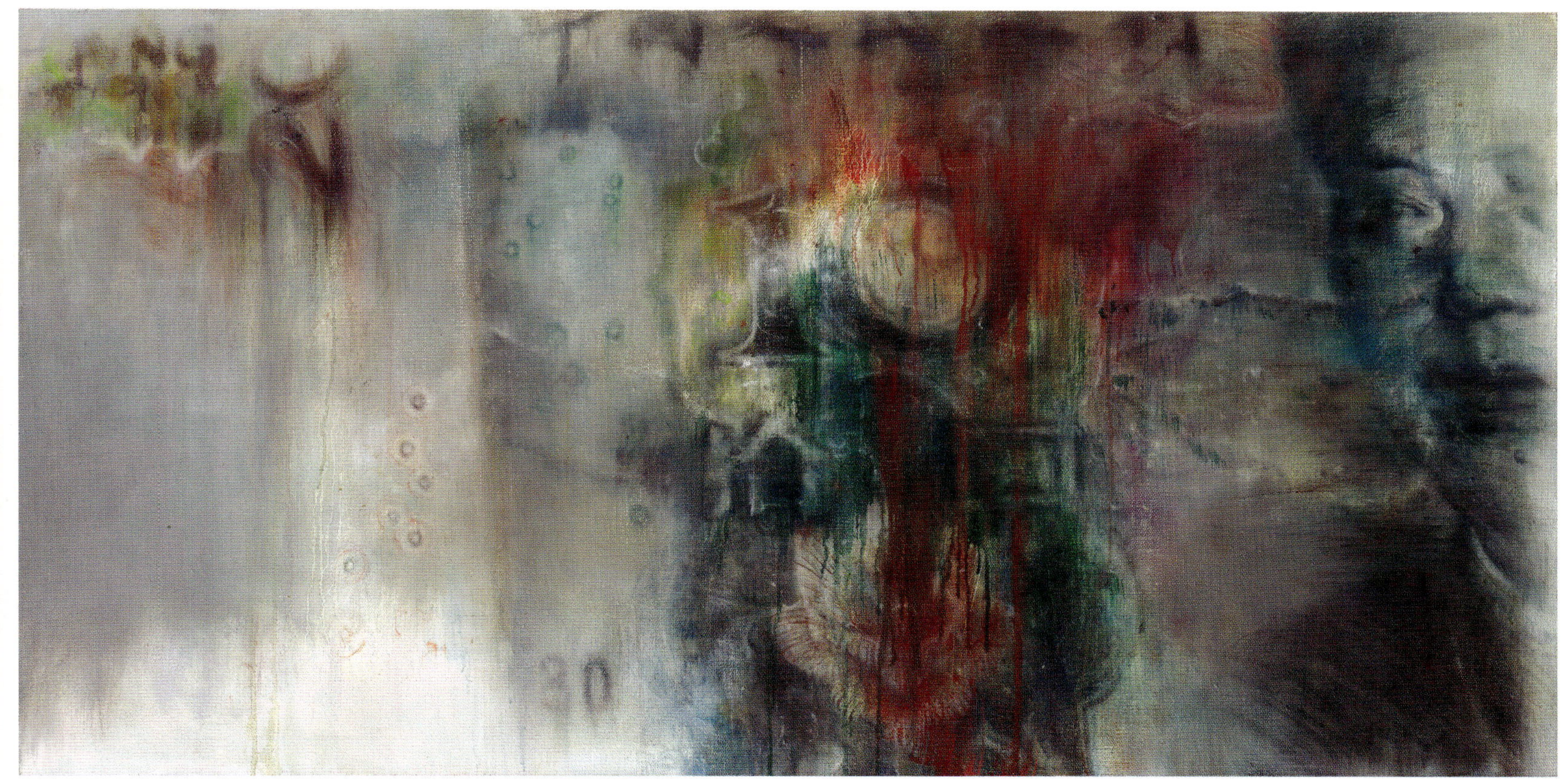

> So it underlines the absurdity of deifying these images. At the end of the day, although they are supposed to be so lofty, they come down to this very plebeian level. These dignified and serious images become dirtied, brought down to a lower, more banal level. I wanted to emphasise the absurd nature of the everyday.[22]

Xie Qi's parents treasure a photograph of the young artist at the age of three or four, earnestly copying a famous painting of a Buddhist deity. She had started even earlier, constantly drawing from the age of two: 'I liked to draw, and I always associated drawing with happiness and pleasure. But at the same time because I came to it very naturally I was always very against the rigidity of drawing classes at school.' She attended a school that was 'very tough, academic and rigid – so constraining.' A free spirit, Xie was determined to follow her older brother to the preparatory high school attached to the Sichuan Fine Arts Academy, knowing there she would experience less emphasis on rote learning and preparing for examinations: 'I had this idea in my mind of the life of an artist. I always identified myself as an artist – even when I was a really little kid. It's also a way of establishing your individuality and your difference, and creating your own identity.'

Her process combines spontaneity and meticulous technique. She usually works in series, across multiple canvases, exploring one particular theme or concept. At the time of writing she was experimenting with portraiture and the still life tradition – objects as simple as cups, bowls, and fruit arranged on a table – in a return to her classical training, and to the Renaissance masters whom she admires. Xie Qi often starts a new work with a photograph, or, in the case of her *RMB* series, with a banknote. She builds an image, then engages in a process of deconstruction, reminding us of Picasso's famous dictum, 'A painting is a sum of destructions.' She explained, 'I do small drawings but I don't sketch every painting or make detailed drawings. I will paint certain realistic elements and then I destroy it by defacing the realism through various techniques.' The surface is layered with paint of different viscosities, and with different kinds of marks. The canvas is rubbed, smeared, scraped back, washed, stained, and overpainted. Each work is a palimpsest: 'I start with realism and then I obliterate it.' She combines technical virtuosity with free experimentation, resulting in an idiosyncratic visual syntax.

In the end, what matters, Xie Qi believes, is not the success or failure of individual works, but her dedication to a consistent, intensely focused practice over a lifetime. It's a romantic

Xie Qi
Ten RMB Yuan 2012
oil on canvas
70 x 150cm
image courtesy the artist and Pékin Fine Arts

notion, revealing her idealism: 'To be a good artist you must have a very strong sense of individualism. The way you live your life – that strong respect for individual expression is what makes you a great artist.' Xie Qi uses the word 'unwavering' to describe the most important quality an artist should possess. She acknowledges that this can be a lonely and difficult path to follow: 'The deeper you look into an artist's work, the more you are going to find a point of loneliness. As an artist you are involved in a very solitary business, and that will inevitably lead to a kind of melancholy.' In an artworld obsessively fixated on the newest, shiniest thing, a world in which fewer students have the patience required to learn the necessary chemistry, the time-consuming and rigorous approach of the painter is not always understood or admired. Current discourses in Beijing are often focused on installation and new media. Xie Qi said:

> Of course this conversation about the death of painting has been going on since the invention of photography. It doesn't really affect what I do because eventually people do come back to the idea that there are some things that you can express in painting that cannot be expressed in any other way. Painting is a very unique visual language – an irreplaceable medium. All these media [photography, video and multimedia] can live side by side with painting and sculpture. They may influence each other but one will not replace the other. Multimedia may change the way you look at the world, and it may influence painting, but it won't eradicate it.

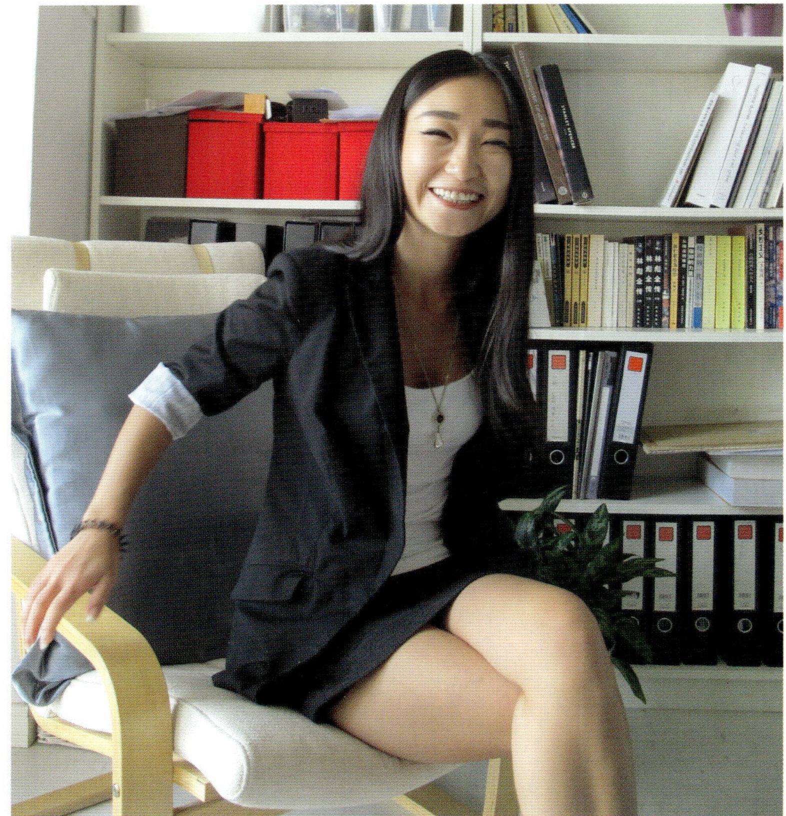

Han Yajuan at home in Beijing, 2013
photograph LG

HAN YAJUAN 韩娅娟

Material Girls and Super Starlets

Han Yajuan is best known for anime-inspired paintings of a new generation of women – 'material girls' in stiletto heels, sporting designer handbags and climbing out of sports cars. Maybe they are the much despised *tuhao*, crassly conspicuous consumers of brand-name labels, or the daughters of high-level party officials flaunting their privilege in an increasingly divided society. Or maybe they represent a generation of young women who please themselves rather than living in Confucian deference to the wishes of their parents. If so, such assertiveness is often labelled as selfish and superficial and likely to lead to the dreadful fate of being a *sheng nu* (leftover woman) before the age of thirty. Despite the gender imbalance created by the One Child Policy and a preference for boys that has resulted in an over-abundance of men seeking wives, contemporary Chinese culture stigmatises women for being over-educated, over-ambitious and financially independent.[23] Han Yajuan's paintings, populated by huge-headed, doll-like female characters, reveal much about contemporary culture. Her work is both a celebration and a critique of her world.

Born in 1980 in Qingdao, Shandong Province, earning her MFA from the Central Academy of Fine Arts in Beijing, she is sometimes described as an artist who embodies the collective unconscious of her generation. Her paintings reveal her interest in Japanese design and animation, and the 'cuteness' prevalent in contemporary Asian pop culture. *Travel Alone* depicts a big-headed cartoon girl climbing into her red sports car wearing Dior glasses. She carries bags labelled Prada and Chanel. Fake or real, they reflect the current Chinese obsession with designer brands as symbols of wealth and success. Han paints young women of her own 1980s generation, *bai fu mei* (literally translated: 'white, wealthy, beautiful') who want it all, and want it now.

Fashion Week represents the frantic busy-ness, but also the emptiness of this world. Luxury goods sales in China amounted to $10.7 billion in 2010, a quarter of the luxury consumption in the world. Despite a crackdown on conspicuous spending in an attempt to rein in corruption, and despite slowing economic growth, by 2015 it is expected to reach $27 billion.[24] China has the youngest luxury consumer community in the world, a reality reflected in Han Yajuan's work.

'I am just trying to present what I see... what exists,' she says. 'Twenty years ago a bicycle was a luxury, but things change. There is so much pressure, the speed [of life] is so fast. I am trying to present my point of view and also give people an opportunity to see their own lives.' Her generation may not have experienced the hardships of the past, but they are experiencing loneliness, amidst all the material comforts of an entirely different kind of society. In sculptural works such as

Super Starlet 6 the cloying cuteness is undercut by a disturbing sense of identity crisis – these doll-like figures are faceless beings, literally from the factory assembly line, 'made in China'.

Earlier works are all about desire – the shiny, lustrous world depicted in advertising and glossy magazines. They feature single female figures, self-absorbed and apparently free from self-doubt. The colours are like the seductive lacquer of nail polish – Han often used jewel inlays and fluorescent colours in her paintings and sculptures between 2005 and 2008. Her female figures avoid any exchange of gaze with their audience, as their eyes are placed so far on the sides of their lollipop-sized heads, making them appear even more self-absorbed. Han talks with nostalgia about her 1980s childhood and the emergence of Chinese cartoons at this time: 'I love cartoons, of course! And those memories and influences are probably there in my work. I use a lot of animation language. [It] influenced me a lot, you can trace it back for a long time, and you can see that in my work, but it's changing,' she says.[25]

My Domain depicts six young girls who cuddle on an improbably large, ornately patterned sofa, like schoolgirls watching TV. When you look more closely you realise that, along with their 'pets' (Han Yajuan often represents young women accompanied by miniature cows as a symbol of femininity) they also have designer-label weaponry – rifles and revolvers labelled 'Chanel' and 'Gucci'. On whom do they plan to take their revenge, these stiletto-heeled divas with sunglasses perched on their heads, coiffed with flowers and glittery barrettes? Similarly in *Cashmere Mafia* these bejewelled creatures – rhinestones from head to toe – embody the fear, expressed in pop songs and on social media, that women have become aggressive harpies who can no longer be controlled. Han has also painted a Chinese version of *Charlie's Angels* in which two angels point guns while the third has a Chinese warrior's sword and wields a red fan like a weapon of mass seduction.

From 2010 Han began to view her world in increasingly complex ways, exploring the possibilities of multiple perspectives. This has resulted in densely detailed paintings presenting an Escher-like multiplicity of angles and viewpoints, a world of sharply fragmented planes, populated by tiny female figures. They are like anthills, where each member of the community scurries about engaged in frantic activity which seems pointless to the human observer peering down at them.

'I am from the Eighties generation', she says, identifying the strictures and limitations of the Chinese education system as a key influence on her thinking. 'My early works are about individualism and uncertainty. Later, I changed my perspective to stand on a higher point and look down upon a whole complex and contradictory world.' When she began to create these elaborate multi-dimensional compositions, she was at first filled with self-doubt:

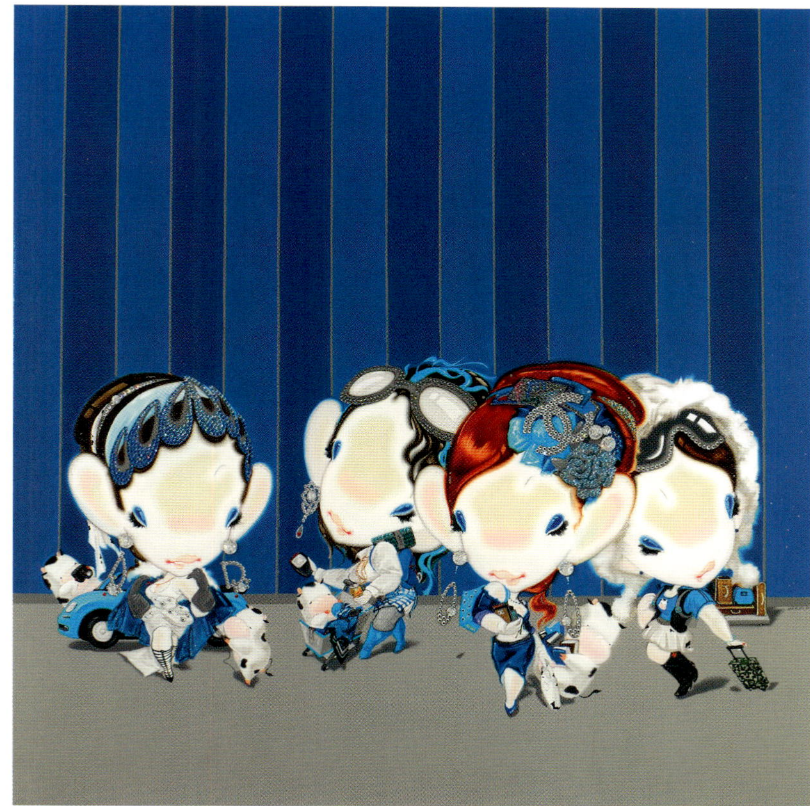

> I am trying to connect doubt and uncertainty with very concrete things. You can see the materialism, you can see the fashion, but this is just recognition. I know why I am doing this. I know what I try to achieve. It is for people who maybe don't have the time to see this, to look at these things.

In works such as *Fashion Ensemble* the tilting planes create a vertiginous sensation of falling. We descend rapidly through a transparent multi-storey building, voyeuristically peering at alien beings engaged in cocktail party gossip, beauty pageants, a photo shoot involving bikinis and Chanel bags, shopping for designer clothes and, at the bottom of the composition, striding from a limousine onto a carpet labelled VIP. At the very top left-hand corner of the painting female figures work at sewing machines and uniformed women unload boxes from a truck labelled 'fashion', an allusion to the complex web of social relationships connecting production and consumption. In Han Yajuan's paintings of privilege and desire the affluence of her 'material girls' is expressed in their purchase of products made by other young girls, in the factories of southern China.

At first glance, Han Yajuan's works may seem as shallow as the characters they depict, but this would be a misjudgement of a thoughtful and intelligent artist. Her parallel universe has much to tell us about our own. Are her female characters victims of their own consumer desire? Or are they the

Han Yajuan
Cashmere Mafia 2009
oil on canvas
150 x 150 cm
image copyright © Han Yajuan

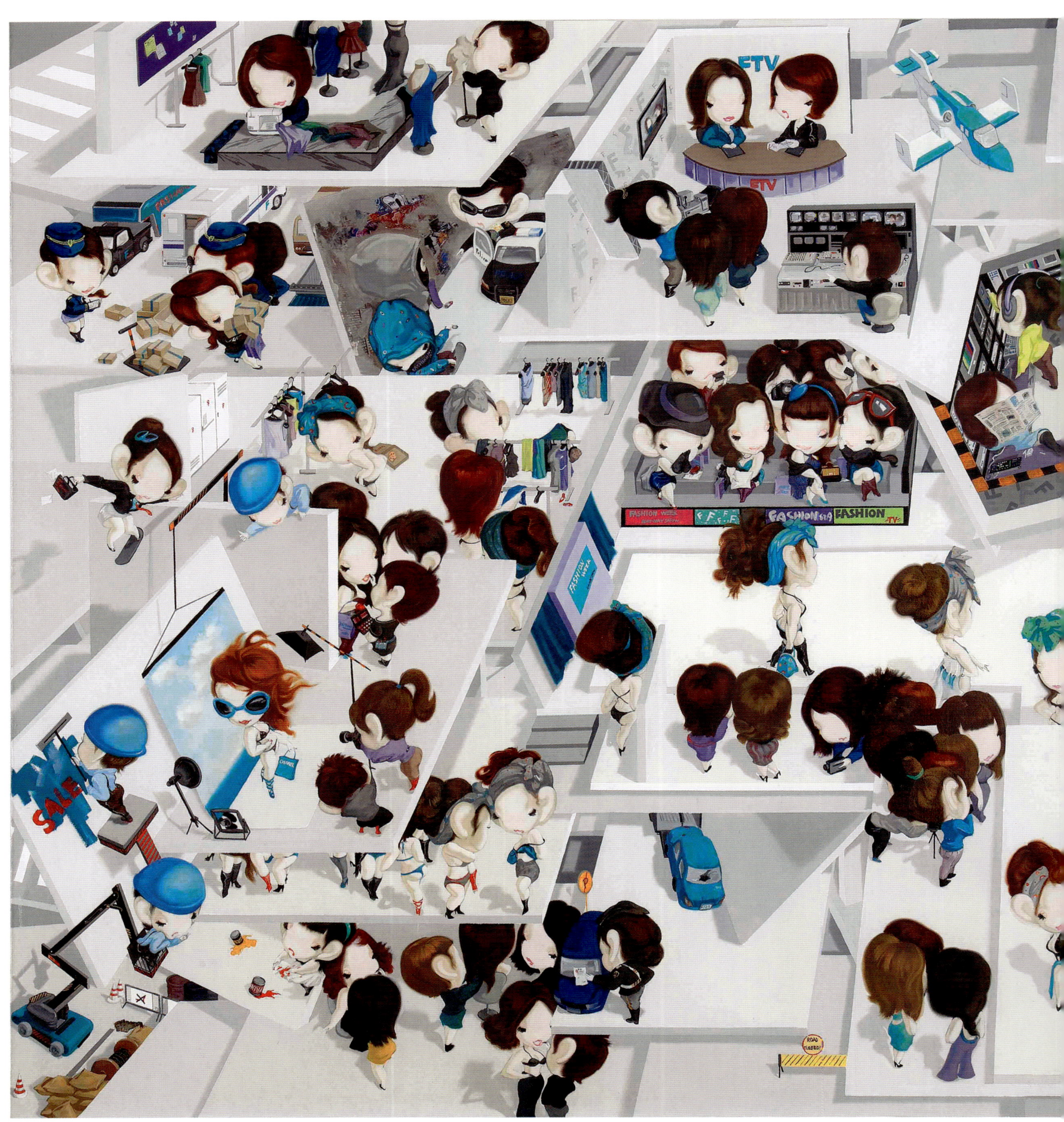

Han Yajuan
Fashion Ensemble 2010
oil on canvas, 180 x 360 cm
image courtesy Klein Sun Gallery, NY and © Han Yajuan

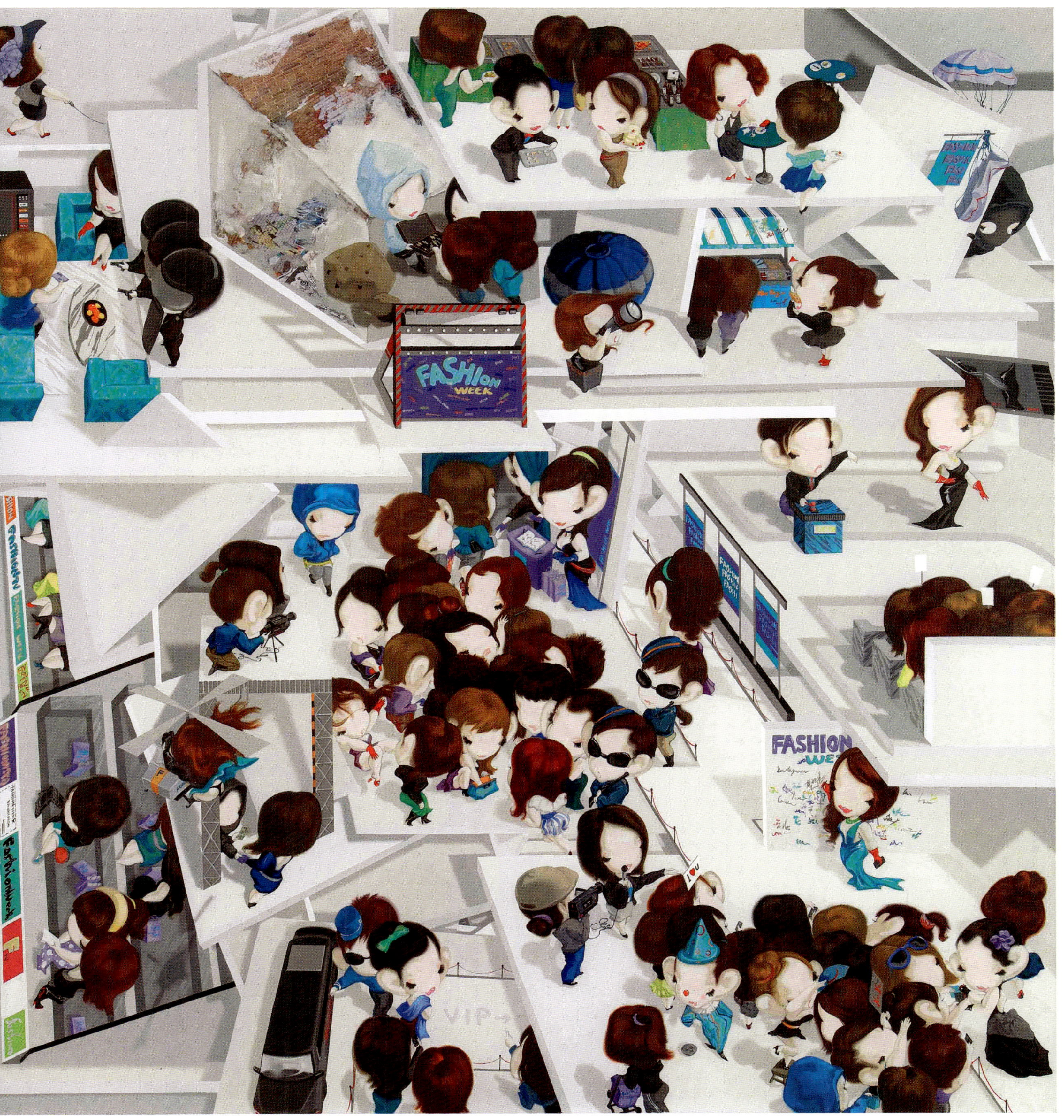
FASHIon WEEK
FASHION
VIP →

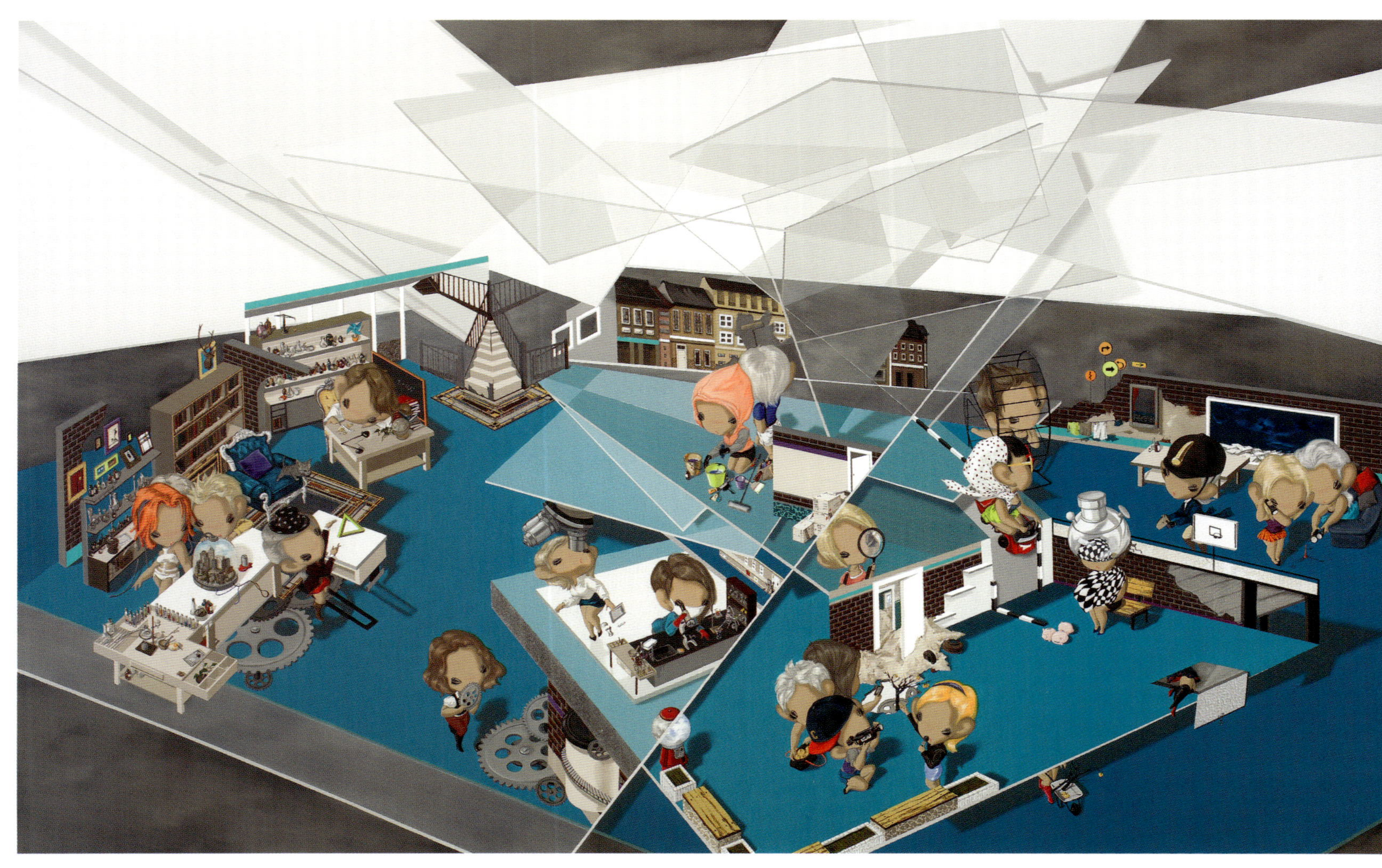

powerful, independent and self-willed creatures of a feminist dream? Celebration, or criticism? The answer, so often the case in China, is equivocal. Han Yajuan's female figures are, in some respects, self-portraits. She is a participant in, as well as an intelligent observer of, the culture in which she lives. Fully aware of the dark side of the glamorous world she depicts – a world of corruption and karaoke bars, mistresses and designer handbags – she is pragmatic: 'From a very primitive perspective it relates to the uncertainties of life – we should pursue the things that make us happy. It's personal. It's about what makes *me* happy. There is definitely a part of me in all those figures... Powerful? No!' she says. 'The most important thing is to be happy about who you are, to be powerful on the inside.' This notion of self-actualisation is the most significant element of her work, the thing that drives Han Yajuan to create and that defines her as a member of a particular generation. She is acutely aware of the fact that her experience is entirely different from the generation that precedes her, and from the one that follows.

Han sees the sharp differences between people born in the three decades after the end of the Cultural Revolution:

> The seventies generation inherited a lot of the traditional culture, they accept what the tradition is. People born in the eighties are struggling to find an identity. It's a time when western culture came more and more into China. They are facing on the one hand the traditional culture and on the other hand the new western ideas. It's a struggle of consciousness, and a contradiction. They like the ideals of the west but have to reconcile that with Chinese tradition. For the nineties generation it's quite different – China was quite open and they were exposed to a lot of new things, it's no longer a struggle for them. My cousins born in the nineties – I can see they are very different from me.

Like many thoughtful, educated Chinese people of her generation, Han looks back a little wistfully to her childhood in a simpler time, yet is very aware of the benefits conferred upon her by the greater freedom and openness of today's society.

Developing sufficient self-confidence to pursue your own path regardless of others' opinions is not easy:

> This might not be a very difficult thing for western people, but for Chinese it's very hard. I notice this from my own life – I have

Han Yajuan
Null Hypothesis 2012
oil on canvas
120 x 200 cm
image copyright © Han Yajuan

Han Yajuan
My Whole World 2008
oil on Canvas
180 x 180 cm
image copyright © Han Yajuan

> many foreign friends who are self-confident and happy with who they are, no matter if they have a poor family, or a horrible background, they are happy and confident. With Chinese friends it is very different. In China there is too much attention about where you come from. When you look at the past, oh my God! Three generations back we were all farmers! And then to care so much about your family, your background – it's incredible how people think like this, caring too much about what other people may think about them rather than about their own individual feelings as a human being on this planet. But I know it's difficult.

Han Yajuan identifies the high-pressure conformity of the Chinese education system as a life experience that impels her to work as she does: 'The education system makes you not free – you don't get the chance or the ability to think, "What do *I* want, as an individual?"' Her multi-dimensional paintings, for which she does no preparatory drawing, could be read as joyless assembly lines, despite the plethora of consumer goods on display. Her tiny figures are miniature cogs in the wheel driving the cycle of production and consumption that makes China rich. *Null Hypothesis* depicts a nightmarish play-room filled with child-like figures dressed in the guise of various adult occupations, playing beside, but not with, each other, an ode to selfishness. There are symbols of science, of industry and of architecture, with a row of faux-European houses like the gated estates of the new rich. There is even a little figure running in a wheel like a pet mouse. It's a bleak vision of a brave new world. The many planes of this self-contained world seem about to shatter like glass, exploding outwards as the fault lines fracture. *Hypothesis Now* likewise represents tiny cartoonish figures engaged in inexplicable activities in a sci-fi space of jagged shards and shiny mirrored reflections, a metaphor for a lost generation seeking an identity through what they can buy.

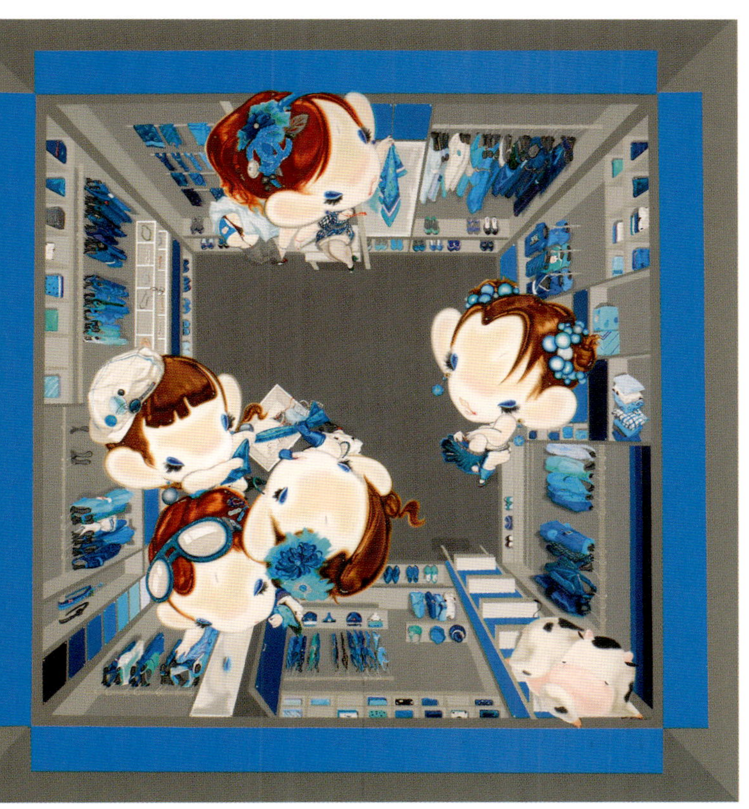

Despite the glitzy Pop appearance of Han's paintings, she is astutely aware of her cultural tradition, alluding to Chinese art history in surprising ways. The *Qingming Scroll* is perhaps the most famous of all traditional Chinese paintings. Originally created by court artists during the Song Dynasty and copied in the Qing, *Along the River During the Qingming Festival* depicts the daily life of people and the landscapes of city and rural areas. Like the frames of a cartoon, unfolding scenes show the lives and activities of all levels of society. In every section of the scroll, tiny people are busy – watching Chinese opera in a theatre, bargaining in the marketplace, fishing on the river banks. Han Yajuan had this scroll in mind when she began to experiment with her complex multi-dimensional series.

From the windows of her apartment and studio, high above a new Beijing suburb, one sees the city and its clogged freeways, railway lines, and high rise apartments laid out below like a toy town, stretching as far as the eye can see. Han Yajuan finds this view 'depressing' but it throws light on the genesis of her compositions of tiny, busy figures in a massively expanding universe of products and interior spaces, represented from an aerial viewpoint. These complex compositions are drawn directly onto the canvas, section by section, a little in the manner of a Renaissance fresco. Han explains:

> I always have a basic structure in my mind. For my earlier work I started with one section, but already I know what other sections or parts I want, and I can see it in my mind. For example, I know I need a person in this part of the painting, I don't know what she looks like or what she is wearing – that comes later as I start to paint it. My compositions make you think they're complex and logical but actually they're illogical!

Whilst fully aware that China is still a patriarchal society, Han Yajuan is inclined to dismiss its effects in her own life. She finds the prejudices expressed about women by an older generation 'hilarious'. Women artists, she says, do experience difficulties that men probably do not:

> They have pressure – but they could also choose not to have pressure! Lots of people ask about women artists. Is that very important? I am a human being, then I am a woman, then I am an artist… It can be difficult for women artists but not just from the art perspective. It is still a male-dominated society and we can't

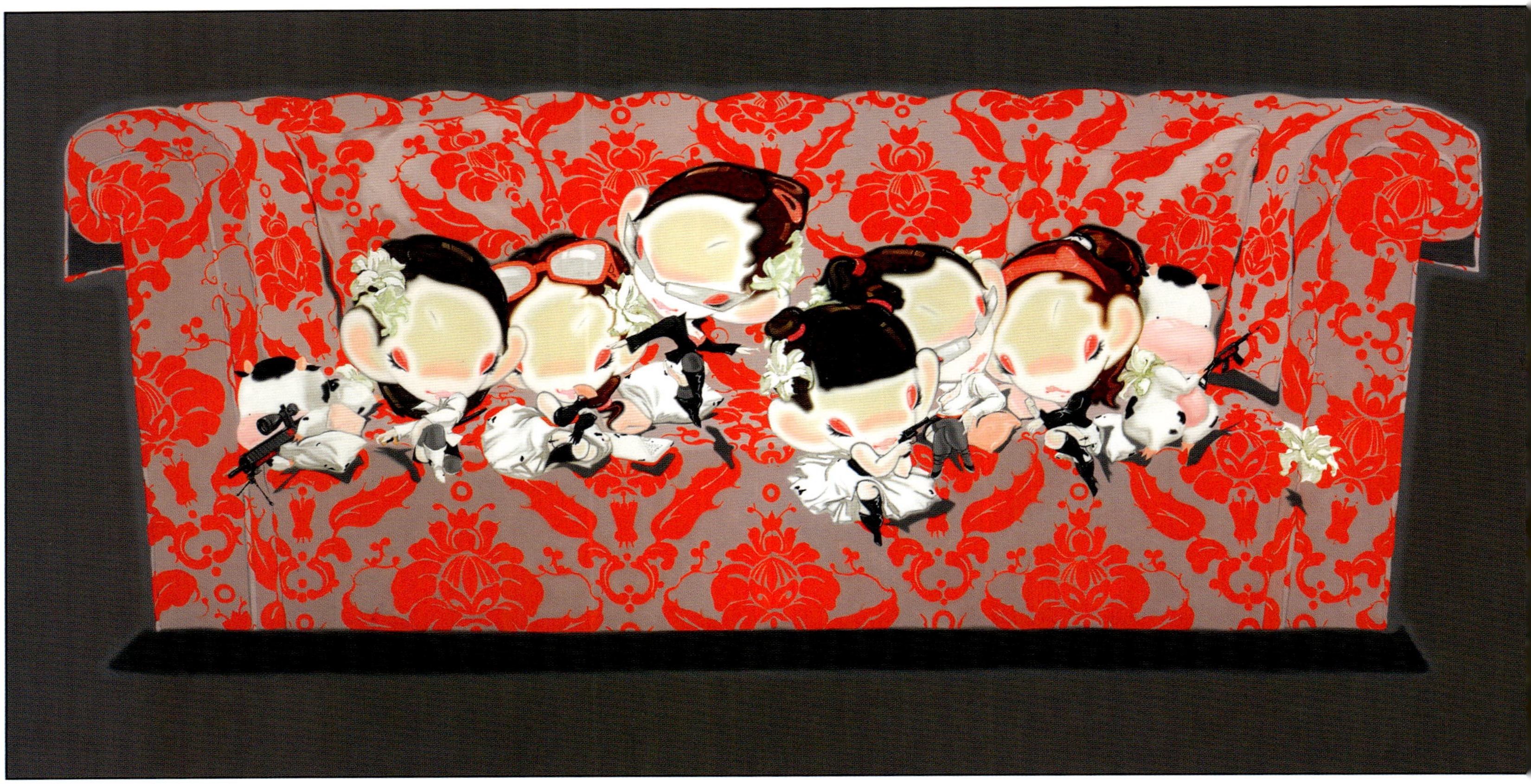

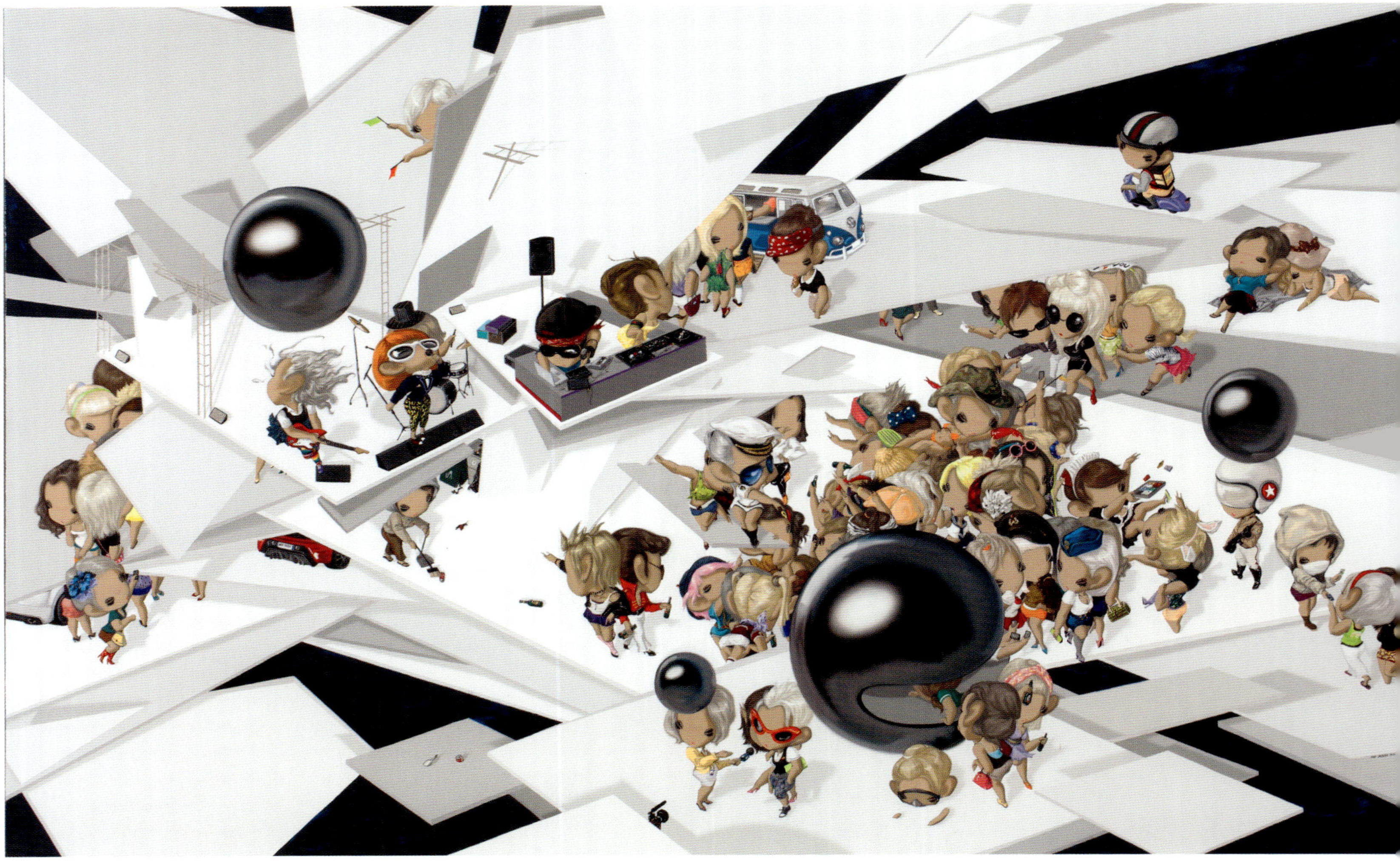

change that. It can also be *not* difficult... as a woman artist you can take advantage of this, and you can have fun.

Han Yajuan is not averse to being interviewed for *Chinese Vogue*, or designing a line of silk scarves printed with her signature 'material girl'.

On round and oval canvases, Han has begun to explore the identity confusion of her own generation, caught between the certainties of a childhood in which equality between social classes, and between genders in a bright revolutionary future were taken for granted, and the very different world in which they entered adulthood. The rapid transition from a collectivist model of social organisation to a dog-eat-dog (in Chinese, '*ren chi ren*' or 'man-eat-man') world of individual ambition has left behind a sense of loss. In these paintings the Young Pioneers in their red scarves and school tracksuits might be either girls or boys, reflecting Han's feeling that she and her peers were not educated about relationships or the roles of men and women. All such expressions of gender and sexuality were hidden from them, resulting in confused and conflicted relationships. Her imagery sometimes refers to recent internet memes or viral '*Weibo*' photographs that appeal to a cynical generation who have come to doubt the universal truths of their youth.

While we talked over strong cups of black coffee – the only coffee I have ever been offered in a Chinese artist's studio – my young translator (who perhaps has a rather more romantic view of art than does a practising artist) suggested that all of Han's work came from her heart. Han Yajuan's denial was swift. 'No!' she said. 'Not from my heart! Everything I create is about my thinking. My work is not from my heart, it's from my mind. And what I hope is that maybe I can provide some little spark of an idea for people who don't have time to see these things.' Her dystopian paradise is revealed In *Perfect Ending*, a densely detailed space of tiny cubicles filled with girls and consumer products – the glistening surfaces of espresso machines, laptops, mobile phones, shoes and handbags. They strike me as extremely sad. A tiny world appears about to implode under its own pressure.

Yu Hong, Xie Qi and Han Yajuan reflect the constantly transforming, contemporary Chinese zeitgeist. Ideas about money, identity, nationhood, relationships and gender shift and turn like shards of coloured glass in a kaleidoscope. Just when you think you have identified a comprehensible pattern it all separates, falling apart to re-assemble in entirely new configurations.

NOTES

1 Clunas, Craig 2009 *Art in China* 2nd edition Oxford University Press (207)
2 Ma Xuedong 2012 'Female Painters of China's Republican Era and the Market for their Works' in *Art Beijing Guide*, vol 40 2012
3 Xu Hung 1993 (transl. Claire Roberts) (ed. Caroline Turner) 'Modern Chinese Art' in *Tradition and Change: Contemporary Art of Asia and the Pacific* University of Queensland Press (118)
4 Wang Keping 1980 quoted by Li Xianting in 'About the Stars Art Exhibition' originally published as 'Guanyu Xingxing Meizhan' in *Meishu (*Art*)* 147 (3) (8–9) Reproduced in Wang, Peggy (ed) 1989 (transl. Donald J. Cohn) *The Stars: Ten Years,* Hong Kong: Hanart 2 and republished in Wu Hung (ed) 2010 *Contemporary Chinese Art: Primary Documents*, MOMA (12)
5 Clunas, Craig, 2009 *Art in China* 2nd edition Oxford University Press (224)
6 Unless otherwise acknowledged all quotes from Yu Hong are from her conversation with the writer in Beijing in April 2014
7 Yu Hong 2011 interviewed by Burris, John for *At Work: 25 Contemporary Chinese artists*, Long River Press
8 Munroe, Alexandra 2011 'Questions for Heaven' in *Yu Hong, Golden Horizon*, catalogue for Shanghai Art Museum, Charta (40)
9 See Chapter 2 for an account of this event
10 Email from Yu Hong to the writer, May 2014
11 ibid.
12 Lu Jie 2011 (transl. Katie Pinke) in *Yu Hong, Golden Horizon* catalogue for Shanghai Art Museum, Charta
13 An interview with the artist, in Jiang Jiehong 2007 *Burden or Legacy: From the Chinese Cultural Revolution to Contemporary Art*, Hong Kong University Press (9)
14 Hao Sheng 2010 'Ten Takes on Chinese Tradition', catalogue essay for *Fresh Ink: Ten Takes on Chinese Tradition,* Museum of Fine Arts Boston (12)
15 Shen Kuiyu and Andrews, Julia F, 2011 'Fresh Ideas, Fresh Ink' in *Yishu* July/August 2011 (84)
16 Yu Hong 2010 'Ladder to the Sky' in *Yu Hong: Golden Sky*, Shanghai Renmin Chubanshe, Shanghai, China (100)
17 Yu Hong 2010 'Reactivating my History: Yu Hong interviewed by Jerome Sans' in *Yu Hong: Golden Sky*, Shanghai Renmin Chubanshe, Shanghai, China
18 Erickson, Britta, 2003 *A Woman's Life: The Art of Yu Hong*, Goedhuis Contemporary, London
19 Email to the writer May 2014
20 Wu Hung (ed) 2010 *Contemporary Chinese Art: Primary Documents*, MOMA (29)
21 Email to the writer, May 2014
22 Unless otherwise acknowledged all quotes from Xie Qi are from her conversation with the writer in Beijing in December 2014
23 Hong Fincher, Leta 2014 *Leftover Women: The Resurgence of Gender Inequality in China*, Zedbooks London presents a discussion of how gender equality is being eroded in a post-socialist China.
24 Sources: *Peoples Daily Online* http://en.people.cn/90001/90778/90860/6991640.html accessed 16 June, World Business on NBC News.com http://www.nbcnews.com/id/30670835/ns/business-world_business/#.VX6q__mqqko accessed 16 June 2015 and McKinsey and Company, various reports www.mckinsey.com
25 Unless otherwise acknowledged all quotes from Han Yajuan are from her conversations with the writer in Beijing in October 2013 and April 2014

Han Yajuan *(top)*
My Domain No. 2 2007
oil on canvas
150 x 300 cm
image copyright © Han Yajuan

Han Yajuan *(bottom)*
Diva Fever Fest 2012
oil on canvas
120 x 200 cm
image courtesy Klein Sun Gallery, NY and © Han Yajuan

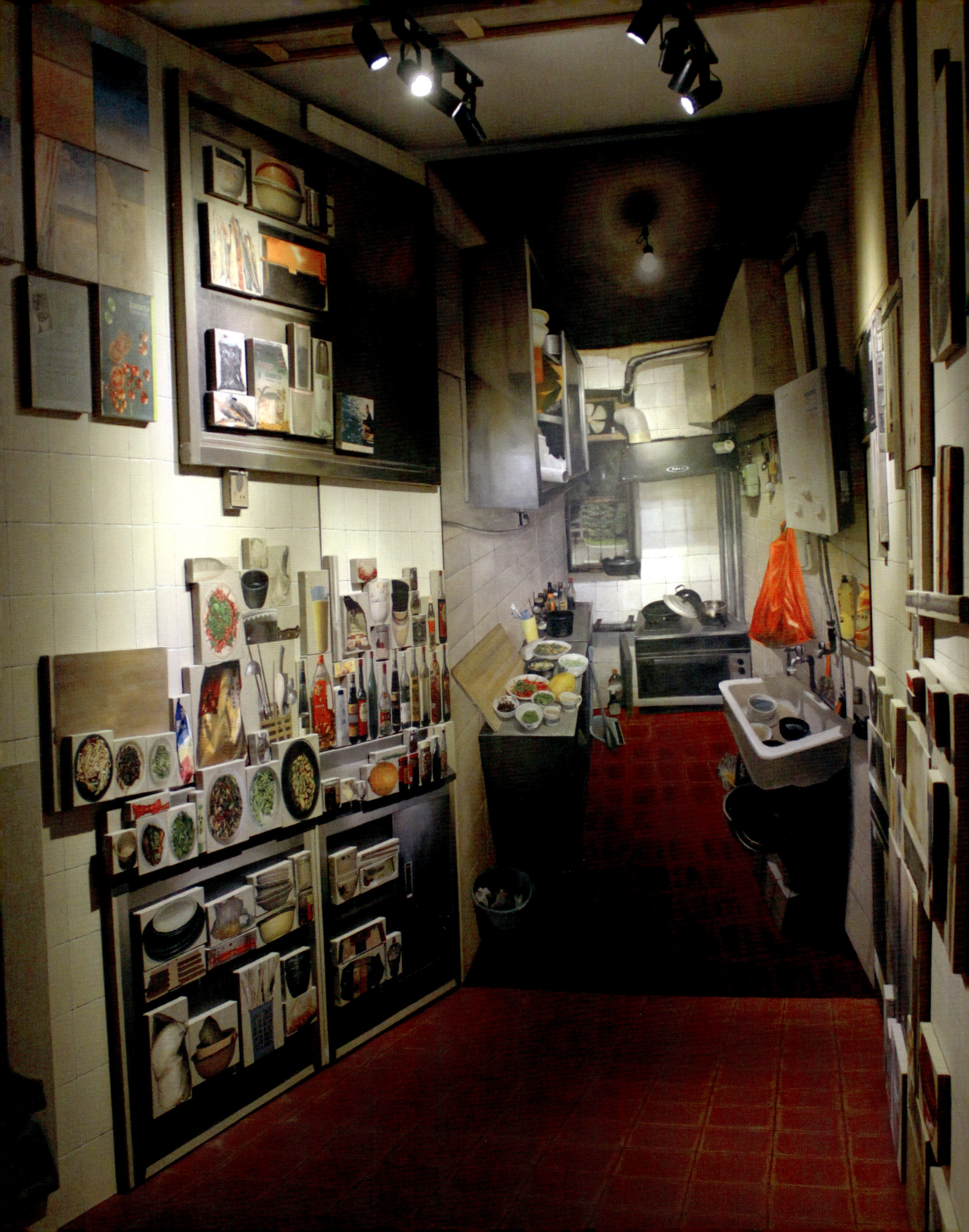

PAST AND PRESENT

Dong Yuan, Wang Zhibo and Huang Jingyuan

The history of 'realist' painting is as complex as anything else in China. From the historical traditions of *gongbi* court painting to Soviet socialist realism, from the 1985 'New Wave' painters to the Pop sensibility which exploded in the 1990s, to the multiplicity of styles today, painting reflects patterns of mutual influence between Europe, America, and China. Historically, realist painting has often been subsumed by the better known tradition of *shui mo*, the ink-on-paper works created by amateur artists of the scholarly literati. However, the continuing influence of both modes of representation are seen in the work of contemporary painters.

The artists in this chapter paint in a manner that is highly realist – even hyper-realist. Dong Yuan reflects on her own and China's past, ruefully examining the rapid transformation of her country, often through a lens of nostalgic reminiscence focused on her grandmother's house. In contrast, Wang Zhibo examines the now. She paints disturbingly dystopian visions of liminal 'non-places', such as hotel lobbies, empty parks, and abandoned public spaces. Huang Jingyuan examines the construction and marketing of culture, specifically critiquing how China presents itself to the world. The practice of each artist can be connected with historical tendencies in both Chinese and western painting. In their works we see elements of the inheritance of Russian and French academic realism, and of an indigenous classical painting style that predated s*han shui* ink painting.

Western forms of realism had been appropriated from the late nineteenth century as signs of modernity – a deliberate departure from a feudal past. To be western was to be for progress and advancement, science and technology. Art historian Francesca Dal Lago explains:

> Travelling to Europe as political envoys... Chinese officials and intellectuals were exposed to the masters of Western oil-painting tradition and confronted with the lack of mimetic functions of Chinese traditional art. Many who travelled during this period mention in their travelogues the experience of viewing Western painting as one of the wonders of the Western world.[1]

As early as 1890 the reformist intellectual and diplomat Xue Fucheng had observed, on discovering the paintings of Raphael, that traditional Chinese paintings were mostly based on the void, but in contrast, 'Western oil painting excels in expressing substance.'[2] The increasing popularity of this *xihua* (western painting) represented a radical departure from tradition. The goal was for Chinese art to be 'as rationalised and modernised as science was.'[3]

At a time when European avant-garde movements were aligning various forms of abstraction and formalism with Utopian socialist ideals, artists in China identified techniques such as perspective, proportion and chiaroscuro as the keys to making Chinese painting 'modern'. Academic realism as taught in France became the standard curriculum of art education across China. 'Realism has been promoted in China as a method of artistic representation for more than a century. During this period it has been employed as the most direct and powerful mode of connecting art to the people,' said the great realist painter Liu Xiaodong.[4]

'If I find any of you painting scholars gazing at waterfalls I shall expel you'

By the 1930s the political winds were shifting. The Chinese Communist Party and the League of Left Wing Artists were advocating a focus on proletarian subjects and 'an art of everyday life.'[5] Mao Zedong's speech to the Yan'an Forum in 1942, when he stressed that art should serve the people, promulgated a particular mode of representation. Soviet socialist realism was henceforth the officially sanctioned style, used in thousands of propaganda posters and paintings glorifying the motherland for the next thirty years. The older Chinese tradition of landscape ink painting was effectively buried. 'Feudal', tainted by the imperial past, by Buddhism and Confucianism, it had no place in the new People's Republic. Famed artist and teacher Feng Zikai told his students, 'If I find any of you painting scholars gazing at waterfalls I shall expel you. You haven't seen them. Don't paint what you don't know.'[6] Critic Wang Chunchen says:

> Realism in China is not entirely an academic issue. Due to the political system of China, it will remain an ideological issue, only with different forms of representation and different degrees of politicization.[7]

Dong Yuan
Kitchen in the Vision 2010
acrylic on canvas (multiple canvases)
installation 280 x 360 x 260 cm
image courtesy the artist and White Rabbit Gallery

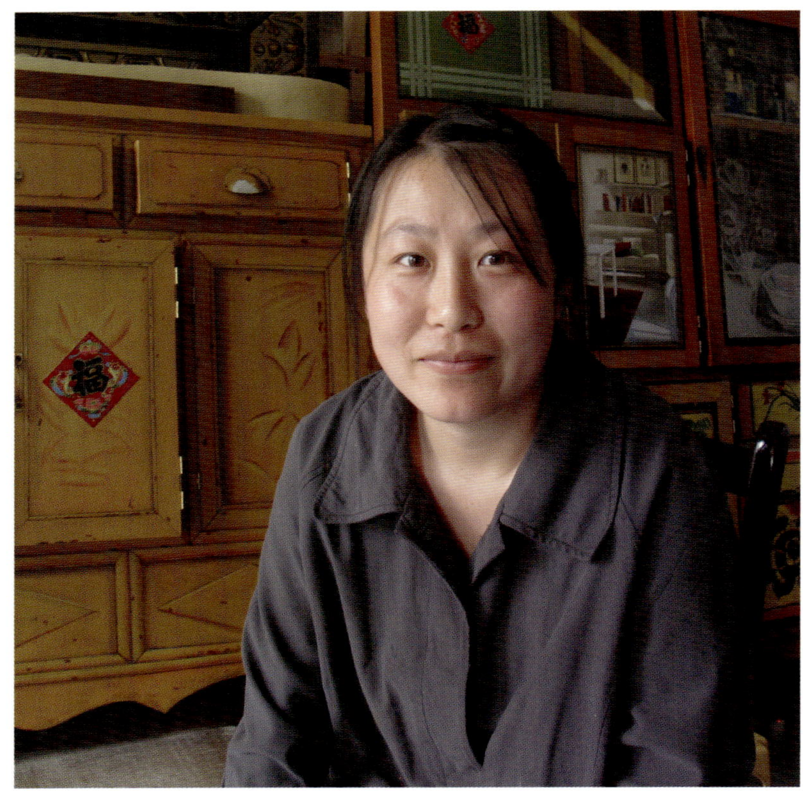

Mao's diktat was formalised in the teaching programs of art academies and fine art work units (*yishu danwei*) after the establishment of the new China. Painters were brought from the Soviet Union to train Chinese artists and art teachers, and Chinese students went to study in Russia and East Germany. Acceptable subjects included workers, farmers and soldiers; dramatic history paintings extolling the Anti-Rightist movement and the Cultural Revolution were popular. 'Realism', in such a context, is clearly unlike its counterpart in western art historical terminology.

There is a much older tradition of realism in China, less well-known in the West than *shui mo* ink-painting or the traditions of the literati. *Gongbi* painting, peaking in the Tang and Song Dynasties, refers to a style which some of its practitioners believe to be the 'true' Chinese painting convention.[8] Representational and narrative, *gongbi* paintings feature detailed and meticulous line drawing rather than a calligraphic mark. Xie He's famous treatise on the art of painting produced in the Six Dynasties period (220–589 AD) emphasised 'fidelity to the object in portraying forms' and 'conformity to kind in applying colours.'[9] The style was eventually overtaken by the more expressive conventions of literati painting, but has continued to exert fascination, with a twenty-first century revival of 'Contemporary *Gongbi*'.

All these threads of realist representation appeared to converge with the new styles that emerged in the 1980s and 1990s. Landscape and figurative painting had been revived after the Cultural Revolution, with artists drawing inspiration from French nineteenth century landscapes and from American painters such as Andrew Wyeth. In reaction to the previous thirty years of ideologically driven paintings of heroic workers and soldiers, epic landscapes featuring single figures became popular.[10] Later, in the 1990s, figures continued to dominate paintings representing the social malaise which followed thirty years of socialist collectivism. Artists such as Zhang Xiaogang, Fang Lijun, Wang Guangyi, and Yue Minjun exemplified a new wave in Chinese art, inspired in part by Western Pop Art and Surrealism, suited to the darkly cynical spirit of the time. The international art market sat up and noticed, and in the popular imagination Chinese contemporary art and realist painting were inextricably linked.

The following conversations reveal how three young artists employ a realist visual language to express responses to their world, and their place within it, in work characterised by the 'substance' that reformist intellectuals such as Xue Fucheng longed for.

DONG YUAN 董媛

Memory and Matter

To visit Dong Yuan you take a long drive from central Beijing, passing new suburbs of shopping malls and apartment complexes, endless construction zones and demolished villages. Past the enormous artist 'village' of Songzhuang, you drive so far that you have entered Hebei Province. 'It's not even Beijing,' my driver muttered as he pulled over to ask directions, at times reversing along an eight-lane highway in order to ask a man carrying vegetables on a bicycle, or a taxi driver. When Dong Yuan realised that I was utterly confused by the identical high-rise apartment buildings in her complex, she came to the entrance to meet me, looking like a red-cheeked, pigtailed girl from a revolutionary propaganda poster, wearing a grey cotton jacket over pyjama pants, accompanied by her dog. Her complete lack of pretentiousness is echoed in her paintings, which celebrate the everyday in all its apparent ordinariness.

Dong Yuan explores the significance of daily life and family relationships, symbolised by domestic spaces and humble possessions, recording all the objects accumulated over a lifetime and referencing the history of still life painting. Past and present collide, as she creates an autobiography with objects. Working on separate small canvases, she develops painted installations, immersive environments, recording her own dramatic journey from a rural childhood that seems, from the distance of adulthood in the smog of Beijing, to have been idyllic.

Born in Shenyang, Liaoning Province in 1984, Dong Yuan moved from her home near the coastal city of Dalian to study

Dong Yuan at home in Beijing, April 2014
photo LG

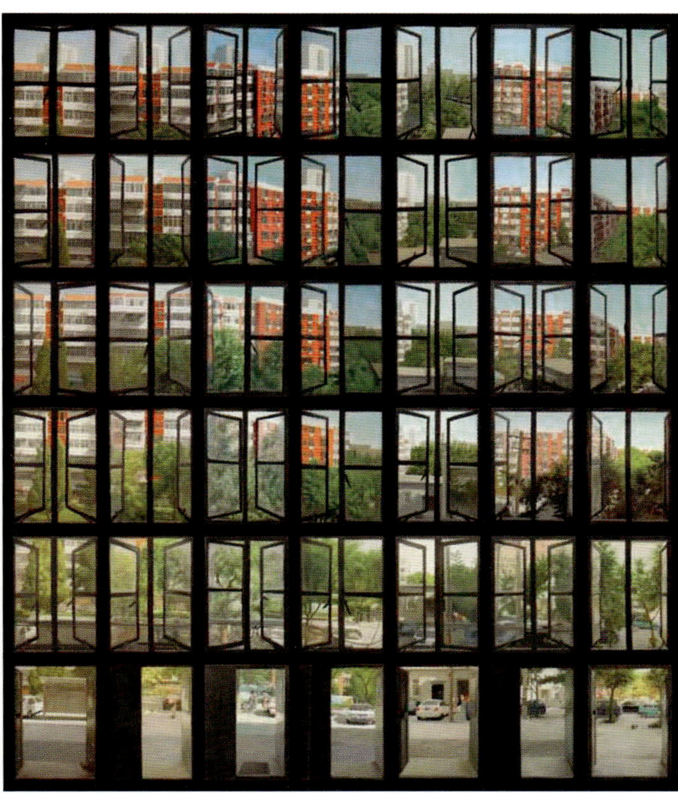

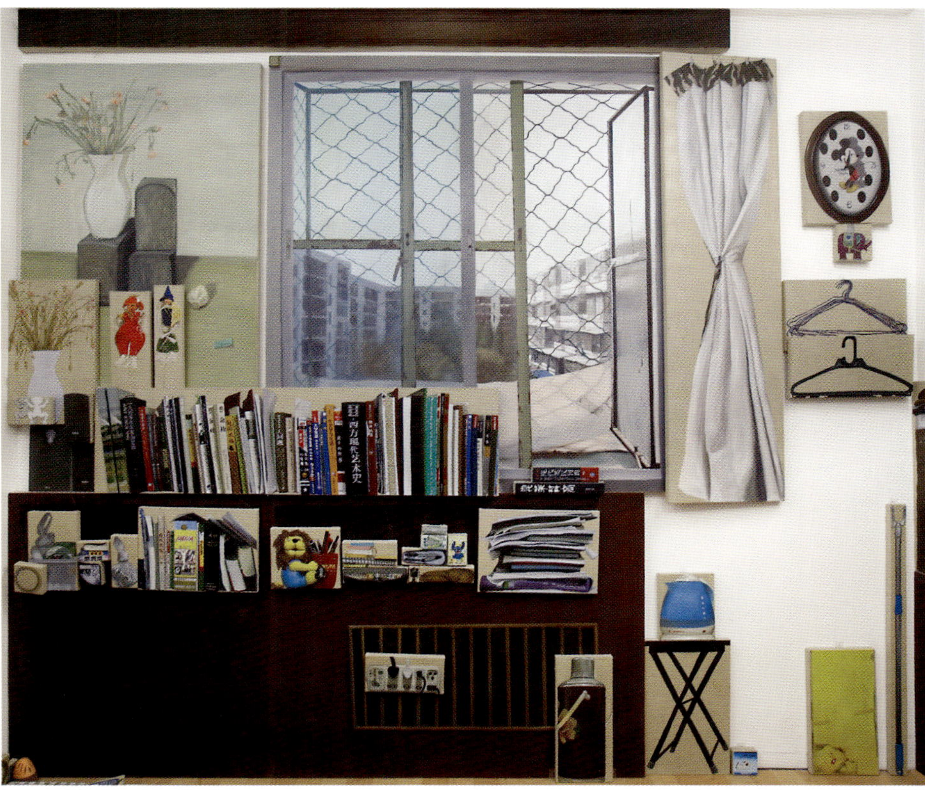

at the Central Academy of Fine Arts in Beijing. In her final years there, inspired by her discovery of Giorgio Morandi, she decided to paint literally everything she owned. As it turned out, by western standards, this was not a lot. Small canvases depict her shoes, hanging jackets, rolled up quilts, books, a rice cooker, a bath towel hanging on the back of a door, a teapot – even a box of tissues. *Home of Paintings* and *Sketch of Family Belongings* record, on fifty-nine and one hundred and eighty six canvases respectively, two apartments in which she lived as a student. With obsessive attention to detail, she renders objects on flat surfaces, sometimes with a Cézanne-inspired aerial perspective, sometimes with a trompe l'oeil illusionism, and then she arranges the canvases in real space.

Later, she painted the view from every stairwell window in her apartment block. The landscape revealed is mundane, especially in comparison with traditional Chinese gardens, or the coastal landscape she remembers from her childhood. She is like an anthropologist of the contemporary city, obsessively documenting her discoveries, posing questions about the nature of modern reality and its rituals. Dong Yuan remembers a different world, measured against her new reality of life in Beijing's suburbs:

> Some of my works have social meanings, like this painting of views through the windows. In the past, in old Chinese houses, especially in the south, people paid a lot of attention to how windows were designed. Normally, through the window you would see a really beautiful view framed. Now, the developers don't even consider whether you can have a view of the outside at all through these little windows. The most terrible thing is that people living in these places don't even see the problem. They don't even look outside. They are too busy and they forget about everything else.[11]

In 2012 Dong Yuan began recreating, in paint, singular object by singular object, the interior of her grandmother's home near Dalian. Like many of her generation, she was largely brought up by her grandparents. Their humble house had been renovated to the point of being unrecognisable and would soon, inevitably, be demolished. Dong Yuan felt strongly that it was her duty and obligation to paint these memories and re-create the place where she had spent the happiest moments of her childhood. Every object and space she recorded was based on a careful plan, checked with other family members who visited her grandmother. She painted each canvas slowly and intensively, one room at a time. Every tiny detail, from the bottle of soy sauce in the kitchen to the potted plants on the windowsill; from her uncle's trousers hanging from a hook on the wall to the cute cartoon stickers that her grandmother hid beneath the approved Mao iconography; from thermos flasks and enamel bowls to stacked flowered quilts: all is exactly as she remembers it from her childhood. Dong Yuan says she is 'fixing it in memory'.

Dong Yuan
Daily Scenes 2009
oil on canvas
42 canvases, each 55 x 40cm
image courtesy the artist and White Rabbit Gallery

Dong Yuan
Sketch of Family Belongings 2008
acrylic on 186 canvases
installation 200 x 360 x 360 cm
image courtesy the artist and White Rabbit Gallery

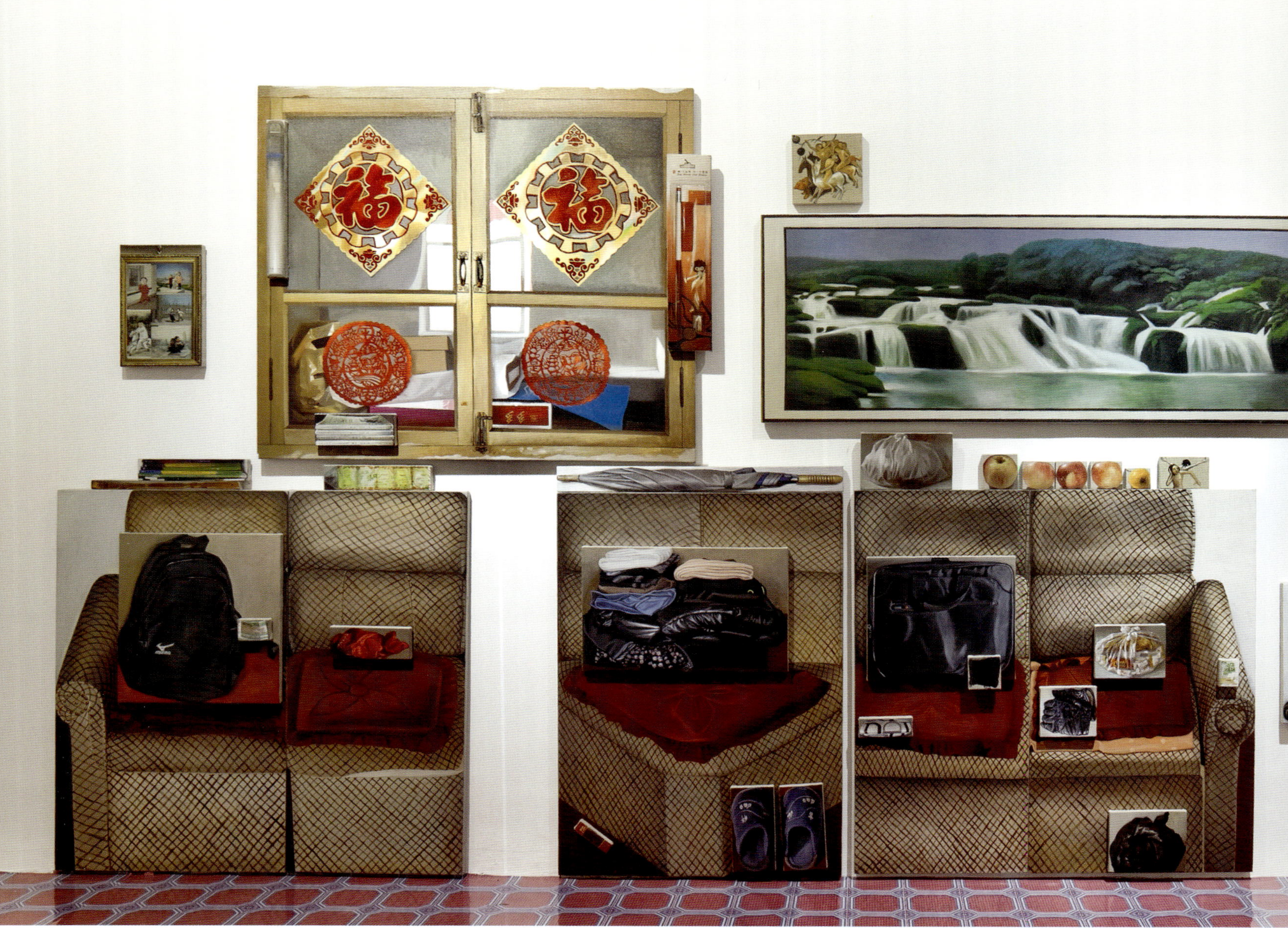

Her rigorous training at the Central Academy of Fine Arts – despite specialisation in Experimental Art, she spent most of her time painting – exposed her to western art history. She immersed herself in the Renaissance. With meticulous realism she records the here and now, a taxonomic process of ordering her world, aiming for the same sharp focus on every detail as a Northern Renaissance master. When all else in life appears temporary and uncertain, her solidly modelled, convincingly rendered forms are a way of keeping chaos at bay.

Installations such as *Grandma's House and Bosch's Garden* are like visual poems honouring the unsung domestic labour of women. They memorialise childhood for her generation, in the way that Cultural Revolution imagery functioned as bittersweet nostalgia for the previous generation. In a similar manner, but without the satirical edge, her work responds to the dramatic pace of change in China. Dong Yuan suspected that non-Chinese people, unfamiliar with her specific cultural references, would be unable to understand her work. She was surprised when I told her some of her paintings had almost brought me to tears, reminding me of the chaotic interiors of my mother's kitchen cupboards, still filled with the utensils, plates and dishes of my 1960s childhood long after she had grown old and forgetful.

Dong Yuan has recorded for posterity the evocative objects of a very particular time and place. These paintings are an elegy to her grandmother, but also to her own younger self:

Dong Yuan
Grandma's House and Bosch's Garden 2013
installation view
dimensions variable
image courtesy the artist

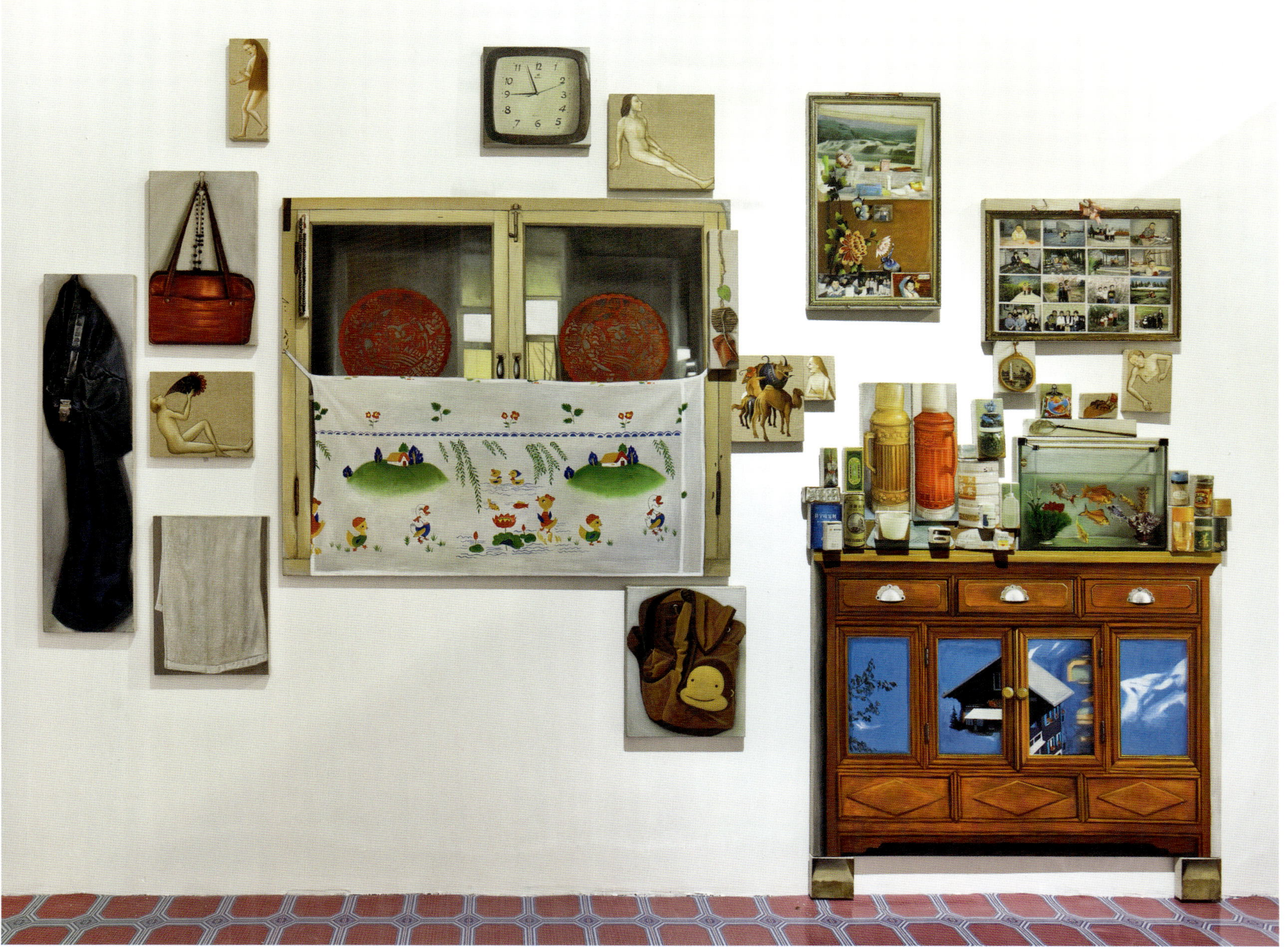

> Grandma's house has four rooms, which are separated into old Uncle's room, the outside, Grandma's room and the back room. Until now it has been the house I liked the most... Every day I could see a busy Grandma... she always tidies the room so it is incredibly clean and pristine. Grandma is so humble, warm-hearted and lovely... Once I arrived at her house I would feel comfort and be at peace.[12]

On my first visit to Dong Yuan's bare apartment in 2012, I found finished and unfinished canvases stacked against every wall. Among them were images of pots and pans, piles of newspapers, an umbrella leaning in a corner – even, on separate canvases, the individual drops of water it left on the floor – bottles and jars in kitchen cupboards, an old radio. By that stage she had completed more than four hundred paintings for an astonishing hyper-real installation. It had taken twelve months and there were still two rooms full of possessions to go. The re-creation of the house in which she spent so much time as a child is a triumphant feat of trompe l'oeil, immensely touching. For the exhibition of this work in Beijing, Dong Yuan wrote:

> For me, Grandma's home gave me a strong feeling of security... it was my 'haven'... But in recent years my Grandma's home is going to be demolished and this kind of stability has quickly disappeared – it's hard to know how many things have to disappear before people find their hearts settled down.[13]

Now the sea is polluted, the beautiful rural roads lined by

Dong Yuan
Grandma's House and Bosch's Garden 2013
installation view
dimensions variable
image courtesy the artist

Dong Yuan *(pages 124–25)*
Kitchen in the Vision (details) 2010
acrylic on multiple canvases
dimensions variable
images courtesy the artist and White Rabbit Gallery

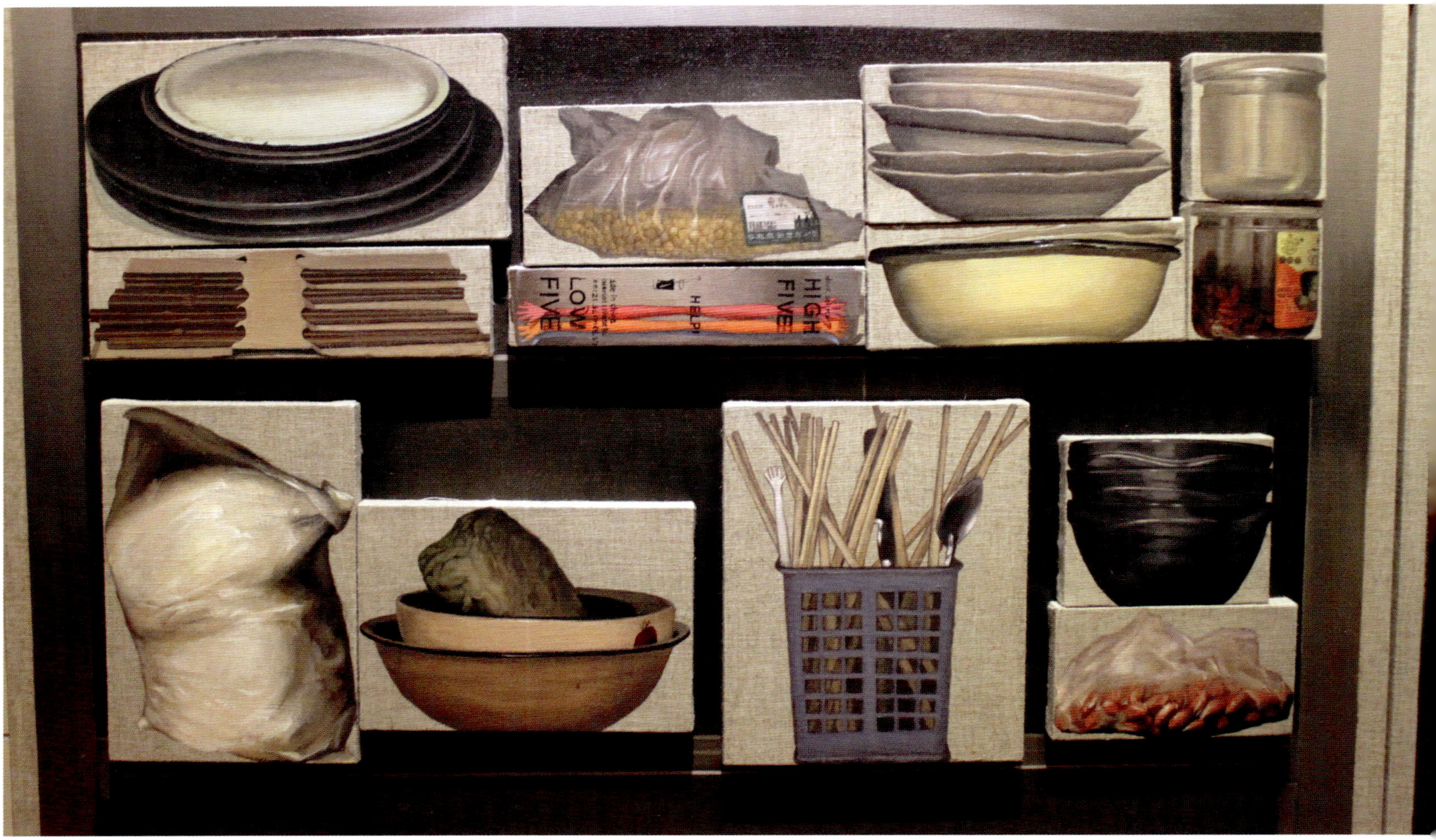

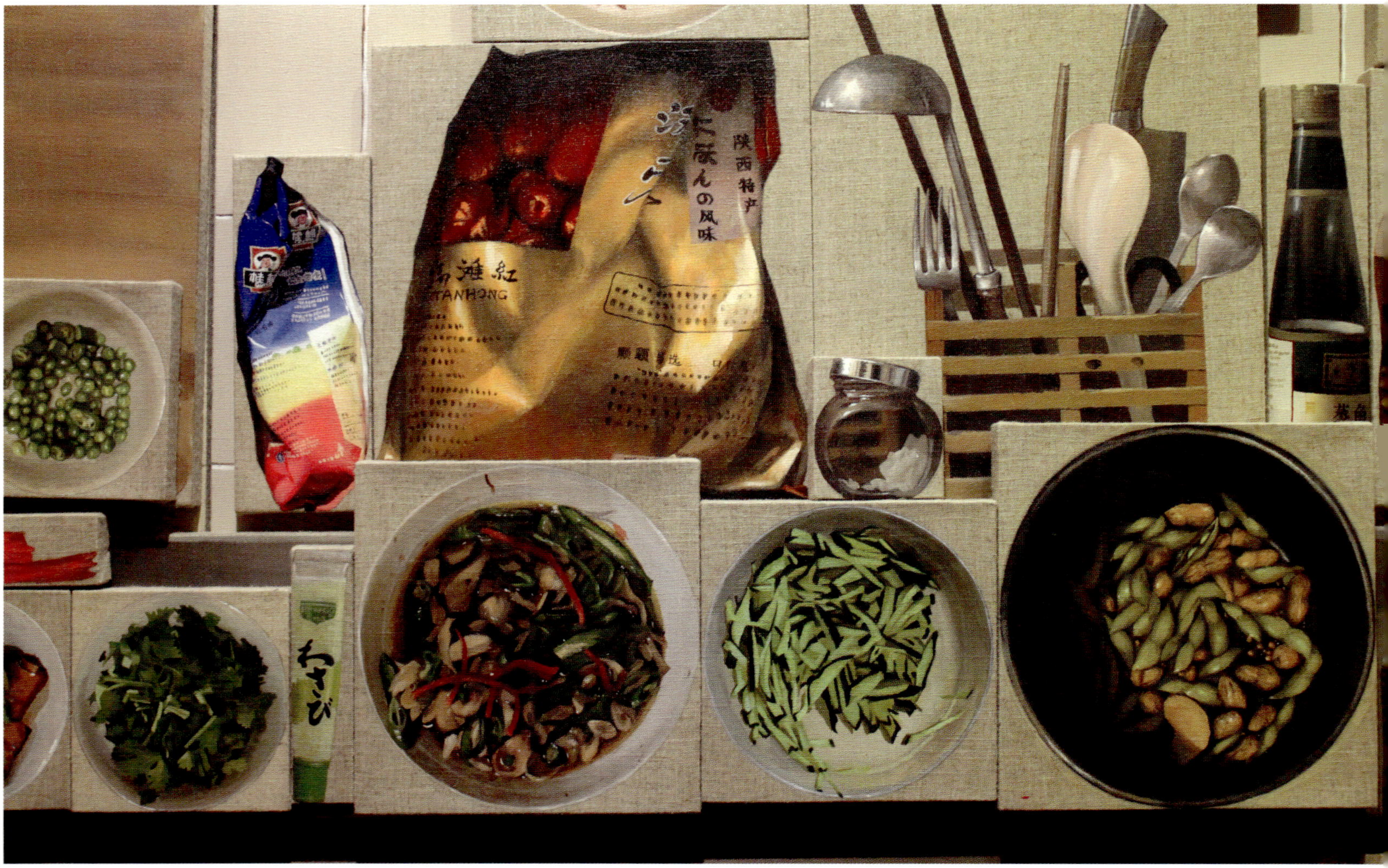

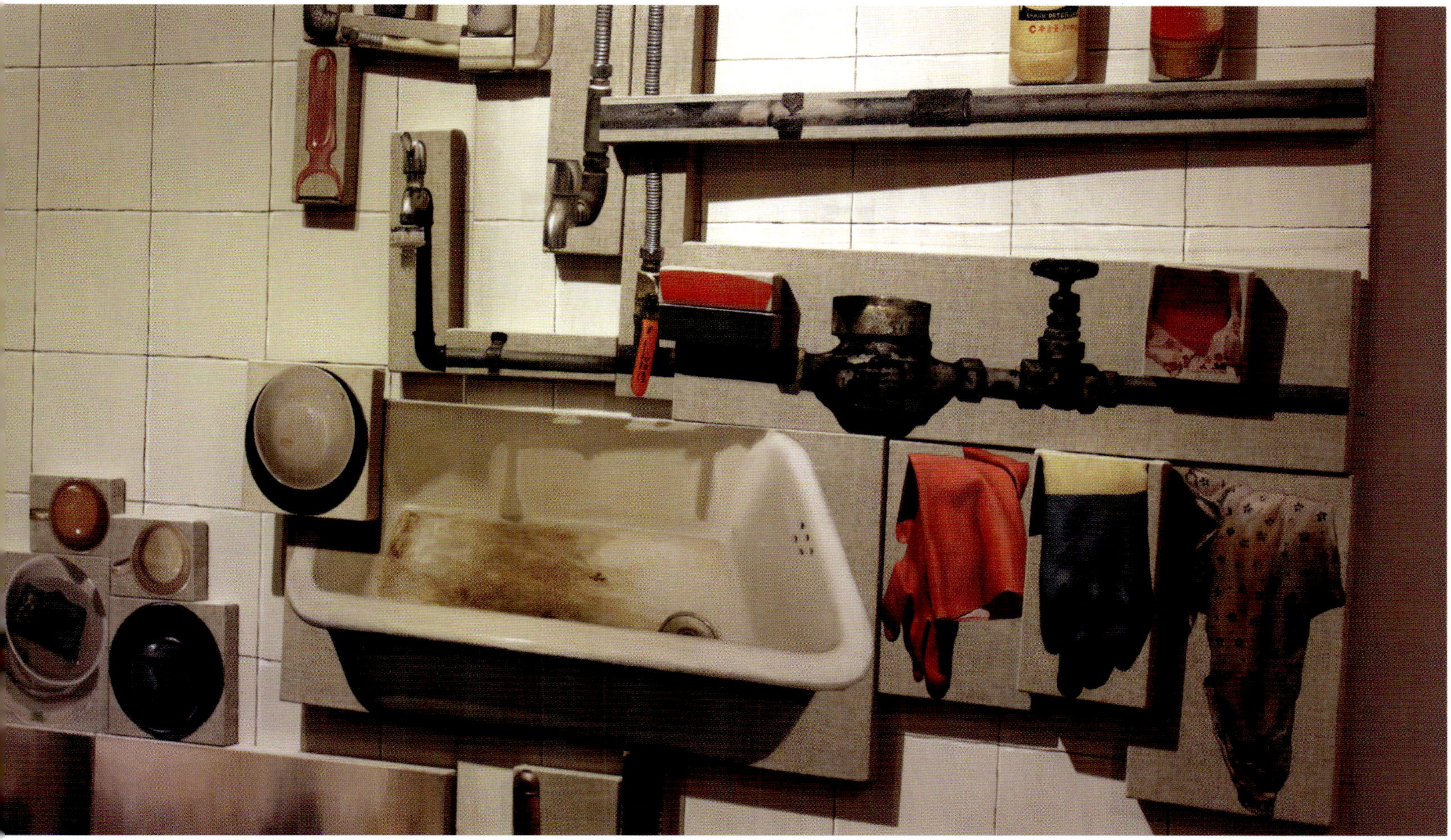

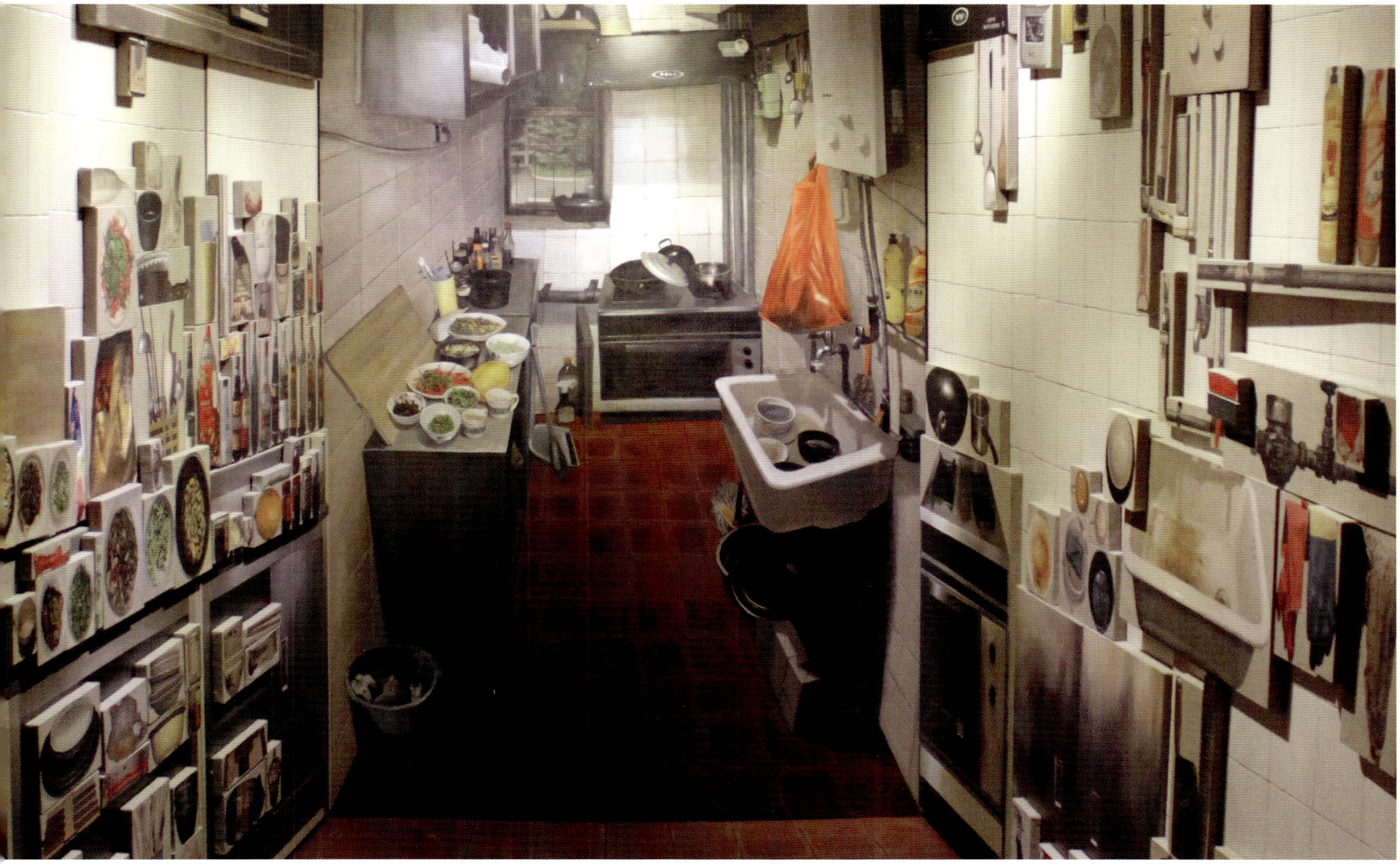

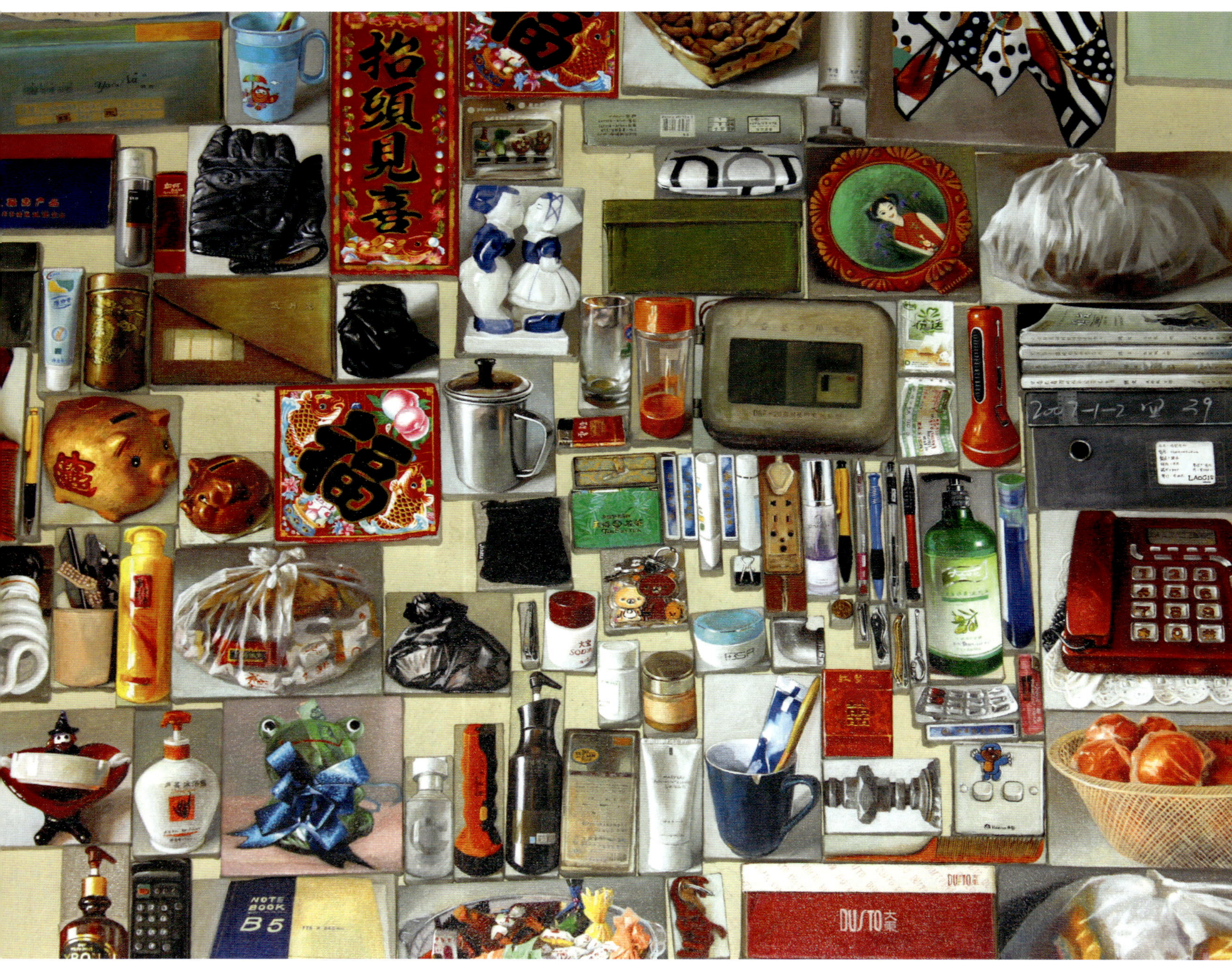

trees are all gone, even the groundwater is contaminated. It has become much too painful to return. Instead, she paints her memories of how it was.

Once finished, there were eight hundred and fifty-five canvases. Dong Yuan had created a surreal combination of the fantasy world imagined by Hieronymus Bosch and the rural world of a Chinese peasant. In thinking of the vanished Eden of her childhood, she referred to Bosch's Garden of Earthly Delights. The gods of happiness, prosperity and longevity were juxtaposed in her Grandma's home with Mao and calendars featuring TV stars. Furniture, teacups, textiles and traditional New Year hanging scrolls intermingle in a glorious jumble. Her paintings explore slippages between illusion and reality, not unlike the medieval painter of angels and demons to whom she had turned for inspiration.

Like Gao Rong's stitched fabric sculptures, Dong Yuan's reflection on the journey from rural village to Beijing is a memorial to tradition and family, a meditation on the transformation of modern China. Apart from her favourite medieval and Renaissance artists, Duchamp is one of the few modern western artists to whom she constantly returns. Her painstaking representations of the contents of her Grandma's cupboards are like a contemporary Chinese version of Duchamp's *Boîte-en-valise*, an exhibition of his life's work in a suitcase.[14]

Dong Yuan
Grandma's House and Bosch's Garden (details) 2013
oil on canvas (multiple canvases)
dimensions variable
image courtesy the artist

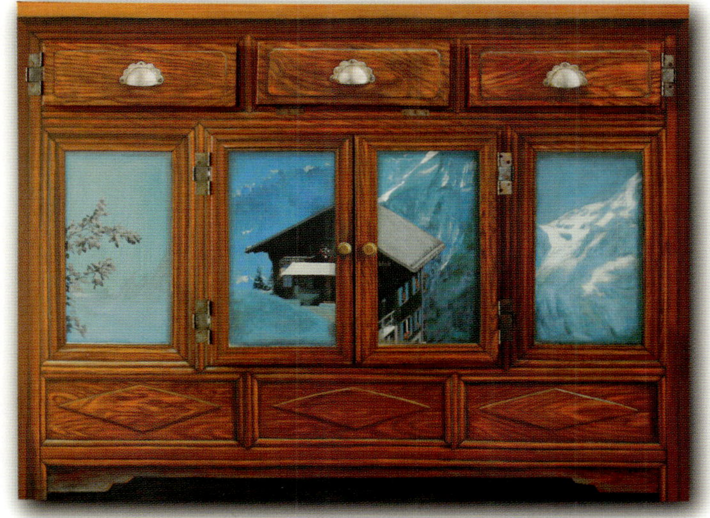

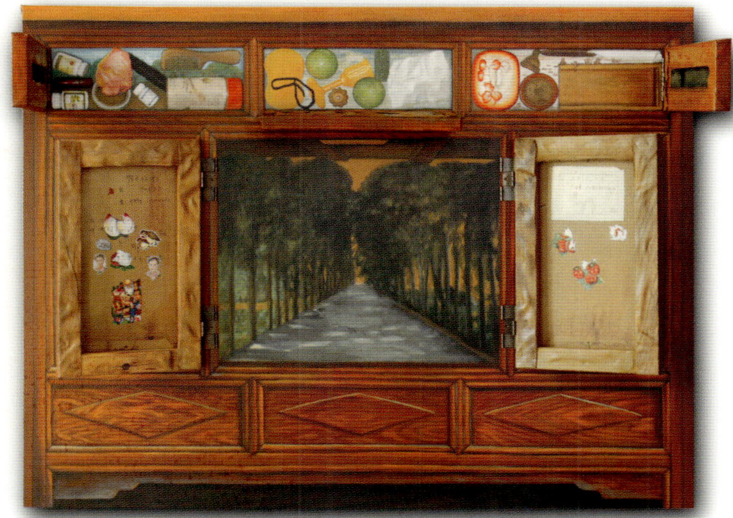

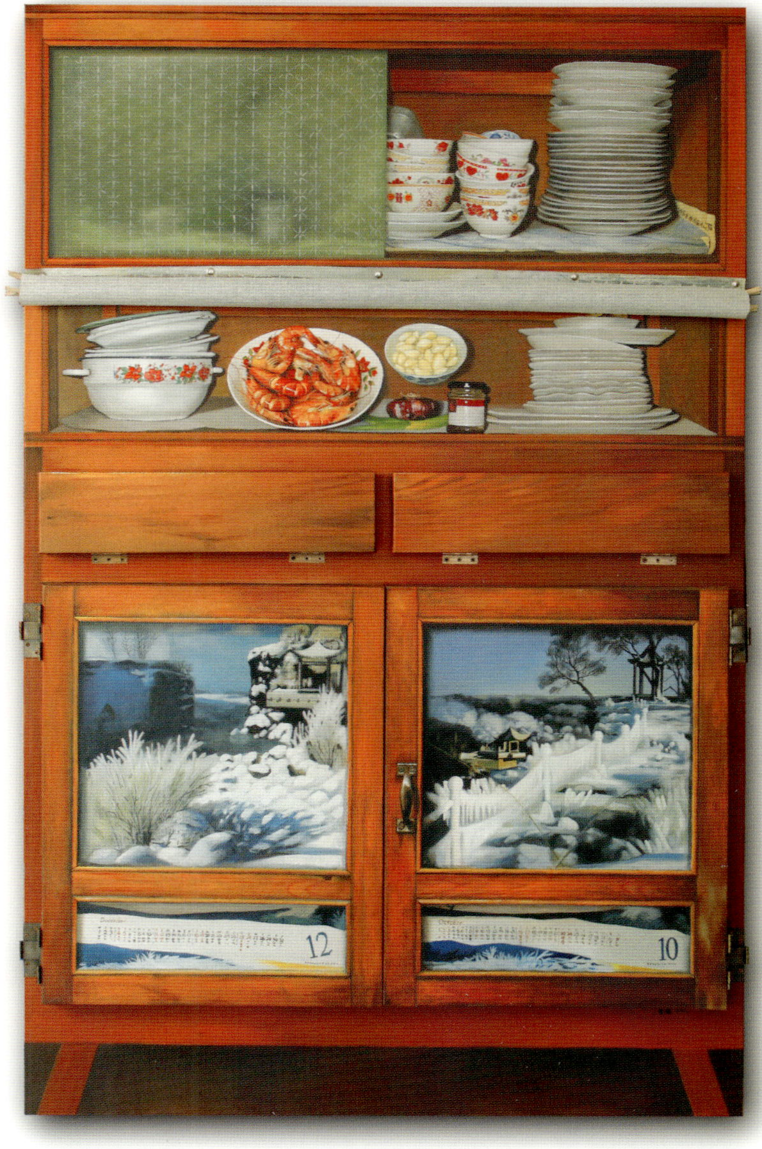

In 2014 Dong Yuan embarked on new three-dimensional approaches to painting, continuing to focus on aspects of her grandmother, Jin Lihua, whom she describes as 'an exquisite person' – always cooking, cleaning and maintaining the traditions of the important festivals that punctuate the year, providing rhythm and comforting ritual. These paintings depict the cupboards, drawers and cabinets in her grandma's home. Multiple canvases are attached to each other, creating complex, intricate 'cabinets of curiosity' with hinged doors that open to reveal their secrets. Inside are painted stacked porcelain noodle bowls, enamel drinking mugs, calendars, a lost roll of sticky-tape and stacked clothing. But there are also tiny landscapes, remembered fields of flowers, fruit trees, flocks of geese, and rooms within rooms. She explains: 'Once I was in my Grandma's house, the things I lacked would be mended… she enabled me to understand what a family was and what a happy home would be like.'[15]

There is sadness lurking beneath the sweetness of these memories as Dong Yuan reflects on her family. She cannot bear to return to the village, to witness the devastating effects of pollution and environmental destruction. At once personal and universal, her work records a way of life which has turned out to be ephemeral.

Dong Yuan
Grandmother's Cabinet No. 3 2014
(shown closed and open)
acrylic on canvas, 90 x 120 cm
images courtesy the artist

Dong Yuan
Grandmother's Cabinet No. 6 2014
(shown partly open)
acrylic on canvas, 156 x 100 cm
image courtesy the artist

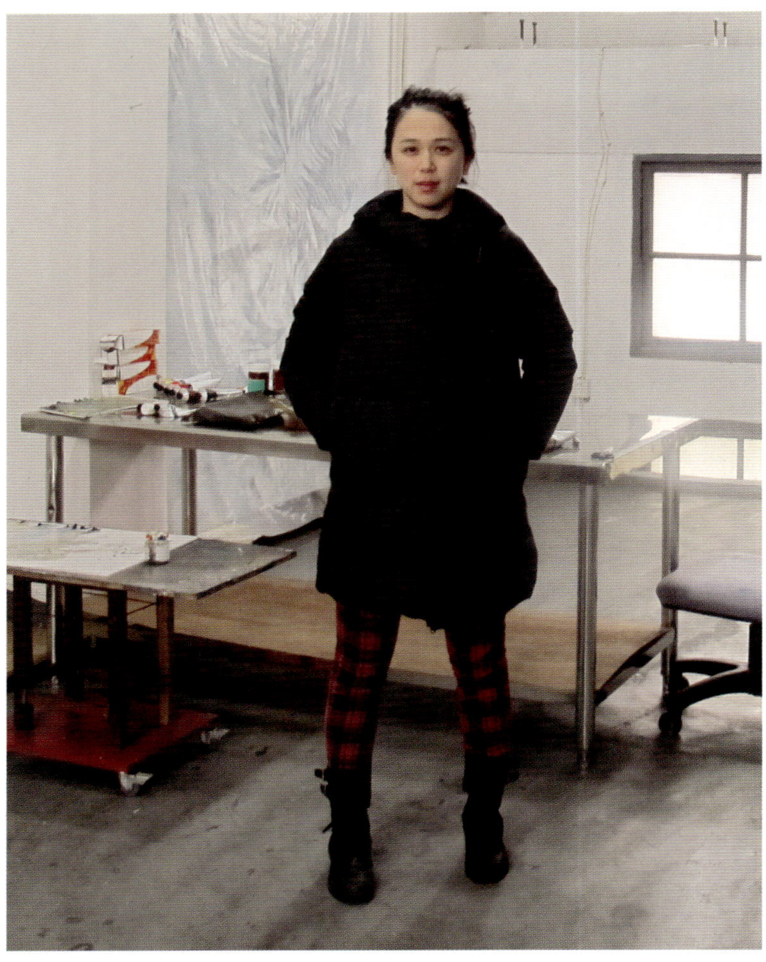

WANG ZHIBO 王之博

Dystopian Visions

Hangzhou-based painter Wang Zhibo draws her inspiration from Chinese and western classical renditions of the sublime, but with a sardonic edge, conveying a disturbing vision of modern China. She creates a world of murky light so ambiguous that one cannot tell if it is day or night, interior or exterior. Unpeopled vistas evoke the grandiose hotel lobbies and shopping-mall interiors of a Chinese metropolis. Constructed with alarming speed by speculative developers, they are often utterly deserted – ghost cities like de Chirico's Turin or Jeffrey Smart's Italian suburbs. *Untitled (Festival)* is far from festive: a rusted metal arch leads to desolate 'scholar rocks' and broken columns; an ambiguous and abandoned place. *Garden* presents a melancholy view of dying potted plants set on rocks in an artificial pond. Wang's paintings represent the landscape within which most city dwellers now live – an international language of the built environment that replaces the idiosyncratic, messy and authentic with manicured, artificial blandness.

Born in 1981 in Wenzhou, Zhejiang Province, Wang Zhibo studied painting at the China Academy of Art in Hangzhou, where she was influenced by significant alumni such as Yang Fudong. Perhaps not coincidentally, Wenzhou was the origin of Chinese landscape poetry and the home of the Song Dynasty 'River and Lake' poets.[16] Their works are a lyrical response to the beautiful landscapes of southern China, seen also in Wang Zhibo's paintings. A line from a poem by Zhao Shixiu conveys the same melancholy ambience:

> The land is quiet, soft is the sound of the fountain
> The climate is cold, red is the setting sun.[17]

Unlike the scholarly poets and painters of the past, however, who glorified the natural world, Wang Zhibo applies her accomplished painterly technique to represent the new landscapes of modern China, its parks, gardens and public spaces. I had travelled to Hangzhou to meet Wang Zhibo in her studio, allowing time to walk around the famed West Lake beforehand. A misty walk through a beautiful – and artificially manicured – vista of water and willow trees provided a fitting introduction to her work.

Wang Zhibo makes deliberate historical references, she says, to reveal the garden as a theme, a concept, found 'in text, in painting, as well as in reality. While the composition of the paintings is influenced by medieval European artworks with an unlimited depth of field and strange perspectives, the garden is also a depiction of a traditional Chinese garden with its awkward humour and a hint of sadness.'[18] Designed as a microcosm of the universe – earth, water, wood and foliage carefully placed in an idealised mirror image of the real world – the Chinese garden traditionally provided repose and aesthetic contemplation for the scholar. Wang Zhibo's tired landscapes of drooping plants, fake rocks, and shallow ponds reveal, rather, a sad simulacrum. The awkwardly placed pots with their stunted shrubs, and the suggestion of drains and grates in the background, represent a slightly comic re-interpretation of the classical ideal. With great control of a subtle palette, she makes us see aspects of the urban world that might otherwise go unnoticed. Adding to their strangeness, her landscapes often include incongruous tropical palm trees, fences, balustrades and empty guardhouses. This is a constructed world. So, too, of course, were the gardens designed by the literati, with their emphasis on vistas seen through arches, latticed pavilions and moon windows, yet Wang Zhibo's twenty-first century landscapes show a world transformed by money and greed.

Expertly blending eastern and western references, Wang Zhibo's landscapes acknowledge that this globalised world is the one that we all now inhabit. The Greek *Discus Thrower* and other allusions to classical statuary appear in *Bases*, silhouetted against dark wintry trees, dry fountains and empty flower beds. In each canvas there are dense, layered areas contrasting with

Wang Zhibo in her Hangzhou studio, December 2014
photo LG

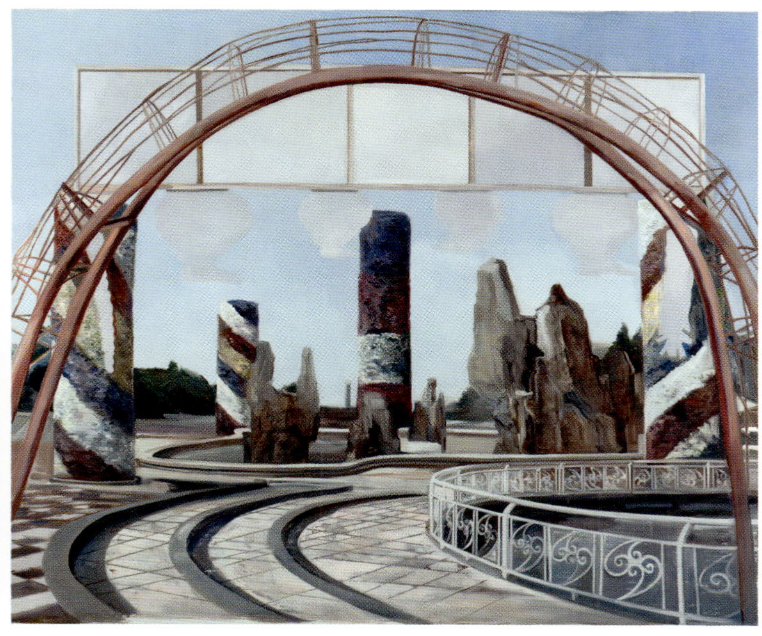

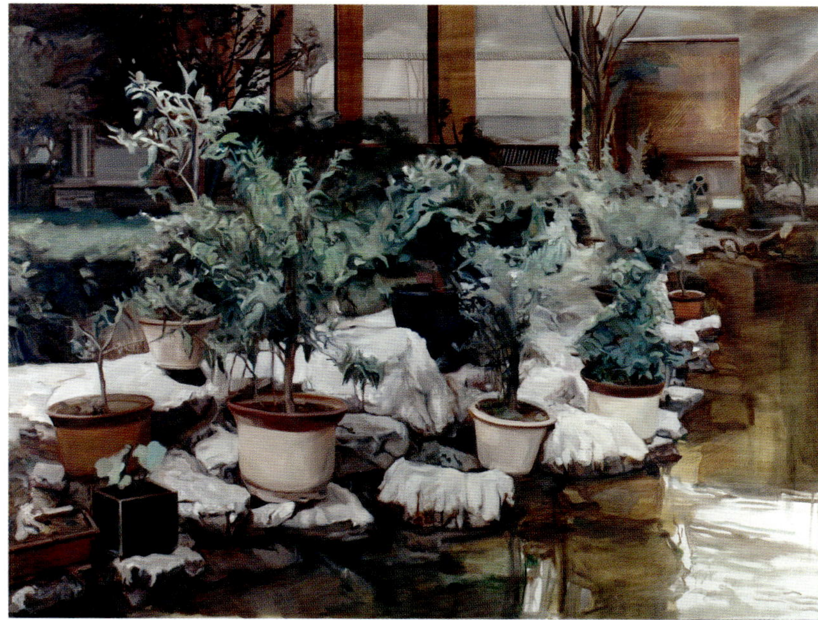

other passages of loose gestural brush marks. Underpinning everything is close observation and superb draughtsmanship. In her paintings of the small guardhouses – like pavilions or tiny temples – at the entries to the gated estates of the newly rich, the tensions between the ideology of the collectivist past and the aspirational present are inescapable. The artist is interested in these juxtapositions. In a characteristic art historical allusion, she paints invented gardens around the guardhouses inspired by the landscapes of Botticelli.

Wang Zhibo became an artist, much to the consternation of her parents, almost by accident:

> When I was young my parents saw that I was very talented. But actually it's a real coincidence that I attended an art class for kids. I learned both Chinese and Western style painting there – even calligraphy. At first I had thought that I wanted to be a writer. But later, when I started learning art, I found it was a better medium for expressing my ideas. And I decided I wanted to be an artist.[19]

Her talent was recognised when she was admitted to the specialist art high school affiliated to the famous art academy in Hangzhou. Like the high school attached to the Central Academy of Fine Arts in Beijing, it is extremely competitive, attracting hopeful students and their parents from all over China. Basic art training is completed at high school, where the curriculum focuses on drawing and mastering the techniques of different painting methods. Wang says, 'It's like playing the piano, and having to practise scales on a daily basis. It's very monotonous. We did figure drawing, still life drawing, perspective and finally a combination of all these things.'

Her parents continued to be anxious: 'My parents are very ordinary Chinese parents. Like any normal parents, they think art is a very unstable profession. They thought I should become a teacher or should have taken a job in a government office.' Wang laughed ruefully. 'So, [at first] they were not very supportive, but they thought I was good at it, so I should do it. And now they are used to it!' Compounding their anxiety, Wang married another painter, Yuan Yuan. In a city where the art scene, unlike Beijing's, is quite small, the two form a supportive alliance, working on different levels of their large studio building, and looking after their small daughter.

Wang Zhibo's paintings are filled with subtle references to works by a range of artists, including Piero della Francesca and Masaccio. She loves their work because of the structure and composition of the paintings, she explains, running across the studio to find a book filled with reproductions of Masaccio's frescoes. She is lost in admiration of the pellucid colour and how the figures, architecture and landscape form a unified whole:

> Masaccio is the painter I admire the most. It's the simplicity of technique. The colours. Some artists focus mostly on their skills, and viewers will admire them for that. But if you can get your idea expressed in a really simple way it's better.

Warhol and Duchamp were the artists who most influenced her as a student and a young painter. 'Because contemporary art began after Duchamp,' she says. 'He is someone from whom I can learn all the time. After a period of time I always go back to him and I learn something new from him. The concepts and ideas are more important than the methods or techniques.'

Wang Zhibo
Untitled (Festival) 2012
oil on canvas, 137 x 180 cm
image courtesy the artist and
Edouard Malingue Gallery

Wang Zhibo
Garden 2013
oil on linen, 150 x 200 cm
image courtesy the artist and
Edouard Malingue Gallery

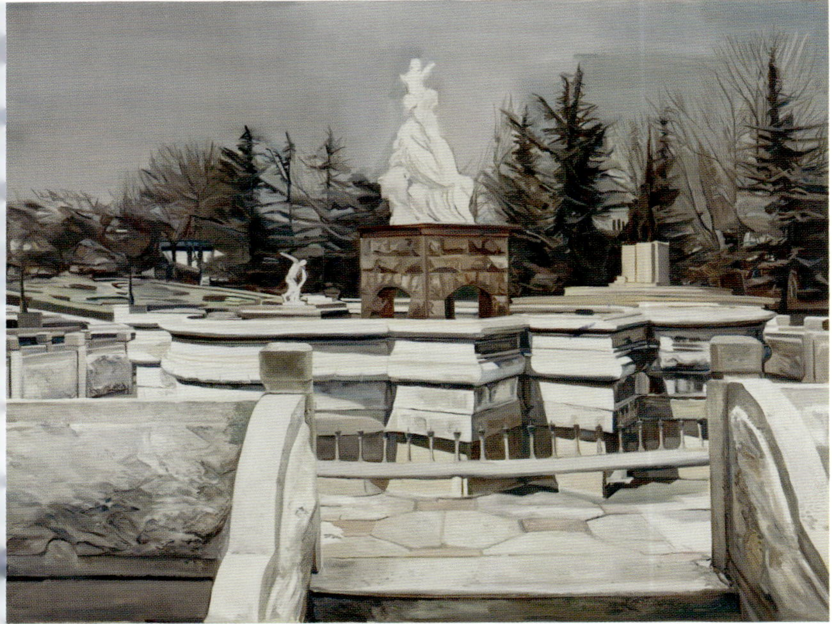

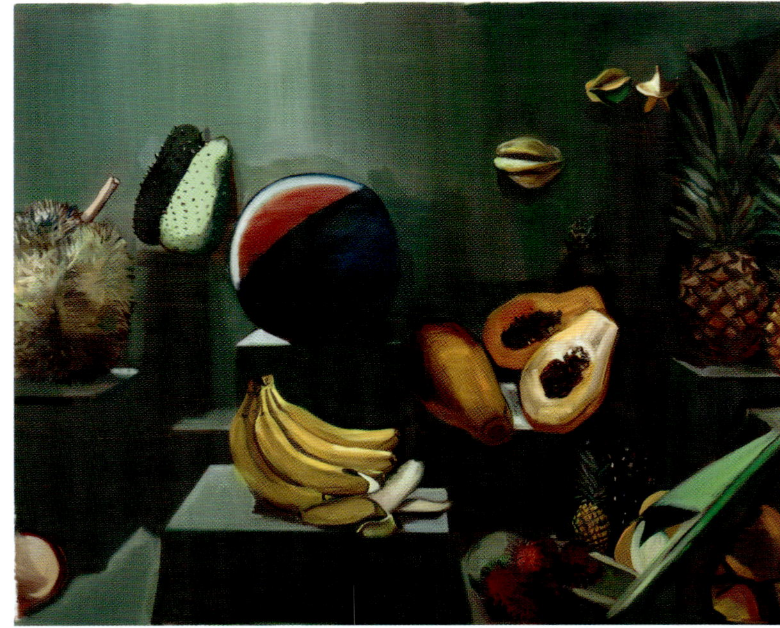

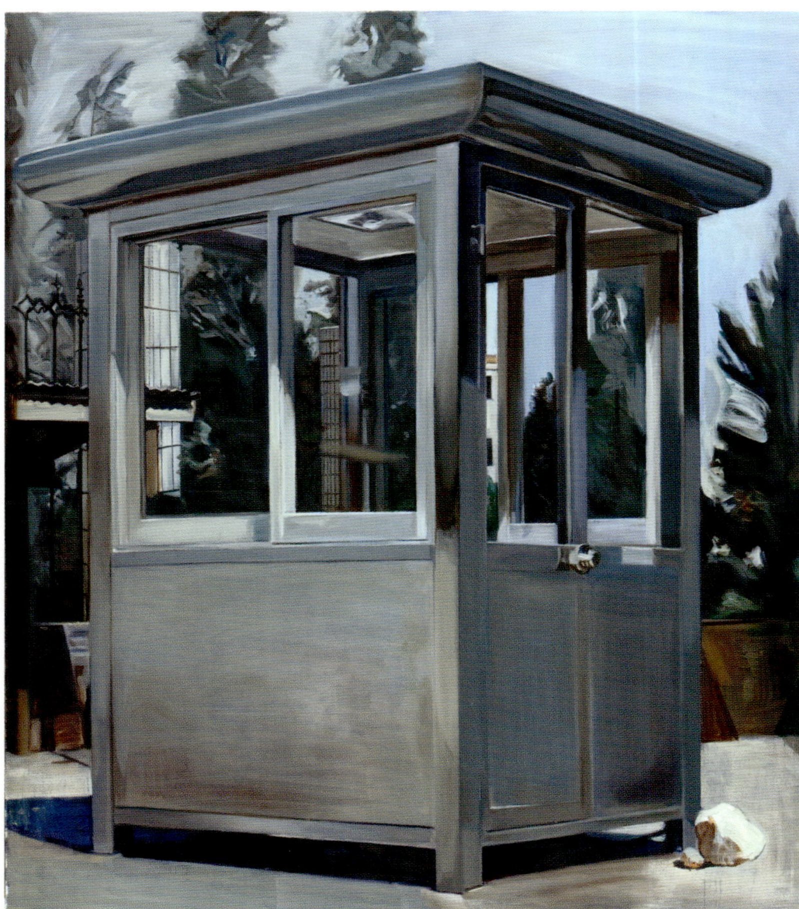

This is an interesting, even surprising, viewpoint for an artist trained in the academic traditions of oil painting, but Wang's feelings echo those of other artists of her generation, as they attempt to reconcile their schooling (which has resulted in superb technical accomplishment) with their desire to make works with complex layers of meaning.

In 2013 Wang Zhibo spent three months in New York. She says:

> Since the end of last year, I have tried to paint something of my own that would bring a new perspective to the world. During my time in New York, I spent numerous days in museums looking at a variety of face shapes depicted in pottery, porcelain and masks. Seeing these faces brought me a totally different feeling to that of the aunts and uncles [old people in the Chinese neighbourhood – not literally aunts and uncles] I would have seen at the local supermarket. The collision between life as it is today and life from the view of history always sends me into a deep trance. It is hard to differentiate between which part is reality and which part is deeply within me. I made some paintings of museum cabinets which included still-life objects.[20]

Ancient Evenings represents a cabinet filled with artefacts from the collections of European and American museums. In the background, behind this wunderkammer, is an arched loggia with a view referencing the sfumato landscape behind the Mona Lisa. In Wang's version, however, it has become a Chinese vista like those observed through the windows of the high-speed train from Shanghai – grey, dry, and punctuated by factory chimneys.

References to the classical traditions of ink painting, as well as the western canon, are evident in Wang's depictions of gardens, rocks and water. She is not sure that this is a deliberate intention:

Wang Zhibo *(top)*
Bases 2012
oil on canvas, 150 x 200 cm
image courtesy the artist and Edouard Malingue Gallery

Wang Zhibo *(bottom)*
Guardhouse 2014
oil on canvas
150 x 134 cm
image courtesy the artist

Wang Zhibo
Potlatch 2014
oil on linen
120 x 160 cm
image courtesy the artist

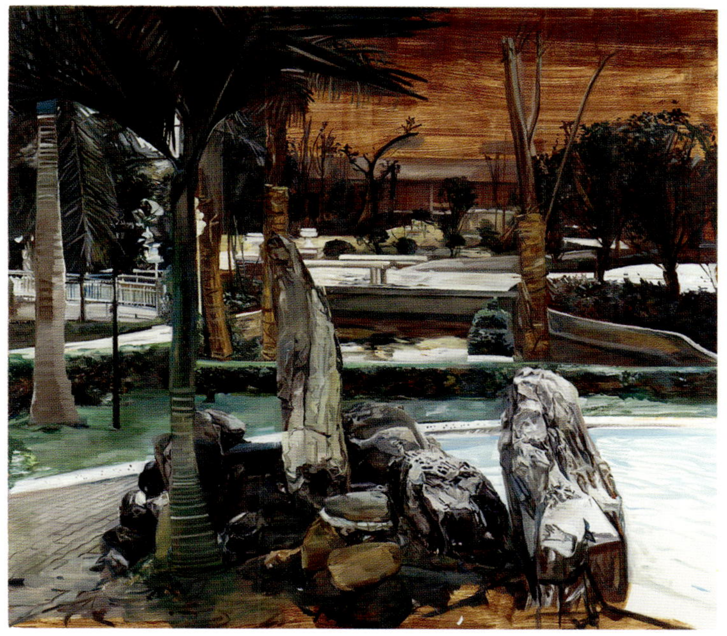

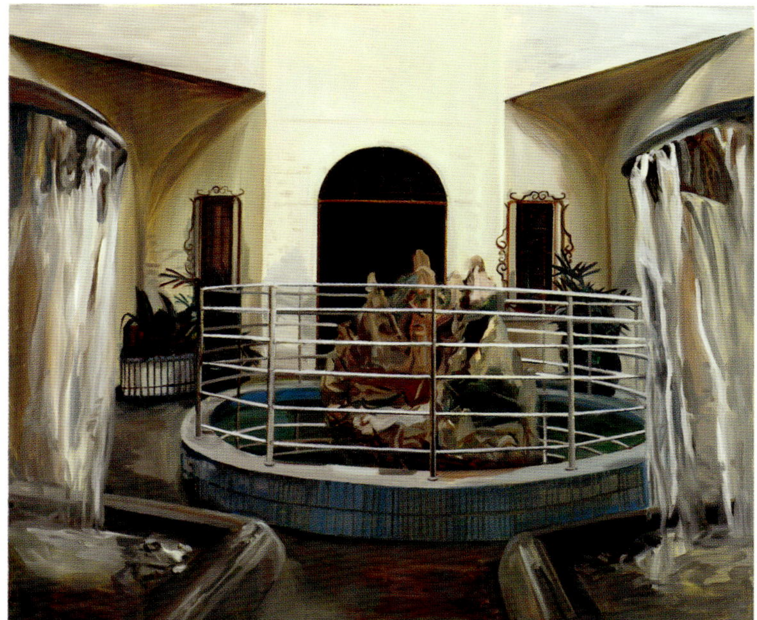

> The standard of beauty in traditional paintings really influenced me, more so than the technique or methods or concepts. [It's] the aesthetic – not the concept. When I am drawing there should be a kind of idea planted into in my painting, which is my own, not one which is based on the concepts of traditional Chinese painting. [She thought for a moment.] Beauty. That is important.

She does not mean a traditional concept of beauty, but rather an individual aesthetic of her own:

> Visual pleasure is not my goal. I want them [my paintings] to be especially rich and detailed. I think that… [in any painting] there should be an entrance for the audience to get into the picture. I try to compress all my ideas into these paintings. With the *Standing Wave* paintings the world [I have depicted] could seem depressing but it's a kind of rational depression. Maybe I unconsciously drifted into a kind of depressing reality. Some of it could be the world today, but some of it is my imagination – the world as it *could* be. It's not [intended as] a kind of depressing mood but rather a rational response.

Wang Zhibo reflects on her birth city of Wenzhou, and how her childhood may have influenced the imagery she uses today. Have the dramatic changes she must witness each time she returns home affected her work? She says:

> I think that is a very good question. Looking back at my childhood, I think that Wenzhou is like a second-tier city, it's not like Beijing or Shanghai. [Therefore] it's missed a lot of the prosperity and still has a countryside flavour. This kind of combination has definitely influenced my work. A lot of my paintings are actually focused on Wenzhou scenery, on what I saw and the changing landscape.

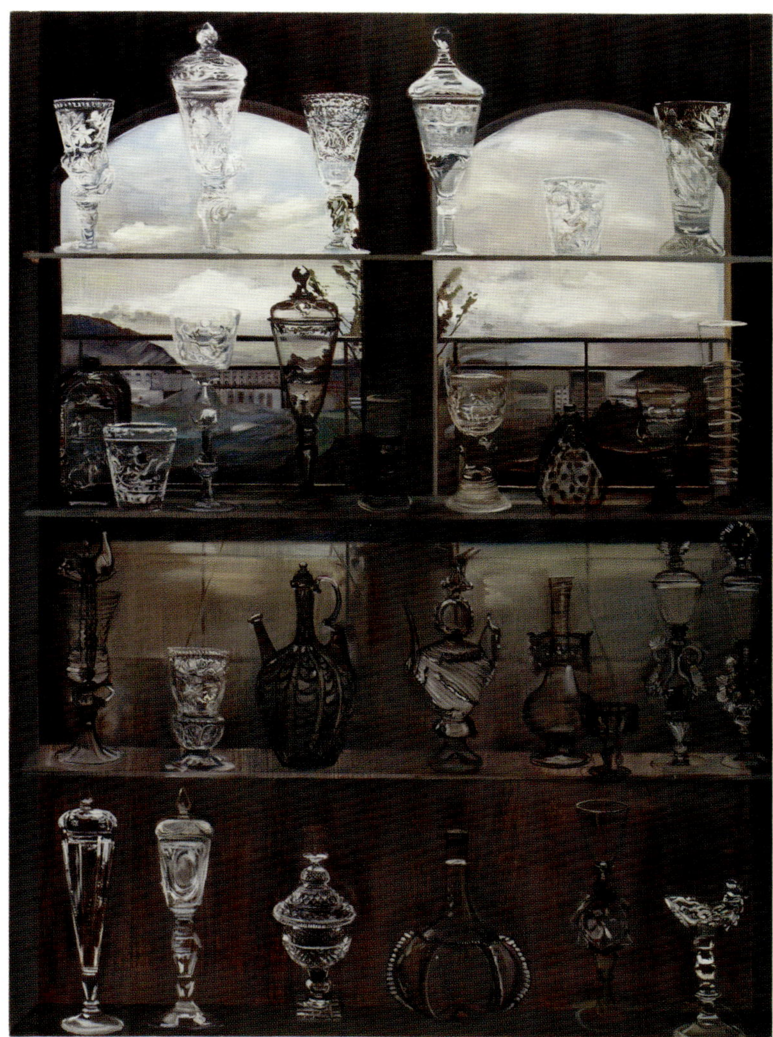

Wang Zhibo
Green Fault 2012
oil on canvas, 157 x 180 cm
image courtesy the artist and
Edouard Malingue Gallery

Wang Zhibo *(top)*
We Just Love The Beauty 2012
oil on canvas, 80 x 96 cm
image courtesy the artist and
Edouard Malingue Gallery

Wang Zhibo *(bottom)*
Ancient Evenings 2013
oil on linen
250 x 187 cm
image courtesy the artist

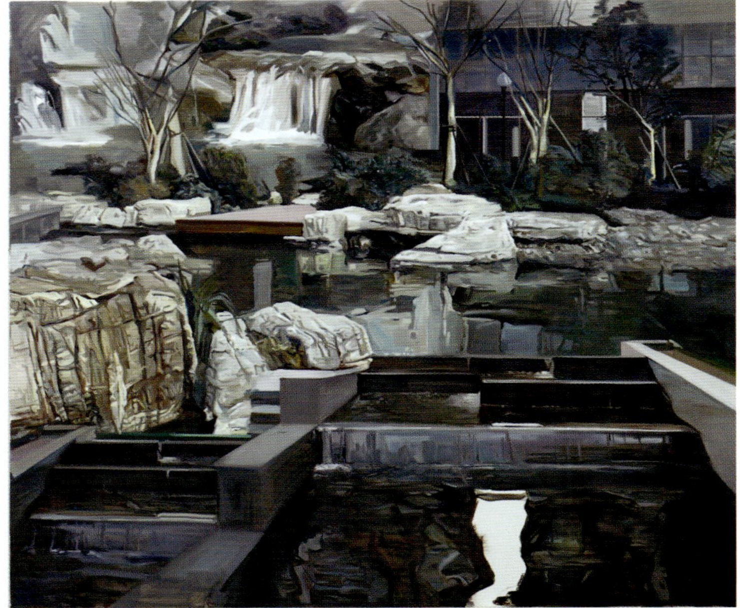

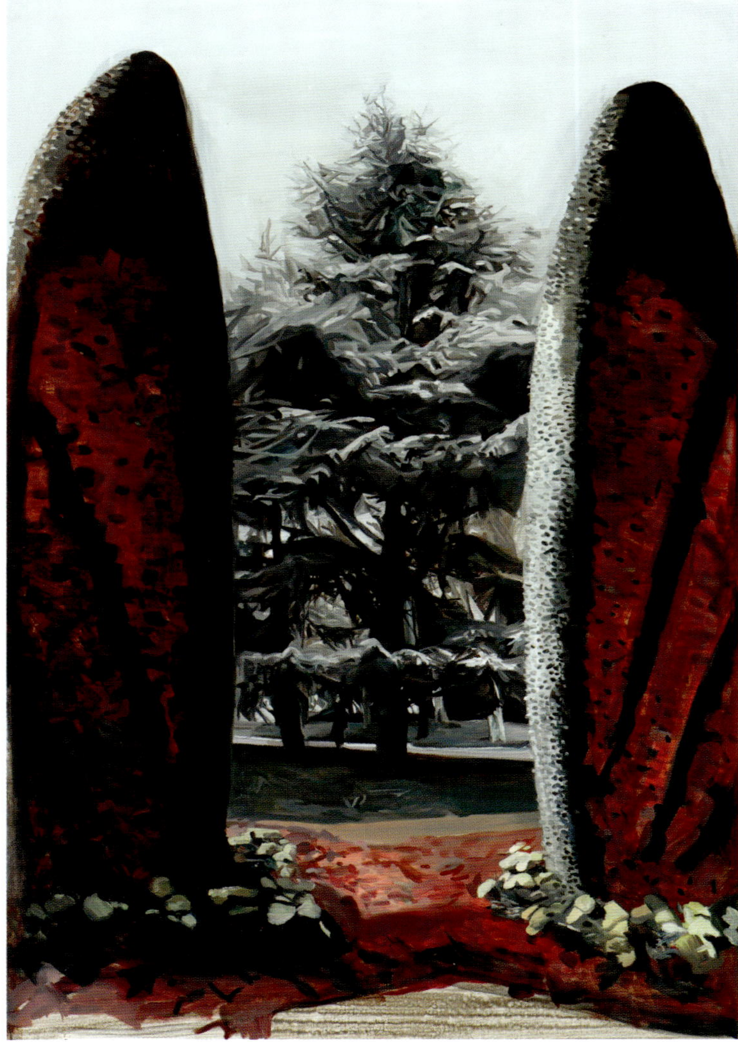

> Some are based on memories and impressions – kind of abstract impressions that I have gathered and concretised. But Wenzhou has also experienced very fast change... It doesn't make me sad, actually. Of course all Chinese people are quite used to daily changes!

She is thoughtful about what distinguishes her generation from the artists who brought Chinese contemporary painting to the attention of international audiences: 'In the 1990s the development of contemporary art mainly focused on expressing the identity of Chinese art in a westernised way. Today is quite different because we can freely express what *we* think and what *our* identities are. We are not limited to expressing a Chinese identity. It is a little bit more mature than just expressing Chinese identity. We give a voice to *our* identity.'

The compressed space in *Red Fault* creates tension. We look through a narrow gap between two enormous rocks framing a fir tree. Wang plays with our expectations of pictorial depth, perspective and illusion. The rocks appear artificial – they could even be fibreglass – and the sky is a soupy polluted grey. There is a sense of foreboding. The symmetry and tight negative spaces of the composition elicit anxiety, whilst Wang's luscious painterly surface and nuanced modulations of colour are a sensory delight.

Wang Zhibo works from memory, from direct observation and from a growing collection of photographs. She collects images of tropical gardens – but artificial ones, like the groupings of palm trees in a shopping mall atrium:

> I always begin with a photo – or lots of photos. And then I draw. Little sketches. Then I plan things like colour before I start on the canvas. Doing the drawings is a little like writing a detective novel where clues are planted in the story. The difference between a painting and a detective novel is that with a painting some things happen unconsciously. We could call it the X-factor. And you always want it to happen! It's a balance between the out-of-control and the in-control. And sometimes you also need luck!

She is describing that agonising balance between knowledge and intuition that every painter knows.

The detective novel analogy suggests that Wang Zhibo is plotting a narrative in each work – albeit an intriguingly ambiguous one. In an interview with Curtis L. Carter for her New York Armory Show exhibition in 2013, the artist likened her practice to that of an anthropologist investigating unknown cultures: 'I believe that the traces and details of daily life are as central to the system of human culture as the original social tools, ornamentations and architectural styles that are researched by anthropologists.'[21] Wang Zhibo's complex compositions represent the shifting relationship between nature and culture in the contemporary world.

Wang Zhibo *(top)*
Untitled (Springs II) 2012
oil on canvas, 151 x 180 cm
image courtesy the artist and Edouard Malingue Gallery

Wang Zhibo *(bottom)*
Red Fault 2012
oil on canvas, 130 x 92 cm
image courtesy the artist and Edouard Malingue Gallery

HUANG JINGYUAN 黄静远

Gossip from Confucius City

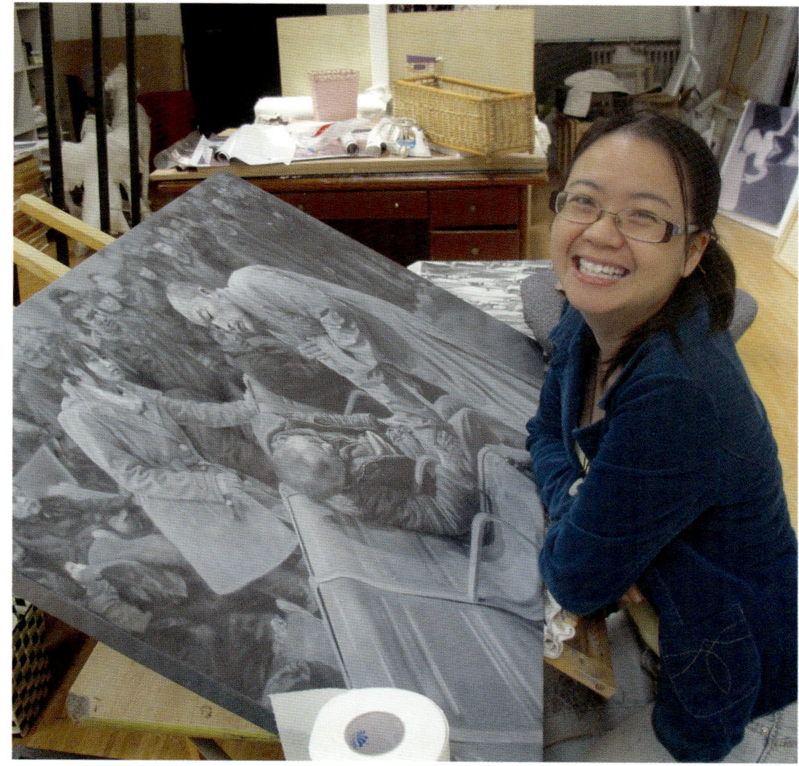

Huang Jingyuan has given a great deal of thought to the dramatic changes in Chinese society. Where Dong Yuan looks back with regret, and Wang Zhibo creates imaginary hybrid places inspired by China's rapid development, Huang Jingyuan focuses on people, politics and propaganda.

Partly educated in Canada and the United States, Huang is a hybrid being. Her atypical Chinese story helps explain her clear-sighted view of the homeland to which she has returned – a clarity that makes viewing her work an uncomfortable, as well as an intriguing, experience. Despite the meticulous realism of their monochrome surfaces, Huang's figurative paintings differ in technique from those of artists trained in Chinese art academies. She does not feel entirely accepted in that world, believing, rightly or wrongly, that some suspicion, some 'foreignness', attaches to her work.

Born in 1979 in Guangxi, she grew up in a small city with a father who practices traditional ink painting. This is not unusual for a Chinese artist, many of whom emerge from families in which image-making and artistic expression are the norm. Many female artists in China are the daughters, sisters or wives of artists. Her choice to study tourism, rather than art, at university may have been her first divergence from an expected path. Her discovery that the nationalistic response of her teachers and fellow students to the 1999 US bombing of the Chinese embassy in Belgrade made her 'uncomfortable' was a sign that she may not be best suited to the career path she had chosen. The anti-American fever was such that one foreign teacher, too afraid to stay on campus, went to the US Embassy for protection. Huang said, 'I didn't want to do that – [use] my individual body to support something in a big angry group. So I just stayed in my dormitory. But after that I was on their blacklist or something and then it confirmed for me that I was not comfortable with what was going on.'[22] Shortly afterwards she went to study in Canada. Huang completed a BFA at Concordia University Montreal, followed by a postgraduate degree at the renowned School of the Art Institute of Chicago.

Years of living away from China in the United States have given Huang a different perspective, which she applies to works representing contemporary China in all its contradictory complexity. An early work, *Transmigrating Inadequacy*, consisted of site-specific murals and architectural elements created from Xerox-printed enlargements of digital scans of photographs of original drawings. Thus the 'original' or 'authentic' is reduced and reproduced again and again, becoming quite different in the process – like a game of Chinese whispers in which the first meaning is lost. Huang explores the validity of reproduction and simulation, and questions 'reality'. She is fascinated by the possibilities of the reproduced image: the original and the shadow. As a diasporic immigrant to North America, she observed with some detachment the way identity is attached to place. Theories of liminality, and the creation of a space which was 'neither this nor that', using techniques which were themselves neither painting nor photography, allowed her to examine experiences of immigration and dislocation. Thus an artist who felt neither Chinese nor American, living in a kind of 'non-place'[23] between cultures, developed a visual language to explore this discomfiting transcultural experience.

Gossip from Confucius City, an ongoing conceptual project for which Huang created a fictitious institute and its museum, furthered her examination of the way China presents itself to the world. Inspired by the state-sponsored Confucius Institute, an arm of Chinese soft diplomacy through which Chinese language and culture is disseminated world-wide, she created a series of paintings which look like black and white photographs. On closer inspection they are revealed to be surreal fictions in which characters act out ambiguous narratives. In this series she painstakingly copied her own small collages in a very small format. Again there is a conscious and deliberate process of distancing – not unlike the way in which images are filtered, manipulated, copied, shared via social media, and recombined again and again in our image-saturated world. The paradox is that the painted version appears hyper-real yet we know it is a fictional world, a

Huang Jingyuan in her Beijing studio, October 2013, photo LG

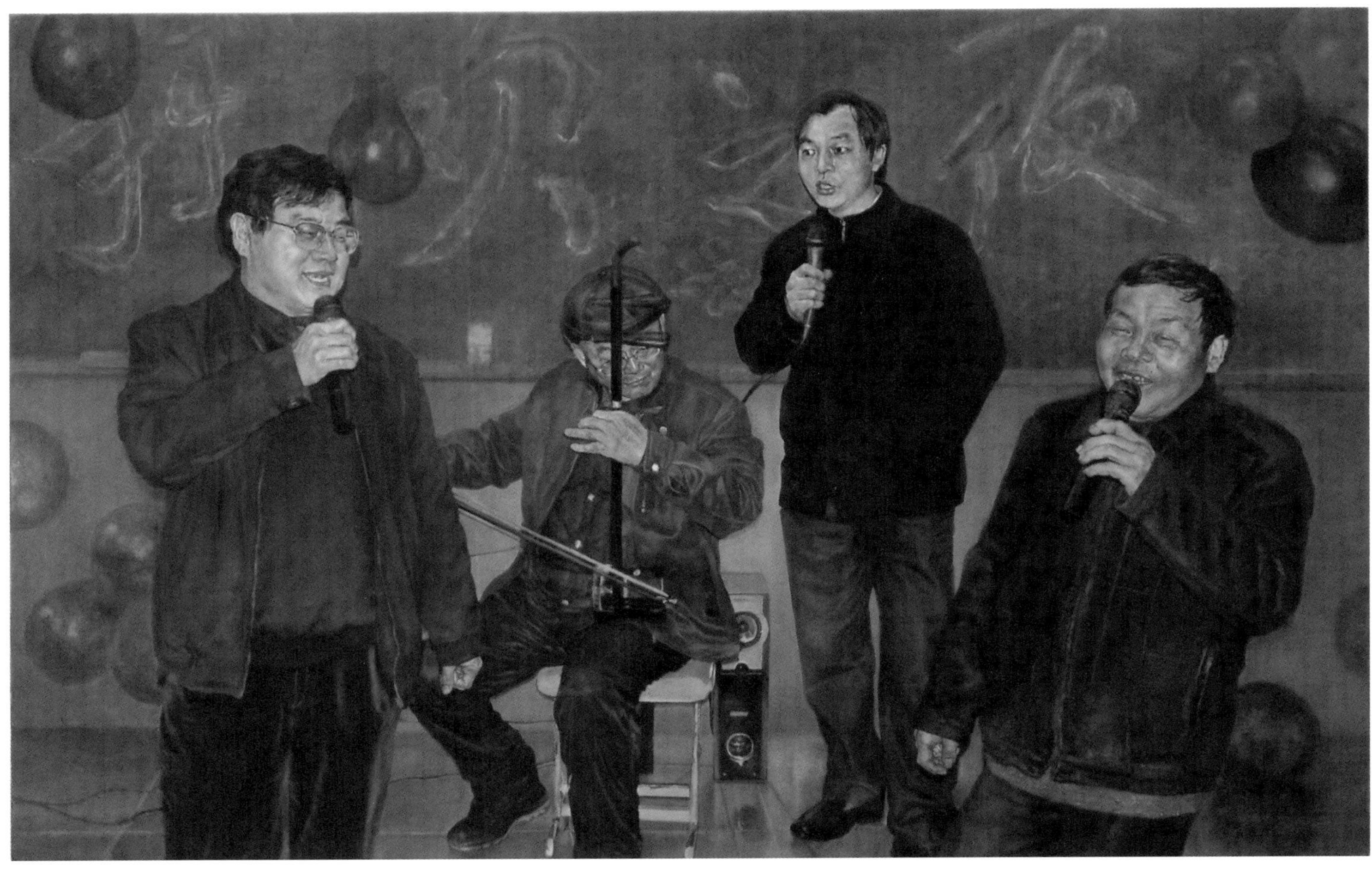

parallel universe of androgynous hybrid western and Chinese creatures, movie stars operating in a constructed reality.

Earlier versions of this work include collages recalling Hannah Höch's dada montages: they emerge from the same iconoclastic desire to puncture dominant social structures. Huang Jingyuan satirises how China represents itself to the west, hyper-inflated and hyperbolic. Any casual viewing of Chinese television will confirm that there is no spectacle considered too 'over the top'. Chinese web sites feature explosions of hectic colour and densely packed text. Hence the gaudy imagery in Huang's work, which combines traditional Chinese motifs such as dragons and peacocks with photographs of grand urban vistas, erotica and scenes of Hollywood excess. She chose the name for her series in 2011 when Ai Weiwei was arrested. 'I think it's interesting to create a fake institution where you can manipulate and export culture and cultural artefacts,' she says. Huang describes this work as a 'transitional project' in her shift from the United States back to living in China, and a necessary process of adjusting from one kind of culture to another: 'I am definitely someone very interested in the logic of how governments want to be seen and how individuals want to be seen.'

Huang is an outsider, looking in at her own culture, and at the same time an insider looking out to the wider world. From this dual position she sees China differently than artists who have never had this experience:

> Now I can ground myself and have a critical mind about what is going on inside China. It [the Confucius City project] can be perceived as a little bit postcolonial, and we are post post-colonial in many ways. That discourse offered lots of opportunities for art outside the canon to be seen, and to initiate a bigger sense of the contemporary world.

I Am Your Agency is a series of monochrome, highly realist paintings sourced entirely from banal photographs found on Chinese web sites. The history of photography in China

Huang Jingyuan
I am your agency No. 24 2013
50 x 80 cm
oil on canvas
image courtesy the artist

is problematic and unique. From the 1950s until the end of the Cultural Revolution, it was controlled by the state, used for propaganda and social control. In the 1980s, during the artist's childhood, ordinary people gained access to the means to document their lives with photographs and began recording family outings, holidays, work picnics, weddings, new babies and even the acquisition of household appliances. However, these amateur snapshots are still curiously formal. People stand in the same pose, always looking straight at the camera. There is little spontaneity of expression. Finding a photograph of her own young parents standing, stiffly formal 'like soldiers', Huang became obsessed with the power of vernacular photography to reveal certain truths. From tens of thousands of ordinary, badly composed and badly shot random images sourced from websites, she selected a small number to reproduce in paint.

Her title asks us to consider who has the 'agency' in the construction and viewing of these images:

> I got to know lots of images from the internet – the accumulation of images from the last five years from vernacular photography, not from photographers. The photos are really bizarre, for example photos of an official from the Propaganda Bureau, taken as a compliment by his staff, or a snapshot of a chicken owned by somebody, or a shirt someone wants to sell on *Taobao* [Chinese e-bay]. It's really a world that is banal and not totally legitimate – not an image you could project on the wall about Chinese people.

Of course these images in themselves are not negative representations of contemporary China. 'You can't see negative images online on Chinese websites, or using a Chinese search

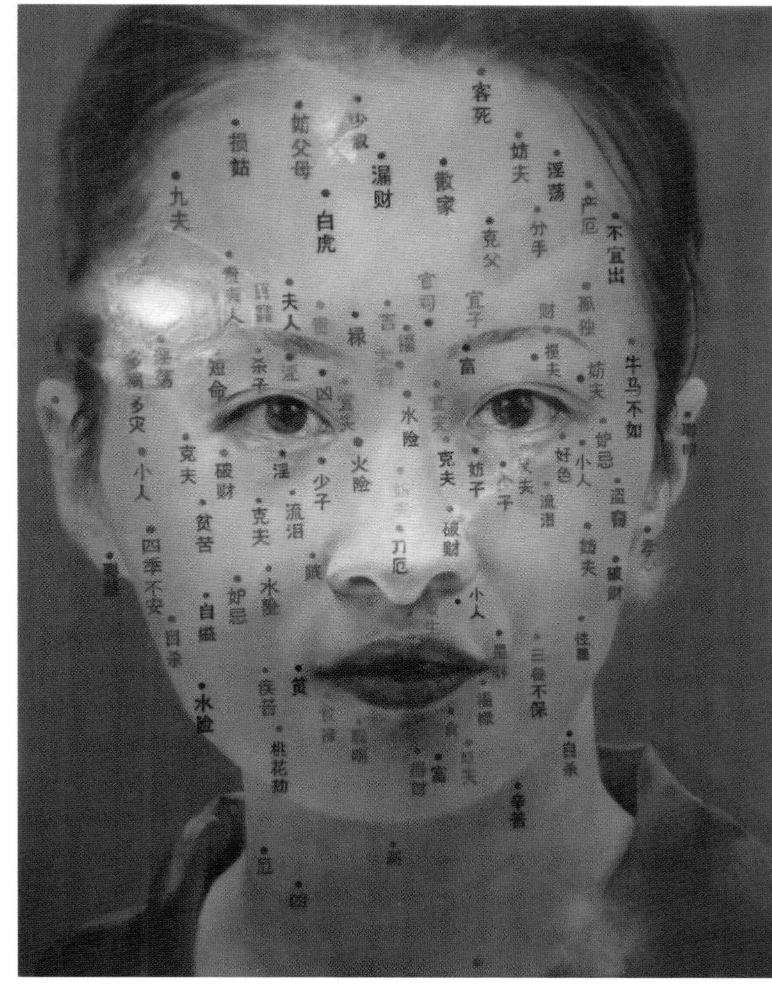

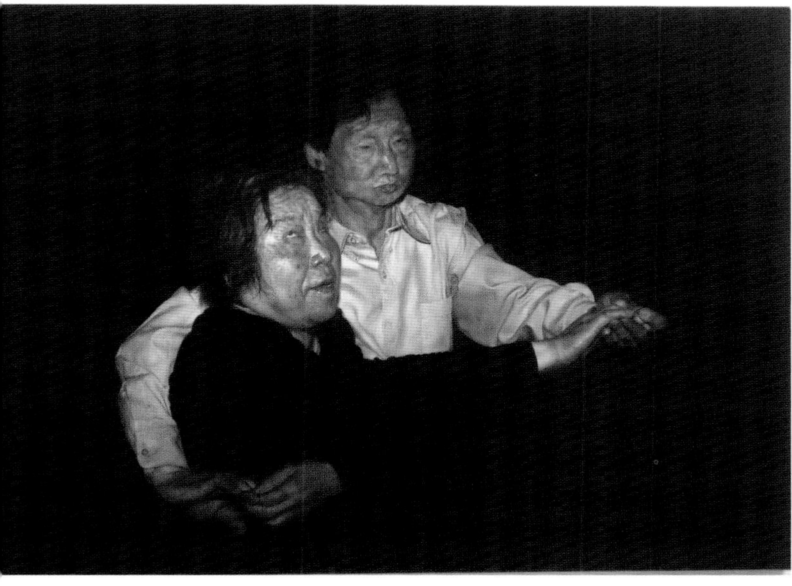

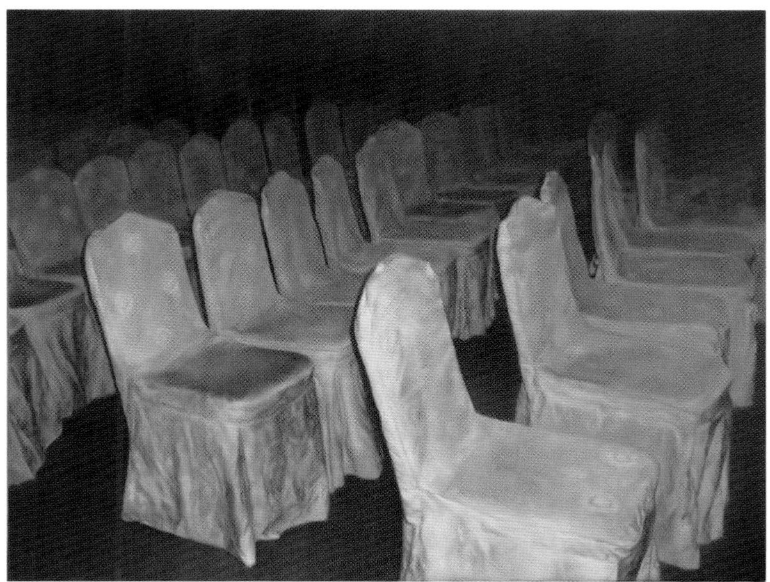

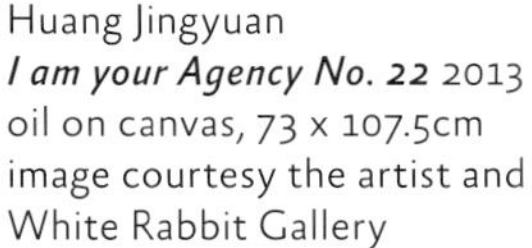
Huang Jingyuan
I am your Agency No. 22 2013
oil on canvas, 73 x 107.5cm
image courtesy the artist and White Rabbit Gallery

Huang Jingyuan *(top)*
I am your Agency No. 20 2013
oil on canvas, 50 x 39cm
image courtesy the artist and White Rabbit Gallery

Huang Jingyuan *(bottom)*
I am your Agency No. 38 2013
oil on canvas, 45 x 59.5cm
image courtesy the artist and White Rabbit Gallery

engine,' she says. But in the transformation from photograph to painting, and then in the carefully considered juxtapositions of pairs and groups of images, subversive meanings emerge. The artist has paired snapshots with more 'official' images to suggest readings which critique the ways in which the Chinese represent themselves, and how we all understand the world mediated through the shadow imagery of photography. It also represents Huang's own 'continuing struggle to disengage from the authority of state media.'[24]

Individual works in the series, such as the empty rows of fabric-skirted chairs in *I Am Your Agency No.38*, suggest many possible readings. Is the wedding banquet cancelled? The official party abandoned? Has something terrible happened here? In fact, Huang found the original photographic image on a badly designed web page advertising chairs available to be hired for functions. The actual meaning of the image is so mundane that it denies our appetite for drama. Other images similarly suggest multiple readings, which in many cases will be undermined by the prosaic reality of advertising photography, or the tools of propaganda. Like the *Da Zi Bao* ('Big Character Posters') of the Cultural Revolution, which at first boldly denounced class enemies, revisionists and landlords, then descended into gossipy accusations of infidelity and 'fornication', photography has descended from the high realm of visual 'truth' to the digitally manipulated and the tacky sales pitch. China is, after all, the country in which provincial authorities routinely doctor photographs for political propaganda purposes, inviting the derision of internet commentators for their often hilariously bad Photoshop skills.

I Am Your Agency No.22, taken from a photograph depicting blind ballroom dancers, evokes pathos and dignity in the intense concentration of the sightless dancers. The beautifully rendered folds of the white shirtsleeve against the deep black of the woman's dress, and the way the figures emerge from a velvety darkness, signify their momentary pleasure in a world of difficulty. It was juxtaposed with a painting taken from a news photograph of political leaders, seated next to each other but looking away. The image is awkwardly revealing, as snapshots of politicians in unguarded moments so often are. Together, the paintings invite us to speculate on the contrast between private and public faces; between those who must navigate the complex and uncertain world of this new China on their own, compared with those who reap all its rewards.

Huang occasionally removes an extraneous detail or further crops an image, but she prefers to work with the compositional infelicities of non-professional photography, finding them intensely revealing. *I am your Agency No. 20* includes her hand-painted camera flare on a woman's face marked with diagrammatic characters. The original clumsy photograph advertised aspects of Chinese medicine. In Huang's hands these vernacular photographs are transformed: new meanings are inscribed upon the original imagery. There is a risk of aestheticizing – even fetishising – such 'found' imagery, a process that 'unmistakably alters their original meanings and value.'[25] Huang is aware that she risks making her found images more beautiful, hence she is determined to show her works as installations in which ambiguous meanings undercut each other.

Today, she says, people have become 'casualties of their own image-in-the-making and their image production is reduced to a self-imposed performance.' In China, this is particularly poignant when one considers the dramatic changes that have taken place in society. On the wall of her parents' bedroom, Huang says, hangs a photograph taken in 1979 in southern China. 'They stand side by side like well-prepared soldiers trying to impress their leaders... I can detect an intimacy that comes from their shared experience as casualties of war.'

Some of her contemporaries have asked, 'Why undertake this laborious and time-consuming process of rendering 'throw-away' ephemeral photographs in paint?' The answer lies in the very meticulousness of the artist's hand, as she works layers of scumbled glazes to create an illusory solidity and reality of form, often in monochrome, in an allusion to the propaganda photographs of that earlier time. Huang continues to grapple with this central conundrum: 'If I can communicate the idea in photographs, then why should I paint it?' Essentially, she concludes, it is about the authority of the image. She invites us to question the truth of what we see. Through their transformation from tiny pixels on a screen, to large black and white prints, finally emerging from her studio as painted canvases, each image becomes something quite different. She chooses vernacular photographs from random websites, searching by category – children singing, domestic workers, women making speeches – because of their very awkwardness: 'I could not begin to take photographs like these – I could not do it! They have to be taken by someone who is indifferent, who is insensitive to the gaze of the women or the subjects.'

Huang Jingyuan is not the only painter to work from found photographs – Lin Jingjing and Yu Hong also seek their source material on the internet. But Huang Jingyuan's intentions are different. She plans her works as installations – paintings are almost always grouped or paired: 'I am interested in images that are ambiguous – like my next series which are images of children, in black and white, and [they are juxtaposed with] images of random objects painted in colour. Not necessarily paired, but grouped.' In the winter of 2014 these works lined the walls of her studio – highly realist monochrome paintings of children playing musical instruments or singing are stacked next to paintings of balloons, eggs, or rabbits coloured in a way that evokes early

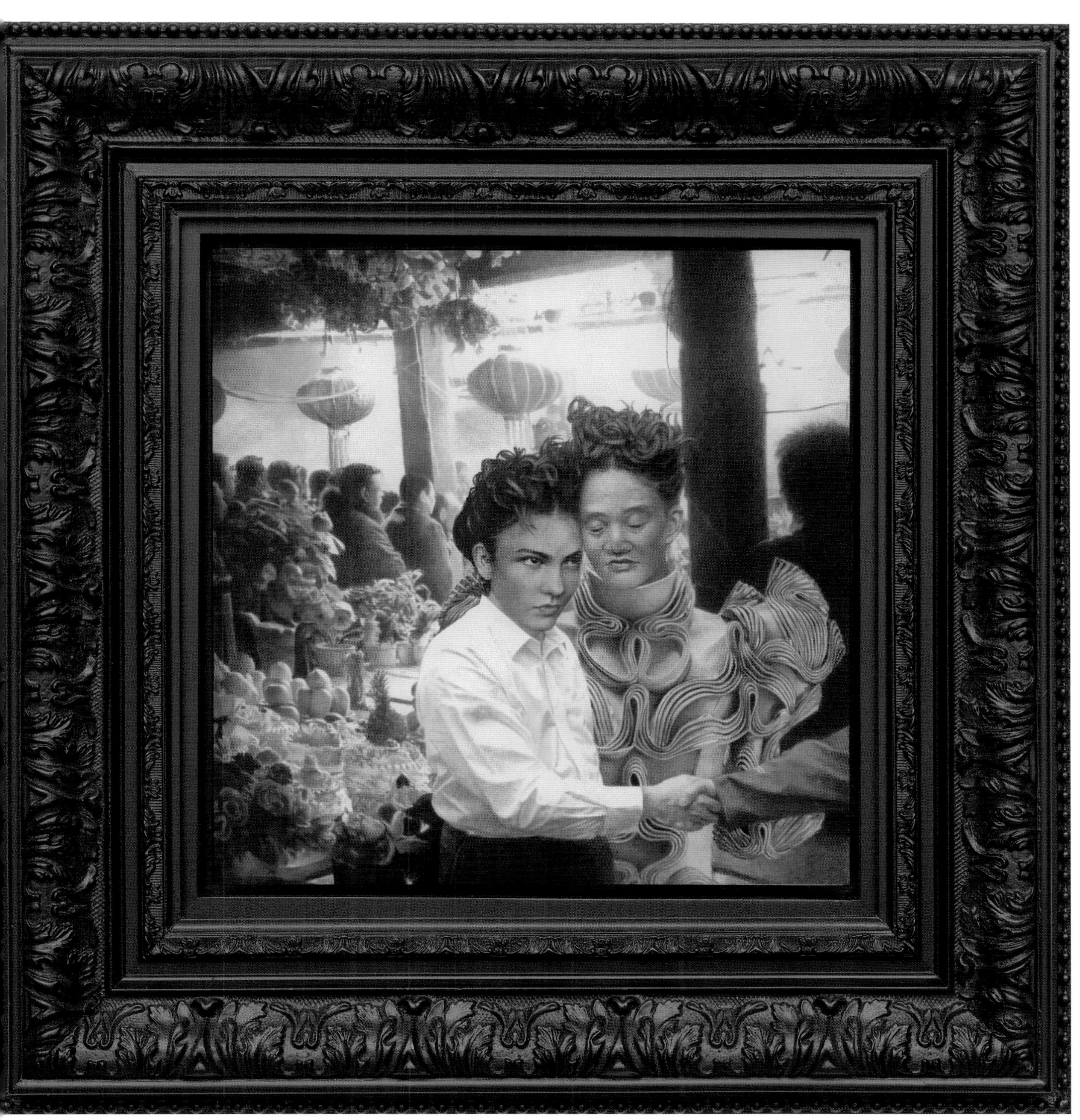

Huang Jingyuan
Gossip from Confucius City 2 2012
acrylic on paper
55 x 55 cm
image courtesy the artist and White Rabbit Gallery

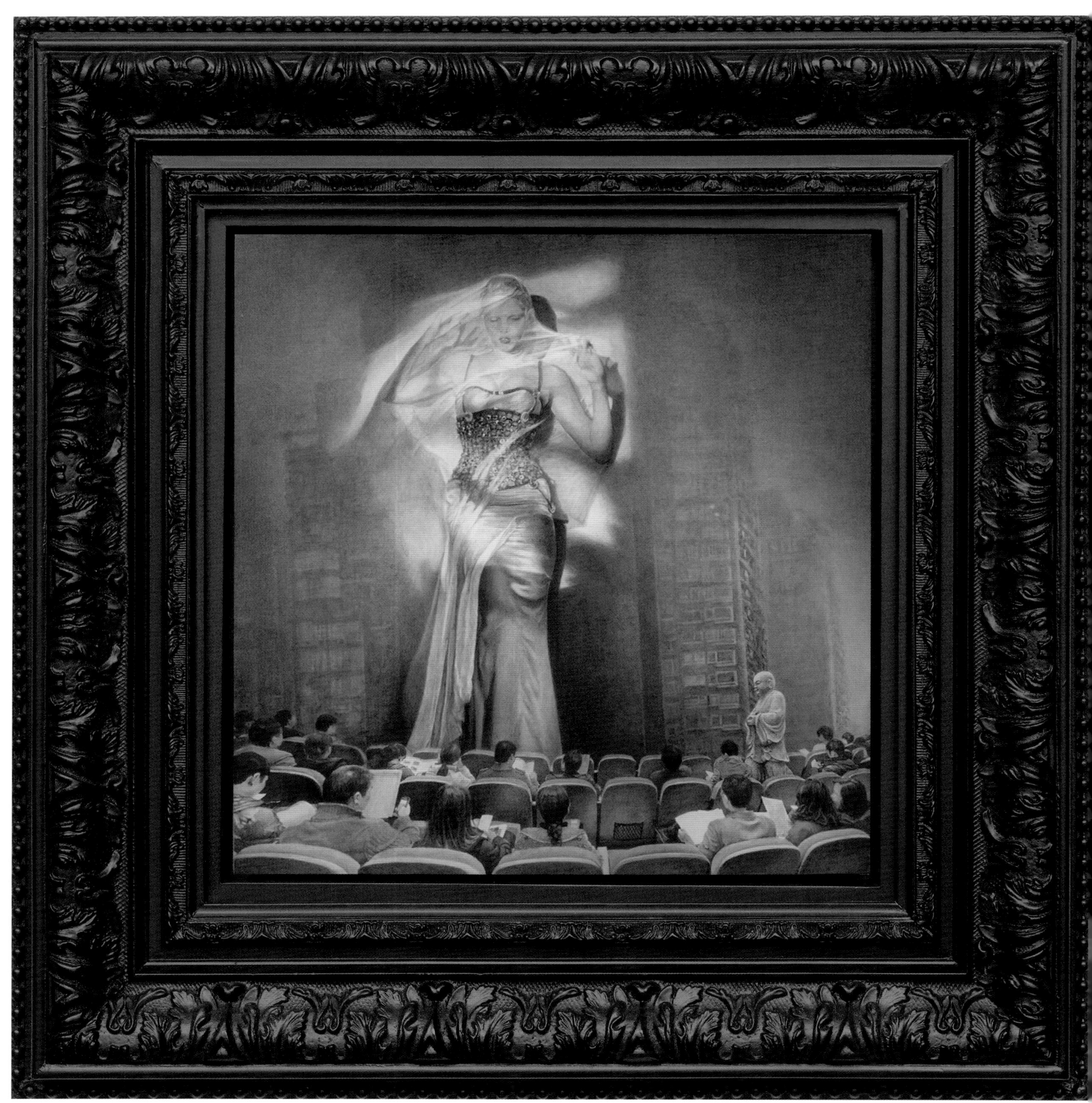

Huang Jingyuan
Gossip from Confucius City 9 2012
acrylic on paper
55 x 55 cm
image courtesy the artist and White Rabbit Gallery

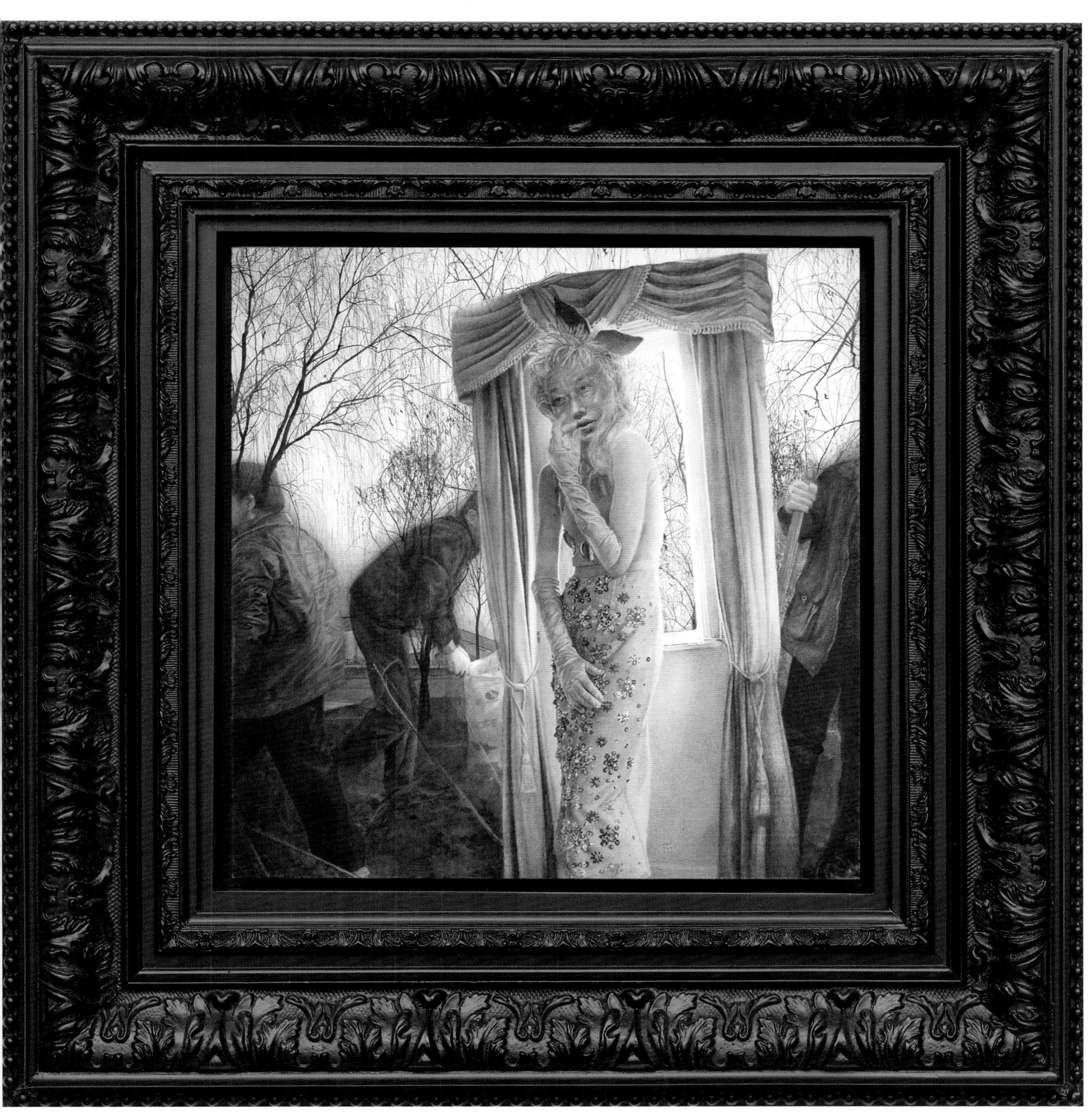

Huang Jingyuan
Gossip from Confucius City 1 2012
acrylic on paper
55 x 55 cm
image courtesy the artist and White Rabbit Gallery

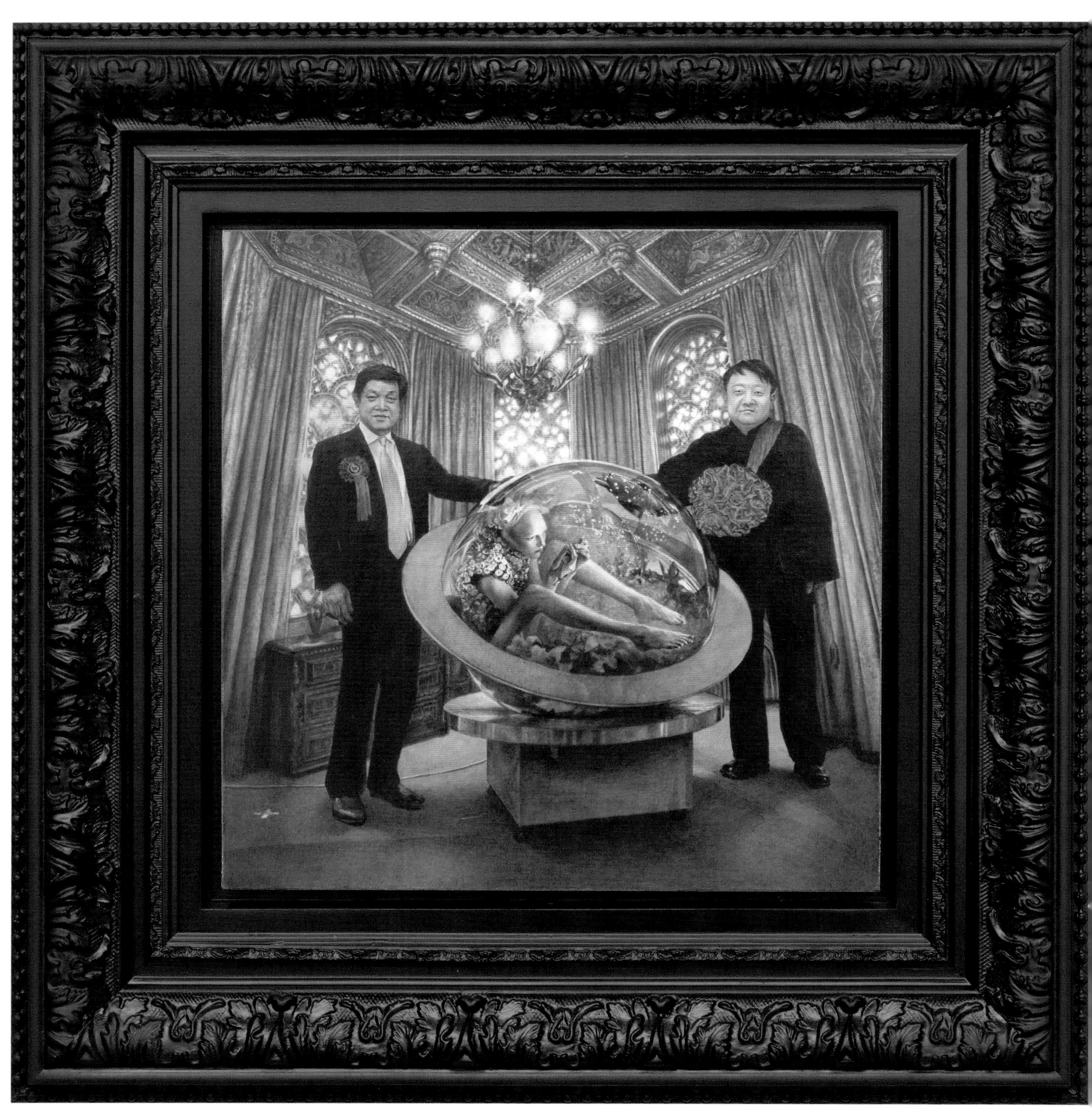

Huang Jingyuan
Gossip from Confucius City 15 2012
acrylic on paper
62 x 62 cm
image courtesy the artist and White Rabbit Gallery

colour photography – things that appear to have no relationship with each other.

Her works reflect an uncomfortable aspect of contemporary China – a globalised and sophisticated culture in which unfettered access to information is still considered a threat. Huang says:

> Things that appear straightforward and obvious when seen by themselves are paired with others that are entirely ambiguous, such that they do not provide exit for each other and one cannot make sense of them. They have *no* relationship with one another. Which one is the reality? Which one is how we define who we are?

A 2014 series juxtaposes photographs of clouds shot from planes with images of middle-aged women. Some are headshots of domestic workers taken from employment websites, some are professional women making speeches, and some are from dating websites. 'They are supposed to show how good life is,' says the artist. 'It's about how women have a decent life, they are respected, they are looking for a job, they are looking for a husband, they are giving a speech! They are in a powerful position, addressing an audience, making political decisions. It's about freedom. Not real freedom – no, it's the opposite! But they are not disenfranchised, I am not making images of weak women.' Huang says the clouds they are paired with signify, 'the sublime, romanticism, and [when clouds are] seen through an airplane – it's modernism! The idea of heaven – totally! Peace, space exploration, the idea that we have another universe. It has all the positive ideas that we see for ourselves. It's about unlimited ideas and a promised future.' Like a modernist idea of progress? 'Exactly! And it's a very sceptical idea of modernism in a postmodern world.'

Ultimately, Huang Jingyuan's body of work is about doubt, an entirely rational response to a world in which things are rarely what they seem.

Dong Yuan, Wang Zhibo and Huang Jingyuan, each in their own way, explore notions of truth – psychological realities, observable appearances, and the ways in which these and other 'truths' may be twisted and re-shaped in the modern world. In China today, just as in the past, 'truth' transforms itself in the currents of the prevailing political winds. Little wonder, then, that artists are interested in examining its nuances and contradictions.

NOTES

1 Dal Lago, Francesca 2009 'Realism as a Tool of National Modernisation in the Reformist Discourses of Late Nineteenth and Early Twentieth Century China' in Anderson, Jayne (Ed) *Crossing Cultures: Migration and Convergence* 32nd Congress of History and Art, Miegunyah Press, Melbourne (847–52) available at https://www.academia.edu/1456859/_Realism_as_a_Tool_of_National_Modernization_in_the_Reformist_Discourse_of_late-19th_and_Early_20th_China accessed 3 August 2014

2 ibid.

3 Gao Minglu 2011 *Total Modernity and the Avant-garde in Twentieth Century Chinese Art* Massachusetts Institute of Technology (37)

4 Liu Xiaodong 1999 *Representing the People* exhibition catalogue, Chinese Arts Centre, Manchester

5 Gladston, Paul 2014 *Contemporary Chinese Art: A Critical History* Reaktion Books London (60)

6 Sullivan, Michael 1996 *Art and Artists of Twentieth Century China* University of California Press (26)

7 Wang Chunchen 2013 'Realism and Contemporary Chinese Art' available at http://www.xzine.org/rhaa/?p=803 accessed 3 August 2014

8 Conversation between the writer and contemporary *gongbi* painter and curator, Jin Sha, in Beijing in December 2012. Jin Sha sees literati painting as a more recent, less truly Chinese, artform

9 Lee, Sherman E 1982 *A History of Far Eastern Art* 4th edition Abrams New York (254)

10 Hill, Katie 2013 'The Elegiac Parkscapes of Wang Zhibo' in *Wang Zhibo: Standing Wave* Edouard Malingue Gallery Hong Kong (41)

11 Unless otherwise acknowledged, all quotes from Dong Yuan are from her conversations with the writer, in Beijing in December 2012 and April 2014

12 Dong Yuan 2013 *A Short History of Everything: Grandma's House and Bosch's Garden* Yang Gallery Beijing

13 ibid.

14 http://www.moma.org/interactives/exhibitions/1999/muse/artist_pages/duchamp_boite.html accessed 4 February 2015

15 Dong Yuan 2013 *A Short History of Everything: Grandma's House and Bosch's Garden* Yang Gallery, Beijing,

16 Fuller, Michael A 2013 *Drifting Among Rivers and Lakes: Southern Song Dynasty Poetry and the Problem of Literary History* Harvard University Asia Center, Harvard University Press

17 Lou Yuming 2011 (transl. Ye Yang) *A Concise History of Chinese Literature* Brill, The Netherlands (547)

18 Email from Wang Zhibo to the writer (transl. Lily Wang) 10 September 2014

19 Unless otherwise acknowledged all quotes from Wang Zhibo are from her conversation with the writer in Hangzhou in December 2014

20 Email from the artist to the writer (transl. Lily Wang) 10 September 2014

21 Carter, Curtis L 2012 'Standing Wave' in *Wang Zhibo: Standing Wave*, Edouard Malingue Gallery, Hong Kong

22 Unless otherwise acknowledged, all quotes from Huang Jingyuan are from her conversations with the writer, in Beijing in October 2013 and December 2014

23 Auge, Marc 1995 *Non-Places: Introduction to an Anthropology of Supermodernity* Verso United Kingdom

24 Laurin, Gordon 2013 'Documenting Photography: New Painting by Jing Yuan Huang' catalogue essay, Force Gallery, Beijing

25 Gomez, Edward, M 2005 'Everybody's Photography' available at http://www.accidentalmysteries.com/essays.html accessed 7 February 2015

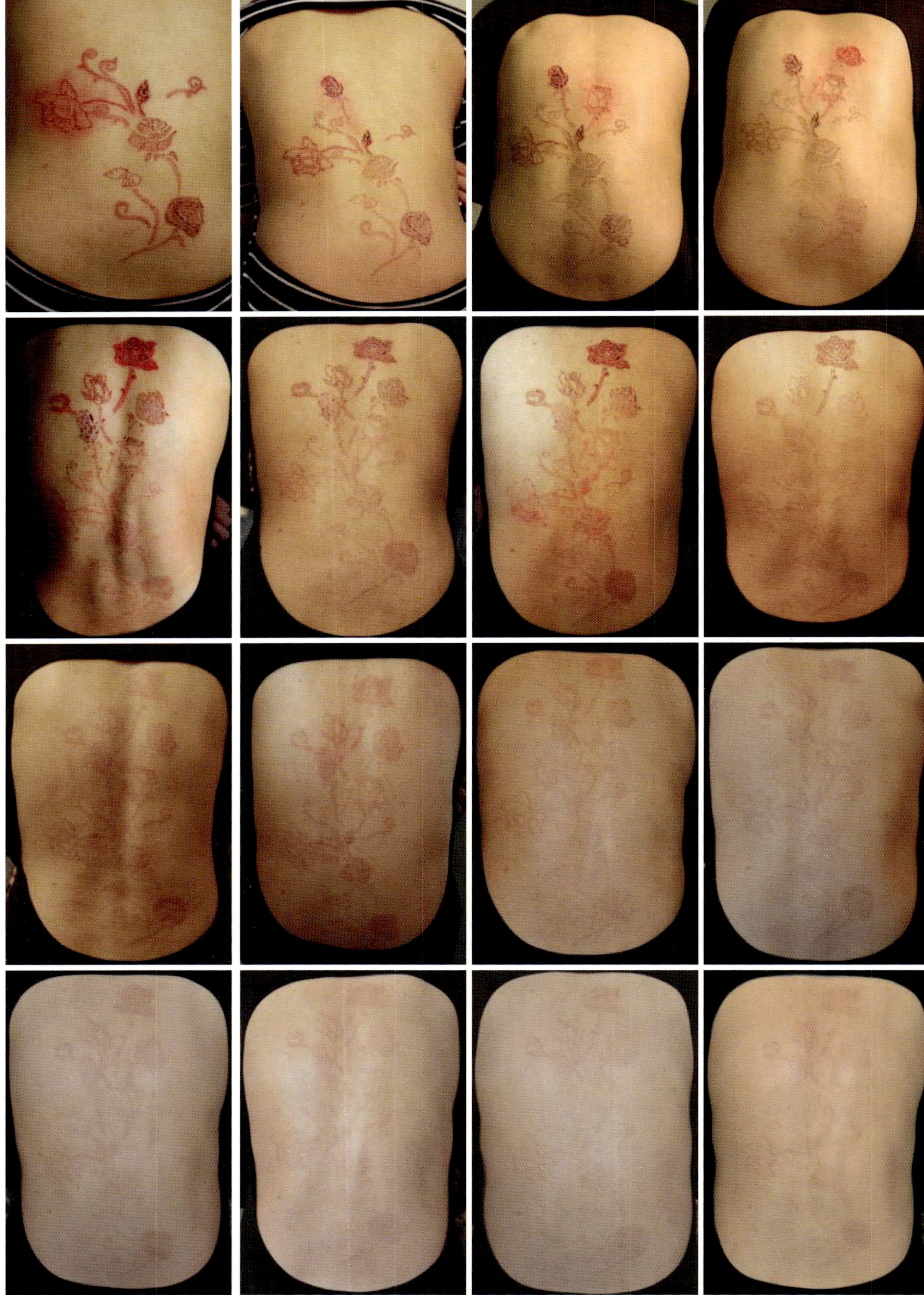

INSCRIPTIONS ON THE BODY

Endurance to Transcendence in Chinese Performance Art He Chengyao, Yingmei Duan and Ma Qiusha, and an introduction to Xu Shanshan

In the bohemian art enclaves of the 1980s, artistic experimentation in Beijing and Shanghai was characterised by violent performance art. It seemed to emerge suddenly, with little precedent, seizing the imagination of artists despite official condemnation and heavy-handed censorship. Influenced by Joseph Beuys and Marina Abramović, artists challenged social, cultural and artistic norms. Chinese performance art entered what some artists describe as a 'golden age' in the late 1990s and early 2000s,[1] and despite the growing popularity of new media it has continued to flourish, inspiring a new generation of young artists. This chapter introduces emerging performance artist Xu Shanshan, and three artists who influenced her developing practice: He Chengyao, Yingmei Duan and Ma Qiusha. Heir to a rich tradition of the performative in Chinese contemporary art, Xu reveals a specifically female approach in the use of her body as the material (literally) of her practice.

Xu Shanshan abandoned painting during her studies at the Central Academy of Fine Arts and began to create work with her own body. The very fact that she was able to do so, and to publicly perform her work for graduation, demonstrates new acceptance of a practice once considered taboo, and banned by the authorities. Using fat extracted by liposuction surgery Xu sculpted flowers, her response to how young women are pressured to conform to accepted standards of physical beauty. She endured having her back tattooed with flowers multiple times without ink, displaying the healing scars in reference to a seminal work by Qin Ga. For his contribution to *Miniature Long March Sites* (2002), interactive art events at various points along the five-thousand mile route across China taken by Mao's army in 1934-35, Qin's back was tattooed with a map of the different stages of the march. In contrast, Xu Shanshan's work emerged from long-buried memories of childhood scars, and the construction of a feminine identity: 'I decided the scars on my body record my process of growth... I used the tattoo to symbolise the way that you create wounds, then the scars eventually disappear, and that is the process of life.' Xu Shanshan believes that in focusing on the private rather than the overtly political, her performance practice is distinct from its avant-garde antecedents.

The development of performance art in China reveals a radical, underground history. After Xiao Lu's gunshots at *China/Avant-garde* in the politically charged year of 1989, Chinese authorities became nervous about the potential for artists' public actions to foment discord, which may of course go some way to explain its continuing popularity. Performance art is still closely monitored,[2] but has been one of the most important features in the rise of 'avant-garde' art in China.

In the traditions of Chinese theatre, and the history of performing arts ranging from courtly musicians and dancers to rustic, raw travelling troupes of actors and acrobats, we can see some of the roots of contemporary performance art practices. From circus to opera, from the elaborate and highly refined to earthy vernacular forms, there are ancient practices underlying contemporary performance art which include shamanism and magic. During the Cultural Revolution all such performances were forbidden, replaced by propagandist political theatre, opera and ballets such as *Red Detachment of Women* (performed for Richard Nixon on his state visit to China.) Critic Richard Vine points out that the carefully choreographed elements of the revolutionary propaganda machine, including 'speeches, rallies, troop reviews, public denunciations, show trials – became the theatre of the Maoist state.'[3]

'To rebel is justified.' —Mao Zedong

Rebellion is a leitmotif in twentieth century Chinese history, from Mao's Long March to Yan'an in 1934 to the *Smash the Four Olds* campaign of the 1960s.[4] 'To rebel is justified,' said

Xu Shanshan
Without Trace 2014
photographic documentation of performance
image courtesy the artist

Mao, in an invitation to schoolchildren during the Cultural Revolution.[5] Red Guards from Tsinghua University's middle school claimed for themselves the fearless character of the Ming Dynasty hero, the Monkey King. '[We] use our magic to turn the old world upside down, smash it into pieces, pulverise it, create chaos, and make a tremendous mess – the bigger the better!' they cried.[6] Order and disorder, chaos and stability, rebellion and obedience are recurring themes in Chinese culture.[7]

After the tumultuous years of 1966–76, artistic responses to social upheaval shifted from *Scar Art* – realistic history paintings recording traumatic events – to a renewed interest in western modernism and, most especially, to notions of anti-art. Artists of the 1980s, according to critic Li Xianting, 'believed in applying modern Western aesthetics and philosophy as a means of revitalizing Chinese culture.'[8] By the 1990s, however, in large part due to the convulsive social revolution of Deng Xiaoping's economic reforms, this had been overtaken by a sense of rupture. Globalisation changed everything. In the artworld, it brought international contemporary art to China, connected by independent artists and curators in dialogue and cultural exchange; the establishment of museums, biennales and international exhibitions. New experimental art forms such as installation and performance provided Chinese artists with an 'international language.'[9]

As we have seen in earlier chapters, the terms 'contemporary', 'avant-garde' and 'postmodern' are problematic in China, and slippages in translation make it difficult to be precise. Wu Hung suggests that the art of the 1980s and 1990s in China – 'a specific historical phenomenon defined by a set of specific factors' – is more properly described as 'experimental art' (*shiyan meishu*).[10] The development of contemporary art (*Zhongguo dangdai yishu*) has been characterised by deliberate combinations of historical Chinese art practices and folk traditions with imagery, styles and techniques derived from international postmodernism. Chinese artists at the end of the twentieth century were in the remarkable position of simultaneously discovering modernist and postmodernist forms and ideas.[11]

Contemporary art in China continues to be influenced by exhibitions both inside and outside China, in an intricate web of global interconnections: internationalist dialogues inform the work of artists everywhere, no less so in the People's Republic. The exhibition of Robert Rauschenberg in Beijing in 1985 – a masterstroke of American soft diplomacy – had a major impact on Chinese artists.[12] Artists who travelled to East Germany, and those taught by returnees from Eastern Europe, were inspired by Joseph Beuys and the Fluxus movement. Gilbert and George visited the experimental East Village artists' enclave in 1993, and Thomas Berghuis recounts how the bemused Englishmen became the audience for an impromptu performance by the radical Ma Liuming.[13] Chinese artists travelling overseas met their European, Australian and American counterparts and their isolation was broken.

As international exhibitions brought western audiences face-to-face with contemporary Chinese art, it became evident that they were presented with a gendered narrative. Curator Britta Erickson points out that most of these exhibitions included few or no female artists.[14] The rare exception to the impression that Chinese contemporary art was an entirely male pursuit was an exhibition at the Frauen Museum in Bonn in 1998, which included twenty-four artists including Yin Xiuzhen. Jia Fangzhou's catalogue essay declares that 'a particular characteristic of the art of Chinese women of the '90s is that it gets rid of male language and explores the value of one's own ego.'[15]

Xingwei Yishu: Shamanic Bodies and 'Disconcerting Events'

Richard Vine identifies an untitled rebellious act of nude painting in 1984 by a very young Wang Peng as perhaps the first performance art in China – like a more chaotic version of Yves Klein's 1960s *Anthropometries* but using the artist's own body rather than naked women.[16] It is as if one of Klein's models had 'gone berserk,' Vine suggests. Paul Gladston, however, believes it was the performance installations staged in Beijing by Hong Kong-based artist Kwok Mang-ho in 1979 that were the game-changer. *Plastic Bag Happenings in China* featured inflated plastic bags strung up in various iconic locations including Tiananmen Square and the Great Wall.[17] The first known video work by an artist from the People's Republic is Zhang Peili's *30 x 30*, filmed in 1988, 'a record of a performance by the artist involving the repeated smashing and sticking-back-together of a mirror measuring 30 x 30 cm.'[18] Following these early examples of performative, Dada-influenced actions, 'behaviour art' (*xingwei yishu*), flourished and spread.

A consistent feature of Chinese performance art is a punishing, ritualised inscription of suffering upon the body. Gao Minglu suggests that the overt violence that characterised performance art in the 1980s revealed, intentionally or not, the 'sorrows and disturbances hidden in the artists' souls as they found themselves straddling cultural epochs and influences while trying to forge a new way.'[19] Zhou Tiehai's 1986 performance *Violence,* in which he stood naked while two other artists punished him by sticking his back with needles, is typical of this genre. Zhou collaborated with an all-male collective founded by Song Haidong in Shanghai, *M Group* ('M' for male), staging events in which performers were bound and beaten by mobs of naked men, in an 'attempt

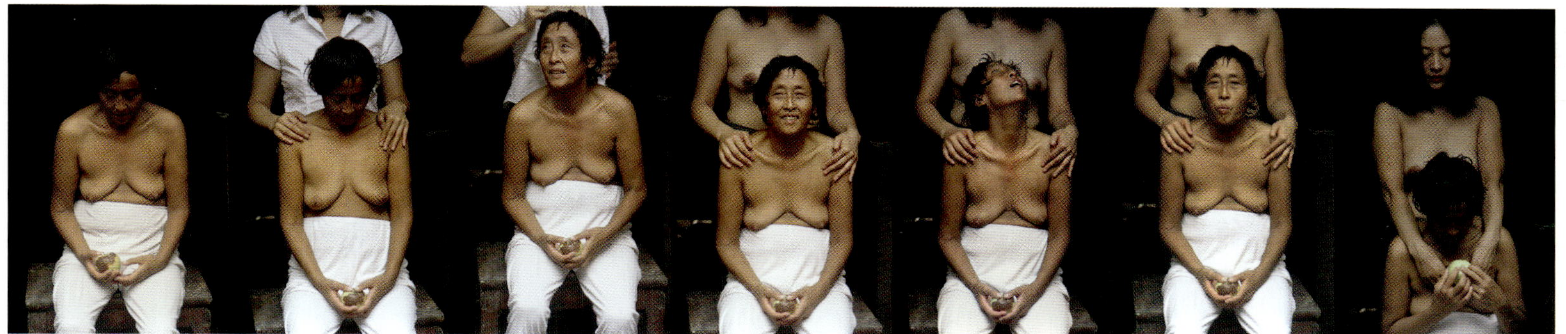

to convey the helplessness of artists and the wounded spirit of art.'[20] These events were often staged in public spaces to taunt the authorities. Their aim was to 'take the most radical avant-garde concepts from Dadaism as a model to destroy the conventional notion of art in the Chinese context, in order to merge with the international contemporary artworld.'[21]

The convention of transgressive endurance performance that developed in the 1980s continued to flourish in the 1990s, despite its essentially clandestine nature. In the bohemian East Village artists' community outside Beijing, Zhang Huan, He Yunchang and Ma Liuming followed a trajectory that intensified from shocking audiences to 'testing their very humanity'.[22] These artists, living in very poor areas, responded to a society increasingly focused on private wealth. They felt they could 'own' nothing but their own bodies, which became their primary material. Existential, ritualised, their work explored shamanism, martyrdom, political violence, and highly contested notions (in a still collectivist society) of the individual.

Art historian Thomas Berghuis classified Chinese performance art into separate categories including 'endurance and transcendence', and 'the body in self-mutilation, masochism or necrophagy'. He even identified, as a separate category, 'disconcerting events'.[23] In *Twelve Square Metres* (1994) Zhang Huan sat in the stench of the public toilet in his village for one hour, naked and covered in honey to attract flies. The villages on the outskirts of Beijing were squalid, polluted places occupied by poor migrant workers. Zhang Huan's act of endurance drew attention to the conditions in which Chinese people were living. In June of the same year, Zhang suspended himself in metal chains from the ceiling of an East Village hut, while his blood from a cut on his body dripped into a heated metal bowl. Like most other such performances, the audience for this event (described by art historian Craig Clunas as 'extreme macho abjection'[24]) was tiny. The police arrived and interrupted proceedings, detaining some artists on the grounds of obscenity.[25]

The relationship between performance artists and the state continued to be tense. On 11 April 2001, the Ministry of Culture released an official policy ordering local authorities nationwide to 'resolutely put a stop to the harmful phenomena of bloody, brutal, obscene spectacles, performed or exhibited in the name of "art".' The exhibition and performance of such art in public was expressly forbidden, as was the display and mechanical reproduction and dissemination of 'video or texts, pictures and other forms' of the works.[26] Despite attempts by the authorities to repress it, transgressive and violent body art continued. In 2008 He Yunchang famously had his own rib surgically removed and made into a piece of jewellery with the addition of four hundred grams of gold.[27]

Back in 1994, however, despite the actions of the police and local authorities, the photographs of Zhang's performance, *65kg* (the artist's body weight), shot by Ai Weiwei, were seen in exhibitions in Japan, Germany and the US within the year: photographs that themselves became highly marketable international art commodities. Outlining his intention for *65kg*, Zhang Huan wrote:

> I had wanted to use iron chains to hang my naked body parallel to the iron rafters, with my suspended body facing the floor. I would experience that state for as long as I could, enduring it for as long as I could hold out... I entertained a momentary thought of hanging from the rafter face to face with a woman and conducting the project together, but I quickly decided against that idea.[28]

Zhang Huan's offhand remark raises the question: where *were* the women while all of this 'disconcerting' activity was taking place? They were not, in fact, entirely absent. Yin Xiuzhen was creating performance works with her husband, Song Dong, whilst continuing to work as a high school art teacher.[29] Yingmei Duan and Zhang Binbin were active participants in East Village events. However, female artists are absent from the narrative as it usually framed. Some exceptions to the overwhelmingly masculine character of the experimental art of this period do exist. This chapter introduces two pioneers of a female performative practice, He Chengyao and Yingmei Duan, and a younger inheritor of that tradition, Ma Qiusha. These artists are developing a new form of embodied performance language to explore important issues and ideas.

He Chengyao
Mama and Me 2001
photograph of performance
image courtesy the artist

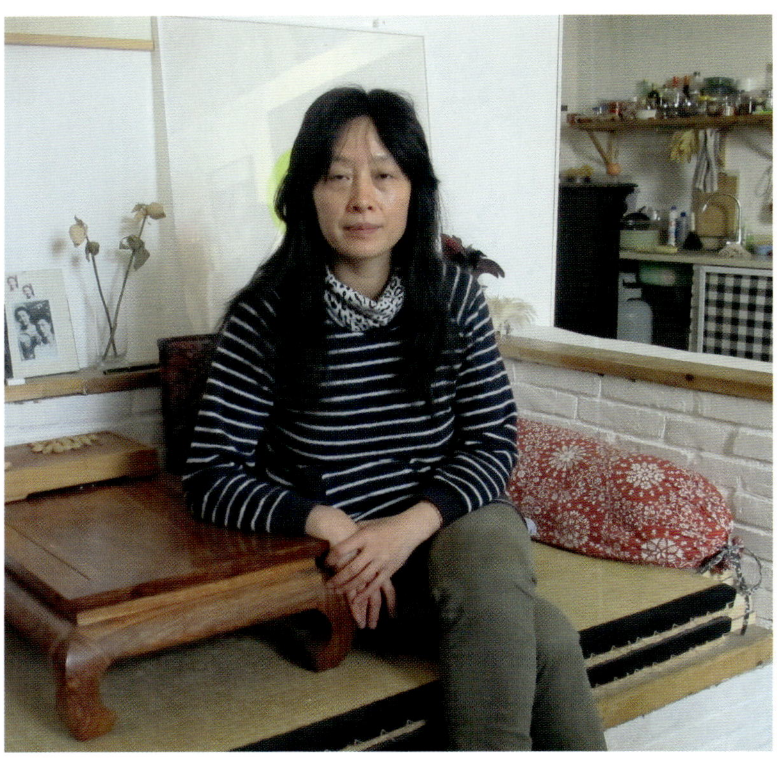

HE CHENGYAO 何成瑶
Body Politic

He Chengyao became instantly notorious in 2001 when she walked topless on the Great Wall of China. Her work was included in *Global Feminisms,* the inaugural exhibition at the Elizabeth A. Sackler Center for Feminist Art at the Brooklyn Museum in 2007, curated by Linda Nochlin and Maura Reilly.[30] At that time He Chengyao said, 'Feminism is a remote topic in my country… China is always a male-dominated world.'[31] Now, however, she acknowledges that the previously male-dominated arena of performance has increasingly become a female space, to the point that for *Meta 2014,* a Performance Art festival staged in Chongqing, almost two thirds of the participating artists were women.[32] He Chengyao herself has made it possible for other women artists to see performative practices as a possible means of expression.

He Chengyao has frequently used her own body to examine the wounds of the past. Born to a teenaged unmarried girl in a poor rural area in 1964, as a child she witnessed the punishments and humiliations visited upon her mother for these transgressions against moral codes, and her subsequent descent into mental illness. She remembers the shame she felt when her mother would manically tear off her clothes in public. Her work often explicitly deals with relationships between mothers and daughters, memory and madness. He Chengyao confronts highly taboo areas head-on, without subterfuge.

Homage to Mother dates from 2001. The artist poses bare breasted, staring ahead, holding a photograph of her mother, who is also topless. From the same year, *Mama and Me* records He's experience of visiting her elderly mother and finding her alone, shirtless, playing with a rotten apple. He Chengyao took off her own shirt and stood behind her, embracing her, the first time that mother and daughter had ever had a picture taken together. Through these works she reaffirmed their relationship and faced the fear of mental illness that had haunted her:

> Before I began performance art… I was avoiding who I was, but after that first performance it was like the veil had been lifted and I had to face who I really am. The same blood runs in my body and my mother's, so my mother really is the source of my creation. My mother suffered during the Cultural Revolution. It was not uncommon for people to commit suicide [as did the artist's grandfather], or to become schizophrenic. So even though my works represent my mother they have a more universal meaning. [I thought that] by exposing this suffering to the world I could forget myself and focus on the bigger picture. It is a healing process. After the series of *Mama and Me,* when I looked back at my previous works I saw myself as a patient. After *Mama and Me* I was cured. I felt really lucky to have art as a kind of healing.[33]

99 Needles (2002), in which the artist stands in front of the camera, clad only in underpants with long acupuncture needles sticking out of her body, recalls the forced treatments her mother was compelled to endure, administered by unqualified rural practitioners. Physical and emotional suffering connects her to the endurance and abasement that is a feature of Chinese performance art: 'I try to use the body to represent the soul as well as flesh, reflecting the culture, politics and economic growth in modern China.'

Nakedness is a recurring theme and symbol. In May 2001, artists and journalists converged by bus at a site one hundred and forty kilometres north of Beijing to see German artist H.A. Schult's installation of life-sized figures constructed of consumer waste. When the semi-naked He Chengyao suddenly appeared in their midst, having spontaneously removed her shirt and continued walking, attention was immediately diverted towards her. Because her impromptu performance was so public, and because it took place at this site – a potent symbol of Chinese nationhood – she attracted considerable media attention, much of it negative. She was accused of being an attention-seeker, and of immorality.[34]

He's Great Wall walk should be seen in the context of numerous performance, installation and conceptual works focused on this iconic site in the 1990s and early 2000s. These range from Xu Bing's 1990 *Ghost Pounding the Wall* to Cai Guo-qiang's 1993 *Project to Extend the Great Wall of China by 10,000 Metres.* Cang Xin (another of the East Village artists) licked

He Chengyao in Beijing,
December 2014
Photo LG

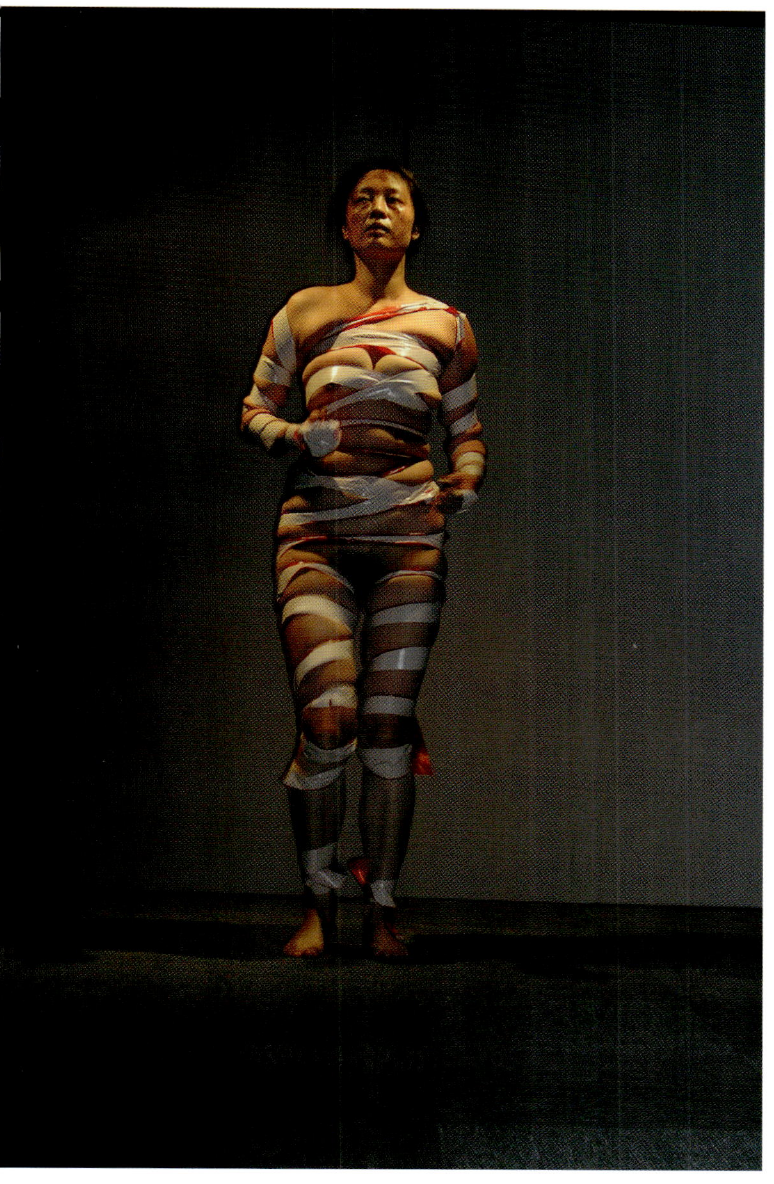

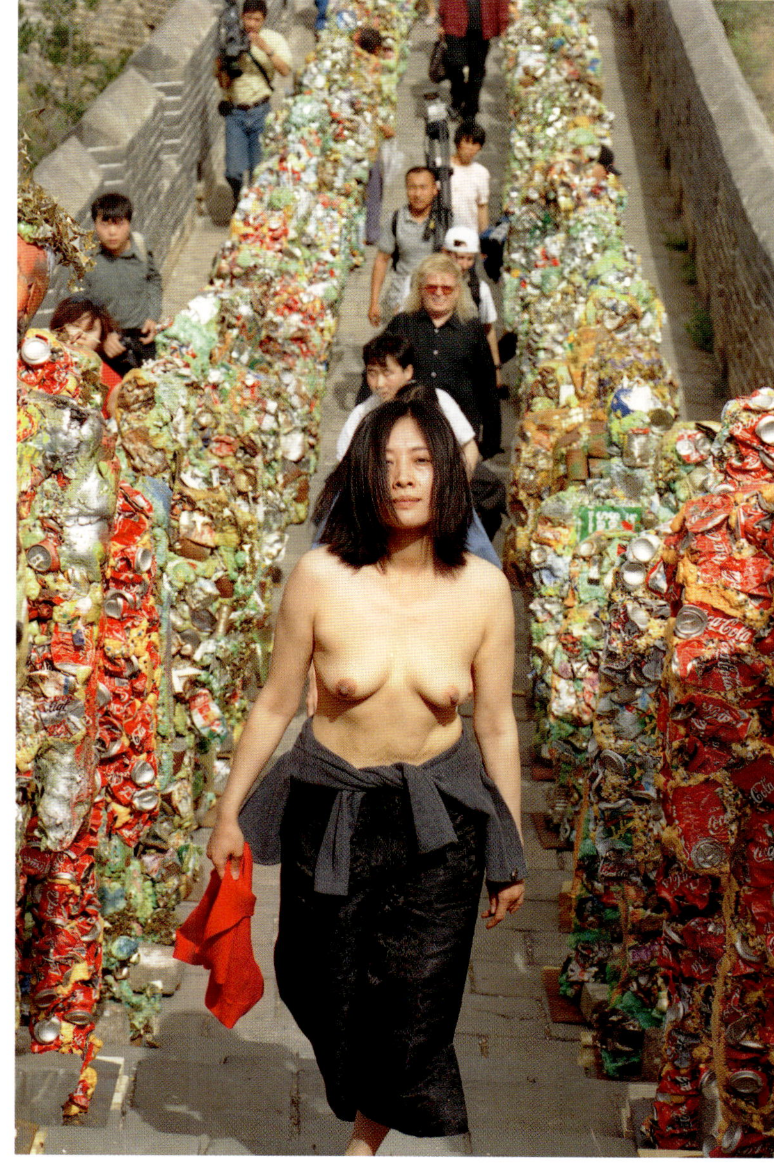

the wall, Ma Liuming walked upon it naked, and in the 1980s Marina Abramović and Ulay had walked its entire length from opposite ends, meeting in the middle. Terry Smith argues that unlike these other artists, for whom the Great Wall is a site of national ideology, 'He Chengyao reconstructed the living space of her childhood' and the shameful memories of her mother's illness, thus the wall itself becomes a symbol of oppressive patriarchy.[35] Her walk, defiant and lonely, became a ceremonial act commenting on her own life, and by extension that of her mother, and of all Chinese women.

Before this moment the notion of public performance art had never occurred to He Chengyao. She had trained as an oil painter in Sichuan Province, arriving in Beijing for postgraduate study at the Central Academy of Fine Arts. She seemed a little bemused by her own younger self as she recalled what happened:

> It was accidental. I had never seen live performance art before – it was only my second year in Beijing. In May there was to be a performance by a German artist on the Great Wall so I decided to go and see it. When I arrived I discovered that it was not after all performance art, it was the artist explaining his installation of about a thousand 1.8 metre figures made of industrial waste, which were lining both sides of the Great Wall so people felt a kind of confinement. It was under those circumstances that I decided to take off my clothes.

In recounting this experience the artist finds it difficult to explain her motivation, but at the time, He Chengyao did not consider her astonishing departure from social norms an artwork. 'Without the subsequent works I would see it only as an accident,' she said. Retrospectively, she gave the piece a

He Chengyao
Public Broadcast Exercises, Shanghai 2004
photograph of performance
image courtesy the artist

He Chengyao
Opening the Great Wall 2001
photograph of performance
image courtesy the artist

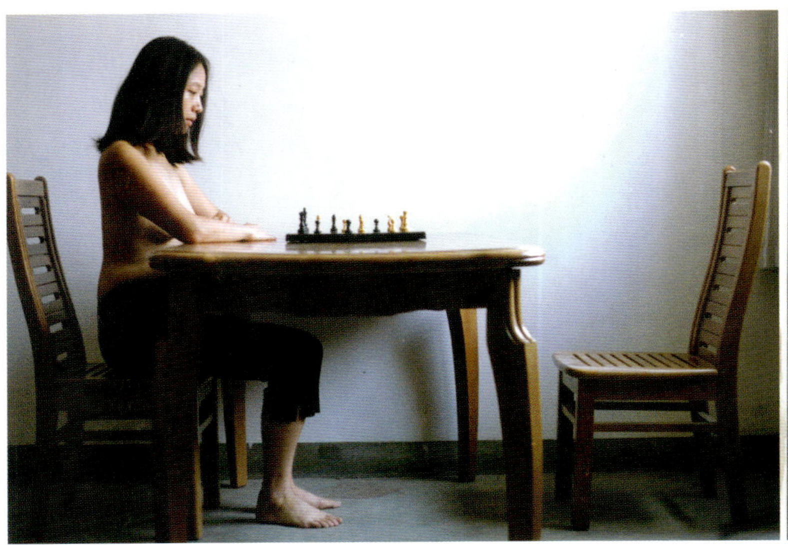

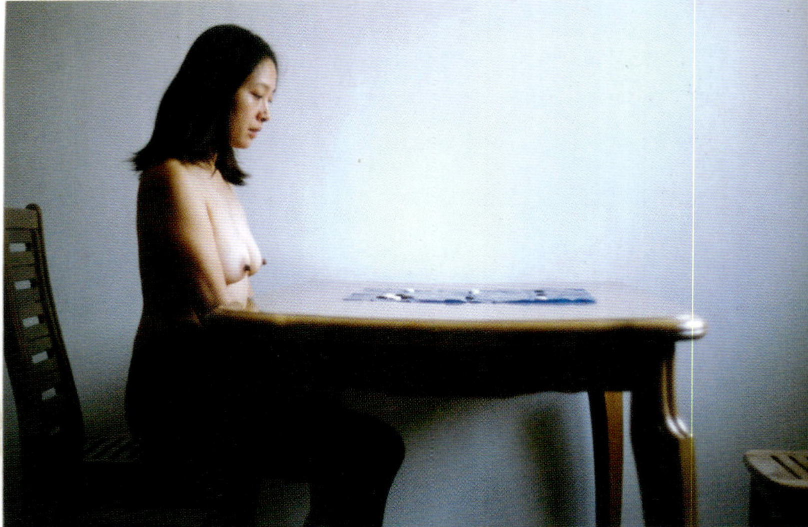

title: *Opening the Great Wall*. Afterwards, even though she was confronted by 'doubt and enmity' she realised the cathartic nature of her action:

> Faced with all this hostility I tried to figure out the reason behind my performance. It was as if I was being controlled by a supernatural power of some kind. I decided [I had] to look inside for answers instead of outside. And I discovered that I had always been trying to avoid or escape from something – and that was from my family and my mother.

Bare-breasted, striding along this symbol of Chinese history, He Chengyao was engaged in a kind of exorcism:

> I think that it was a very important and defining moment in my art practice as it was the start of my performance work. I had studied oil painting, a very traditional and conservative practice, but I felt that performance might be a more straightforward and immediate way of expressing myself.

He Chengyao had previously described her paintings as 'bourgeois, fuzzy, romantic, sentimental.'[36] She yearned to find a different way to express herself: 'At that time artists did not have much experience of performance art and it was not taught in the art schools. All our experiences came from a few books with some pictures – a very indirect experience. It [performance art] was an entirely new possibility for me.' Her cathartic action was important for the artist personally, but it was also significant in the story of Chinese contemporary art. Wu Hung believes that He Chengyao 'simultaneously challenged a supreme national symbol and the male-dominated world of Chinese performance art.'[37] He Chengyao stopped painting shortly afterwards:

> I thought that there was something between my real feelings and thoughts, and the paintings that I made, so they were not a very good way of expressing myself. Performance was more real, more immediate and more powerful. The more I dug deep into myself and into my heart, the more I realised that I had to present the experiences of my generation, my mother's generation and even my grandmother's generation to the world. It didn't matter to me whether there were any exhibitions or not, it was like a calling.

In 2004 she created *Public Broadcast Exercises*, performing naked the calisthenics that were once mandatory for all Chinese schoolchildren, bound in red and white tape which sometimes snapped or fell off. 'The point is to be bound,' she says. The tapes were wrapped around the artist's body with the sticky side out, and as she strained to pull her limbs apart the tearing sound signifies the painful ripping of flesh. 'I feel that the works I do are for my grandmother, for my mother. Not for myself,' she said in a New York Times interview. 'I feel they are speaking through my body and I have to speak for them. They don't have the opportunity.'[38]

He Chengyao resists defining her work as feminist. Like many Chinese artists she is uncomfortable with the term, seeing feminism as a western philosophy that does not speak to the Chinese experience of collectivism: 'We need to recognise the distinction between men and women, but there is [should be] no difference in their rights... what we are trying to achieve is equality of *all* people, not only for women... . First of all there are no basic human rights in China. So there are no foundations for us to pose the question for women's rights. The first task would be to champion universal rights for all Chinese people.'

He Chengyao is entirely aware of the implications and possible consequences of using her own naked body, in a

He Chengyao
With Marcel Duchamp as My Opponent 2001
two photographs, each 53 x 80 cm
image courtesy the artist

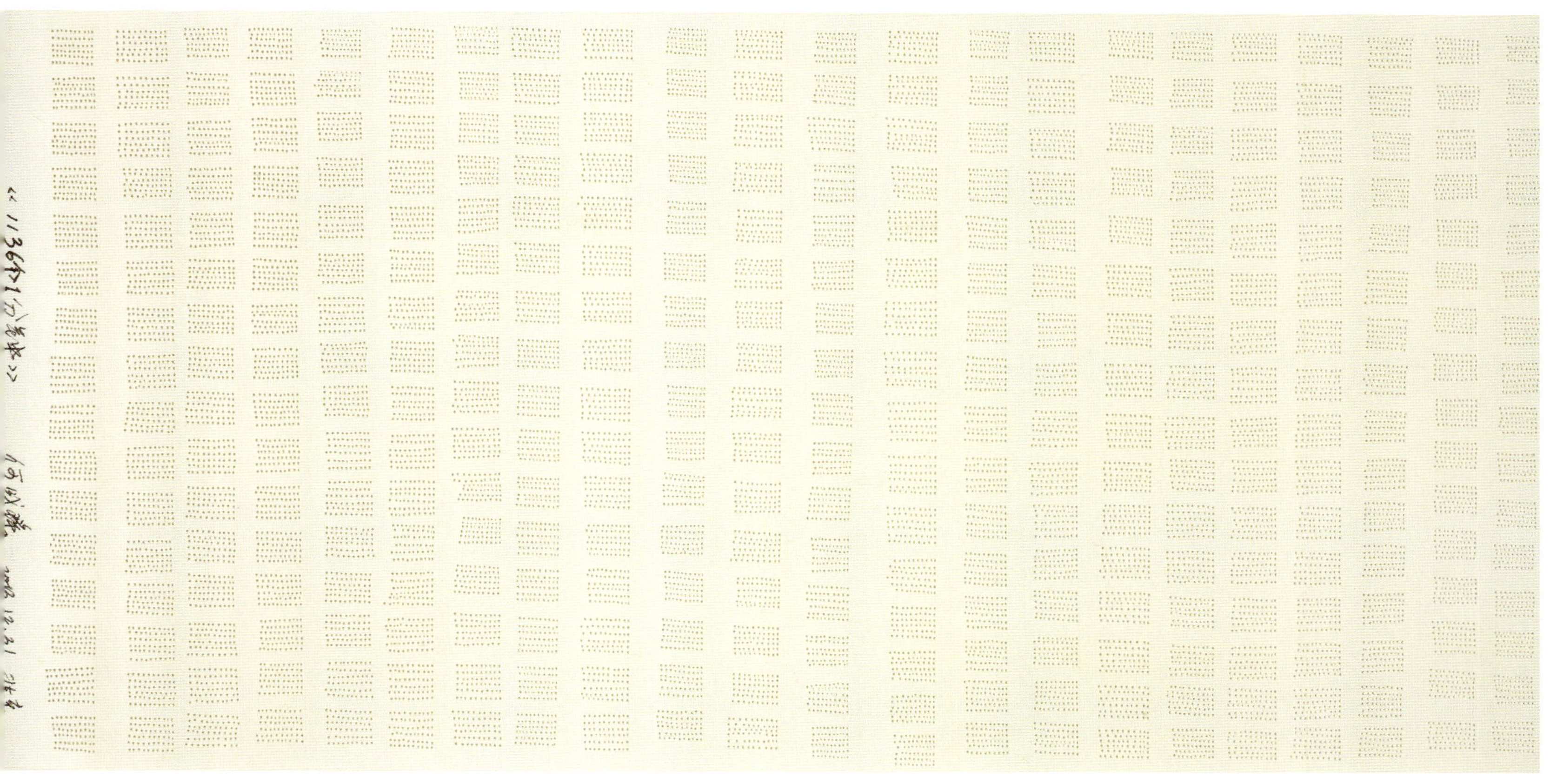

society where nudity is still taboo. She thinks of her work as universal. It is personal, first and foremost, but her own female body symbolises all humanity. Filled with psychological metaphor and ritualised enactments of pain, her work is open to multiple interpretations. In addition to mining the rawness of family history and individual suffering, she knowingly references the history of conceptual and performance art. When she began post-graduate study in 2000 she discovered the work of Marcel Duchamp and Joseph Beuys:

> Their ideas are so important to Chinese artists. Duchamp's conceptual art and Beuys' social sculpture, and his belief that everyone is an artist, were really important to me, as well as to other Chinese artists. Beuys' ideas [in particular] seemed very democratic and I agreed with him that art has very healing properties. I imitated one of his works using a photograph of my mother.

In *Homage to Mama* (sometimes entitled *Salute to Mama*), she holds a photograph of her mother upraised, appropriating Beuys' 1964 action in which he held a crucifix in one hand, with the other raised in salute. Her upper body is naked and her face painted with red fluid. The artist has said this was enacted in gratitude to Beuys for showing her that art could be cathartic.[39]

With Marcel Duchamp as My Opponent shows the artist, bare breasted, playing chess in her apartment opposite an empty chair, as if placed for the absent French artist. In the second of two paired images, she and her invisible artistic mentor play the Chinese game of Go. The work refers to an event in 1963. The Pasadena Art Museum held a retrospective of Duchamp's work, and photographer Julian Wassner proposed a photo-shoot in which Duchamp would play chess with a nude female art student. The artist agreed, and the pair sat in front of *The Bride Stripped Bare by her Bachelors, Even* and played several games.[40] Thus He Chengyao literally inserts her own body into the canon of art history – a provocative act Duchamp himself would have appreciated. She questions the western dominance of contemporary art:

> Every artist and intellectual in China has a kind of identity crisis trying to find out who we really are. After Reform and Opening so many books on philosophy and art came from the west that we became more familiar with western culture than with our own.

In 2006, in Manchester, He Chengyao presented a work reflecting on the commodification of the art object and the fetishisation of the female body. *Auction of Very Personal Possessions* invited the audience to bid on an undisclosed item belonging to the artist. When they entered the room they discovered that the possession in question was the artist's hair. She knelt beside a table, her long black plait stretched behind her on a white tablecloth. The auctioneer lit a candle, explaining

He Chengyao
1,136 Minutes 2013
pierced paper
image courtesy the artist

that the winner would be the last person whose bid was received before the flame went out. The cutting of hair implies many things: sacrifice, punishment, subjugation – sometimes even freedom. The severance of Chinese hair, however, particularly in a western context, has other uncomfortable connotations of the removal of Chinese pigtails.[41] A member of the audience described the artist's presentation of her long hair as 'a scenario that evoked an execution.'[42] Hair is deeply personal – a woman's hair is considered beautiful and erotic, so much so that some cultures require it to be covered, but hair may also evoke horror or disgust.

He Chengyao's performance invited audiences to question the role of the artist in the art marketplace, at a time when the international demand for contemporary Chinese art was booming. The work alluded to gender and power relationships, within China and elsewhere, and to binaries of Oriental versus western culture. Chinese-born British performance artists Cai Yuan and JJ Xi (the same artists who notoriously tried to jump on Tracey Emin's bed in 1999 and urinate into Duchamp's *Fountain* at the Tate Modern in 2000) were the successful bidders, and were instructed to cut off her hair close to her scalp with a pair of scissors while she stared impassively at them. It took ten excruciating minutes.

In April 2012 He Chengyao travelled to Tibet, where she stayed in a Buddhist monastery for twelve months, a transformative experience. 'I was the only teacher who was not a lama,' she said. 'I was surprised to find they could live so peacefully and so happily in conditions that were very simple and not at all prosperous. They spent most of their time in sutras – prayers – for the sick people in the village and for the dying. The Tibetan villagers also live a very simple life, in the fields, harvesting their crops. They did not seem interested in material wealth. After that I discovered my own way of finding my true self through meditation. I am trying to discover the ultimate meaning of my own life.'

He Chengyao's work now is based on time. She pierces white scrolls of rice paper with an acupuncture needle, once each second, measuring the seconds with a metronome. She says:

> To live in this world is to solve problems every day, both big and small problems. Life in this way can seem meaningless. But it's like the lamas chanting sutras, it is in this process of solving problems [this meaninglessness] that meaning presents itself. After Tibet I realised I wanted to spend my life in my own way. Before that I was a patient trying to cure myself but afterwards I was completely cured. Now I am a Buddhist.

He Chengyao's new practice is both meditation and mark-making. The body is still present – the actions of the artist, bent over her paper and measuring out breaths and seconds, are now embedded in each work.

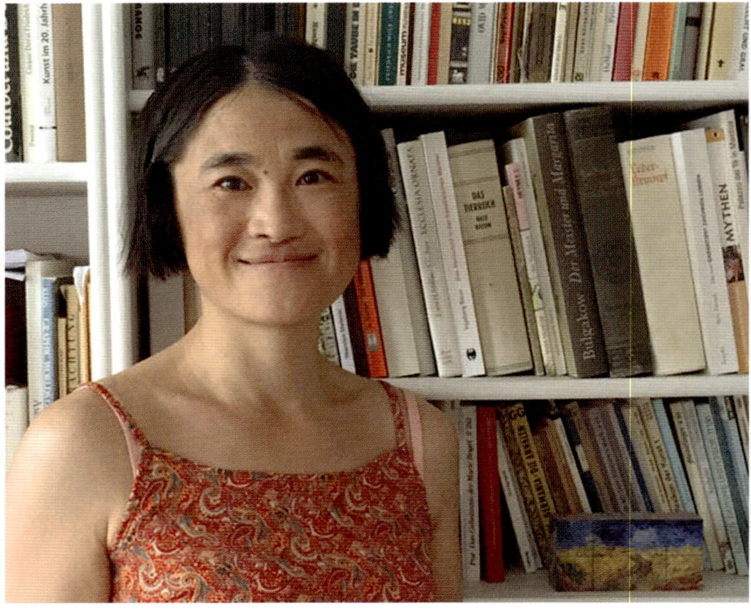

Yingmei Duan
image courtesy the artist

YINGMEI DUAN 段英梅

A Curious Observer

Yingmei Duan was one of only two women artists who lived in Beijing's East Village at the height of its 1990s radicalism. She worked in Beijing as a freelance artist until 1998. Duan no longer lives in China, making her something of an exception among artists selected for this book,[43] however, she is significant due to her participation in the early years of avant-garde art. Her practice is founded upon the twin influences of Beuys and Abramović, both of whom have been important catalysts for Chinese artists.

Duan has lived in Germany for many years, returning to China only to visit her parents and extended family, so in lieu of a studio visit a long Skype conversation about her work was followed by emails and social media exchanges, in which she explained how she came to be involved in the 1990s cauldron of experimentation and innovation:

> In 1993 I moved to the East Village in Beijing. The reason I went there was because I fell in love with a man living there. At the time it was just a group of young, passionate people, all away from their homes, trying to find a new life and develop their artworks. With time some of them came to performance art. I was one of the two female artists living there and part of the East Village artist's community; Zhang Binbin was the other female artist. At that time I was very young and naive, and living in the East Village gave me more opportunities to learn more about art and human life. They [the male artists] all treated me like a younger sister.[44]

In 1995 she participated in the legendary performance of stacked naked artists, *To add one meter to an anonymous mountain*. Like other artists recalling this time, she is a little wistful:

> I remember before we made the performance on the mountain, we tried to set it up in an interior space. We ended up deciding on performing on a mountain, and the performance began with each of the artists being weighed by Kong Bu. He then ordered the artists determined by weight and they began to build a human mountain by lying on top of each other. The heaviest lay down first, and the lightest lay down last.
>
> At that time there were not many galleries or museums, it was very seldom that artists sold their art, and most of them also very rarely thought about selling. We all had similar life conditions – even though we did not have much money we felt very happy and lucky. At that time Chinese art was dominated by traditional mediums – painting, sculpture and printmaking. We did not have much information about foreign countries.

Even though the authorities frowned on western influences in popular culture and fashion, young people were adept at circumventing such restrictions. 'When I was in the East Village, there are so many interesting memories... we often went to Zuoxiao Zuzhou's room to enjoy listening to American rock and roll music from the 1960s.[45] Each time I went to Zhang Huan's house, there was always a lot of communication and discussion concerning art and exchanging ideas.' She thinks of this as a happy, exciting time, when everyone seemed filled with energy: 'My most vivid memories come from all the different people I met when I was in Beijing.'

Duan travelled to Germany for a solo painting exhibition in 1995, then returned to China. Unhappy with her life in Beijing, she returned to Germany in 1998. In 2000 she began studying with Marina Abramović, Birgit Hein and Christoph Schlingensief at the prestigious fine arts college, the 'Hochschule fuer Bildende Kuenste Braunschweig'. She has lived in that small city ever since.[46]

Her practice is gentle and reflective, evident in *The Circle Dream*, created to bridge the gulf between herself and her family. She writes:

> Since I moved to Germany, I've been missing my family quite a lot. We call each other very often. They are always worried about my health and my living here. When we discuss art and money, we always disagree. There seems to be an insurmountable divide between us when it comes to this particular issue. They have always wished that I would be able to make a living from my art and become wealthy. Whenever we talk about this there is an element of reverse psychology and we often end up fighting. From their point of view I'm not practising Filial Piety to the same extent as my brothers and sisters. I've been very upset about this for quite some time.[47]

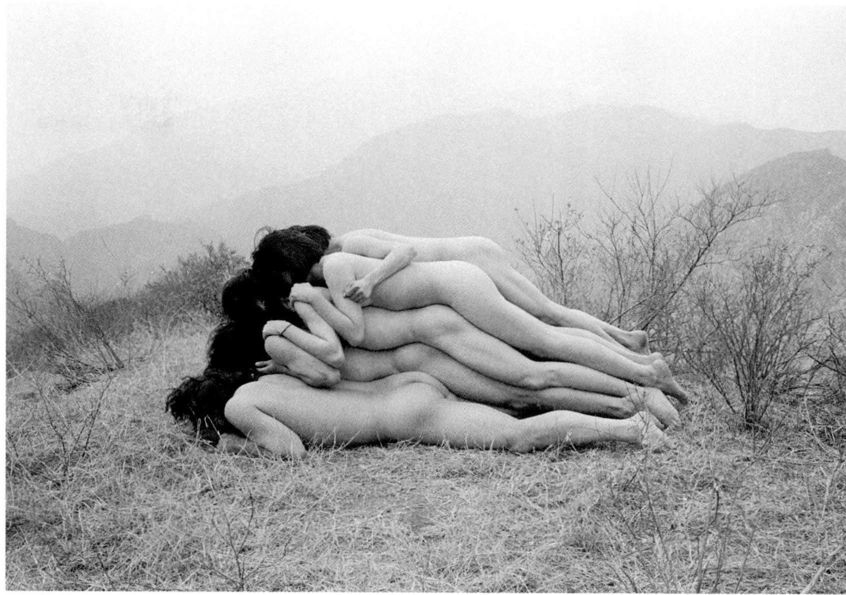

Zhang Huan, Yingmei Duan and other artists from Beijing's East Village
To Add One Meter to an Anonymous Mountain 1995
black and white photograph of a collaborative performance
by the Beijing East Village artists, 104 x 154 cm
image courtesy Yingmei Duan, photograph Lü Nan

In this work the artist and her family communicate through letters and paintings, on Skype, and also meet in person. She questions the distinction between art and life, between artist and audience.

Duan is not especially interested in exploring ideas about gender. Like He Chengyao, she prefers to think of herself as a 'human being first and foremost', and believes that her work relates to universal experiences. In 2011 she said:

> I think of myself as a woman in particular in only a few of my performances. Most of the time, I consider myself to be a normal human being, generally interested in how one can express one's feelings. I haven't researched the changing role of women in China in the last fifteen years, and I haven't considered that change to be significant in my work. But it is a very interesting question and one that I would like very much to pay attention to moving forward.[48]

Duan's most pessimistic thoughts about being a woman relate to age. Her separation from her ageing parents makes her anxious and drives some ongoing projects, such as *The Circle Dream*. She worries about them, telling Asia Art Archive, 'As a Chinese, my darkest idea is: one day in the future, I will go to visit my parents, but they will already have died.' Living away from China and family is not easy. '*The Circle Dream* has been a very significant work in my life,' she says. 'It has united my art with my family. Previously the two were very separate. However, involving my family in a collaborative project has been a great bonding experience. It gave us the opportunity to open up conversations between

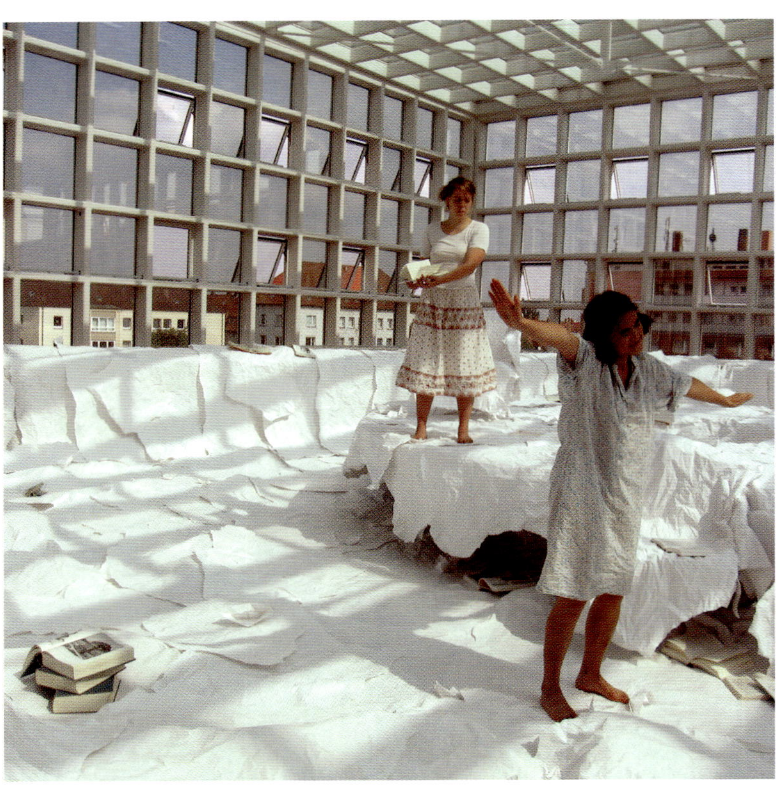

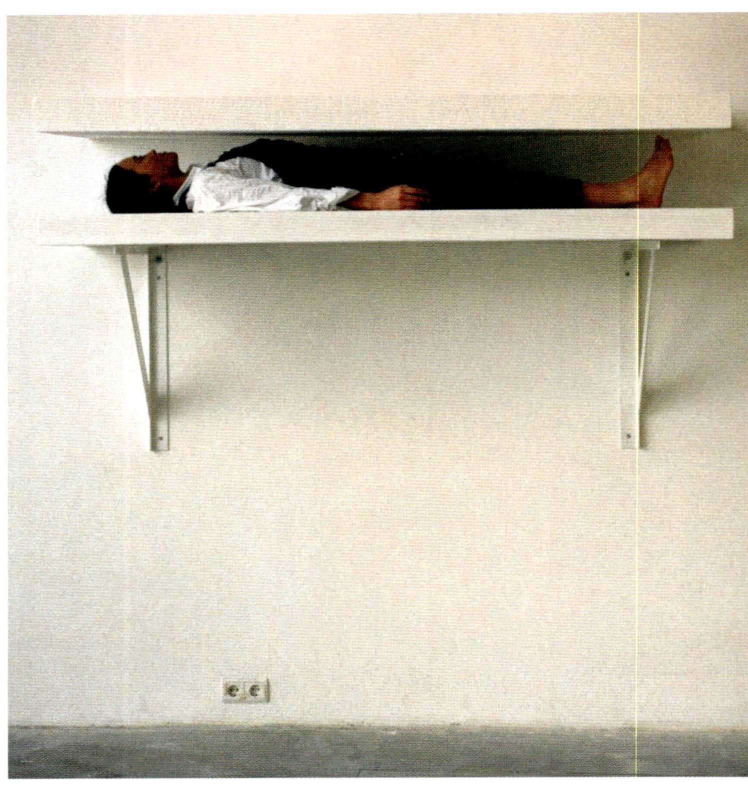

us. With time our conversation was not only about art, but more normal family life topics. According to their feelings and interests we tried to find interesting topics for conversation, [and] during this work's development our relationship improved a lot.'

Like other diasporic artists, the question of 'Chinese-ness' is complex and her ideas about this aspect of her identity continue to change:

> I actually do not think about my identity in these terms. Each person can find his or her own "paradise island", so I found my paradise in Germany... If I go really deep into your question and answer you with rational consideration, of course I am Chinese because it's where I grew up for twenty-seven years, and it's my heritage. Chinese culture and life has influenced me greatly and always plays an important role in my whole life. However, living in Germany for so many years has also influenced me. In addition, I have been able to travel a great deal around the world, experiencing many different places, culture and people along the way. So I see myself as a combination of different influences.

Love is tied to obligation in Chinese culture and in her own life:

> Filial piety is a traditional virtue in China and can be found in all aspects of life, which permeates every Chinese person's blood... This theme inspired another work, and the inspiration came from family disagreements about art, money, etcetera. I hope that the work *Filial Piety* which I did with fellow artist Feng Weidong can help me understand my family better and at the same time let my family learn more about me and my art... At first, this work was calculated to last for one year. During this year we communicated with our families in different ways, such as letters, chatting, paintings and so on. However, I found that a year was not long enough so I decided to continue this work without time limits until our relationship improved. My family did not want to be recorded by video or other mediums, so our collaboration is via face-to-face conversation or online using Skype.

For Yingmei Duan there is little separation between art and what other people call 'life'. Duan describes her work as DLAP (Daily Live Art Performance). Her interactions with audiences, and her research about where she will enact each new work, are vital to its construction. She describes her practice as a form of questioning – for the artist and for the audience.

In Britain in 2010, in a Sheffield hospice for terminally ill children, Duan began a project based on conversations with the children, their families and the staff. She said:

> Performance art should not be bound to galleries, museums, and festivals; it can also happen in daily life. I am a performance artist and, at the same time, a researcher. Using my performances to connect with different parts of society has become a very important part of

Yingmei Duan, with Julia Dick and Ulrich Reinhardt
HBK, My Last Lesson 2006
live performance
Braunschweig University of Art, Germany
image courtesy the artist, photograph Jürgen Bernhard Kuck

Yingmei Duan
In Between 2004
live performance and installation
Hochschule fuer Bildende Kuenste Braunschweig, Germany
image courtesy the artist, photograph Chengwu Luo

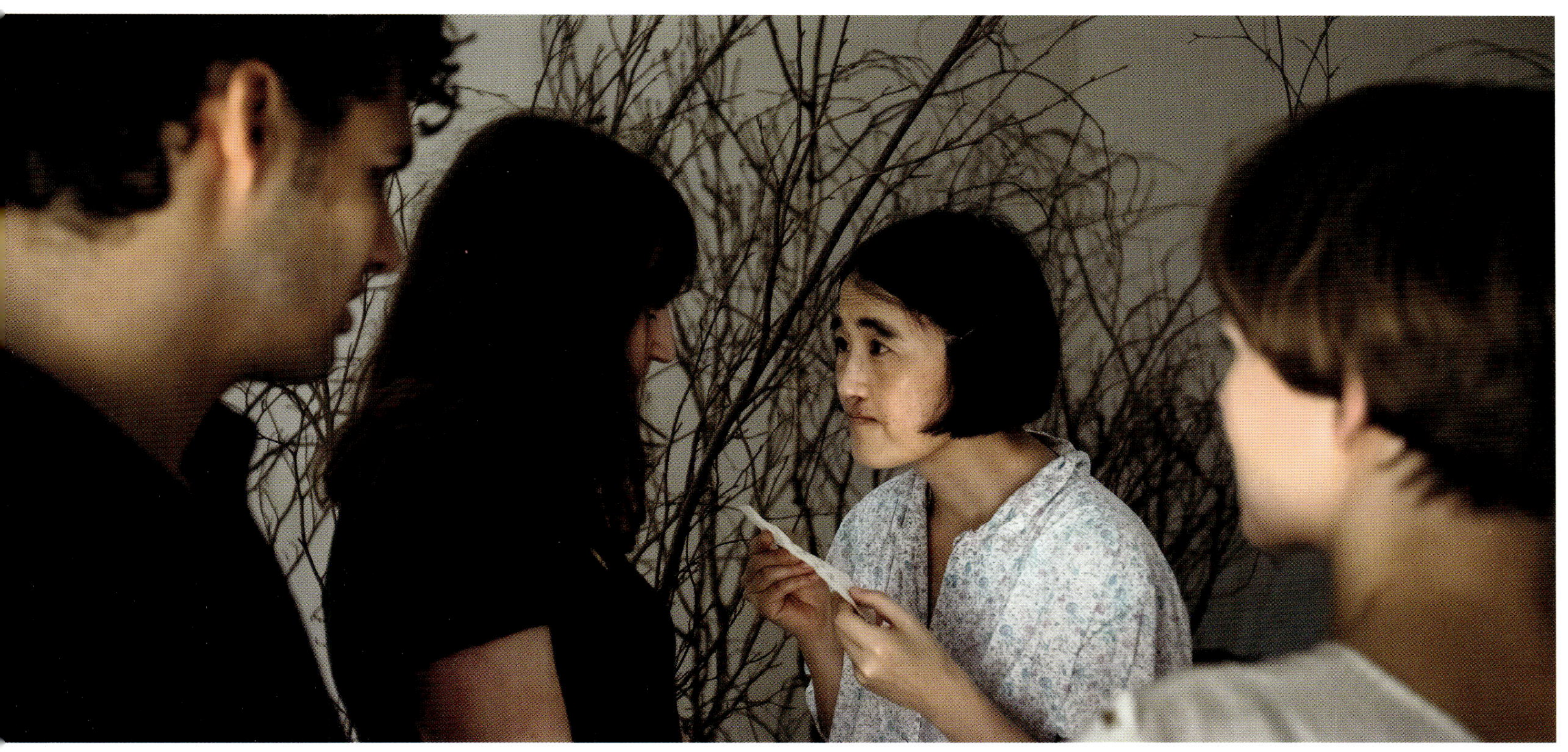

> my work. I am always interested in doing social projects. In *Yingmei at Bluebell Wood Children's Hospice*, I worked both as an artist and a volunteer. Bluebell Wood Children's Hospice is a fascinating institution, offering a place for children with terminal conditions and their families to come to relax and have fun. Most of the children at Bluebell will die before they reach adulthood. Observing, helping, chatting, and researching were an important part of my process while I was there. I enjoyed my time there very much, despite its being challenging. The life of each child looked like a fairy tale.[49]

The endpoint of this process was the production of twenty-four paintings made in collaboration with the patients – a permanent legacy – and two books of fairytale stories based on the children she had met there.

For *The Art of Change: New Directions from China*, at London's Hayward Gallery in 2012, Yingmei Duan presented three static works previously shown in Germany: *Sleeping, Patience* and *In Between*. In each work white shelves are attached to the walls. The first contains a woman in a sleeping bag, the second a woman sandwiched between two shelves, and the third a woman with her head poking through a hole. They were performed by actors to Duan's instructions. There is a Samuel Beckett-like absurdity in these pieces, a reference to Minimalist sculpture, and a deep sense of stillness. An ongoing concern in her work is sleep and the recumbent body, evoking unconsciousness and even death. She is interested in *wei wu wei* – 'action without action' – a Taoist concept deeply connected with Chinese culture.

In conversation, and in many of her performance works, Duan presents a persona of childlike wonder, but her work has a darker side. In *Sleepwalker* (2002) the artist wakes, as if from a trance, and slowly stands up. She moves towards the audience as if sleepwalking. Suddenly, she slaps the face of a member of the audience, then walks on as if oblivious. In another work, the effect is dependent on a sense of shock: 'In 2001, I did an interactive live performance entitled *Clown*, where I made up my face like a clown. I grinned stiffly at the audience and, with a contorted animal-like face, I laughed right into people's faces, moving past them very slowly. The feeling conveyed in that situation was anything but funny.'[50]

At the At the 19th Biennale of Sydney in 2014 Duan performed *Happy Yingmei*, inspired by Oscar Wilde's fairy tale *The Happy Prince* – a story about a golden statue that befriends a swallow. Together they bring happiness to others, in life as well as in death. She describes the performance:

> Through a small doorway one steps into Duan's poetic fairy tale wonderland, which is enacted in a forest glade. In the forest glade one hears different sounds like wind, water dripping and Yingmei herself is crouching down on a tree stump, she is also sometimes making sounds... Yingmei is going (but slowly) and handing out many wishes which are written on small folded pieces of paper, which she opens and gives to the audience, making eye contact.[51]

Yingmei Duan
Happy Yingmei 2012
Hayward Gallery, London
live performance and sound installation
image courtesy the artist, photograph Alexander Newton

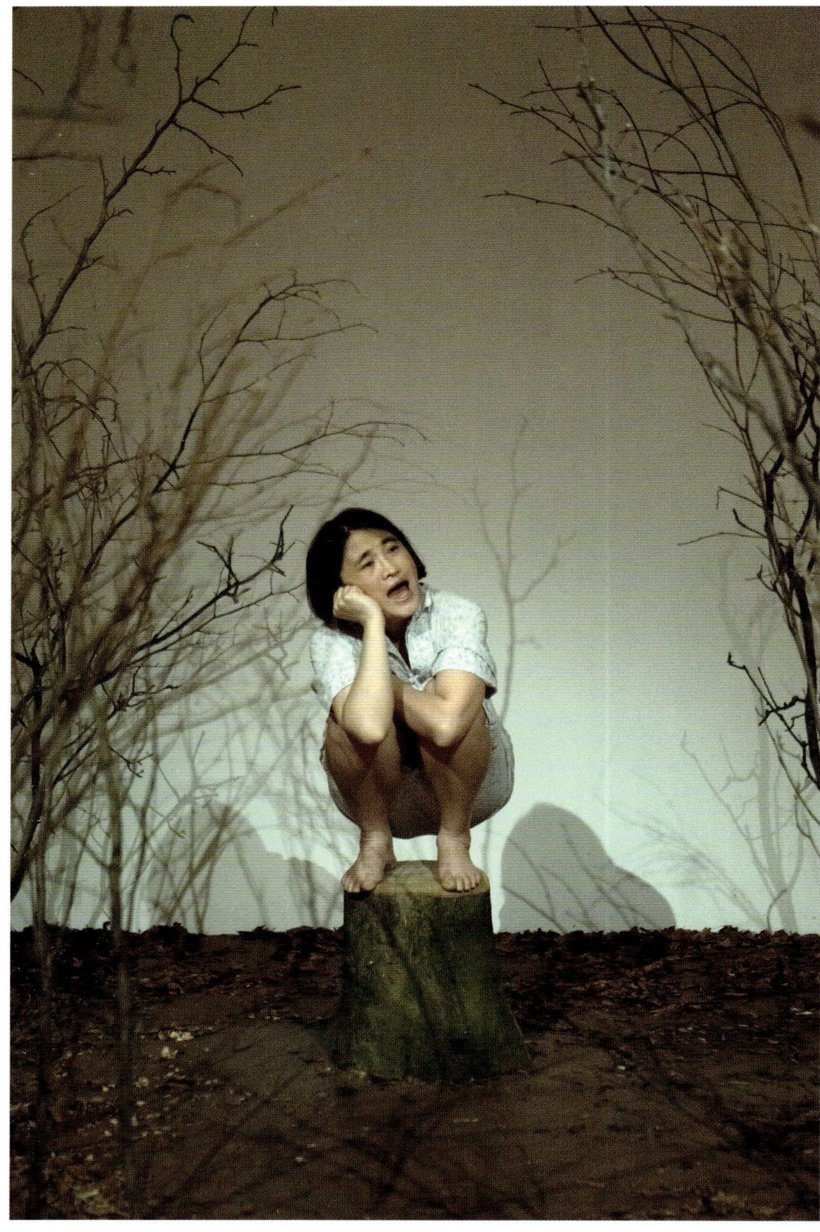

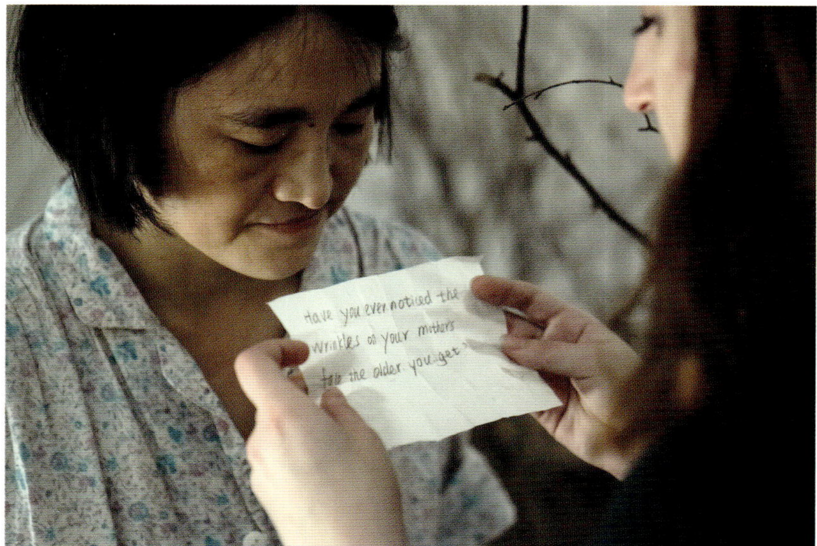

Duan inhabited a small forest inside the Art Gallery of New South Wales, where she could be found singing softly and handing 'prophecies', wishes or instructions to visitors. You might be handed a slip of paper reading, 'Go to the church and ask them why religion is not free' or 'Watch the sky tonight and make a wish' or 'Have you ever noticed the wrinkles on your mother's face?' Intended to inspire reflection, the whimsical texts are instructional, yet not didactic. Art historian Jacqueline Millner believes the work is part of a resurgence of performance art in response to the dominance of the digital in the twenty-first century, and a new revitalisation of feminist concerns in contemporary art.[52]

In November 2014 Duan presented two performances at the Heixiangning Art Museum in Shenzhen, in an exhibition of work by Chinese women artists living and working outside of China. In *Observer* Yingmei Duan scrutinises the audience, while the audience simultaneously observes her. She is both performer and spectator: 'The audience enters the exhibition; they look around with curiosity and suddenly notice a woman far up above – on the wall. It is Yingmei. She sits on a little platform. Yingmei pulls her legs to her body to appear very small and watches the people with concentration through her large glasses. Quietly she rests on the platform, which is just big enough for her to sit on. She wears everyday clothes and over her shoulder is carrying a white linen bag, which is full of things, as if she was on her way to an appointment or had just come back from shopping.'[53]

Room 2 involved the audience more directly: '[It] involves the audience entering an empty room – they experience an environment of white walls and they can hear sounds coming from the walls. The audience cannot see pieces by me but instead can imagine my works by listening to the audio. The sound describes different artworks in various mediums such as installation, photography and performance. During the course of the exhibition this work is constantly in development. The audio changes daily so the audience always experiences new works. Some materials like paper, pencils and so on will be provided for the audience to use to create their own artworks in response to their feelings and imagination inspired by the audio. Their artworks will be presented on the walls or on the floor outside of the empty room.'

Yingmei Duan's works reference family relationships, memories, dreams and fairy tales. Like her contemporaries in Beijing's East Village, Yingmei Duan employs a sophisticated internationalist visual language, inflected by her Chinese heritage. Being distant from her homeland and her family has focused her attention on aspects of culture such as filial love and reciprocal obligation. The barrier between performer, artist and audience becomes a porous membrane, as light and transparent as a lantern.

Yingmei Duan
Happy Yingmei 2012
Hayward Gallery, London
live performance and sound installation
image courtesy the artist, photograph Alexander Newton

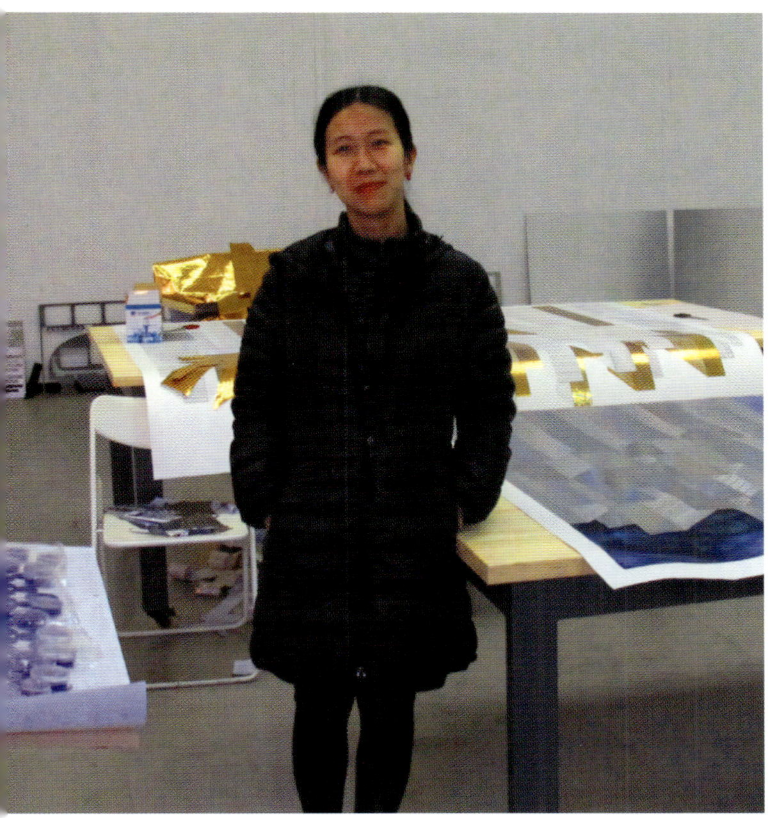

Ma Qiusha in her Beijing studio, December 2014, photo LG

MA QIUSHA 马秋莎

Membranes and Memory

Born in Beijing in 1982, Ma Qiusha grew up in the centre of the city, in a traditional '*hutong*' courtyard house. She is a 'true' Beijinger, proud of this familial link to her city. In 2005, after graduating from the Digital Media Department of the Central Academy of Fine Arts, she headed to New York to complete her MFA at Alfred University. *From No. 4 Pinguanli to No.4 Tianqiaobeili*, which brought her a degree of notoriety in 2007, shows the artist speaking at length about her childhood. Expressionless, she recounts how her mother pressured her to study art, and to excel at school. She was constantly exhorted to do better, to *be* better. After a while you see that she is speaking with more and more difficulty, repeatedly swallowing. She appears to have an obstruction in her mouth. At the end of her monologue, when she removes the object, you realise she has been speaking with a razorblade on her tongue, and her mouth is filled with blood. The metaphor of the blade is horrifyingly immediate, evoking self-mutilation and sadism. Ma Qiusha presents the voice of the one-child generation, at once indulged and pressured, the products of an enormous social experiment and its unintended consequences.

She is quick to point out that we should not assume that the narrative in the video is a form of unmediated autobiographical truth:

> Is it a made-up story or a true living experience? [Actually] it's just a kind of archetype. It's the eighties generation – it's typical of what we experienced in our childhood. I try to manifest this experience in a virtual self.[54]

Despite this disavowal, her monologue expresses a deeply felt personal truth, albeit exaggerated for the sake of dramatic effect. It is a bleak view of childhood, in which her earliest experiences of art were joyless, even punishing. 'I am not suggesting that it is either positive or negative – without one there is not the other. There was happiness as well as sorrow in my childhood,' says the artist. But as an only child, and a daughter, the pressure to succeed, to bring honour to the family and make her parents' lives meaningful, was relentless.

Ma considers that her focus on pain and endurance in her performance and video works is different in nature from the work of artists of the previous generation:

> I think that [artists such as] Zhang Huan are excellent but we have different starting points. He was challenging the extremities of the human body. But my work cannot be analysed [so] logically. When I have a new idea or a strong opinion I have to wait until I find the most suitable form of expression. It might take months or even a year to find it. I cannot really explain why I used the razor blade, except that when I returned from America I had a bitterness in my mouth but I had to keep smiling. There is a contrast in this work – the razor in your mouth causes physical pain but the story I am telling is about mental pain.
>
> The parents of children born in the 1980s experienced the Cultural Revolution as they grew up. They lacked education and missed so many opportunities, so they have a strong desire for their children to really achieve something. And, of course, in Chinese culture you must live up to the expectations of your parents. So for children born in the eighties there is a really heavy burden. It's a really complicated issue, because it is not only because of desire and ambition that the parents want their children to achieve, it is also all mixed up with love and so many other elements.

In 2011, when her work was shown at Beijing's Ullens Centre for Contemporary Art, she wrote, 'Though I love my mother deeply, that love is often fraught with pain.'[55]

Blades and acts of cutting appear often in Ma Qiusha's work. For *All My Sharpness Comes From Your Hardness* (2011), the artist filmed herself being dragged behind a car, wearing ice skates that scrape and slice across the road surface as she zig-zags back and forth, sharpening the blades. We see only her legs and feet, from the viewpoint of a camera attached to the roof of a small vehicle. Shot on the road leading to her grandparents' home, the source of so many of her childhood memories, the video is excruciating to watch, but curiously

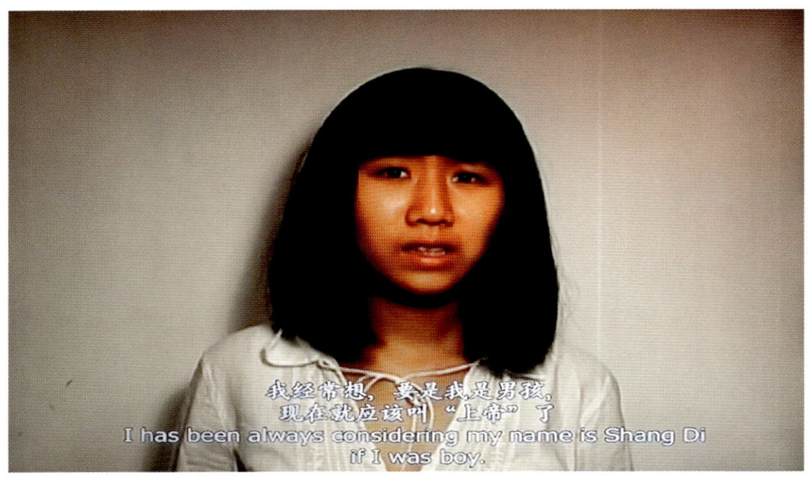

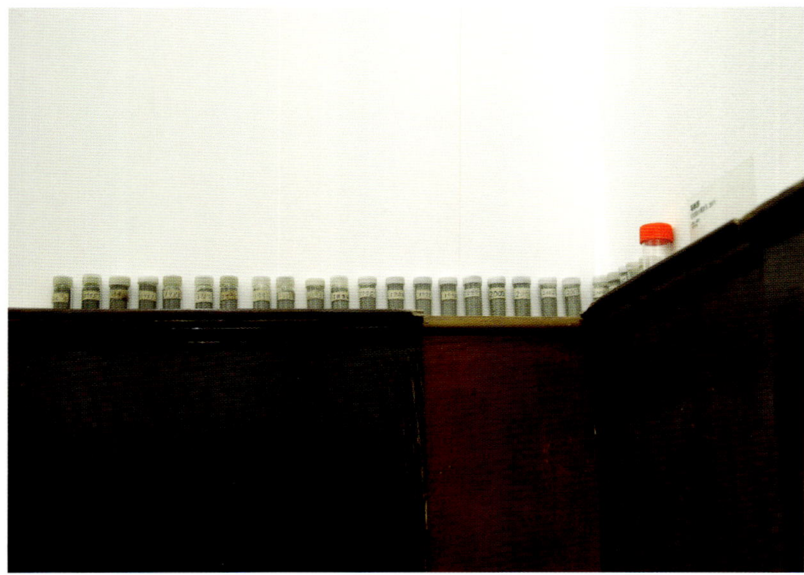

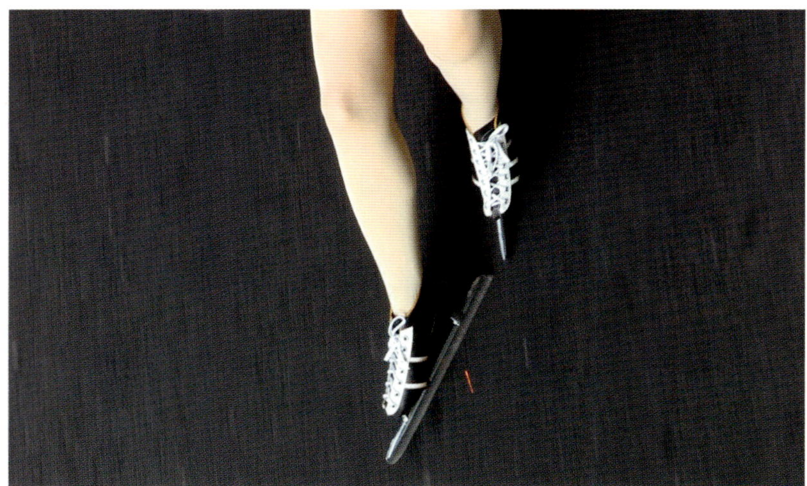

compelling. Like most of Beijing's traditional *hutongs*, subject to the constant demolition and redevelopment transforming the face of China, the neighbourhood is utterly changed. The work successfully conveys the agony of growing up, coming to terms with your own limitations and those of your family. The blades of her skates screech and scrape across the gravelly surface, creating a disturbing sense of futility and hopelessness. Ma Qiusha wrote, 'The pavement races underfoot, grinding against the blades of the skates. The blades grow sharper and sharper, until finally, they become knives. Real knives.'[56]

As a child, Ma Qiusha and a neighbourhood friend were taught by the eminent artist Song Dong. At that time Song and his wife, Yin Xiuzhen,[57] lived nearby, in another old courtyard house in downtown Beijing. In 2011 he curated an exhibition at the Ullens Center for Contemporary Art of his own work and the work of his two young protégés. In his exhibition statement, Song Dong wrote:

> In 1980, China's one-child policy went into effect. In 1982, Ma Qiusha was born. In 1984, Wang Shang was born. In 1989, the year I turned 23, I began teaching art to Ma Qiusha, age 7, and Wang Shang, age 5. In the 22 years since, our relationship has progressed through three stages: teacher/pupil, friends and colleagues/fellow artists. The teacher/pupil relationship was mutual: right from the start, we studied together and learned from each other. Our relationship as friends was wide-ranging: I formed a deep bond with both the kids and their families... We all grew up in a similar environment, Beijing's hutongs. But an era of great changes has led us to very different lives. Different family environments made us different people, and gave us different futures...[58]

Ma Qiusha's work is grounded in that Beijing childhood. She will not explain what she learned from those early experiences with Song Dong, except to say, somewhat elliptically, 'The most important [thing] is that I learned how to behave in society,' but, like her mentor, she explores familial bonds and personal history. *Two Years Younger Than Me* (2011) is an installation consisting of her grandfather's beard shavings, which he inexplicably collected in glass jars for twenty-seven years. They had a fraught relationship: 'He is the only member of my family that I had ever had a quarrel with. Normally Chinese grandparents really indulge their grandchildren. But my grandfather saw his granddaughter as an equal and was very strict with me. We would fight about everything – even over what TV show to watch.' Ma Qiusha's grandmother told her not to hate her grandfather. Very unusually he was the only child in his family so he had experienced great loneliness and sadness. When he died, Ma Qiusha could not bear to see his humble possessions discarded. She said of her installation:

Ma Qiusha *(top)*
From No. 4 Pinguanli to No.4 Tianqiaobeili 2007
video 7 min 54 sec
image courtesy the artist

Ma Qiusha *(middle)*
Two Years Younger Than Me 2011
beard shavings, bottles
dimensions variable
image courtesy the artist

Ma Qiusha *(bottom)*
All My Sharpness Comes From Your Hardness 2011
single-channel video 25 min 29 sec
image courtesy the artist

> That was created in 2011 when my grandfather passed away – [by that time] he had collected twenty-seven bottles of beard shavings. In that year I was twenty-nine so that is where the title came from. These beard shavings were really significant and precious to my grandfather, more than bank accounts or money! When I was a child he would put the shavings in a piece of A4 paper, and put it in the bottle and then lock it away in a cupboard. He did this for twenty-seven years. It was like a ritual. No-one ever asked him why he did it and so now we just guess. Maybe it was because of the fear of the times. From the loneliness of life. He didn't do it when he was young, when his beard would have been black, but when it was already grey. As the only child in his family he had to face his life and his death alone and perhaps this was the cause of his fear. When you are alone you tend to be more sensitive to the change of time and may exaggerate the feeling more than when you are in a crowd.

These bodily relics are like traditional Chinese ancestor portraits, objects of veneration, but also a source of uncomfortable memories and regrets. Ma said:

> When he passed away his children were throwing away his stuff, seemingly trivial things. I saw the bottles of beard shavings and sadness overwhelmed me. I thought that none of his children understood what was dear to him, so I decided to get them back. They are very beautiful. Especially the change of colour from dark grey to white.

She doesn't see these vials of hair as found objects, but rather as talismanic, possessed of a mystical quality: 'For me, my grandfather's beard shavings are not personal objects, not even to be regarded as objects', she explained. 'It's something about a mysterious or divine sign in mind.' After his death, she felt they were a bridge between two single lonely children of two different generations.[59] Ma Qiusha explores mutual relationships, memories and changing states.

Ma's focus is the everyday: the mundane events of a childhood, skates on a road, beard shavings collected in a bottle. She creates alchemical magic with these seemingly banal materials, making the ordinary into something extraordinary. In *Red/White/Yellow* (2011) she froze bodily fluids – blood, milk and urine – in condoms and then recorded on video their change of state from solid to liquid over twenty-four hours. There are references to the global discourses of contemporary art: to Damien Hirst's processes of embalming; to Andres Serrano's *Piss Christ (1987)*; to Marc Quinn and his 1991 self-portrait made of his own frozen blood; yet Ma Qiusha's distinct voice is evident. Her video was exhibited with a grid-like installation of three ordinary chest freezers, placed in the centre of the gallery. *To S* contained carrots, cucumbers and yams which the artist had spent hours trimming and cutting in order to make them conform to a standard measurement. They suggest the same resistance to conformity and standardisation as her recitation of the pressures of her childhood. There is a meticulous, obsessive focus in her practice, not unlike the compulsive collecting of her grandfather. Banal objects or apparently random moments take on a new significance under her gaze.

In a 2009 performance work one hundred people in thin white cotton clothing were stitched together and then had to tear themselves apart. Ma Qiusha is interested in membranes: the thin, metaphorical membranes separating individuals in a family, and the literal, such as the condoms containing bodily fluids in *Red/White/Yellow*. The *Fog* series is inspired by a different kind of membrane – the cheap lace curtains with which people living so close to their neighbours in tiny, higgledy-piggledy courtyard houses could maintain a modicum of privacy. She makes works on paper as a starting point for video productions. 'Works on paper are kind of the source of inspiration for me,' she says. Stacked in her studio, they appear dark, mysterious and minimalist. 'It looks very abstract and there is a line across the paper, but when you look more closely you can see the relief pattern that is like lace,' she said. A pattern emerges from the darkness, made by painting watercolours over lace laid onto the paper. A line slices across each minimalist composition. The repeated motif of cutting and slashing represents the ripping apart of the past and present:

> It's like in traditional hutong family houses where there is little privacy and buildings are really close together, so people hang lace curtains to cover and hide things. You can see out, but people cannot see in. It's from traditional hutong life. It's kind of brilliant I think, because lace is really cheap. When I was a child I did not have many toys but I thought the patterns of the moving sun through the lace curtains and the moving shadows across the room were really interesting. It was this experience in my childhood that made me more sensitive to photographs and to images. And the light of the moon coming through the curtains onto my bed at night was like a lullaby.

Like He Chengyao, Ma Qiusha has moved from more literal representations of personal and cultural history to a metaphorical and poetic form of transcendence.

The performative practices of these women reflect deeply embodied psychological wounds and the physical and emotional restrictions they have experienced, quite distinct from the works of the male artists of the 1990s. In the years since He Chengyao's mother experienced scorn and hostility for bearing a child outside marriage, much has changed in China. But sexuality, gender, and the expected roles of women are still highly contested in both public and private discourses.

NOTES

1 Performance artist Yang Zhichao, in conversation with the writer, 16 May 2015, at Sherman Contemporary Art Foundation, Sydney

2 Performance art is often identified with actions intended to disrupt social harmony, as in the case of the five feminist activists arrested and detained prior to International Women's Day 2015 – apparently because they had planned to pass out anti-sexual harassment fliers on buses , and had previously campaigned for more female public restrooms with an 'occupy the men's room' protest http://foreignpolicy.com/2015/03/17/they-are-the-best-feminist-activists-in-china-detained-why/ accessed 12 April 2015

3 Vine, Richard 2011 *New China New Art* Prestel Verlag, Munich, London (76–77)

4 See Chapter 3 for a more detailed account of the 'Smash the Four Olds' campaign

5 Wright, David, *Party Slogans*, The Society for Anglo-Chinese Understanding available at http://www.sacu.org/slogans.html accessed 3 September 2014

6 Jiang Jiehong 2008 *New Art From China: The Revolution Continues* Saatchi Gallery, Rizzoli, New York (106)

7 Gittings, John 2006 *The Changing Face of China, From Mao to Market* Oxford University Press, Oxford (60)

8 Li Xianting 2008 quoted by Wu Hung, *Making History (Wu Hung on Contemporary Art)* Timezone 8 Beijing, (16)

9 Wu Hung 2008 *Making History (Wu Hung on Contemporary Art) Timezone 8* Beijing (17)

10 ibid. (37)

11 Smith, Terry 2011 *Contemporary Art: World Currents* Laurence King Pty Ltd, London (154). Smith explains that while some artists were rediscovering modernist abstraction, others were responding to 'the sudden plethora of ideas flooding in from the west, not least the critical constellations of Postmodernism and Poststructuralism.'

12 Wu Hung 2014 *Contemporary Chinese Art: A History 1970s–2000s* Thames and Hudson, UK (59)

13 Berghuis, Thomas 2006 *Performance Art in China* Timezone 8, Beijing (102–04)

14 Erickson, Britta 2002 'The Reception in the West of Experimental Mainland Chinese Art of the 1990s in Contemporary Chinese Art' in Wu Hung, with Peggy Wang (eds) *Primary Documents* MOMA 2010 (361) excerpted from a text originally published in *Reinterpretation: A Decade of Experimental Chinese Art 1990–2000* (ed Wu Hung) Guangzhou: Guangdong Museum of Art, 2002 (105–12)

15 Jia Fangzhou 1998 (transl. Doris Symons) 'Chinese Women Artists of the 20th Century' in *Die Halfte des Himmels: Chinesische Kunstlerinnin* Frauen Museum Bonn (160–63)

16 Vine, Richard 2011 *New China New Art* Prestel Verlag, Munich London New York (77–78)

17 Gladston, Paul 2014 *Chinese Contemporary Art: A Critical History* Reaktion Books U.K (95)

18 ibid. (111)

19 Gao Minglu 2011 *Total Modernity and the Avant-garde in Twentieth Century Chinese Art* Cambridge MIT Press (216–17)

20 Gao Minglu 1999 'Conceptual Art with Anti-conceptual Attitude: Mainland China, Taiwan and Hong Kong, 1999' in Chiu, Melissa and Genocchio, Benjamin (eds) 2011 *Contemporary Art in Asia: A Critical Reader* MIT Press, Cambridge Massachusetts (277–83)

21 Gao Minglu 2011 *Total Modernity and the Avant-garde in Twentieth Century Chinese Art* Cambridge MIT Press (216–17)

22 ibid. (278–84)

23 Berghuis, Thomas 2006 *Performance Art in China* Timezone 8, Beijing

24 Clunas, Craig 2009 *Art in China* 2nd edition Oxford University Press, Oxford (232)

25 Wu Hung 2014 *Contemporary Chinese Art: A History 1970s–2000s* Thames and Hudson, London (199)

26 Kovskaya, Maya 2010 'Public Action Art and Performative Interventions in the Chinese Public Sphere' in *Mayday Magazine* Issue 2 Winter 2010 available at http://maydaymagazine.com/issue2scholarkovskayapublicactionart.php accessed 13 January 2015

27 Fok, Sylvia 2013 *Life and Death: Art and the Body in Contemporary China* Intellect Books, Bristol, UK (79)

28 Zhang Huan, quoted in *Contemporary Chinese Art: Primary Documents* MOMA 2010 (186) originally published as 'Guanyu 65 kg de zishu' in Leng Lin 2000 (transl. Lee Ambrozy) *Shi Wo (It's Me)* Beijing: China Federation of Literary and Art Circles Publishing (150–52)

29 Lau, Joyce Hor-Chung 2011 'Bringing A Woman's Touch to the Chinese Art Scene' *New York Times*, 20 January 2011 available at http://www.nytimes.com/2011/01/21/arts/21iht-women21.html?pagewanted=all accessed 2 September 2014

30 Global Feminisms featured Lin Tianmiao and Yin Xiuxhen (see Chapter 3) and the Australians Fiona Foley, Tracey Moffatt and Patricia Piccinini. Curator Maura Reilly's stated intention was to show the work of artists 'whose work visually manifests their identities (socio-cultural, political, economic, racial, gender, and/or sexual) in myriad innovative ways...' and at the same time to challenge the 'monocultural, so-called first-world feminism that assumes a sameness among women.' See Reilly, Maura 2007 'Towards Transnational Feminism' in *Global Feminisms: New Directions in Contemporary Art* (Brooklyn Museum) Merrell London, New York (15)

31 http://www.brooklynmuseum.org/eascfa/feminist_art_base/gallery/chengyao_he.php accessed 3 September 2014

32 He Chengyao curated this event in November 2014 and recounted her astonishment at the proportions of women artists represented in her conversation with me the following month.

33 Unless otherwise acknowledged all quotes from He Chengyao are from her conversation with the writer in Beijing in December 2014

34 Welland, Sasha Su-Ling 2007 (transl Mao Weidong) 'Opening the Great Wall' in *Pain in Soul: Performance Art and Video Works by He Chengyao* Shanghai Zendai Museum of Modern Art (59)

35 Smith, Terry with Okwui Enwezor and Nancy Condee (eds) 2008 *Antinomies of Art and Culture: Modernity, Postmodernity* Duke University Press (147–48)

36 He Chengyao 2007 interviewed by Zhang Na, in *Pain in Soul: Performance Art and Video Works by He Chengyao*, Shanghai Zendai Museum of Art (25)

37 Wu Hung 2014 *Contemporary Chinese Art: A History 1970s–2000s* Thames and Hudson, UK (195)

38 Tatlow, Didi Kirsten, 'She. Herself. Naked. The Art of He

Chengyao' *New York Times*, Sinosphere Blog, 20 January 2014 http://sinosphere.blogs.nytimes.com/2014/01/20/she-herself-naked-the-art-of-he-chengyao/?_php=true&_type=blogs&_php=true&_r=0 accessed 10 September 2014

39 Wah Man, Eva Kit 2011 'Expression Extreme and History Trauma in Women Body Art in China (sic): The Case of He Chengyao', in Bittner Wiseman, Mary and Liu Yuedi (eds) *Subversive Strategies in Contemporary Chinese Art* Brill, Leiden Netherlands (171–80)

40 Welland, Sasha Su-Ling 2007 (transl Mao Weidong) 'Interpreting He Chengyao's Opening the Great Wall' in *Pain in Soul: Performance Art and Video Works by He Chengyao* Shanghai Zendai Museum of Modern Art (60)

41 For example, Chinese miners at the 1861 Battle of Lambing Flat in NSW had their pigtails forcibly cut off http://www.migrationheritage.nsw.gov.au/exhibition/objectsthroughtime/lambingflatsbanner/ accessed 8 January 2015

42 http://www.realtimearts.net/article/issue77/8331 presents a first-hand account of the event, accessed 8 January 2015

43 I do not attempt to deal with diasporic artists, although many artists in the book, including Lin Tianmiao, Yin Xiuzhen, Huang Jingyuan and Bingyi have lived, studied and worked for extensive periods outside China, and Chen Lingyang lives in France. For a comprehensive discussion of diasporic Chinese artists see Chiu, Melissa 2006 *Breakout: Chinese art outside China*, Charta, Milan, New York

44 Unless otherwise acknowledged all quotes from Yingmei Duan are from her conversation with the writer on Skype 11 October 2014, and subsequent emails

45 Zuoxiao Zuzhou is a famous underground rock musician, novelist and artist, renowned for gritty lyrics. He is a friend and collaborator of Ai Weiwei

46 An email to the writer, 26 January 2015, confirmed the sequence of events

47 http://www.yingmei-art.com/en/works/yingmei accessed 15 October 2014

48 Yingmei Duan interviewed by Asia Art Archive's Ian Cheng and Fiona He in May 2011 http://www.aaa.org.hk/Diaaalogue/Details/1015 accessed 16 October 2014

49 ibid.

50 ibid.

51 http://www.yingmei-art.com/en/works/wish accessed 15 October 2014

52 Millner, Jacqueline 2014 'Yingmei Duan and the Feminists Giving Contemporary Art a Makeover', in *The Conversation* available at http://theconversation.com/yingmei-duan-and-the-feminists-giving-contemporary-art-a-makeover-19341 accessed 15 October 2014

53 http://www.hanmigallery.co.uk/news/news-2014/yingmei-duan-heixiangning-art-museum-shenzhen/ accessed 8 January 2014

54 Unless otherwise acknowledged, all quotes from Ma Qiusha are from her conversation with the writer, in Beijing in December 2014

55 Ma Qiusha http://www.beijingcommune.com/EnNewXQ.aspx?ID=89 accessed 8 January 2015

56 ibid.

57 See Chapter 3 for an account of Yin Xiuzhen's practice

58 Song Dong http://www.beijingcommune.com/EnNewXQ.aspx?ID=89 accessed 8 January 2015

59 Ma Qiusha, for her 2013 solo exhibition in Manchester, reviewed by Carol Huston for *This is Tomorrow* Contemporary Art Magazine 8 February 2013 http://thisistomorrow.info/articles/ma-qiusha accessed 29 May 2015

Ma Qiusha
Fog No. 9 2012
watercolour on paper
136 x 153 cm
image courtesy the artist

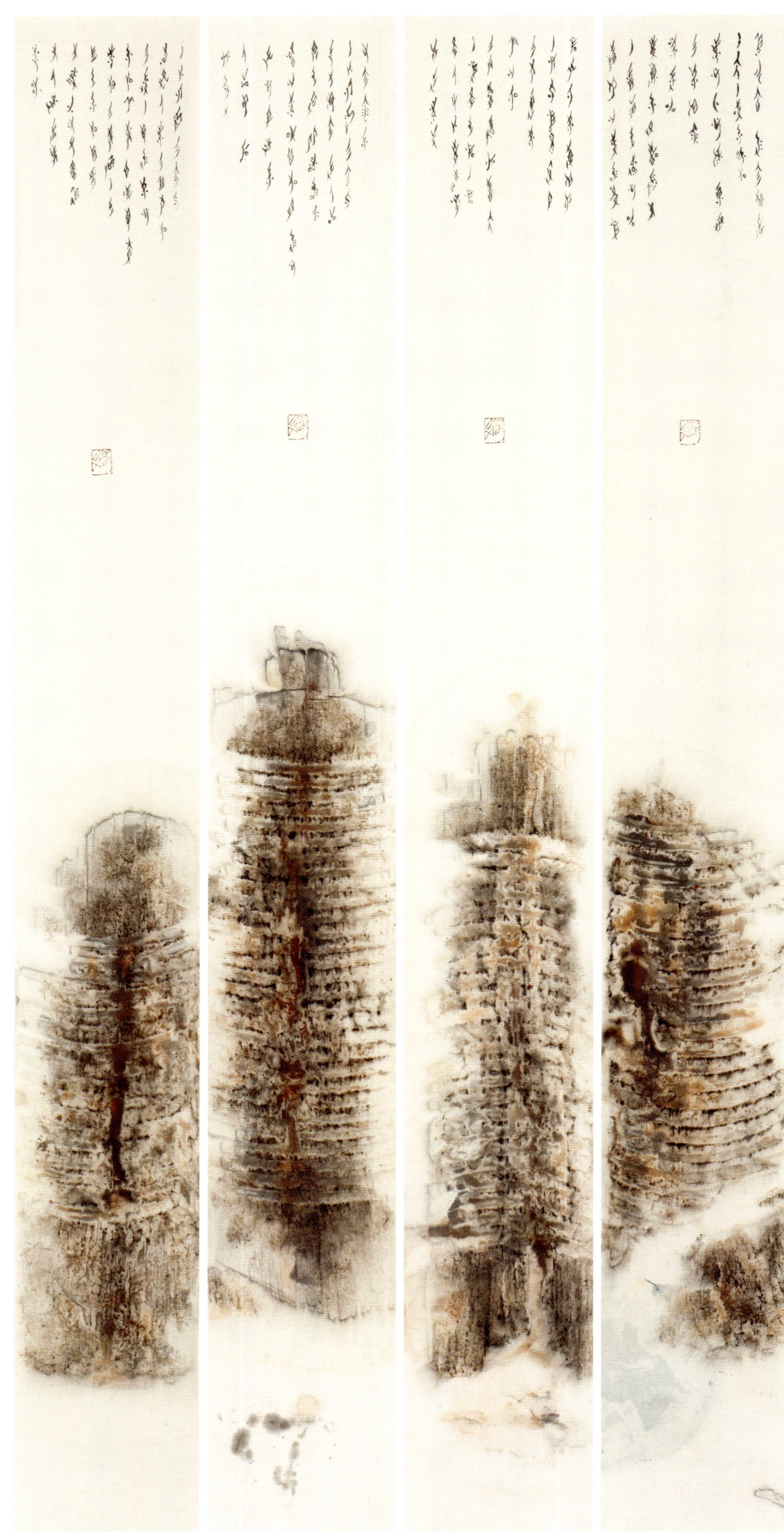

NÜSHU: A SECRET LANGUAGE OF WOMEN

Tao Aimin and Ma Yanling

Holding my brush to write this letter, two streams of tears flow
Of the thousand hardships I've suffered, nobody knows.
—Nüshu text

This chapter examines the work of two artists who have been influenced by their discovery of an obscure, exclusively female traditional language – the 'secret' script of *Nüshu*, once used in remote areas to communicate between women in the villages of Jiangyong County, Hunan Province. It was in a sense, a performative practice, a language which could only be fully understood when chanted aloud. Unknown to the outside world until the 1980s, discovered just as it was disappearing, the origin of this unique script is shrouded in mystery. It is likely that *Nüshu* evolved in this isolated part of a rural province from the female occupation of embroidery, as its slanting strokes were stitched on fans, handkerchiefs, and hand-woven belts, and in cloth-bound books given to brides.[1]

At the intersection between oral and written culture, *Nüshu* texts often took the form of wedding lamentations, mournful litanies of female endurance. Long narrative songs were chanted aloud, in what the scholar Anne McLaren describes as 'a private domain of fantasy and self-assertion, consolation and misery.'[2] Marriage is presented as a terrible fate:

> Once I lived in my parental home
> Now I go downstairs sobbing
> A knife cuts my heart.[3]

Bridal laments were part of a ritualised expression of sorrow as the bride prepared to leave her parents and her village for what may have seemed a fearful, uncertain future.

Often embroidered onto dowry items, *Nüshu* script was also used to write messages in *San Zhao Shu* – cloth-bound booklets created by mothers to give to their daughters, or by women to give to their closest female friends, their 'sworn sisters', on the occasion of their marriage. One such fragment is found in a translated *Nüshu* lament, *Her Own Story by He Huanshi of Baishui*, the tale of a widowed mother and daughter which includes the words:

> I write this letter myself on a paper fan
> the misery of mother and daughter is found on this fan.[4]

Some historians have interpreted these texts as a transgressive female culture in which encoded messages of resistance subvert conventional expectations of proper female behaviour.[5] However, despite the feisty heroines of some tales written in *Nüshu*, they tend to represent gender roles as fated, and women as powerless to change them. The emphasis is on duty at the expense of individual desire, reinforcing Confucian norms of obedient submission to familial authority.[6] *Nüshu* provided a permissible space for women to articulate their sorrow and anger at the stoic endurance of suffering expected of them. The writing of the texts was an act of catharsis:

> It shouldn't have been that we came in this life wrong as girls
> Red plums on the tree, a useless branch.[7]

The script is visually distinctive, with slanting hook-like characters entirely different from written forms of Mandarin, and the texts represent the voices of women who were otherwise anonymous; invisible to history. *Nüshu* created a 'place and a society of sworn sisters in which women's lives are valued and celebrated.'[8] In all other ways, their silence was taken for granted. The *Nüshu* texts often feature strong courageous heroines who must cope with the weakness or duplicity of men, providing an insight into a hidden history. They are a rich source of inspiration for some contemporary artists working at the intersection of performance, painting and printmaking in China today, who have seen these discourses as transformative responses to the sufferings of women and their lack of autonomy, in the present as well as in the past.

Tao Aimin
In an Instant 2010–11
ink and pigment on rice paper
each panel 300 x 18 cm
image courtesy the artist

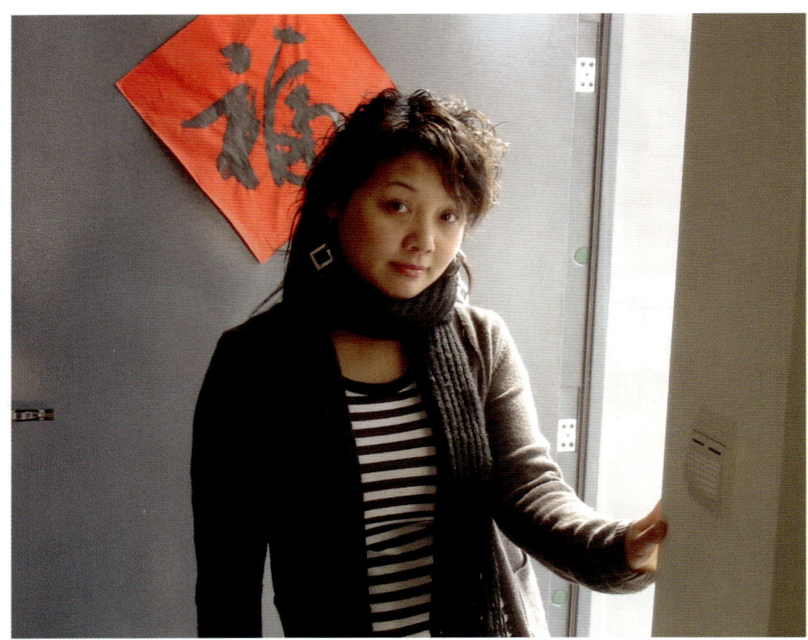

TAO AIMIN 陶艾民

Book of Women

Tao Aimin documents the hard lives of rural women in her paintings, prints, video works and sculptural installations. A distinctive hallmark of her practice is her use of traditional wooden washboards. These humble objects, superseded by the washing machine in all but the poorest villages, appear as found objects and are sometimes employed as printing blocks, becoming a key symbol in her work. Bearing witness to the repetitive and exhausting domestic labour of generations of Chinese women, Tao's works are like monuments to anonymous wives, mothers and grandmothers.

In recent years she became determined to learn more about *Nüshu,* which, like the artist herself, originated in remote regions of Hunan Province. In 2008 she made a pilgrimage to the most rural and isolated villages of Jiangyong County, hoping to find someone who might still be familiar with this ancient female calligraphy. Braving snowbound roads in late winter, she found one very old woman who was able to read and understand the script. Since that encounter, the slanting *Nüshu* characters have become a motif and signifier in her own work.

Tao Aimin lives and works far from Beijing in a rural area near the Great Wall, and her story is intriguing, like a mythical quest, complete with an indefatigable heroine who allowed nothing to deflect her determination to become an artist. Like He Chengyao, Tao's family background is an unlikely one for a contemporary artist. Born in 1974 in rural Hunan Province, she remembers a childhood of feeding chickens, fetching water, collecting eggs, picking fruit from the family's orange orchard, and generally running free. The path she travelled towards establishing an artistic career was filled with unexpected twists and turns, traversing vast physical distances across China, requiring astonishing stamina and fortitude.

Her journey, filled with adversities and, ultimately, victory over unfortunate circumstances, resembles a classic Chinese tale. Tao Aimin is an engaging narrator:

> I have a very big family, but none of them work in the art field. My father is an artisan – he creates furniture – so maybe we could say that is a kind of art. [But] I always loved to paint. In middle school I was interested in art, literature and poetry. When I was sixteen years old I edited a book of poetry just for myself. The name was *The Dream of a Sixteen Year Old.* All the poems are full of vicissitudes! [*Tao Aimin laughed and agreed that* **all** *poetry written by teenagers is likely to be filled with angst and drama.*] I did a lot of painting at that time, and there was a painting teacher I liked very much. I painted with oil paint, watercolour, acrylic – everything! Then I got into the senior high school that specialises in painting. [*She laughed again.*] I didn't do too well in Maths or English, so I specialised in art![9]

Her family didn't actively discourage her, but they did not know what to make of her unusual determination to follow a path unlike that mapped out for a young girl in rural China.

After graduating from high school Tao wanted to study art at university. However, in the punishingly competitive Chinese education system, she was faced with an almost insurmountable obstacle: 'I tried the college entrance exams two or three times but I could not succeed.' An organisation in her hometown advertised success assisting students to gain acceptance to the most prestigious art colleges, such as the Central Academy of Fine Arts in Beijing, and the China Academy of Art in Hangzhou. She took classes and continued to hope. This organisation moved all over China – an indication of the huge demand for places and the difficulty of Tao's project. She travelled too:

> I went to a lot of places in China with them. To Hangzhou, [where] I tried to get into the China Academy of Art. I lived in a basement that cost five yuan for one night. I went to Wuhan and slept on the benches in the railway station. When I woke up I was covered in dew!' She was so determined, she says, 'because I loved painting so much. I wanted so much to improve myself.

When Tao Aimin was just twenty she came to Beijing alone, stubbornly refusing to acknowledge that her goal was impossible. She said:

> I failed over and over again to be accepted into any college. But then I came back to Beijing and got into a college that had no

Tao Aimin
image courtesy the artist

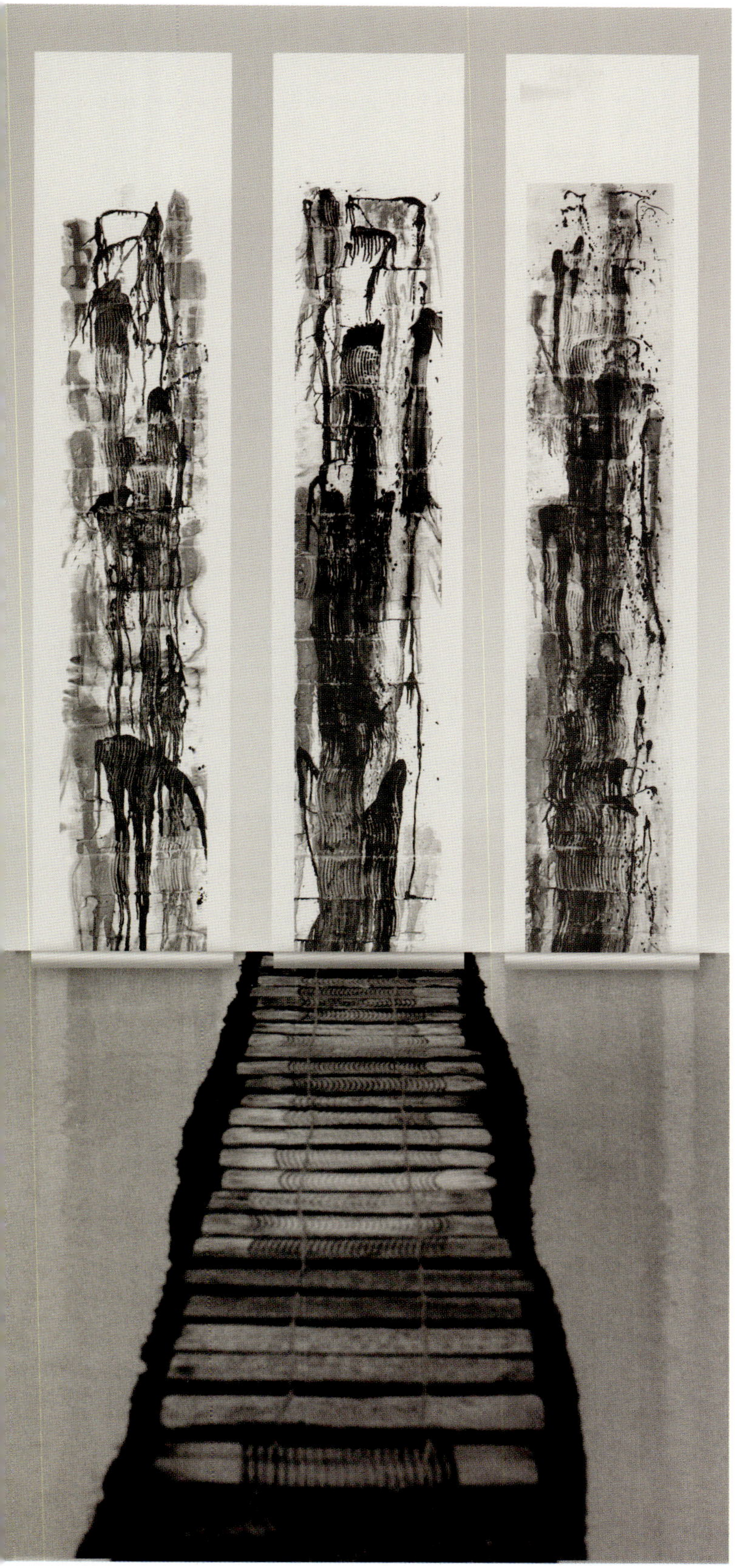

Tao Aimin
High Mountains and Flowing Water 2007
washboards, ink, paper
installation view
image courtesy the artist

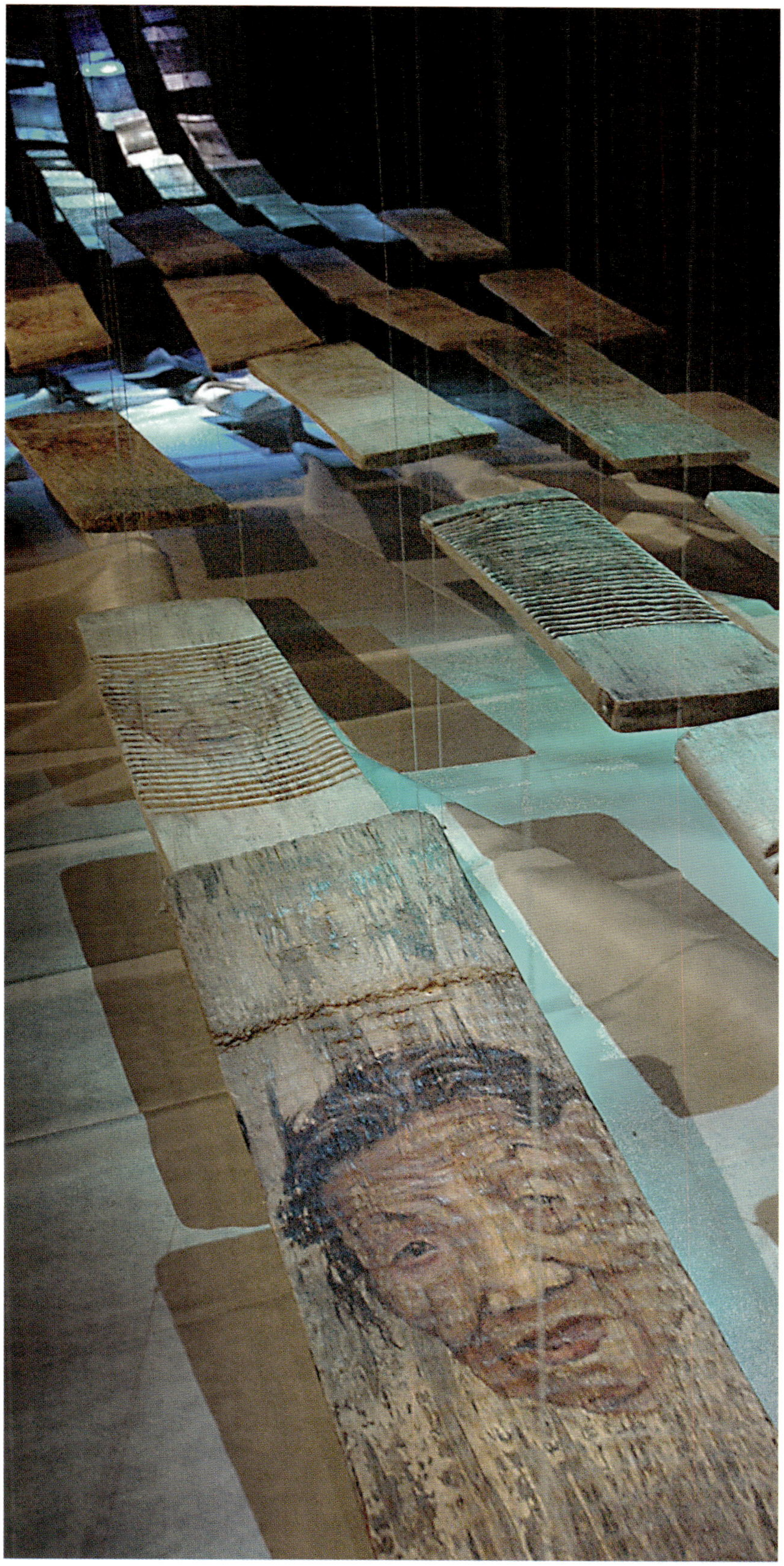

Tao Aimin
River of Women 2005
washboards, paint
installation view, dimensions variable
image courtesy the artist

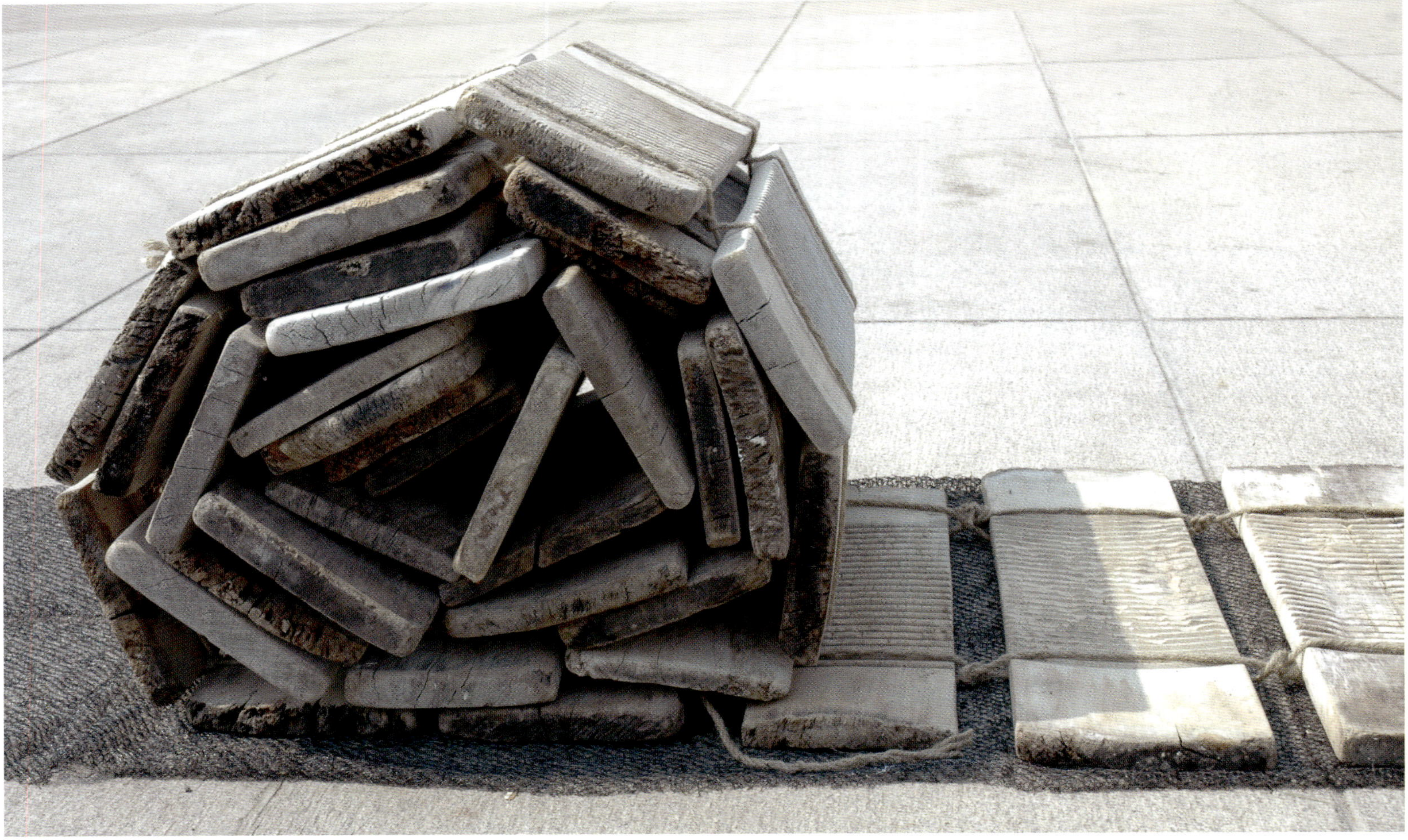

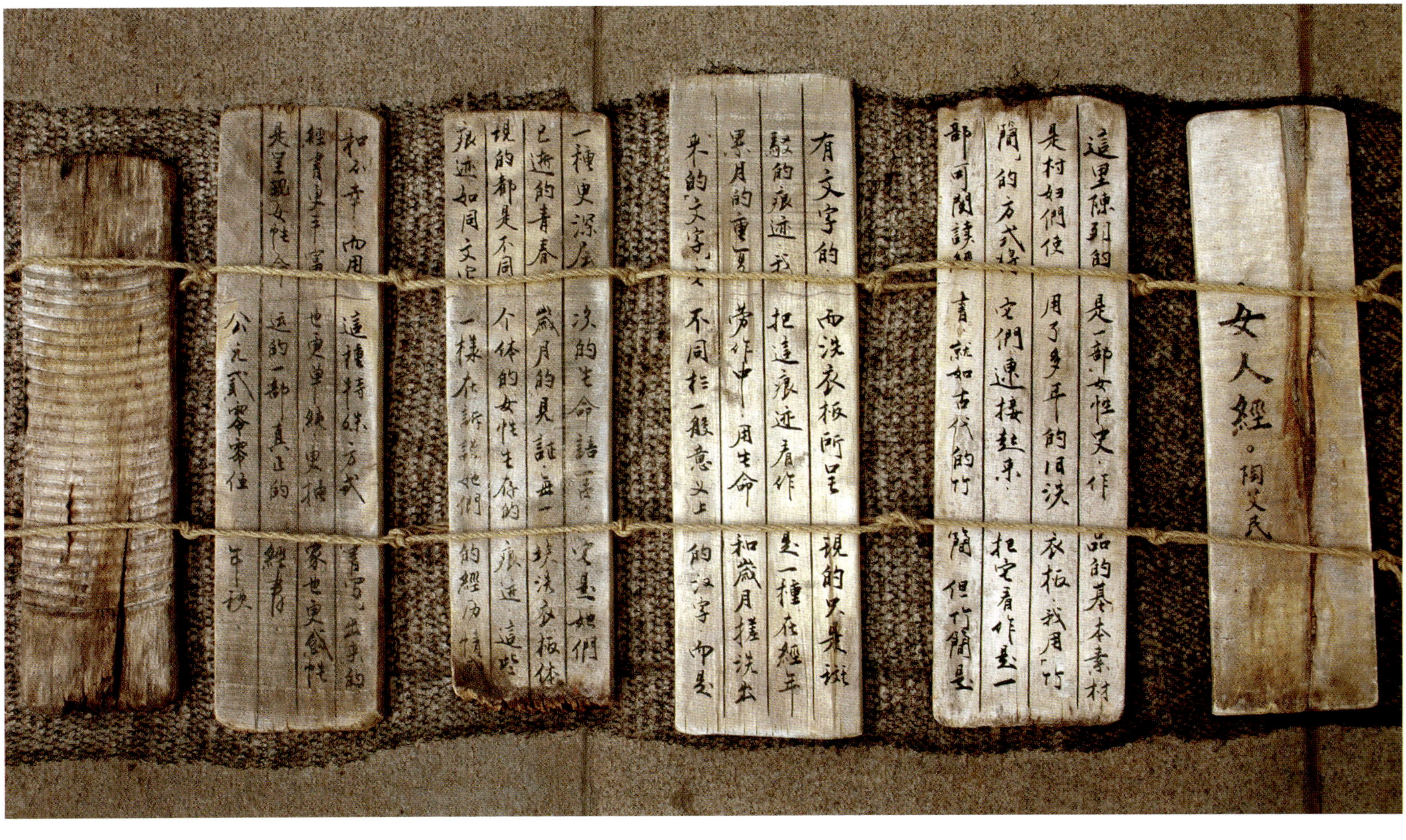

entrance exam. After two years I quit that school because I still wanted to go to university. I tried three art colleges in Beijing but I failed to get into any of them. I went to Fujian and finally I got into the Huaqiao University through their entrance exam. From Hunan to Fujian I travelled by train for three days, standing up with a suitcase, all by myself. The train went through a lot of tunnels, and I kept thinking, "This is really far."

From Hunan's capital of Changsha to Xiamen in Fujian Province is a journey of almost nine hundred kilometres by car, a journey which would seem far longer to a young girl travelling alone in one of the cheapest 'hard sleeper' carriages.

In 1999 Tao graduated from the Fine Arts Department of National Huaqiao University, later studying at Beijing's Central Academy of Fine Arts, which had always been her dream. Tao Aimin's father was happy for her to travel to seek opportunities beyond her hometown. There was a little subterfuge involved, however. In her first semester Tao enrolled in a design degree, but found she didn't enjoy it. She changed her major to Chinese painting without telling her family. 'That was the first time I touched the brush and ink,' she says, and it was a revelation. The traditions of ink painting have been at the heart of her practice ever since. Even today her father believes that she graduated with a design qualification: 'He still thinks I studied design! He thought a designer would be able to make a good living, whereas the path of an artist is much more uncertain,' said Tao.

When Tao tells her father that her work is exhibited within and beyond China now, 'He is still negative. In his opinion I should pay more attention to family. He always thinks that for a happy family a child is the most important thing. He thinks I am not successful because I do not have a child. He believes women should pass on the bloodline.' The pressure to marry, bear a child and continue the family line is immense in China.

After Tao Aimin graduated her father insisted upon her immediate return to her hometown, and found her a job. A free spirit, she stayed for one month and then went straight back to Beijing, where she has remained ever since. After a few years juggling the demands of a teaching position with her own practice, she was accepted into a course at the Central Academy of Fine Arts. She was, at long last, in the place that she had dreamed of for so many years. It was not as she had hoped: 'I really didn't like it at all! They had so many rules and restrictions which limited me a lot. I had worked for such a long time to get there, and then when I finally got in I found out how it worked and it was really quite a disappointment.' Despite the fact that CAFA did not live up to her expectations, in 2001 Tao graduated from the Assistant Lecturer Training Class in the Mural Painting Department.

Following this disillusionment Tao realised that her unique vision, based on her own experiences, was driving her to make work unlike that of her peers. This was ultimately to take her back to a significant aspect of her identity. 'I grew up in a very rural environment,' she says. 'There was an orange orchard in front of my house, and my grandfather called himself the master of the orchard. This simple and natural environment of the countryside influenced me a lot.' Hunan culture and customs are imprinted on her work and her ideas: 'I grew up with my grandparents. My childhood was happy but memories of Hunan Province always influence how I think. My grandparents were very proud of the true *'Chu'* Hunan culture,[10] and my grandfather believed very strongly in Taoism. Actually, [people thought of him as] a Taoist priest – but not a real one! And my grandpa also did some incantations. When somebody died the local people would hold a ceremony and my grandfather would sing mantras and write songs for other people to sing at funeral ceremonies. This is Chu culture. This is folk culture. And there would be paintings and embroideries made in the place where the ceremony happened.'

A vivid memory of her grandparents, as was customary, making their own coffins, haunts her dreams. They stood for years in the family's main room like 'big black pieces of furniture.' Asked if seeing the coffins every day seemed strange or frightening, Tao hesitated, then said:

> Sometimes frightening, yes, but basically they were treated as pieces of furniture. And when my grandmother died I watched as she was put into her coffin, and later I did a lot of work about this strong memory. Since I was a child this ceremony has always appeared in my dreams. I was very close to my grandparents and they influenced me a lot. When I was studying at CAFA some years ago we went sketching outside the city, and I went to the tombs to draw. And my classmates all thought I was crazy because I knelt down on the ground in the dusk, into the evening, and drew these tombs.

The tomb drawings have their echo in Tao Aimin's important first series and installations. In *River of Women* and *Book of Women* she used wooden washboards, collected from hundreds of rural women over many years, to create works reminiscent of tombstone rubbings. She went to villages all over the countryside, engaging women in conversation, and asked them to give her their washboards. When they heard that she wanted to incorporate their domestic work into her artwork and record stories of their lives, they responded enthusiastically. Since her encounter with the very old woman with bound feet who gave her the first washboard, she has collected more than a thousand of these artefacts of female history, recording the details of each owner. The first, Mrs Wang, her landlady and her friend, treated Tao Aimin like a

Women's Book 2005
installation of washboards
dimensions variable
image courtesy the artist

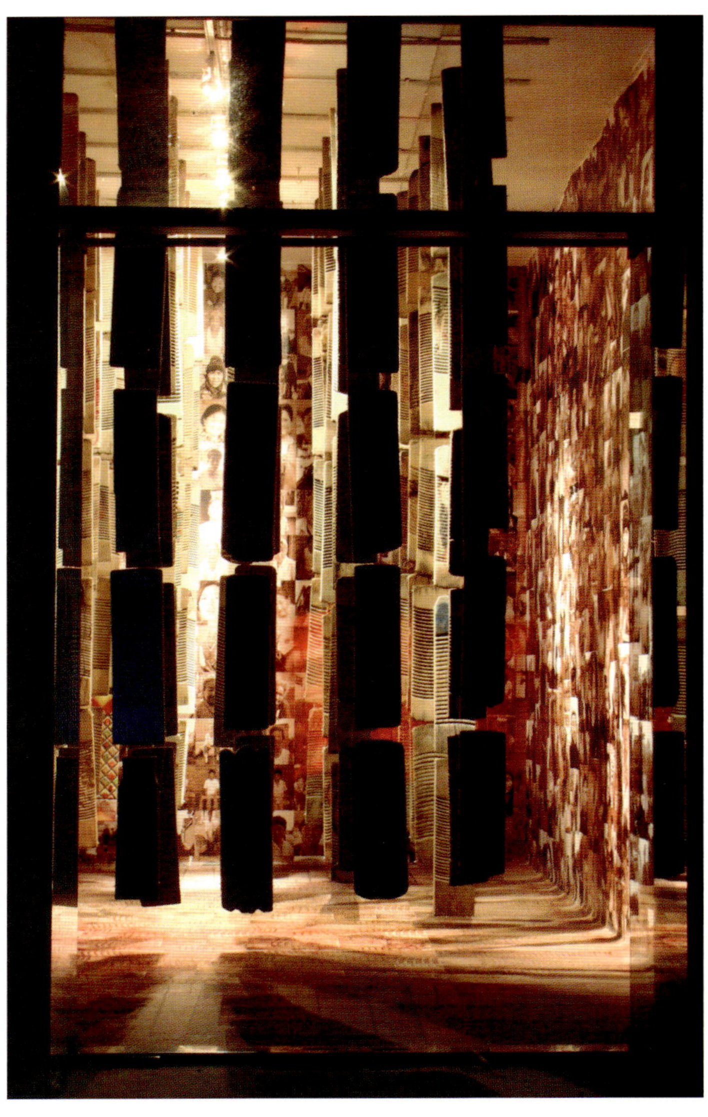

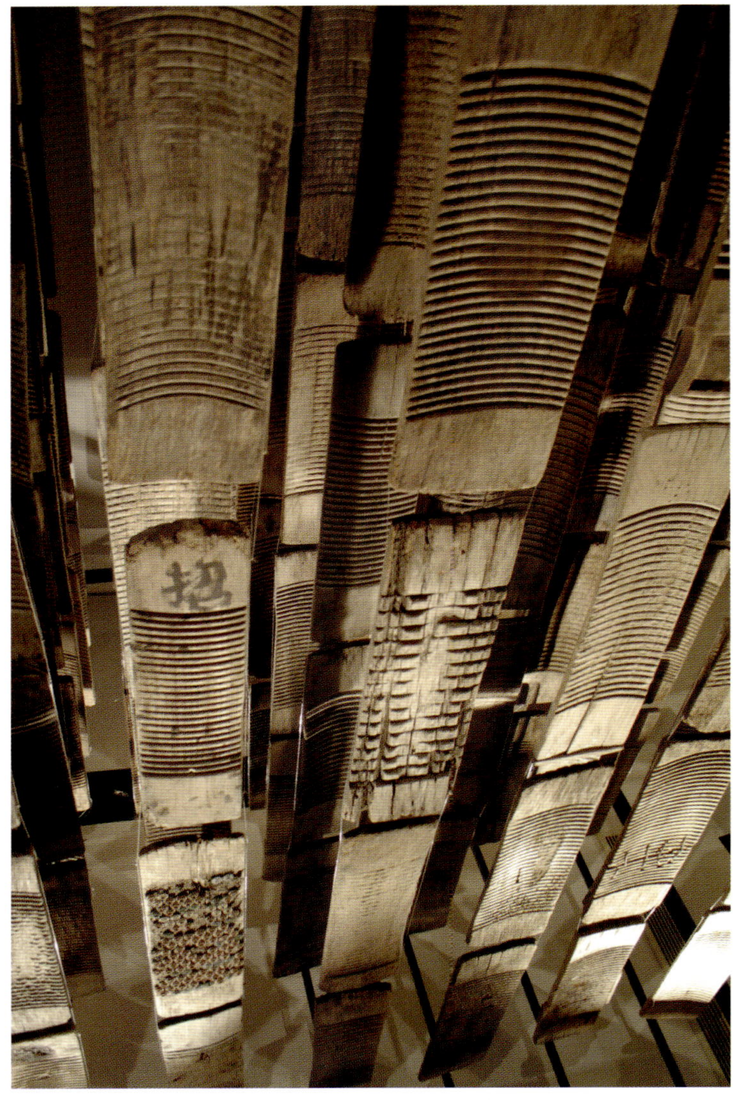

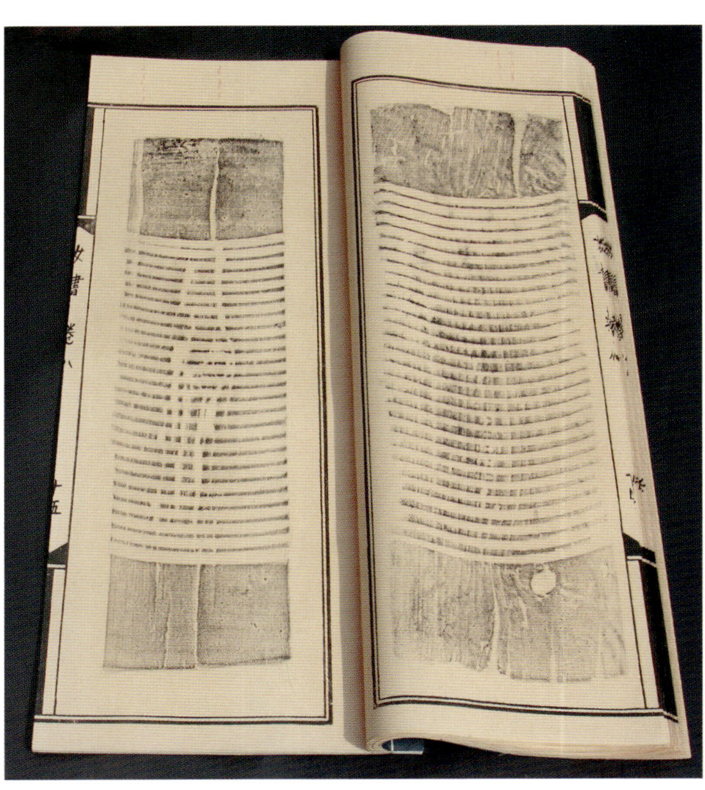

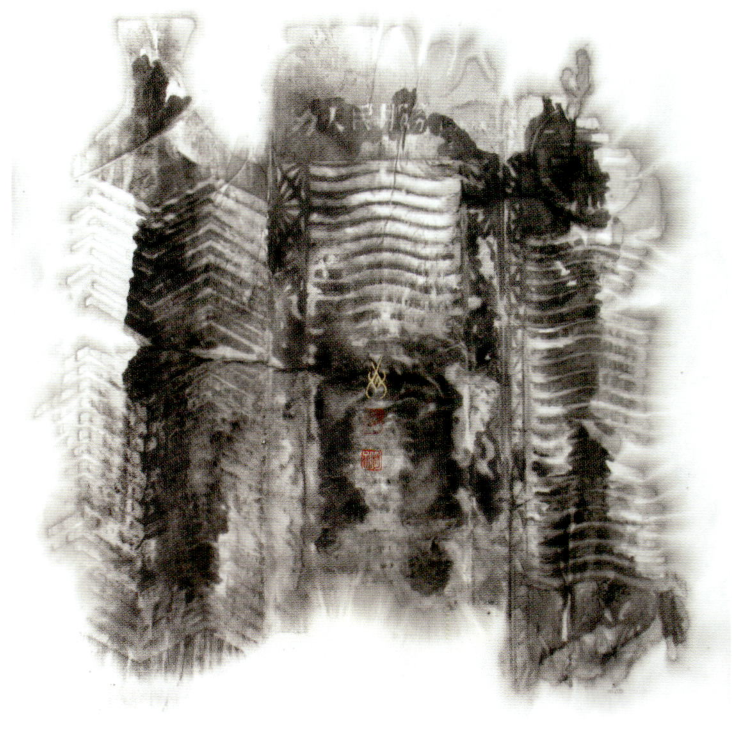

grand-daughter until her death at the age of ninety-nine. Tao has made a substantial video about Mrs Wang's life, a hybrid form of art and social history. The idea of using washboards came from direct experience:

> It was because of my mother and my mother-in-law. Because in my family my father held all the power, and my mother is a very traditional woman. Since I was a child my mother was very diligent and dedicated in washing everybody's clothes. Even now she washes for the grandchildren. She is so diligent that she is very thin, she has become like a washing board herself. I want to free her from doing this – I don't want her to do all these things. But she believes it is her duty... My mother-in-law was also this kind of woman. She passed away a few years ago and right up until she died she was washing in this traditional way.

Before they were married, her mother-in-law would travel from her own village to wash Tao's husband's clothes. Once they married and bought a washing machine, this act of love for her son was superseded by new technology. At that time, in 2004, Tao Aimin had no immediate plans to apply her developing ideas about the nature and significance of female labour to the production of artworks, but it remained at the back of her mind.

River of Women consists of more than sixty washboards, hung like a slatted bridge from ceiling to floor in an undulating line. On each board she painted a portrait of its previous owner's lined face. Audiences entering the installation would hear the recorded sound of a washing machine churning endlessly through its cycles, reminding us of the loss of this way of life. Curator Maya Kovskaya describes works such as *River of Women* and *Riverbed* as 'an archive of silent histories – the multiple and seemingly invisible realities of the vast majority of women in history, even today, who labour in obscurity until they pass from this world.'[11]

For *Women's Book* Tao constructed a line of washboards strung together with twine and unrolled across the floor, reminiscent of ancient tomes made from bamboo slabs. Each washboard is like the page of a book, its worn grooves forming an unreadable calligraphy made by the hands of the illiterate rural woman who used it every day. A kind of braille, a physical knowing born of endlessly repeated actions, is the same as a written language, says the artist. In the past, without photographic documentation, diaries or letters, the washboard belonging to a poor, illiterate woman might be the only significant possession that remained after her death, mute record of the labour that had occupied her days. Tao Aimin wrote:

> Here is a display of the history of women... a deeper life language, it is the witness of their past youth. Each piece traces individual women and the traces are a text that tells of their experiences, emotions and misfortunes... This is a vision beyond literal language. It is the fate of women.[12]

She does not, however, see herself as a feminist artist:

> I don't want to define myself in this way. I care about women and am sensitive to ideas about female destiny. I care about humanity, both male and female. It's not like how westerners think of feminism – as an absolute. Maybe you can say I have a feminist perspective because all my works are about women, but I think that the works should speak for themselves. The works can speak and the artist shouldn't.

Washed Relics is a large sculptural installation of stacked upright washboards, like prehistoric standing stones, with the solemn power of a memorial. It consists of two hundred and eighty washboards, all in their original state – some broken and wired together, some with pieces or strips of rubber nailed to them, some with traces of handwritten names. All possess historical significance, says the artist. They hang on a three-metre high metal frame, in neat columns. The subtle variations on the surface of each worn and weathered board create dramatic shadowed patterns. A large mirror symbolising water reflects the washboards, which are now witnesses of a vanished era.

Tao Aimin began to see other possibilities in these quotidian objects. Using the washboards like woodblocks or collagraph plates (or perhaps, in the ancient Chinese tradition of making rubbings from stone stele), she inked them up and printed them. She calls this 'ink language'. The prosaic becomes poetic. Ridges and grooves, now printed as positives and negatives, emulate the lines of printed text on a page. Black ink emphasises the worn, split and scarred surfaces of the timber. Tao Aimin feels a strong connection with the lives of the women she met in her travels to different rural villages, and the stories she collected. 'The boards are marked by the passage of their lives,' she says.[13] They are beautiful objects, their scarred and splintered surfaces a testament to the labour of women washing clothes for their families – a lifetime of work. Organised into grids as sculptural structures, or used to create expressive works on paper with black ink, they are given a new life.

In considering the significance of ink and brush, Tao Aimin says, 'I tried to mix the ink painting with the washboard works and expand the possibilities of mixing these two things. I am Chinese therefore I always loved ink painting. I studied it in college, and now I use the washboards as prints and rubbings. By using rubbing I can produce an effect – because the washing board is usually in the water, so the effect of the ink print is

Tao Aimin *(top left)*
A Woman's Long March 2006
installation view
dimensions variable
image courtesy the artist

Tao Aimin *(top right)*
Washed Relics 2006
installation
dimensions variable
image courtesy the artist

Tao Aimin *(bottom left)*
The Secret Language of Women (014 Volume 8 Text 15) 2008
ink on ricepaper and traditional Chinese bookbinding
image courtesy the artist

Tao Aimin *(bottom right)*
Women's Book (Nüshu) 2009
ink on paper
image courtesy the artist

like water, and women's destiny is also like water.' Tao denies she is part of the current 'New Ink' movement in China:

> I don't want to follow this trend. I loved ink painting long before this ink painting "fever". I started to do my ink painting prints in 2007. I think you should create your work according to the work itself. It should be what is appropriate to your idea.

As Tao Aimin collected washboards in travels to rural villages outside Beijing, she documented the lives of the women that she met, fixing their aged bodies and wrinkled faces in video and still photographs, collecting their stories before they could be lost. It has become an anthropological art project, revealing much about community, relationships, familial connections and power. In 2008, she began to extend the project when she discovered the strange historical anomaly of *Nüshu* script, which enthralled her. For Tao Aimin, who had revealed her own independence and strong will with every step of her life's journey, the appeal of this secret language was irresistible. Describing the appearance of *Nüshu* texts she said, 'The characters are solid and sharp. They demonstrate the independent spirit and strong will of the women.'[14] *Nüshu* script interested her for several reasons:

> Firstly because I think the washing boards are a kind of language and *Nüshu* is also a language. Secondly because it is from Hunan Province and from close to my hometown. Thirdly because it is about women. I found it very mysterious so I wanted to research it and find out more. They created books called *San Chao Shu* from blue cloth... secret and hidden from men. At a girl's wedding her mother passed the book to the daughter and the sisters to each other. They comfort each other and express their worries, they give each other the books as gifts. And after a woman passed away her books had to be burned. Like burning paper money at a funeral.

She described this voyage of discovery for the catalogue of her 2010 exhibition *Riverbed*:

> During Spring Festival, 2008, I made an arduous journey in a snow storm to Pumei Village in Jiangyong to find a woman who understands and uses this language. Yi Youqi was eighty-three years old and very delightful. She showed me her handkerchief and belt embroidered with the characters from the language. She had a strong accent that I could not fully understand... Later she showed me a garden in a clearing hidden by bamboo trees. A path of oval shaped pebbles made characters in the language of women...[15]

In 2014, sitting in a smoky café in the 798 Art District, the artist revealed more details:

> I went in heavy snow and terrible traffic with my younger brother. Actually it's not that far, but we travelled by bus for a long time. We stayed overnight and then changed buses and travelled all around this snow covered mountain. The place where you can find *Nüshu*, Jiangyong, is on an island. In winter the mountains block it and make it inaccessible. In the past you would have had to take a boat. But now there are bridges. I had read a book about an old, old woman and I tracked her down and stayed at her house. She could sing and embroider this language. The last person who could write *Nüshu* had passed away a long time ago. She [this woman] could not write it, but she could sing and read it. At night we sat around the fire and she sang the *Nüshu* songs for the whole night. About her whole life experience. Like a kind of release. This was fantastic, it was like an exchange of spirit.' After this experience, she said, 'I produced a work named simply *Nüshu*. I merged this language with the language of the washing board. Just like the washing boards, *Nüshu* is telling stories about women's toil.

Since 2010, Tao Aimin has sought ways to combine these female languages (*Nüshu* script and washboards) with the important Chinese language of ink painting. Art historian Maxwell A. Hearn has pointed out that throughout Chinese history, 'Artists have used ink to write or draw on every conceivable surface.'[16] In exploring the infinitely expressive possibilities of marks made with ink and brush, and extending that practice to printed marks made with ink applied to the tactile surfaces of her collected washboards, Tao Aimin contributes to a significant aspect of Chinese contemporary art, reinventing ancient art practices. By working with ink, she continues the scholarly tradition of thousands of years of Chinese history. By using calligraphy, Tao makes a historical connection valued by many contemporary artists in China today. Calligraphy endures as a vital element in the work of artists ranging from Gu Wenda and Xu Bing through to the dada-esque antics of the Guangdong based Yangjiang group, who write calligraphy while drunk, or copy pages from Marx's *Das Kapital* in Chinese characters and then rip them up and play football on them. The calligraphic mark, and the connection between language and artistic expression, is an enduring practice despite cultural disruptions, misinterpretations and re-imaginings of such traditions over the course of the last fifty years.

In Tao Aimin's scrolls and books the traces of ink on washboards and the marks made by the act of printing suggest the mountains and misty waterfalls of literati landscape painting. By choosing the secret female script of *Nüshu* as her calligraphy, however, Tao Aimin's practice is a radical departure from the ink painters of the past and from today's artists who are reinventing the tradition. She inserts a language invented by anonymous, unlettered rural women into the rarefied canon of the Imperial scholarly tradition, bringing a largely unacknowledged female history into the light of day.

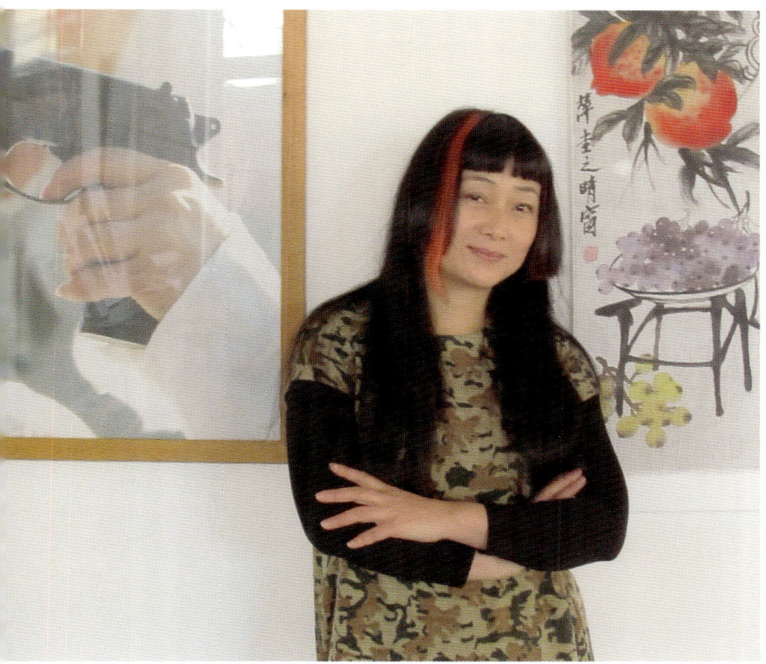

Ma Yanling in her studio, Songzhuang, November 2013, photo LG

MA YANLING 马嬿泠

Sweetness and Bitterness

Painter and performance artist Ma Yanling lives and works in a tranquil house and studio in Songzhuang, once a poor farming village on Beijing's outskirts, now home to thousands of artists.[17] The diverse and apparently contradictory elements of her practice highlight the complex experiences of her generation.

Born in Hubei Province in 1966, at the start of the Cultural Revolution, Ma Yanling came to adulthood during the turbulent late 1980s, experiencing the alternating greater and lesser freedom of expression that characterised this era. Her family's property had been confiscated during the Cultural Revolution and her grandparents were outcast, reviled as despised landlords; her grandfather died in prison. As a result of these bitter formative experiences, Ma looks back to earlier periods in Chinese history, pre-1949, for the nostalgic imagery of her paintings. She thinks deeply about the position of women and the ways that an authoritarian state has defined identities and constrained relationships. 'Mao Zedong destroyed this country,'[18] she says bitterly. When she discovered *Nüshu* she found a way to give voice to some of these feelings in a more direct manner, through performance practice.

Ma Yanling is best known for her paintings of beautiful women – Hollywood movie stars such as Audrey Hepburn and the ubiquitous Marilyn, and Shanghai divas of the 1930s. Meditations on celebrity and glamour, at their heart lie dark secrets and sorrow. One of her subjects is Mao Zedong's wife, Jiang Qing, who had been a famous actress in her youth, long before she became Madame Mao, and the most hated woman in China as a leader of the 'Gang of Four'. Another features Ruan Lingyu, a famed movie star of the 1930s. Pursued by the tabloids and with an unravelling private life, she committed suicide at the age of twenty-four, reputedly (although its authenticity is disputed) leaving a suicide note that read, 'Gossip is a fearful thing.' Three hundred thousand people followed her coffin through the streets of Shanghai.[19]

Ma is passionately interested in ancient Chinese cultural history, revering the work of traditional ink painting masters such as Ba Da Shenren, and practising calligraphy every day. She applies fine brush strokes derived from the eighteen styles of traditional calligraphy over the entire surface of her canvases, creating a net-like grid partially shrouding the features of her subjects. They look through her meticulous brush-strokes as if through a fine curtain, behind which the painful realities of their lives remain obscured. Curator Li Xianting described how her 'leaf vein' strokes, knitting and weaving across the canvas, create a 'veil of silk.'[20] The painter must hold her breath and draw each line with one sweep of the brush. If even one stroke was flawed it would reduce all her previous labour to nothing. Like the ink paintings of the literati, 'Fluent or hesitating, supple or straight, all these strokes represent the artist's spirit.'[21]

'Lines in Chinese art are like the bones in a human body.'

Ma Yanling graduated from Xiangfan University Institute of Fine Arts in 1989. There she studied traditional *gong bi* (highly realistic) painting styles and the traditions of calligraphy. She developed purely abstract canvases in which floating grids of fine lines shimmer over neutral fields. It was not until 2003, when Li Xianting included her work in an exhibition of twenty artists working with the brush in a Chinese manner at Beijing's *Tokyo Art Projects* Gallery, that she found her characteristic iconography. She paints from photographs, sometimes applied as giclée prints onto canvas and worked over with paint, in oil or acrylic. Then she applies repeated highly controlled fine brush strokes across the surface, using the bai miao technique, blurring the faces of her beautiful subjects as if veiling them with sadness. The term *bai miao* (translated as 'plain drawing') describes line drawing without shading, as seen in Tang Dynasty paintings, requiring great skill and discipline. She sees her work as a merging of *gong bi* and *shui mo* (water/ink) traditions:

> Lines are the basis of Chinese painting. If you excel in that you can do either style of painting. There is no clear line between *gong bi* and *shui mo*. You can trace *gong bi* back to the Tang Dynasty and the Dunhuang wall paintings. *Gong bi* is all about line. Lines in Chinese art are like the bones in a human body. So as an artist you need to be successful in *gong bi* because it is like the backbone of Chinese art.

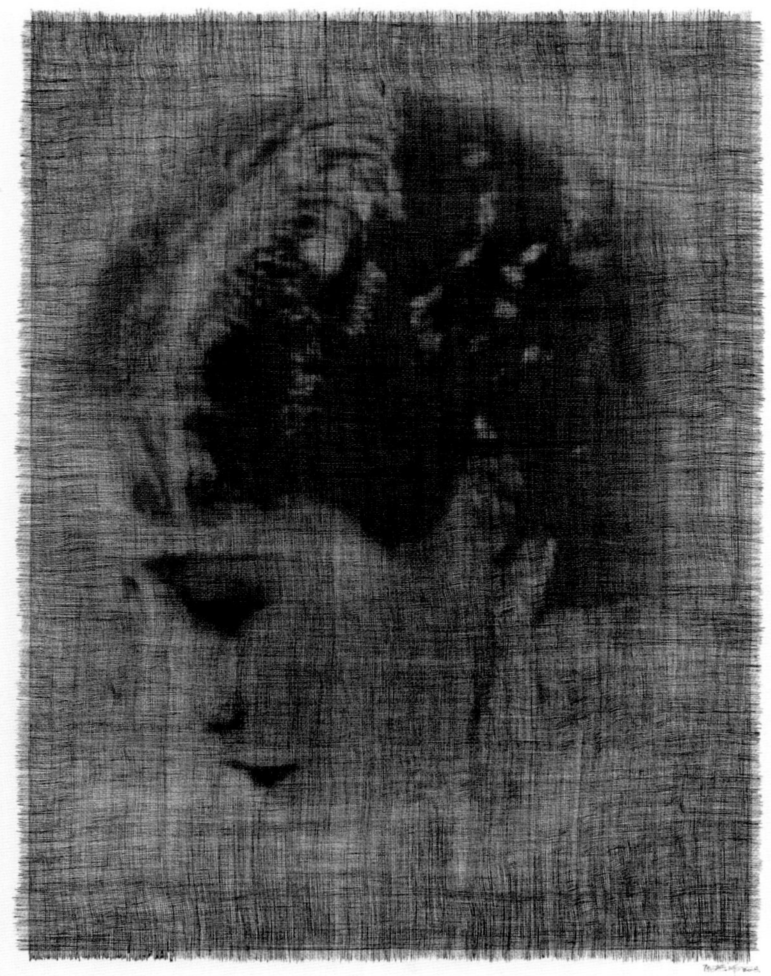

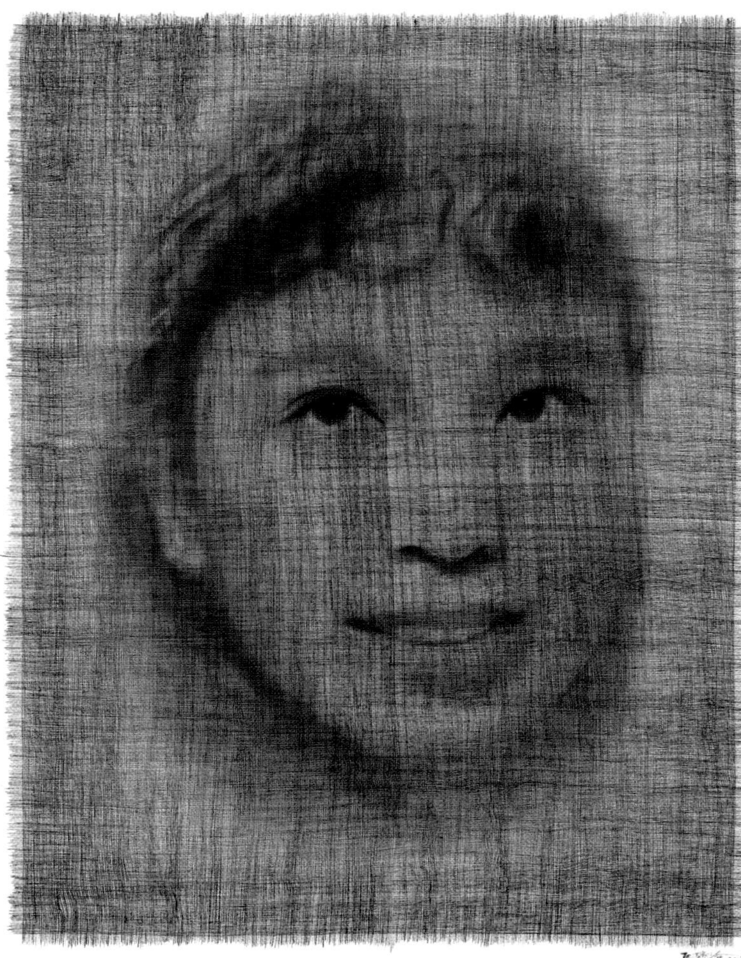

Ma Yanling is representing a captive form of beauty, expressing her belief that the feminine spirit cannot express its 'true nature' in a patriarchal culture. Her paintings evoke the flower houses of Qing Dynasty Shanghai, elegant brothels in which graceful and cultivated courtesans lived lives of quiet despair. She is interested in what lies beneath the polished surface. Just as Wang Guangyi incorporated Western brands (Coca Cola, Kodak, Marlboro) into his appropriations of heroic Cultural Revolution propaganda posters, in order to suggest the similarities between political ideology and mass-manufactured commodities,[22] so too Ma Yanling examines notions of beauty, glamour and femininity via the appropriated kitsch imagery of Shanghai vintage pin-up girls. In each there is a subversive intent.

Drawn to stories of the pre-revolutionary past, and classical Chinese literature, Ma sees women from the past as more refined, more highly educated in the arts, and (perhaps in a form of wishful thinking) more 'free'. She does, however, identify the women she depicts as 'commodities', captive to the desires of others. Jiang Qing, a woman still despised by those who remember the Gang of Four, was 'just an actress, brainwashed by Mao,' says Ma. Yearning for a past that she imagines was free and beautiful, she expresses regret for the way her generation grew up with parents who 'devoted themselves to the country' and were unaware of the emotional needs of their own children. Family relationships and trust between people were destroyed by ideology, and the fallout continues to this day.

In her revulsion for the revolutionary period Ma Yanling expresses nostalgia for a China she never experienced. She looks back to the Tang Dynasty paintings that she admired as a student, and to early Chinese cinema, encountered during later study at the Beijing Film Institute in 2000. Both were forbidden territory during the Maoist era. She said, 'I want to show the perfect image of women and also the free heart. As women we need to have our free ideas and also be independent. I want to express my own ideas and feelings through my artworks of these women.' The beautiful faces around her studio looking through their veils of disciplined brush marks are relics – faint traces of women whose existence was defined entirely by others.

Ma Yanling
Ruan Lingyu 2008
acrylic and Chinese ink on canvas
100 x 80 cm
image courtesy the artist and
White Rabbit Gallery, Sydney

Ma Yanling
Jiang Qing 2008
acrylic and Chinese ink on canvas
100 x 80 cm
image courtesy the artist and
White Rabbit Gallery, Sydney

In her daily studio practice Ma stands over a table applying her intricate grid of fine lines with great precision. Despite the popular culture nostalgia of her chosen subject it is a meditative act, quietly performed in silence and solitude. Ma Yanling is aware of a certain paradox at the heart of these codified representations of femininity. She is regretful that collectors often see the beauty in her works but not their underlying sadness. On the one hand she expresses a romantic view of feminine subjectivity, longing for the perceived 'refinement, grace and elegance' of women in pre-revolutionary China. On the other hand, particularly in her performance works, she recognises the brutal realities of how women have been silenced. Ma believes young women are much more powerful and 'more straightforward' than her own generation. As a mother, however, she sees continuing problems: today's young women, usually single children, have been brought up by overly controlling parents who themselves had poor experiences of family life during the Cultural Revolution.

A contrasting aspect of her practice is revealed by large photographs of confrontational performance works. They show the artist holding a gun to her own head in Tiananmen Square, and near the Forbidden City, an echo of those famous gunshots of Xiao Lu's in the National Art Museum in 1989, and a reference to acts of terror in the present day. Ma Yanling saw Ma Qiusha's live performance *No.4 Pingyuanli to No.4 Tianqiaobeili* in which the younger artist describes the psychological and societal pressures of her life as a razor blade cuts her tongue and blood fills her mouth.[23] She found it horrifying and compelling. It made her think about the experiences of her own daughter's generation: 'I saw a performance by a young artist who was talking with very blurred words and nobody could understand her. And then we saw she was holding a knife (blade) inside her mouth. Their words do not count in front of their parents, that's why she was holding a knife in her mouth – because she does not have the right to express her own ideas in front of her parents.'

The implied contradiction in Ma Qiusha's performance, between physical and psychological pain, is similarly found in the *Nüshu* texts. When Ma Yanling discovered *Nüshu* she saw it as a metaphor for everything she wanted to say about relationships between women, and about female experience. She is interested in how young girls were introduced by older women to a culturally sanctioned form for the expression of dissatisfaction. In her performance art, ostensibly so different to her painting, Ma Yanling writes – sometimes explicitly using *Nüshu* characters – on her own body and the bodies of other women, making works that confront audiences with ideas about sexuality, menstruation, female fertility and violence. Knowing that *Nüshu* letters received from a sworn sister, or from a mother to a daughter, would usually be

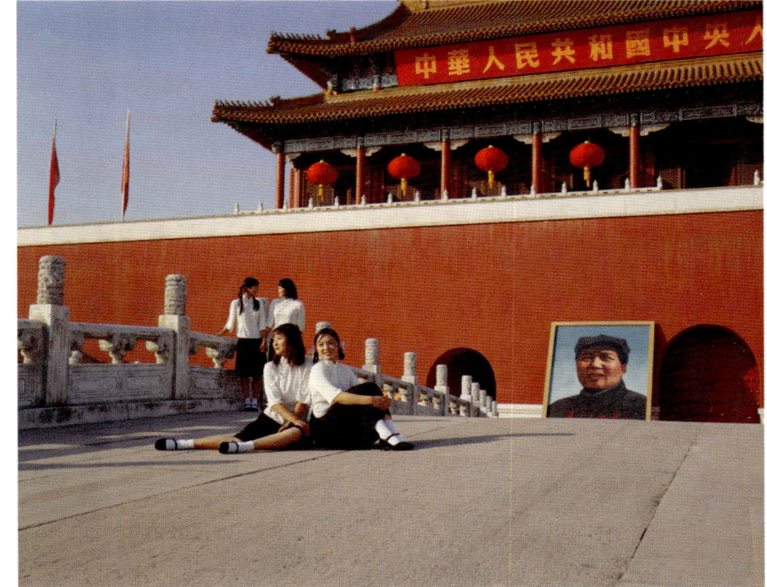

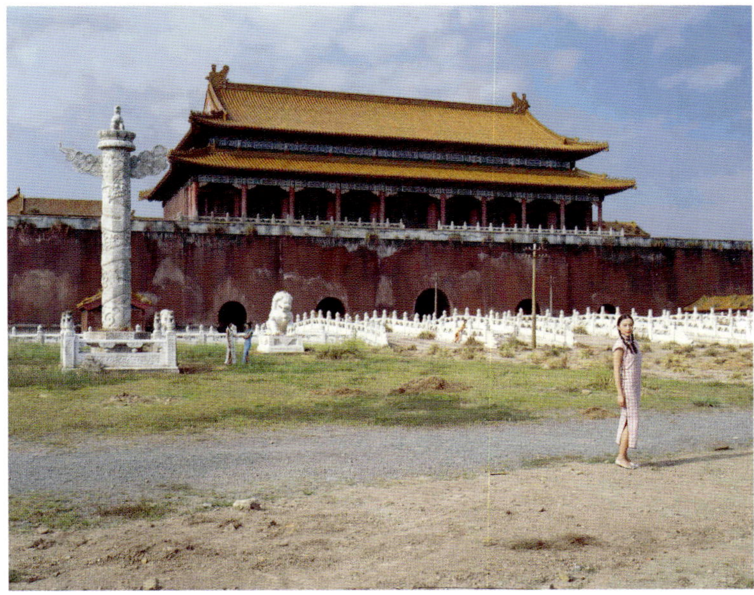

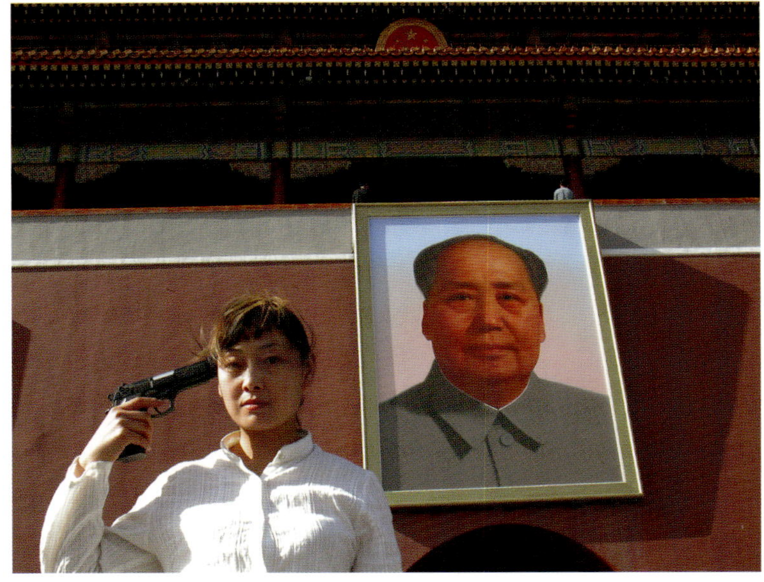

Ma Yanling
Tiananmen 1949 2009
Tiananmen 1945 2007
Gun 2007
photographs, each 80 x 100 cm
images courtesy the artist

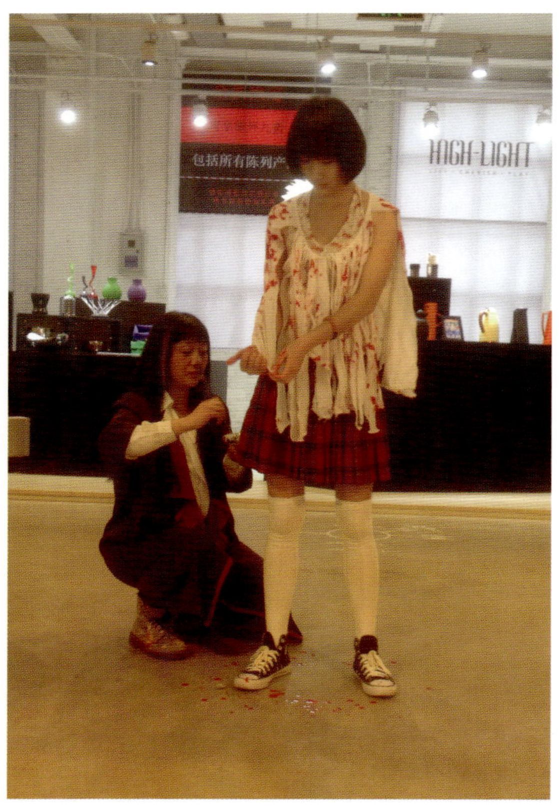

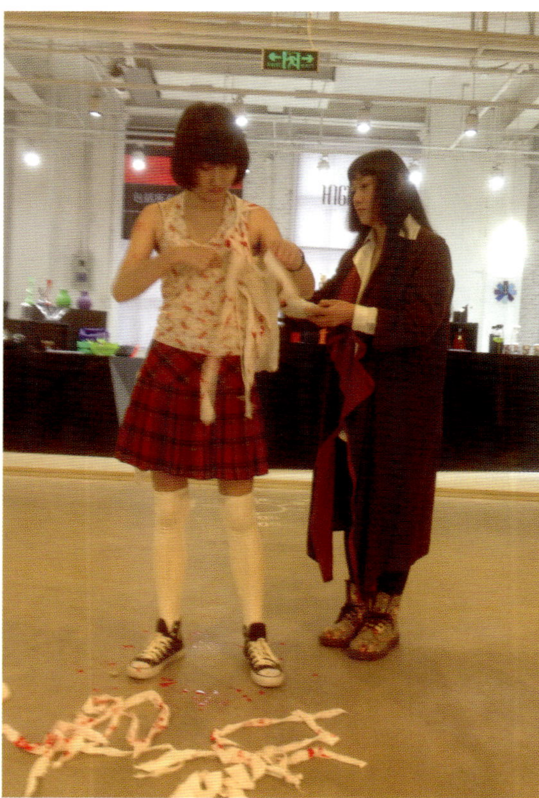
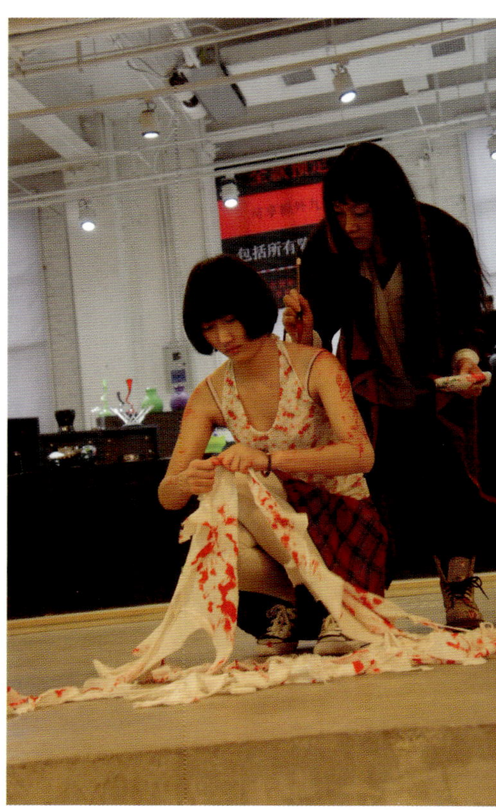

destroyed after being read, thus keeping their contents, and the forms of the language itself, entirely secret, Ma Yanling developed a performance in which she and her art student daughter wrote in *Nüshu* script on each other's skin: 'We read it and then wiped it away – so it is like you wipe away the language, and then you wipe away the possibility to inherit this language.' In another work the clothes worn by the artist and her daughter were stitched together, joining the two, and they had to wield scissors to release themselves from these bonds. 'I sew people together, then cut them apart,' she says.

The two elements of her practice (commercially successful paintings and challenging performance art, documented with video and photography) apparently so disparate, are linked by her interest in the hidden history of women in China, and by a sense of loss and regret which emanates from every painting and photograph. Ma explores the profound relationships between women, most particularly between mothers and daughters. She identifies the connecting thread that runs through all of her work as her interest in the ancient female written language.

Ma Yanling was a young artist in the early 1990s, moving in artistic circles in Beijing, aware of the growing success of a new wave of figurative and pop-inspired painters, in what was an overwhelmingly male artworld. Perhaps little has changed. Ma sees the artworld in which she moves as unambiguously patriarchal. Asked if it is more difficult for a woman artist than for a man to be successful here in China, she says:

> Ah it's very hard! After all it is still a male-dominated society in China. Very hard! *Very* hard! You have to give birth to the children and still make your own art… [There is a] lack of attention for women artists – plus men can go out to drink with their friends and women have to stay at home to look after the family.

She hopes it will change, but the desired change is slow in coming. She says:

> Lots of women artists, when they try to struggle for their own success they get hurt and have to work alone with no support. I feel very lucky. I have my husband and my daughter and I think I am pretty successful. Actually, that is also the reason why so many women artists create some surprising and shocking works – because the loneliness they reveal is more powerful.

Ma navigates this complex territory by the strategic division of her practice into two distinct, but connected elements. She is clear-sighted about creating paintings for a particular market, for collectors who love their nostalgia and glamour, although this is not to deny the layers of meaning with which they are imbued. She is also highly aware of combining a western modernist (and postmodernist) idiom with Chinese tradition: 'Of course, I learned Chinese painting *and* oil painting at high school, both Chinese and western techniques, [although] people then paid more attention to Western art. I myself liked Chinese painting more, that was my interest.'

Ma Yanling
Woman's Book (Nüshu) 2014
documentation of performance,
images courtesy the artist

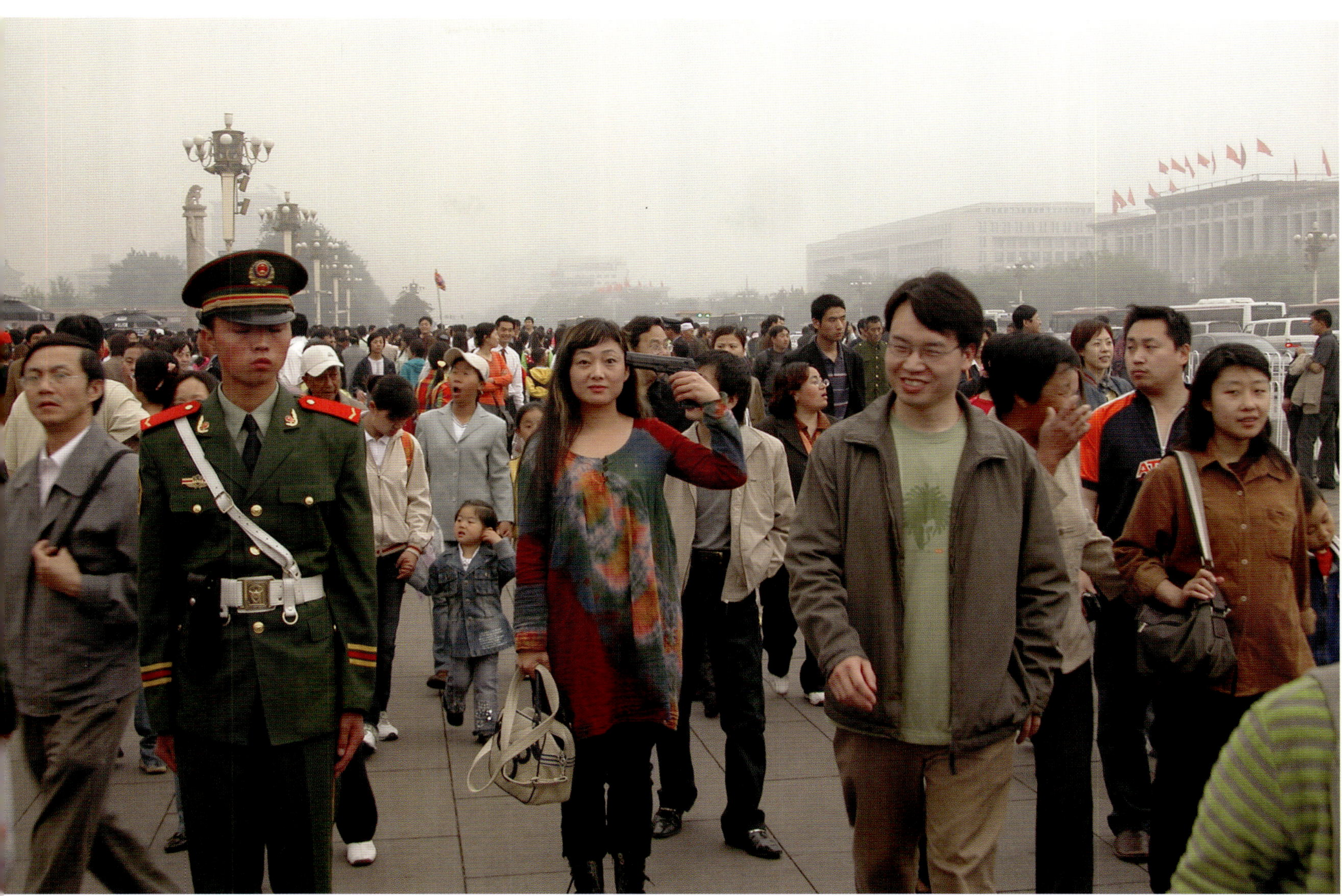

This distinguishes her from her peers, who were exploring the expanding possibilities of western art, reintroduced to China as a result of Deng Xiaoping's policies of Reform and Opening. Ma Yanling, however, was less seduced by western ideas. At that time she was not interested in abstraction or the blurring of media boundaries exemplified by Rauschenberg, shown in Beijing in 1985. For Ma, a journey to Xi'an with her classmates to see the ancient stone tablets and copy their calligraphy was much more inspirational: 'Now there are too many tourists, so you can no longer get access to those things, but at that time you could get very close and actually touch the tablets – you could really feel this is calligraphy from the Tang Dynasty, and you could feel the Tang Dynasty in those words.'

Later, Ma Yanling developed a love for cinema and photography, moving away from painting for a period: 'I thought it was more appealing to show life and direct emotions through the lens of the camera.' Her photographs of women on an abandoned film set – a pre-1949 Tiananmen Square – are highly cinematic. They appear to be frames cut from a filmic narrative, imbued with mystery. Hidden beneath the surface beauty is the uncomfortable truth that her female subjects are objects of desire. Just as the net of brushed fine lines in her paintings veils the faces of her subjects, the girls in her photographs are often posed with faces averted; 'romantic' images onto which a host of interpretations can be projected. All people see is the external glamour but, 'they are controlled by other people, they don't have any power over their own lives,' says the artist. The schoolgirls in one such image are reminiscent of Cui Xiuwen's photographs of young girls dwarfed by the monumental architecture of the Forbidden City's walls and gates. She is reflecting on her own girlhood, and bitter memories of a collectivist, conformist culture she now despises.

Ma Yanling's performance work has often focused on social control, exemplified by her 2007 *Gun* series. In the years after

Ma Yanling
Beijing 2007
photograph, 80 x 100 cm
image courtesy the artist

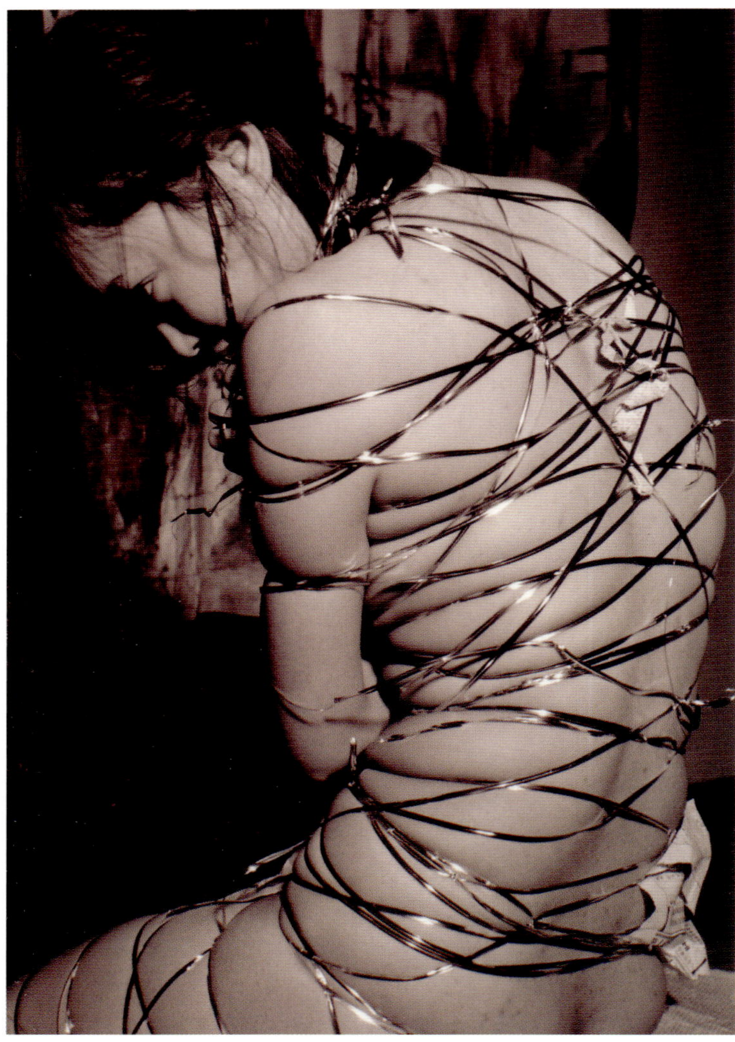

the SARS epidemic, and in the lead-up to the 2008 Beijing Olympics, she created a series of 'interventions' in the public domain, pointing a realistic replica gun at her own head in crowded places of national significance. These disturbing and theatrical mock suicide attempts, like experimental theatre interventions in the public sphere, were at least in part inspired by her interest in the work of Marina Abramović. She especially admires Abramović's collaborative work with Ulay, seeing a parallel with her own feelings about the difficulties of communication between men and women.

After the horrors of 9/11, the pervasive fear of SARS in 2002–04, and the destruction wrought upon the city in the years leading to the 2008 Olympics, Ma Yanling saw how sudden violence could transform an ordinary urban space into a locus of tragedy. She covertly brought a replica gun into crowded public arenas including the Beijing subway and – with the inevitable result of her arrest, subsequent detention and release – Tiananmen Square, in front of Mao's portrait. She would suddenly produce the gun, hold it to her own head, and a collaborator would photograph the result. The resulting images reveal the anxiety evident in public spaces after 9/11. They are also particular to the Chinese context, suggesting an awareness of constant surveillance, overt and covert. Her work is prescient – these images have even greater resonance today, in a world of unexpected terrorist attacks in city centres.

Although Ma Yanling explicitly denies any connection, it is difficult not to see a relationship between this series and Xiao Lu's notorious 1989 performance work, *Two Gunshots Fired at the Installation, Dialogue*, in the National Art Museum close to Tiananmen Square.[24] By taking a (replica) gun into Tiananmen Square – a powerful symbol of Chinese nationalism and tragic history – suggesting she was about to suicide under the image of Mao Zedong, Ma Yanling, like Xiao Lu before her, was metaphorically firing at the heart of Chinese political authority. Her arrest did not come as a surprise, even though her gun was a fake. What does it mean, however, that the implied threat of violence is directed at the artist herself? Ma sees this body of work, in which she performs the role of 'the terrorist', and her photographic series of women on an abandoned movie set representing Tiananmen in the pre-1949 past, as part of an ongoing secret female Chinese history. Like her paintings these images reveal a paradox: despair underlying beauty and grace.

'Morse Code for Women.'

Ma Yanling works within the convention of Chinese avant-garde endurance performance. In *Suitcase Series* the artist's naked body is tightly bound with plastic tape or silk ribbons, creating grotesque patterns in her flesh reminding us of the *Public Broadcast Exercises* performances of He Chengyao, an artist of the same generation.[25] After being bound, Ma Yanling crams herself into small spaces such as cupboards and suitcases, representing the violence often meted out to uncooperative women. Metaphors of bondage and confinement, they are intentionally feminist expressions of dissent.

In a performance work presented in 2009 in Japan she wrote *Nüshu* characters on sanitary towels and handed them to the audience, who were, she says, very reluctant to take them, revealing fear and disgust at even the suggestion of menstrual blood, despite its actual absence. In a series of collaborative performances with her own daughter and other female artists she continues to use *Nüshu* script as a female language, describing it as 'Morse Code for women.' Female secrets recur in Ma Yanling's work: the secret ways women were forced to operate in a world which confined them to the domestic sphere and denied them a voice in public discourse; the secrecy which pervades politics and public life in China even today; and the coded communications – and miscommunications – between generations of Chinese women.

Ma Yanling
Untitled 2004
photographic documentation of performance
image courtesy the artist

In the Confucian classic *Book of Rites*, one poem concludes, 'Women should not take part in public affairs; they should devote themselves to tending silkworms and weaving.'[26] Ma Yanling 'speaks bitterness' in her performances, not unlike the chanted bridal laments and Third Day Missives of the *Nüshu* texts passed between women. Tao Aimin honours the lives and labour of generations of rural women, speaking for those who cannot. Each artist explicitly identifies her work as a form of language, a potent image in a cultural history that traditionally denied women a voice in the discourse.

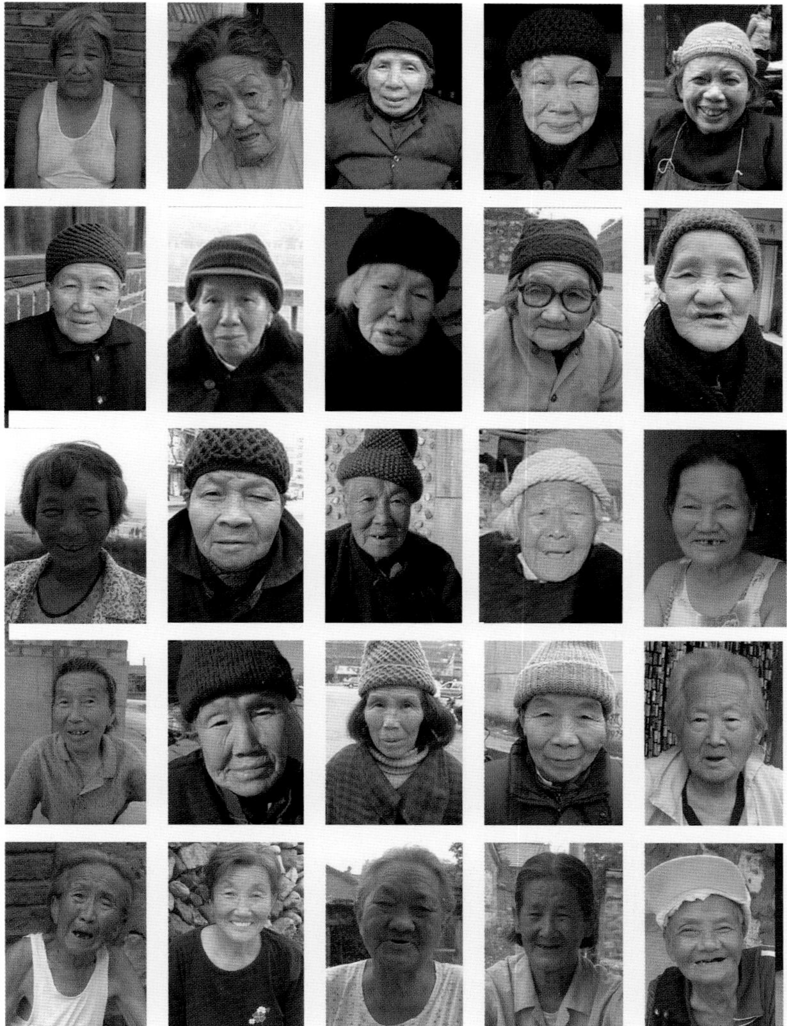

Tao Aimin
Process of Collection 1
photographic documentation of the artist's
interviews with rural women
image courtesy the artist

NOTES

1 For a more detailed analysis of the history and influence of *Nüshu*, see Guest, L 2015 'Secrets, Sorrow and the Feminine Subjective: *Nüshu* References in the Work of Contemporary Chinese Artist Ma Yanling, *Journal of Contemporary Chinese Art* 2 (1) (45–63) Intellect Books, UK
2 McLaren, A 1996 'Women's Voices and Textuality: Chastity and Abduction in Chinese *Nüshu* Writing' *Modern China* 22 (4) (382–416)
3 ibid.
4 Broussard, JT 2008 '*Nüshu*: A Curriculum of Women's Identity' *Transnational Curriculum Inquiry* 5 (2) available at http://nitinat.library.ubc.ca/ojs/index.php/tci accessed 28 June 2014
5 Radner, J N 1993 *Feminist Messages: Coding in Women's Folk Cultures* Chicago: Urbana University of Illinois Press
6 Idema, WL 2009 *Heroines of Jiangyong: Narrative Ballads in Women's Script* University of Washington Press Seattle
7 Silber, C. 1994 'From Daughter to Daughter-in-Law in the Women's Script of Southern Hunan' In: C. K. GIlmartin, G. Hershatter, L. Rofel & T White (eds) *Engendering China: Women, Culture and the State* Harvard Contemporary China Series Boston (47–68)
8 Lee, L. L 2004. 'Pure Persuasion: A Case Study of *Nüshu*, or "Women's Script" Discourses' in *Quarterly Journal of Speech*, 90(4) (403–21)
9 Unless otherwise acknowledged all quotes from Tao Aimin are from her conversation with the writer in Beijing in December 2014
10 During the 1st millennium BC, the city of Changsha was the centre of the southern part of the Yangtze River valley state of Chu. 'Chu Culture' has been connected to ideas about shamanic religious rituals which included ecstatic states and 'poetic lamentations'. See Cook, Constance A and Major, John S 1999 *Defining Chu: Image and Reality in Ancient China* University of Hawai'i Press, USA (169)
11 Kovskaya, Maya 2010 'Life Passes Like the Song of Water' in *Riverbed* catalogue, Onemoon Gallery Beijing, also found on the author's website, available at http://www.mayakovskaya.com/publications/riverbed.php accessed 15 January 2015
12 Tao Aimin, 2005, texts and Artist Statements provided to the writer and translated from the Chinese
13 Fenichel, Luna 2006 An interview with Tao Aimin for *New York Arts* 1 December 2006 available at http://www.nyartsmagazine.com/?p=3892 accessed 13 January 2015
14 Tao Aimin 2010 'The Secret Language of Women' in *Riverbed* catalogue, Onemoon Gallery Beijing
15 ibid.
16 Hearn, Maxwell K 2013 'Ink Art: An Introduction' in *Ink Art: Past as Present in Contemporary China* The Metropolitan Museum of Art, New York (13)
17 Artist Guo Jian, speaking at The University of Sydney and China Studies Centre symposium *Contemporary Artists in China: how they operate between freedom and restriction* 30 July 2015, said that he believed there were 20,000 artists living and working in Songzhuang
18 Unless otherwise acknowledged all quotes from Ma Yanling are from her conversations with the writer in October and November of 2013
19 and http://gbtimes.com/life/ruan-lingyu-media-killed-movie-star accessed 11 January 2015
20 Li Xianting 2011 'Clouding the Passions of Yore' in *Ma Yanling: Timeless Elegance* Dialogue Space Gallery Beijing
21 ibid.
22 in Wang Guangyi's 1990s Political Pop *Great Criticisms* series of paintings
23 See Chapter 7 for an account of this work and of Ma Qiusha's practice
24 See Chapter 2 for a full account of the incident in 1989 at the opening of the *China/Avant-garde* exhibition, when Xiao Lu fired a gun into her own sculpture
25 See Chapter 7 for an account of the development of performance art in China and the practice of He Chengyao
26 Available online at http://asiasociety.org/women-traditional-china accessed 12 April 2015

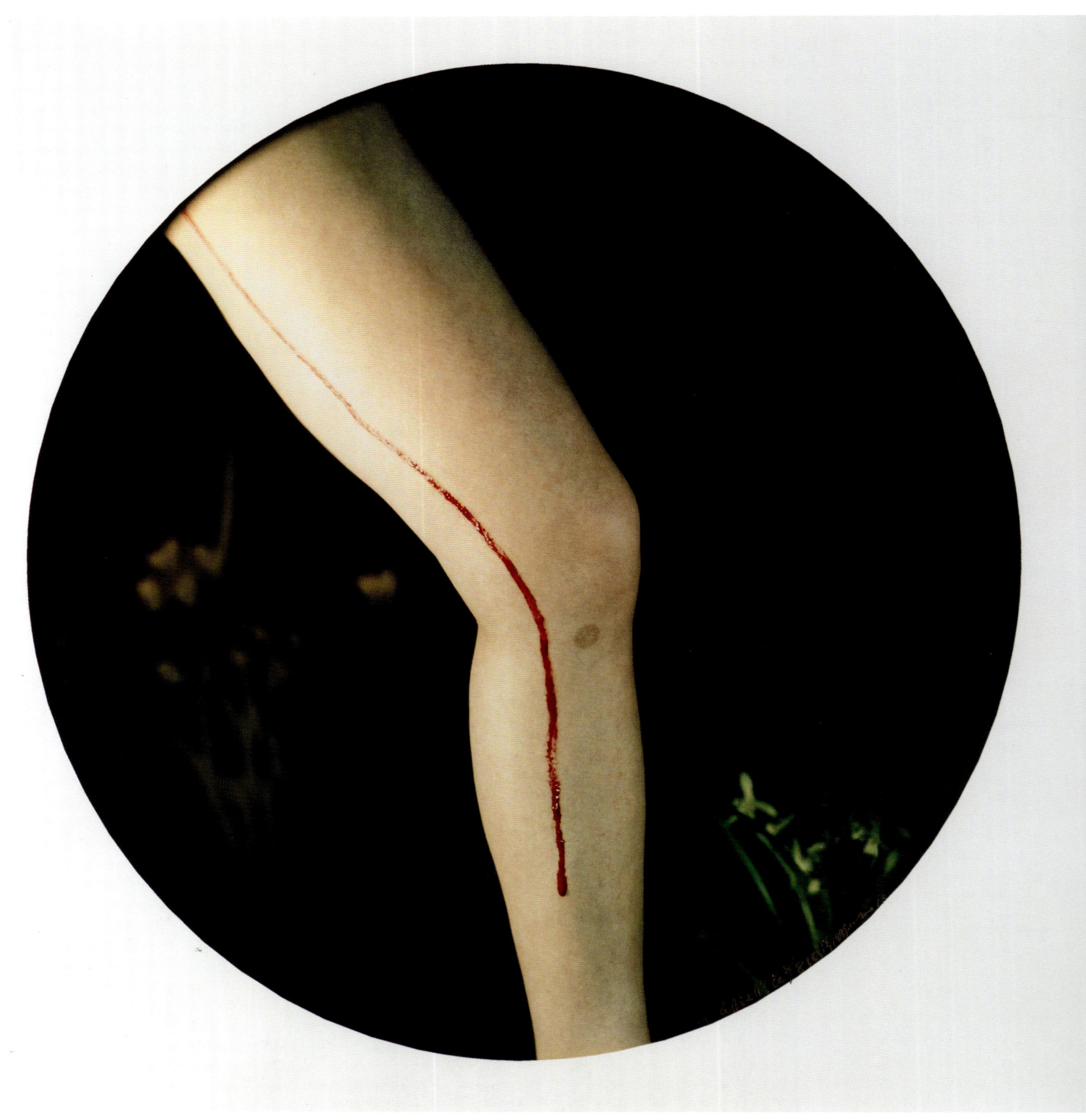

A WINDOW OPENS

Chen Lingyang, Zhou Hongbin, Liu Shiyuan and Fang Lu

From the first moments of the newly formed People's Republic in 1949, Mao Zedong and his government understood the power of photography. News photographers had recorded the war with Japan and the dramatic struggles of Mao's troops against Chiang Kai-shek's Nationalists, and photographers would play a significant role in the new China, too, their work understood as a political task shaping the new nation. In 1953 Mao Songyou, a photographer working for the Xinhua News Agency, called for 'photographic workers to increase the beauty of their images such that they "sing the praise of [New China]."' [1] Those who seized the reins of political power quickly recognised that photographs could influence people and move their emotions. It took much longer, however, for photography to be understood and accepted as art. Only relatively recently have artists, curators and collectors recognised its aesthetic potential.

The development of Chinese photography is inextricably connected with the tumultuous history of modern China. William Henry Fox Talbot and Louis Daguerre invented the photographic process in 1839, the year the First Opium War erupted. In 1842 the new 'calotype' process recorded China's humiliation at the hands of colonial powers after the Treaty of Nanking, which conceded the island of Hong Kong to Britain and established other treaty ports.[2] The first British Governor of Hong Kong presented a photographic portrait of himself and his family to the Guangdong Governor General, Qi Ying, who requested a reciprocal photographic portrait from the Emperor – the earliest evidence of official Chinese contact with photography. By 1846 foreigners had set up photographic studios in Hong Kong, and by the 1870s Chinese-owned studios had opened in treaty ports such as Shanghai. At first they were suppressed by the Qing government, seen as spreading western culture.

By the end of the nineteenth century photographic portraiture was widespread and popular. Art historian Claire Roberts refers to portraits 'printed onto slivers of stone, ivory, porcelain or silk – materials that were more robust than glass – and [carried] the spirit of the person into the future.'[3] Even the imperial court was immortalised in this way, when the formidable Empress Dowager Cixi demanded a photograph, staged in the impressive surroundings of the Hall of Happiness and Longevity at the Summer Palace, as she approached her seventieth birthday. Photographs from the time demonstrate a theatrical staging of their subjects, employing Chinese symbols of prosperity and longevity. It had taken less than fifty years for an entirely new visual medium to be adapted to a particularly Chinese mode of expression.

Early in the twentieth century, the artistic potential of the medium attracted intellectuals who thought it could forge an identity for a modern nation. Before the Japanese invasion of Shanghai in August 1937, a number of amateur fine-art photographic groups flourished, organising exhibitions and producing catalogues and magazines.[4] But the days of this cosmopolitan milieu of photography enthusiasts, amateur practitioners and professional photographic studios catering to the middle and upper classes were numbered, and after the defeat of the Nationalists, photography was to play an important role in the propaganda machine of the new People's Republic. For almost thirty years there was almost no vernacular, unofficial photography, until the mid-1980s when increasing wealth and greater openness made cameras and film available to ordinary people.

Photography resurfaced into the contemporary art sphere in the 1980s and 1990s, but it would take years for photography to be considered an art form equal to painting and sculpture. Many experimental photography journals were banned after the disruptions of 1989, and the fledgling photographic renaissance was stalled. As late as 1993 an important exhibition, *China's New Art Post-1989,* made no reference to photography.[5] In 1994, Ai Weiwei, Xu Bei, Zeng

Chen Lingyang
Twelve Flower Months – July: Orchid 1999
c-type photograph
50 x 50 cm
image courtesy the artist and White Rabbit Gallery

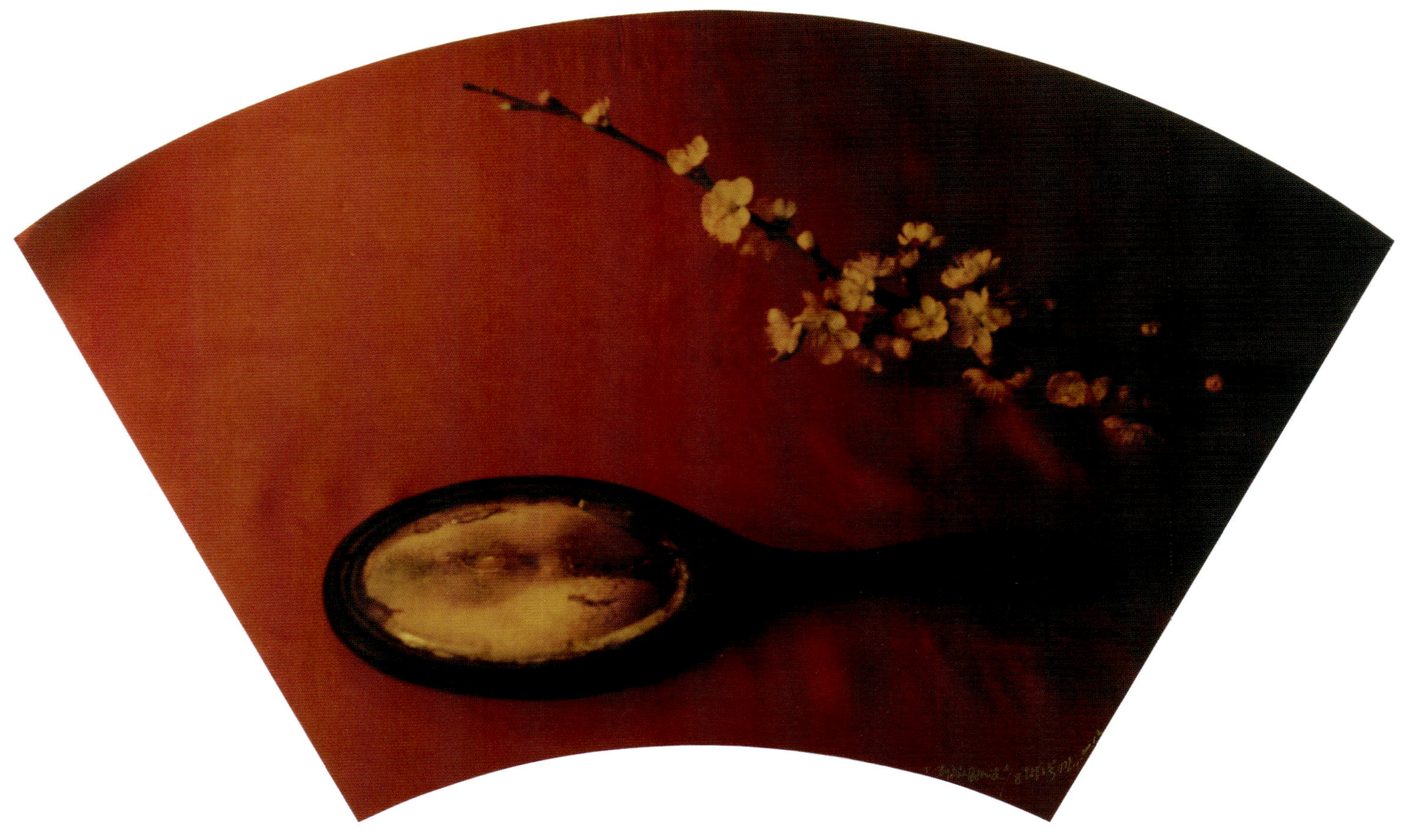

Xiaojun and Zheng Hui secretly published *The Book with the Black Cover* featuring experimental photography, and an approach known as 'Conceptual Photography' took flight.[6] Artists freely adapted Western idioms, appropriated the language of Chinese painting, and satirised their Maoist past. In the process they created something entirely Chinese, and, as writer Peter Yeoh has argued, 'decentred the medium from its Western orthodoxy.'[7]

'A Window Suddenly Opens.' *—Rong Rong*

'Conceptual' photography developed in the fiercely experimental East Village. As artists documented each other's actions, some began to focus more on the camera than on their performances or installations. In 1996 photographer Rong Rong (who, with his Japanese artist/photographer wife, Inri, established the influential *Three Shadows Photography Art Centre* in Beijing, in a courtyard building designed by Ai Weiwei) published the third issue of avant-garde journal *New Photo,* with an introduction stating, 'When CONCEPT enters Chinese photography, it is as if a window suddenly opens in a room which has been sealed for years.'[8] The metaphor of a suddenly-opened window applies to all avant-garde art, after thirty years of repression, but is especially apt in relation to photography, due to its association with state power and the questionable veracity of propaganda photographs.

Photography began to merge with painting, sculpture, performance and installation, and boundaries between media became porous. Following that first generation of avant-garde artists, a new generation experimented with digital media and video.

In 2004 Wu Hung, together with Christopher Phillips, from New York's International Center of Photography, organised *Between Past and Future: New Photography and Video From China,* a survey show that toured internationally, bringing Chinese photography to new audiences. Phillips told writer Peter Yeoh, 'What really interested me in Chinese photography is the fact that most artists and photographers didn't understand the history of Western art or have a strong grasp of the history of Asian art. They thought everything was available and that they can mix and match, slam everything together according to their own imagination, and produced either absolutely kitsch results or just extraordinarily surprising and unparalleled results.'[9] These qualities – an imagination unhindered by theoretical frameworks or historical precedent, inspired by the freedom to innovate after years of heavy-handed control – distinguish Chinese approaches to the medium.

Some emerging art photographers focused on the body. For Zhang Huan, Huang Yan and Chen Lingyang, the artist's body becomes a metaphor for the landscape, history and culture of China itself, sometimes literally 'written' on their skin. Others

Chen Lingyang
Twelve Flower Months – March: Peach 1999–2000
c-type photograph
42 x 71 cm
image courtesy the artist and White Rabbit Gallery

explored bitter memories of the recent past or re-examined distant tradition and history. Younger artists are reinventing the medium with a greater awareness of international photographic discourses, whilst maintaining the imaginative freedom that has characterised the rise of a Chinese photographic and video practice. For even the youngest, however, the compulsory uniformity of the collectivist past lies just beneath the individualist expressions of the present-day.

These themes and preoccupations are found in the work of each artist in this chapter. Chen Lingyang's *Twelve Flower Months* appropriates traditional floral symbols, subverting the imagery with overt references to female cycles, using her own body, and glimpses of her genitalia, in each image. Zhou Hongbin takes landscape and animal motifs from traditional Chinese painting to create Utopian dream-like images. Fang Lu is interested in ritual, examining her Chinese identity from the perspective of an artist educated in the United States. Young artist Liu Shiyuan divides her time between Beijing and Copenhagen. She is interested in notions of beauty, of ritual, and the emotive possibilities of the photographic image, but far less interested in the past than artists of an older generation. Despite their immersion in international discourses, each artist references – overtly, or in more hidden, coded ways – Chinese traditions.

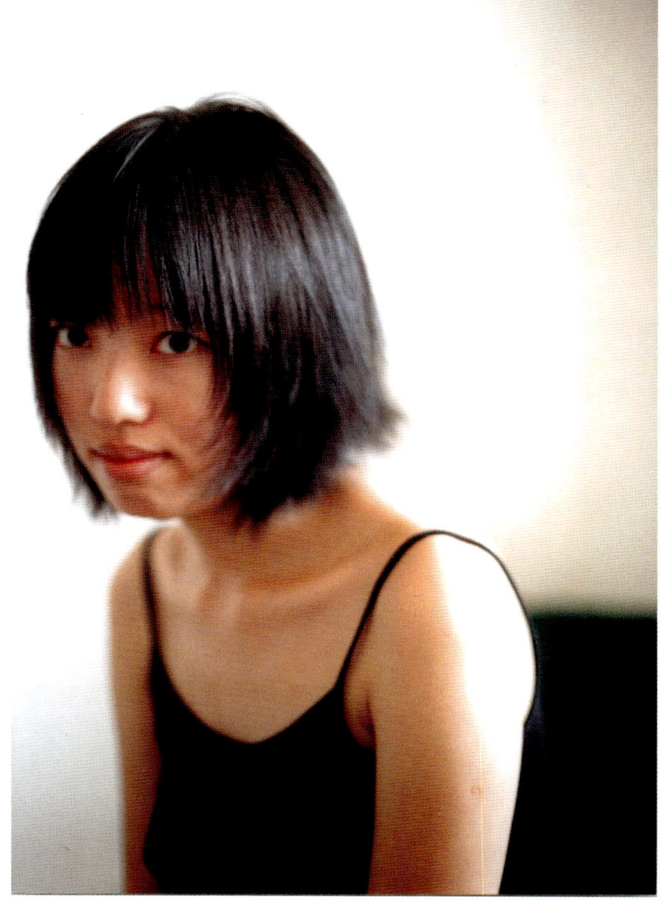

CHEN LINGYANG 陈羚羊

Twelve Flower Months

Born in 1975 in Yiwu, Zhejiang Province, and educated at the Central Academy of Fine Arts in Beijing, Chen Lingyang's work is often described as 'brave'. Her first publicly exhibited work, *Scroll*, was a roll of toilet paper, painted as a classical scroll might have been, with what seemed at first to be misty mountains, clouds and water. In reality, the paper was stained with her own dark menstrual blood. Shown in 1999 in the Yunfeng Gallery, inside the old Imperial Archives adjacent to the Forbidden City, the ancient solemnity of the surroundings made the abject nature of the work seem even more transgressive. Some may have interpreted her actions as an unsubtle satire of the masculine traditions of the literati, but art historian Wu Hung suggests it 'reinterprets the hand scroll medium and its inherent temporality based on a woman artist's knowledge of her own body.'[10]

Reminiscent of feminist artworks of the 1970s such as Carolee Schneemann's notorious 1975 performance, in which she pulled a long scroll of paper from her vagina and read aloud from it, or the vagina imagery of Judy Chicago's *The Dinner Party Project* (1974-79), Chen's practice focused obsessively for a time on menstruation. Art writer Jinli He distinguishes Chen Lingyang's work from the American artists: 'Chen's work, rooted in her cultural sensibility, expresses a totally different statement of women's desires and conditions...' arguing that a specifically Chinese allusion to Taoist concepts of yin and yang in Chen's work is more important than its apparent feminism.[11]

Chen Lingyang followed *Scroll* with *Twelve Flower Months*, a series of photographs completed over the course of a year recording her menstrual cycle. The artist's own body and bleeding genitalia are reflected in antique mirrors, with the traditional flower representing each calendar month. The representation of the naked body was never an established convention in Chinese art, which in itself marks out Chen Lingyang's practice as a reaction against literati traditions, despite her use of their garden iconography. By photographing her own genitals Chen Lingyang challenges Chinese taboos against nudity and a generalised cultural disgust about menstrual blood. Her images are deliberately provocative, exploring a subject still hidden and secret.

The photographs are beautiful – glimpses of body parts are lit in chiaroscuro against a black background, framed as if seen through the moon windows of a classical Chinese garden. Warning against interpreting such works through a western feminist paradigm, Jinli He interprets the contrast between the closed nature of the boudoir, a private and eroticised female space, and the openness of the work's central motif of the body, as a cultural expression of yin and yang:

Chen Lingyang
photograph courtesy the artist

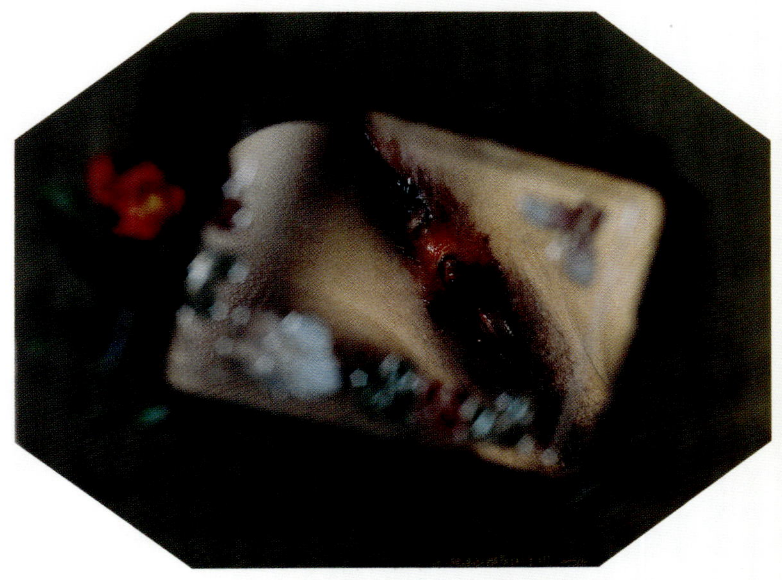

The open blossom and the opened body in the reflected mirror and the gaze of the camera all emphasize the idea of openness. But this openness is not a strong, open statement as is clearly expressed in Chicago and Schneemann's works, rather it implies a continuity of nature and culture.[12]

Chen Lingyang no longer lives and works in Beijing, having moved to Paris following her marriage. It is widely believed that she has stopped making art. What remains is a significant body of work from the turn of the century revealing an artist courageously using her own body and its functions to make beautiful and arresting images.

From her new world in Paris, far from the heady experimental days of Beijing at the end of the nineties, Chen Lingyang responded thoughtfully and in detail to my questions. She explicitly denies a feminist intention:

> I am not a feminist in the sense of having the ideas first, and then finding some creative means to communicate them through an artwork. I just have something to express, and then I find a suitable expressive means to do it. I have my own creative motivation. Viewers can interpret my work from their own perspective, whether feminist or not... As an artist, I hope that my work has the ability to stimulate the viewer.[13]

Chen maintains viewers have the right to interpret her work in many ways, just as she, the artist, has the right to 'create my own work freely and interpret it frankly.' [14]

Chen Lingyang
Twelve Flower Months – May: Pomegranate 1999–2000
c-type photograph
41 x 56 cm
image courtesy the artist and White Rabbit Gallery

Despite her disavowal of a consciously feminist intent, her work was linked to a surge of interest in 'female' and 'feminist' representations in China in the 1990s. Photomedia and video artist Cui Xiuwen, in her collaboration with the *Sirens* group, often focused on representations of the body, and sexual desire.[15] In 2000 the female critic and curator, Jiang Mei, wrote:

> Chinese feminist art of the 1990s on the whole is characterised by intimate private space... self-contentment, self-cultivation and attainment... Chinese female artists rarely participate in the debates that are taking place on the international [level] or employ artistic means to express their views of contemporary international or local politics, society or culture.[16]

Certainly, Chen's work has been curated and 'read' in a variety of ways: her photographs were included in Ai Weiwei's infamous 2000 *Fuck Off* exhibition in Shanghai, which included Zhu Yu's documentation of a performance in which he (allegedly) cooked and ate a human foetus. This was one way of interpreting Chen's work: performative, iconoclastic, deliberately shocking, confronting social norms. In Chinese, this exhibition was called *An Uncooperative Attitude*. A very different reading of the *Twelve Flower Months* was conveyed by Chen's inclusion in a show of work by female artists in New York in 2004. *Who Am I? Chinese Contemporary Art by Chinese and Chinese-American Women Artists* was intended to address 'important questions posed by contemporary Chinese female artists whose work explores the themes of personal, cultural, and artistic identity.'[17] From the distance of more than fifteen years, Chen's work appears more dreamily self-absorbed than flagrantly provocative.

Chen told art historian Zhao Chuan that she combined ideas from traditional village interpretations of Taoism with her own thoughts:

> Our ancestors had a crude saying, 'The Tao is everywhere, even in excrement.' But I used the motif of menstruation. The fact that I'm affected by the physiological phenomenon of menstruation is of course because of the gender I was born with. This is also why, since its first exhibition, this artwork has been considered a feminist work of art.[18]

She deliberately staged her photographs in a dimly lit, classical boudoir setting. The antique mirror in each image is an attempt to see the truth reflected, she says. Because the backgrounds are so dark, the spectator sees him or herself reflected in the glossy photographic paper, an allusion to the voyeuristic impulse. Chen Lingyang is aware of the contradiction in her work. Intending to establish a new field of vision with a 'visual irritation' between the image of menstruating female genitalia

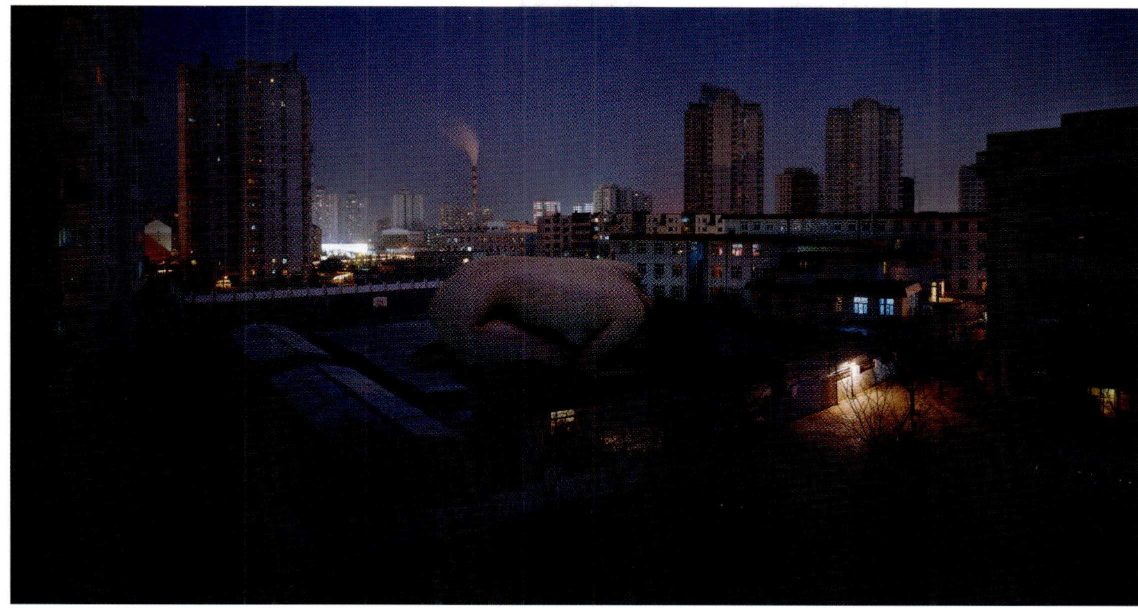

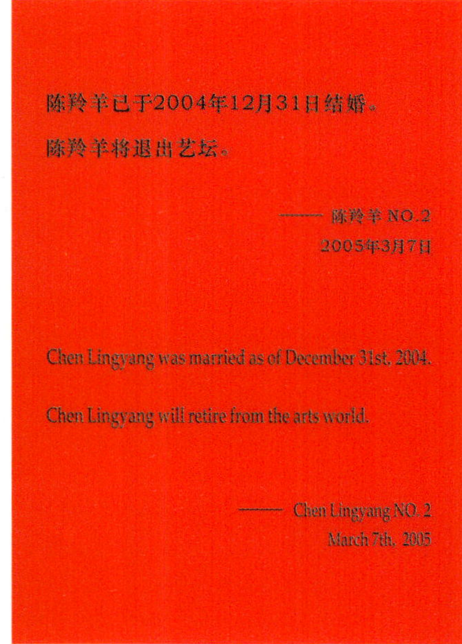

陈羚羊已于2004年12月31日结婚。

陈羚羊将退出艺坛。

—— 陈羚羊 NO.2
2005年3月7日

Chen Lingyang was married as of December 31st, 2004.

Chen Lingyang will retire from the arts world.

—— Chen Lingyang NO. 2
March 7th, 2005

and ideals of classical Chinese beauty, she suspects that what she established instead is 'the pleasure of voyeurism,'[19] evoking the traditional sequestration of wives and concubines in an almost entirely enclosed female world.

There is a suggestion of cruelty in these images; in the trickle of blood running down the artist's pale bare leg and in her awareness of being watched. The flower as a metaphor representing female sex organs is a familiar one, and has particular associations here, evoking Qing Dynasty 'flower houses' – brothels for beautiful, highly cultured courtesans. The idea for this work came to Chen in 1999, when, after graduating from the Central Academy of Fine Arts, she was unemployed and a little lonely. She spent time observing the patterns of nature – time passing, the changing seasons, and the rhythms of her own body. 'I observed the daily cycle from dawn to dusk, I noticed the slow growth of plants, and I paid attention to the gradual changes in the weather,' she told Zhao Chuan. Gradually she became completely absorbed in recording her own menstrual cycle, a specifically female experience of temporality. The *Twelve Flower Months* are like old master paintings: their luminous chiaroscuro hints at secrets partially revealed. We look firstly at the timber frame, then through the white paper frame with its traditional Chinese shape, then through the frame of the mirror. We are gazing into a secret world, just as the audience may peer at Titian's *Venus of Urbino* in her boudoir. The difference, of course, is that Titian's self-aware beauty gazes back at us, whilst Chen Lingyang is entirely absorbed in watching herself.

In the late 1990s Chen Lingyang chose photography as her medium, believing it was the most appropriate means to express her conceptual intentions, but she did not think of herself as a specialist photographer. She used film to avoid any suspicion of digital manipulation or collaging of imagery. 'Photography can show a precise moment in time and can best convey the impression of being a genuine document – although photographs can also deceive,' she told Zhao Chuan.[20] In comparison with painting, with photography she was 'starting from the real.'[21] In an email she added, 'I think traditional film photography [in contrast to digital media] has a characteristic that solidifies a particular instant of time and space.'[22]

In 2002 she produced a series entitled *25.00* in reference to an imaginary, impossible hour. Digital images, lit in a spectral, vivid blue, depict the artist's own nude body, a giantess lying across the rooftops of city buildings against the night sky. Chen says:

> This 'giantess' is not really very brave, and so she will only freely change her size and make these kinds of gestures when the clock strikes 25:00. Very often, the real world and the male world get mixed up in my mind. They both come from outside me; they both exist very forcefully, with initiative, power and aggression. Facing these two worlds, I often feel that I am weak and helpless, and don't know what to do. But just being alive means that I cannot avoid them, not even for one day. I wish that every day there could be a certain time like 25:00, when I could become as large as I like...[23]

The impossible desire for the clock to strike twenty-five is a wistful yearning for freedom. Jinli He interprets the nude female figures in these works as submissive, representing the symbiotic relationship between nature and culture, woman

Chen Lingyang
25.00 No. 1 2002
digital photograph
image courtesy the artist

Chen Lingyang
Chen Lingyang No. 2 Leaving the Art Scene 2005
document supplied to the writer by the artist and reproduced with permission

and metropolis. I see them differently. Female power is barely contained, *25.00* seems to suggest, and could wreak devastation if the giantess awoke from her slumber.

When she began to conceptualise *Twelve Flower Months* as an artwork, rather than merely as a hiatus after graduation, Chen became intrigued by Taiwanese/American performance artist Tehching Hsieh.[24] Most of his performance projects were notarised and monitored by lawyers, and in 2000, he stopped making art altogether. Chen Lingyang was especially interested in Hsieh's control of a specific, twelve-month time. She wanted to do something similar that connected her with the rhythms of the natural world. Hsieh's practice may also have provided the impetus for Chen Lingyang to officially record her own decision to stop making art in 2005.

Prior to this she had created an alternate persona with which to comment on her work. She became 'Chen Lingyang' and 'Chen Lingyang 2'. It was this second alter-ego who signed the declaration informing the world that, upon the occasion of her marriage, Chen Lingyang was withdrawing from art practice. She says, 'In 2005 I took the initiative to give up the identity of the artist and an art career.' She had come to realise that making art, and participating as a professional artist in what she describes as 'the operating system' of the arts, are two entirely separate things: 'I wanted to see if, without a professional artist's identity, art and I would become a totally private matter.'[25] Does 'Chen Lingyang 2' still speak for the artist? She says, 'For now, both the art of Chen Lingyang and Chen Lingyang 2 are an entirely personal state of affairs.'[26]

Many questions remain. Does Chen Lingyang still make art, in a more private capacity? Have 'Chen Lingyang' and 'Chen Lingyang 2' become entirely distinct beings? The artist clarified her intentions in an email:

> My final artwork, *Chen Lingyang No. 2 Leaving the Art Scene,* was used to mark my retirement from the art scene. It was a direct piece of work with a touch of feminism. The real reason for my departure is of course not due to marriage or children, although I'm guessing a lot of people would conclude that. The artwork has a strong flavour of irony and ridicule. I specifically used the words retiring from the 'art scene' to make reference to the fact that the term 'art scene' was commonly referred to in the entertainment industry.

Chen says she has separated the functions of 'professional artist' (one who makes public works and participates in arts operational systems), and art as a private transaction between artists. 'So I never left the art, but abandoned the professional artist's identity and transactions,' she says.[27] Whether her two identities are still separate but coexisting, like conjoined twins, is a matter for speculation. The artist is maintaining her silence.

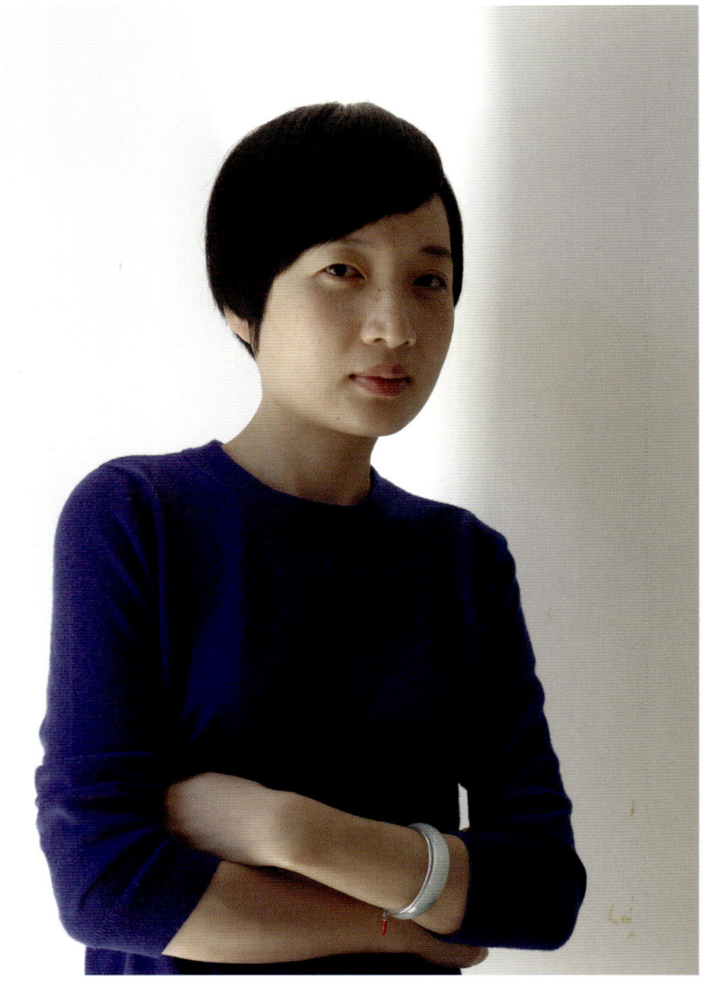

ZHOU HONGBIN 周宏斌

A New Utopia

Born in 1978 in Zhangzhou, Fujian Province, photographer and sculptor Zhou Hongbin transforms and subverts the motifs of classical ink painting. The literati believed that ink painting was a vehicle for personal expression, like their beautiful and refined calligraphy. Zhou Hongbin's work reveals something of that same sensibility – even at times the same imagery of misty mountains, bamboo and water – but using new technologies with rather different intentions.

In 'moon window' photographs of rabbits swimming underwater she playfully reinvents traditional imagery. The *Aquarium* series depicts the artist's pet rabbits swimming energetically through a mysterious watery world, a liminal no-place where the impossible becomes possible. Zhou maintains that the rabbits (beloved pets) enjoy their brief immersion in a tank of water, but adds that you have to pull them out and dry them off very quickly – with a hairdryer – so they don't catch cold. Other works in the series represent her own pregnant

Zhou Hongbin
photograph courtesy the artist

Zhou Hongbin *(top)*
Theatre 2
giclée print
image courtesy the artist
and China Art Projects

Zhou Hongbin *(bottom left)*
Crane (***Utopia-Illusion*** series) 2014
giclée print, 90 x 90cm
image courtesy the artist
and China Art Projects

Zhou Hongbin *(bottom right)*
Parrots (***Utopia-Illusion*** series) 2014
giclée print, 90 x 90cm
image courtesy the artist
and China Art Projects

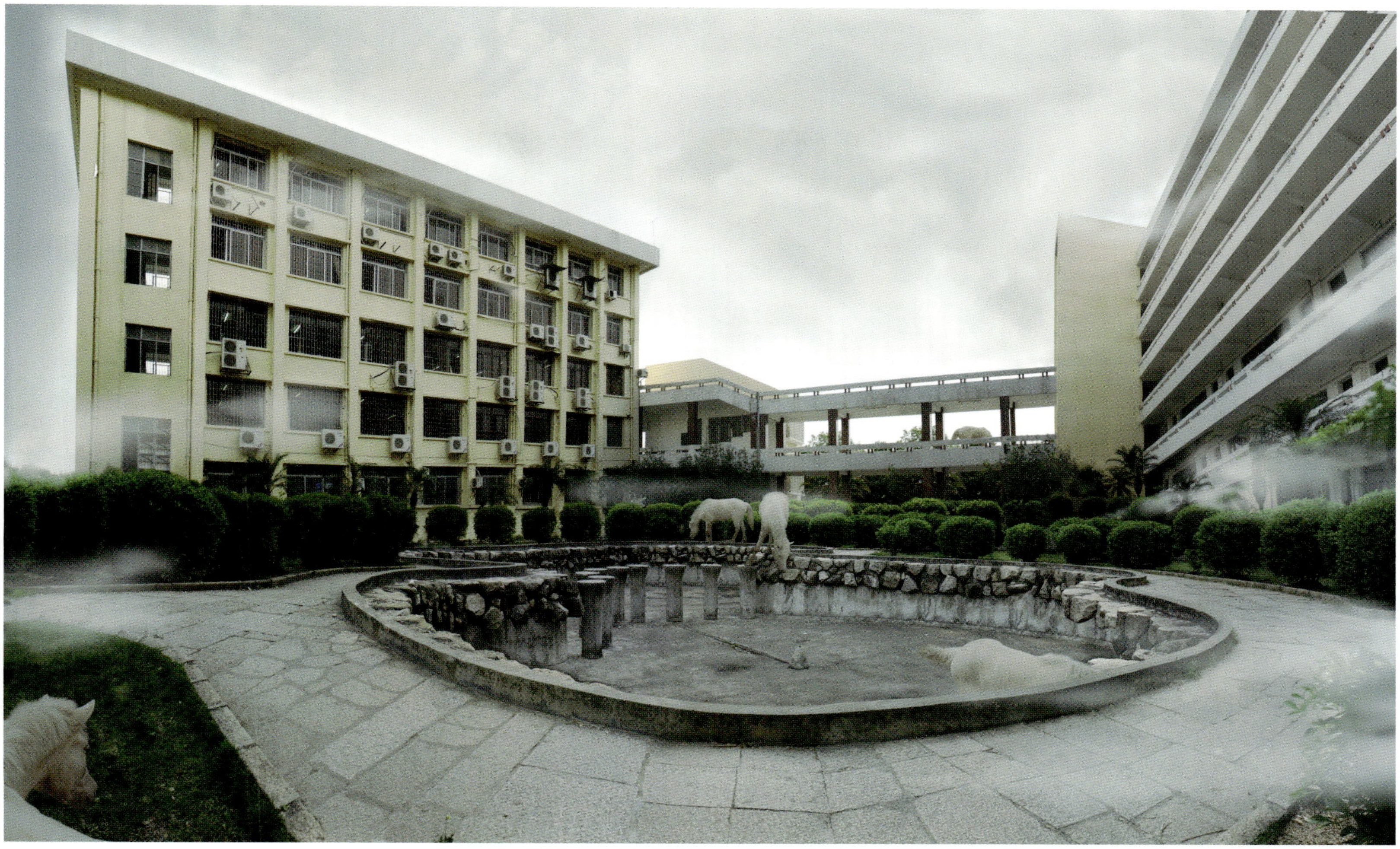

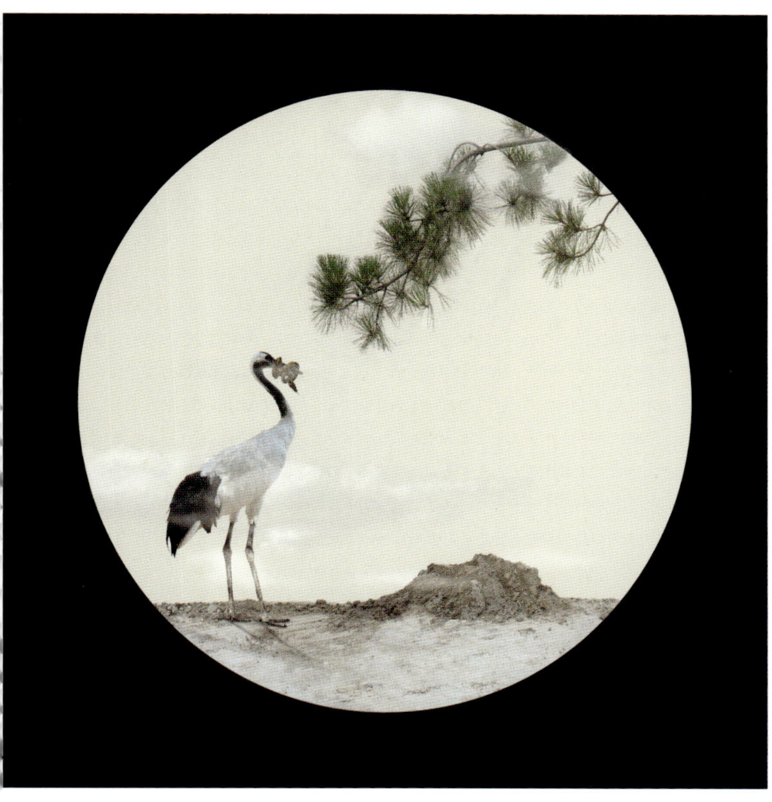

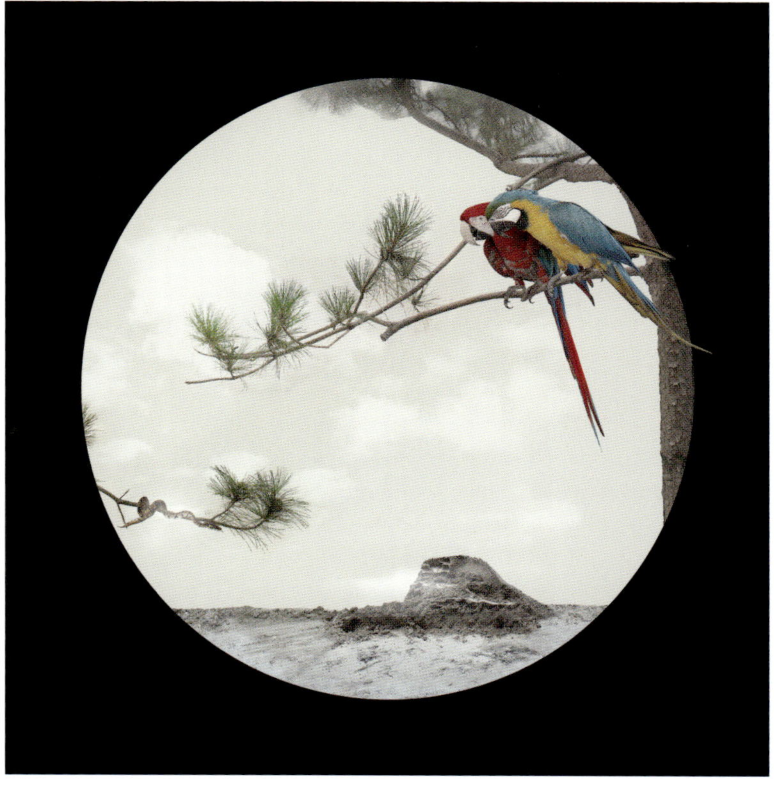

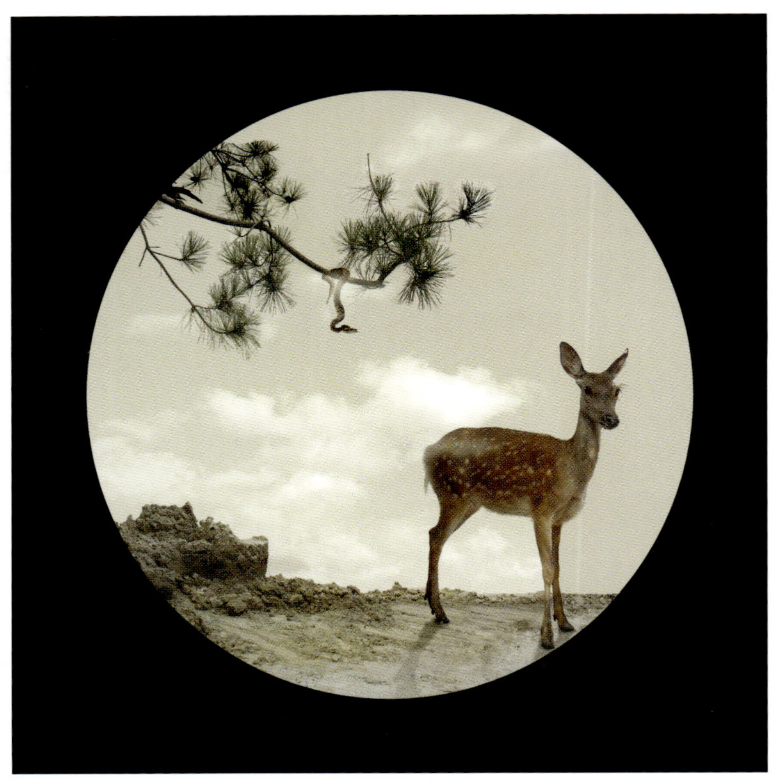

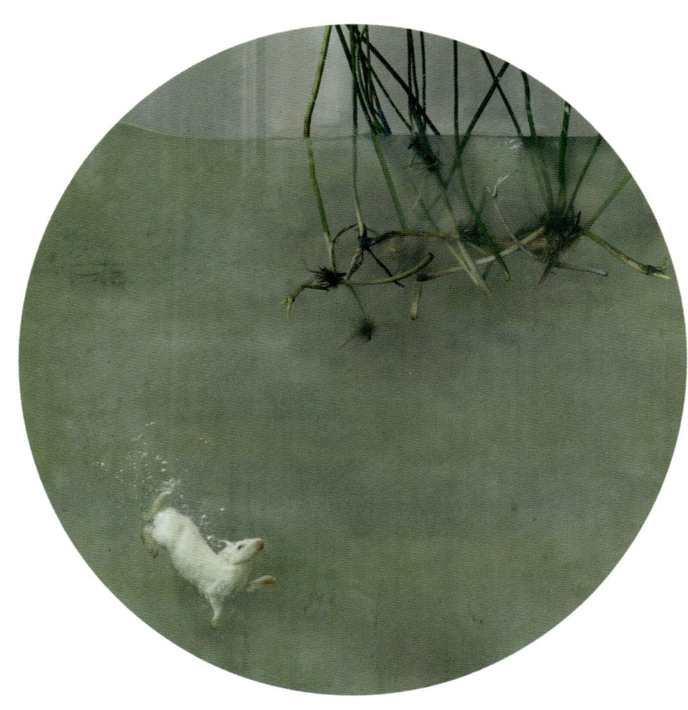

body, floating weightlessly as if adrift on the current. They are ecstatic images. Zhou said:

> Expecting a child, I was experiencing a new sense of life and death and I wanted to record that. The water is the source of life, and in every series I make there is a little change. In this work there is a light, which symbolises the light of hope. When you swim you can feel less burdened.[28]

Utopia – Illusion unveils an ideal world, far from the Chinese urban environment of constant demolition. Zhou aims to create:

> lovely and pure thoughts... and avoid the conflict of reality. Economic growth has had an impact on everybody's life. People have this sense of urgency to find their path. And a sense of great uncertainty. [In contrast] my work has a quietness – it is my response to the problems in society. It also relates to the tradition of ink painting, which has a similar quiet and peaceful atmosphere.

Despite her desire to create beautiful imagery, Zhou says Damien Hirst is an artist she much admires. Rather surprisingly, it is *The Physical Impossibility of Death in the Mind of Someone Living* (1991), the notorious shark floating in its tank of embalming fluid, which she particularly loves. She agrees that Hirst's focus on mortality and decay is different to her own: 'I think that this is the difference between male and female artists. Men look to shock and have powerful artworks, but artworks by women are more delicate and gentle.' This traditional notion of femininity – and feminine art – was reiterated by many artists, an attitude I came to expect in any Chinese discussion of feminism. The yin/yang binary of masculinity versus femininity is deeply entrenched, only very recently beginning to be challenged by a younger generation of women.

Zhou's digitally manipulated Utopian images always feature animals. In addition to rabbits ('very smart creatures in Chinese folk tradition!' Zhou says), deer, tigers, horses, snakes, peacocks and cranes symbolise human qualities, including the artist herself. Embodiments of the feminine, they are inserted into the invented classical landscapes of the literati tradition. There is a photographic precedent. A pioneer nineteenth century photographer, Liang Shitai, began to take photographs of Prince Chun, Yihuan, father of the Guangxu Emperor, in the 1860s. Some are conventionally documentary, but others are poetic. One depicts the prince in a peony garden with three eunuchs. A photograph from 1887 entitled *Seventh Prince Feeding Deer, Stamped with his Seals* shows the prince holding a branch from a pine tree, a tame deer feeding from his hand. Both deer and pine are symbols of longevity. The photograph is stamped with his royal seals, as if it were a painted scroll. Art historian Claire Roberts describes it as a 'performance-based representation that simulates a traditional painting, but using live subjects in combination with the latest technology for image making.'[29] This faded nineteenth

Zhou Hongbin
Deer **(*Utopia-Illusion*** series) 2014
giclée print, 90 x 90cm
image courtesy the artist
and China Art Projects

Zhou Hongbin
Aquarium 2008
giclée print, 120 cm diameter
image courtesy the artist
and China Art Projects

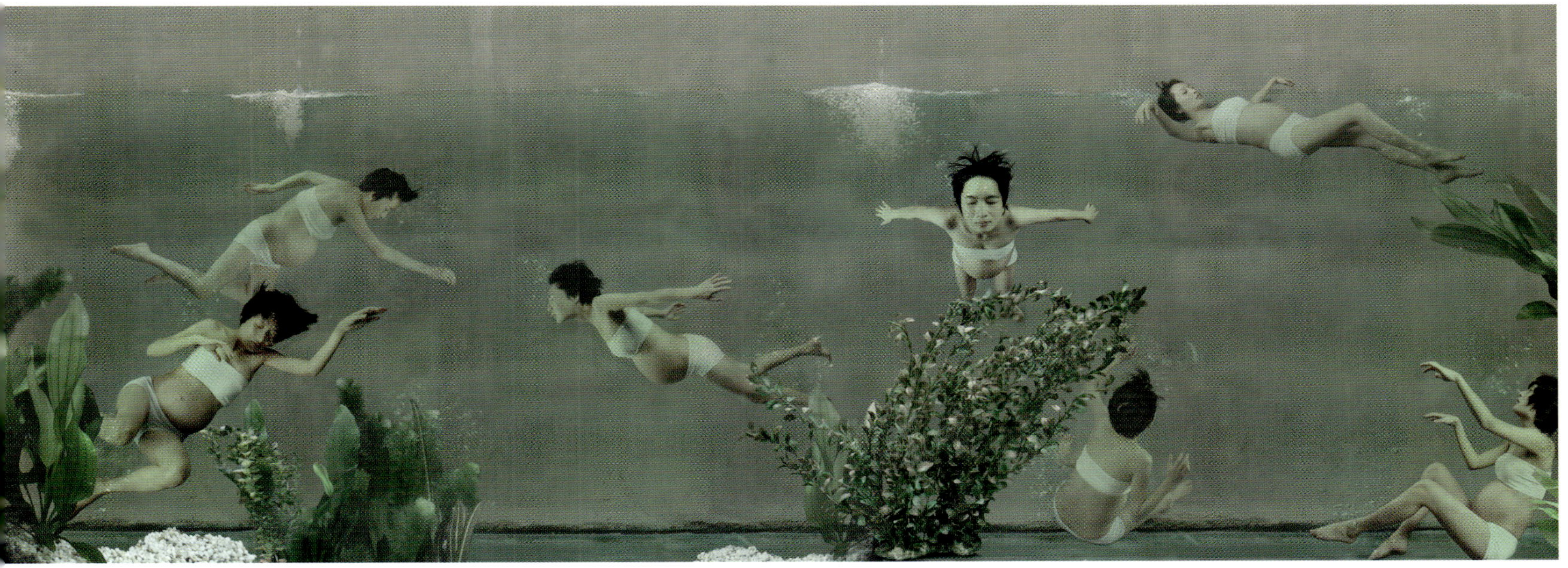

century albumen print reveals the same wistfulness as Zhou Hongbin's imaginary Eden.

Many Chinese artists are exploring the relationships between human beings and the natural world, sensing the fragility of coexistence in the barrage of media reports of pollution, species extinction, and environmental destruction. Described by artist/critic Sheng Qi as 'somewhere else... familiar and strange at the same time',[30] Zhou's surreal watery landscape is her instinctual response to the fragmentation of the contemporary world. About her *Secret Garden* series, depicting white horses in eerily deserted urban landscapes, she says, 'I want to transform the public space into [a] strange feeling...to re-build a mirror for women's inner world... a last habitat of women in the complicated city, sensitive and fragile.'[31]

Zhou Hongbin seeks quietness and serenity: 'When I was studying at CAFA I really didn't know what I wanted to do, and [at that time] the rapid growth in the economy made everyone feel uneasy. I didn't have a really clear goal. As I got closer to what I wanted to do my works became more and more quiet and serene. I also started to do some installations and some sculpture...When I had my child I experienced a very subtle change in my heart – I began to value things around me more and to have more gratitude. I am keen on finding the lovely things in life. In a Utopian world one must be true to oneself and express oneself freely. In my world right now this is my state, and I can follow this dream and express my own ideas. So perhaps I am living in my Utopia!'

There is a dark shadow in Zhou's paradise, however. The snake in *Utopia Illusion: Crane* alludes to temptation in the Garden of Eden. Beneath the apparently peaceful landscape lurks something frightening. Her dream-like photographs question what is real and what is imagined. Zhou is interested in Baudrillard's theories of the simulacrum. At a time when digital photography produces such a convincing replica of reality, we know, even as we look at photographic images and accept them as 'real' that they may be totally constructed. In the twenty-first century we have come to doubt the veracity of every image.

Zhou Hongbin has begun to make sculptures, producing works fabricated to her specifications. Rabbits make another appearance, frolicking through stainless steel structures, but she has become more interested in pure abstraction in both sculpture and photography, echoing decisions made by other artists such as Cui Xiuwen and He Chengyao. Strong, simple forms may be read in a variety of ways. A series of works made in different sizes, in stainless steel or copper, *Pagoda* suggests the biblical story of the Tower of Babel: the confusion of language and its potential for misunderstanding and conflict. These works also reference Chinese Buddhist stupas, says the artist, in a deliberate layering of eastern and western historical allusion.[32] The simplicity is echoed in abstract photographs that evoke the early twentieth century Modernist pioneers of the medium. Zhou says, 'I like abstract and simple works, because I hope that our life can be simple.'

Zhou Hongbin
Aquarium II (1) 2010
giclee print, 78 x 220 cm
image courtesy the artist
and China Art Projects

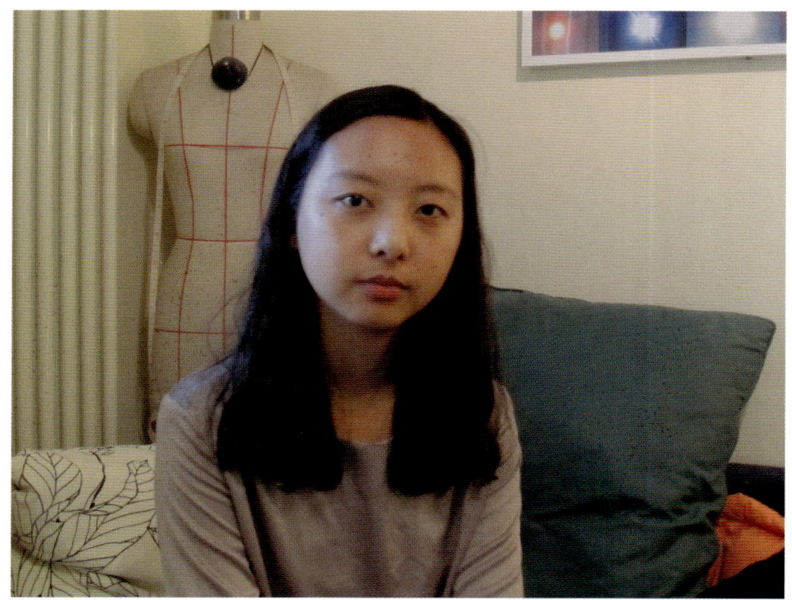

LIU SHIYUAN 刘诗园

The Edge of Vision

Liu Shiyuan was educated partly in China and partly in the United States. Married to a Danish composer and musician, she lives between Beijing, New York and Copenhagen. This leaves her, she says, in the uncomfortable position of feeling like an outsider everywhere:

> Working across three countries has influenced me a lot. I am doing something really very much related to cultural differences, very different to artists based in Beijing. They don't really go out [of China]. Artists here are all talking about how China is now. Because I am outside the wall I can see it from another angle, and I can see there is something beyond that. From the first moment I travelled I saw there are a lot of things that we share – there are not *so* many differences between cultures... Then the second thing I noticed is, yes, there *are* many differences, but not in the ways that people think.[33]

The assumptions made about Chinese art in the west, and western art in China, and how the artist herself is perceived by both Chinese and non-Chinese as straddling two cultures, intrigue her. Interviewed by art critic Iona Whittaker in 2012 she said:

> I have lived in Beijing, New York and Copenhagen. Through my art practice, I try to release myself from the discourse of cultural difference. I have come to question the very notion. This is in part because I find it increasingly difficult to point out fixed social norms that are exclusive to specific locations. I work with an awareness of cultural differences to make art that shows the overlap between cultures in order to communicate a globalized view of the world.[34]

Born in Beijing in 1985, Liu's early talent ensured that she followed the expected path to the high school affiliated with the Central Academy of Fine Arts, and to CAFA for a degree in New Media. She was given her first camera at the age of eight, but hated photography because a strict teacher focused on 'boring' technical aspects of camera craft. At that early age, she sought out dark subject matter, she says, rather than the expected happy and beautiful subjects: 'When I was eight years old I looked for bad things to take photographs of, like car accidents.' Later, in high school, the focus of her training was on painting. She said, 'I was the best artist in the middle school, so if there was only one student who was going to get into CAFA, that would be me!' Later, however, she realised that places for students who did not have to sit for the gruelling entrance examination were allocated on a political basis (in China everything comes back to *guanxi* – connections and reciprocal obligations) and Liu was never in the running due to her father's 'bad family background' – the Cultural Revolution continues to haunt people even today. Reflecting on this early art education, Liu Shiyuan says:

> Our education was Russian style – in realistic oil painting. I can paint something that looks as real as a photograph. Then I thought, if I can do that, I might as well just make photography! But you never know, I might come back to painting when I am maybe seventy years old.

Liu travelled to the United States for postgraduate study where she was disconcerted to find that students in New York were expected to speak critically about their own work, an entirely unfamiliar experience:

> In the beginning they always wanted me to talk about my work and I had to do it. In CAFA we don't talk about our work, we just say '*blah*' and become friends with our professors! Once you translate the work into language you pin it down a lot. I said to my professor, 'I don't want to talk about my work, I *cannot* do it!' [But] in the end I learned how to talk about my art practice in New York. Now I can write a pretty good statement about my work in English. And if you want me to I could talk about it for eight hours!

I had no doubt this was true – Liu is voluble, articulate and thoughtful in three languages.

Liu Shiyuan bridges her two worlds of life in Beijing with her family and a different life in Copenhagen with aplomb, but she is always aware of cultural nuances and slippages. In Beijing, Liu and her husband live in the tiny one-roomed apartment where she grew up, allocated to her father by his work-unit. It is hard to imagine a smaller space for a family of three people. Now, her parents own two other apartments,

Liu Shiyuan at home in Beijing, October 2013, photo LG

Liu Shiyuan *(top)*
A Conversation with Photography (details) 2012
installation, dimensions variable
images courtesy the artist

Liu Shiyuan *(middle)*
As Simple as Clay 2013
installation views, c-type photographs, dimensions variable
images courtesy the artist

Liu Shiyuan *(bottom)*
We Were Never Alone, Never Bored 2014
inkjet prints, apple, pear
dimensions variable
images courtesy the artist

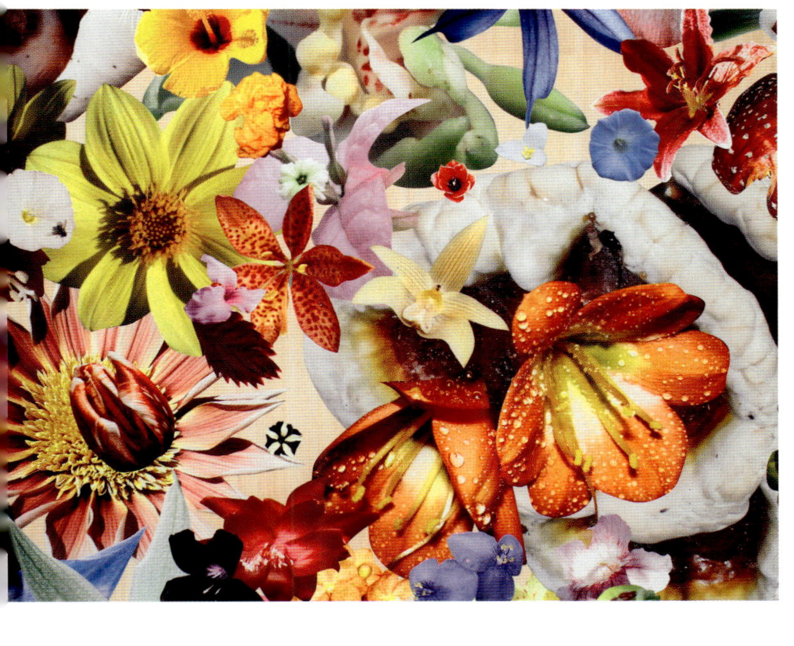
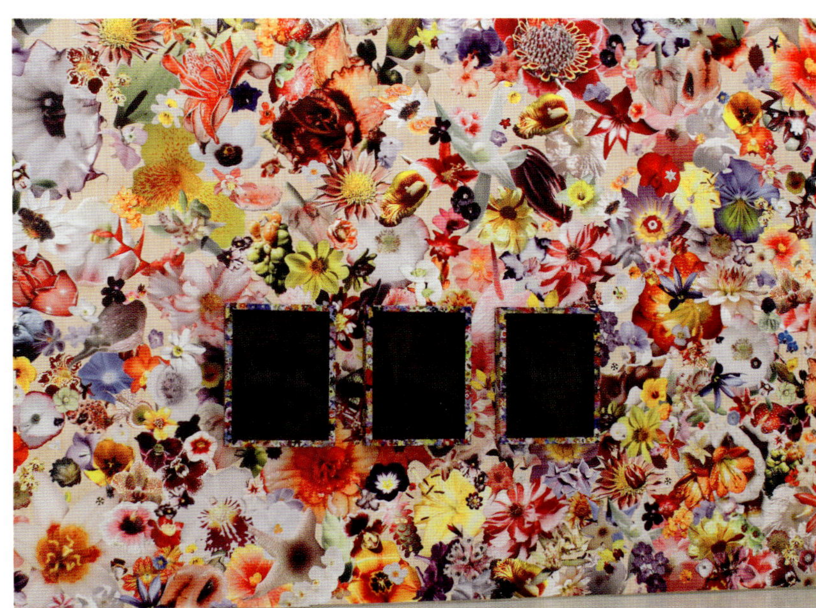
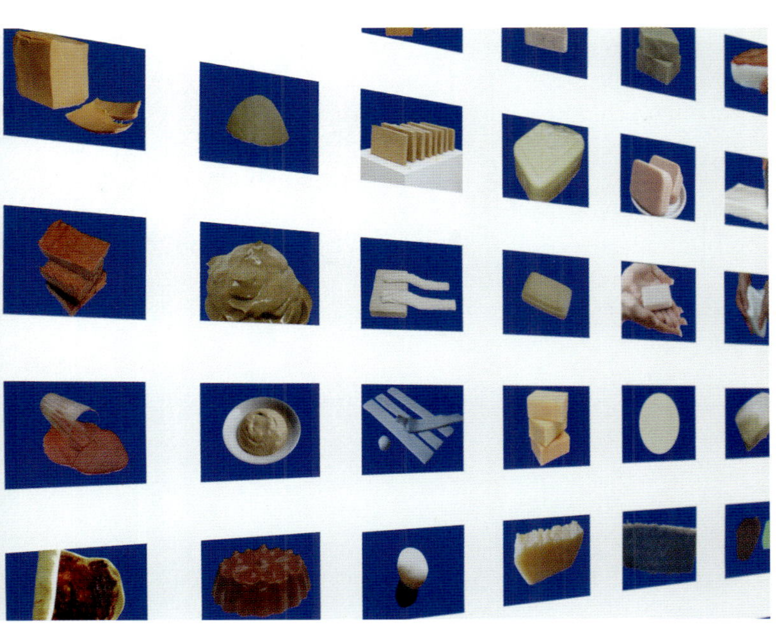
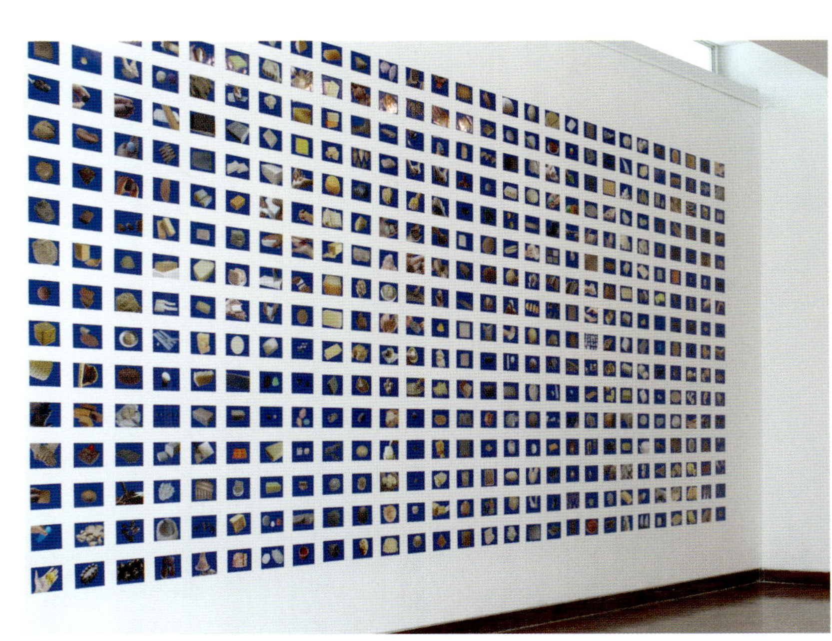
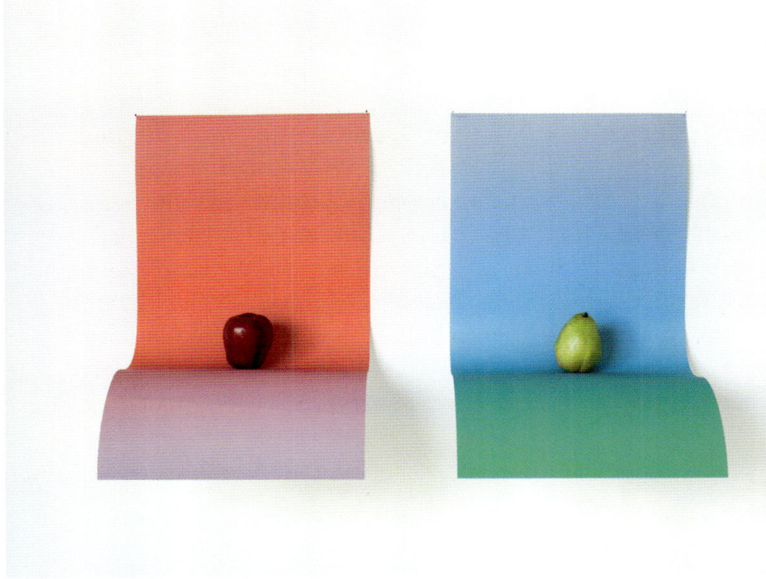
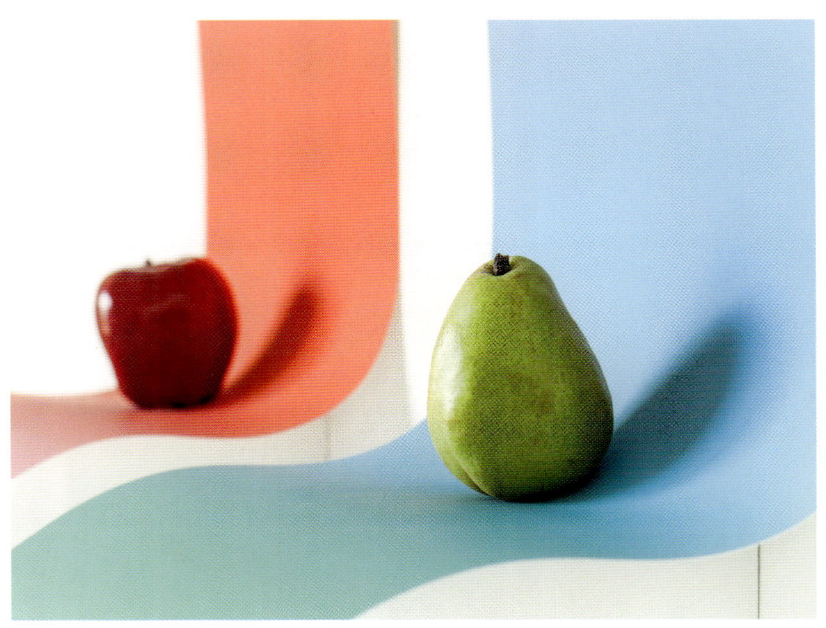

one in the southern part of Beijing and another on the outskirts, 'right on the edge of the map,' says the artist. Her parents worry that she does not have a stable income, and that she has married a musician. In part their anxiety is based on their personal history:

> My father is from a very rich family – they were super rich during the Qing Dynasty. During the Cultural Revolution – boom! My father had a terrible childhood. His parents were sent to the countryside. At five years old he was forced to do work in the fields. Even after I was born in 1985 people still said bad things about his family background. Even today people in his company say things like that – it's terrible when you think about it. He joined the party to give me and my mum a good life, but he is happy I married a foreigner to have a different kind of life, and another option if things are bad again... But he worries that I don't have a job with a salary. He says two people cannot both do art, one person must earn some money!

When she was living in New York, Liu perceived it as a much tougher city for an artist that Beijing. In fact, she says, her Chinese artist friends kept calling, exhorting her to return: '[They] said "Shiyuan, this is the last train from the eighties and nineties – you must come back and get on this train or you will miss it!"' Liu believes – and her group and solo shows attest – that the continued interest in young emerging artists in Beijing is a result of the immense popularity and celebrity attached to those artists who broke new ground in the late 1980s and 1990s:

> People are interested in new things and new artists. I think the galleries here are very open, more than in the States. I think the galleries [in Beijing] are more concerned with the work itself, not with the artist, or whether they are female or male. Whereas in New York the competition is much more intense and people still think you are a young emerging artist when you are thirty-five! I don't feel pressure because I am just doing what I am doing, and I want to just keep doing it and continue my work. I think that success will come if my work is good enough. If the work is good it will bring its own opportunities.

Much of her work is about uncertainty and flux. She makes us doubt our perceptions of the world and, indeed, the medium of photography itself. Influenced by the work of Penelope Umbrico (her teacher at the School of Visual Arts in New York) who created an installation of images of the sun sourced from Flickr, Liu Shiyuan has often turned to the internet for her source material. For her first solo show in Beijing, in 2012, she found the floral imagery she wanted for the installation *A Conversation with Photography* by searching Google using terms like 'cliché flowers' and 'disgusting flowers'. The result was a wall entirely covered with densely layered exotic flora. *A Conversation with Photography* disrupts our expectations with its shifting focus and ambiguities of scale. Three frames decorated with the same flowers are installed at eye level. Look inside and you see nothing but tinted glass, the flowers on the wall behind, and perhaps a reflection of yourself. This digital collage of tropical blooms plays with our assumptions of photographic veracity, creating a surreal and incoherent – almost psychedelic – experience. Liu is interested in the relationship between language and images. Is what you find on Google an objective truth? How do the algorithms of search engines manipulate our experiences? Notions of truth have become ever more slippery and elusive, she believes.

Re-en-act (2012) features images of expensive, opulent jewellery (sourced from Google) arranged on what appears to be the green felt of a billiard table, or the roulette table in a casino. Liu does not want these images read in a simple, singular way, as an obvious critique of extremes of wealth, rather, she says, she is 'making something beautiful' that may be interpreted in multiple ways – or perhaps not at all.

As Simple as Clay (2013) was developed during a period in Denmark when, without the obligations of family, a gallery to represent her, or a job to go to, she was bored and at a loose end. She decided to make art – maybe even deliberately bad art. A trip to an art supply store provided her with raw materials for the installation – a bag of clay. She says:

> I was expressing a cross-cultural idea about the boundaries of culture – the process of making work and its cross-cultural nature. I noticed that there is a lot of overlap between cultures. That's the essence of human beings – mostly people are the same. So I was trying to find the things that are different.

She translated the word 'clay' into different languages, exploring how people used it and thought about it in different cultures.

Liu began to collect images of clay and clay-like substances like ice-cream, tofu, butter, and soap, making the background of each image blue to erase any context. She said, 'I feel like there is something that all people in the world are doing together. It's a little bit sad, that installation. When some people join their hands together and try to make something together it makes me cry...The materials are just waiting for people to make them into something.' The final installation consisted of one thousand, one-hundred-and-forty photographs, an attempt to evoke the energy and emotion of creative work. The artist says it 'presents a cross-cultural ideal in the sense that the boundaries of culture are both present and obliterated.'[35]

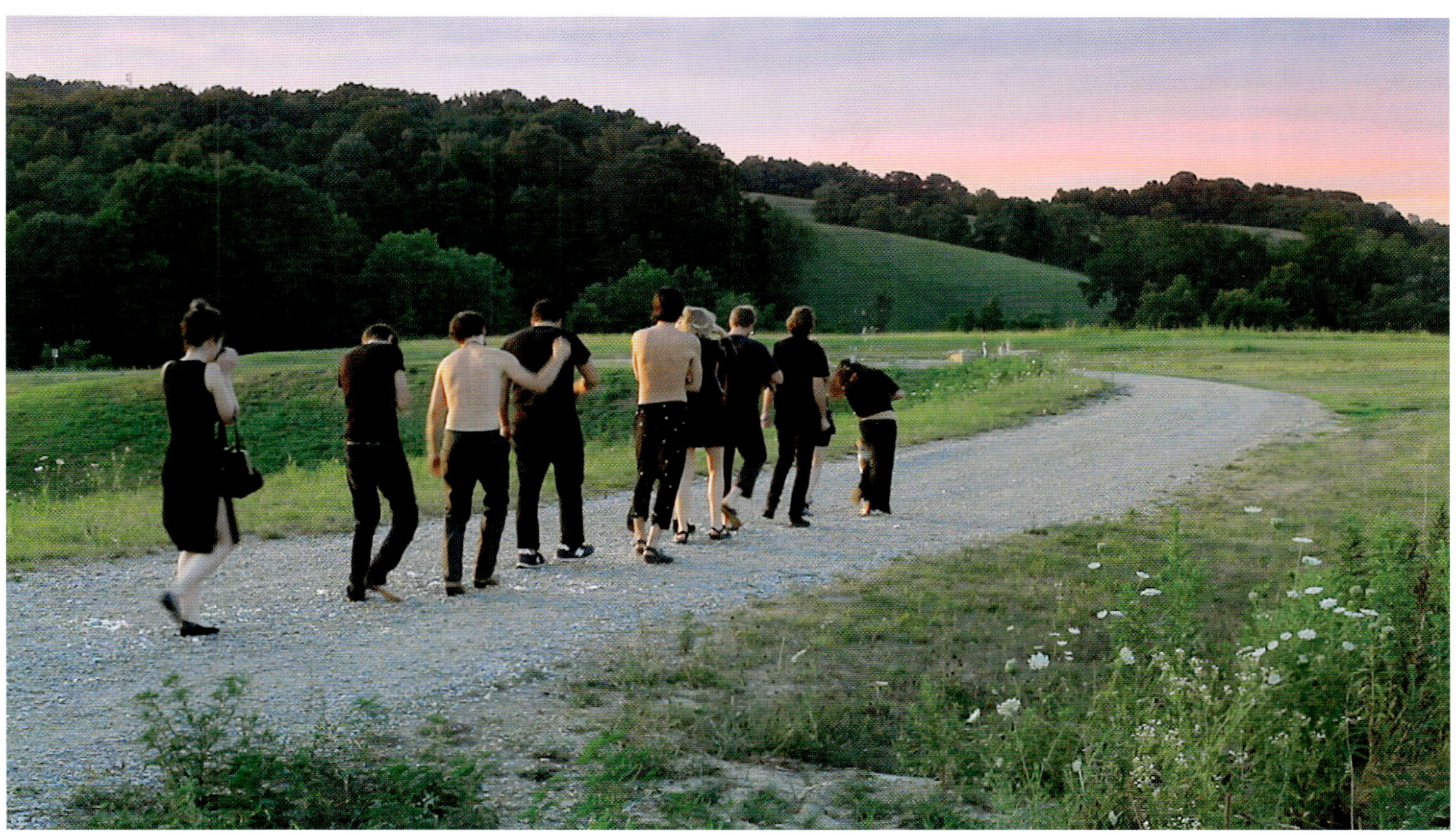

Liu Shiyuan is playing a complicated linguistic and visual game. 'Art has to be beautiful, in my opinion,' she says. 'I am currently very interested in the standards of beauty.'[36] Her ideas of beauty are unconventional, found in the everyday world of supermarket packaging and advertising, rather than in any 'high art' notions of taste:

> I like the images in supermarket catalogues, I think there are some very good photographs. I cut them out and stick them in my notebook. Why is beauty so important? My beauty is different from 'arty' beauty. My understanding of beauty is about truth and honesty and daily life. I want to put everything into my work – philosophy, art history, beauty. [For me] it is more about *why* do I do it? What am I doing? It is all about the idea.

Seeking a visual language that transcends assumptions about visual culture, Liu strips away narrative through the use of found images, making 'camera-less photography' and 'footage-less' video.

Like other Chinese artists who spend time overseas, she feels some discomfort when fellow artists or curators accuse her of being too 'western':

> I think my work is related to Chinese culture, but not in a political way. In my work I don't tell you all of my thoughts, I hide a little bit – I hide half! I think this is traditionally Chinese. You make it be little-by-little, step-by-step… I don't want my work to be too conceptual. I hate work that is just one idea – it's so boring, why not just say it! I think this is something I learned from my teacher in the States [Penelope Umbrico] – it's thinking about *who* takes pictures, *why* take pictures…There is something about traditional photography that is magic, but now the magic is being lost.

Liu Shiyuan watches BBC wildlife documentaries and they provide inspiration for video works:

> For example, the nature documentary might be about lions or tigers, and they use beautiful images of sunsets, and other beautiful footage in between to make it narrative, and sometimes they even use the same footage in different documentaries!

Her practice is dedicated to exposing narratives of this kind as cultural artefacts. In works such as *Sunrise*, she disrupts assumptions and challenges cinematic conventions. We think we are seeing a long shot of the ocean before dawn, with

Liu Shiyuan
The Edge of Vision or
The Edge of the Earth 2013
single-channel video, 6 mins
image courtesy the artist

ocean sound effects. When the camera pulls back we realise it is in fact a television screen transmitting feedback from the camera. She describes it as 'a piece of misunderstanding video work.'[37] What she likes about video, she says, is that 'it is just a bunch of still images strung together.'

The Edge of Vision or The Edge of the Earth has a soundtrack in which one of the artist's friends imitates David Attenborough's hushed wildlife documentary voice over ambiguous landscape footage from China, Denmark and the United States. Some is the artist's own footage, shot over a long period of time in her journeying between cultures, but other elements are sourced from the web. She complicates the relationship between the artist, the audience and the work, 'opening up a space for us to explore the cultural, moral and ethical discourses embedded in the genre of documentary.'[38] Her interest in liminality and fluidity may well come from her own sense of being nowhere, in a space between cultures: 'I am very interested in the things that are in between. Maybe because I am myself somehow in between.' *Beyond the Pale*, Liu's 2014 solo show at Andersen's Contemporary Gallery, Copenhagen, presented 'found' floral imagery once again, in a sculptural installation that explored how audiences engage with unfolding sequences of associations and visual/neural connections. Meaning is elusive here, as in earlier installations, but the experience is a sensory and aesthetic delight. Liu Shiyuan's work requires us to suspend our instinctive drive to interpret and categorise.

Liu represents a new generation of artists, who not only work across cultures and forms, but deliberately undermine and challenge their boundaries. She is immersed in international debates about photography and image-making. She represents a new generation of artists, who not only work across cultures and forms, but deliberately undermine and challenge boundaries. Where other photographers seek to reinvent and subvert traditional forms such as ink painting, Liu sees that as 'wearing your Chinese identity on the outside.' Artists of her generation no longer have to do this in order to be accepted outside of China, she says. Nevertheless, she still identifies herself as primarily a Chinese artist:

> Of course! I am Chinese, I am trained at CAFA. I am a Chinese artist. If I say that to other artists here in China, they think, 'Oh OK, you are an artist' but if I say that to westerners they say, 'Oh, you are like Ai Weiwei.' Why do I say I am a Chinese artist? Firstly because I have a Chinese passport, I am Chinese. In China, people think my work is not sufficiently Chinese. But when I show my work outside out of China in the west, people think it is something quite new and something they have never seen before... I think our works are more individual than the older generation. We have different ways – I want my work to be strong [too], but our strategy is quite different... to be strong, it must be honest to ourselves.

Liu Shiyuan believes that today, the boundaries between China and the west are more fluid than in the past. 'I think that in 1985, the year that I was born, China was [finally] open and everyone got so excited,' she says. 'The older generation really wanted the west to see China. For us, the traditional Chinese culture is on the inside of our body, it is not on the surface for everyone to see.'

Caught between different identities, Liu Shiyuan faces contradictory expectations: 'When I am living in Europe I see America. When I am in America I see China. I am outside everything. I have a really big responsibility towards art history. I really have to care about that, and I think my work has to be beautiful. I think about everything in that way.'

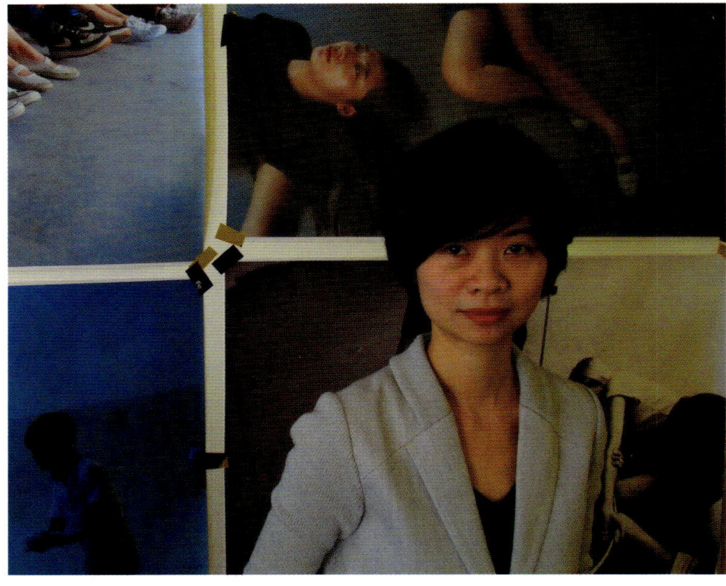

FANG LU 方璐

Lovers are Artists

An empty shopping trolley engulfed in flames slides sideways across the cement floor of an abandoned building. The long shot dissolves to close-ups of young faces, screaming. There is no sound except an amplified heartbeat and electronic noise. Later, the same young people goose-step in formation around the empty space with an Alsatian dog on a tight leash, throwing what appear to be tear gas canisters, engaging in ritualised forms of hand-to-hand combat. This is Fang Lu's video *No World*, which employs the language of film to consider how public actions become theatrical performances. Far from spontaneous expressions of authentic selfhood, Fang Lu suggests that in an age of mediated imagery, the desire to record and curate each of life's moments,

Fang Lu in Beijing, December 2014, photo LG

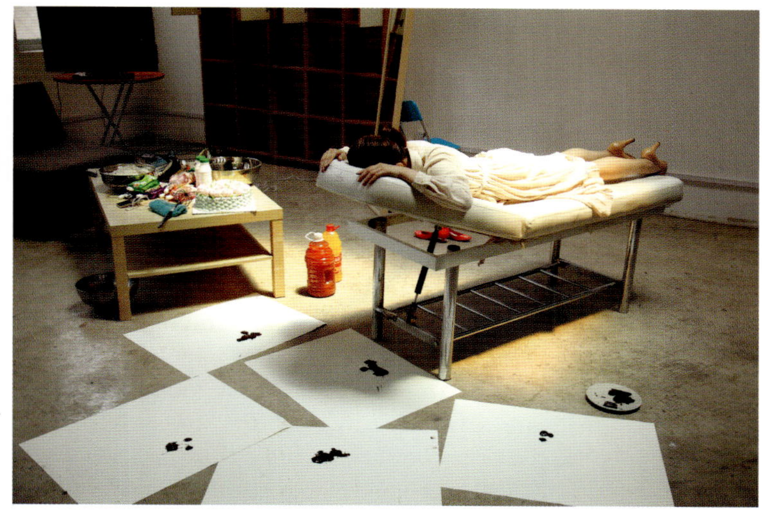

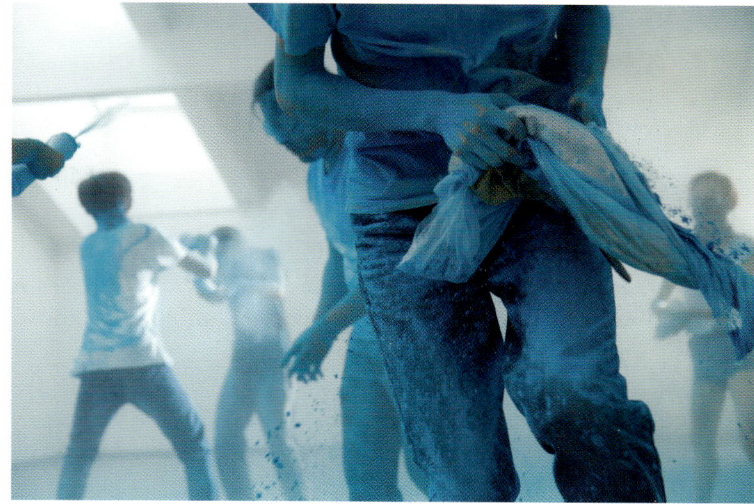

always with the possibility of instantaneous internet fame, our actions are intensely choreographed, like a video game.

Shot in an abandoned art museum in Songzhuang, using non-actors, *No World* explores what happens when people are continually observed. She is interested in the effects of surveillance, but says:

> I am more interested in the behaviour of people in front of the camera. Perhaps in our everyday life now we all perform for the camera even *without* the presence of the camera. I am more interested in the people who are in front of the camera, not behind the camera... This new work [is] about a group of people living in this house, and the activities of their everyday life are what you would often only see when people go on public protests on the news. They turn it into a kind of self-training or a kind of game, so the video shows the routines of their day.[39]

In the final scenes the participants are shown, in a paradoxically beautiful blue and purple light, destroying a car with shovels and baseball bats. Shards of glass fly through the air as windows and headlights are violently smashed. In November and December 2014, while Fang Lu was editing and then showing this work in the *2014 OCAT-Pierre Huber Art Prize Shortlist Exhibition* at OCT Contemporary Art Terminal Shanghai, the world (including the Chinese mainland) was galvanised by just such a public protest. News and social media video footage of students occupying the streets of Hong Kong in what became known as 'the Umbrella Revolution' was making it through the 'Great Firewall' of internet censorship, providing dramatic imagery of chaos and conflict. Fang's work makes no reference to these real events, but rather creates a dreamlike evocation of violence and the ever-present possibility of entropy and the collapse of social order.

Fang Lu is interested in the rituals of the everyday; in how individuals construct performative identities. *Cinema* presents us with a single female protagonist in an empty theatre. Her actress is simultaneously the film director, producer, star and audience. The seven-channel video installation zooms in on her face to reveal subtle emotional shifts, and we witness her changing emotions. There are uncomfortable suggestions of narcissism in her self-absorbed isolation. The cocooned experience of watching a movie on the big screen, from a red velvet seat in a dark cinema, is replaced with a discomfiting sensation of surveillance. The artist suggests that we now collude in self-surveillance, through our obsessive documentation of our own lives in social media.

Like photography, the moving image arrived in China from the west in the nineteenth century. By the 1930s, Shanghai was the centre of a thriving film industry, with multiple studios and glamorous movie stars, but facing Japanese invasion, the industry moved to Hong Kong. After 1945, film, like photography, became a vital instrument for Maoist propaganda, and during the Cultural Revolution the only films made were heavy-handed political dramas. In the mid-1980s, a group of idealistic film-makers graduated from the Beijing Film Academy, simultaneous with the rise of the '85 'New Wave' artists. Video in an art context was pioneered by artists such as Wang Jianwei, Hu Jieming and Zhang Peili. An explosive mix of new technical knowledge, influences from abroad (including Nam June Paik, Bill Viola and Bruce Nauman), and the influx of popular culture from diverse sources, provided the impetus for the Chinese avant-garde to experiment, pastiche and invent.

Fang Lu is of a new generation for whom the language of video is entirely unremarkable. Unlike Liu Shiyuan, who resists any tendency towards narrative, Fang Lu plays with narrative and non-narrative, scripted and unscripted, in her works. She left her home city of Guangzhou immediately after high school to study in the United States, first in the Graphic Design department of the School of Visual Arts in New York, before completing an MFA in the New Genres department at the San Francisco Arts Institute in 2007. Fang's transition

Fang Lu
Lovers Are Artists Part 2 2012
video, 11 mins 50 secs
image courtesy the artist

Fang Lu
No World 2014
single-channel video
18 mins, sound, 16:9
image courtesy the artist

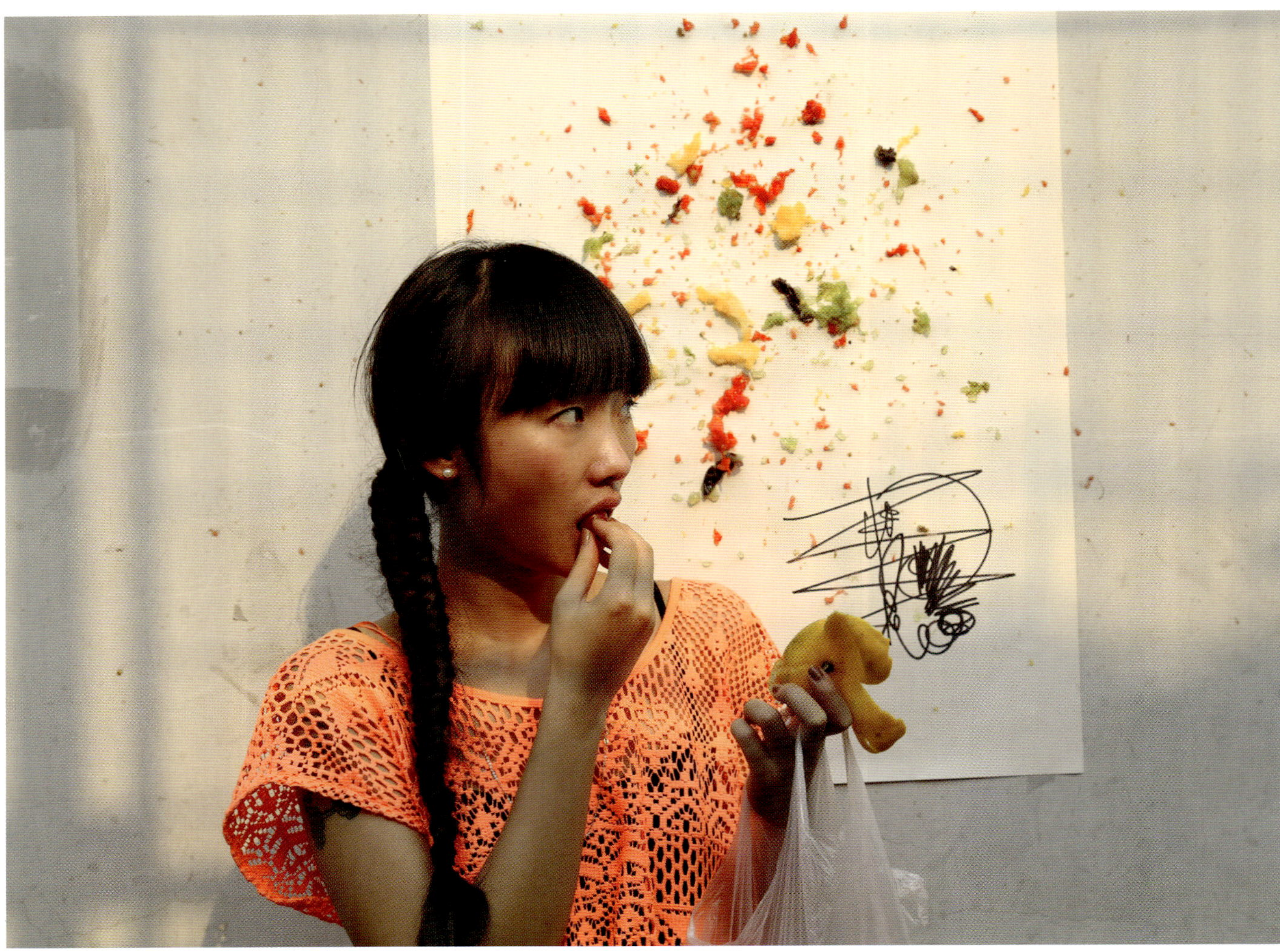

from Guangzhou to San Francisco, and then to Beijing via Baltimore and New York, has impacted her work in profound ways. She explained her intentions with the multi-channel work *Cinema*:

> There are different sides to this work. I was really thinking that the cinema is a place we never give up, even though the medium has changed so much, and now we can see everything online and on DVDs. People still love to go to movie theatres. It's a magic place, besides the content – you have two hours being really passive, in the dark, and just completely absorbed in what is in front of you. A video work is probably the complete opposite – you want the viewer to make the decision to stay, you do not want to force them to stay and watch. It's [about] a social phenomenon too, about how people understand themselves, about how people represent themselves to others. People send photos all the time, using social media – that reflects the way that people understand themselves... so I wanted to make a work that in some way could put all these ideas into this moment, and this person [the protagonist of the video] could be everything. She is an audience, but she is also performing, and she is creating this image.

Generally Fang Lu attempts to break down expectations of narrative, cinematic structure and film language. This is a little different:

> I think the quality of the work is very filmic. It was realised by having all these cameras in this very small theatre in Beijing. It's not really a cinema, it's usually used for small stage shows. Everything is controlled by the control panel, there is no cameraman.

A major production involving multiple cameras, the work was to some extent a carefully choreographed sequence, although the main 'actress' was encouraged to improvise:

> This process of performance was through her [the main character's] improvisation. The quality of the image was something that seduced her to perform as well, because the image was just so beautiful. Every one of us working on shooting the film, we each went to sit in her place and look at the screen in front of us and we all fell in love with the image, because all the cameras and the lighting created such a sense of beauty.

Fang Lu
Lovers Are Artists Part 1:
Amorous Acts 2012
4-channel video installation with still images, silent
image courtesy the artist

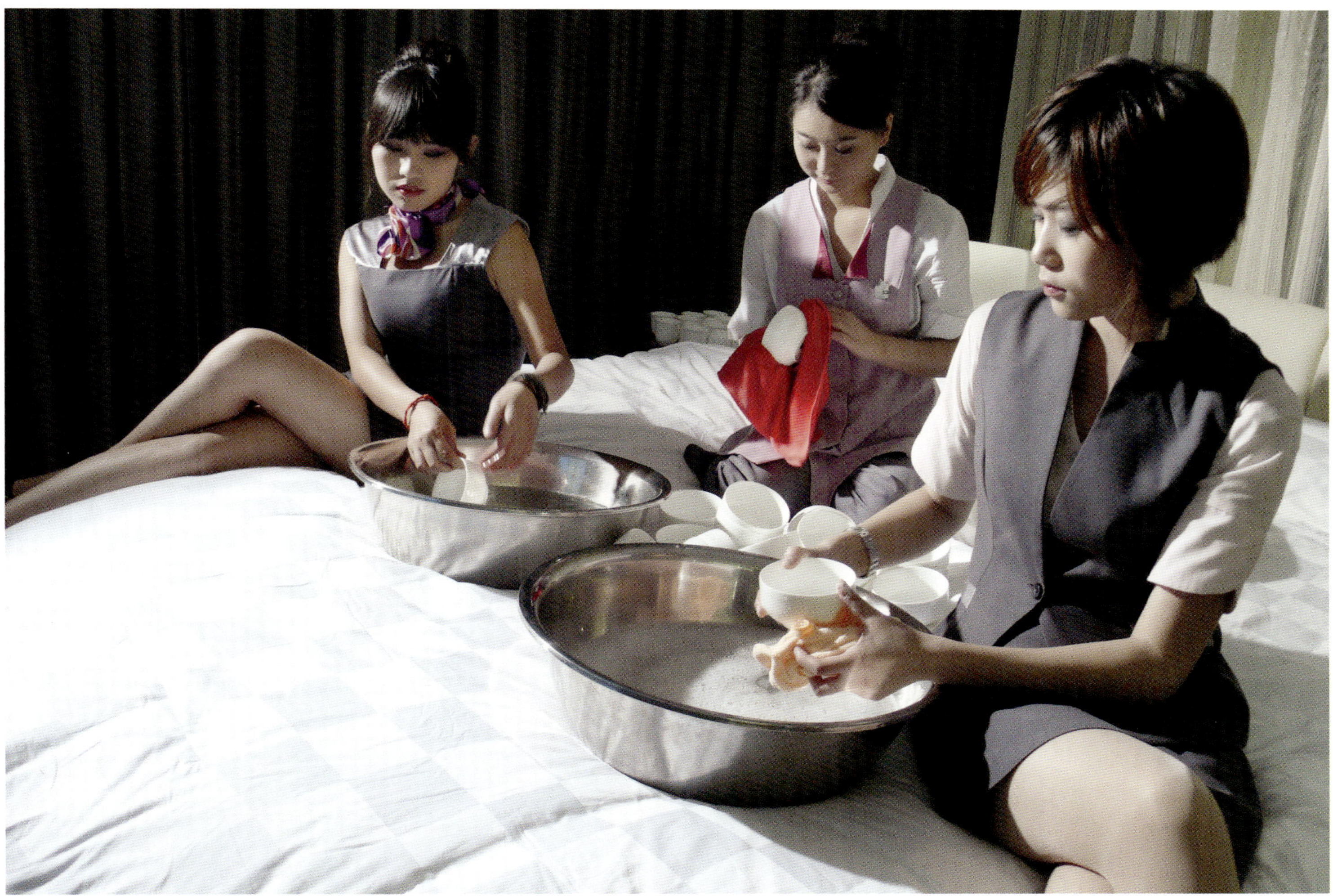

Housework Ritual shows female hotel staff acting out bizarre versions of the repetitive work of their daily lives, including washing red and green peppers in the hotel bathrooms, and washing-up cups and plates whilst seated on the crisp linen of the bed. The performance took place in the swish surroundings of a new boutique hotel in Xi'an. Fang explains:

> That was a piece that started me creating a series of similar works using food and domestic activities. I was given this opportunity to make a work in a hotel that was about to open. A group of artists were invited to use the hotel in whatever way we wanted. So we were living there, and I saw the women at the front desk just standing there, so beautiful, like a plastic display. And I was thinking, 'OK, when they get home they will do all this housework and it will have nothing to do with this work they are doing all day, just standing there like plastic dolls.' So I wanted these same staff to perform work that they might do in a domestic setting, but it doesn't lead to any final product – it maybe makes a mess, or it just creates only a cycle of continuously working... I invited female staff who work in a hotel to 'perform' housework in various locations within the hotel. These normally internalized activities are ritualised performance[s] in the video, repetitive and with no result from their labour. The aesthetic of women in our society is often separated from the everyday labour they engaged in, and these works are often identified as actions that are internal, domestic and with no transcendental value. This video takes out the functionality from the housework and uses it to create ritual and aesthetic.

For *Automatic Happenings* the artist prepares food timed by an alarm clock. Food recurs in a number of her works – shopping for it, preparing it, eating it and cleaning up after it. *Lovers Are Artists Part 1: Amorous Acts* was presented at the tiny Arrow Factory, a shopfront gallery in the Beijing hutongs. The series of still images, presented as slides, depicts a young girl employed in mundane activities such as shopping for vegetables and eating yogurt. Her activities become more and more bizarre and nonsensical, merging fantasy and reality. Four slideshows were compiled from thousands of images shot in the old courtyards and lanes of the neighbourhood around Arrow Factory. Fang Lu's young, lovesick protagonist

Fang Lu
Housework Ritual 2009
HD video
10 mins 58 secs
image courtesy the artist

exemplifies the irrationality of love. Typical of the 'meta' nature of her practice, the work does not obscure the method of its construction. As Pauline Yao's text for the exhibition noted:

> *Amorous Acts* draws explicit attention to the methods and means of its own making, namely an awareness of the camera and its conflicted role as both "objective" witness and a tool capable of manipulating emotions to elicit new forms of experience.[40]

In *Lovers Are Artists Part 2* the female protagonist is given the role of 'Someone in Love' and she occupies the space of 'An Artist's Studio'. The agony of love and the agony of art are analogous – and equally irrational.

Fang Lu's father teaches traditional Chinese painting at the Guangzhou Academy of Fine Arts, and all her cousins have followed an expected path through its painting department. She broke with family tradition when she decided to study overseas:

> I really didn't know what to do [after I left high school]. I actually applied for a design major in the United States...I had seen that Chinese painting is developed in such a way that students follow the teacher, and the students are told exactly what to do. Even my father fixes the paintings for his students! And I realised I just didn't find my freedom in painting or drawing at all.

She knew she wanted to do something related to art or design:

> I went to the high school attached to the Guangzhou Art Academy. In [that] high school you have to go through a lot of very rigid, very painful drawing and painting classes, looking at objects and painting them realistically. I could do it – I wasn't the top of the class, but I could pass everything. But I didn't *love* it. I felt I didn't want to draw or paint any more. That realism became a restraint, I couldn't really paint anything outside of what I could see. When I went to New York I started visiting museums and it was the first time I had ever seen contemporary art – and especially video art. I was quite shocked, and it was quite liberating to see, 'Oh, there is another kind of art!' I remember, I went to PS1 – that was the place [where] I thought 'Wow!' You are in this old public school and you see Pipilotti Rist! I just remember going in some room and seeing TV monitors on the floor and cables everywhere. It was really dark with just the light coming from the TV monitors.

Immediately after 9/11, Fang Lu was studying in Baltimore, visiting Manhattan's museums and galleries whenever possible, then transferring to New York to complete her undergraduate degree. Despite the heightened tensions of the time, Fang felt comfortable in the United States, having had no real expectations except what she knew from Hollywood movies. Her mother rang every day, begging her to come home, but she was enjoying her newfound freedom. Empowered by the sense that she could follow any direction she chose, she took music classes and learned to make video for her design projects:

> Later on I decided to take a fine art course more seriously, and I went to San Francisco. I never really used my Graphic Design [training] as anything more than a set of standards that I can use. I never saw myself as a designer and I was making video work all that time. Video was a medium in which I could make things happen! I see it as an initiator to generate things that don't really happen in real life. And it's liberating because you are not facing a blank white canvas, which I feel is a very frightening thing. With video I never have that fear at all.

Fang Lu was stimulated by the experience of a very different culture:

> Did it change me? Yes, I think quite a lot – I was at the age that you really form your understanding of the world, and so there were many moments when I felt that what I knew before was completely wrong, and that there was so much more to see and to learn.

Living in New York, and later in San Francisco, made her reflect on her Chinese culture. She says:

> When I was in San Francisco I did a series of works called *News Reenactments*. At that time I was reading a lot of news about China, and they were the kind of news items that were really small and mundane, things that don't really matter at all. It was a way to understand the place that you come from, but from a distance. So when I went back to China I had some scripts based on some of these mundane news items that I had read online, and I then created them back home on the street as small performances in front of the camera. In those early works I performed in my own work – it felt like a very natural beginning, and I think it partly came from the influences of the older generation of video artists. I was very eager to experiment with doing works without any materials – just the camera and myself.

The return to China after completing her MFA seemed, at first, quite uncomplicated. Some artists, including Huang Jingyuan, Ma Qiusha and Liu Shiyuan found that transition challenging. They felt an uncomfortable sense of separation from their own culture, and experienced some suspicion from other artists. Fang says, 'I didn't find that,' but she tells a story about participating in a panel discussion with other artists, not really knowing the topic:

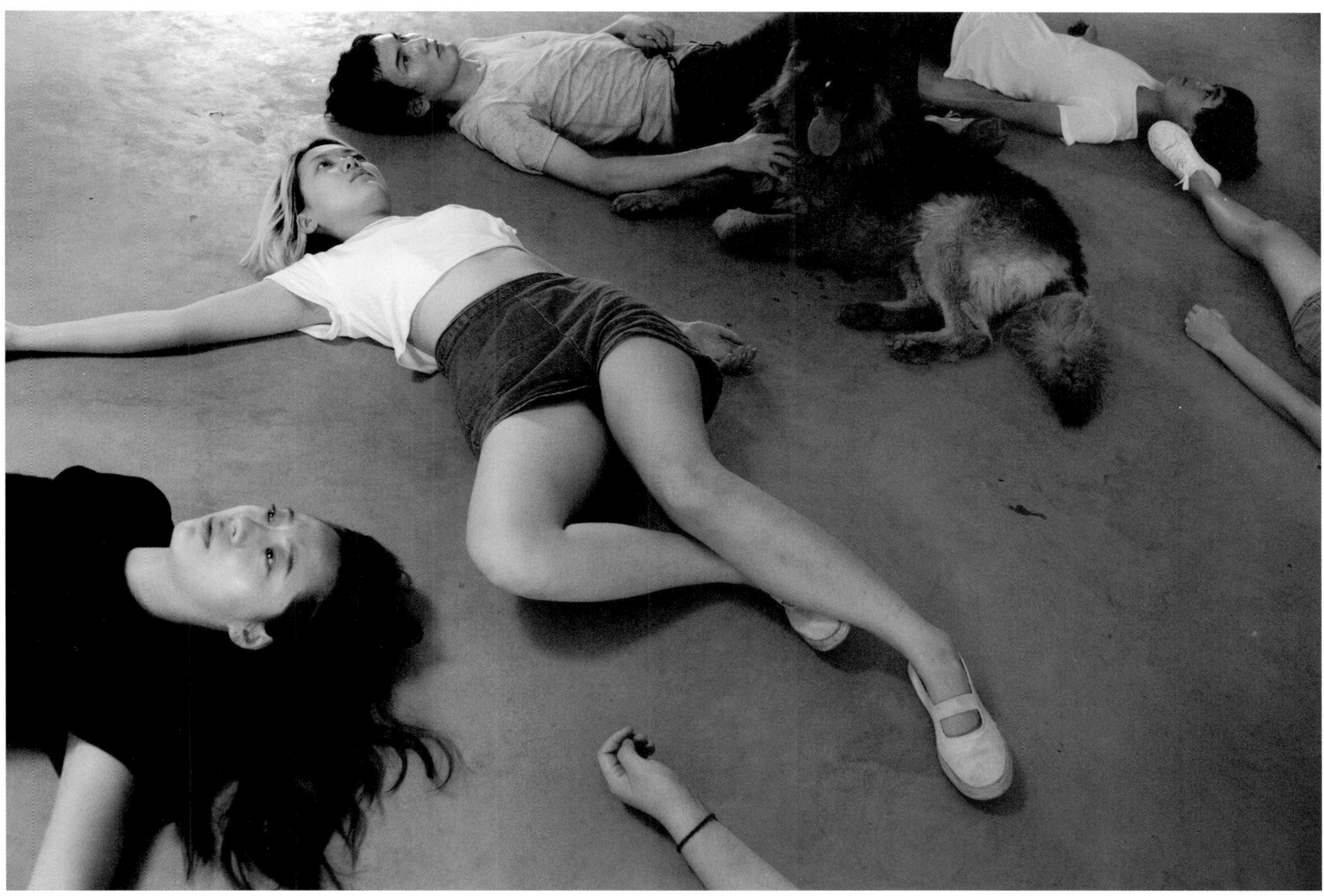

> When I went I realised it was actually about artists who study abroad and then come back to China. That was the first time I realised how different people thought our identity might be. I think they assumed that artworks have a place; that art is rooted; that art practice grows out of a particular location... But if an artist is living in multiple places, then they think that the artist might not be able to find that place, to be rooted [in their own culture].

For Fang Lu, notions of the cultural specificity of art belong in the past. Did those artists on her discussion panel believe that people who have lived and worked abroad have lost their truly Chinese identity?

> If so they are referring to an older generation of Chinese artists. Like from the time before people could travel, and if someone came back from abroad they would be sharing information. Today, everyone already knows everything from the internet and from magazines, like if there is an exhibition in, say, *White Cube*, we already know about that!

Artists of Fang's generation are connected to a global art world, plugged in to current discourses through the internet and social media. Their connection to Chinese history and tradition is different from the previous generation: they see themselves as global beings. In *No World* Fang Lu explores a universal theme born in an age of mediated images, in which people train themselves through repetitive actions, and 'everyday life is gaming.'[41]

Fang Lu's main concerns about art in China today are not, as many westerners would expect, about censorship, or the tendency towards self-censorship. With some regret, she feels she may have missed the best, most exciting days of contemporary Chinese art. Explaining this, Fang referred to her work, *Lovers Are Artists,* and its representation of the boredom and banality of the everyday:

> For me this was a slightly bold statement, to say that if you are in love you are an artist. It also came from Roland Barthes' book [*A Lover's Discourse*], and it reflects my frustration with art practice

Fang Lu
No World 2014
single-channel video
18 mins, sound, 16:9
image courtesy the artist

now, which is becoming safer and safer. Like you can't really see something crazy and chaotic anymore! Even if there *is* something crazy it will be safely in a gallery. And I think this really reflects an attitude to life. People don't really want to talk about love. They would not consider it a wise or logical subject to discuss. People want to talk about cars, or houses, or auctions. And I think that is why people are not making such interesting art, because you don't find many lovers any more... and also the gallery system is pushing artists too hard to make work valuable and commercially saleable, in certain forms. Of course art should be in the commercial world in order to circulate and to be self-sustaining. But I think it is the gallery's responsibility to push the work, but not to push the artists to make work in certain ways.

Does she see the craziness and wildness of falling in love – the huge risk involved – as analogous to making art? She says:

> Yes! But also, being in love is very wasteful – wasteful of time and wasteful of money. And people don't want to engage themselves in that way. People are very pragmatic, career driven, wanting to be established, wanting to have a relationship that is beneficial to their career.

Fang believes that you don't have to look back as far as the experimental days of the 1990s to see a very different Beijing art scene: 'Even before the Olympics people say it was wild, with quite a lot of freedom.' A number of artists speak wistfully of the days before there was an art market in China, seeing it as 'pure' in a way that is impossible now, in a time of career-driven and financially highly successful professional artists. In the end, though, this is a separate issue from Fang Lu's desire to make work driven by her fascination with how meanings are generated by images, exploring the self-consciousness and artificiality of contemporary life.

Fang Lu, Chen Lingyang, Zhou Hongbin and Liu Shiyuan make internal truths visible. Hidden bodily realities of female experience; dreams and desires; the forging of identities in the ebb and flow of a society still in the process of radically reshaping itself: all these things inform their practice. Entirely aware of the history of their chosen medium, and its relationship to theories of meaning, they exploit the possibilities of photography and video to present a heightened reality. In the words of Claire Roberts, they are 'conjuring images from darkness and light'[42] to express the uncertainty and doubt of the contemporary world.

NOTES

1 Mao Songyu 1953 *Xinwen Sheying* (News Photography) Shanghai, 1953 (3–4)
2 Roberts, Claire 2013 *Photography and China*, Reaktion Books, London
3 ibid. (32)
4 ibid. Early twentieth-century journals and magazines included *Zhonghua Sheying Zazhi* (The Chinese Journal of Photography), *Chenfeng* (Dawn Wind), and *Feiying* (Flying Eagle)
5 *China's New Art Post-1989* was seen first in Hong Kong before travelling to Australia and the USA
6 Yeoh, Peter 2012 'Eastern Exposure' *Glass* Autumn 2012
7 ibid.
8 ibid. Peter Yeoh quotes Rong Rong's introduction for the third issue of *New Photo*
9 ibid.
10 Wu Hung 2014 *Contemporary Chinese Art* Thames and Hudson, London UK (230)
11 He, Jinli 2014 'Continuity and Evolution: The Idea of "Co-creativity" in Chinese Art' *ASIANetwork Exchange* Spring 2014 21 (2) available at file:///C:/Users/Louise/Downloads/112-807-1-PB.pdf accessed 10 February 2015
12 ibid.
13 Chen Lingyang, in an email to the writer, 9 February 2015
14 Chen Lingyang 2013 interviewed by Zhao Chuan in Huber, Jorg and Zhao Chuan (eds) *The Body at Stake: Experiments in Contemporary Chinese Art and Theatre*, Institute for Critical Theory, Zurich University of the Arts
15 see Chapter 1 for a discussion of Cui Xiuwen
16 Roy Forward 2006 quotes Jiang Mei in *Reclaiming Their Bodies: Contemporary Chinese Women Artists* ShanghART Gallery Shanghai, ShanghART Web. Nov. 2010. Available at http://www.shanghartgallery.com/galleryarchive/texts/id/433 accessed 10 February 2015
17 Karetsky, Patricia Eichenbaum 2004 *Who Am I?* Chinese-American Arts Council, Inc. Gallery 456 New York available at http://www.karetzky.com/whoami-text.htm accessed 10 February 2015
18 Chen Lingyang 2013 interviewed by Zhao Chuan in Huber, Jorg and Zhao Chuan (eds) *The Body at Stake: Experiments in Contemporary Chinese Art and Theatre*, Institute for Critical Theory, Zurich University of the Arts
19 ibid.
20 ibid.
21 ibid.
22 Chen Lingyang in an email to the writer, 9 February 2015
23 Chen Lingyang, quoted by He, Jinli 2014 in 'Continuity and Evolution: The Idea of "Co-creativity" in Chinese Art' *ASIANetwork Exchange* Spring 2014, 21 (2) available at file:///C:/Users/Louise/Downloads/112-807-1-PB.pdf accessed 10 February 2015
24 For *One Year Performance 1978–1979* (also called *Cage Piece*) the artist locked himself into a small wooden cage which contained only a wash basin, lights, a bucket and a single bed. For twelve months he was not permitted to speak, read, write or watch television. Food was delivered, and waste removed. A single photograph was taken each day to document the project. Later, he spent one year outside, not entering any building or enclosed space. For *One Year Performance 1985–1986 (No Art Piece)* Hsieh made no art, saw no art, did not read or speak about art, and did not enter any museum or art gallery.
25 Chen Lingyang, in an email to the writer, 9 February 2015 (transl. Lily Wang)
26 Chen Lingyang, in an email to the writer, 11 February 2015

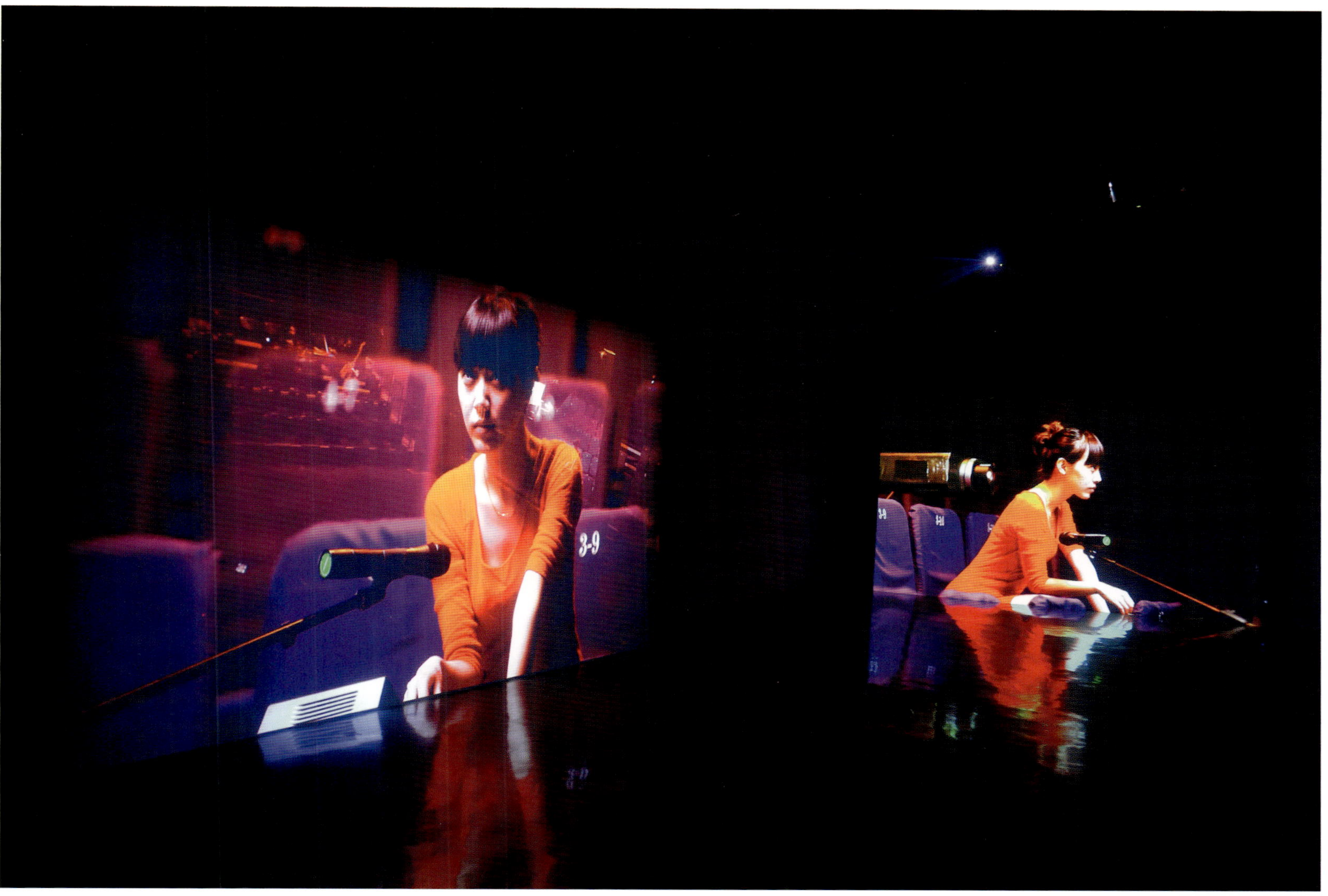

27 Chen Lingyang, in an email to the writer, 9 February 2015, (transl. Lily Wang)
28 Unless otherwise acknowledged all quotes from Zhou Hongbin are from her conversation with the writer in Beijing in December 2014
29 Roberts, Claire 2013 *Photography and China*, Reaktion Books, London, UK (34)
30 http://www.chinaartprojects.com/zhou-hongbin-essay/ accessed 5 April 2015
31 Zhou Hongbin, Artist's Statement http://www.chinaartprojects.com/zhbstatement/ accessed 12 April 2015
32 Zhou Hongbin, in an email to the writer, 9 February 2015
33 Unless otherwise acknowledged all quotes from Liu Shiyuan are from her conversations with the writer in Beijing in October 2013, November 2013 and April 2014
34 Liu Shiyuan spoke to Iona Whittaker for *Randian* in 2013 on the occasion of her first solo Beijing Show at Whitespace Gallery available at http://www.randian-online.com/np_feature/video-artist-series-liu-shiyuan/ accessed 8 February 2015
35 http://shiyuanliu.com/assimpleasclay-mainpage.html accessed 8 February 2015
36 Liu Shiyuan spoke to Iona Whittaker for *Randian* in 2013 on the occasion of her first solo Beijing Show at Whitespace Gallery http://www.randian-online.com/np_feature/video-artist-series-liu-shiyuan/ accessed 8 February 2015
37 http://shiyuanliu.com/sunrise.html accessed 8 February 2015
38 http://shiyuanliu.com/edge-mainpage.html accessed 8 February 2015
39 Unless otherwise acknowledged all quotes from Fang Lu are from her conversation with the writer in Beijing in December 2014
40 Yao, Pauline 2012 *Amorous Acts* available at http://www.fanglu.net/criticism.php?textid=11&lang=en accessed 11 February 2015
41 Fang Lu, on 'No World' http://www.fanglu.net/noworld.php accessed 12 February 2015
42 Roberts, Claire 2013 *Photography and China* Reaktion Books 2013 UK (183)

Fang Lu
Cinema 2013
video installation, 7 channels,
19 mins 19 secs, sound, 16:9
image courtesy the artist

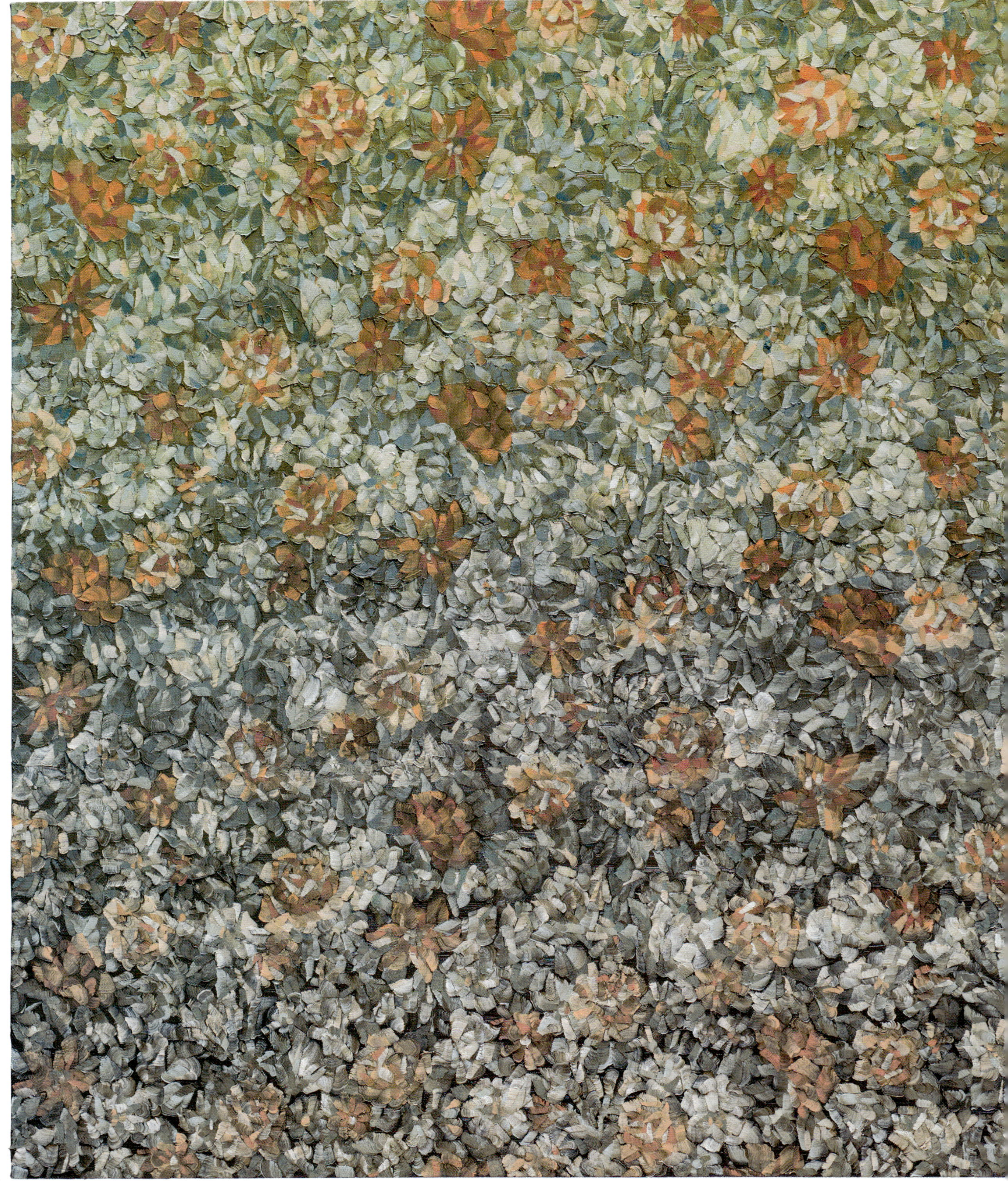

BLURRED BOUNDARIES

Liang Yuanwei, Li Shurui, and Qin Fengling

Chinese artists are capable of astonishingly irreverent and eclectic feats of invention and reinvention, overturning conventions and blurring boundaries. You trained as a painter? Why not reinvent yourself as a performance artist, or make installations? You made your name as a photographer? That's no reason not to venture into bronze sculpture, or textiles, or to experiment with ceramics. Artists can work on an industrial scale, taking advantage of cheap labour and material costs, although some choose not to do so, preferring to exercise craft traditions. The atmosphere in the big art centres of Beijing, Shanghai and Chongqing is almost febrile. Artist 'villages' grow and change so fast that they appear to be metastasizing. The construction of everything – from superhighways to fast train lines, from gigantic shopping malls to whole new cities – is on fast forward. Artists and curators play with a postcolonial mash-up of eclectic theories and influences.

The artists in this final chapter exemplify two significant aspects of Chinese art practice: inventive playfulness, and a deep reluctance to be confined or pigeonholed. Liang Yuanwei is a painter who has also created installations and whose first exhibited work was a notorious series of photographs, produced as an act of defiance after a gallerist to whom she had shown her paintings told her, 'There are already too many female painters. Why don't you become a photographer?' Li Shurui invented her own technique whilst still a student in Chongqing, using an airbrush to make paintings that break the boundaries of the two-dimensional picture plane. At that point she had never seen – or even heard of – any other artist making paintings in this way, and some of her peers found the idea of a woman artist using such 'masculine' gadgetry confronting. Qin Fengling, in contrast, describes her painting technique in domestic terms – she says it's like cooking, or cake decorating. What connects these diverse artists is their defiance of expectation. They are in a continual process of reinvention and renewal, and in this they are absolutely typical of contemporary art in China today.

Liang Yuanwei
Untitled 2013 13 2013
oil on linen
140 x120 cm
image courtesy the artist and Pace London

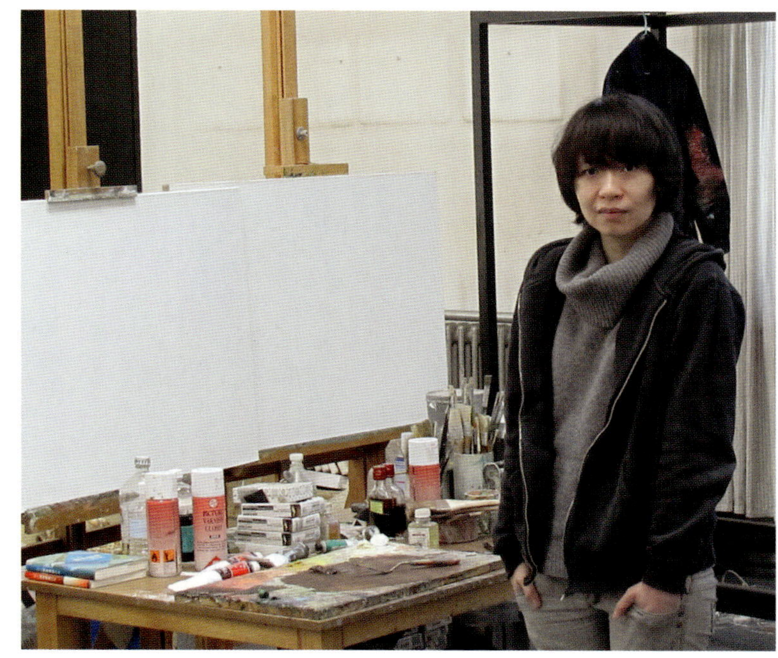

Liang Yuanwei in her Beijing studio, 2012
photo LG

LIANG YUANWEI 梁远苇

A Piece of Life

Liang Yuanwei was one of the first female artists I met who was willing to speak frankly about the frustrations particular to women in the Chinese art world. That first 2011 journey to an artists' village in Beijing's northern outskirts was memorable – my driver and translator argued constantly over the map, and the driver was unhappy about taking his new car on the dusty unpaved roads. After we arrived, he spent an hour polishing his car with a handkerchief, muttering to himself. In December 2012, eighteen months later, I visited Liang Yuanwei again, after she had controversially represented China at the

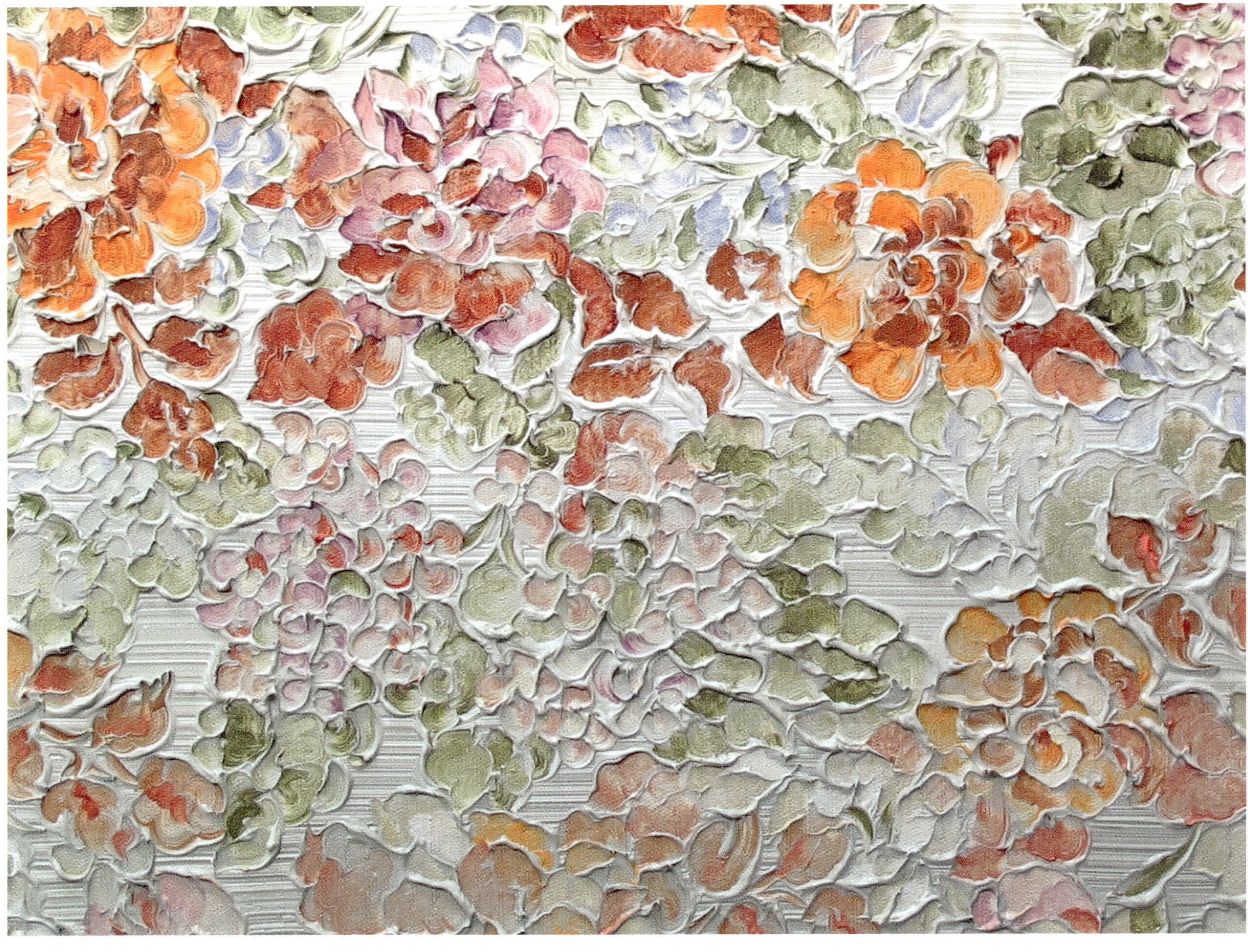

2011 Venice Biennale. This time, there were new roads leading to *Heiqiao* (Black Bridge) Artists' Village. The following year, I had a third conversation with the artist about new directions in her work, before her solo show at Pace Gallery in London. Liang picked me up from outside the 798 Art District in her new car and the journey took about ten minutes. Our conversation was punctuated by calls to her mobile phone from estate agents – she was negotiating to buy an apartment. Change is swift in China.

Known for richly textured impasto paintings, produced in an unusual technique that the self-taught painter invented, Liang Yuanwei's early canvases simulate patterned cloth – checked, striped, or intricately flowered like traditional quilts. She collected fabric remnants from friends and relatives, some with a personal significance and attached to memories, others of a deliberately banal nature, like striped flannelette sheets or pyjamas. Her meticulous technique results in a recreation of these textiles, an effect reminiscent of modernist 'all-over' abstraction.

For the series *Piece of Life* she recreated the colours, patterns and textures of her chosen fabric samples, working slowly and laboriously, section by section. The paintings suggest the domestic and the homely; the labour of generations of Chinese women. *Through the Glass* is intended to suggest the slow unrolling of a bolt of silk, iridescent threads glinting in the light reflecting from its surface. Her signature technique of painting each work slowly and carefully from the top to the bottom of the canvas allows her to gradually shift from light to dark. Her practice is deliberate, controlled and meditative, underpinned by her reading of philosophy and knowledge of Chinese and western art history. In particular, Liang admires painters such as Agnes Martin and Ad Reinhardt, with

Liang Yuanwei
Study for Piece of Life 2008
oil on canvas
image courtesty the artist
photo LG

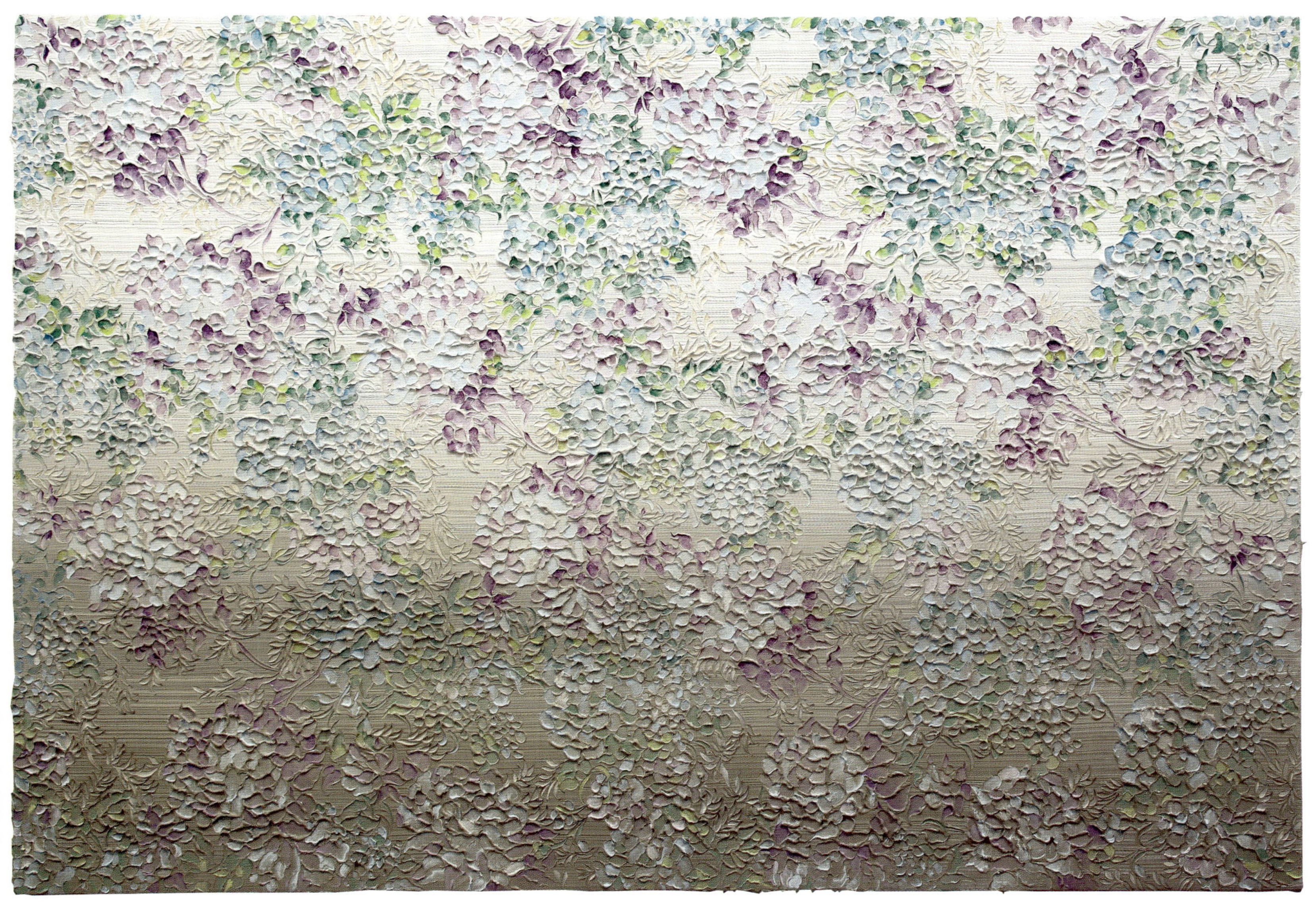

whom she showed in *Beijing Voice: Leaving Realism Behind*, at Pace Gallery in 2011. The curators of this exhibition, which included works by Mark Rothko and Bridget Riley, identified a growing tendency towards abstraction in Chinese art. But, 'Unlike the pure abstraction of the West, these abstract forms are backed by a strong sense of life and temporality. They imbue a pure form with an almost meditative spirituality and everyday emotions.'[1] In recent years there has been a new interest in the possibilities of painterly abstraction in China. However, as critic Richard Vine points out:

> The Chinese avant-garde's quick leap over modernism has deprived abstraction of the pioneering status it holds in western art history. For experimental painters in the PRC, coming onto the scene some eight decades after the emergence of such work abroad, abstraction was just one more handy option among many.[2]

Liang Yuanwei says it would be incorrect to see her as a painter in the tradition of artists focused entirely on their mastery of technique. In contrast, her painting practice is a kind of performance art:

> [Each] painting is a part of a project, they are not separate paintings in themselves. They kind of record a performance, a performance that I did every day as I looked at the original garment. You can see how in this painting that I did in 2008... I painted from the top to the bottom, and every day I finished a section. I did the background colour very thick and then I had to finish every section each day before it dried. The colours changing from the top to the bottom give the effect of light reflecting, like a piece of silk. That is a kind of design – a project which is already designed in my mind. Then I treat every day's labour like a kind of recording.[3]

Liang Yuanwei
Through the Glass 3–3 2011
oil on linen
65 x 95 cm
image courtesy the artist and Beijing Commune

This is painting as a performative act, Liang agrees. 'So then, when the performance is finished, I have a completed piece of silk...the painting is just a record of the performance.' The repetitive labour of their production echoes the labour of the worker in the home or the factory. 'Actually,' says the artist, 'That is the interesting part of my work because I treat my body like a machine to do the repetition, I limit my body, so it makes the result very complex and very subtle, because I am human and I must make some mistakes...'

Liang Yuanwei worked in this way for more than five years, refining her laborious process of applying paint in small sections of the canvas. She says:

> The physical work every day, the labour, is more than the meaning of the painting, whether it is good or bad. It cannot be corrected – as the paint dries it cannot be changed...so it is a little bit different, the concept is different. Because in those paintings I cannot correct any mistakes if something is not perfect... I have to paint every day, but I didn't treat it as painting. For every large painting, I have one small study. I used them as a kind of exercise. So that is a sort of conflict, a different kind of thinking than that of a painter. I do some handwork but I didn't trust the hand itself.

Despite the luscious surfaces of her canvases, with their seductive renderings of nostalgic fabrics, her work is conceptually driven. There is a cool, considered and slightly ironic intent behind her sensuous manipulation of the plastic and tactile qualities of paint. The canvases in the *Piece of Life* series satirise high modernist 'all-over' painting, replacing the serious masculine angst of American mid-century abstraction with domestic textiles as sewn and worn by ordinary women. There is also a hint at Chinese history and tradition, and the significance of embroidery and textiles in the imperial past.

Born in 1977 in Xi'an, Shaanxi Province, Liang Yuanwei came to Beijing with her parents and was educated there, graduating from the Design Department of the Central Academy of Fine Arts. She was a reluctant student of design – her father would not permit her to study Fine Arts, fearing the unpredictable and financially precarious life of the artist. Liang Yuanwei remembers painful early experiences as a self-taught painter forced to 'lose face' by persuading undergraduates to show her how to stretch a canvas. She had to develop a thick skin and 'act tough', she says, fighting for acceptance in the testosterone-fuelled Beijing art scene, at a time when the art market was at its most volatile, and even young emerging artists were viewed as potential rock stars. She learned how to deal with gallery directors, such as the one who famously told her in 2005 that she had better become a photographer as 'there are already too many female painters'. Her response, a series of photographic self-portraits, *Don't Forget to Say You Love Me When You Fuck Me*, is a parody of erotically charged photographs of women, featuring the artist herself as the pouting object of the male gaze.

Liang Yuanwei acknowledges artists who have been significant to her, including sculptor Eva Hesse and painters Luc Tuymans, Sigmar Polke and Gerhard Richter. In 1995 some CAFA tutors returned to China from Berlin, bringing with them new ideas about art, and introducing her to the work of Joseph Beuys. This informed her developing practice as an installation artist interested in working with found objects and non-art materials. She realised that the ideas underpinning her work were as important as the materials and techniques with which they were constructed:

> Art practice is like building houses, where different people use many different materials and construction methods. My paintings are my own little universe of materials, purposes and techniques.

A year and a half later I made my way to *Heiqiao* to visit Liang Yuanwei again, to ask how her selection for the 2011 Venice Biennale had changed her. She seemed wary. 'Feminism is just a word, generated from Western systems,' she said, with a degree of bitterness. 'There is no feminism in China.' Venice left her feeling wounded, and a little disillusioned. The space she was given to install her work was small, dark and difficult, and she attracted criticism from curators and critics for 'not being Chinese enough'. She said, 'I was chosen because I was young and female, to make China look good. My gender, my age and my background were more important than my work.'

Her plan for the Venice work was appealingly simple. Each of the artists proposing work for the China Pavilion was asked to represent one of the five pervasive Chinese flavours or scents: tea, lotus, medicinal herbs, incense, and the unmistakeably pungent and intoxicating white spirit, *baijiu*. Liang, and a number of other female artists, were asked to present the curators of the China Pavilion with proposals relating to baijiu, perhaps in an ironic gender inversion, because it is associated so firmly with male rituals of boozy banquets. Her proposal was accepted, and she was invited to install it in Venice. She decided to pump the alcohol through rubber tubes in and around large metal barrels. The movement of the fermented liquid created a loud soundscape in the echoing space, as the spirit splashed into the metal, and developed an increasingly rancid smell over time. Wine spurted from three lumbar puncture needles at the top of rubber hoses into metal basins, and then pumped back up to continuously repeat the process. Her chosen material – the liquid spirit – was authentically Chinese, representing 'high mountains and water streaming', that staple of traditional ink painting. Baijiu is made from crops (usually sorghum) and thus also represents the farmers and the countryside.

Liang Yuanwei
Piece of Life 2008
28 x 24 cm
oil on linen
image courtesy the artist and Beijing Commune

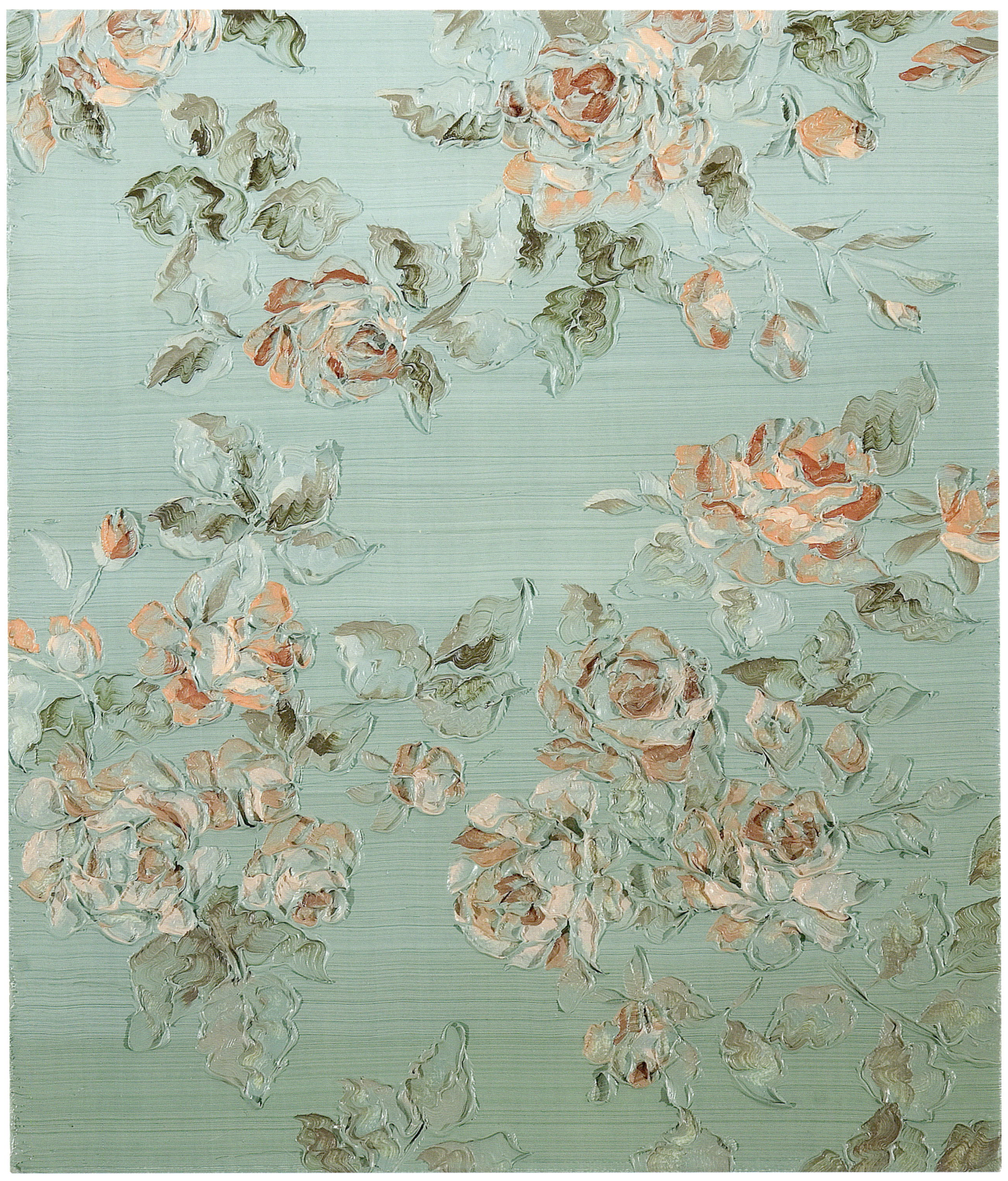

After Venice Liang Yuanwei travelled in Europe and then stayed in Germany for three months, immersing herself in the contemporary art culture of Berlin and visiting *Documenta 13* in Kassel, which proved an epiphany. She was struck by the approaches to the curation of contemporary art in Europe; the embedding of criticality into the practices of both artists and curators. Liang spent a year studying, thinking, writing and observing the differences between the Chinese and European art worlds. 'I found the problems I am facing as a woman artist [in China] are very different to the issues faced by artists internationally,' she said. 'Women artists in China, especially women artists over the age of thirty-five, are in the minority. Things are still very unequal and there appears to be no change.' Her time away from China was important, allowing her to think deeply about new ideas.

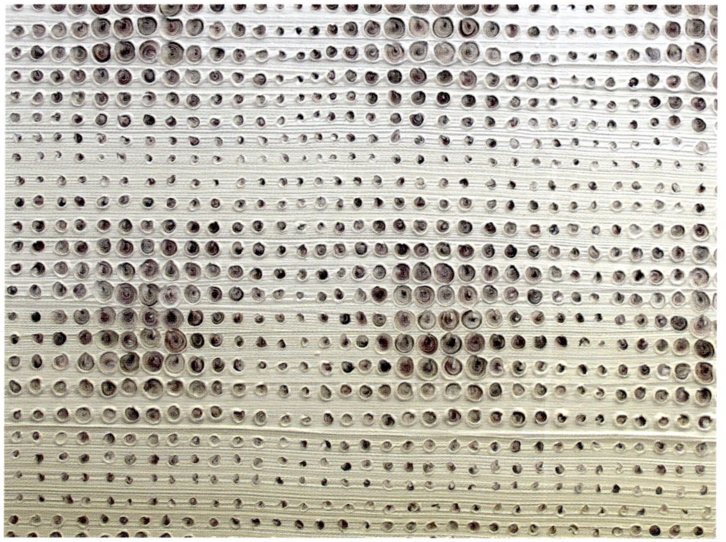

Returning to Beijing, Liang Yuanwei re-evaluated her earlier approach to painting, beginning work on a series of canvases featuring goldfish in seething complex patterns, a development of diptych works presented in her earlier *Golden Notes* exhibition at Beijing Commune in 2010. Liang had always been interested in the science of colour, and she began to experiment with lipstick as a painting pigment – strong reds and pinks applied to crumpled paper in drawings of geometric precision. The colours change over time as they fade from strong reds to softer browns. They opened up a new avenue:

> This is kind of a project for me, which I developed into a solo exhibition called *Pomegranate*, including about thirty-five lipstick on paper works, about four oil paintings, and some paintings [directly] onto the wall using house paint.

The wall paintings were instructional works based on Pantone colours. Liang asked a designer friend to use the *Pantone Color Matching System* to replicate her chosen shades of lipstick into one hundred and twenty paint samples, applied to the wall in rows. Reviewing the show, art writer Fiona He saw an allusion to Mark Rothko's shimmering colour fields – a plausible interpretation, as the artist often refers to Rothko in conversation.[4] As a teenager, she says, 'Mark Rothko was my idol.' She especially loves the Rothko chapel in Houston, where the paintings form an integral part of the architectural space: the relationship between her own works and the spaces they inhabit is significant.

Each of her paintings forms part of an installation; they are not singular works. 'I began my art career with installation, even still in college, and my first exhibition also was installation,' she says. One of these early works, *Salt Series, Little Clocks* (2007), is an installation made up of things that might be found in a woman's bag or wardrobe. A row of small shelves displays these quotidian objects – a pair of canvas shoes, a watch, an envelope, a bank book, a packet of cigarettes. A woman's shirt, slightly crumpled, hangs on the wall. Tiny, moving watch hands are attached to each object, almost invisible until you look closely. It suggests how we waste time in the everyday minutiae of a life: all those seconds, minutes and hours spent on truly unimportant things. The installation packs the punch of a *Vanitas*, despite its unassuming appearance.

Early works such as this were very personal, based on her own life. Now, she says, her work has changed: 'I used to be more interested in the material, and now it's more conceptual.' Her experimentation with unorthodox materials has provided a new freedom. The soft and insubstantial nature of marks made by lipstick is as far from the heavy texture of oil paint as one can imagine:

> As in the lipstick paintings, everything [now] is very loose and free, experimental work. But in my so-called mature oil painting it is a very completed system which I felt I did not have the right to break myself. The lipstick works taught me how to follow the feelings of my physical body. [And] gave me a kind of reason for doing oil painting in this contemporary art scene. Because I began with installation and I use oil painting as material.

Over ten years working mostly with oil paint, she had begun to feel she had lost the most interesting aspect of this material, in some ways overwhelmed by a consciousness of *the problem of painting*:

> I treat [oil paint] as a medium which I have to have a good reason to use in this contemporary world. [Actually] when I first started oil

Liang Yuanwei
Study for Piece of Life 2008
oil on canvas
image courtesy the artist
photo LG

Liang Yuanwei
Piece of Life 14 2008
oil on canvas
162 x 130 cm
image courtesy the artist and White Rabbit Gallery

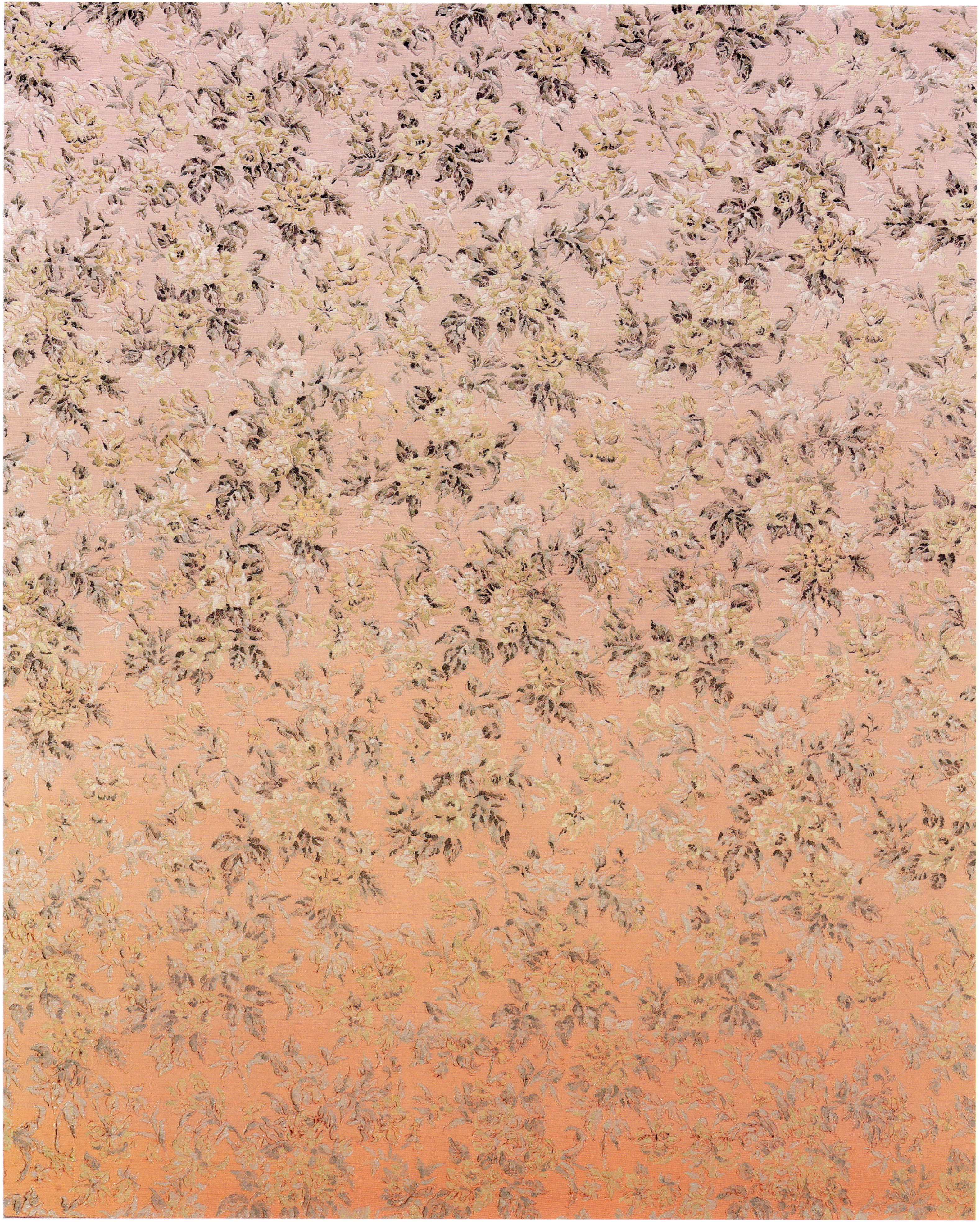

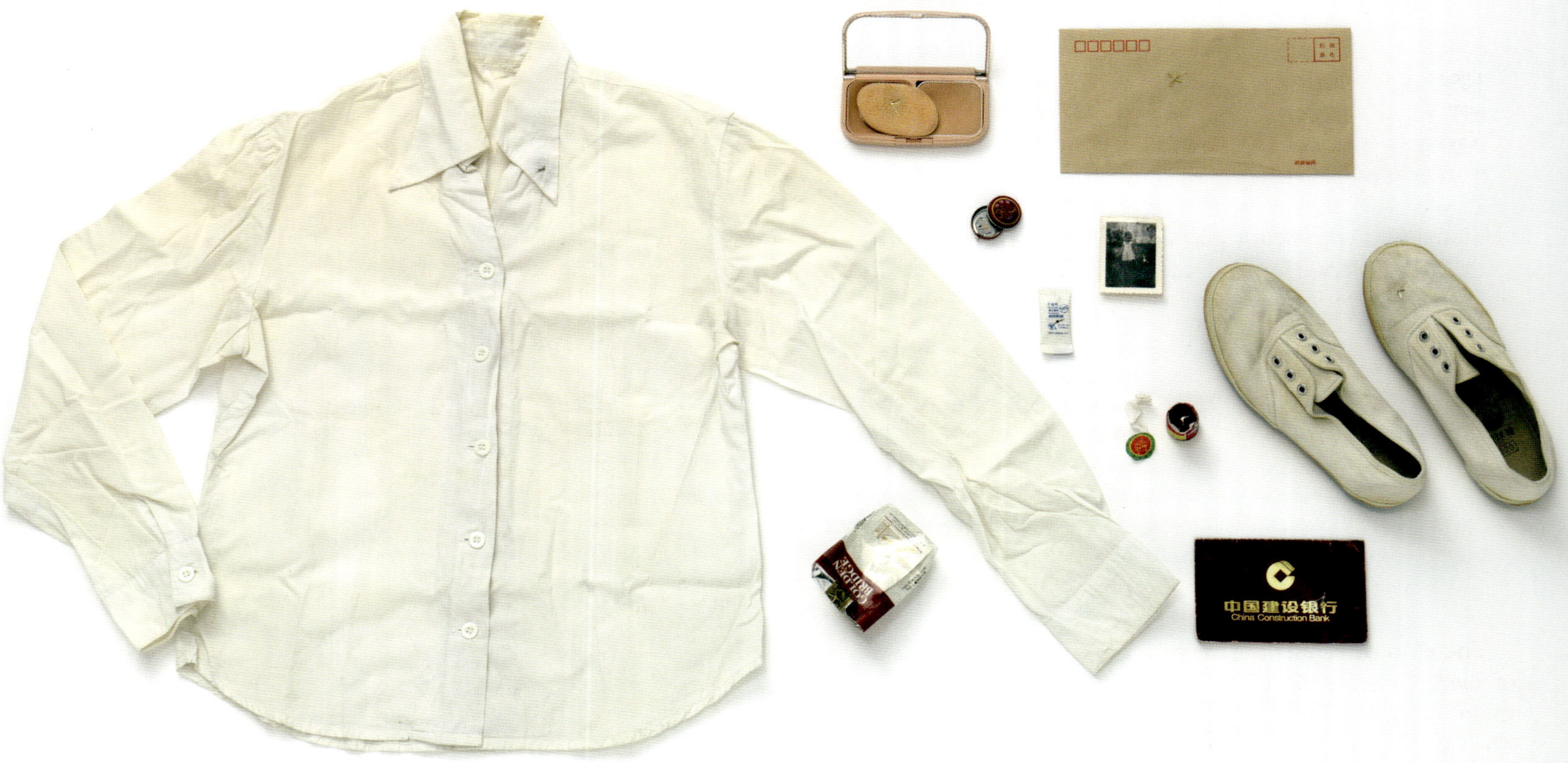

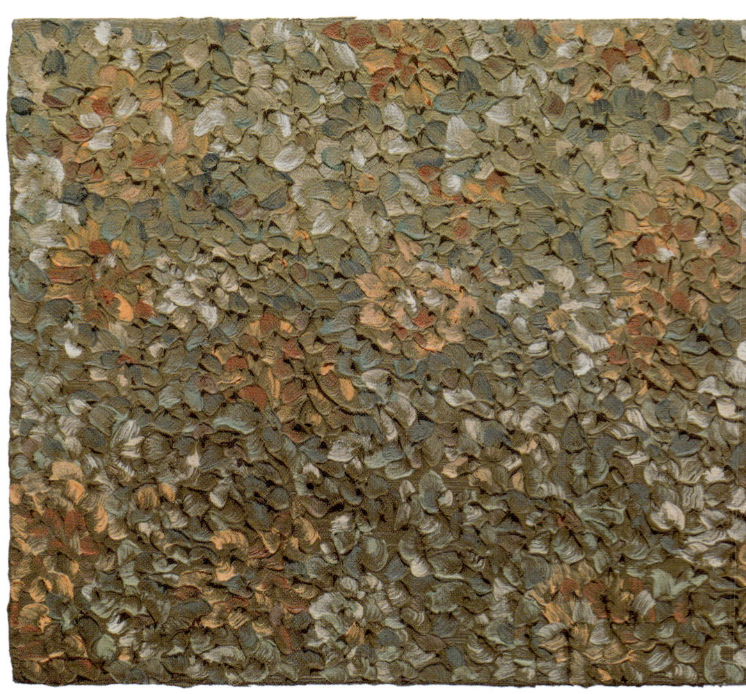

Liang Yuarwei *(top)*
Salt Series Little Clocks 2007
mixed media
dimensions variable
image courtesy the artist
and White Rabbit Gallery

Liang Yuanwei *(bottom left)*
Piece of Life 18 2008
oil on canvas
170 x 200 cm
image courtesy the artist
and White Rabbit Gallery

Liang Yuanwei *(bottom right)*
Untitled 2013 4 2013
oil on linen
30 x 40 cm
image courtesy the artist
and Pace London

painting, because it is a kind of outdated tradition, I thought I needed a good reason. But now, although I am using oil paint in a traditional way, the concept I am expressing is modern. It's like whether you are playing according to the contemporary rules... I have always liked oil painting but I also want to do something different.

Liang Yuanwei's work may appear 'western' at first glance, with its deliberate nod to modernist abstraction. Yet it is underpinned by a deep awareness of Chinese culture and tradition, both artistic and philosophical. Liang says:

My painting includes labour, beauty and skill, and some mixed cultural information under that. It is very easy to see my painting in a western construct of culture, but inside it is a very eastern feeling... There are complex things hidden in the works. There are many paradoxes, [for example] the Chinese atmosphere versus the western construct, and also the flexibility of painting by hand versus the repetitive patterns in the painting.

The 'eastern' element in the paintings is not merely a function of Liang's choice of culturally specific fabrics to replicate, or the philosophical reading with which she imbues her practice. The quiet, concentrated act of painting one small section of canvas at a time, slowly and deliberately, working in the same manner every day, is more like the practice of a Renaissance fresco painter than a gestural abstract artist. There is an echo of the literati tradition too; the careful acquired knowledge of the scholarly calligrapher painting a scroll in his study.

In fact, Liang's *Golden Notes* exhibition was likened by Chinese critics to Song Dynasty *Bird and Flower* painting in its suggestion of fleeting, ephemeral moments of sensual pleasure.[5] Yet the artist herself sees it as a kind of field painting, an immersive experience for both artist and audience:

Like colour field. Or Mark Rothko. There is a big influence from art outside of China. I speak about change [after her year away from China] in terms of changes inside myself, which comes before the art. Before I went to Europe, when I looked at western paintings I looked [just] at the technique, but now when I look at them I see them in their context of time and place – their social context. In Venice I was in the group show in the China Pavilion, and was part of a group including more important figures than me. So it was no longer just me in my studio doing works about my own life. It became a more public action. My work [now] is concerned about other artists' work and about our culture and about politics.

Preparing for a solo show, *The Tension Between a Bow and an Elephant,* at Pace London in 2014, Liang studied the late works of Cézanne, an artist she admires for his insistence on the act of seeing, the process of perception. Her palette of earthy tones and subtle greenish blues evokes Cézanne's depictions of Mont Saint Victoire, although she is also interested in how Chinese artists of the Northern Song period used colour. Painting has not come easily to her, despite the lush tactile surfaces of her canvases. She views the act of painting as a battle with 'both governable and ungovernable forces'[6] and a process of constant decision-making. The title of the exhibition emerged from a vivid dream in which the artist saw herself taking aim at an elephant with a bow, but not shooting the arrow. When she woke, she realised that this image represented her feelings about painting: the inevitable tension between what works and what doesn't; between the patience required to paint her canvases slowly, section by small section and her desire to visualise the finished work; between the flat paintings and the architectural spaces in which they are hung; between the large and small works presented as diptychs. 'It's all about tension,' she says.[7]

Surrounded by paintings old and new in Liang Yuanwei's studio in the winter of 2012, the table in front of us littered with dog-eared books of art and philosophy, the artist's cat plaintively winding around our legs, she reflected on the changes in her life and her practice: 'Everything now is connected – both memory and future. I now think more about the relationship between myself as the artist, my work and the world. I have become a curator of myself.'

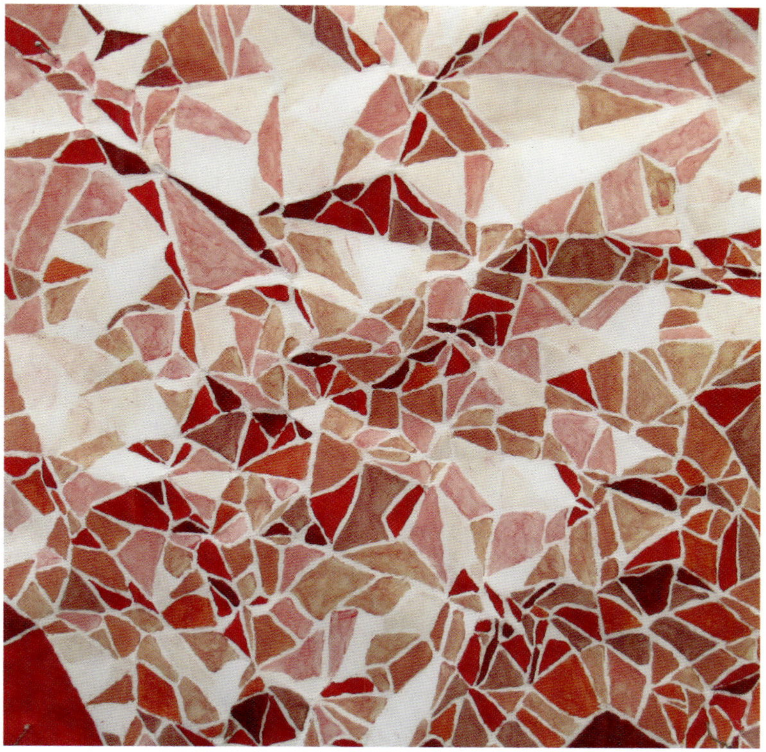

Liang Yuanwei
study for ***Pomegranate*** 2012
lipstick on paper
image courtesty the artists
photo LG

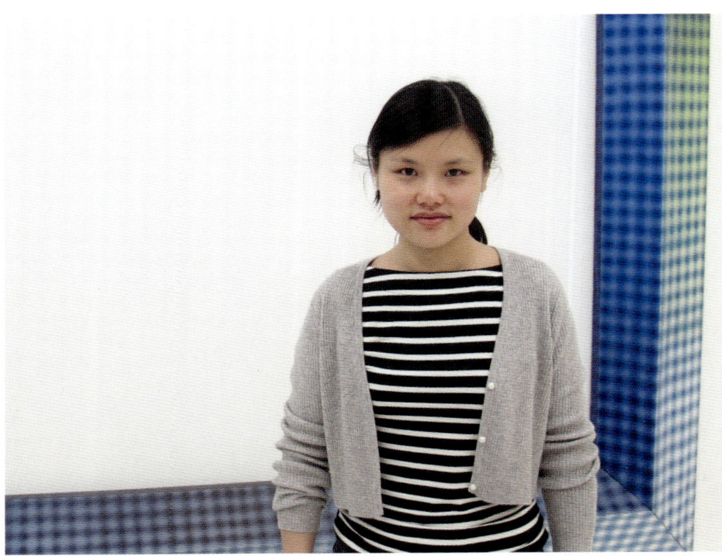

LI SHURUI 李姝睿

Light and Space

When Li Shurui was a teenager, her mother wanted her to leave school to work for the massive State Grid electricity company, just as every other member of her family had done: a government job was a key to stability and security in uncertain, rapidly changing times. Li had other ideas, and she persisted in following what must have seemed a crazy dream, firstly to the high school attached to the Sichuan Academy of Fine Arts, then to the Academy itself, and finally to Beijing, a pilgrimage destination for artists in the early years of the twenty-first century.

Li Shurui knew from earliest childhood that she wanted to be an artist, despite having no family connections with art or the art world, and her talent was identified when she was still in elementary school. She says:

> My mother was proud of this, thinking maybe it made me a bit special. She supported me in my education. But when I was fifteen, I had to make a big decision about whether to go to the school for the electricity company, to train as a worker, or whether to apply for the high school for the Sichuan Fine Arts Academy. I wanted to run away... My family life was not so good at that time. All my decisions were, in a way, against my mum's wishes. She could not really push me to go to the training school, though – because I didn't go to the exam! [*Here she laughs, with a hint of triumph.*] My parents had already been divorced for ten years, and my father said I could go [to the specialist art high school], so it was two against one. My mum said, 'OK, but when you graduate and you have no income, no food, no place to stay – all I can give you is one room, and a meal. So you have to take all the responsibility for this decision. If you don't want to be middle class, then that is your responsibility.' But it wasn't really such a big decision for me, even though I was only fifteen.[8]

Her parents remain to this day a little mystified about their daughter's occupation. In an interview for Phaidon's *Vitamin P2* Li Shurui said, 'When I entered art school she [my mother] thought I would paint Chinese landscapes and make a living from it, but when she heard that I was doing this thing called "contemporary art" she couldn't understand it and was rather perturbed.'[9] Li thinks art must be in her DNA: 'I guess it must have been my destiny to become an artist since an unrealistic childhood ambition was enough to counterbalance all of the things that should have forced me into some other profession or role in society.'[10]

Born in 1981, Li grew up in the grey-green clinging mists of Chongqing, a city at the confluence of two rivers whose damp humidity and lack of sunshine is famed throughout China. She was trained in the distinctive Sichuan tradition of painting, although her mature practice is abstract rather than figurative. When we met in April 2014, in the midst of the installation of her solo show at White Space Gallery in Beijing's Caochangdi, we talked about her emergence from the relative obscurity of the provinces as a young artist with a distinctive practice. She agrees that her work reflects the particular history of painting in Sichuan Province:

> Yes! Last year I did some painting with pigments mixed with green. This green colour is the tradition of the Sichuan Fine Arts Academy. Chongqing is a very green city – we don't see sunshine usually. It's very misty and foggy. We have a standard for green colour – make it pure, not dirty... The green colour is a Sichuan aesthetic. Maybe from history? I think [actually] it's about weather – every day it surrounds you, and it controls your behaviour and the way you look at everything.

Li has fond memories of passionate discussions about art and life whilst she and her fellow art students ate hotpot with their professors, in true Sichuan style. Her art education encouraged independence, rather than slavish imitation of the work of a 'master teacher':

> In my school we don't have the idea of learning from a particular teacher. Our teachers encourage us to do something different from themselves. They tell you the truth, like people to people... The teachers say, 'Do anything, but don't be like me.' Teachers and students drink tea together every day, and at night they drink beer and eat hotpot. It makes you feel relaxed. Sometimes I didn't want to go to class and the teacher would just say, 'OK, just give me something to show that you are not just having fun all day.'

Li Shurui at Whitespace Beijing, April 2014
photo LG

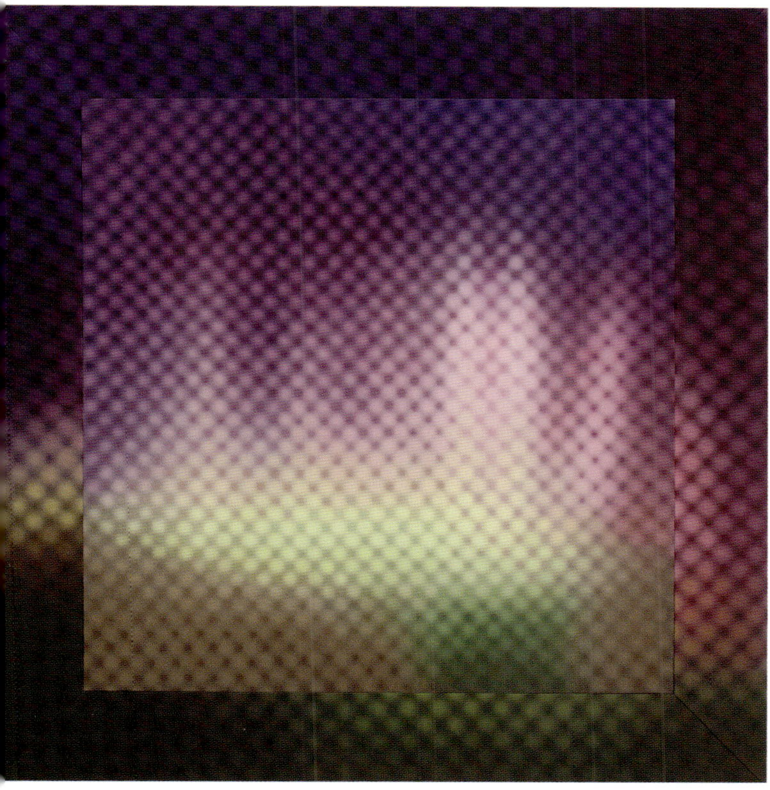

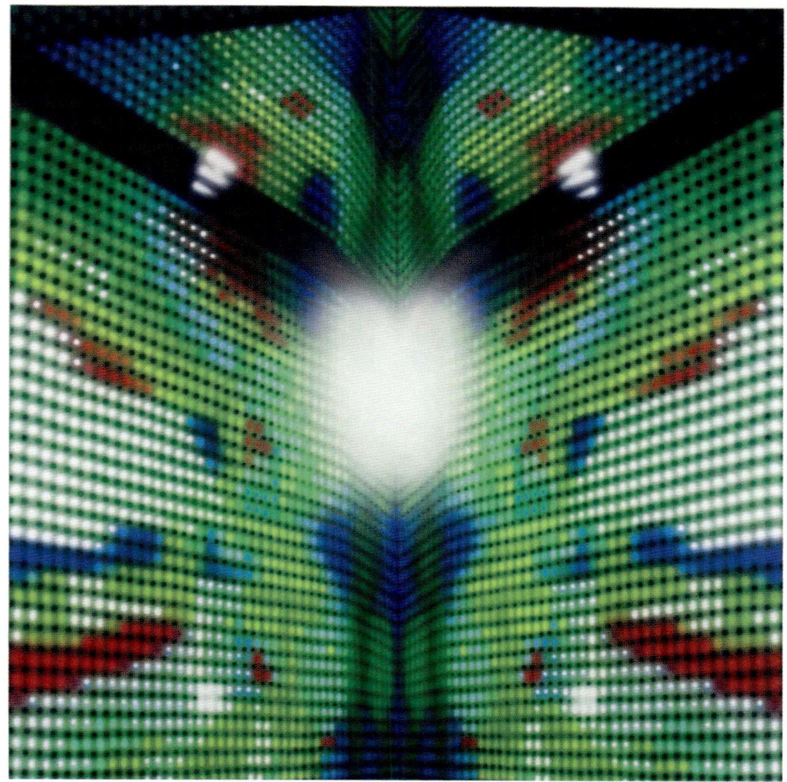

Chongqing today is a 'mega-city', a very different place than the hometown of her childhood memories. Li said:

> Old Chongqing where I grew up is not really so big. There are two rivers, and the main city is in the middle... Now, it's [become] like cities everywhere in China... It's kind of a sad thing, you cannot find where you grew up. My grandma's house now is a public park. They just don't like the old houses, they want to demolish them and put on a new face. There are three layers of memory – the first is everything from your childhood that you cannot find. The second is from teenage years – you can find some of those things. The third thing is now. I feel bored with living in the city now, [even] Beijing. Every city should have a different face, but now they build every city so they all look exactly the same. The advertising is the same, the people eat the same food, shopping malls are the same...

Li Shurui graduated in 2004, after returning rather reluctantly to Chongqing from an exploratory trip to Beijing. She has always been a fiercely independent character, and she yearned for Beijing in much the same the way that Chekhov's three sisters yearned for Moscow. It appeared to her that all the excitement, glamour and action for an emerging artist, all the possibility, all the promise, was to be found there, far from the mists of her hometown. The celebrated curator Pi Li gave a talk to the students at the art academy about the avant-garde scene in Beijing, intensifying Li Shurui's desire:

> Back in 2003 – 2004, Beijing was really a wonderland for us. The first time I was here [in Beijing] was in about 2001 – there was no 798 art district, no galleries, nothing. I met artists like Shi Qing, and what they were doing really impressed me. [Their work] really made you think. They were really amazing... So I decided I had to be there, in Beijing. I told my mum in second year I didn't want to finish my education. I told her, 'I want to go to Beijing now.' She said, 'When you wanted to go to the art high school instead of the trade school I agreed. When you wanted to go to the art academy I agreed. And now you want to give up?' She threatened to jump out of the window from the nineteenth floor. I felt I couldn't wait. Everything happened here – how can I wait? But I earned some money first, and I arrived in 2004.

At first sight Li Shurui's style, defined by her skilful application of airbrush techniques, seems a homage to the Op Art of the 1960s, influenced by artists such as Victor Vasarely or Bridget Riley. In fact, she had never heard of these artists, nor seen examples of their work, until long after she had established her own style of optical airbrush painting. Li says:

> I didn't really know Pop or Op Art when I started. Later, two friends who had studied art history came to the studio and said, 'Oh, are you doing Pop now?' and I said, 'What is that?' Our education system was from Russia, we didn't learn about all that. The western art they introduced to us is very realist.

Li Shurui
I am not ready 2013
acrylic on canvas
250 x 250cm
image courtesy the artist and White Space Beijing

Li Shurui
Lights No. 95 2009
acrylic on canvas
210 x 210 cm
image courtesy the artist and White Space Beijing

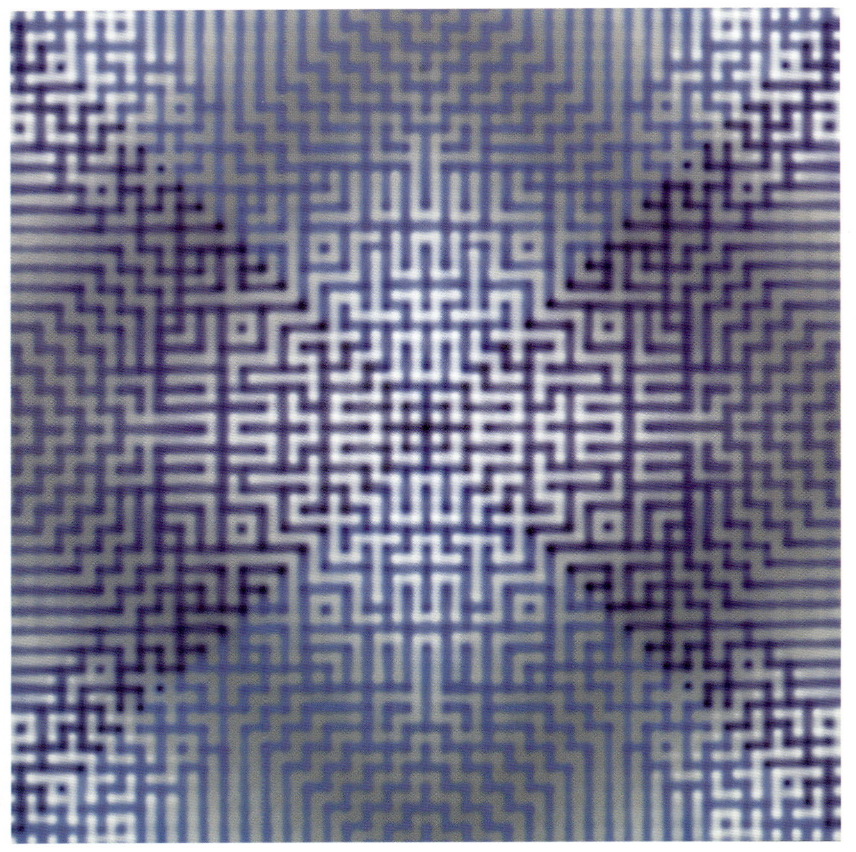

Li tried to remember the western artist that they learned about, finding a picture of Andrew Wyeth's *Christina's World* (1948) on her mobile phone. 'We knew a very little about modern art, but Pop or Op art I had never heard of.' Her work springs from a different motivation than that of modernist op artists in Europe or America. Art critic Bao Dong said:

> Li relies not on technique and knowledge but experience and intuition, and her work seeks to arouse not a pure reaction in the optic nerve but more the viewer's grasp of a kind of experiential state. In this sense, we might call her work 'Lyrical Op Art'... representations of objective experiences from life and not simply figures and colour schemes.[11]

Karen Smith, the distinguished critic, curator and Chinese art expert, suggests that Li's work fits firmly into the zeitgeist (in Chinese, the *Shidai Jinsheng*) of contemporary China:

> ... her expansive canvases are to the nation's twenty-first century, boom-and-bust, design-accoutred and technology-rich culture what psychedelia was to pockets of Western art that flourished in the 1960s.

Li Shurui
Allodoxaphobia No. 2 2014
acrylic on canvas
210 x 210 cm
image courtesy the artist and White Space Beijing

Smith characterises the key quality of Li Shurui's work as a kind of 'delirious escapism.'[12] Indeed, there is an intoxicating energy in these canvases, evocative of youthful extremes of emotion and sensory experience.

Li's almost accidental discovery of the airbrush dates back to her student days. She had been exhibiting photographs and installations throughout her final year, but for the graduating exhibition thought that if she showed paintings, she might be able to sell them, and make enough money to get to Beijing:

> I hadn't done so much painting in my studies, and had not been so interested in it. But I felt like I wanted to copy the images from a Hollywood movie – an explosion – and I thought maybe an airbrush would give me that [effect]. So I asked people how to use it. They said, 'Just practise!' and they told me how to wash the tools. An airbrush was so expensive at that time. I borrowed the money from my mum, and she said, 'You always want more money, more money, more money! *Why* do you want to buy this?' But she did [give me the money], and I practised. It was trial and error.

Li Shurui felt like a pioneer, exploring new territory, engaged in a process of constant invention. She began to see that each canvas formed part of an installation. Whilst still a student, she had participated in the celebrated *Long March Project*, in which Chinese and international artists re-traced the steps of the arduous journey undertaken by Mao's Communist forces on their retreat across China to Yan'an in 1934–35, creating site-specific and performative works in different locations along the route.[13] Li said:

> In 2002 I did an installation as part of the *Long March Project*. Judy Chicago was there and she was the host of the whole event. I did an installation with twenty mosquito nets hanging from bamboo. That work was the really the beginning of my system.

She was not so interested in the notion of feminist art at that time, nor does she think now that there should be any 'specialness' attached to art by women. However, her participation in this significant event was a first introduction to the cultural exchanges of international contemporary art, with their inevitable politics, pressures and difficulties. By all accounts this event, at Lugu Lake in Yunnan Province, seems to have been fraught with communication difficulties, disagreements, extreme weather, and sickness. Some participants fell ill, resulting in the presence of a local shaman at one point, and others departed. There were arguments and personality clashes.

The original plan articulated by curators Qiu Zhijie and Lu Jie was for twelve female Chinese artists to participate alongside Chicago at Lugu Lake in a work entitled, *If Women Ruled the World*. Lu Jie's record of the event suggests:

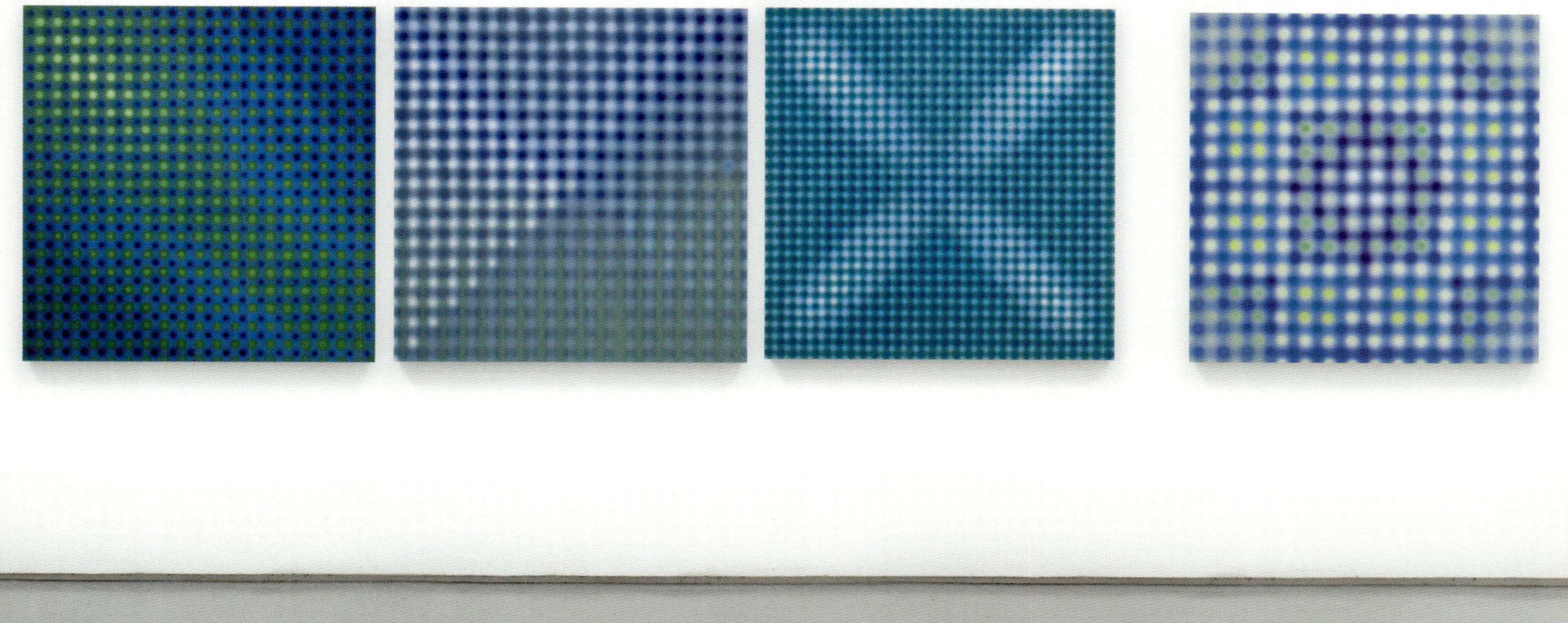

Lu Jie and Qiu Zhijie began to doubt their authority, as men, to pick twelve artists, and recommended to Chicago that the limit of twelve artists be removed and the proposal exhibition opened to the more than thirty artists who offered submissions, with the proposals to be printed on Tibetan-style prayer flags. This plan won Chicago's consent, and she quickly began making such a flag for her own work. Afterwards, some artists expressed their discontent that they could only display proposals at Lugu Lake, and their sincere hope that they could actually realize works on-site. Lu Jie and Qiu Zhijie decided to forgo their curatorial prerogative and allow all those artists who had submitted proposals and wanted to realize works to do so.[14]

The project was made more difficult by language barriers and cultural misunderstandings, which Chicago alludes to in a letter to participants: 'It was an extremely challenging task to work cross-culturally and from such a distance away and I think we did extremely well. Despite the language problem, we were able to connect with each other in a way that speaks highly about women's abilities to cooperate, even under difficult circumstances.'[15]

Li Shurui was not entirely seduced by Chicago's notion of a 'kingdom of women', but the event started her thinking about the imagery of the net, and the possibilities of three-dimensional forms in space. The 'system' that she identifies in her practice centres on her exploration of light. Flickering, artificial, psychedelic, her paintings suggest the raw excitement of the urban nightscape, and were originally inspired by the lighting effects in a Beijing nightclub. She realised that she had no interest in painting 'things' in the manner of painter Chen Wenbo, for whom she worked as a studio assistant; rather, she wanted to make works about perception itself. She is fully aware of what distinguishes her work from the previous, 'New Wave' generation of Chinese painters, most of whom worked in forms of figuration:

> I have two keywords. One is light. The other is space. In 2002 nobody was doing things like this in China, and I had no opportunity to see what people were doing outside China. We had no internet and not many books...When I came to Beijing I worked in Chen Wenbo's studio. He was a unique painter at that

Li Shurui
Sky Light Nos. 13–16 2012
acrylic on canvas
each 90 x 90 cm
image courtesy the artist and White Space Beijing

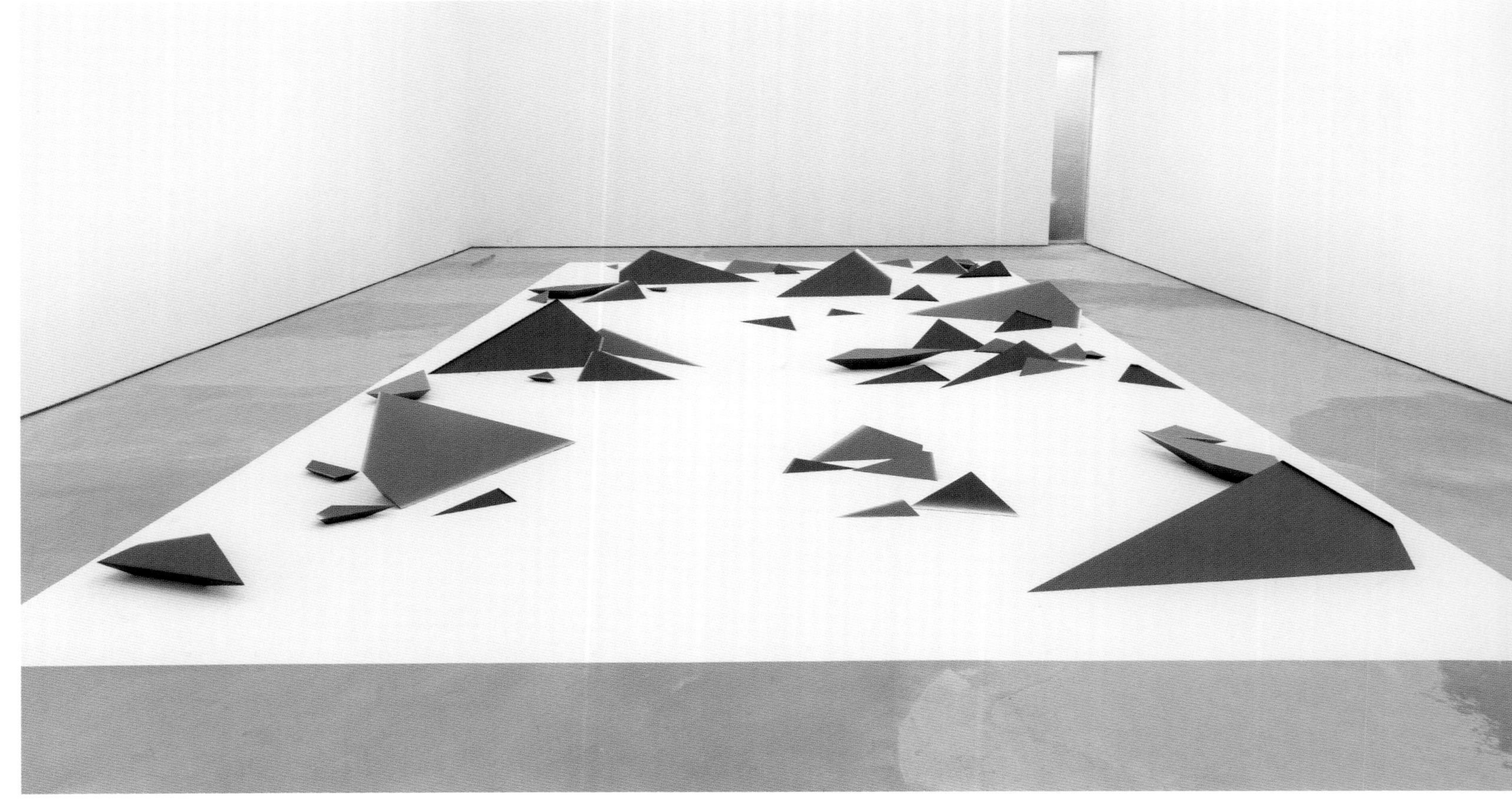

> moment, doing paintings about light on objects, [but] I wanted to go beyond his system, doing paintings of light on nowhere, just the light itself. I tried one painting in 2005, just the light...It felt weird, nobody was doing this.

Despite her initial uncertainty, Li persisted with her experim-entation, using colour to intuitive effect in works that create ambiguous spaces that make you feel as if you have entered a different dimension, or arrived at a new plane of consciousness.

Like other painters of her own and the preceding generation, for Li Shurui the way contemporary Chinese art developed after the death of Mao Zedong, and the influx of foreign ideas during the 'Reform and Opening' period, presents both advantages and handicaps. She says, 'As an abstract painter you are doing something very different. In China there is no language of modernism, as everything happened at once in the 1980s.' The artist describes her brain as a 'constantly jumping circuit board',[16] as she seeks new ways to express her responses to light and space. She explained how she developed her abstract language, following an education in which she transitioned from figurative painting to photography, multi-media and installation:

> After 2005 I had to think more about why I was painting in this way. In 2006 I was working in a gallery, and I had many chances to go to the nightclub where we would take the artists. I took photos of the LED screen with my mobile phone. Then I thought, I could copy this image with my airbrush skill. It's light itself, not light *on* something. When I had [enough] money I built a small studio and started my own things. From that moment I had found the way.

From recreating Hollywood images of explosions seen on a TV screen, she began to look at light in a more abstract and cerebral manner, breaking the boundaries of the two-dimensional picture plane, with installations of paintings that respond to our digital, image-saturated age. By photographing the dots made by LED lights on a screen, then reproducing them in paint using the mechanical tool of an airbrush, she highlights the insubstantial nature of reality, its slipperiness and ephemerality. Viewing works such as her series of *Light* paintings, you doubt the information sent to your own optic nerve, as the blurred softening of edges created by the airbrush renders all forms and spaces ambiguous. They are beautiful and accomplished works, but the experience is slightly discomfiting.

Although her paintings appear to be firmly embedded in an internationalist language of abstraction, Li Shurui says her

Li Shurui
Sharp 2013–14
aluminium, paint
dimensions variable
image courtesy the artist and White Space Beijing

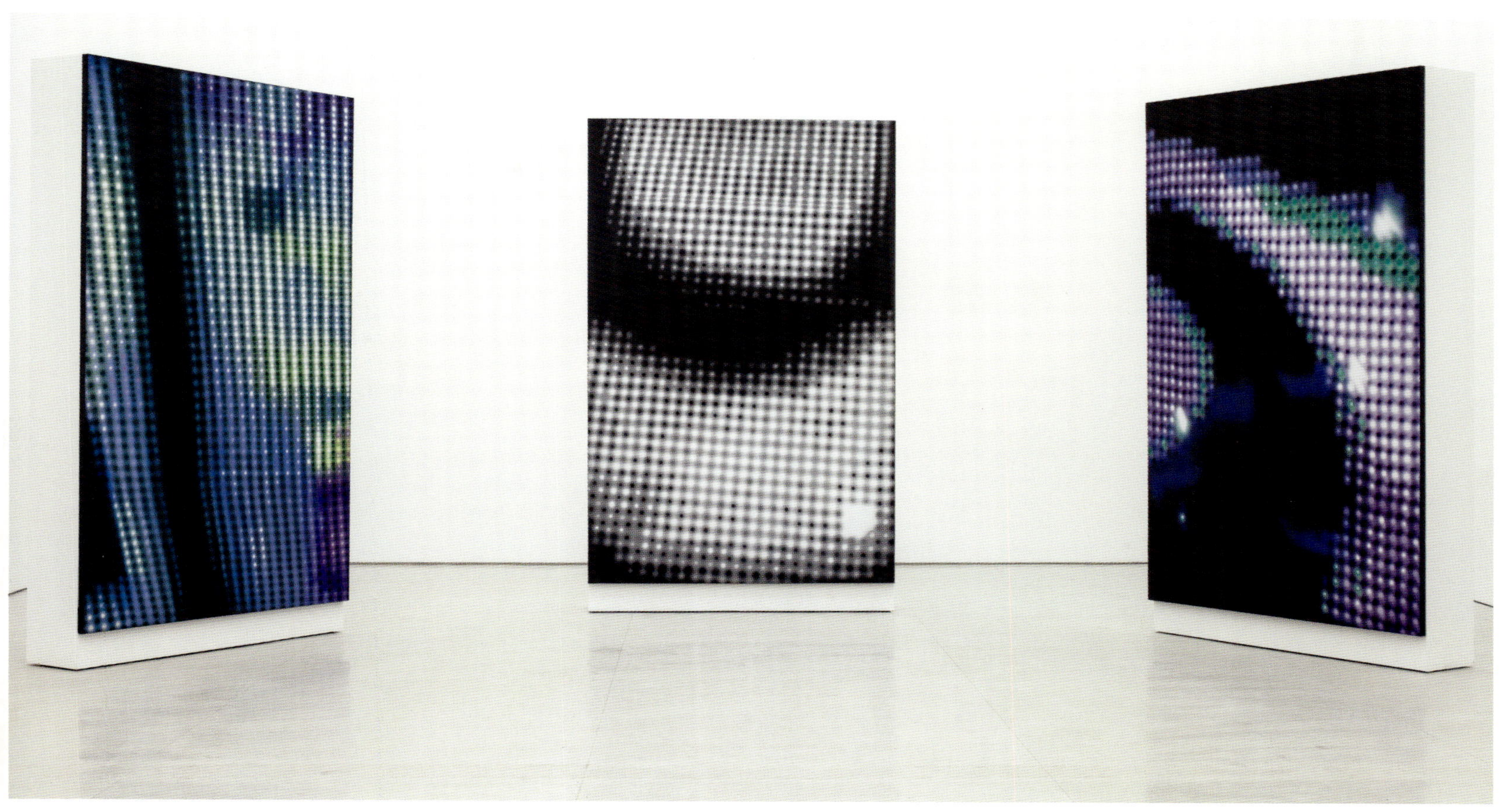

work is connected to her experiences painting with Chinese ink and learning *shu fa* (calligraphy) from childhood. She says:

> Now, so many artists of my generation return to tradition – we love to drink tea and to write calligraphy. We feel like that is the most comfortable way to live. Just natural. Even though my work doesn't look Chinese, but on the inside… some collectors ask me why I do this kind of work and I say I really don't know, maybe it's in my DNA. I grew up in the traditional language.

Her paintings evolve from objects and experiences related to vision – broken mirrors, solar flares, pixilated screens, reflected and refracted images, neon and LED lights. Bao Dong, quoting Lyotard, suggests that she is 'representing the unrepresentable.'[17]

Li Shurui's 2014 exhibition at White Space Gallery developed her 'system' further. Although the artist talks about her deliberate lack of planning and her intuitive response in front of the canvas, these works blur conventional boundaries between painting and sculpture. *Sharp* consists of fifty-seven gunmetal grey forms scattered on the gallery floor like machine remnants from an accident in space, brightly painted edges emphasising their blade-like quality. She flirts with the conventions of Minimalism and Hard-edge Abstraction, yet in an ironic inversion she denies this formalism with her insistence that we see her work in a Chinese context. Her intention is to provide an experience so physically immersive that it becomes emotive as well as perceptual, referencing the dramatic transformation of China in the past thirty years. Perhaps Li Shurui's works, inspired by electric lights, and the flickering 'circuit board' of the artist's cerebral cortex, represent her escape from a lifetime working for the electricity company.

Monadology, her second solo show in Beijing, presented four paintings as well as the fifty seven sculptures scattered across the floor. They are like blades, or knives. The title of the exhibition refers to the ideas of Gottfried Leibniz, the seventeenth-century philosopher and mathematician. He defined the Monad as 'the single most irreducible metaphysical unit, fundamental to the makeup of everything in the universe… Timeless by nature, monads are reciprocally bound to space-time and influence the formation of overall perception.'[18] Arcane references to obscure philosophers aside, there is no doubting the artist's obsessive concentration on theories of perception, space, the senses and the larger questions of human existence. Li Shurui's work is all about seeing, in the broadest sense – not what we see, but how we see.

Li Shurui
Light89*, *Light90*, *Light88 2009
acrylic on canvas
each 300 x 200 cm
image courtesy the artist and White Space Beijing

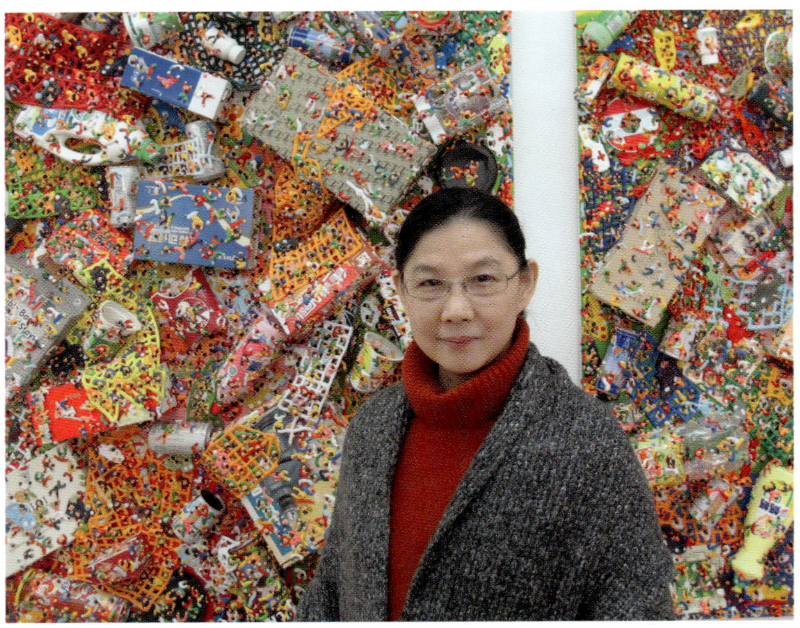

QIN FENLING 秦风玲

Social Fairy Tales

The studios and tranquil domestic spaces inhabited by self-taught painter Qin Fengling and her husband, celebrated artist Wang Luyan, are filled with their own paintings and sculptures, carved temple doors and traditional ceramics, and an eclectic mix of modern design and ornate antique Chinese and European furniture. Wang's stainless steel marching figures are juxtaposed with his monumental paintings and Qin's sculptural canvases of red flags, targets and tiny tumbling figures. It is a far cry from the hutong courtyard house where they began their married life in a few cramped rooms, which rapidly became so cluttered with Wang's paintings and materials that they often had to work outside.

Qin Fengling is modest, almost self-effacing, insisting that she really doesn't think of herself as an artist at all, despite exhibitions in major Beijing and international galleries and a loyal group of collectors. Born in 1957, growing up during the Cultural Revolution, she never intended to become an artist, working briefly in a clothing factory after she left school. Once she married Wang Luyan in 1984 she believed her major responsibility was to take care of her husband, serve tea and meals to his artist friends, and keep domestic order.

Wang Luyan was a key member of the 'Stars' group of artists in the late 1970s, and a participant in their important exhibition in 1979.[19] After they married, in the heady days of an emergent Beijing art scene, Qin Fengling was surrounded by artists at the cutting edge of the Chinese avant-garde, participating in their impassioned discussions about art, philosophy and politics. She says, 'From what I remember of that period of time, every time my husband or one of his friends went to an art exhibition they would joke to each other, "You should bring your toothbrush with you, as you must be prepared to be arrested."' That nascent period of contemporary art in China was a dangerous time, but an exciting one. Artists believed they were at the forefront of a new kind of society. Qin says, 'At that time we lived in the centre of Beijing, in Dongsi, near the National Art Museum, so lots of artists gathered in our house. Many later became very famous artists, critics or curators, including Wang Guangyi, Li Xianting and Huang Du. And sometimes they would argue. My role was to feed them, to cook for them. That was one responsibility. My other responsibility was to moderate when they were arguing. When they were too noisy I had to hush them!' Qin remembers trying to make them keep the noise down so the police would not arrive and arrest them for having a rowdy 'illicit' gathering.

Far from seeing herself as an artist, she says, 'I was being a good assistant to my husband, and focused on his art, so I wanted to be a helping hand for him.' Eventually Qin developed enough confidence to paint herself. 'It's really the influence of my husband,' she said. 'I had always loved painting as a hobby. My father worked for the State Council [a government organisation in charge of cultural communication between China and foreign countries] so when I was young I had the opportunity to see many exhibitions of foreign artists, even including Picasso.' When she saw these western modernist paintings – the first that had been shown in China since the establishment of the People's Republic – she was intrigued but unmoved. They were interesting, she decided, but of no immediate personal relevance: 'I thought that the beauty in Picasso's art was very different from my life in the hutongs when I was a child.' But the *idea* of art formed by these early experiences remained a centrally important element of her thinking. So much so, she says, laughing, that:

> When I was looking for someone to marry I decided I had to find a painter! When I met my husband he was doing some oil paintings. He doesn't actually have a lot of formal training either – he tried to enter CAFA but he failed the politics part of the entrance exam! It was only when I met my husband that I began to get any knowledge of art. My husband was always painting, and he encouraged me, always.[20]

This was a time, almost unimaginable today, when there were no opportunities for artists to exhibit or sell their art, and where your politics, or your 'bad family background', could keep you out of university. Artists exhibited their

Qin Fengling in Beijing, October 2013
photo LG

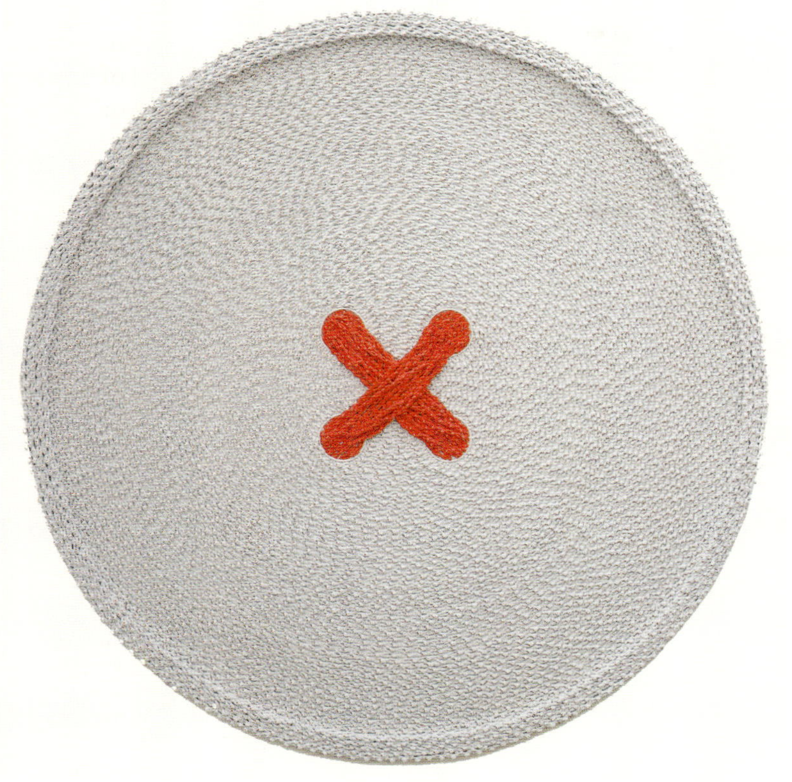

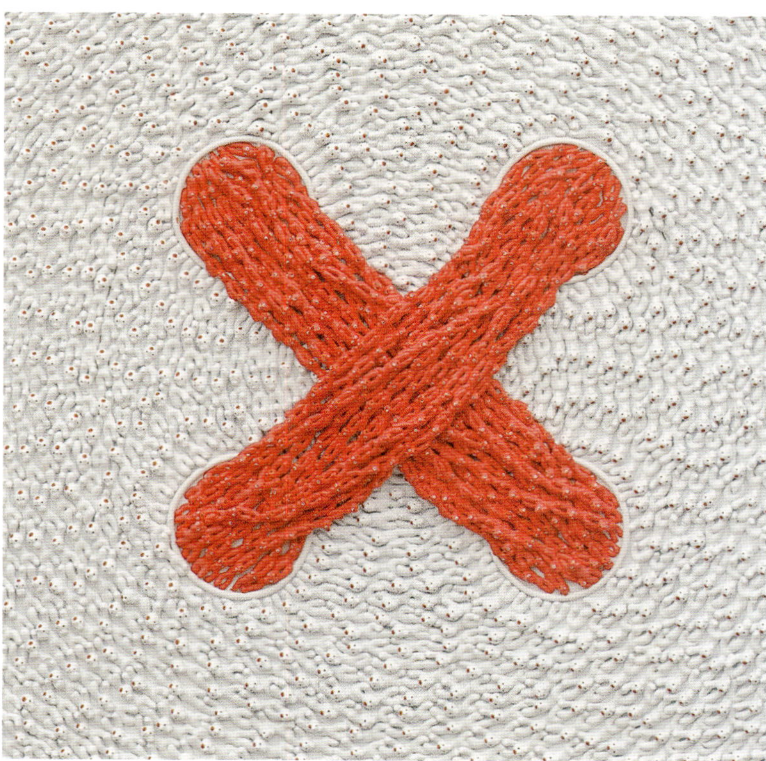

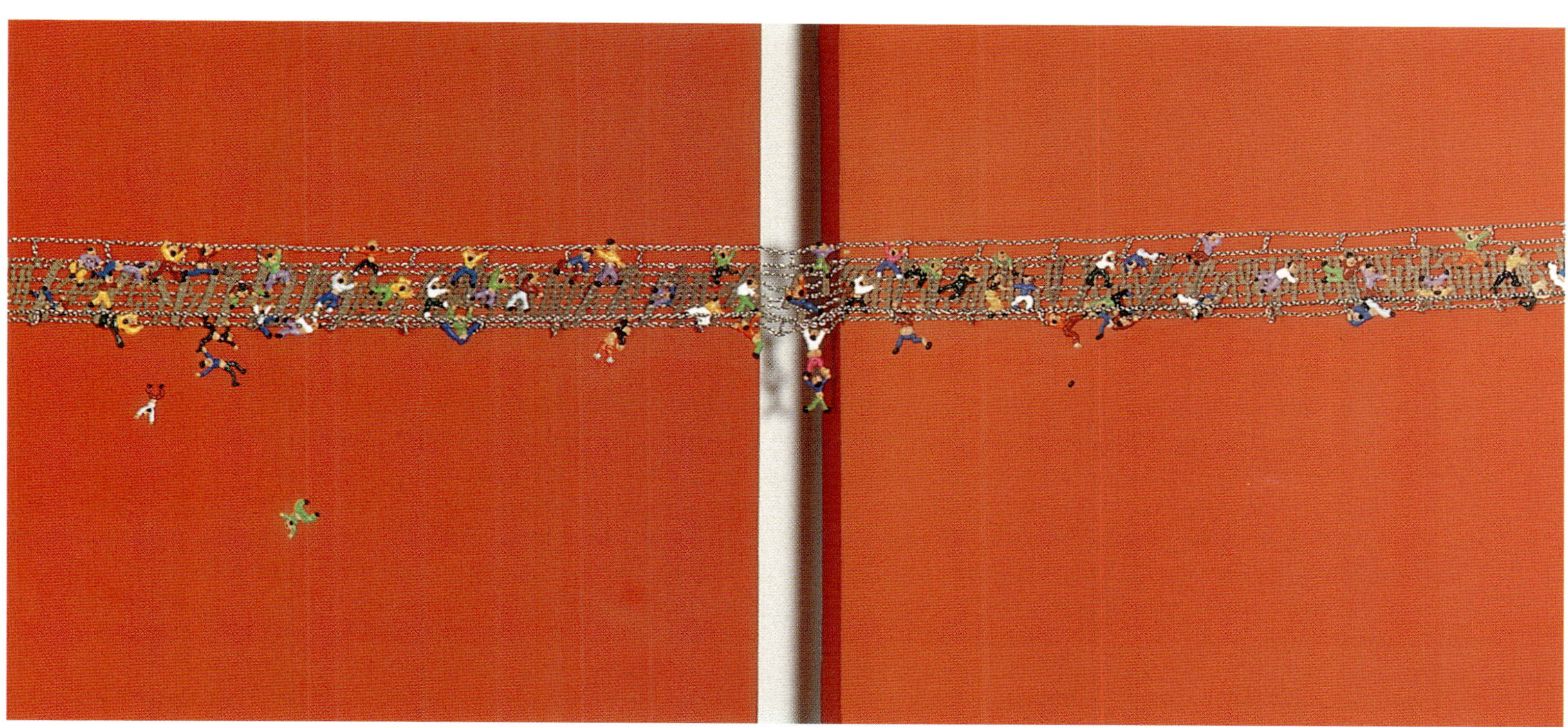

Qin Fengling *(top: work and detail)*
Button 2008
acrylic on canvas
150 x 150 cm
image courtesy the artist

Qin Fengling *(bottom)*
New Iron Chain Bridge (detail) 2007
acrylic on canvas
75 x 615 cm
image courtesy the artist

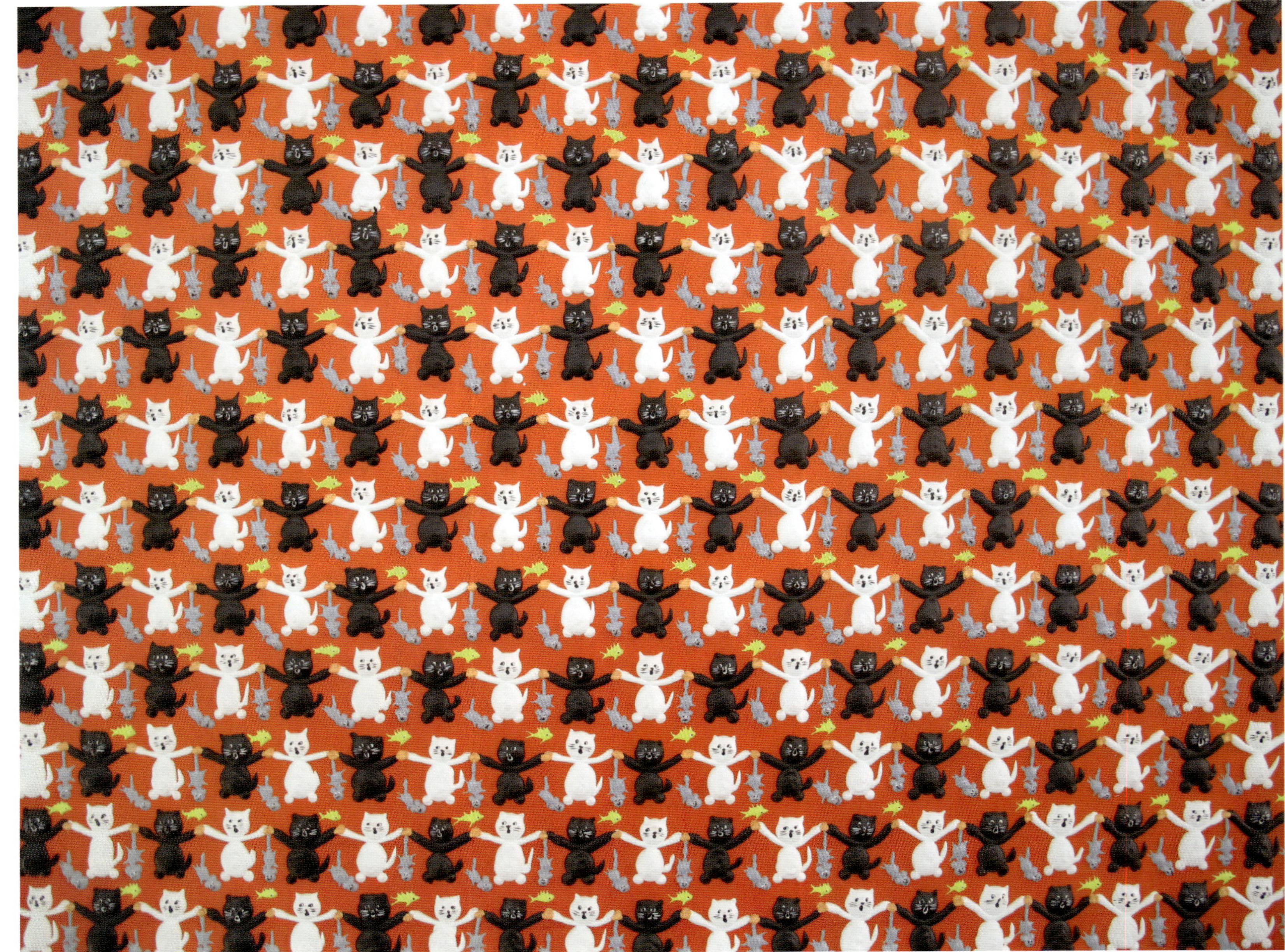

paintings to each other, and to a handful of foreign friends, in their own apartments and the apartments and hotel rooms of western diplomats. Until the Red Gate Gallery was established by Australian Brian Wallace in 1991, there were no private galleries in Beijing. Qin Fengling pointed out that she and her friends had little access to art books or magazines, except for the official magazine *Meishu* (Fine Art) edited by Li Xianting.[21] Word of mouth and the passing from one hand to another of precious foreign books and journals was how artists discovered what might be happening in the rest of the world.

Qin Fengling listened carefully as the male artists spoke, and after a while she gained the confidence to join their discussions: 'I thought at that time I was like a student in their classroom.' Watching Wang Luyan manipulate paint in his studio, she became interested in colour, texture and form. Qin began to make art in her own right in 1985, with Wang Luyan's support, at first 'painting on anything available, such as paper or newspaper, whatever.'[22] With Wang Luyan encouraging her to express her thoughts in the medium of paint, Qin began to use her experiences of cooking and baking, applying these skills to painting prolifically in an idiosyncratic self-devised style, manipulating the plasticity of acrylic paint to create sculptural figures crowding the surfaces of her canvases.

At first her artmaking was an entirely private pursuit, secondary to her role as studio assistant to her husband. Her early paintings were abstract explorations of colour, in

Qin Fengling
White Cats Black Cats 2006
acrylic on canvas
one of four panels, each 90 x 120 cm
image courtesy the artist

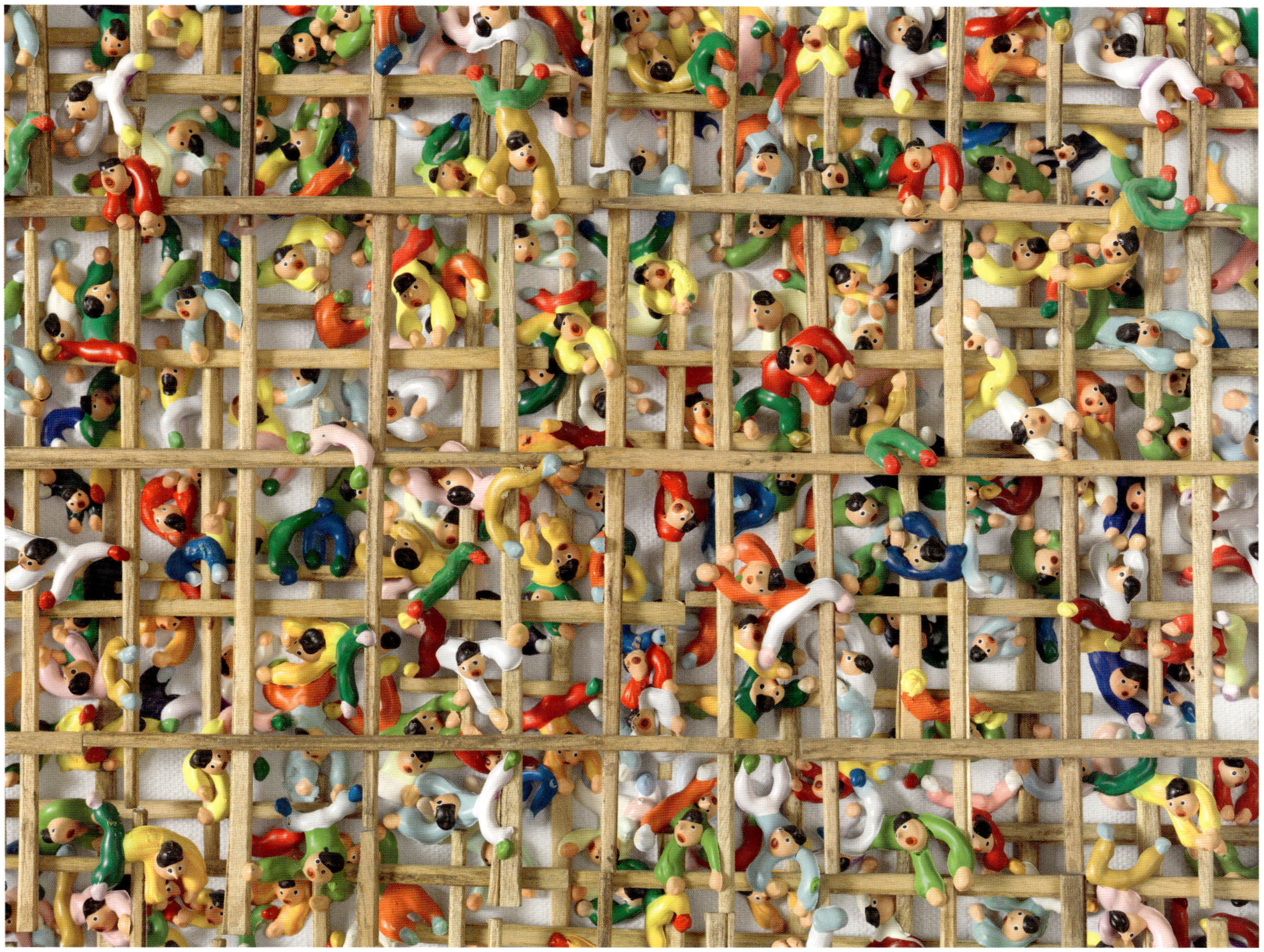

response to Wang's non-figurative work of that time, but she gradually developed a technique that lies halfway between figuration and abstraction, and halfway between painting and sculpture. By 1985 she was painting seriously:

> Back then there were a lot of artworks displayed in our house, I didn't have children, and I was helping my husband as his assistant – his palettes and brushes were all over the place -and Wang Luyan encouraged me to try painting. He said that my lack of formal training might turn out to be an advantage. He said that he himself didn't use much of what he learned at school, so it can be a good thing to paint without an art education... he encouraged me to express my thoughts in my own way.

Qin Fengling began to develop her own unique approach, squeezing acrylic paint directly from the tube into blobs on the canvas, manipulating the plastic paint into the required shapes of tiny human figures, animals, cars, or machinery and then painting eyes, mouths and small details on once the lumpy surface had dried. When she speaks about her method she says it is more like cooking than like any conventional form of art production. I suggested to the artist that she has created an entirely new kind of painting. Qin shook her head and demurred:

> You praise me too much! You can see a lot of the figures in my paintings look like candies or cookies – they resemble what a

Qin Fengling
Scaffold (detail) 2008
acrylic on canvas, wood sticks
200 x 250 cm
image courtesy the artist and White Rabbit Gallery

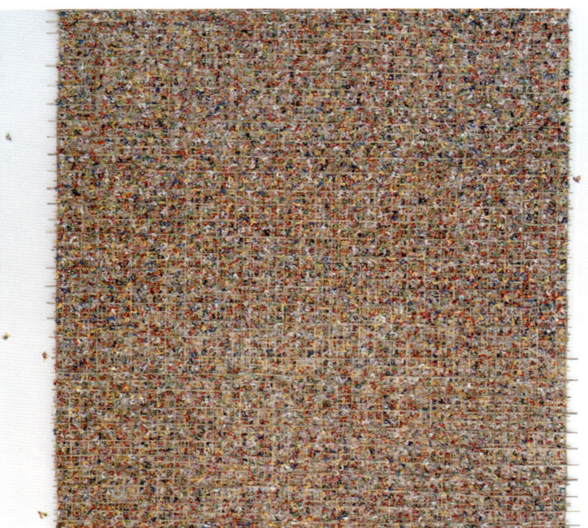

housewife creates in her kitchen. I even use a baking tray, except I am not baking, I am allowing the figures to dry at room temperature.

This unusually domestic approach to her practice owes something to Chinese traditions of painting. Qin Fengling says:

> The traditional influence is like an imprint. It comes from the environment you live in, and it's inevitable that everyone will have this. Some people transform and convert this into poetry, others into architecture, in my case into paintings. A typical housewife transforms these influences using egg and sugar and turns them into biscuits. In my case I use acrylic paint and they become paintings.

Almost more sculpture than painting, her works blur boundaries: between two dimensions and three; between 'naive' art and narrative painting; between a language of colour and pattern, and figuration. Qin Fengling identifies her husband, Wang Luyan, as the major influence on her work; her first teacher and her most important supporter. But she has also acknowledged the influence of other artists, in particular Zhu Jinshi, who also paints with a heavy impasto. 'Luyan's paintings are very thin and Jinshi's paintings are very thick, but both of their paintings are full of strength,' she told critic Wang Baoju in a 2008 interview.[23]

Once she began to paint she was unstoppable. Memories, observations, sardonic political references and quirky, affectionate responses to China past and present, were squeezed from tubes of brightly coloured paint onto canvas after canvas. Every canvas is crowded with hundreds of tiny figures, her response to a past era of collectivism and conformity. She first showed her work publicly in 2005, when curator Huang Du discovered her work and included her in an exhibition of eight artists at White Space Beijing, *Painting Unrealism*. He believed that her work 'reached the real nature of painting.'[24]

At first sight, other than her references to the loss of individualism within the collective masses, there would appear to be no overtly Chinese style or content in her work. However, New York art critic Robert C. Morgan identifies the tactile nature of her paintings as Taoist in nature, exemplifying the opposing forces of yin and yang. Just as Liang Yuanwei's impasto canvases reference Song Dynasty masterworks and Li Shurui reinvents the painting traditions of Sichuan Province, on a subterranean level Qin Fengling's works reveal an aspect of Chinese culture: 'the touch, the calligraphic nuance that finally transmits the message: the tactile and virtual are one.'[25] Without a foundation of drawing, she had to seek other ways to create her imagery, organising her tiny figures into rows, grids and complex patterns to create unified compositions, and bright primary colours to engage the viewer. She said:

> As long as there are the arms of the small figure, then it is rational, as long as there is the small face with nose and eyes, they form the picture. Why should I make drawings there all the time? I neither have such foundation, nor do I have to present what I want to express in that way.[26]

I asked, 'At what point in this long process of learning and experimenting did you finally define yourself as a practising artist?' She shook her head in denial, and uttered the definitive Chinese 'no.' The word *meiyou* is a little slippery. It can mean 'don't have', 'cannot', 'did not' 'will not' 'have not' or 'not at all' depending on the circumstances, and you hear it a lot in China:

> *Meiyou*! No! I don't define myself in this way. Even now I do not define myself as an artist. I feel I am just using art as my own

Qin Fengling
Scaffold 2008
acrylic on canvas, wood sticks
200 x 250 cm
image courtesy the artist and White Rabbit Gallery

Qin Fengling
Red 2006
acrylic on canvas
150 x 250 cm
image courtesy the artist and White Rabbit Gallery

> language to communicate with society – everyone should find their own way to be able to do this. I have lived in this society for fifty years and I have an obligation to communicate my ideas about social interaction in some way.

Qin Fengling's subject is society, the complex interrelationships of people and systems that she describes as 'social structure.' She sources her ideas from newspaper and TV stories, and her own experiences of a changing world: traffic jams, social conflict, terrible waste, pollution and over-consumption. One might imagine that her use of bright primary colours, and the play-doh tactile quality of her surfaces, would create cheerful works of child-like optimism. There is a much darker undercurrent here, however. Qin Fengling's hundreds of little figures on each canvas are almost, but not quite, identical – a reminder of the collectivist ideology of her youth, a system that created obligatory conformist identities as obedient servants of the Motherland. Her miniature people struggle to escape chains, grids and scaffolding, are trapped in horrendous traffic, scramble through construction sites, or tumble over each other in a reminder of the sheer enormity of China's population. Wang Baoju interprets these works as depicting Chinese social history:

> The scenes of the grand parade, the Junior Red Guards that are saluting, the people riding bikes, the faces of desires that belong to those who want to make fortunes quickly by "going into business", the people residing in the high buildings...the notion of being submerged by the crowd, the feelings of being controlled without independence and of losing one's individual consciousness... As a witness of time, you have written the history and the transformation of the society by your work.[27]

Red, with its field of innumerable tiny red soldiers, rifles held in readiness, reveals the claustrophobic paranoia of a world of military parades and the massing of troops – hundreds of identical figures in uniform, their individual desires subsumed by the necessity of conformity. *Scaffold* further breaks down the two-dimensional picture plane. A chaotic wriggling mass of tiny figures clambers over a grid-like structure made of wooden sticks, trampling over each other in the race to get ahead, up the ladder of success. Some fall, or are thrown, whilst others cling precariously. The work is both humorous and anxiety-provoking.

Qin Fengling is a gentle and humble person, yet a sardonic humour lurks beneath her placid exterior. *White Cats, Black Cats* is a reference to Deng Xiaoping's famous phrase from the Reform and Opening period. 'It doesn't matter whether the cat is black or white, as long as it catches mice it is a good cat,' is usually interpreted in relation to Deng's pragmatic pursuit of economic reform at the apparent expense of Marxist ideology. Qin's version suggests the absurdity of all forms of political theorising. Nor is she interested in feminism, at least not in its western guise, explaining that she believes the hardest thing is to find a way to express yourself. Once you have found that language, it doesn't matter whether you are male or female.

In 2006 her work was selected for an exhibition of female artists from China and Norway at Beijing's Today Art Museum, exploring the provocative question: 'What if Ibsen's Nora left her family to pursue her own desires?' The curator, Wang Baoju, wrote about the evolution of a subjective female identity in China, stating, 'In China today it is a luxury to talk about feminism and post-feminism because there is a bigger topic, which is humanity, above women. In our times, what's more important is humanism.'[28] This is a view that is often expressed in relation to a Chinese feminism. It emerges from a twentieth century history in which men and women were expected to work together to forge the Chinese socialist Utopia, in which gender distinctions were almost erased, and expressions of sexuality suppressed. Qin Fengling focuses on what she identifies as the pressing issues of her own time: greed, aspirational materialism, pollution, over-crowded cities and a loss of identity. She says:

> As for the subjects of my artworks, as a contemporary artist I am supposed to reflect on the problems in my environment. An artist's job is to raise the questions, and it is for scientists to solve them. So I raise the questions. As an artist I show the influence that society has on me. I hope I won't be seeing this many problems! But the problems I am trying to reflect now are things like the lack of security in modern society, inequality, and how the common people and the less fortunate are sometimes wronged by the government – these problems worry me and make me very uncomfortable.

She has previously said that Chinese society leaves 'scars and brands on you, together with shocks and memory. As long as your brain works, you can never erase these things.'[29]

Qin Fengling finds her inspiration in the kitchen, the supermarket, the street and in her observations of the ordinary events of her domestic sphere. It would be a mistake, however, to see her as a naïve painter. One of the larger-than-life figures in her artistic circle in the 1980s was the Political Pop painter Wang Guangyi, and there is a Pop sensibility in Qin's works too. She says, 'My paintings are very close to daily life.' Social Fairy Tales? In their quirky combination of humour and social observation, and their quiet puncturing of the absurdity of the contemporary world, they are more Brothers Grimm than comforting bedtime story.

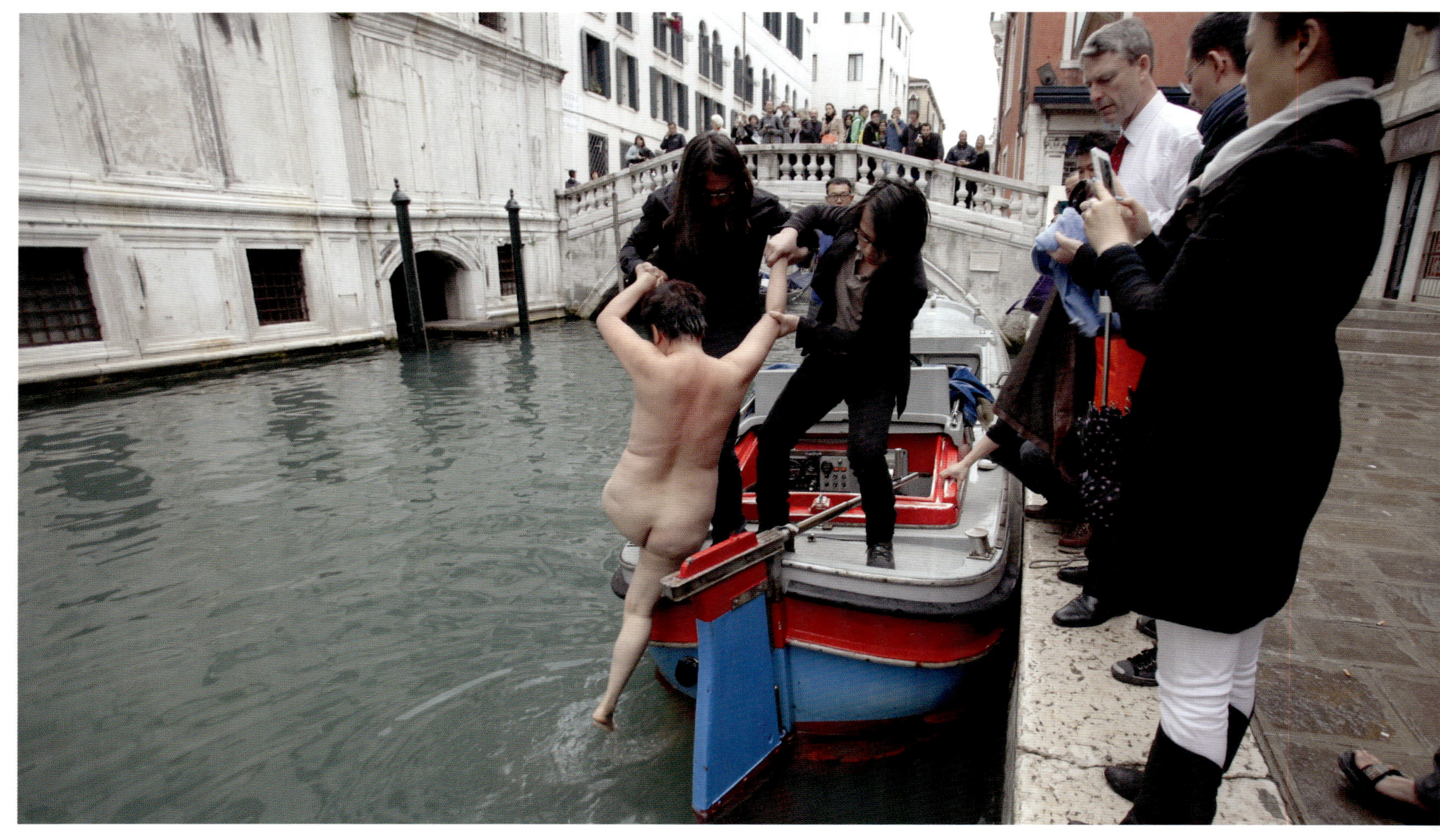

EPILOGUE

Xiao Lu 肖鲁 and Yu Ji 于吉

The moment when a young Xiao Lu took up a gun and fired two shots into her own installation at the *China/Avant-garde* exhibition in 1989 marked a point of departure for the development of contemporary art in China, and for discussions of the role for women artists in an emerging avant-garde. Today, Xiao's performative practice has continued to shock audiences, most recently challenging perceptions about the older female body with a controversial naked dip in Venice's Grand Canal.

Xiao Lu proposed a performance for the 2013 Venice Biennale, *Purged,* in which she planned to swim naked in the canal, covered with mud dug out of another Grand Canal, the one linking Beijing with Hangzhou. She was refused permission on the grounds that nudity is not permitted in the surrounds of the Diocesan Museum. The proposed performance was part of the exhibition *Grand Canal*, which included her installation of papers stained with toxic fluids extracted from her body via Daoist massage, juxtaposed with containers of sludge from China's Grand Canal. Despite the ban on her performance, Xiao Lu stripped off her clothes during the opening ceremony and jumped into the canal regardless. She explained her intention as asking the question, 'Is God dead?'

Of greater significance is a 2011 performance *Tang Poetry – Chinese Medicine – Copying – Time*. For eighty-four days, using traditional Chinese medicine as her ink, Xiao Lu copied the *Three Hundred Tang Dynasty Poems*. She describes this as an act of meditation upon her changing life, growing older and calmer, working in a more extended temporal manner, creating rituals. Things may not get easier, but they do get quieter.

Meanwhile, artists of the younger generation, born in the 1980s and early 1990s, have left the twentieth century behind them and are dealing with the issues of what might just as well be a different country, a different culture. As they enter what seems to some an uncertain future, they too look back over their shoulders to examine their own childhoods and the very different life experiences of their parents and grandparents.

In December 2014 I walked through Shanghai streets filled with over-the-top Christmas decorations – a tangible indication of a changing society – to meet young sculptor Yu Ji in her artist-run space in the French Concession district. She is pushing traditional forms of figurative sculpture into the realms of performance art, exploring her interest in the body

Xiao Lu
Purged 2013
performance (Xiao Lu is pulled from the Grand Canal, Venice, onto a boat)
image courtesy the artist
photo Wen Cheng

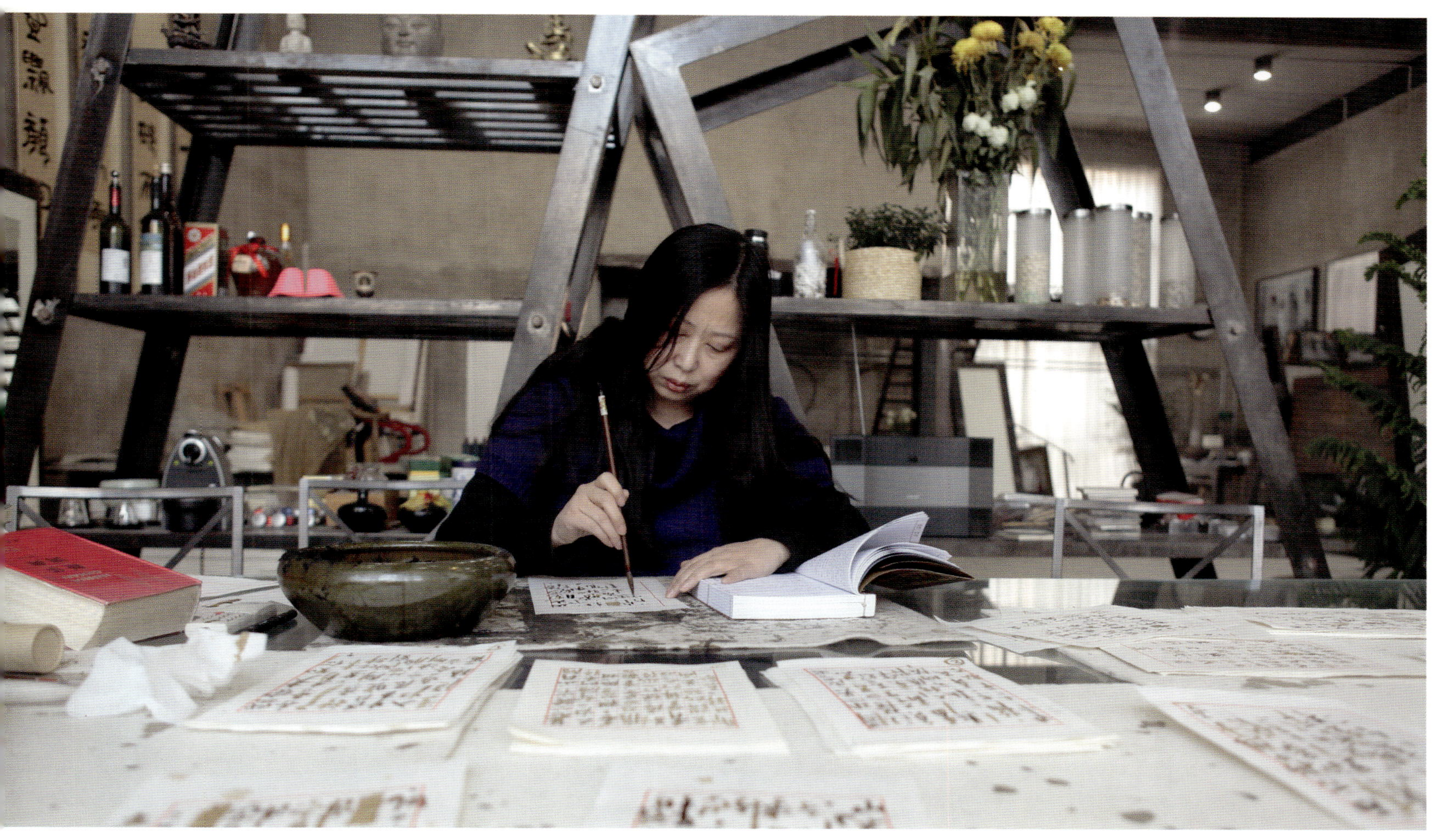

occupying space, notions of public and private space, and the experience of physical sensation. Born in Shanghai in 1985, she studied with the sculptor Liu Jianhua at Shanghai University's Fine Arts Academy. From the beginning her main subject has been the body. But, 'The body is a mainstream subject. Many artists use this theme, so the big question for me is "Where is your entry point?"' she says. To that end she has collaborated with the experimental Shanghai political collective, *Grass Stage Theater Group*. She is interested in inviting audiences to literally enter her work, to create a physical intervention in the artwork itself.

An early work began with a collection of used bars of soap with which different people of all ages and backgrounds had washed their bodies. Yu Ji made plaster casts of these ephemeral, worn and humble objects, representations of time and memory. Complex, layered meanings are embedded in her material choices, and in the strong physical presence of her installations. The Arte Povera movement interests her; she likes to use simple inexpensive materials such as concrete and plaster. This has been partly out of necessity, as a student and then as a young artist just beginning to make her way, but it is also a distinct aesthetic and conceptual choice. Yu Ji admires the 'social sculpture' of Joseph Beuys and the installation works of the German artist Wolfgang Laib; his use of materials such as wax, milk and pollen intrigue her.

Yu Ji's *Flesh in Stone* series of truncated cement figures held to the wall by iron bands is inspired by the amputated limbs and battered torsos of Classical sculpture from the ancient world, and the Buddhist statuary of the Mogao caves along the silk route. She is interested in the connection between art and daily life, exemplified by *Public Space*, an installation based on the very particularly Chinese experience of the communal public toilet. The fragile tiles, private yet exposed, were made of plaster, and they crumbled into dust as the audience walked over them. Like so many other artists of her generation, and the generation before hers, she is dealing with the fragile nature of memory.

Contemporary China has abandoned the collectivist past and embraced the aspirational future: it is the 'age of ambition', according to New Yorker reporter Evan Osnos, when the national narrative is 'splintering into a billion stories – stories of flesh and blood, of idiosyncrasies, of individual struggles.'[30] At the first artist dinner I attended in Beijing, early in 2011, three male artists sat wreathed in cigarette smoke at one end

Xiao Lu
Tang Poetry, Chinese Medicine, Copying, Time 2011
performance at Huantie Studio Beijing
image courtesy the artist
photo Yang Chao

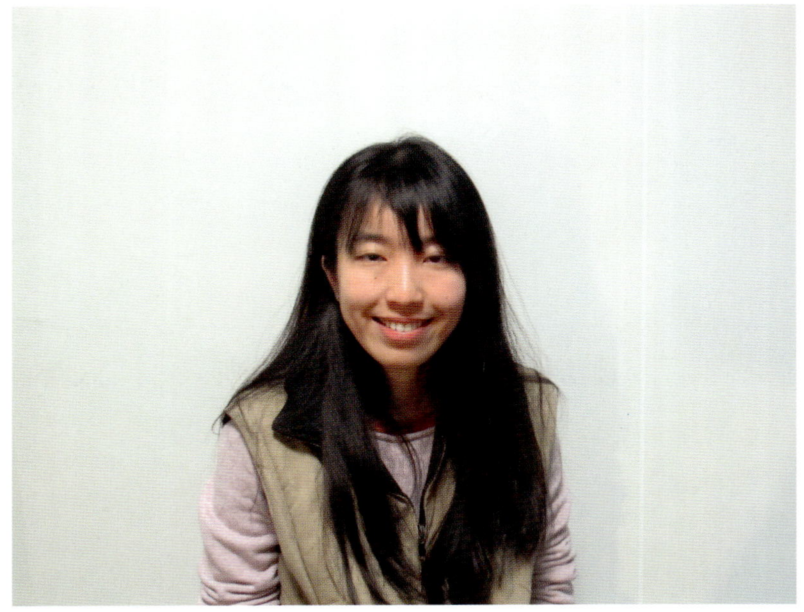

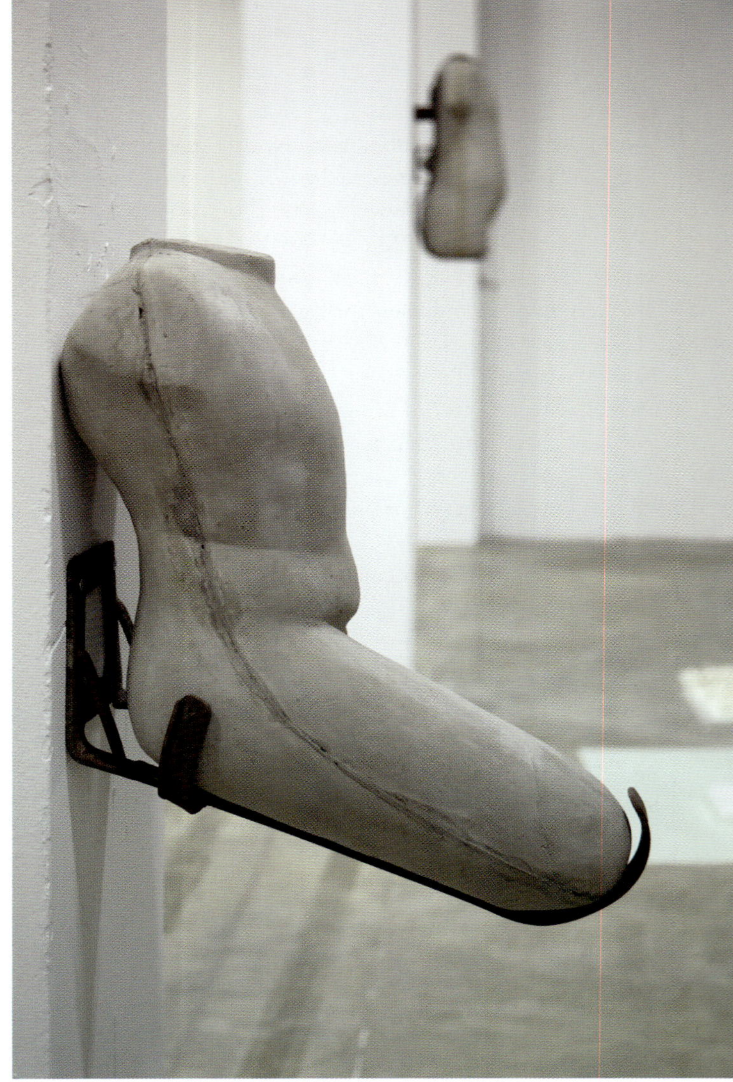

of the table. Like rock stars in their leather jackets, they were fussed over by their pretty girlfriends. Everyone listened when they spoke. The women didn't speak at all. I left to hail a taxi, thinking, 'Well, Dorothy, you're not in Kansas anymore!' From that moment onwards, I wanted to peer beneath veneers of westernisation and globalisation, through barriers of language and culture, in an attempt to explore the new realities of this 'new China'. I wanted to hear the voices of those silent women.

The women artists who generously invited me into their homes and studios, sharing their stories and ideas – about art, marriage, parenthood, politics and spirituality among other things – exemplify a dramatic cultural shift. The different generations have entirely distinct experiences, but all are dealing with change, coming to terms with the past. The broader past, the 'grand narrative' of China, as much as their own, their mother's, and their grandmothers', form the background to their perceptions of the world and the work they create. They have invented new forms, and new visual languages with which to express their reality, and they have reinvented old ones. In so many ways, they are 'holding up half the sky'.

NOTES

1 Pace Gallery Press Release for *Beijing Voice: Leaving Realism Behind* http://www.pacegallery.com/beijing/exhibitions/11178/beijing-voice-2011-leaving-realism-behind accessed 15 January 2015
2 Vine, Richard 2011 *New China New Art* Prestel Verlag, Munich, London New York (38)
3 Unless otherwise acknowledged all quotes from Liang Yuanwei are from her conversations with the writer in Beijing in March 2011, December 2012 and October 2013
4 He, Fiona 2013 'Liang Yuanwei at Beijing Commune' in *Artforum* April 2013, available at http://www.beijingcommune.com/EnArtText.aspx?ID=52 accessed 17 February 2015
5 Leng Lin 2010 *Liang Yuanwei Golden Notes* Beijing Commune, 798 Art District Beijing, November 2010 – January 2011. Available at http://www.beijingcommune.com/Uploads/UploadsExhibitionFile/4b1b5b89ca6e491f8e2a3f6db75e1dbd.pdf accessed 28 February 2015
6 Pace London http://www.pacegallery.com/london/exhibitions/12656/liang-yuanwei accessed 23 February 2015
7 ibid.
8 Unless otherwise acknowledged all quotes from Li Shurui are from her conversation with the writer in Beijing in April 2014
9 Interviews with artists for *Vitamin P2: New Perspectives in Painting* Phaidon, London, 2011 available at http://au.phaidon.com/agenda/art/articles/2011/november/29/inside-the-mind-of-li-shurui/ accessed 1 March 2015

Yu Ji, Shanghai, December 2014
photo LG

Yu Ji
Flesh in Stone 2 2013
cement, iron
dimensions variable
image courtesy the artist

10 ibid.

11 Bao Dong 2010 'Freedom and Nothingness: the Art of Li Shurui/ Optical Lyricism: the Art of Li Shurui' available on the artist's website http://www.lishurui.com/article/-freedom-and-nothingness/ accessed 1 March 2015

12 Smith, Karen 2011 in *Vitamin P2: New Perspectives in Painting* Phaidon, London and New York (184)

13 Lu Jie 2005 *The Long March Project,* a presentation at the Vancouver Art Gallery on 12 October 2005 in conjunction with the exhibition *Classified Materials: Accumulations, Archives, Artists* available at http://fillip.ca/content/the-long-march-project accessed 14 June 2015

14 http://www.longmarchproject.com/e-progess6-1-1.htm accessed 1 March 2015

15 http://longmarchproject.com/e-progess6-3.htm accessed 1 March 2015

16 Interviews with artists for *Vitamin P2: New Perspectives in Painting* Phaidon, London, 2011 available at http://au.phaidon.com/agenda/art/articles/2011/november/29/inside-the-mind-of-li-shurui/ accessed 1 March 2015

17 Bao Dong 2010 'Freedom and Nothingness: the Art of Li Shurui/ Optical Lyricism: the Art of Li Shurui' available on the artist's website http://www.lishurui.com/article/-freedom-and-nothingness/ accessed 1 March 2015

18 'Li Shurui: Monadology' (author uncredited) 2014 Whitespace Gallery, Beijing available at http://www.whitespace-beijing.com/ExhView.asp?language=en&id=88 accessed 1 March 2015

19 See Chapter 2 for an account of the 'Stars' group in the late 1970s.

20 Unless otherwise acknowledged all quotes from Qin Fengling are from her conversation with the writer, in Beijing in October 2013

21 *Art Asia Pacific* Issue 71 provides a thorough account of this significant figure in Chinese Contemporary Art, available at http://artasiapacific.com/Magazine/71/OffThePageLiXianting (accessed 3 March 2015) Li Xianting graduated from CAFA in 1978 and was one of the most vocal supporters of the Stars Group. He edited '*Meishu*' from 1978 – 80. From 1985 – 89 he edited the magazine '*Zhongguo Meishubao*' which promoted contemporary art. With Gao Minglu he was one of the organisers of the 1989 *China/Avant-garde* exhibition (see Chapter 2) but after 1989 he focused on independent critical and curatorial projects. More information is available at http://contemporary_chinese_culture.academic.ru/435/Li_Xianting accessed 3 March 2015

22 Qin Fengling 2007 'The Lyric But Cruel Social Fairy Tale: Dialog (sic) Between Wang Baoju and Qin Fengling in *Qin Fengling,* White Space Beijing and Timezone 8, Beijing

23 ibid.

24 Huang Du 2007 'Painting Beyond Touch: On the Possibilities of the 'New Painting' and Recent Works by Qin Fengling' in *Qin Fengling,* White Space Beijing and Timezone 8, Beijing

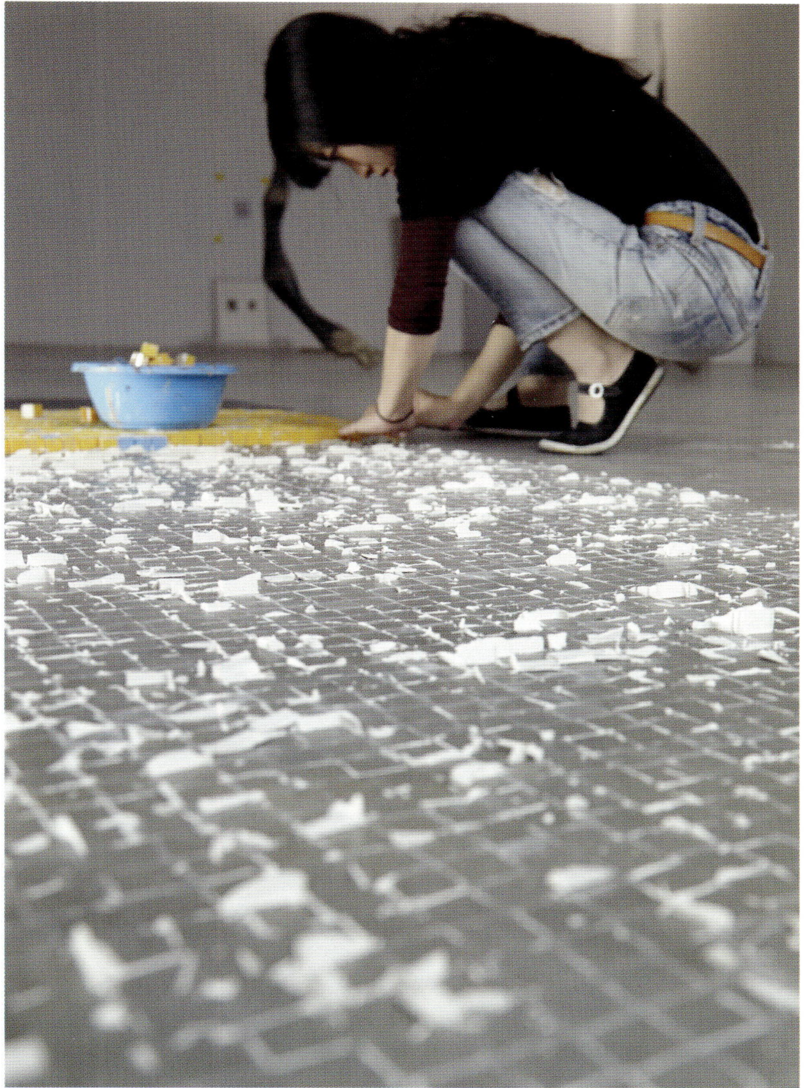

25 Morgan, Robert. C 2008 'Qin Fengling: Just A Part of Life', catalogue essay for *Multitude* Kasia Kay Art Projects and David Parker Fine Arts Chicago

26 Qin Fengling 2007 in 'The Lyric But Cruel Social Fairy Tale: Dialog (sic) Between Wang Baoju and Qin Fengling, in *Qin Fengling* White Space Beijing and Timezone 8, Beijing

27 Wang Baoju 2007 'The Lyric But Cruel Social Fairy Tale: Dialog (sic) Between Wang Baoju and Qin Fengling, in *Qin Fengling* White Space Beijing and Timezone 8, Beijing

28 Wang Baoju 2006 'The Self-Possessed Subject: Women's Attitudes and Positions in the Post-Nora Age' cataolgue essay, *Post Nora* Today Art Museum, Beijing

29 Qin Fengling 2007 'The Lyric But Cruel Social Fairy Tale: Dialog (sic) Between Wang Baoju and Qin Fengling, in *Qin Fengling* White Space Beijing and Timezone 8, Beijing

30 Osnos, Evan 2014 *Age of Ambition: Chasing Fortune, Truth and Faith in the New China,* Farrer, Strauss and Giroux, New York

Yu Ji
installing ***Silence Practice***
Palais de Tokyo, Paris, 2014
image courtesy the artist

ACKNOWLEDGEMENTS

The process of writing this book has been quite an adventure. A notorious sign in the Beijing Zoo says, in its English translation, 'Beware, lest suddenness happens!' In my travels to China over a period of five years, and in my encounters with Chinese artists, curators, collectors, educators and writers, there has been much that is sudden, surprising – even extraordinary. Not least, the process of researching and writing the book has changed me in unexpected ways. In this mid-life transition from teacher to writer, there have been many individuals and institutions whose support and encouragement have been instrumental in the gestation of this book.

Firstly, I am profoundly grateful to Judith Neilson for her support. From generously lending me some of her own personal books and catalogues, advising me about the chaotic creative frenzy that I would discover in China, connecting me with artists in her collection, and supporting the publication of this book, she has encouraged me throughout the process. I must also thank the staff of the White Rabbit Gallery, most especially Phyllis Rowlinson and David Williams, whose enthusiasm and assistance have been so much appreciated. From the exhibitions of works from Neilson's extensive collection of contemporary Chinese art, to the (excellent) dumplings in its teahouse and the quiet space of its library, Neilson's White Rabbit Gallery has become a focal point in Sydney for anyone interested in contemporary China.

Margaret Bishop and John Dunn of Piper Press took a chance on a novice writer – their encouragement, patience and attention to detail as they guided me through the process have been unwavering, and I am enormously grateful to them. To Julie Ewington, editor extraordinaire, whose encouraging advice and keen eye for my occasionally purple prose has helped me to become a better writer: thank you. The final shape of the book owes much to your guidance. Professor Ian Howard and Associate Professor Kerry Thomas of the University of New South Wales commented on draft chapters, and their encouragement and sage advice were extremely helpful. I am also indebted to the Principal and Executive of Loreto Kirribilli for providing a period of study leave in 2013, and for their affirming support of my work.

To my friends and colleagues – I owe you thanks for your forbearance, as you listened patiently to my endless talk about China, and for your belief in me. And to my Beijing friend, Kendra, who shared some of my art adventures, and listened to my tall tales over many bowls of noodles and glasses of wine – we had fun! I thank my excellent translators in Beijing and Shanghai, who spent many, many cold hours in artists' studios with me, patiently making sure that there were no misunderstandings due to slippages in communication across barriers of language. Any errors of interpretation are entirely my own. In particular, to those who helped me on repeated occasions in Beijing – Shasha, Hermione, Ellen and Cindy, I am most grateful for your diligent and careful work. To my students, who responded with passionate interest when I introduced them to contemporary Chinese art – our time together gave me so much pleasure, and I loved sharing my research with you.

Without a scholarship in 2011, however, I may never have summoned up the courage to go to China at all: the opportunities afforded by the NSW Premier's Kingold Creative Arts Travelling Scholarship significantly changed my life. Brian Wallace, whose Red Gate Gallery in Beijing has played a pivotal role in the development of the contemporary art scene in China, has provided immersive opportunities for artists and writers through a residency program, and I was fortunate to have a Red Gate residency on two occasions. Without that opportunity, this book would not exist. Tony Scott, of China Art Projects, made me welcome in Beijing, and provided my first entrée into artists' studios. He is a great friend to me, to Chinese artists, and to China.

Other helpful gallerists, curators and researchers in the investigative phase included Rebecca Catching, Diana Freundl, Martin Kemble, Shasha Liu and Monika Lin in Shanghai, and Meg Maggio in Beijing. Apart from assisting me to connect with artists, they provided me with a sounding board, and shared their own observations about the position of women in the Chinese artworld. I must also thank galleries and organisations who have assisted with permission to reproduce works by a number of artists: Klein Sun Gallery in New York, Pace Gallery in Beijing and London, Beijing Commune, White Space Gallery, Edouard Malingue Gallery (Hong Kong),de Sarthe Gallery Beijing, China Art Projects and Pékin Fine Arts.

To my family – John, Sarah and Annie Peachman, whose support, encouragement and unconditional love has kept me going through more than a few dark nights of the soul – this book is dedicated to you. In reading early drafts, Annie's valiant efforts to cure me of my adjective addiction and John's explanations of how not to use semi-colons may have failed, but it was not their fault.

Finally, I thank all the artists in this book for welcoming me into their studios and giving me the opportunity to tell their stories. It has been an enormous privilege.

—Luise Guest

PUBLISHED WORKS

Some of the material in this book has appeared in different forms in a number of online publications and websites; in *Artist Profile*; and in the *Journal of Contemporary Chinese Art*. In particular, a profile of artist Gao Rong was published in *Artist Profile* in August 2014; interviews and articles featuring Bingyi (13August 2014), Cao Fei (8 May 2014) and Ma Yanling (5 March 2014) appeared in *Creative Asia* (www.creative-asia.net), interviews and articles featuring Liang Yuanwei, Lin Tianmiao and Shi Zhiying have appeared in *The Culture Trip* (www.theculturetrip.com) and an article entitled 'Ten Contemporary Chinese Women Artists You Should Know' (Bu Hua, Cui Xiuwen, Dong Yuan, Gao Rong, Han Yajuan, Huang Jing Yuan, Wang Zhibo, Xie Qi, Yu Ji, Zhou Hongbin) was published in January 2014; reviews of exhibitions by Gao Ping, Huang Jingyuan and Lin Tianmiao have appeared in *The Art Life* (www.theartlife.com.au) as has an article, 'Material Girls, Super Starlets and Girls With Swagger' featuring the work of Han Yajuan, Bu Hua and Ma Yanling (15 November 2013); 'Material Practices: Stitching, Fabric and Textiles in the Work of Contemporary Chinese Artists' was published in *Daily Serving* (www.dailyserving.com) on 10 January 2014 featuring Lin Tianmaio, Lin Jingjing, Gao Rong and Yin Xiuzhen; 'Holding Up Half the Sky: an Interview with Lin Tianmiao' was published in *Daily Serving* (www.dailyserving.com) on 11 December 2012; 'In Grandmother's House', a discussion of the work of Gao Rong and Dong Yuan, was published in *Randian* http://www.randian-online.com/ on 25 March 2013; and 'Secrets, Sorrows and the Feminine Subjective: Nüshu References in the work of Contemporary Artist Ma Yanling' was published in the *Journal of Contemporary Chinese Art 2 (1)* (JCCA) Intellect Books, United Kingdom in July 2015.

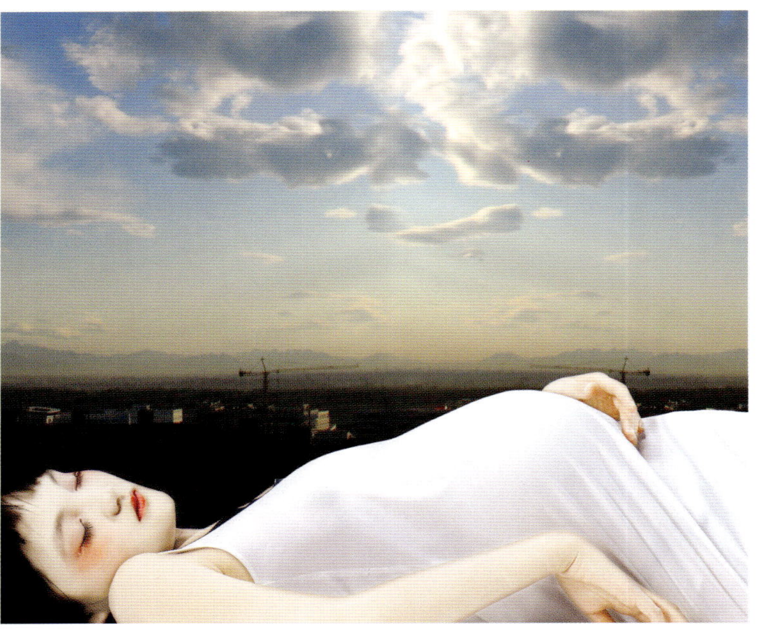

Cui Xiuwen
Angel No. 13 2006
type c photograph
100 x 119.5 cm
images courtesy and © Cui Xiuwen